Rational Choice Theory

Schools of Thought in Sociology

Series Editor: John Urry
Professor of Sociology
Lancaster University

For greater convenience, a cumulative index to all titles in this series will be published in a separate volume.

Rational Choice Theory

Edited by

Peter Abell

Professor
London School of Economics and Political Science

An Elgar Reference Collection

Published by
Edward Elgar Publishing Limited
Gower House
Croft Road
Aldershot
Hants GU11 3HR
England

Edward Elgar Publishing Company
Old Post Road
Brookfield
Vermont 05036
USA

British Library Cataloguing in Publication Data
Rational choice theory. − (Schools of thought in sociology,
  no. 8).
  1. Sociology. Theories
  I. Abell, Peter *1939−* II. Series
  300.1

Library of Congress Cataloguing in Publication Data
Rational choice theory/edited by Peter Abell.
    p. cm. − (Schools of thought in sociology : v. 8) (An Elgar
reference collection)
  Includes bibliographical references.
  1. Sociology−Methodology. 2. Social exchange. 3. Choice
(Psychology) 4. Game theory. I. Abell, Peter, 1939−
II. Series. III. Series: An Elgar reference collection.
HM24.R34 1991
301'.01−dc20   91−9912
                                                            CIP

Printed in Great Britain at the University Press, Cambridge

ISBN 1 85278 321 4

Contents

Acknowledgements

The editor and publishers wish to thank the following who have kindly given permission for the use of copyright material.

American Association for the Advancement of Science for article: R. Axelrod and W.D. Hamilton (1981), 'The Evolution of Cooperation', *Science*, **211**, 1390–1396.

American Journal of Economics and Sociology for article: E.E. Williams and M.C. Findlay (1981), 'A Reconsideration of the Rationality Postulate', *American Journal of Economics and Sociology*, **40**(1), 17–36.

American Psychological Association for article: D. Kaheneman and A. Tversky (1984), 'Choices, Values and Frames', *American Psychologist*, **39**, 341–350.

American Sociological Association for article: R.A. Emerson (1962), 'Power-Dependence Relations', *American Sociological Review*, **27**(1), 31–41; P.E. Oliver and G. Marwell (1988), 'The Paradox of Group Size in Collective Action: A Theory of Critical Mass II', *American Sociological Review*, **53**, 1–8; A.L. Stinchcombe (1986), 'Reason and Rationality', *Sociological Theory*, **4**, 151–166; D. Friedman and M. Hechter (1988), 'The Contribution of Rational Choice Theory to Macrosociological Research', *Sociological Theory*, **6**, 201–218.

Basil Blackwell for article: A. Carling (1987), 'Exploitation, Extortion and Oppression', *Political Studies*, **35**, 173–188.

British Sociological Association for articles: A. Heath (1968), 'Economic Theory and Sociology: A Critique', *Sociology*, **2**, 273–292; P. Abell (1977), 'The Many Faces of Power and Liberty', *Sociology*, **11**, 3–24.

Center for Migration Studies for article: M. Hechter, D. Friedman and M. Appelbaum (1982), 'A Theory of Ethnic Collective Action', *International Migration Review*, **16**(2), 412–439.

Elsevier Science Publishers B.V. for article: G. Marwell and R.E. Ames (1981), 'Economists Free Ride, Does Anyone Else?', *Journal of Public Economics*, **15**, 295–310.

General Systems Science Foundation for articles: J.G. Harsanyi (1962), 'Measurement of Social Power, Opportunity Costs, and the Theory of Two-Person Bargaining Games', *Behavioral Science*, **1**, 67–80; J.G. Harsanyi (1962), 'Measurement of Social Power in *n*-Person Reciprocal Power Situations', *Behavioral Science*, **7**, 81–91; R. Hardin (1971),

'Collective Action as an Agreeable *n*-Prisoner's Dilemma', *Behavioral Science*, **16**, 472–481.

Gordon and Breach Science Publishers, Inc. for article: K. Kosake (1986), 'A Model of Relative Deprivation', *Journal of Mathematical Sociology*, **12**(1), 35–48.

Kluwer Academic Publishers for articles: J. Elster (1982), 'Marxism, Functionalism and Game Theory', *Theory and Society*, **11**, 453–482; G.A. Cohen (1982), 'Reply to Elster, Marxism, Functionalism and Game Theory', *Theory and Society*, **11**, 483–495; J.E. Roemer (1982), 'Methodological Individualism and Deductive Marxism', *Theory and Society*, **11**, 513–520.

Mancur Olson for his article: M. Olson (1968), 'Economics, Sociology and the Best of All Possible Worlds', *Public Interest*, **Summer**, 96–118.

University of Chicago Press for articles: G.C. Homans (1958), 'Social Behaviour as Exchange', *American Journal of Sociology*, **63**, 597–606; J.S. Coleman (1986), 'Social Theory, Social Research and a Theory of Action', *American Journal of Sociology*, **91**(6), 1309–1335; D.D. Heckathorn (1988), 'Collective Sanctions and the Creation of Prisoner's Dilemma Norms', *American Journal of Sociology*, **94**, 535–562; H. Margolis (1981), 'A New Model of Rational Choice', *Ethics*, **9**, 265–279.

Every effort has been made to trace all the copyright holders but if any have been inadvertently overlooked the publishers will be pleased to make the necessary arrangement at the first opportunity.

The publishers wish to thank the Library of the London School of Economics and Political Science for their assistance in obtaining these articles.

Introduction

Adopting even a flexible conception of rational choice (action) as *the* foundational idea for a contemporary sociological theory has not until recently attracted more than a handful of adherents. Despite some near contemporary seminal works by Homas (1958), Blau (1964) and Olson (1965), the imprint of Parson's (1937) authority, in roundly rejecting 'rationality', has taken its toll. Indeed, for many the very essence of the sociological enterprise has been, and still is, to understand the motives or purposes lying behind 'irrational' actions and to incorporate these into a systematic theory. Yet for others, coming from very diverse intellectual traditions, the whole vocabulary of motives is dismissed as irrelevant. On the one hand, 'motives' are always construed as *post hoc* rationalizations, and all we are entitled to examine are the entrails of a rationalizing discourse. On the other hand, the generative capacity of 'structures' disembodied from motives and rational calculation are the building blocks of a social science. Neither of these traditions has, in my view, proved particularly successful, nor have attempts to glue them together with an infusion of obscuring neologisms.

There are, however, signs that a re-evaluation of rational action theory is underway. Marxists have rediscovered the rational choice foundations of the Master's theories (Elster, 1985; Roemer, 1982) and others are re-exploring the boundaries of a conception which is, of course, as old as social science itself (Boudon, 1981; Coleman, 1990; Cook, 1987; Fararo, 1989). Why this should now be so will, no doubt, entertain future historians – assuming the revival is more than yet one more passing whim. But, I suspect the reason is fairly evident, namely the almost complete failure of the established theoretical traditions – be they marxist or non-marxist, functionalist or non-functionalist, interactionist or non-interactionist, structuralist or non-structuralist – to provide a framework for the systematic deductive modelling of that complex realm called 'social reality'.

Some will immediately cavil at the objective of 'deductive modelling' itself. Words of justification are consequentially called for. No doubt, models where testable propositions can be validly deduced from a series of clearly stated axioms, hypothesizing more or less latent complex multiple-actor mechanisms, have both their aesthetic and parsimonious appeals, and may be sought for these reasons only. But neither matters of aesthetics or parsiomony are at the heart of things. Rather, deductive models become indispensable when dealing with complex systems of human interaction, and where consequences (intended or otherwise) are dependent upon the *strategic calculation* of many individuals. Such systems were, of course, precisely what Parsons (1937) had in mind, notwithstanding his rejection of an overly rationalistic perspective. The only way to start to model complex n-actor ($n > 1$) systems is by making bold assumptions about (a) the motives/objectives/utilities/preferences, etc., of the actors, and (b) their *strategic possiblities* given the situation (resources constraints, etc.) they find themselves in, and then to deduce their consequential actions and the ultimate outcomes. It is the latter which provide a test of the theory. Rational action and interaction (i.e. game) theories are, of course, well designed to deductively model systems of this sort and, as long as we are prepared to adopt a sufficiently flexible conception of 'rationality' itself, they should be at a premium in social theory though, it must be said, not infallible (see below).

A quite natural retort to these claims is, of course, to question the implied exogeneity of both 'motives' and 'strategic possibilities'. Surely, many would say, the way in which these elements themselves are fashioned is of central concern to the sociologist! This is certainly true, and any theoretical perspective worth its salt will ultimately have to face up to this challenge, rendering both elements theoretically endogenous. As far as I am aware there is, as yet, little achievement in this direction (though see Emerson, 1987), but there is no reason to suppose that the endogenization of actors 'preferences' (and their constituitive elements, beliefs, values and socialized affects), and the possibilities they face cannot be fruitfully brought within the ambit of rational interaction analysis. They are themselves, after all, best modelled as the consequences (intentional or otherwise) of prior complex patterns of interaction, which may be locally quite rational though globally (i.e. in terms of unintended consequences) often much less so. But all of this must be for the future.

A good example of the style of reasoning, which takes both preferences and strategic opportunities as exogenous, is to be found in Boudon's model of the often remarked upon, but apparently counterintuitive, relationship between increasing rates of social mobility and increasing relative deprivation (Boudon, 1981). Surely nothing could be more irrational? But not so, Kosaka's elegant development of this model is to be found in this volume (Kosaka, 1985). There, he shows how individuals, acting in an entirely rational manner, (i.e. in terms of subjective expected utility maximization) will generate a curvilinear relationship between relative deprivation and rates of mobility. I believe this paper provides us with an exemplar of what sociological theory should look like. Clear assumptions leading deductively to interesting and testable conclusions.

But such explicit modelling of this sort, based in this case upon a subjective expected utility framework, is only the pinnacle of rational action analysis, and it should not be concluded that all applications need to be as tightly constructed as this. Many of the examples of rational choice/action theorizing which follow are conceptually really quite far from this approach. Indeed, though I could have filled the following pages with examples of this nature I have resisted the temptation by including a spectrum of papers exhibiting the breadth of the approach. They vary from the substantive to the philosophical, from the experimental to the historical, from the micro to the macro, and exhibit a marked variation in technical complexity.

It is perhaps useful to record here that rational action models are sometimes going to fail. It would be absurd to maintain their exclusive legitimacy; they will occasionally be found not to account for the known facts and are, thus, open to refutation. This is one of their undoubted strengths. Although it is ultimately an empirical matter as to the explanatory scope of rational action models, it is my impression that a vast proportion of human interaction will prove in one form or another to be open to analysis by them. Such models, except in the face of very strong contrary evidence, should always be the natural first resort for the aspiring social theorist. This is partly because even in default they offer us some help in understanding what is going on. To see how consequences don't follow from rationally (or reasoned) actions/interactions is to invite an explanation which takes this failure as a starting point. It is in this sense that rationality, as a normative theory, has a privileged claim to our attention.

A rational action framework can all too easily be stymied at the outset by imposing upon it either a far too restrictive or a too liberal picture of what it entails. This is not the place to enter into the technical niceties, as these have been debated repeatedly elsewhere (Luce and Raiffa, 1957) and much of the finesse in these debates is not likely to have an appreciable impact upon how we begin to construct genuine deductive sociological theories. Perhaps the best way to get an initial grip on what matters is to set out a very general framework for theory construction under the aegis of rational action/choice precepts. It would take the following from when designed to explain a specified outcome (which may be rather simple or a highly complex set of events):

(i) Assume the actors who are responsible for generating the outcome (which may not be intended but only a consequence of what is intentionally brought about) to be rationally *self-interested* in a transparent manner given their (exogenous) *objective resources* and (exogenous) *preferences/utilities*.

(ii) Model the structure of the actors *interdependencies* in the sense that the *outcome* depends *jointly* upon what each does. Thus each actor has to take account of what others do (will do, are likely to do and, if appropriate, have done in the past). Such modelling will usually define a feasible set of actions for each actor (i.e. their possibility sets).

(iii) In the light of (i) and (ii), determine the courses of action each actor will (rationally) pursue. If these are not unique then specify their ranges of actions (e.g. multiple equilibria).

(iv) Thus, predict the outcome(s) and test these against descriptions of the outcomes one wishes to explain. Of course, if the model possesses no unique outcome then all one can require is that the event in question is amongst the set of possible outcomes predicted by the model.

(v) If this simple model fails, construct further models which might involve one or more of the following possibilities:
   (a) relax the assumption of self-interest, introducing richer utility/preference functions (e.g., altruism, malice, indifference, envy, etc.);
   (b) relax the assumption of objectively calculated resources introducing subjective beliefs about resources;
   (c) relax the assumption of an objectively calculated set of feasible actions, introducing subjective beliefs about what is feasible.
   (d) recompute the structure of interdependencies.

When either (a), (b) or (c) are seen to hold then this will inevitably prompt a further question as to why this should be so. Answers to these questions might also be couched in terms of rational action precepts. But as I intimated above, theory building of this sort is for the future.

It is only if this very general framework fails to provide the answers we seek that we should then reach for an alternative theoretical framework. Some may well feel, though, a framework as flexible as this loses much of its value. After all, if we are willing to entertain a 'utility/preference function' containing any suitably selected argument, is this not in practice tantamount to entertaining a tautology? Will we not always, *post hoc*, be able to find some motive/preference which will fit the case? There would be some considerable merit in this line of reasoning if the precepts of rational action theory were to be used in isolation to predict (retrodict) individual actions. When, however, these are conjoined with those describing the structure of actors' interdependencies (interactions) then the argument loses much of its force. *The distinctive contribution of sociological theory is, in practice, to model these structures.* If each of us responded in isolation (i.e., without calculating what others will do) to a parametric environment, then there would be little necessity for sociological theories which attempt to link human actions to realised events: though there would still be a need to theorise about the genesis of preferences, values and beliefs, etc.

Foundations

The selected papers in this volume are categorized under three headings. The first, *Foundations*, contains six papers which, I hope, give some impression of the intellectual roots of modern approaches to rational action and exchange in sociological theory.

Homans (1958) – 'Social Behavior as Exchange' – was written "to honor the memory of Georg Simmel", surely in many ways the founder of exchange and rational choice theory in sociology. Homans aspires to clarify the relationships amongst four bodies of theory: "behavioural psychology, economics, propositions about the dynamics of influence, and propositions about the structure of small groups." He explicitly adopts an exchange perspective, and grounds his psychology on Skinnerian operant conditioning. This latter aspect will not bring him many friends in sociology, but much of what he has to say does not depend crucially upon this particular grounding. The paper brings out both the salient features of the exchange perspective and Homans insistence upon 'social approval' as a near universal human motive. It introduces the ideas of benefits and costs of alternative courses of action and declining marginal effects, along with a conception of balance or equilibrium in an exchange. From the standpoint of the general framework outlined above the key idea arises when Homans writes: ". . . not only does he (i.e. any actor) seek a maximum himself (in exchange) but tries to see to it that no one in the group makes more profit than he does". I doubt if this is anywhere near universally correct, but it does capture well what I have termed the structure of interdependence between actors. Here, actors not only keep an eye on bilateral rates of exchange (if indeed they can exert control at all, they may face a market situation where the rates of exchange are, in effect, parameters), but also what implication their exchange might have elsewhere in the 'group'. Consequently, we would encounter very complex patterns of strategic calculation – though Homans does not pursue them in his paper. Nevertheless, it is precisely this sort of structure which provides an analytical challenge for the social theorist.

Emerson's 'Power-Dependence Relations', published four years later than Homan's paper, takes up the theme of balance in reciprocal power relations. Though the details of his treatment of the concepts have subsequently attracted much critical comment, the paper remains a classic in the field. Like Homans, Emerson seeks to integrate a large body of research into a unified model with deductive properties. He equates the power of A over B with the extent to which B is dependent upon A in pursuit of his/her valued goals (taken as exogenous). A situation is 'balanced' when A and B are equivalently dependent, and 'imbalanced' otherwise. Emerson's treatment of the strategies for reducing imbalance are at the core of his thinking, and raise a number of issues which have subsequently come to dominate exchange theory. He constructs a picture of power relations which is essentially sociological in the sense that the power balance between A and B is not usually isolated but embedded in a potential *network* of such relations. This observation, as Emerson shows, provides a simple entré to coalition formation which in a more elaborated formulation has become a central issue in rational action theory. Though Emerson does not place his analyses in a game-theoretic framework it is clear that it invites such a placement. If, for instance, A is disproportionately dependent upon B in a network where other dependencies can be established, but at a cost, then the bargaining inherent in such a system is manifest. Here, once again, we have a structure of interdependence which lies at the centre of our earlier formulated framework.

The next two papers, both by Harsanyi ('Measurement of Social Power, Opportunity Costs, and the Theory of Two Person Bargaining Game', and 'Measurement of Social Power in *n*-Person Reciprocal Power Situations') move us directly into game-theoretic formulations in a way that complements and extends Emerson's work. Although both of these papers are more technically demanding than many of the others in this volume, they reward close reading, and the mathematics involved is reasonably straightforward. I have included both of them, first, because they interrelate, second, because they set standards of clarity in exposition which are rare in more traditional sociological writings in this area, and, third, because they introduce some central ideas of game-theory. One of the unfortunate features of contemporary sociology is the way in which the technical writings on the concept of power (and its close cognates) have had little or no impact upon mainstream writings. For example, in an otherwise exemplary essay Lukes (*Power a Radical View*, 1974) fails even to mention the work of Harsanyi.

The contribution I have chosen by Olson, which follows, may well strike some as a rather odd selection ('Economics, Sociology, and the Best of all Possible Worlds'). It was made for two reasons: first, Olson must be represented because his book *The Logic of Collective Action* (1965) has proven to be one of the most seminal works in sociological theory in recent times, and its imprint will be evident in many of the subsequent papers in this volume; second, because in the paper I have chosen, Olson raises the whole issue concerning the appropriateness of 'economic perspectives', which are closely allied to rational action theory, in sociological theorizing. Furthermore, he puts the Hobbsian problem of social order in a rather novel light and, in so doing, provides an elementary introduction to the distinction between private and public goods. A distinction which has become central to the theory of collective action in both the Marxist and non-Marxist traditions.

Peter Blau published his influential work *Exchange and Power in Social Life* in 1964. It is now regarded as a minor classic of its genre, and certainly served to put the exchange version of rational action theory on the map. I have chosen, however, to introduce Blau's work through the critical eyes of Anthony Heath ('Economic Theory and Sociology: a Critique') a then young economist who, though impressed with Blau's contribution, is critical of much of his technical detail. What Heath so effectively demonstrates is how careful we have to be when trying to incorporate ideas from other disciplines into our own. Blau, as Heath so ably shows, makes a number of elementary mistakes, and though they do not invalidate all of the sociologist's conclusions, they do give cause for concern. Heath raises a number of perennial problems, amongst which those of measurement and aggregation are prominent. What I think is important in Heath's paper, along with his painstaking reconstruction of Blau's basic exchange framework, is his rejection of Blau's assumptions that, first, people behave 'atomistically' and, second, as a consequence, 'group' action can be understood by mere aggregation. In this sense, Blau's framework is a step back from Homans and Emerson. As

I suggested above, it is largely because this atomistic assumption is false that we need the helping hand of sociological theory.

Hardin's paper takes up the issue of collective (i.e., group) action directly. 'Collective Action as an Agreeable *n*-Prisoners' Dilemma' is prompted by Olson's earlier referred to book. It is important because it brings out the connections between the Prisoners' Dilemma game, the problem of public goods and collective action. This is perhaps one of the most fruitful connections to have been made in sociological theory in recent decades, the ramifications of which are many but have, for example, inspired much neo-Marxist writing (e.g., see Elster below).

Theoretical Critique and Development

James Coleman's 'Social Theory, Social Research and a Theory of Action' hardly mentions rational action theory at all, but constitutes a sustained plea for the incorporation of what he terms 'purposive action' into sociological theorizing. He laments the fact that Parsons failed in this respect in his post-1937 writings. It fits into the present volume for a number of reasons. First, it provides a very general approach to types of explanation (macro to micro, micro to micro and macro to macro) which is entirely in accord with the framework I tried to promote earlier, and which has subsequently guided Coleman's work on the rational action foundations of social theory (*Foundations of Social Theory*, 1990). Second, it sketches the variety of ways in which we might begin to conceive of the strategic structuring of individual actions. Third, it begins to address the problem of the generation of normative systems within the framework of rational action theory.

The following paper by Williams and Findlay is a critical one ('A Reconsideration of the Rationality Postulate: Right Hemisphere Thinking in Economics'). Grounding their argument in the well established distinction between the cognitive properties of the right and left hemispheres of the brain, they regard assumptions of rational maximization, in either a restrictive and more general form (e.g., Simon's bounded rationality) as unwarrantable in accounting for most of human affairs. Whilst one might find it difficult to agree with all of the authors strictures, the paper is useful in that it takes us towards a psychologist's perspective on these matters, and it may turn out that 'right hemisphere' thinking is an important ingredient in determination (shaping) of preferences on utilities (i.e., their theoretical endogenization). It is too early to be certain about this, but those of us who advocate an emphasis upon reasoned action and belief at the foundation of social theory must be prepared to address the issues which Williams and Findlay raise.

John Elster has over the last decade established a deservedly enviable reputation as an exponent of rational action theory in the social sciences, often with a Marxian flavour. Of the many insightful papers he has published in this period I have chosen for inclusion here his 'Marxism, Functionalism, and Game Theory'. It has the great merit of raising, in a very accessible manner, many of the issues he has written upon more extensively elsewhere (e.g., functionalism and methodological individualism). He also takes issue with Cohen's functionalist interpretation of Marx's theory of historical materialism. I have, therefore, also included Cohen's response to Elster. This, though brief, sets forth the substance of Cohen's elaborate treatment of the theory (*Karl Marx's Theory of History*, 1978). John Reomer also commented upon Elster, and I have included his contribution to the debate – 'Methodological Individualism and Deductive Marxism'. Although also brief, the paper makes a strong plea for a game-theoretic approach to class theory. A plea which has had some considerable impact upon sociology, if not in a very technical sense, at least in a descriptive sense through the work of E.O. Wright (*Classes*, 1985). I hope the inclusion of this and a subsequent piece by Reomer (see below) will encourage the reader who is not to become acquainted with Roemer's book (*A General Theory of Exploration and Class*, 1982). It is surely a modern classic in the tradition of rational action theory.

The paper by Friedman and Hechter ('The Contribution of Rational Choice Theory to Macrosociological Research') takes us away from the sometimes arcane world of Marxist sociology. They set out what they term a 'skeletal model' of rational choice, involving the impact of preferences, opportunity costs and institutional constraints upon 'social outcomes'. The model is illustrated by reference to a large number of empirical studies which provides the main reasons for the inclusion of the paper in this volume. Anybody wishing to assess the worth of the general approach would not go far wrong by following up the leads which these authors provide. The paper is also salutory in reminding us, in the closing section, about the limitations of rational choice theory. The authors speak of 'fiddling with the behavioural assumptions of rational choice theory'. This is precisely what Kahneman and Tversky ask us to do.

Kahneman and Tversky's 'Choices, Values, and Frames' introduces in an easily assimable form the essentials of their celebrated 'prospect theory'. Rational choice theorists had, until the advent of Kahneman and Tversky's work, accepted the standard precepts of subjective utility theory when analysing decisions under risk. The importance of prospect theory is that it shows that a number of the assumptions of this theory do not provide an adequate description of real world behaviour. The precepts of prospect theory will, as a consequence, often provide a better starting point for the sociological model builder, and also widen the purview of rational action theory. The paper included here provides the bare bones of Kahneman and Tversky's theories. The interested reader will have to progress to their more technical expositions referred to at the end of their paper.

Margolis ('A New Model of Rational Choice'), though an economist, raises a fundamental sociological issue: how can situations where individuals show a commitment to collectives (e.g., organizational or group altruism) of one sort or another, best be modelled? He constructs his analysis in a way that offers a potential solution to the 'public goods' (collective action) problem we have already encountered in earlier papers. Whether or not Margolis' allocation rules will prove useful in accounting for all situations where group commitments arise, only research will show. But what is important is the manner in which he systematically models conflicting motives (of S. and G. Smith), and is able to engage with some of the perennial problems of collective action. With Kahneman and Tversky, Margolis extends the reach of rational action theory. Again, readers wishing to take things further can consult Margolis' book (*Selfishness, Altruism and Rationality: a theory of social choice*, 1982). Stinchcome, 'Reason and Rationality' makes a case for the distinction in his title – reasoned action is a broader category than rational action.

The final paper in this section is by myself ('The Many Faces of Power and Liberty'). I have included it because whilst placing the analysis of power within a rational action framework where preferences are exogenous it opens up the line of attack whereby they may be made endogenous. The paper also introduces the important philosophical contribution of G.H. Von-Wright, who insists that the practical-syllogism plays a role in the social sciences which parallels that of the covering-law or hypothetico-deductive model in the natural sciences (Von Wright, 1972).

Applications: Theoretical and Empirical

In the third section of the volume I have selected papers which, in one way or another, evidence the analytical power of the rational action framework.

The section opens with a paper by Kosaka ('A Model of Relative Deprivation'). Building upon an earlier paper by Raymond Boudon, Kosaka constructs a model which has all the hallmarks of the general framework being promoted in this volume. Clear axioms, a structure of actor interdependence, and outcomes which may be tested against experience. The most interesting feature of the model is the deduction of the often noted relationship of increased relative deprivation with increased mobility.

Axelrod and Hamilton ('The Evolution of Cooperation') bring us back to the prisoner's dilemma, public goods and collective action. In a beautifully crafted paper the authors show us how co-operation between rational agents can emerge as an evolutionary stable strategy when there are opportunities for repeated interactions between the agents. Axelrod's subsequent book (*The Evolution of Co-operation*, 1984), developing this theme further, has gained much critical approval. Both the paper included here and the book are witness to the power of rational action theory in coming to grips with a series of classic problems about social order.

Carling ('Exploitation, Extortion and Oppression') takes up a 'rational choice' approach to the interrelationship between the closely allied concepts he introduces in his title. Along with Roemer, Cohen and Elster, authors we have already encountered, are sources of inspiration.

The following and final papers come from a rather different intellectual tradition. Marwell and Ames ('Economists Free Ride, Does Anyone Else?') report upon a series of experiments to test the free-rider hypothesis in the provision of collective goods. I have included this paper partly because it illustrates the use of experimental techniques in this area, but also because it shows how assumptions about free-riding may well have to be treated with some considerable caution. Oliver and Marwell ('The Paradox of Group Size in Collective Action: a Theory of the Critical Mass II') take up a related issue, namely Olson's theoretical derivation that free-riding increases with group size and, thus, large groups face greater problems in procuring collective goods. These authors take issue with the generalizability of this conclusion. If the costs of a collective good rise with the number who benefit, then Olson's conclusion is correct. If, however, costs do not vary with size, then the converse is true. This simple observation enables Oliver and Marwell to account for a number of empirical findings (e.g., size of riots) which appear to conflict with Olson's theory. Here we have a very good example of theoretical elaboration whence a powerful general theory (Olson's) is refined to account for diversity in the empirical world.

Heckathorn ('Collective Sanctions and the Creation of Prisoners' Dilemma Norms') addresses a further issue in connection with collective action. Externally imposed collective sanctions (as opposed to individually focused sanctions) can lead to the emergence of norms amongst those subject to the sanctions which enforce the mandate of the external agent.

However, such sanctions can mobilize individuals against the agent. It appears from Heckathorn's analysis that the likely response is sensitive to group size and prior cohesion.

The final paper ('A Theory of Ethnic Collective Action') by Hechter, Friedman and Appelbaum demonstrates the analytical power of rational action theory in accounting for the frequency of ethnic collective action. It is particularly instructive to follow the confrontation they offer between 'structural' and 'rational choice' theory. By incorporating organizational variables (surrounding resource mobilization) they are, in their analytic endeavours, conforming to the general framework which I tried to promote in the opening section of this introduction. The organization of actions implies strategic (i.e., actor interdependent) calculation, and this is what sociological theory should be about.

Conclusion and Invitation

It has not proved easy to select the papers included in this volume. I could rather easily have arrived at a very different selection indeed. For instance, it would have been possible to slant the selection in a more substantive or a more technical direction, or I could have given it a more philosophical appearance. There is a wealth of material in the literature which would have enabled me to take any one of these tacks – particularly the philosophical one. Furthermore, I could have multiplied the length of this introduction by entering into a critical assessment of each of the papers included. I have not attempted this, not because I am persuaded by everything my selected authors have to say – that certainly would be far from the truth. Rather, I feel criticism should take place whilst one is attempting to actually use, extend or reject the ideas and models presented. Since I believe that the art of sociological theory building will always involve making rather drastic conceptual simplifications and compromises, I find debates about the right- or wrong-headedness of a particular model or approach *in abstracto* somewhat of an irrelevance. This accounts for the absense of selections from the 'philosophical' literature on matters of rational action and choice. Moreover, this literature has been anthologized very effectively elsewhere (e.g., Hollis and Lukes, 1982).

References

R. Axelrod (1984), *The Evolution of Co-operation*, New York, Basic.

P. Blau (1964), *Exchange and Power in Social Life*, New York, Wiley.

R. Boudon (1981), *The Logic of Social Action: an introduction to sociological analysis*, Boston, Routledge and Kegan Paul.

G.R. Cohen (1978), *Karl Marx's Theory of History: a defence*, Oxford, Oxford University Press.

J.S. Coleman (1990), *Foundations of Social Theory*, Cambridge, MA, Harvard University Press.

K.S. Cook (1987), *Social Exchange Theory*, Newbury Park, CA, Sage.

J. Elster (1985), *Making Sense of Marx*, Cambridge, Cambridge University Press.

R.M. Emerson (1987), 'Toward a Theory of Value in Social Exchange' in: K.S. Cook *op.cit.*

T.J. Fararo (1989), *The Meaning of General Sociological Theory*, Cambridge, Cambridge University Press.

M. Hollis and S. Lukes (eds.), (1982), *Rationality and Relativism*, Oxford, Blackwell.

G. Homans (1958), 'Social Behaviour as Exchange', *American Journal of Sociology*, **65**, 597–606.

K. Kosaka (1985), 'A Model of Relative Deprivation', *Journal of Mathematical Sociology*, **12**(1), **35**(1), 35–48.

R.D. Luce and H. Raiffa (1957), *Games and Decisions*, New York, Wiley.

S. Lukes (1974), *Power: A radical view*, London, Macmillan.

H. Margolis (1982), *Selfishness, Altruism and Rationality: a theory of social choice*, Cambridge, Cambridge University Press.

M. Olson (1965), *The Logic of Collective Action*, Cambridge, MA, Harvard University Press.

T. Parsons (1937), *The Structure of Social Action*, New York, McGraw-Hill.

J. Roemer (1982), *A General Theory of Exploitation and Class*, Cambridge, MA, Harvard University Press.

G.H. von Wright (1972), 'On So-Called Practical Inference', *Acta Sociologica*, **15**, 39–53.

E.O. Wright (1988), *Classes*, London, Verso.

Part I
Foundations

[1]

SOCIAL BEHAVIOR AS EXCHANGE

GEORGE C. HOMANS

ABSTRACT

To consider social behavior as an exchange of goods may clarify the relations among four bodies of theory: behavioral psychology, economics, propositions about the dynamics of influence, and propositions about the structure of small groups.

THE PROBLEMS OF SMALL-GROUP RESEARCH

This essay will hope to honor the memory of Georg Simmel in two different ways. So far as it pretends to be suggestive rather than conclusive, its tone will be Simmel's; and its subject, too, will be one of his. Because Simmel, in essays such as those on sociability, games, coquetry, and conversation, was an analyst of elementary social behavior, we call him an ancestor of what is known today as small-group research. For what we are really studying in small groups is elementary social behavior: what happens when two or three persons are in a position to influence one another, the sort of thing of which those massive structures called "classes," "firms," "communities," and "societies" must ultimately be composed.

As I survey small-group research today, I feel that, apart from just keeping on with it, three sorts of things need to be done. The first is to show the relation between the results of experimental work done under laboratory conditions and the results of *quasi-* anthropological field research on what those of us who do it are pleased to call "real-life" groups in industry and elsewhere. If the experimental work has anything to do with real life—and I am persuaded that it has everything to do—its propositions cannot be inconsistent with those discovered through the field work. But the consistency has not yet been demonstrated in any systematic way.

The second job is to pull together in some set of general propositions the actual results, from the laboratory and from the field, of work on small groups—propositions that at least sum up, to an approximation,

what happens in elementary social behavior, even though we may not be able to explain why the propositions should take the form they do. A great amount of work has been done, and more appears every day, but what it all amounts to in the shape of a set of propositions from which, under specified conditions, many of the observational results might be derived, is not at all clear—and yet to state such a set is the first aim of science.

The third job is to begin to show how the propositions that empirically hold good in small groups may be derived from some set of still more general propositions. "Still more general" means only that empirical propositions other than ours may also be derived from the set. This derivation would constitute the explanatory stage in the science of elementary social behavior, for explanation *is* derivation.[1] (I myself suspect that the more general set will turn out to contain the propositions of behavioral psychology. I hold myself to be an "ultimate psychological reductionist," but I cannot know that I am right so long as the reduction has not been carried out.)

I have come to think that all three of these jobs would be furthered by our adopting the view that interaction between persons is an exchange of goods, material and non-material. This is one of the oldest theories of social behavior, and one that we still use every day to interpret our own behavior, as when we say, "I found so-and-so rewarding"; or "I got a great deal out of him"; or, even, "Talking with him took a great deal out of me." But, perhaps just be-

[1] See R. B. Braithwaite, *Scientific Explanation* (Cambridge: Cambridge University Press, 1953).

597

cause it is so obvious, this view has been much neglected by social scientists. So far as I know, the only theoretical work that makes explicit use of it is Marcel Mauss's *Essai sur le don*, published in 1925, which is ancient as social science goes.[2] It may be that the tradition of neglect is now changing and that, for instance, the psychologists who interpret behavior in terms of transactions may be coming back to something of the sort I have in mind.[3]

An incidental advantage of an exchange theory is that it might bring sociology closer to economics—that science of man most advanced, most capable of application, and, intellectually, most isolated. Economics studies exchange carried out under special circumstances and with a most useful built-in numerical measure of value. What are the laws of the general phenomenon of which economic behavior is one class?

In what follows I shall suggest some reasons for the usefulness of a theory of social behavior as exchange and suggest the nature of the propositions such a theory might contain.

AN EXCHANGE PARADIGM

I start with the link to behavioral psychology and the kind of statement it makes about the behavior of an experimental animal such as the pigeon.[4] As a pigeon explores its cage in the laboratory, it happens to peck a target, whereupon the psychologist feeds it corn. The evidence is that it will peck the target again; it has learned the behavior, or, as my friend Skinner says, the behavior has been reinforced, and the pigeon has undergone *operant conditioning*. This kind of psychologist is not interested in how the behavior was learned: "learning theory" is a poor name for his field. Instead,

[2] Translated by I. Cunnison as *The Gift* (Glencoe, Ill.: Free Press, 1954).

[3] In social anthropology D. L. Oliver is working along these lines, and I owe much to him. See also T. M. Newcomb, "The Prediction of Interpersonal Attraction," *American Psychologist*, XI (1956), 575–86.

[4] B. F. Skinner, *Science and Human Behavior* (New York: Macmillan Co., 1953).

he is interested in what determines changes in the rate of emission of learned behavior, whether pecks at a target or something else.

The more hungry the pigeon, the less corn or other food it has gotten in the recent past, the more often it will peck. By the same token, if the behavior is often reinforced, if the pigeon is given much corn every time it pecks, the rate of emission will fall off as the pigeon gets *satiated*. If, on the other hand, the behavior is not reinforced at all, then, too, its rate of emission will tend to fall off, though a long time may pass before it stops altogether, before it is *extinguished*. In the emission of many kinds of behavior the pigeon incurs *aversive stimulation*, or what I shall call "cost" for short, and this, too, will lead in time to a decrease in the emission rate. Fatigue is an example of a "cost." Extinction, satiation, and cost, by decreasing the rate of emission of a particular kind of behavior, render more probable the emission of some other kind of behavior, including doing nothing. I shall only add that even a hard-boiled psychologist puts "emotional" behavior, as well as such things as pecking, among the unconditioned responses that may be reinforced in operant conditioning. As a statement of the propositions of behavioral psychology, the foregoing is, of course, inadequate for any purpose except my present one.

We may look on the pigeon as engaged in an exchange—pecks for corn—with the psychologist, but let us not dwell upon that, for the behavior of the pigeon hardly determines the behavior of the psychologist at all. Let us turn to a situation where the exchange is real, that is, where the determination is mutual. Suppose we are dealing with two men. Each is emitting behavior reinforced to some degree by the behavior of the other. How it was in the past that each learned the behavior he emits and how he learned to find the other's behavior reinforcing we are not concerned with. It is enough that each does find the other's behavior reinforcing, and I shall call the reinforcers—the equivalent of the pigeon's corn—*values*, for this, I think, is what we

SOCIAL BEHAVIOR AS EXCHANGE 599

mean by this term. As he emits behavior, each man may incur costs, and each man has more than one course of behavior open to him.

This seems to me the paradigm of elementary social behavior, and the problem of the elementary sociologist is to state propositions relating the variations in the values and costs of each man to his frequency distribution of behavior among alternatives, where the values (in the mathematical sense) taken by these variable for one man determine in part their values for the other.[5]

I see no reason to believe that the propositions of behavioral psychology do not apply to this situation, though the complexity of their implications in the concrete case may be great indeed. In particular, we must suppose that, with men as with pigeons, an increase in extinction, satiation, or aversive stimulation of any one kind of behavior will increase the probability of emission of some other kind. The problem is not, as it is often stated, merely, what a man's values are, what he has learned in the past to find reinforcing, but how much of any one value his behavior is getting him now. The more he gets, the less valuable any further unit of that value is to him, and the less often he will emit behavior reinforced by it.

THE INFLUENCE PROCESS

We do not, I think, possess the kind of studies of two-person interaction that would either bear out these propositions or fail to do so. But we do have studies of larger numbers of persons that suggest that they may apply, notably the studies by Festinger, Schachter, Back, and their associates on the dynamics of influence. One of the variables they work with they call *cohesiveness,* defined as anything that attracts people to take part in a group. Cohesiveness is a value variable; it refers to the degree of reinforcement people find in the ac-

tivities of the group. Festinger and his colleagues consider two kinds of reinforcing activity: the symbolic behavior we call "social approval" (sentiment) and activity valuable in other ways, such as doing something interesting.

The other variable they work with they call *communication* and others call *interaction.* This is a frequency variable; it is a measure of the frequency of emission of valuable and costly verbal behavior. We must bear in mind that, in general, the one kind of variable is a function of the other.

Festinger and his co-workers show that the more cohesive a group is, that is, the more valuable the sentiment or activity the members exchange with one another, the greater the average frequency of interaction of the members.[6] With men, as with pigeons, the greater the reinforcement, the more often is the reinforced behavior emitted. The more cohesive a group, too, the greater the change that members can produce in the behavior of other members in the direction of rendering these activities more valuable.[7] That is, the more valuable the activities that members get, the more valuable those that they must give. For if a person is emitting behavior of a certain kind, and other people do not find it particularly rewarding, these others will suffer their own production of sentiment and activity, in time, to fall off. But perhaps the first person has found their sentiment and activity rewarding, and, if he is to keep on getting them, he must make his own behavior more valuable to the others. In short, the propositions of behavioral psychology imply a tendency toward a certain proportionality between the value to others of the behavior a man gives them

[5] *Ibid.,* pp. 297–329. The discussion of "double contingency" by T. Parsons and E. A. Shils could easily lead to a similar paradigm (see *Toward a General Theory of Action* [Cambridge, Mass.: Harvard University Press, 1951], pp. 14–16).

[6] K. W. Back, "The Exertion of Influence through Social Communication," in L. Festinger, K. Back, S. Schachter, H. H. Kelley, and J. Thibaut (eds.), *Theory and Experiment in Social Communication* (Ann Arbor: Research Center for Dynamics, University of Michigan, 1950), pp. 21–36.

[7] S. Schachter, N. Ellertson, D. McBride, and D. Gregory, "An Experimental Study of Cohesiveness and Productivity," *Human Relations,* IV (1951), 229–38.

and the value to him of the behavior they give him.[8]

Schachter also studied the behavior of members of a group toward two kinds of other members, "conformers" and "deviates."[9] I assume that conformers are people whose activity the other members find valuable. For conformity is behavior that coincides to a degree with some group standard or norm, and the only meaning I can assign to *norm* is "a verbal description of behavior that many members find it valuable for the actual behavior of themselves and others to conform to." By the same token, a deviate is a member whose behavior is not particularly valuable. Now Schachter shows that, as the members of a group come to see another member as a deviate, their interaction with him—communication addressed to getting him to change his behavior—goes up, the faster the more cohesive the group. The members need not talk to the other conformers so much; they are relatively satiated by the conformers' behavior: they have gotten what they want out of them. But if the deviate, by failing to change his behavior, fails to reinforce the members, they start to withhold social approval from him: the deviate gets low sociometric choice at the end of the experiment. And in the most cohesive groups—those Schachter calls "high cohesive-relevant"—interaction with the deviate also falls off in the end and is lowest among those members that rejected him most strongly, as if they had given him up as a bad job. But how plonking can we get? These findings are utterly in line with everyday experience.

PRACTICAL EQUILIBRIUM

At the beginning of this paper I suggested that one of the tasks of small-group research was to show the relation between the results of experimental work done under laboratory conditions and the results of field research on real-life small groups. Now the

latter often appear to be in practical equilibrium, and by this I mean nothing fancy. I do not mean that all real-life groups are in equilibrium. I certainly do not mean that all groups must tend to equilibrium. I do not mean that groups have built-in antidotes to change: there is no homeostasis here. I do not mean that we assume equilibrium. I mean only that we sometimes *observe* it, that for the time we are with a group—and it is often short—there is no great change in the values of the variables we choose to measure. If, for instance, person A is interacting with B more than with C both at the beginning and at the end of the study, then at least by this crude measure the group is in equilibrium.

Many of the Festinger-Schachter studies are experimental, and their propositions about the process of influence seem to me to imply the kind of proposition that empirically holds good of real-life groups in practical equilibrium. For instance, Festinger *et al.* find that, the more cohesive a group is, the greater the change that members can produce in the behavior of other members. If the influence is exerted in the direction of conformity to group norms, then, when the process of influence has accomplished all the change of which it is capable, the proposition should hold good that, the more cohesive a group is, the larger the number of members that conform to its norms. And it does hold good.[10]

Again, Schachter found, in the experiment I summarized above, that in the most cohesive groups and at the end, when the effort to influence the deviate had failed, members interacted little with the deviate and gave him little in the way of sociometric choice. Now two of the propositions that hold good most often of real-life groups in practical equilibrium are precisely that the more closely a member's activity conforms to the norms the more interaction he receives from other members and the more liking choices he gets from them too. From

[8] Skinner, *op. cit.*, p. 100.

[9] S. Schachter, "Deviation, Rejection, and Communication," *Journal of Abnormal and Social Psychology*, XLVI (1951), 190-207.

[10] L. Festinger, S. Schachter, and K. Back, *Social Pressures in Informal Groups* (New York: Harper & Bros., 1950), pp. 72-100.

SOCIAL BEHAVIOR AS EXCHANGE 601

these main propositions a number of others may be derived that also hold good.[11]

Yet we must ever remember that the truth of the proposition linking conformity to liking may on occasion be masked by the truth of other propositions. If, for instance, the man that conforms to the norms most closely also exerts some authority over the group, this may render liking for him somewhat less than it might otherwise have been.[12]

Be that as it may, I suggest that the laboratory experiments on influence imply propositions about the behavior of members of small groups, when the process of influence has worked itself out, that are identical with propositions that hold good of real-life groups in equilibrium. This is hardly surprising if all we mean by equilibrium is that all the change of which the system is, under present conditions, capable has been effected, so that no further change occurs. Nor would this be the first time that statics has turned out to be a special case of dynamics.

PROFIT AND SOCIAL CONTROL

Though I have treated equilibrium as an observed fact, it is a fact that cries for explanation. I shall not, as structural-functional sociologists do, use an assumed equilibrium as a means of explaining, or trying to explain, why the other features of a social system should be what they are. Rather, I shall take practical equilibrium as something that is itself to be explained by the other features of the system.

If every member of a group emits at the end of, and during, a period of time much the same kinds of behavior and in much the same frequencies as he did at the beginning, the group is for that period in equilibrium. Let us then ask why any one member's behavior should persist. Suppose he is emitting behavior of value A_1. Why does he not let his behavior get worse (less valuable or reinforcing to the others) until it stands at $A_1 - \Delta A$? True, the sentiments expressed by others toward him are apt to decline in value (become less reinforcing to him), so that what he gets from them may be $S_1 - \Delta S$. But it is conceivable that, since most activity carries cost, a decline in the value of what he emits will mean a reduction in cost to him that more than offsets his losses in sentiment. Where, then, does he stabilize his behavior? This is the problem of social control.[13]

Mankind has always assumed that a person stabilizes his behavior, at least in the short run, at the point where he is doing the best he can for himself under the circumstances, though his best may not be a "rational" best, and what he can do may not be at all easy to specify, except that he is not apt to think like one of the theoretical antagonists in the *Theory of Games*. Before a sociologist rejects this answer out of hand for its horrid profit-seeking implications, he will do well to ask himself if he can offer any other answer to the question posed. I think he will find that he cannot. Yet experiments designed to test the truth of the answer are extraordinarily rare.

I shall review one that seems to me to provide a little support for the theory, though it·was not meant to do so. The experiment is reported by H. B. Gerard, a member of the Festinger-Schachter team, under the title "The Anchorage of Opinions in Face-to-Face Groups."[14] The experimenter formed artificial groups whose members met to discuss a case in industrial relations and to express their opinions about its probable outcome. The groups were of two kinds: high-attraction groups, whose members were told that they would like one another very much, and low-attraction groups, whose

[11] For propositions holding good of groups in practical equilibrium see G. C. Homans, *The Human Group* (New York: Harcourt, Brace & Co., 1950), and H. W. Riecken and G. C. Homans, "Psychological Aspects of Social Structure," in G. Lindzey (ed.), *Handbook of Social Psychology* (Cambridge, Mass.: Addison-Wesley Publishing Co., 1954), II, 786–832.

[12] See Homans, *op. cit.*, pp. 244–48, and R. F. Bales, "The Equilibrium Problem in Small Groups," in A. P. Hare, E. F. Borgatta, and R. F. Bales (eds.), *Small Groups* (New York: A. A. Knopf, 1953), pp. 450–56.

[13] Homans, *op. cit.*, pp. 281–301.

[14] *Human Relations*, VII (1954), 313–25.

members were told that they would not find one another particularly likable.

At a later time the experimenter called the members in separately, asked them again to express their opinions on the outcome of the case, and counted the number that had changed their opinions to bring them into accord with those of other members of their groups. At the same time, a paid participant entered into a further discussion of the case with each member, always taking, on the probable outcome of the case, a position opposed to that taken by the bulk of the other members of the group to which the person belonged. The

TABLE 1

PERCENTAGE OF SUBJECTS CHANGING TOWARD SOMEONE IN THE GROUP

	Agree-ment	Mild Disagree-ment	Strong Disagree-ment
High attraction....	0	12	44
Low attraction....	0	15	9

TABLE 2

PERCENTAGE OF SUBJECTS CHANGING TOWARD THE PAID PARTICIPANT

	Agree-ment	Mild Disagree-ment	Strong Disagree-ment
High attraction....	7	13	25
Low attraction....	20	38	8

experimenter counted the number of persons shifting toward the opinion of the paid participant.

The experiment had many interesting results, from which I choose only those summed up in Tables 1 and 2. The three different agreement classes are made up of people who, at the original sessions, expressed different degrees of agreement with the opinions of other members of their groups. And the figure 44, for instance, means that, of all members of high-attraction groups whose initial opinions were strongly in disagreement with those of other members, 44 per cent shifted their opinion later toward that of others.

In these results the experimenter seems

to have been interested only in the differences in the sums of the rows, which show that there is more shifting toward the group, and less shifting toward the paid participant, in the high-attraction than in the low-attraction condition. This is in line with a proposition suggested earlier. If you think that the members of a group can give you much—in this case, liking—you are apt to give them much—in this case, a change to an opinion in accordance with their views—or you will not get the liking. And, by the same token, if the group can give you little of value, you will not be ready to give it much of value. Indeed, you may change your opinion so as to depart from agreement even further, to move, that is, toward the view held by the paid participant.

So far so good, but, when I first scanned these tables, I was less struck by the difference between them than by their similarity. The same classes of people in both tables showed much the same relative propensities to change their opinions, no matter whether the change was toward the group or toward the paid participant. We see, for instance, that those who change least are the high-attraction, agreement people and the low-attraction, strong-disagreement ones. And those who change most are the high-attraction, strong-disagreement people and the low-attraction, mild-disagreement ones.

How am I to interpret these particular results? Since the experimenter did not discuss them, I am free to offer my own explanation. The behavior emitted by the subjects is opinion and changes in opinion. For this behavior they have learned to expect two possible kinds of reinforcement. Agreement with the group gets the subject favorable sentiment (acceptance) from it, and the experiment was designed to give this reinforcement a higher value in the high-attraction condition than in the low-attraction one. The second kind of possible reinforcement is what I shall call the "maintenance of one's personal integrity," which a subject gets by sticking to his own opinion in the face of disagreement with the group. The experimenter does not mention this reward, but I cannot

SOCIAL BEHAVIOR AS EXCHANGE 603

make sense of the results without something much like it. In different degrees for different subjects, depending on their initial positions, these rewards are in competition with one another: they are alternatives. They are not absolutely scarce goods, but some persons cannot get both at once.

Since the rewards are alternatives, let me introduce a familiar assumption from economics—that the cost of a particular course of action is the equivalent of the foregone value of an alternative[15]—and then add the definition: Profit = Reward — Cost.

Now consider the persons in the corresponding cells of the two tables. The behavior of the high-attraction, agreement people gets them much in the way of acceptance by the group, and for it they must give up little in the way of personal integrity, for their views are from the start in accord with those of the group. Their profit is high, and they are not prone to change their behavior. The low-attraction, strong-disagreement people are getting much in integrity, and they are not giving up for it much in valuable acceptance, for they are members of low-attraction groups. Reward less cost is high for them, too, and they change little. The high-attraction, strong-disagreement people are getting much in the way of integrity, but their costs in doing so are high, too, for they are in high-attraction groups and thus foregoing much valuable acceptance by the group. Their profit is low, and they are very apt to change, either toward the group or toward the paid participant, from whom they think, perhaps, they will get some acceptance while maintaining some integrity. The low-attraction, mild-disagreement people do not get much in the way of integrity, for they are only in mild disagreement with the group, but neither are they giving up much in acceptance, for they are members of low-attraction groups. Their rewards are low; their costs are low too, and their profit—the difference between the two—is also low. In their low profit they resemble the high-attraction, strong-disagree-

[15] G. J. Stigler, *The Theory of Price* (rev. ed.; New York: Macmillan Co., 1952), p. 99.

ment people, and, like them, they are prone to change their opinions, in this case, more toward the paid participant. The subjects in the other two cells, who have medium profits, display medium propensities to change.

If we define profit as reward less cost, and if cost is value foregone, I suggest that we have here some evidence for the proposition that change in behavior is greatest when perceived profit is least. This constitutes no direct demonstration that change in behavior is least when profit is greatest, but if, whenever a man's behavior brought him a balance of reward and cost, he changed his behavior away from what got him, under the circumstances, the less profit, there might well come a time when his behavior would not change further. That is, his behavior would be stabilized, at least for the time being. And, so far as this were true for every member of a group, the group would have a social organization in equilibrium.

I do not say that a member would stabilize his behavior at the point of greatest conceivable profit to himself, because his profit is partly at the mercy of the behavior of others. It is a commonplace that the short-run pursuit of profit by several persons often lands them in positions where all are worse off than they might conceivably be. I do not say that the paths of behavioral change in which a member pursues his profit under the condition that others are pursuing theirs too are easy to describe or predict; and we can readily conceive that in jockeying for position they might never arrive at any equilibrium at all.

DISTRIBUTIVE JUSTICE

Yet practical equilibrium is often observed, and thus some further condition may make its attainment, under some circumstance, more probable than would the individual pursuit of profit left to itself. I can offer evidence for this further condition only in the behavior of subgroups and not in that of individuals. Suppose that there are two subgroups, working close together in a factory, the job of one being somewhat different from that of the other. And suppose that the members of the first complain and say: "We are getting the same pay as they are. We ought to get just a couple of dollars a week more to show that our work is more responsible." When you ask them what they mean by "more responsible," they say that, if they do their work wrong, more damage can result, and so they are under more pressure to take care.[16] Something like this is a common feature of industrial behavior. It is at the heart of disputes not over absolute wages but over wage differentials—indeed, at the heart of disputes over rewards other than wages.

In what kind of propostion may we express observations like these? We may say that wages and responsibility give status in the group, in the sense that a man who takes high responsibility and gets high wages is admired, other things equal. Then, if the members of one group score higher on responsibility than do the members of another, there is a felt need on the part of the first to score higher on pay too. There is a pressure, which shows itself in complaints, to bring the *status factors*, as I have called them, into line with one another. If they are in line, a condition of *status congruence* is said to exist. In this condition the workers may find their jobs dull or irksome, but they will not complain about the relative position of groups.

But there may be a more illuminating way of looking at the matter. In my example I have considered only responsibility and pay, but these may be enough, for they represent the two kinds of thing that come into the problem. Pay is clearly a reward; responsibility may be looked on, less clearly, as a cost. It means constraint and worry—or peace of mind foregone. Then the proposition about status congruence becomes this: If the costs of the members of one group are higher than those of another, distributive justice requires that their rewards should be higher too. But the thing works both ways: If the rewards are higher, the costs should

be higher too. This last is the theory of *noblesse oblige*, which we all subscribe to, though we all laugh at it, perhaps because the *noblesse* often fails to *oblige*. To put the matter in terms of profit: though the rewards and costs of two persons or the members of two groups may be different, yet the profits of the two—the excess of reward over cost—should tend to equality. And more than "should." The less-advantaged group will at least try to attain greater equality, as, in the example I have used, the first group tried to increase its profit by increasing its pay.

I have talked of distributive justice. Clearly, this is not the only condition determining the actual distribution of rewards and costs. At the same time, never tell me that notions of justice are not a strong influence on behavior, though we sociologists often neglect them. Distributive justice may be one of the conditions of group equilibrium.

EXCHANGE AND SOCIAL STRUCTURE

I shall end by reviewing almost the only study I am aware of that begins to show in detail how a stable and differentiated social structure in a real-life group might arise out of a process of exchange between members. This is Peter Blau's description of the behavior of sixteen agents in a federal law-enforcement agency.[17]

The agents had the duty of investigating firms and preparing reports on the firms' compliance with the law. Since the reports might lead to legal action against the firms, the agents had to prepare them carefully, in the proper form, and take strict account of the many regulations that might apply. The agents were often in doubt what they should do, and then they were supposed to take the question to their supervisor. This they were reluctant to do, for they naturally believed that thus confessing to him their inability to solve a problem would reflect on their competence, affect the official ratings he

[16] G. C. Homans, "Status among Clerical Workers," *Human Organization*, XII (1953), 5–10.

[17] Peter M. Blau, *The Dynamics of Bureaucracy* (Chicago: University of Chicago Press, 1955), 99–116.

made of their work, and so hurt their chances for promotion. So agents often asked other agents for help and advice, and, though this was nominally forbidden, the supervisor usually let it pass.

Blau ascertained the ratings the supervisor made of the agents, and he also asked the agents to rate one another. The two opinions agreed closely. Fewer agents were regarded as highly competent than were regarded as of middle or low competence; competence, or the ability to solve technical problems, was a fairly scarce good. One or two of the more competent agents would not give help and advice when asked, and so received few interactions and little liking. A man that will not exchange, that will not give you what he has when you need it, will not get from you the only thing you are, in this case, able to give him in return, your regard.

But most of the more competent agents were willing to give help, and of them Blau says:

A consultation can be considered an exchange of values: both participants gain something, and both have to pay a price. The questioning agent is enabled to perform better than he could otherwise have done, without exposing his difficulties to his supervisor. By asking for advice, he implicitly pays his respect to the superior proficiency of his colleague. This acknowledgment of inferiority is the cost of receiving assistance. The consultant gains prestige, in return for which he is willing to devote some time to the consultation and permit it to disrupt his own work. The following remark of an agent illustrates this: "I like giving advice. It's flattering, I suppose, if you feel that others come to you for advice.[18]

Blau goes on to say: "All agents liked being consulted, but the value of any one of very many consultations became deflated for experts, and the price they paid in frequent interruptions became inflated."[19] This implies that, the more prestige an agent received, the less was the increment of value of that prestige; the more advice an agent gave, the greater was the increment of cost

of that advice, the cost lying precisely in the foregone value of time to do his own work. Blau suggests that something of the same sort was true of an agent who went to a more competent colleague for advice: the more often he went, the more costly to him, in feelings of inferiority, became any further request. "The repeated admission of his inability to solve his own problems . . . undermined the self-confidence of the worker and his standing in the group."[20]

The result was that the less competent agents went to the more competent ones for help less often than they might have done if the costs of repeated admissions of inferiority had been less high and that, while many agents sought out the few highly competent ones, no single agent sought out the latter much. Had they done so (to look at the exchange from the other side), the costs to the highly competent in interruptions to their own work would have become exorbitant. Yet the need of the less competent for help was still not fully satisfied. Under these circumstances they tended to turn for help to agents more nearly like themselves in competence. Though the help they got was not the most valuable, it was of a kind they could themselves return on occasion. With such agents they could exchange help and liking, without the exchange becoming on either side too great a confession of inferiority.

The highly competent agents tended to enter into exchanges, that is, to interact with many others. But, in the more equal exchanges I have just spoken of, less competent agents tended to pair off as partners. That is, they interacted with a smaller number of people, but interacted often with these few. I think I could show why pair relations in these more equal exchanges would be more economical for an agent than a wider distribution of favors. But perhaps I have gone far enough. The final pattern of this social structure was one in which a small number of highly competent agents exchanged advice for prestige with a large number of others less competent and in which the less

[18] *Ibid.*, p. 108.　　　[19] *Ibid.*, p. 108.　　　[20] *Ibid.*, p. 109.

competent agents exchanged, in pairs and in trios, both help and liking on more nearly equal terms.

Blau shows, then, that a social structure in equilibrium might be the result of a process of exchanging behavior rewarding and costly in different degrees, in which the increment of reward and cost varied with the frequency of the behavior, that is, with the frequency of interaction. Note that the behavior of the agents seems also to have satisfied my second condition of equilibrium: the more competent agents took more responsibility for the work, either their own or others', than did the less competent ones, but they also got more for it in the way of prestige. I suspect that the same kind of explanation could be given for the structure of many "informal" groups.

SUMMARY

The current job of theory in small-group research is to make the connection between experimental and real-life studies, to consolidate the propositions that empirically hold good in the two fields, and to show how these propositions might be derived from a still more general set. One way of doing this job would be to revive and make more rigorous the oldest of theories of social behavior—social behavior as exchange.

Some of the statements of such a theory might be the following. Social behavior is an exchange of goods, material goods but also non-material ones, such as the symbols of approval or prestige. Persons that give much to others try to get much from them, and persons that get much from others are under pressure to give much to them. This process of influence tends to work out at equilibrium to a balance in the exchanges. For a person engaged in exchange, what he gives may be a cost to him, just as what he gets may be a reward, and his behavior changes less as profit, that is, reward less cost, tends to a maximum. Not only does he seek a maximum for himself, but he tries to see to it that no one in his group makes more profit than he does. The cost and the value of what he gives and of what he gets vary with the quantity of what he gives and gets. It is surprising how familiar these propositions are; it is surprising, too, how propositions about the dynamics of exchange can begin to generate the static thing we call "group structure" and, in so doing, generate also some of the propositions about group structure that students of real-life groups have stated.

In our unguarded moments we sociologists find words like "reward" and "cost" slipping into what we say. Human nature will break in upon even our most elaborate theories. But we seldom let it have its way with us and follow up systematically what these words imply.[21] Of all our many "approaches" to social behavior, the one that sees it as an economy is the most neglected, and yet it is the one we use every moment of our lives—except when we write sociology.

HARVARD UNIVERSITY

[21] *The White-Collar Job* (Ann Arbor: Survey Research Center, University of Michigan, 1953), pp. 115–27.

[2]

POWER-DEPENDENCE RELATIONS

RICHARD M. EMERSON

University of Cincinnati

A simple theory of power relations is developed in an effort to resolve some of the ambiguities surrounding "power," "authority," "legitimacy," and power "structures," through bringing them together in a coherent scheme. After defining a reciprocal power-dependence relation, attention is focused upon properties of balance and "balancing operations" in such relations. The theory dictates exactly four generic types of balancing process, and discussion of these leads directly into processes of group formation, including the emergence of group norms, role structure and status hierarchy, all presented as the outcome of balancing tendencies in power relations. Within the framework of this theory, authority appears quite naturally to be legitimized power, vested in roles, and "legitimation" is seen as a special case of the coalition process through which norms and role-prescriptions are formed. Finally, through treating both persons and groups as actors in a power-network (two or more connected power-dependence relations) the door is opened for meaningful analysis of complex power structures. Brief reference is made to findings from two experiments pertaining to hypotheses advanced in this theory.

JUDGING from the frequent occurrence of such words as *power, influence, dominance* and *submission, status* and *authority,* the importance of power is widely recognized, yet considerable confusion exists concerning these concepts.[1] There is an extensive literature pertaining to power, on both theoretical and empirical levels, and in small group [2] as well as large community contexts.[3] Unfortunately, this already large and rapidly growing body of research has not achieved the cumulative character desired. Our *integrated* knowledge of power does not significantly surpass the conceptions left by Max Weber.[4]

This suggests that there is a place at this moment for a systematic treatment of social power. The underdeveloped state of this area is further suggested by what appears, to this author, to be a recurrent flaw in common conceptions of social power; a flaw which helps to block adequate theoretical development as well as meaningful research. That flaw is the implicit treatment of power as though it were an attribute of a person or group ("X is an influential person." "Y is a powerful group," etc.). Given this conception, the natural research question becomes "Who in community X are the power *holders*?". The project then proceeds to rank-order persons by some criterion of power, and this ordering is called the *power-structure*. This is a highly questionable representation of a "structure," based upon a questionable assumption of *generalized power*.[5]

It is commonly observed that some person X dominates Y, while being subservient in relations with Z. Furthermore, these power relations are frequently intransitive! Hence,

---

[1] See the Communications by Jay Butler and Paul Harrison on "On Power and Authority: An Exchange on Concepts," *American Sociological Review,* 25 (October, 1960), pp. 731–732. That both men can be essentially correct in the points they make yet fail to reconcile these points, strongly suggests the need for conceptual development in the domain of power relations.

[2] Among many studies, see Ronald Lippitt, Norman Polansky, Fritz Redl and Sidney Rosen, "The Dynamics of Power," *Human Relations,* 5 (February, 1952), pp. 37–64.

[3] Floyd Hunter, *Community Power Structure,* Chapel Hill: University of North Carolina Press, 1953.

[4] Max Weber, in *The Theory of Social and Economic Organization,* New York: Oxford University Press, 1947, presents what is still a classic formulation of power, authority and legitimacy. However, it is characteristic of Weber that he constructs a typology rather than an organized theory of power.

[5] See Raymond E. Wolfinger, "Reputation and Reality in the Study of 'Community Power'," *American Sociological Review,* 25 (October, 1960), pp. 636–644, for a well taken critical review of Floyd Hunter's work on these very points. The notion of "generalized power" which is not restricted to specific social relations, if taken literally, is probably meaningless. Power may indeed be generalized across a finite set of relations in a power network, but this notion, too, requires very careful analysis. Are you dealing with some kind of halo effect (reputations if you wish), or are the range and boundary of generalized power anchored in the power structure itself? These are questions which must be asked and answered.

to say that "X has power" is vacant, unless we specify "over whom." In making these necessary qualifications we force ourselves to face up to the obvious: power is a property of the social relation; it is not an attribute of the actor.[6]

In this paper an attempt is made to construct a simple theory of the power aspects of social relations. Attention is focused upon characteristics of the relationship as such, with little or no regard for particular features of the persons or groups engaged in such relations. Personal traits, skills or possessions (such as wealth) which might be relevant to power in one relation are infinitely variable across the set of possible relations, and hence have no place in a general theory.

THE POWER-DEPENDENCE RELATION

While the theory presented here is anchored most intimately in small group research, it is meant to apply to more complex community relations as well. In an effort to make these conceptions potentially as broadly applicable as possible, we shall speak of relations among *actors*, where an actor can be either a person or a group. Unless otherwise indicated, any relation discussed might be a person-person, group-person or group-group relation.

Social relations commonly entail *ties of mutual dependence* between the parties. A *depends* upon B if he aspires to goals or gratifications whose achievement is facilitated by appropriate actions on B's part. By virtue of mutual dependency, it is more or less imperative to each party that he be able to control or influence the other's conduct. At the same time, these ties of mutual dependence imply that each party is in a position, to some degree, to grant or deny, facilitate or hinder, the other's gratification. Thus, it would appear that the power to control or influence the other resides in control over the things he values, which may range all the way from oil resources to ego-support, depending upon the relation in question. In short, *power resides implicitly in the other's dependency.* When this is recognized, the analysis will of necessity revolve largely around the concept of dependence.[7]

Two variables appear to function jointly in fixing the dependence of one actor upon another. Since the precise nature of this joint function is an empirical question, our proposition can do no more than specify the directional relationships involved:

> *Dependence (Dab).* The dependence of actor A upon actor B is (1) directly proportional to A's *motivational investment* in goals mediated by B, and (2) inversely proportional to the *availability* of those goals to A outside of the A-B relation.

In this proposition "goal" is used in the broadest possible sense to refer to gratifications consciously sought as well as rewards unconsciously obtained through the relationship. The "availability" of such goals outside of the relation refers to alternative avenues of goal-achievement, most notably other social relations. The costs associated with such alternatives must be included in any assessment of dependency.[8]

If the dependence of one party provides the basis for the power of the other, that power must be defined as a potential influence:

> *Power (Pab).* The power of actor A over actor B is the amount of resistance on the part of B which can be potentially overcome by A.

Two points must be made clear about this definition. First, the power defined here will not be, of necessity, observable in every interactive episode between A and B, yet we suggest that it exists nonetheless as a potential, to be explored, tested, and occasionally employed by the participants. Pab will be

---

[6] Just as power is often treated as though it were a property of the person, so leadership, conformity, etc., are frequently referred to the personal traits of "leaders," "conformers" and so on, as if they were distinguishable types of people. In a sociological perspective such behavior should be explicitly treated as an attribute of a relation rather than a person.

[7] The relation between power and dependence is given similar emphasis in the systematic treatment by J. Thibaut and H. H. Kelley, *The Social Psychology of Groups,* New York: John Wiley and Sons, 1959.

[8] The notion of "opportunity costs" in economics is a similar idea. If an employee has alternative employment opportunities, and if these opportunities have low associated cost (travel, etc.), the employee's dependence upon his current employer is reduced.

empirically manifest only if A makes some demand, and only *if* this demand runs counter to B's desires (resistance to be overcome).. operational definition must make reference to *change* in the conduct of B attributable to demands made by A.

Second, we define power as the "resistance" which can be overcome, without restricting it to any one domain of action. Thus, if A is dependent upon B for love and respect, B might then draw A into criminal activity which he would normally resist. The reader might object to this formulation, arguing that social power is in fact restricted to certain channels. If so, the reader is apparently concerned with legitimized power embedded in a social structure. Rather than begin at this more evolved level, we hope to derive legitimized power in the theory itself.

The premise we began with can now be stated as Pab=Dba; the power of A over B is equal to, and based upon, the dependence of B upon A.[9] Recognizing the reciprocity of social relations, we can represent a power-dependence relation as a pair of equations:

$$Pab=Dba$$
$$Pba=Dab.$$

Before proceeding further we should emphasize that these formulations have been so worded in the hope that they will apply across a wide range of social life. At a glance our conception of dependence contains two variables remarkably like supply and demand ("availability" and "motivational investment," respectively).[10] We pre-

fer the term *dependency* over these economic terms because it facilitates broader application, for all we need to do to shift these ideas from one area of application to another is change the motivational basis of dependency. We can speak of the economic dependence of a home builder upon a loan agency as varying directly with his desire for the home, and hence capital, and inversely with the "availability" of capital from other agencies. Similarly, a child may be dependent upon another child based upon motivation toward the pleasures of collective play, the availability of alternative playmates, etc. The same generic power-dependence relation is involved in each case. The dependency side of the equation may show itself in "friendship" among playmates, in "filial love" between parent and child, in "respect for treaties" among nations. On the other side of the equation, I am sure no one doubts that mothers, lovers, children, and nations enjoy the power to influence their respective partners, within the limit set by the partner's dependence upon them.

Finally, because these concepts are meant to apply across a wide variety of social situations, operational definitions cannot be appropriately presented here. Operational definitions provide the necessary bridge between generalizing concepts on the one hand, and the concrete features of a specific research situation on the other hand. Hence, there is no *one* proper operational definition for a theoretical concept.[11]

BALANCE AND IMBALANCE

The notion of reciprocity in power-dependency relations raises the question of equality or inequality of power in the relation. If the power of A over B (Pab) is confronted by equal opposing power of B over A, is power then neutralized or cancelled out? We suggest that in such a balanced con-

---

[9] In asserting that power is based upon the dependency of the other, it might appear that we are dealing with *one* of the bases of power ("reward power") listed by John R. P. French, Jr. and Bertram Raven, "The Bases of Social Power," *Studies in Social Power*, D. Cartwright, editor, Ann Arbor, Michigan: Institute for Social Research, 1959. However, careful attention to our highly generalized conception of dependence will show that it covers most if not all of the forms of power listed in that study.

[10] Professor Alfred Kuhn, Department of Economics, University of Cincinnati, has been working on a theory for power analysis soon to be published. The scheme he develops, though very similar to the one presented here, is put together in a different way. It is anchored more tightly to economic concepts, and hence its implications lead off in different directions from those presented below.

[11] Many different operational definitions can serve one theoretical concept, and there is no reason to require that they produce intercorrelated results when applied in the same research situation. While the controversies surrounding "operationalism" have now been largely resolved, there remains some confusion on this point. See, for example, Bernice Eisman, "Some Operational Measures of Cohesiveness and Their Interrelations," *Human Relations*, 12 (May, 1959), pp. 183–189.

dition, power is in no way removed from the relationship. A pattern of "dominance" might not emerge in the interaction among these actors, but that does not imply that power is inoperative in either or both directions. A *balanced* relation and an *unbalanced* relation are represented respectively as follows:

$$Pab = Dba \qquad Pab = Dba$$
$$\| \quad \| \qquad \quad \vee \quad \vee$$
$$Pba = Dab \qquad Pba = Dab$$

Consider two social relations, both of which are balanced, but at *different levels* of dependence (say Loeb and Leopold, as compared with two casual friends). A moment's thought will reveal the utility of the argument that balance does not neutralize power, for each party may continue to exert profound control over the other. It might even be meaningful to talk about the parties being controlled by the relation itself.

Rather than cancelling out considerations of power, reciprocal power provides the basis for studying three more features of power-relations: first, a power advantage can be defined as Pab minus Pba, which can be either positive or negative (a power disadvantage); [12] second, the *cohesion* of a relationship can be defined as the average of Dab and Dba, though this definition can be refined; [13] and finally, it opens the door to the study of *balancing operations* as structural changes in power-dependence relations which tend to reduce power advantage.

Discussion of balancing tendencies should begin with a concrete illustration. In the unbalanced relation represented symbolically above, A is the more powerful party because B is the more dependent of the two. Let actor B be a rather "unpopular" girl, with puritanical upbringing, who wants desperately to date; and let A be a young man who occasionally takes her out, while dating other girls as well. (The reader can satisfy himself about A's power advantage in this illustra-

tion by referring to the formulations above.) Assume further that A "discovers" this power advantage, and, in exploring for the limits of his power, makes sexual advances. In this simplified illustration, these advances should encounter resistance in B's puritanical values. Thus, when a power advantage is *used,* the weaker member will achieve one value at the expense of other values.

In this illustration the tensions involved in an unbalanced relation need not be long endured. They can be reduced in either of two ways: (1) the girl might reduce the psychic costs involved in continuing the relation by redefining her moral values, with appropriate rationalizations and shifts in reference group attachments; or (2) she might renounce the value of dating, develop career aspirations, etc., thus reducing A's power. Notice that the first solution does *not* of necessity alter the unbalanced relation. The weaker member has sidestepped one painful demand but she is still vulnerable to new demands. By contrast, the second solution alters the power relation itself. In general, it appears that an unbalanced relation is unstable for it encourages the use of power which in turn sets in motion processes which we will call (a) cost reduction and (b) balancing operations. [14]

COST REDUCTION

The "cost" referred to here amounts to the "resistance" to be overcome in our definition of power—the cost involved for one party in meeting the demands made by the other. The process of cost reduction in power-dependence relations shows itself in many varied forms. In the courting relation above it took the form of alteration in moral attitudes on the part of a girl who wanted to be popular; in industry it is commonly seen as the impetus for improved plant efficiency and technology in reducing the cost of production. What we call the "mark of oppression" in the character structure of members

[12] J. Thibaut and H. H. Kelley, *op. cit.,* pp. 107–108.

[13] This definition of cohesion, based upon dependency, seems to have one advantage over the definition offered by Leon Festinger, *et al., Theory and Experiment in Social Communication,* Ann Arbor: Research Center for Group Dynamics, University of Michigan Press, 1950. The Festinger definition takes into account only one of the two variables involved in dependency.

[14] The "tensions of imbalance," which are assumed to make an unbalanced relation unstable, are closely related to the idea of "distributive justice" discussed by George C. Homans, *Social Behavior: Its Elementary Forms,* New York: Harcourt, Brace and World, Inc., 1961. All of what Homans has to say around this idea could be fruitfully drawn into the present formulation.

of low social castes (the submissive and "painless" loss of freedom) might well involve the same power processes, as does the "internalization of parental codes" in the socialization process. In fact, the oedipal conflict might be interpreted as a special case of the tensions of imbalance in a power-dependence relation, and cost reduction takes the form of identification and internalization as classically described. "Identification with the aggressor" in any context would appear to be explainable in terms of cost reduction.

In general, *cost reduction* is a process involving change in values (personal, social, economic) which reduces the pains incurred in meeting the demands of a powerful other. It must be emphasized, however, that these adjustments do not necessarily alter the balance or imbalance of the relation, and, as a result, they must be distinguished from the more fundamental *balancing operations* described below. It must be recognized that cost reducing tendencies will take place even under conditions of balance, and while this is obvious in economic transactions, it is equally true of other social relations, where the "costs" involved are anchored in modifiable attitudes and values. The intense cohesion of a lasting social relation like the Loeb-Leopold relation mentioned above can be attributed in part to the cost reduction processes involved in the progressive formation of their respective personalities, taking place in the interest of preserving the valued relation. We suggest that cost reducing tendencies generally will function to deepen and stabilize social relations over and above the condition of balance.

BALANCING OPERATIONS

The remainder of this paper will deal with balancing processes which operate through changes in the variables which define the structure of the power-dependence relation as such. The formal notation adopted here suggests *exactly four generic types* of balancing operation. In the unbalanced relation
$$\begin{array}{c} Pab = Dba \\ \vee \qquad \vee \end{array}, \text{ balance can be restored either by}$$
$$Pba = Dab$$
an increase in Dab or by a decrease in Dba. If we recall that *dependence* is a joint function of two variables, the following altera-

tions will move the relation toward a state of balance:

1. If B reduces motivational investment in goals mediated by A;
2. If B cultivates alternative sources for gratification of those goals;
3. If A increases motivational investment in goals mediated by B;
4. If A is denied alternative sources for achieving those goals.

While these four types of balancing operation are dictated by the logic of the scheme, we suggest that each corresponds to well known social processes. The first operation yields balance through motivational withdrawal by B, the weaker member. The second involves the cultivation of alternative social relations by B. The third is based upon "giving status" to A, and the fourth involves coalition and group formation.

In some of these processes the role of power is well known, while in others it seems to have escaped notice. In discussing any one of these balancing operations it must be remembered that a prediction of which one (or what combination) of the four will take place must rest upon analysis of conditions involved in the concrete case at hand.

In the interest of simplicity and clarity, we will illustrate each of the four generic types of balancing operation in relations among children in the context of play. Consider two children equally motivated toward the pleasures of collective play and equally capable of contributing to such play. These children, A and B, form a balanced relation if we assume further that each has the other as his only playmate, and the give-and-take of their interactions might well be imagined, involving the emergence of such equalitarian rules as "taking turns," etc. Suppose now that a third child, C, moves into the neighborhood and makes the acquaintance of A, but *not* B. The A-B relation will be thrown out of balance by virtue of A's decreased dependence upon B. The reader should convince himself of this fact by referring back to the proposition on dependence. Without any of these parties necessarily "understanding" what is going on, we would predict that A would slowly come to dominate B in the pattern of their interactions. On more frequent occasions B will find himself deprived of the pleasures A can offer, thus slowly coming to sense his own dependency more acutely. By the same token A will more frequently find B saying "yes" instead of "no" to his proposals, and he will gain increased awareness of his power over B. The growing self-images of these children will surely reflect and perpetuate this pattern.

OPERATION NUMBER ONE: WITHDRAWAL

We now have the powerful A making demands of the dependent B. One of the processes through which the tensions in the unbalanced A-B relation can be reduced is *motivational withdrawal* on the part of B, for this will reduce Dba and Pab. In this illustration, child B might lose some of his interest in collective play under the impact of frustrations and demands imposed by A. Such a withdrawal from the play relation would presumably come about if the other three balancing operations were blocked by the circumstances peculiar to the situation. The same operation was illustrated above in the case of the girl who might renounce the value of dating. It would seem to be involved in the dampened level of aspiration associated with the "mark of oppression" referred to above.

In general, the denial of dependency involved in this balancing operation will have the effect of moving actors away from relations which are unbalanced to their disadvantage. The actor's motivational orientations and commitments toward different areas of activity will intimately reflect this process.

OPERATION NUMBER TWO: EXTENSION OF POWER NETWORK

Withdrawal as a balancing operation entails subjective alterations in the weaker actor. The second operation takes place through alterations in a structure we shall call a *power network*, defined as two or more *connected* power-dependence relations. As we have seen in our illustration, when the C-A relation is connected through A with the A-B relation, forming a simple linear network C-A-B, the properties of A-B are altered. In this example, a previously balanced A-B relation is thrown out of balance, giving A a power advantage. This points up the

general fact that while each relation in a network will involve interactions which appear to be independent of other relations in the network (e.g., A and B are seen to play together in the absence of C; C and A in the absence of B), the internal features of one relation are nonetheless a function of the entire network. Any adequate conception of a "power structure" must be based upon this fact.

In this illustration the form of the network throws both relations within it out of balance, thus stimulating one or several of the balancing operations under discussion. If balancing operation number two takes place, *the network* will be extended by the formation of new relationships. The tensions of imbalance in the A-B and A-C relations will make B and C "ready" to form new friendships (1) with additional children D and E, thus lengthening a linear network, or (2) with each other, thus "closing" the network. It is important to notice that the lengthened network balances some relations, but not the network as a whole, while the closed network is completely balanced under the limiting assumptions of this illustration. Thus, we might offer as a corollary to operation number two: Power networks tend to achieve closure.[15]

If the reader is dissatisfied with this illustration in children's play relations, let A be the loan agent mentioned earlier, and B, C, . . . N be home builders or others dependent upon A for capital. This is the familiar monopoly situation with the imbalance commonly attributed to it. As a network, it is a set of relations connected only at A. Just as the children were "ready" to accept new friends, so the community of actors B, C, . . . N is ready to receive new loan agencies.

---

[15] The notion of closed versus open networks as discussed here can be directly related to research dealing with communication networks, such as that reported by Harold J. Leavitt, "Some Effects of Communication Patterns on Group Performance," *Journal of Abnormal and Social Psychology*, 46 (January, 1951), pp. 38–50, in which the limiting assumptions involved in this discussion are fully met by experimental controls. In discussing those experiments in terms of the concepts in this theory we would consider each actor's dependence upon other actors for *information*. A formal treatment of such networks is suggested by A. Bavelas, "A Mathematical Model For Group Structure," *Applied Anthropology*, 7 (Summer, 1948), pp. 16-30.

Balancing operation number 2 involves in all cases the *diffusion* of dependency into new relations in a network. A final illustration of this principle can be found in institutionalized form in some kinship systems involving the extended family. In the case of the Hopi, for example, Dorothy Eggan has described at length the diffusion of child dependency among many "mothers," thus draining off much of the force of oedipal conflicts in that society.[16] We have already suggested that oedipal conflict may be taken as a special case of the tension of imbalance, which in this case appears to be institutionally handled in a manner resembling operation number two. This is not to be taken, however, as an assertion that the institution evolved as a balancing process, though this is clearly open for consideration.

It is convenient at this juncture to take up balancing operation number 4, leaving number 3 to the last.

OPERATION NUMBER FOUR: COALITION FORMATION

Let us continue with the same illustration. When the B-C relation forms, closing the C-A-B network in the process of balancing, we have what appears to be a coalition of the two weaker against the one stronger. This, however, is not technically the case, for A is not involved in the B-C interactions; he simply exists as an alternative playmate for both B and C.

The proper representation of coalitions in a triad would be (AB)-C, (AC)-B, or (BC)-A. That is, a triadic network reduces to a coalition only if two members unite as a single actor in the process of dealing directly with the third. The difference involved here may be very small in behavioral terms, and the distinction may seem overly refined, but it goes to the heart of an important conceptual problem (the difference between a closed "network" and a "group"), and it rests upon the fact that two very different balancing operations are involved. The C-A-B network is balanced through the addition of a third relation (C-B) in operation number two, but it is still just a power network. In operation number 4 it achieves

[16] Dorothy Eggan, "The General Problem of Hopi Adjustment," *American Anthropologist*, 45 (July-September, 1943), pp. 357-373.

balance through collapsing the two-relational network into one group-person relation with the emergence of a "collective actor." Operation number two reduces the power of the stronger actor, while number 4 increases the power of weaker actors through collectivization. If the rewards mediated by A are such that they can be jointly enjoyed by B and C, then the tensions of imbalance in the A-B and A-C relations can be resolved in the (BC)-A coalition.

In a general way, Marx was asking for balancing operation number 4 in his call to "Workers of the world," and the collectivization of labor can be taken as an illustration of this balancing tendency as an historic process. Among the balancing operations described here, coalition formation is the one most commonly recognized as a power process. However, the more general significance of this balancing operation seems to have escaped notice, for the typical coalition is only one of the many forms this same operation takes. For this reason the next section will explore coalition processes further.

THE ORGANIZED GROUP

We wish to suggest that the coalition process is basically involved in all organized group functioning, whether the group be called a coalition or not. We believe this illuminates the role which power processes play in the emergence and maintenance of group structure in general.

In the typical coalition pattern, (AB)-C, A and B constitute a collective actor in the sense that they act as one, presenting themselves to their common environment as a single unit. A coalition, as one *type* of group, is characterized by the fact that (a) the common environment is an actor to be controlled, and (b) its unity is historically based upon efforts to achieve that control. Now, all we need do to blend this type of group with groups in general is to *dehumanize* the environmental problem which the group collectively encounters. Thus, instead of having the control of actor C as its end, the group attempts to control C in the interest of achieving X, some "group goal." Now, if C also aspires toward X, and if C is dependent upon the group for achieving X, C might well be one of the group members—any member. Thus, in a three-member group we have three coalition structures as *intra-group* relations, each representable as ([AB]-C)-X, with A, B and C interchangeable.

The situation involved here is reminiscent of the rapidly forming and reforming coalitions in unconsolidated children's play groups. As the group consolidates, these coalitions do not drop out of the picture; they become stabilized features of group structure, and the stabilization process is identical with "norm formation." In fact, the demands made by (AB) of C in the power process within ([AB]-C) are exactly what we normally call *group norms* and *role-prescriptions*. Such norms are properly viewed as the "voice" of a collective actor, standing in coalition against the object of its demands. This reasoning suggests an idealized conception of group structure, based upon two types of collective demands:

(1) *Role-Prescriptions.* Specifications of behavior which all group members expect (demand) of one or more but not all members.

(2) *Group Norms.* Specifications of behavior which all group members expect of all group members.

Certain actions, when performed by some member or members, need not be performed by all other members to properly facilitate group functioning. These will tend to be incorporated in role-prescriptions, which, taken together, provide a division of labor in a role structure. Roles are defined and enforced through a consolidation of power in coalition formation. Likewise with group norms. Thus, the structure of a group (its norms and prescriptions) will specify the makeup of the coalition a member would face for any group-relevant act he might perform.

This conception of group structure is idealized in the sense that it describes complete consensus among members, even to the point of group identification and internalization of collective demands (members expect things of themselves in the above definitions). Balancing operations, along with cost reduction, should move group structure toward this ideal.

AUTHORITY

It should be clear that in introducing conceptions of group *structure* we have in no way digressed from our discussion of power *processes*, for the emergence of these structural forms is attributed directly to operation number four, closely resembling coalition formation. Even the most formalized role-prescription is properly viewed as the "voice" of all members standing as a coalition in making its demand of the occupant of the role. Whenever a specific member finds occasion to remind another member of his "proper" job in terms of such prescriptions, he speaks with the *authority* of the group behind him; he is "authorized" to speak for them. In this sense, every member has authority of a kind (as in civil arrest), but authority is usually used to refer to power vested in an office or role. The situation is basically the same, however, in either case. The occupant of such a role has simply been singled out and commissioned more explicitly to speak for the group in the group's dealings with its members. That authority is *limited* power follows from logical necessity when role-prescriptions are treated as they are here. A dean, for example, can force faculty member A to turn in his grades on time because the demand is "legitimate," that is, supported by a coalition of all other faculty members joining with the dean in making the demand. If that dean, however, were to employ sanctions in an effort to induce that member to polish the dean's private car, the "coalition" would immediately re-form around the faculty member, as expressed in role-prescriptions defining the boundary of "legitimate power" or authority. The dean's authority is power contained and restricted through balancing operation number four, coalition formation.

The notion of legitimacy is important, for authority is more than balanced power; it is *directed* power which can be employed (legitimately) only in channels defined by the norms of the group. A person holding such authority is commissioned; he does not simply have the right to rule or govern—he is obliged to. Thus, authority emerges as a transformation of power in a process called "legitimation," and that process is one special case of balancing operation number four.[17]

---

[17] The process of legitimation has sometimes been described as a tactic employed by a person aspiring

Earlier in this section we referred to the common phenomenon of rapidly forming and re-forming coalitions in children's play groups. Our reasoning suggests that it is precisely through these coalition processes that unifying norms emerge. These fluctuating coalitions can be taken as the prototype of organized group life wherein the tempo of coalition realignment is accelerated to the point of being a blur before our eyes. Stated more accurately, the norms and prescriptions define implicitly the membership of the coalition which would either support or oppose any member if he were to perform any action relevant to those norms.

OPERATION NUMBER THREE: EMERGENCE OF STATUS

One important feature of group structure remains to be discussed: status and status hierarchies. It is interesting that the one remaining balancing operation provided in this theory takes us naturally to the emergence of status ordering. Operation number three increases the weaker member's power to control the formerly more powerful member through increasing the latter's motivational investment in the relation. This is normally accomplished through giving him status recognition in one or more of its many forms, from ego-gratifications to monetary differentials. The ego-rewards, such as prestige, loom large in this process because they are highly valued by many recipients while given at low cost to the giver.

---

to power or trying to hold his power, rather than a process through which persons are granted restricted power. For example, C. Wright Mills states: "Those in authority attempt to justify their rule over institutions by linking it, as if it were a necessary consequence, with widely believed in moral symbols, sacred emblems, legal formulae. These central conceptions may refer to god or gods, the 'vote of the majority,' 'the will of the people,' 'the aristocracy of talent or wealth,' to the 'divine right of kings,' or to the allegedly extraordinary endowments of the ruler himself. Social scientists, following Weber, call such conceptions 'legitimations,' or sometimes 'symbols of justification.'" (*The Sociological Imagination*, New York: Oxford University Press, 1959, p. 36). Whether we view the process of legitimation in the context of the *formation* of such collective conceptions, or in the context of calling upon them to justify action, the process is fundamentally that of mobilizing collective support to oppose those who challenge power. Power so supported is authority, and the process fits the general model of coalition formation.

The discussion of status hierarchies forces us to consider *intra*-group relations, and how this can be done in a theory which treats the group in the singular as *an* actor. The answer is contained in the idealized conception of group structure outlined above. That conception implies that every intra-group relation involves at once every member of the group. Thus, in a group with members A, B, C, and D, the relations A-B, A-C, etc. do not exist. Any interactions between A and B, for example, lie outside of the social system in question unless one or both of these persons "represents" the group in his actions, as in the coalition pattern discussed at length above. The relations which do exist are (ABCD)-A, (ABCD)-B, (ABCD)-C and (ABCD)-D as a minimum, plus whatever relations of the (ABCD)-(AB) type may be involved in the peculiar structure of the group in question. Thus, in a group of N members we have theoretical reason for dealing with N *group-member* relations rather than considering all of the $\frac{N(N-1)}{2}$ possible member-member relations. Each of these group-member relations can now be expressed in the familiar equations for a power-dependence relation:

$$Pgm_i = Dm_ig$$
$$Pm_ig = Dgm_i.$$

To account for the emergence of a status hierarchy within a group of N members, we start with a set of N group-member relations of this type and consider balancing operations in these relations.

Let us imagine a five member group and proceed on three assumptions: (1) *status* involves differential valuation of members (or roles) by the group, and this valuation is equivalent to, or an expression of, Dgm_i; (2) a member who is highly valued by the group is highly valued in other *similar* groups he belongs to or might freely join; and (3) all five members have the same motivational investment in the group at the outset. Assumptions 2 and 3 are empirical, and when they are true they imply that Dgm and Dmg are inversely related across the N group-member relations. This in turn implies a state of imbalance of a very precarious nature so far as group stability is concerned.

The least dependent member of a group will be the first to break from the group, and these members are precisely the most valued members. It is this situation which balancing operation number three alleviates through "giving status" to the highly valued members, thus gaining the power to keep and control those members.

These ideas are illustrated with hypothetical values in Table 1, with imbalance represented as power advantage (PA). Balancing operations will tend to move PA toward zero, as shown in column 6 after the highly valued members A and B have come to depend upon the group for the special rewards of status, and in column 9 after the least valued members D and E have withdrawn some of their

taches to member roles), it is notably difficult to rely upon a functional explanation. Is the pitcher more highly valued than the center fielder because he is functionally more important or because good pitchers are harder to find? Is the physicist valued over the plumber because of a "more important" functional contribution to the social system, or because physicists are more difficult to replace, more costly to obtain, etc.? The latter considerations involve the availability factor. We suggest here that the *values* people use in ordering roles or persons express the dependence of the system upon those roles, and that the *availability* factor in dependency plays the decisive part in historically shaping those values.[18]

TABLE 1. HYPOTHETICAL VALUES SHOWING THE RELATION BETWEEN DGM AND DMG IN A GROUP WITH FIVE MEMBERS

	Before Balancing			After Operation #3			After Operation #1		
	1	2	3	4	5	6	7	8	9
Member	Dgm	Dmg*	PAgm**	Dgm	Dmg	PAgm**	Dgm	Dmg	PAgm**
A	5	1	—4	5	5	0	5	5	0
B	4	2	—2	4	4	0	4	4	0
C	3	3	0	3	3	0	3	3	0
D	2	4	2	2	4	2	2	2	0
E	1	5	4	1	5	4	1	1	0

* Assuming that all members have the same motivational investment in the group at the outset, and that highly valued members (A and B) are valued in other groups as well.

** Power Advantage PAgm=Dmg—Dgm.

original motivational investment in the group. The table presents three stages in status crystallization, and the process of crystallization is seen as a balancing process. The final stage (columns 7, 8, and 9) should be achieved only in groups with very low membership turnover. The middle stage might well be perpetual in groups with new members continually coming in at the lower levels. In such "open" groups, status striving should be a characteristic feature and can be taken as a direct manifestation of the tensions of imbalance. In the final stage, such strivers have either succeeded or withdrawn from the struggle.

Among the factors involved in status ordering, this theory focuses attention upon the extreme importance of the *availability* factor in dependency as a determinant of status position and the values employed in status ordering. In considering Dgm (the relative value or importance the group at-

CONCLUSION

The theory put forth in this paper is in large part contained implicitly in the ties of mutual dependence which bind actors together in social systems. Its principal value seems to be its ability to pull together a wide variety of social events, ranging from the internalization of parental codes to society-wide movements, like the collectivization of labor, in terms of a few very simple principles. Most important, the concepts involved are subject to operational formulation. Two

[18] "Motivational investment" and "availability," which jointly determine dependency at any point in time, are functionally related through time. This is implied in our balancing operations. While these two variables can be readily distinguished in the case of Dmg, they are too intimately fused in Dgm to be clearly separated. The values by which a group sees a given role as "important" at time 2, evolve from felt scarcity in that role and similar roles at time 1.

CHOICE IN INTERPERSONAL RELATIONS 41

experiments testing certain propositions discussed above led to the following results:

1. Conformity (Pgm) varies directly with motivational investment in the group;
2. Conformity varies inversely with acceptance in alternative groups;
3. Conformity is high at both status extremes in groups with membership turnover (see column 5, Table 1);
4. Highly valued members of a group are strong conformers *only if* they are valued by other groups as well. (This supports the notion that special status rewards are used to hold the highly valued member who does not depend heavily upon the group, and that in granting him such rewards power is obtained over him.);
5. Coalitions form among the weak to control the strong (balancing operation number three);
6. The greatest rewards within a coalition are given to the less dependent member of the coalition (balancing operation number three, analogous to "status giving").

Once the basic ideas in this theory have been adequately validated and refined, both theoretical and empirical work must be extended in two main directions. First, the interaction process should be studied to locate carefully the factors leading to *perceived* power and dependency in self and others, and the conditions under which power, as a potential, will be employed in action. Secondly, and, in the long run, more important, will be study of *power networks* more complex than those referred to here, leading to more adequate understanding of complex power structures. The theory presented here does no more than provide the basic underpinning to the study of complex networks. There is every reason to believe that modern mathematics, graph theory in particular,[19] can be fruitfully employed in the analysis of complex networks and predicting the outcome of power plays within such networks.

---

[19] F. Harary and R. Norman, *Graph Theory as a Mathematical Model in the Social Sciences.* Ann Arbor: Institute for Social Research, 1953. An effort to apply such a model to power relations can be found in John R. P. French, Jr., "A Formal Theory of Social Power," *The Psychological Review,* 63 (May, 1956), pp. 181–194.

[3]

This paper tries to extend the concepts of amount of power and strength of power to n-person reciprocal power situations, where all u participants have some power over one another and over the joint policies of their group. Intuitively, the amount of a person's power is a measure of the probability of his being able to achieve adoption of joint policies agreeing with his own preferences; while the strength of his power is a measure of the strength of the incentives he can provide for the other participants to agree to his policy proposals, and more generally, the strength of his bargaining position against the other participants. To define the strength of power the paper uses the author's bargaining model for the n-person game. The measure obtained in this way can be regarded as a generalization of the power measure of Shapley and Shubik.

MEASUREMENT OF SOCIAL POWER IN n-PERSON RECIPROCAL POWER SITUATIONS

by John C. Harsanyi

Australian National University, now at Wayne State University

INTRODUCTION

THE preceding paper argued that social power must be defined in terms of five dimensions: the *costs*, the *strength*, the *scope*, the *amount*, and the *extension* of this power. A distinction was made between unilateral and reciprocal (or bilateral) power situations. The former are situations in which a given person A is in a position to determine, by his own unilateral decision, the incentives he will provide for another person B to comply with his wishes, and also the degree of compliance he will try to enforce. The latter are situations in which both parties have the ability to exert pressure on each other, and in which the incentives provided by A and, even more important, the degree of compliance he will try to enforce, therefore become matters of explicit or implicit bargaining between the two parties. Certain simple mathematical relationships between the *strength* and the *amount* of A's power over B were established, both for unilateral and for bilateral power situations.

In *unilateral* power situations, the generalization of these results to the n-person case is quite straightforward. As a matter of fact, the situation where one given individual A

has unilateral power over several individuals $B_1, \ldots, B_k$ is already covered in the preceding paper. Thus it is sufficient to consider the case where several individuals $A_1, \ldots, A_k$ simultaneously have some power over the same individual B. Here it is natural to define the *amount* of joint power that $A_1, \ldots, A_k$ have over B with respect to some action X as the *net increase* in the probability of B's actually performing action X because of the intervention of $A_1, \ldots, A_k$. On the other hand, the *strength* of their joint power may be defined as the algebraic sum of the strength of every A_i's separate power over B (giving a negative sign to the strength of the power of any individual A_i who may try to prevent B from performing action X). It is easy to see that under these definitions Theorem I (and I') retains its validity.

However, the model of bilateral power cannot be directly extended to n-person *reciprocal* power situations, where more than two individuals are able to exert pressures and counterpressures upon one another. To analyze situations of this latter type, the Zeuthen-Nash theory of two-person bargaining must be replaced by a theory of n-person bargaining. The bargaining model for the n-person co-operative game (Harsanyi, 1960;

81

82   JOHN C. HARSANYI

for an earlier version, see Harsanyi, 1959) which will be used is an *n*-person generalization of the Zeuthen-Nash theory. (It is also a generalization of the Shapley [1953] value for the *n*-person game, in that it extends a certain modified form of the Shapley value from the special case of games with transferable utility, originally considered by Shapley, to the general case.)

To make the model of bilateral power more readily amenable to generalization for the *n*-person case, the measure for the *amount* of power possessed by each participant must be slightly modified. The amount of *A*'s power over *B* (that is, *A*'s power over *B*'s *individual policy*) with respect to some action $\overline{X}$ to be performed by *B* was defined as the net increase Δp in the probability of *B*'s actually performing action $\overline{X}$ because of *A*'s intervention. Now a new measure, the amount of *A*'s power over *A* and *B*'s *joint policy* with respect to some controversial issue $X = (X_A, X_B)$, is defined as the probability p of *A*'s being able to get the joint policy X_A adopted when *A* favors this policy X_A and *B* favors a different policy X_B.

Clearly the old model is a special case of the new one, as the controversial issue between *A* and *B* may be that *B* would prefer *not* to perform some action $\overline{X}$ which *A* wants *B* to perform. If we denote by $\overline{X}^*$ *A*'s possible action of *tolerating* *B*'s failure to perform action $\overline{X}$, then the joint policy X_A preferred by *A* will involve *B*'s performing action $\overline{X}$ and *A*'s *not* performing action $\overline{X}^*$, whereas the joint policy X_B preferred by *B* will involve *B*'s *not* performing action $\overline{X}$ and *A*'s performing action $\overline{X}^*$.

Quantitatively these two measures for the amount of *A*'s power are related as follows. Suppose that, without *A*'s intervention, *B* would perform action $\overline{X}$ with probability p_1; but because of *A*'s intervention, and as a result of mutual agreement between the two parties, *B* increases the probability of his performing action $\overline{X}$ to p_2. Then the amount of *A*'s power *over B* (i.e., *A*'s power over *B*'s *policy* concerning action $\overline{X}$) would be the difference $\Delta p = p_2 - p_1$. On the other hand,

the amount of *A*'s power over *A* and *B*'s *joint policy* would be defined as the *conditional probability* p of *B*'s performing action X, given that on the present occasion he would not perform action $\overline{X}$ without *A*'s intervention (because a controversial issue between *A* and *B* exists only on occasions where *B* would not perform action X without *A*'s intervention). This conditional probability is $p = (p_2 - p_1)/(1 - p_1)$.

It is easy to see that our new measure for the amount of *A*'s power is simply a normalized version of the old measure. For in any particular situation where p_1 is given, the new measure p is proportional to the old measure Δp, as $p = \Delta p/(1 - p_1)$. But while Δp varies[1] between 0 and $1 - p_1$, the new measure p varies between 0 and 1. (However, our main concern will be with the *n*-person analogue of the case where *A*'s and *B*'s preferences are completely opposed with respect to some particular action $\overline{X}$, i.e., where $p_1 = 0$. Then of course $p = \Delta p$ and the two measures coincide.)

DEFINITIONS OF THE AMOUNT OF POWER IN THREE TYPES OF n-PERSON SITUATIONS

Case A. Single preferences and no compromise policies

Power relations become relevant in a social group when two or more individuals have conflicting preferences and a decision has to be made as to whose preferences shall prevail. Thus special theoretical interest attaches to the extreme case where *n* individuals have preferences so dissimilar that no two of them agree in preferring some particular policy X_i to some other policy X_j, and where no "pure" compromise policies (i.e., policies having the nature of *pure strategies*) exist among the policies preferred by different individuals.

---

[1] To simplify our analysis, we disregard the case of negative power, where $\Delta p < 0$, i.e., where *A*'s intervention actually *decreases* the probability of *B*'s performing action $\overline{X}$ which *A* wants him to perform. (This can occur only as a result of *A*'s seriously misjudging the situation. For if he knew the effects of his intervention, he always could achieve at least a *zero* amount of power by simply refraining from any intervention.)

This can be represented by the following model. There are n individuals, called $1, \ldots, n$. Each individual i prefers a different joint policy X_i, but is completely indifferent among all alternative policies $X_j, X_k, \ldots$ preferred by various other individuals $j, k, \ldots$ (This we shall call the *single preferences* assumption. Its purpose is to rule out the possibility that two or more individuals *jointly* prefer some policy X_i over some alternative policy X_j. For instance, suppose to the contrary that while individual 1's first preference is policy X_1, he is not indifferent between policy X_2 (favored by individual 2) and policy X_3 (favored by individual 3), in that his second preference goes to X_2 and his third preference to X_3. Here 1 and 2 will *jointly* prefer X_2 to X_3, contrary to our assumption.)

Let v_{ij} be the utility that individual i assigns to joint policy X_j. By the single preferences assumption we can write

$$v_{ij} = \begin{cases} w_i & \text{if } i \neq j \\ w_i + x_i & \text{if } i = j \end{cases} \qquad (1)$$

It will also be assumed that between any policy X_i, favored by i, and any policy X_j, favored by j, there is no pure compromise policy X_k that would be preferred by *both* individuals to the policy favored by the *other* individual. (This will be called the *no compromise* assumption). This implies that all possible joint policies other than the policies $X_1, \ldots, X_n$ representing the first preference of one of the n individuals, are inefficient policies and can be disregarded. Therefore we shall identify the controversial issue at stake among the n individuals with the n-tuple $X = (X_1, \ldots, X_n)$.

In this situation it is natural to define the *amount* of individual i's power over the *joint policy* of all n individuals as the probability p_i of his being able to get his favorite joint policy X_i adopted by all individuals. Of course, $\Sigma p_i = 1$. We shall write $\bar{\bar{p}}$ for the probability vector $\bar{\bar{p}} = (p_1, \ldots, p_n)$.

Case B. Multiple preferences and no compromise policies

There are again n individuals, with each individual i giving his *first* preference to a different[2] joint policy X_i. But now each individual i may also have definite preferences between policies X_j and X_k, even if $j, k \neq i$ (*multiple preferences* assumption).

We shall still assume, however, that $X_1, \ldots, X_n$ are the only efficient policies (*no compromise* assumption).

We may again try to define individual i's power as the probability p_i of his being able to get policy X_i accepted. But for most purposes this probability will not be an adequate measure of his power. If, e.g., out of three possible policies, individual 1 assigns 10 units of utility to policy X_1, 9 units of utility to policy X_2, and 1 unit of utility to policy X_3, we shall not be able to assess the magnitude of his power if we know only that he has a 10 per cent chance of getting X_1 adopted and do not know how the remaining 90 per cent probability is distributed between policies X_2 and X_3.

Thus we may call p_i, the probability of individual i's favorite policy X_i being adopted by the whole group, the *amount* of i's *specific power*, because it measures his power to determine exactly the nature of the specific policy to be adopted by the group. (Again, $\Sigma p_i = 1$.) For most purposes, however, we need a different measure.

A more satisfactory measure will be the whole probability vector $\bar{\bar{p}} = (p_1, \ldots, p_n)$ giving the probabilities for the adoption of each of the alternative policies $X_1, \ldots, X_n$. This may be called the *vector measure* for i's power.

But we can also define a more satisfactory scalar measure as follows. Let v_{ij} again denote the utility that individual i assigns to joint policy X_j. Suppose that X_k is the policy alternative least preferred by i so that

$$v_{ik} = \min_j v_{ij} = w_i. \qquad (2)$$

We define $x_{ij} = v_{ij} - w_i$. Then for each policy x_j we can write

$$v_{ij} = w_i + x_{ij} \qquad (3)$$

with $x_{ik} = 0$ for the least-preferred policy X_k.

---

[2] As to the case where two individuals i and j prefer the *same* policy $X_i = X_j = X_{ij}$, see Footnote 3 below.

Let $Y(\bar{p})$ be the prospect corresponding to the probability vector $\bar{p}$, i.e., the prospect that adoption by the group of joint policies $X_1, \ldots, X_n$ has the probabilities $p_1, \ldots, p_n$ respectively. The expected utility value to individual i of prospect $Y(\bar{p})$ will be

$$y_i = w_i + \sum_j p_j \, x_{ij}. \qquad (4)$$

In order to compare Case B with Case A, we may also consider certain simpler hypothetical prospects $\bar{Y}_i(\bar{p}_i)$ which would involve only two possibilities: adoption of policy X_i, most preferred by i, and adoption of policy X_k, least preferred by i, the former having probability $\bar{p}_i$ and the latter having probability $1 - \bar{p}_i$. The expected utility value to i of any such hypothetical prospect $\bar{Y}_i(\bar{p}_i)$ would be

$$\bar{y}_i = w_i + \bar{p}_i \, x_{ii}. \qquad (5)$$

There will be a unique prospect $\bar{Y}_i(\bar{p}_i)$ which would have the same utility value to individual i as prospect $Y(\bar{p})$, making $\bar{y}_i = y_i$. This $\bar{Y}_i(\bar{p}_i)$ will correspond to the probability

$$\bar{p}_i = \sum_j p_j \, x_{ij}/x_{ii}. \qquad (6)$$

This hypothetical two-way prospect $\bar{Y}_i(\bar{p}_i)$ may be said to measure the value to i of the n-way prospect $Y(\bar{p})$, and the corresponding probability $\bar{p}_i$ may be used as a scalar measure of individual i's power. What $\bar{p}_i$ measures is not i's power to get the group to adopt some specific joint policy X_i; this is measured by p_i, the amount of i's *specific* power. Rather, $\bar{p}_i$ measures i's power to get the group to adopt *some* policy reasonably satisfactory to him, even if this policy is not necessarily the policy *most preferred* by him. This quantity $\bar{p}_i$ we shall call the amount of i's *generic* power over the group's joint policy. For most purposes it represents the best scalar measure for the amount of i's power.[3]

[3] If two individuals i and j prefer the same policy $X_i = X_j = X_{ij}$, we of course have only one probability p_{ij} for the adoption of policy X_{ij}, instead of having two separate probabilities p_i and p_j for the adoption of X_i and X_j. This probability p_{ij} may be regarded as a measure for the amount of *joint* specific

Of course in Case A previously considered, $\bar{p}_i = p_i$, and the amount of i's power (without qualification), the amount of i's *specific* power, and the amount of i's *generic* power, are all the same thing.

Case C. Multiple preferences and possible compromise policies

Finally, we shall consider the more general case where the number of efficient alternative policies available is $n + m$, i.e., is greater than n, the number of individuals.[4] Policies $X_1, \ldots, X_n$ will represent the first preferences of individuals $1, \ldots, n$. Policies $X_{n+1}, \ldots, X_{n+m}$ will not represent any individual's first preference, but they still may be adopted as joint policies by the n individuals (or they may be used with positive probability weights in the jointly randomized mixed strategy adopted by them) because they may represent a suitable compromise among the conflicting interests of different individuals.

In Case C, individual i's power can again be measured by the amounts of his specific or generic power, or by the vector measure for the amount of his power. But there are the following differences. The amounts of specific power, p_i, for the n individuals now need not add up to unity (because some probability now may be allocated to policies other than $X_1, \ldots, X_n$). The vector measure $\bar{p}$ for the amount of power now is an $(n + m)$-vector, not an n-vector as in Case B.[5]

power of these two individuals. (We cannot regard p_{ij} as a measure for each individual's separate specific power, because if we counted p_{ij} two times, the specific-power measures of all n individuals would not add up to unity.) On the other hand, using equation (6), we can define separate measures for the amounts of *generic* power, $\bar{p}_i$ and $\bar{p}_j$, possessed by the two individuals. If, apart from their common first preference for policy X_{ij}, their utility functions for the various policy alternatives are otherwise not identical, then we actually may have $\bar{p}_i \neq \bar{p}_j$.

[4] For a situation where the number of policy alternatives is smaller than the number of individuals, see Footnote 3.

[5] But this $(n + m)$-vector will normally have no more than n nonzero components (and in most cases is likely to have much fewer than that). Let $v_j = (v_{1j}, \ldots, v_{nj})$ be the vector of the utilities that individuals $1, \ldots, n$ associate with each policy

Finally, in Case C the amount of *i*'s *specific* power is an even less satisfactory measure for his power than it was in Case B, and the use of the amount of his *generic* power will become even more necessary. (For instance, if the *n* individuals agree to adopt some particular compromise policy, say, with probability 1; then every individual will have zero amount of *specific* power, as he had to give up all his chances to achieve his own favorite policy. At the same time, the compromise actually adopted may very well be highly satisfactory to all of them, giving all of them a near-unity amount of *generic* power.)

DEFINITION OF THE STRENGTH OF POWER

As Cases A and B are special cases under Case C, we shall define the strength of each participant's power for the *general* Case C, and shall later mention some of the simplifications applying in special cases.

The *n* participants will have more or less conflicting interests concerning a certain controversial issue $X = (X_1, \ldots, X_{n+m})$, i.e., concerning how much probability p_j to allocate to each of the $(n + m)$ policy alternatives X_j. Therefore we shall assume that these probabilities p_j will be determined by explicit or implicit bargaining among the *n* participants.[6] By definition, the amount of indi-

vidual *i*'s specific power will be simply p_i. By equation (6), the amount of his generic power, $\tilde{p}_i$, will also be defined in terms of the probabilities p_j. Thus both of these measures for each individual's power can be regarded as results of bargaining among these individuals.

The outcome of this bargaining will depend on two main factors. One is the physical and legal ability of each individual or coalition of individuals to carry through certain policies independently of the consent of other individuals, which we shall call the *independent power* of this individual or coalition. (For instance, in many policy-making bodies a simple or qualified majority coalition of the members will have full independent power to decide on policies.) The other factor is the ability of each individual, or coalition of individuals, to provide incentives (i.e., rewards and penalties) for other individuals to give their consent to policies favored by this individual or coalition, which we shall call the *incentive power* of this individual or coalition. (For instance, a minority which could not decide policies by its own rights may be able to bribe or intimidate the majority into consenting to its policy proposals.)

My bargaining model for the *n*-person game—on the assumption that each participant's behavior will satisfy certain rationality postulates—predicts the outcome of bargaining among the *n* participants in terms of all individuals' and all possible coalitions' independent power and incentive power. Thus the *theoretically predicted value* of the amount of a given individual *i*'s *generic power*, $\tilde{p}_i$, can be regarded as a measure of the *strength* of *i*'s *bargaining position*, or of his power to get some policy alternative reasonably acceptable to him adopted by the group. This quantity I propose to call the *strength* of individual *i*'s power.[7] (I propose to use the theoretically predicted value of $\tilde{p}_i$, the amount of *i*'s generic power, rather than the predicted value of p_i, the amount of *i*'s *specific* power,

---

alternative X_j. Let us call a set of policies X_j, X_k, . . . linearly independent if the corresponding utility vectors $\overline{u}_j$, $\overline{u}_k$, . . . are linearly independent. Then no efficient probability mixture of the policy alternatives $X_1, \ldots, X_{n+m}$ can use more than *n* linearly independent policies with nonzero probability weights. Moreover, any efficient utility vector that can be attained by a probability mixture of more than *n* linearly dependent policies can also be attained by a mixture of *at most n* linearly independent policies. Therefore there is never any advantage in using a probability mixture of more than *n* different policies.

[6] In the real world, of course, the bargaining parties will usually trade in statistical *frequencies*, not in *probabilities* as such. That is, if no direct (i.e., pure) compromise policy is available, they will reach an indirect compromise by letting one party have his way on one occasion and another party on another occasion, with frequencies dependent on each party's bargaining position. But reinterpreta-

tion of our model in terms of frequencies rather than probabilities tends to make little difference to our conclusions (see pages 72-73).

[7] A more exact definition will be given below (see equation [27]).

because for reasons already indicated I consider $\bar{p}_i$ as being a much better measure for i's power than p_i.)

We shall consider a bargaining situation of the following kind. The n individuals agree to adopt the jointly randomized mixed strategy $\bar{\bar{p}}$ assigning the probabilities $p_1, \ldots, p_{n+m}$ to the *policy alternatives* $X_1, \ldots, X_{n+m}$. By equation (4), strategy $\bar{\bar{p}}$ will yield for individual i the expected utility

$$y_i = w_i + \sum_{j \in M} p_j \, x_{ij} \qquad (7)$$

where $M = (1, \ldots, n + m)$.

At the same time, the n participants also agree on a reward strategy ϱ, under which each individual i will give each other individual j a *reward* R_{ij} in order to get j to agree to a strategy $\bar{\bar{p}}$ favorable to i. (Of course, some or all of these rewards R_{ij} may be nil.) These rewards may take the form of money, commodities, power in *other* fields (i.e., concessions concerning controversial issues other than X—this restriction is necessary to avoid double counting), etc.

Let r_i be the total *net* utility gain that individual i obtains as a result of reward strategy ϱ.[8] The total utility payoff of individual i as a result of strategies $\bar{\bar{p}}$ and ϱ will be

$$u_i = w_i + r_i + \sum_{j \in M} p_j \, x_{ij}. \qquad (8)$$

We also need a set of notations to describe the situation that would arise if the n individuals could not agree on the joint strategies $\bar{\bar{p}}$ and ϱ, in particular to describe the situation that would arise if the n individuals split into two opposing coalitions S and $\bar{S}$, the former having s members and the latter having $\bar{s} = n - s$ members.

We shall assume that, in case of a conflict

between coalitions S and $\bar{S}$, coalition S would have the choice among the policy alternatives $X_1, \ldots, X_{n+m}$ with probability π^s, while coalition $\bar{S}$ would have the choice among these alternatives with probability $\pi^{\bar{s}} = 1 - \pi^s$. If the choice were made by coalition S, alternative X_i would be selected with probability q_i^s; if the choice were made by coalition S, alternative X_i would be selected with probability $q_i^{\bar{s}}$. Hence, in case of a conflict between coalitions S and $\bar{S}$, the total probability of X_i being selected would be

$$p_i^s = p_i^{\bar{s}} = \pi^s q_i^s + (1 - \pi^s) q_i^s. \qquad (9)$$

If policy alternatives $X_1, \ldots, X_{n+m}$ have probabilities $p_1^s, \ldots, p_n^s{}_{+m}$ associated with them, equation (4) would give individual i the expected utility

$$y_i^s = w_i + \sum_{i \in M} p_i^s \, x_{ij}. \qquad (10)$$

We shall also assume that in the event of a conflict between coalitions S and $\bar{S}$, coalition S would use the retaliatory as well as defensive conflict strategy ϑ^s, while coalition $\bar{S}$ would use the conflict strategy $\vartheta^{\bar{s}}$. To a given member i of coalition S, the conflict strategies ϑ^s (of which he would be a participant) and $\vartheta^{\bar{s}}$ (of which he would be a target of attack) would cause the total *net* utility loss t_i^s. Thus t_i^s would be the total net *cost* to i of a conflict between S and $\bar{S}$ (if, to avoid double counting, we disregard the losses that i would suffer because the conflict might change the probabilities associated with the various policy alternatives X_i).[9]

Thus the total payoff to individual i in case of a conflict between S and $\bar{S}$ would be

---

[8] When all rewards R_{ij} happen to be *independent goods* for both the giver i and the receiver j, i.e., when they are neither complementary nor competitive goods, then we can analyze each net utility gain r_i into an algebraic sum of the separate utilities of all rewards received, and the separate utility costs of all rewards given away, by individual i. But in general such analysis is not possible because these quantities are not simply additive.

[9] Again, in special cases we may be able to analyze t_i^s into a sum of the *losses* that i would suffer by the opposing coalition's conflict strategy $\vartheta^{\bar{s}}$, and of the *costs* to him of his own coalition's conflict strategy ϑ^s. The latter in turn may possibly admit of analysis into the costs of retaliatory actions against members of the opposing coalition, the costs of defensive measures, the costs of subsidies (rewards) to be paid to members of his own coalition *less* the value of subsidies he receives from them, etc. But in general such analysis is not possible because these items are not simply additive.

$$u_i^s = w_i - t_i^s + \sum_{j \in M} p_j^s x_{ij}. \quad (11)$$

Under these assumptions, according to my bargaining model (Harsanyi, 1960, equa-

tion [8·7]) the n individuals will agree on such strategies $\overline{\overline{p}}$ and ϱ which will give each individual i the final utility payoff u_i, defined by the generalized Shapley-value expression:

$$u_i = w_i + z_i \cdot \frac{1}{n} (1 + R) +$$

$$+ z_i \cdot \sum_{\substack{s \ni i \\ S \subset N}} \frac{(s-1)!(n-s)!}{n!} \left[(P^s - P^{\bar{s}}) - (T^s - T^{\bar{s}}) \right] \quad (12)$$

where N denotes the set $N = (1, \ldots, n)$, and where $z_1, \ldots, z_n$ are certain variables,[10] whereas

$$R = \sum_{k \in N} \frac{r_k}{z_k} \quad (13)$$

$$P^s = \sum_{k \in N} \sum_{j \in M} \frac{p_j^s x_{kj}}{z_k} \quad (14)$$

and

$$T^s = \sum_{k \in N} \frac{t_k^s}{z_k}. \quad (15)$$

The quantities x_{kj} are the constants defined by equations (2) and (3). On the other hand, the variables of form z_i, r_i, p_i^s, t_i^s are defined implicitly in terms of a set of simultaneous optimizational equations[11] (equations $(\alpha\alpha)$, $(\beta\beta)$, and (γ) to (η) in Harsanyi, 1960), whose numerical solution in general requires an iterative procedure.

In special cases, however, a more direct approach is possible. In particular, in Case A it is often possible to treat the assumed bargaining game as a game with (locally) *transferable utility*,[12] owing to the participants'

ability to redistribute probability, by mutual agreement, between different policy alternatives X_i and X_j. In Case A, equation (8), in view of equation (1), takes the simple form

$$u_i = w_i + r_i + p_i x_i. \quad (16)$$

In order to obtain transferable utility, we have to subject all individuals' utility functions to linear transformations, by choosing the quantities x_i as the new units of measurement for each individual i's utility. The transformed value of u_i will be

$$u_i' = \frac{w_i + r_i}{x_i} + p_i. \quad (17)$$

Summing these quantities, we obtain

$$\sum_{i \in N} u_i' = \sum_{i \in N} \frac{w_i + r_i}{x_i} + 1 \quad (18)$$

which is a constant independent of the probabilities p_i and so satisfies the transferable-utility requirement.

Similarly, equation (11), in view of (1), now takes the simple form

$$u_i^s = w_i - t_i^s + p_i^s x_i. \quad (19)$$

The transformed value of u_i^s will be

$$(u_i^s)' = \frac{w_i - t_i^s}{x_i} + p_i^s. \quad (20)$$

Summing these quantities, in view of (9), we obtain

$$\sum_{i \in S} (u_i^s)' = \sum_{i \in S} \frac{w_i - t_i^s}{x_i} + \pi^s \sum_{i \in N} q_i^s =$$

$$= \sum_{i \in S} \frac{w_i - t_i^s}{x_i} + \pi^s. \quad (21)$$

---

[10] They are the reciprocals of the quantities a_1, ... , a_n, which I have called the *weights* of the game (Harsanyi, 1960).

[11] By an *optimizational* equation I mean an equation containing the *max* and/or the *min* operator(s).

[12] We speak of a game with *transferable utility* if any player i can transfer money or other values (or can transfer power in our case) to any other player j in such a way that the *sum* of their utilities (as well as the utilities of all other players) remains *constant* because j's utility gain is exactly equal to i's utility loss.

The last equality applies because in Case A coalition S will obviously distribute all probability among the policies X_i favored by its own members i so that

$$\sum_{i \epsilon S} q_i^S = 1. \tag{22}$$

We see that the summation in equation (21) also yields a constant independent of the probabilities q_i^S, and so satisfies the transferable-utility requirement.

However, the possibility of utility transfers satisfying equations (20) or (21) is restricted by the fact that the probabilities p_i and q_i^S can never become negative. For our purposes it is sufficient if the transferable-utility requirement is *locally* satisfied in the neighborhood of the solution payoff vector $u = (u_1, \ldots, u_n)$ of the game, which will be so if the equilibrium values for all n probabilities $p_1, \ldots, p_n$ are positive (i.e., nonzero).[13] In actual fact, it can be shown that the method to be discussed always furnishes the correct solution in any situation under Case A where it yields positive or zero values for all probabilities $p_i = \tilde{p}_i$. But when our method gives negative values for some of the p_i's, then the whole solution (including those p_i's for which we have obtained positive or zero values)

must be recomputed by means of the general iterative method not assuming transferable utility.

In cases where the transferable-utility assumption is admissible, equation (12) can be supplemented by the following simple equilibrium conditions:

$$z_i = x_i \qquad i = 1, \ldots, n \tag{23}$$

$$R = \max_\rho R (\rho) \tag{24}$$

$$T^S - T^{\bar{S}}$$
$$= \min_{\vartheta^S} \max_{\vartheta^{\bar{S}}} [T^S (\vartheta^S, \vartheta^{\bar{S}}) - T^{\bar{S}} (\vartheta^S, \vartheta^{\bar{S}})] \tag{25}$$

Moreover, by (22), (1), and (23), we have

$$P^S = \pi^S. \tag{26}$$

(In the general case without transferable utility, we obtain equilibrium conditions fairly similar to (24) and (25). But the *max* and *min* operators are subject to constraints involving some of the other variables, in such a way that the constraints together form a non-recursive circular system. This nonrecursiveness generally necessitates the use of an iterative procedure for finding the solution.)[14]

From equations (12), (8), and (6), we obtain the predicted value of $\tilde{p}_i$, the amount of individual i's generic power, as

$$\tilde{p}_i = \frac{z_i}{x_{ii}} \left[\frac{1}{n} + \sum_{\substack{S \ni i \\ S \subset N}} \frac{(s-1)!(n-s)!}{n!} (P^S - P^{\bar{S}}) \right] +$$

$$+ \frac{z_i}{x_{ii}} \left[\frac{1}{n} \left(R - \frac{r_i}{z_i} \right) - \sum_{\substack{S \ni i \\ S \subset N}} \frac{(s-1)!(n-s)!}{n!} (T^S - T^{\bar{S}}) \right] \tag{27}$$

[13] More exactly, the transferable-utility requirement must be satisfied also for each coalition S in the neighborhood of the vector $\bar{u}^S$ formed out of the conflict payoffs u_i^S of all members i of coalition S. This in turn requires that the equilibrium values (as defined by equations $(\alpha\alpha)$, $(\beta\beta)$, and (γ) to (η) of my 1960 paper) of the probabilities q_j^S for each $j \epsilon M$, and for each $S \subset N$, should be nonnegative.

[14] In cases B and C, also, the solution of the game takes a simpler form when the solution uses n different policy alternatives X_j with nonzero probabilities p_j. (By Footnote 5 the solution never has to use more than n different policies, but of course it

may use a smaller number of them.) Then the n variables z_i become the roots of the following set of n simultaneous equations, linear in the reciprocals of the unknowns:

$$\sum_{i \epsilon S} \frac{x_{ij}}{z_i} = 1 \qquad \text{for each } j \epsilon J$$

where J is the set of all j corresponding to a policy X_j actually used. The equilibrium values of R and of the T^S's are again determined by equations (24) and (25). But the equilibrium values of the P^S's are now determined by conditions more complex than equation (26).

The expression on the right of this equation is what we propose to call the *strength of* individual *i's power*.

Let us consider the meaning of this mathematical expression more closely. If we interpret equation (14) in the light of equation (6), we can see that each variable P^s is essentially a weighted sum of the amounts of *generic power* that the various members of coalition S would possess in case of a conflict between coalitions S and $\bar{S}$. Similarly, by equation (13), the variable R is a weighted sum of the net *rewards* r_i that the different individuals would receive from one another in case of full agreement. Finally, by equation (15), each variable T^s is a weighted sum of the *penalties* (or conflict costs) that the members of coalition S would suffer in case of a conflict between coalitions S and $\bar{S}$.

Accordingly, the first term on the right of equation (27) is a weighted sum (of a constant $1/_n$ and) of the amounts of generic power that individual i and his coalition partners would possess in various possible conflict situations, less a weighted sum of the amounts of generic power that members of the opposing coalitions would possess. This term can be regarded as a measure of the *net strength* of individual *i's* (and of his potential allies') *independent power*, i.e., of his ability to implement his policy preferences without the consent, or even against the resistance, of various individuals who may oppose him (and of his ability to prevent the latter from implementing their policy preferences without his consent).

On the other hand, the second term is a weighted sum of the net rewards that all other individuals would obtain in case of full agreement, and of the net penalties that they would suffer in various possible conflict situations if they opposed individual i, less a weighted sum of the net reward that individual *i* would obtain if full agreement were reached, and of the net penalties that he and his coalition partners would suffer in conflict situations. This term can be regarded as a measure of the *net strength* of individual *i's incentive power*, i.e., of his ability to provide incentives (or to use incentives provided by nature or by outside agencies) to induce other

participants to consent to implementing his own policy preferences.

Finally, the *sum* of these two terms, i.e., the whole expression on the right of equation (27), which we have called the *strength of i's power*, can be taken as a measure for the full strength of *i's bargaining position*, or of his power to get his policy preferences satisfied within the group, based both on his independent power and on his incentive power. (Under the models in the preceding paper for 2-person situations involving either unilateral power or reciprocal power, A had no independent power with respect to action X to be performed by B, as A was unable to perform an action of B's in place of B. The only way A could get an action of B's performed was to provide incentives for B to perform it. Hence the total strength of A's power over B was simply equal to the strength of his incentive power. But in *n*-person reciprocal power situations we need a more general definition for the strength of a person's power, admitting the strength of his independent power as a separate term.)

We have derived the mathematical expression defining the strength of an individual's power from a bargaining model for the *n*-person game, based on certain specific rationality postulates. But the above analysis shows that this expression is a suitable measure for the strength of each participant's *bargaining position* or *power* even in situations where the participants do not follow the rationality postulates of this bargaining model. (Of course, in such situations the observed *amount* of each participant's generic power will usually *not* be equal to its theoretically predicted value, i.e., to the *strength* of this participant's power.) To put it differently, the rationality postulates of our bargaining model are based on the assumption that all participants will use the strategical possibilities open to them in the best possible and most rational ways. In empirical situations this assumption will not always be fulfilled. But what the outcome would be if all participants did make full rational use of their strategical possibilities will still be a question of great theoretical interest; because the answer to this question will help us to assess quantitatively *what their strategical possibilities actually are,* i.e., what each participant's objective *bargaining position* is, even if the actual outcome does not correspond very closely to the different participants' objective bargaining positions.

To sum up our results, we now state our: *Theorem III.*[15] In *n*-person reciprocal power situations, if the participants follow the rationality postulates of the writer's bargaining model for the *n*-person game, then the *amount* of each participant's *generic power* will tend to be equal to the *strength* of his power, defined as the sum of the strength of his *independent power* and the strength of his *incentive power.*[16]

RELATIONSHIP BETWEEN OUR STRENGTH-OF-POWER CONCEPT AND THE SHAPLEY-SHUBIK MEASURE FOR POWER

Shapley and Shubik (1954) have proposed a quantitative measure for the power of each participant in a committee system, e.g., in a constitutional structure. (For instance, they have found that under the U.S. Constitution the power indices for the President, for an individual senator, and for an individual congressman are in the proportion of 350:9:2.) In our notations, their power index can be defined as

$$p_i^* = \frac{1}{n} + \sum_{\substack{S \ni i \\ S \subset N}} \frac{(s-1)!(n-s)!}{n!} \left(\pi^s - \pi^{\bar{s}} \right) \qquad (28)$$

which is identical with our measure for the *strength* of individual *i*'s *independent power* alone in Case A (cf. equations [23], [26], and [27]).

Shapley and Shubik's power measure is based on the Shapley value for the *n*-person game (Shapley, 1953), while our strength-of-power concept is based on our own bargaining model for the *n*-person game. But in view of the very close mathematical relationship between our bargaining model and the Shapley value, it is not surprising that our

---

[15] For easier reference I am calling this Theorem III, to follow Theorems I and II of the preceding paper.

[16] Theorem III is a direct generalization of Theorem II. But formally there is no full parallelism, because in Theorem II the strength-of-power measure has to be multiplied by a factor 1/2 while in Theorem III no multiplication is necessary. This is so because we have found it convenient to incorporate the factor 1/*n* (corresponding to factor 1/2 of Theorem II) into the expression we have chosen to define the strength of a person's power in *n*-person situations.

We do not have to add a qualification, as we did in the cases of Theorems I and II, concerning the range of variation of the amount of generic power (viz. that $0 \leqslant \bar{p}_i \leqslant 1$), because under the definition given the strength of a person's power always remains within the required range.

strength-of-power concept and their power index are also closely related.

Of course, the intuitive interpretation Shapley and Shubik give to their power index is not the same that we have given to our measure for the strength of independent power, in that their power index is supposed to express (roughly speaking) the *a priori* probability that a given participant *i* will have the *decisive vote* in getting policy proposals finally accepted. But Shapley and Shubik are fully aware of the fact that their power index admits of a number of alternative intuitive interpretations—in effect, they point out that any intuitive interpretation consistent with the axioms defining the Shapley value would necessarily lead to numerically the same power index.

But even at an intuitive level it is possible to translate their definition in terms of our own model. Let us consider the case of *n* individuals each of whom wants to have the decisive vote on some particular policy problem. Let us also make the following two restrictive assumptions:

1. Each of the *n* participants would be perfectly indifferent as to who should have the decisive vote in case he could not have it himself.

2. None of the *n* participants can provide any incentives for the other participants.

Assumption 1 brings the situation under our Case A, while assumption 2 makes the strength of each participant's incentive power equal to zero.

We may consider that the Shapley-Shubik model deals with the special case corresponding to these assumptions. Given these assumptions, both our strength-of-power measure and the Shapley-Shubik power index for a given individual *i* are defined as being equal to the probability p_i that the decisive vote will be cast by this individual *i*. Moreover, both our own model and the Shapley-Shubik model yield for this probability the value $p_i = p_i^*$ defined by equation (28). Thus, under these assumptions their power measure and ours coincide.

In short, the Shapley-Shubik power measure can be regarded as that special case of our own strength-of-power concept where the *single-preferences* and the *no-compromise* assumptions of Case A are satisfied, and where at the same time the *incentive power* of every participant is *nil* (or is disregarded).

That is, compared with the Shapley-Shubik measure, our own strength-of-power measure has the advantage of taking account of the effects that the *incentive power* of various participants has on each participant's power position. For instance, if the participants' utility functions are sufficiently known then our measure makes it possible to compute the increase in the American President's strength of power (and the corresponding decrease in the strength of the power of the Congress), due to a given amount of patronage that he can promise to senators and congressmen, or due to a given amount of influence with the electorate he can promise or threaten to mobilize at the next election for the Congress, etc.

Our strength-of-power measure can also take account of the effects of alliances and party alignments among the participants. Under Case A this can be done only by assuming that the very act of co-operation with the other members of a given possible coalition *S* would be a source of direct utility or disutility to certain individuals *i*, with corresponding effects on the values of the quantities t_i^s and T^s.[17] But under Cases B and C, alliances and party alignments can be represented also by similarities among the policy preferences of various participants. In the analysis of most empirical situations one will presumably need both of these methods for representing alliances among the participants. (Shapley and Shubik [1954, pp. 791-792] take account of party alignments by noting the possible discrepancies between their theoretical measure and an analogous empirical measure they introduce, but the existence of a party structure does not enter into their theoretical measure as such.)

Finally, our strength-of-power measure can also take account of improvements in *all* participants' power positions when suitable *compromise policies* are discovered, which may increase the chances, for all participants at the same time, of a reasonably satisfactory outcome (Case C).

REFERENCES

Harsanyi, J. C. A bargaining model for the co-operative *n*-person game. In A. W. Tucker and R. D. Luce (Eds.), *Contributions to the theory of games*, IV. Princeton: Princeton Univ. Press, 1959, Pp. 325-355.

Harsanyi, J. C. A simplified model for the *n*-person cooperative game, 1960 (hectographed). Available from author on request.

Harsanyi, J. C. Measurement of social power, opportunity costs, and the theory of two-person bargaining games, *Behav. Sci.*, 1962, 1, Pp. 67-80.

Shapley, L. S. A value for *n*-person games. In H. W. Kuhn and A. W. Tucker (Eds.), *Contributions to the theory of games*, II. Princeton, Princeton Univ. Press, 1953, Pp. 307-317.

Shapley, L. S., & Shubik, M. A method for evaluating the distribution of power in a committee system. *Amer. Polit. Sci. Rev.*, 1954, 48, 787-792.

(Manuscript received April 17, 1961)

[17] The pairs of opposing coalitions *S* and $\bar{S}$ in my bargaining model are assumed in general to be based merely on *tactical considerations*. But some particular coalitions of course may also exhibit emotional ties and/or similarities in policy preferences among their members. This fact in our model would find expression in the utility functions of the relevant individuals.

[4]

Several authors have recently suggested measuring social power in terms of its effects; that is, in terms of the changes that A can cause in B's behavior. This paper argues that an adequate measure of power must also contain information on the two parties' opportunity costs—the costs to A of acquiring or using his power over B, which the paper calls the costs of A's power; and the costs to B of noncompliance, which measure the strength of B's incentives to compliance, and which the paper calls the strength of A's power over B. For bilateral power situations, where both parties can exert pressure on each other, a somewhat different game-theoretical measure for the strength of A's power is developed.

MEASUREMENT OF SOCIAL POWER, OPPORTUNITY COSTS, AND THE THEORY OF TWO-PERSON BARGAINING GAMES

by John C. Harsanyi

Australian National University, now at Wayne State University

INTRODUCTION

RECENT papers by Simon (1957), by March (1955, 1957), and by Dahl (1957) have suggested measuring person A's power over person B in terms of its actual or potential *effects*, that is, in terms of the changes that A causes or can cause in B's behavior.[1] As Dahl puts it, A has power over B to the extent to which "he can get B to do something that B would not otherwise do" (1957, p. 203).

As Simon and March have obtained very similar results, I shall restrict myself largely to summarizing Dahl's main conclusions. Dahl distinguishes the following constituents of the power relation:

(a) the *base* of power, i.e., the resources (economic assets, constitutional prerogatives, military forces, popular prestige, etc.) that A can use to influence B's behavior;

(b) the *means* of power, i.e., the specific actions (promises, threats, public appeals, etc.) by which A can make actual use of these resources to influence B's behavior;

[1] I am indebted to Professor Jacob Marschak, of U.C.L.A., and to Professors Herbert A. Simon and James G. March, of Carnegie Institute of Technology, for helpful discussions on this and related topics.

(c) the *scope* of power, i.e., the set of specific actions that A, by using his means of power, can get B to perform; and finally

(d) the *amount* of power, i.e., the net increase in the probability of B's actually performing some specific action X, due to A's using his means of power against B (1957, pp. 203-205).

If A has power over several individuals, Dahl adds a fifth constituent:

(e) the set of individuals over whom A has power—this we shall call the *extension* of A's power.

Dahl points out that the power of two individuals can be compared in any of these five dimensions. Other things being equal, an individual's power is greater: (a) the greater his power base, (b) the more means of power available to him, and the greater (c) the scope, (d) the amount, and (e) the extension of his power. But Dahl proposes to use only the last three variables for the formal definition and measurement of social power. He argues that what we primarily mean by great social power is an ability to influence many people (extension) in many respects (scope) and with a high probability (amount of power). In contrast, a large power base or numerous means of power are not direct measures of the extent of the influence or power that one person can exert over other persons; they are only instruments by which great power can be achieved and maintained, and are indicators from which we can normally *infer* the likely possession of great power by an individual.

Among the three variables of scope, amount, and extension, amount of power is the crucial one, in terms of which the other two can be defined. For the scope of A's power over B is simply the set of specific actions X with respect to which A has a nonzero amount of power over B, i.e., the set of those actions X for which A can achieve a nonzero increase in the probability of these actions actually being performed by B. Similarly, the extension of A's power is the set of specific individuals over whom A has power of nonzero scope and amount.

While the amount of power is a difference of two probabilities, and therefore is directly given as a *real number*,[2] all other dimensions of power are directly given as lists of specific objects (e.g., a list of specific resources, a list of specific actions by A or by B, or a list of specific individuals over whom A has power). But Dahl and March suggest that at least in certain situations it will be worthwhile to develop straight numerical measures for them by appropriate aggregating procedures—essentially by counting the number of comparable items in a given list, and possibly by assigning different weights to items of unequal importance (e.g., we may give more "marks" for power over an important individual than for power over a less important one) (March, 1957, pp. 213-220). In other cases we may divide up a given list into several sublists and may assign a separate numerical measure to each of them, without necessarily aggregating all these numbers into a single figure. That is, we may characterize a given dimension of power not by a

single number, but rather by a set of several numbers, i.e., a vector. (For instance, we may describe the extension of President de Gaulle's power by listing the numbers [or percentages] of deputies, of army officers of various ranks, of electors, etc., who support him, without trying to combine all these figures into one index number.)

TWO ADDITIONAL DIMENSIONS OF SOCIAL POWER

A quantitative characterization of a power relation, however, in my view must include two more variables not mentioned in Dahl's list:

(f) the opportunity costs to A of attempting to influence B's behavior, i.e., the opportunity costs of using his power over B (and of acquiring this power over B in the first place if A does not yet possess the required power), which we shall call the *costs* of A's power over B; and

(g) the opportunity costs to B of refusing to do what A wants him to do, i.e., of refusing to yield to A's attempt to influence his behavior. As these opportunity costs measure the strength of B's incentives for yielding to A's influence, we shall call them the *strength* of A's power over B.[3]

More precisely, the *costs* of A's power over B will be defined as the *expected value* (actuarial value) of the costs of his attempt to influence B. It will be a weighted average of the net total costs that A would incur if his attempt were successful (e.g., the costs of rewarding B), and of the net total costs that A would incur if his attempt were unsuccessful (e.g., the costs of punishing B).

Other things being equal, A's power over B is greater the smaller the costs of A's power and the greater the strength of A's power.

Both of these two cost variables may be

---

[2] But as the probability that B will actually perform a specific action X suggested by A will in general be different for different actions X and for different individuals B, the total amount of A's power (or even the amount of A's power over a given individual B) will also have to be described by a vector rather than by a single number, except if some sort of aggregation procedure is used.

[3] Of course, instead of taking the opportunity costs (i.e. the net disadvantages) associated for B with noncompliance, we could just as well take the net advantages associated for him with compliance —they both amount to the same thing.

expressed either in physical units (e.g., it may cost A so many bottles of beer or so many working hours to get B to adopt a given policy X; and again it may cost B so many bottles of beer or so many years' imprisonment if he does not adopt policy X), in monetary units (e.g., A's or B's relevant costs may amount to so many actual dollars, or at least may be equivalent to a loss of so many dollars for him), or in utility units. (In view of the theoretical problems connected with interpersonal comparisons of utility, and of the difficulties associated with utility measurement even for one individual, in practice the costs and the strength of power will usually be expressed in physical or in monetary units.[4] But for the purposes of theoretical analysis the use of utility costs sometimes has important advantages, as we shall see.)

Unlike the power base and the means of power, which need not be included in the definition of the power relation, both the costs of power and the strength of power are essential ingredients of the definition ' of power. A's power over B should be defined not merely as an ability by A to get B to do X with a certain probability p, but rather as an ability by A to achieve this at a certain total cost u to himself, by convincing B that B would have to bear the total cost v if he did not do X.

THE COSTS OF POWER

One of the main purposes for which social scientists use the concept of A's power over B is for the description of the policy possibilities open to A. If we want to know the situation (or environment) which A faces as a decision-maker, we must know whether he can or cannot get B to perform a certain action X, and more specifically how sure he can be (in a probability sense) that B will

[4] A good deal of recent experimental work shows that it is possible, at least under certain conditions, to measure the utilities that a given individual assigns to various alternatives. Interpersonal comparisons of utility can also be given operationally meaningful interpretation (Harsanyi, 1955, pp. 316-320). Note, however, that the main conclusions of this paper, in particular Theorems I and II, do not require interpersonal utility comparisons.

actually perform this action. But a realistic description of A's policy possibilities must include not only A's ability or inability to get B to perform a certain action X, but also the *costs* that A has to bear in order to achieve this result. If two individuals are in a position to exert the same influence over other individuals, but if one can achieve this influence only at the cost of great efforts and/or financial or other sacrifices, while the other can achieve it free of any such costs, we cannot say in any useful sense that their power is equally great. Any meaningful comparison must be in terms of the influence that two individuals can achieve at comparable costs, or in terms of the costs they have to bear in order to achieve comparable degrees of influence.

For instance, it is misleading to say that two political candidates have the same power over two comparable constituencies if one needs much more electioneering effort and expenditure to achieve a given majority, even if in the end both achieve the same majorities; or that two businessmen have the same power over the city government if one can achieve favorable treatment by city officials only at the price of large donations to party funds, while the other can get the same favorable treatment just for the asking.

Of course, a power concept which disregards the costs of power is most inaccurate when the costs of using a given power become very high or even prohibitive. For instance, suppose that an army commander becomes a prisoner of enemy troops, who try to force him at gun point to give a radio order to his army units to withdraw from a certain area. He may very well have the power to give a contrary order, both in the sense of having the physical ability to do so and in the sense of there being a very good chance of his order being actually obeyed by his army units—but he can use this power only at the cost of his life. Though the scope, the amount, and the extension of his power over his soldiers would still be very great, it would clearly be very misleading in this situation to call him a powerful individual in the same sense as before his capture.

More generally, measurement of power

merely in terms of its scope, amount, and extension tends to give counterintuitive results when the possessor of power has little or no real opportunity to actually use his power. For example, take the case of a secretary who has to compile various reports for her employer, according to very specific instructions which leave her little actual choice as to how to prepare them. Suppose that her employer then uses these reports as a basis for very important decisions.[5] Physically she could exert considerable influence on her employer's policies by omitting certain pieces of information from her reports, or including misleading information. In this sense, the scope and the amount of her power over her employer is considerable. But normally she will have little opportunity for using this power, and social scientists would hardly wish to describe her as a powerful individual, as they would have to do if they used Dahl's power concept without modification.

In terms of our own power concept, however, the secretary in question has little real power if all dimensions of her power are taken into account. Though she does have power of great scope and great amount over her employer, this fact is normally more than offset by the very high costs of using her power. If she intentionally submits misleading reports she probably will be found out very soon and will be dismissed and/or punished in other ways. Moreover, if she is a loyal employee such flagrant violation of her instructions would in itself involve very high disutility costs to her.

To conclude, a realistic quantitative description of *A*'s power over *B* must include, as an essential dimension of this power relation, the costs to *A* of attempting to influence *B*'s behavior.

THE STRENGTH OF POWER

While the costs of power must be included in the definition of our power concept in order to ensure its descriptive validity, the variable of *strength* of power must be included to ensure the usefulness of our power concept for explanatory purposes.

As March (1955, pp. 431-432) has pointed

5 I owe this example to Professor Jacob Marschak.

out about the concept of influence, one of the main analytical tasks of such concepts as influence or power (which essentially is an ability to exert influence) is to serve as *intervening variables* in the analysis of individual or social decision-making. Therefore we need a power or influence concept which enables us in the relevant cases to explain a decision by a given private individual or by an official of a social organization, in terms of the power or influence that another individual or some social group has over him. But fundamentally, the analysis of any human decision must be in terms of the variables on the basis of which the decision-maker concerned actually makes his decision —that is, in terms of the advantages and disadvantages he associates with alternative policies available to him. In order to explain why *B* adopts a certain policy *X* in accordance with *A*'s wishes, we must know what *difference it makes* for *B* whether *A* is his friend or his enemy—or more generally, we must know the *opportunity costs* to *B* of not adopting policy *X*. Hence, if our power concept is to serve us as an explanatory intervening variable in the analysis of *B*'s decision to comply with *A*'s wishes, our power concept must include as one of its essential dimensions the opportunity costs to *B* of noncompliance, which measure the strength of *B*'s incentives to compliance and which we have called the strength of *A*'s power over *B*.

For instance, if we want to explain the decision of Senator Knowland to support a certain bill of the Eisenhower administration we must find out, among other things, which particular individuals or social groups influenced his decision, and to what extent. Now suppose that we have strong reasons to assume that it was President Eisenhower's personal intervention which made Senator Knowland change his mind and decide to support the bill in question. Then we still have to explain *how* the variables governing the Senator's decision were actually affected by the President's intervention. Did the President make a promise to him, i.e., did he attach new *advantages*, from the Senator's point of view, to the policy of supporting the bill? Or did the President make a threat, i.e., did he attach new *disadvantages* to the policy of opposing the bill? Or did the President supply new information, pointing out certain already *existing* advantages and/or disadvantages associated with these two policies, which the Senator had been insufficiently aware of before? In any case we must explain how the President's intervention increased the opportunity costs that Senator Knowland came to associate with opposing the bill.

If we cannot supply this information, then the mere existence of an influence or power relationship between President Eisenhower and Senator Knowland will not *explain* the latter's decision to support the bill. It will only pose a *problem* concerning this decision. (Why on earth did he comply with the President's request to support the bill, when it is known that he had many reasons to oppose it, and did actually oppose it for a while?)

There seem to be four main ways by which a given actor *A* can manipulate the incentives or opportunity costs of another actor *B*:

1. *A* may provide certain *new* advantages or disadvantages for *B*, subject to *no condition*. For instance, he may provide certain facilities for *B* which make it easier or less expensive for *B* to follow certain particular policy objectives desirable to *A*. (For example, country *A* may be able to induce country *B* to attack some third country *C*, simply by supplying arms to *B*, even if *A* supplies these arms "without any strings attached"—and in particular without making it a condition of her arms deliveries that *B* will actually attack *C*.) Or *A* may withdraw from *B* certain facilities that could help *B* in attaining policy objectives undesirable to *A*. More generally, *A* may provide for *B* goods or services complementary to some particular policy goal *X*, or competitive to policy goals alternative to *X*, so as to increase for *B* the net utility of *X*, or to decrease the net utility of its alternatives; or *A* may achieve similar results by depriving *B* of goods or services either competitive to *X* or complementary to its alternatives.[6]

2. *A* may set up *rewards* and *punishments*, i.e. *new* advantages and disadvantages subject to certain *conditions* as to *B*'s future behavior.

3. *A* may supply *information* (or misinformation) on (allegedly) already *existing* advantages and/or disadvantages connected with various alternative policies open to *B*.

4. *A* may rely on his legitimate *authority* over *B*, or on *B*'s personal *affection* for *A*, which make *B* attach *direct disutility* to the very act of disobeying *A*.

Of course, in a situation where *A* has certain power over *B*, either party can be mistaken about the true opportunity costs to him of various alternatives. Therefore both in discussing the costs of *A*'s power over *B*, and in discussing the strength of his power, we must distinguish between *objective* costs and *perceived* costs—between what these costs actually are and what the individual bearing these costs thinks them to be. For the purpose of a formal definition of the power relation, the *costs* of *A*'s power over *B* have to be stated as the *objective* costs that an attempt to influence *B* would actually entail upon *A*, while the *strength* of *A*'s power over *B* has to be stated in terms of the costs of noncompliance as *perceived* by *B* himself. The reason is that the costs of *A*'s power serve to describe the objective policy possibilities open to *A*, whereas the strength of *A*'s power serves to explain *B*'s subjective motivation for compliant behavior. (Of course, a full description of a given power situation would require listing both objective and perceived costs for both participants.)

THE STRENGTH OF POWER, AND THE AMOUNT OF POWER IN DAHL'S SENSE

Clearly, in general the greater the *strength* of *A*'s power over *B*, the greater will be *A*'s

---

[6] Case 1 is discussed in somewhat greater detail

because power based on providing services or disservices without any conditions attached is often overlooked in the literature. For our purposes, the distinction between unconditional advantages or disadvantages on the one hand, and conditional rewards or punishments on the other hand, is important because the latter lend themselves to *bargaining* much more easily than the former do.

amount of power over B with respect to action X. The relationship between these two variables will take a particularly simple mathematical form if the strength of A's power is measured in *utility* terms, i.e., in terms of the disutility costs to B of noncompliance.[7]

We shall use the following model. A wants B to perform action X. But B associates disutility x with doing X. Nevertheless B would perform X with probability p_1 (i.e., would adopt the mixed strategy $s[p_1]$ assigning probability p_1 to doing X and probability $[1 - p_1]$ to not doing X), even in the absence of A's intervention.[8] B would adopt this strategy because if he completely refused to do X (i.e., if he adopted the mixed strategy $s[0]$) he would obtain only the utility payoff u_0 —; while if he did X with probability p_1 (i.e., if he adopted strategy $s[p_1]$), then he would obtain the higher utility payoff u_1, making his total expected utility $u_1 - p_1 x > u_0$.

Now A intervenes and persuades B that B will obtain the still higher utility payoff u_2 if he agrees to do action X with a certain probability $p_2 > p_1$ (i.e., if he adopts strategy $s[p_2]$), making his total expected utility $u_2 - p_2 x$. In view of this, B does adopt strategy $s[p_2]$.

Under these assumptions, obviously the *amount* of A's power over B will be the difference $\Delta p = p_2 - p_1$, while the *strength* of A's power over B will be the difference $u_2 - u_1$. As $p_2 \leq 1$, we must have $\Delta p \leq 1 - p_1$. Moreover, by assumption (cf. Footnote 7); $\Delta p \geq 0$.

If B tries to maximize his expected utility,[9] then he will adopt strategy $s[p_2]$ only if

$$u_2 - p_2 x \geqq u_1 - p_1 x, \qquad (1)$$

that is, if

$$\Delta p = p_2 - p_1 \leqq \frac{u_2 - u_1}{x} = \frac{\Delta u}{x}. \qquad (2)$$

This gives us:

Theorem 1. The maximum *amount* of power that A can achieve over B with respect to action X tends to be equal to the *strength* of A's power over B (as expressed in utility units) divided by the disutility to B of doing action X—except that this maximum amount of power cannot be more than the amount of power corresponding to B's doing action X with probability *one*.

The strength of A's power over B divided by the disutility to B of doing X may be called the *relative strength* of A's power over B. Accordingly, we obtain:

Theorem 1'. The maximum *amount* of power that A can achieve over B with respect to action X tends to be equal to the *relative strength* of A's power over B with respect to action X (except that, again, this maximum amount of power cannot be more than the amount of power corresponding to B's doing action X with probability one).

Of course, in the real world we seldom observe B to use a randomized mixed strategy of form $s[p]$, in a literal sense. What we do find is that, if we watch B's behavior over a series of comparable occasions, he will comply with A's wishes in some proportion p of all occasions and will fail to comply in the remaining proportion $(1 - p)$ of the occasions. Moreover, the disutility to B of compliant behavior will vary from one occasion to another. Hence if B wants to comply with A's wishes in pn cases out of n then, other things being equal, he will tend to select those pn cases where compliance is associated with the smallest disutility to him. For example, suppose that a U.S. senator, with political attitudes rather different from the administration's, decides to vote for the president's legislative program often enough to avoid at least an open break with the administration. Then he is likely to select for his support those administration bills which are least distasteful to him and to his constituents. This means that the total disutility to B of a given

---

[7] To simplify our analysis, in what follows we shall be concerned only with the case where A is able to influence B in the intended direction, i.e., has a nonnegative amount of power over him. (A can have a negative amount of power over B only if he seriously misjudges the situation, because otherwise he can always make the amount of his power at worst *zero*, by simply refraining from intervention.)

[8] We follow Dahl in considering the more general case where B would do action X with some probability p_1 (which of course may be zero), even in the absence of A's intervention.

[9] On the assumption of expected-utility maximization, see Marschak (1950; 1954, Section 1).

strategy $s[p]$ (which now has to be defined as a strategy involving compliance in *proportion p* of all cases) will tend to increase somewhat more than proportionally as p increases, because should B decide to increase the frequency of his compliant behavior he would have to include a higher fraction of "difficult" cases.

Accordingly, if we restate our model in terms of empirical *frequencies*, rather than theoretical *probabilities*, we must expect that the maximum *amount* of power that A can achieve over B will increase somewhat less than in proportion to increments in the *strength* of A's power over B (measuring this strength now in terms of the *average* utility value of B's incentives for compliance over all occasions). But our Theorem I is likely to retain at least its approximate validity in most empirical situations.[10]

POWER IN A SCHEDULE SENSE

We have just seen that the greater the strength of a person's power over other persons the greater the amount of his power over them tends to be. But likewise, the greater the strength of a person's power over other people, the greater both the scope and the extension of his power over these people. That is, the stronger incentives he can provide for compliance, the larger the number of specific actions he can get other people to perform for him will be, and the larger the number of individuals he can get to perform these actions.

But while the scope, the amount, and the extension of his power are all functions of the *strength* of his power over all individuals, the strength of his power is itself a function of the *costs* of power he is prepared to bear.

The greater efforts and sacrifices he is prepared to make, the stronger incentives for compliance he will be able to provide and the greater will be the strength of his power over them.

Therefore, a given individual's power can be described not only by stating the specific values of the five dimensions of his power (whether as single numbers, or as vectors, or as lists of specific items), but also by specifying the mathematical *functions* or *schedules* that connect the costs of his power with the other four dimensions. When power is defined in terms of the specific values of the five power variables we shall speak of power in a *point* sense, and when power is defined in terms of the functions or schedules connecting the other four power variables with the costs of power we shall speak of power in a *schedule* sense.[11]

Power in a schedule sense can be regarded as a "production function" describing how a given individual can "transform" different amounts of his resources (of his working time, his money, his political rights, his popularity, etc.) into social power of various dimensions (of various strengths, scopes, amounts, and extensions). The commonsense notion of social power makes it an *ability* to achieve certain things—an ability that the person concerned is free to use or to leave unused. It seems to me that this notion of power as an ability is better captured by our concept of power in a schedule sense than it is by the concept of power in a point sense. (The latter seems to better correspond to the commonsense notion of actually exerted *influence*, rather than to that of power as such.)

If a person's power is given in a mere schedule sense, then we can state the specific values of his five power dimensions only if we are also told how much of his different resources he is actually prepared to use in order to obtain social power of various dimensions—that is, if besides his power schedules we know also his *utility function*. Whereas his power defined in a schedule sense

---

[10] More exactly, in most unilateral power situations. The distinction between unilateral and bilateral power situations will be discussed below.

Note that in empirical applications based on a *frequency* interpretation, a further complication may arise owing to the fact that the utilities to A, and the disutilities to B, of a set of several compliant actions $X_1, \ldots, X_k$ by B may *not* be simply *additive* (as they may have the nature of complementary or of competitive "goods" from A's point of view, and/or the nature of complementary or of competitive "evils" from B's point of view).

[11] In analogy to the distinction in economic theory between demand or supply in a point sense and in a schedule sense.

indicates the conditions under which his environment is ready to "supply" power to him, it is his utility function which determines his "demand" for power under various alternative conditions.

BILATERAL POWER AND THE "BLACKMAILER'S FALLACY"

So far we have tacitly assumed that, in situations where A has power over B, A is always in a position to determine, by his unilateral decision, the incentives he will provide for B's compliance, as well as the degree of compliance he will try to enforce. Situations in which this is actually the case may be called unilateral power situations. But it very often happens that not only can A exert pressure on B in order to get him to adopt certain specific policies, but B can do the same to A. In particular, B may be able to press A for increased rewards and/or decreased penalties, and for relaxing the standards of compliance required from him and used in administering rewards and penalties to him. Situations of this type we shall call bilateral or reciprocal power situations. In such situations, both the extent of B's compliant behavior (i.e., the scope and the amount of A's power over B) and the net incentives that A can provide for B (i.e., the net strength of A's power over B) will become matters of explicit or implicit *bargaining* between the two parties.

Of the four ways in which A can increase his strength of power discussed previously, we tend to obtain unilateral power situations in cases 1, 3, and 4, where A's power over B is based on providing *unconditional* advantages or disadvantages for B, on conveying information or misinformation to him, or on having legitimate authority over B and/or enjoying B's personal affection (though there are also exceptions where these cases give rise to bilateral power). For example, it is usually largely a matter for A's personal discretion whether he provides certain facilities for B, whether he discloses certain pieces of information to him, or whether he gives him an order as his legitimate superior. In case 2, on the other hand, when A's power over B is based on A's ability to set up rewards and/

or punishments for B *conditional* upon B's behavior, normally we find bilateral power situations (though again there are important exceptions).[12] Here B can exert pressure on A by withholding his compliance, even though compliance would be much more profitable than noncompliance. He may also be able to exert pressure on A by making the costs of a conflict (including the costs of punishing B for noncompliance) very high to A.

For bilateral power situations Theorem I and Theorem I' do not hold true. For these conclusions have been completely dependent on the assumption that if a certain strategy s_1, involving some given degree of compliance by B, is more profitable to B than any alternative strategy s_2 involving a lesser degree of compliance (or none at all), then B will always choose strategy s_1 and will never choose strategy s_2—not even as a result of dissatisfaction with the terms A offers in return for B's co-operation. While in unilateral power situations this assumption is perfectly legitimate (as it amounts to no more than assuming that B tries to maximize his utility or expected utility), in bilateral power situations this assumption would involve what I propose to call the "blackmailer's fallacy" (Harsanyi, 1956, p. 156).

A would-be blackmailer A once argued that as he was in a position to cause damage worth \$1,000 to a certain rich man B, he should be able to extract from B *any* ransom r short of \$1,000, because after payment of $r < \$1,000$, B would still be better off than if he had to suffer the full \$1,000 damage.

But this argument is clearly fallacious. By similar reasoning, B could also have argued that A would accept *any* ransom r larger than nil, because after accepting a ransom $r > \$0$, A would still be better off than if no agreement were reached and he did not receive anything at all. What both of these arguments really show is that in any bargaining between two rational bargainers, the outcome must fall between what may be called

---

[12] Viz. in cases when A is able to persuade B that he, A, has irrevocably committed himself in advance to not making any concessions to B. See Schelling (1956, pp. 282-287), Harsanyi (1961).

the two parties' *concession limits*, which are defined by each party's refusal to accept any agreement that would make him actually worse off than he would be in the conflict situation. But the two arguments in themselves say nothing about where the two parties' agreement point will actually lie *between* these two limits. They certainly do not allow the inference that this agreement point will actually coincide or nearly coincide with one party's concession limit.[13] (Only if we know the two parties' attitudes towards risk-taking, and in particular towards risking a conflict rather than accepting unfavorable terms, can we make any predictions about where their agreement point will lie between the two concession limits.)

Either party's actual behavior will be a resultant of two opposing psychological forces. On the one hand, for example, *B* will admittedly have some incentive for agreeing to any ransom payment less than \$1,000. But *B* will also know that *A* will likewise have some incentive for accepting any ransom payment greater than zero, and this fact will make *B* expect to get away with a ransom payment of much less than \$1,000. This expectation in turn will provide *B* with some incentive to resist any ransom payment too close to \$1,000. Any realistic theory of *B*'s behavior must take full account of *both* of these psychological forces—both of *B*'s motives for compliance, and of the reasons which make him expect some concessions on *A*'s part which will render full compliance on his own part unnecessary.

THE ZEUTHEN-NASH THEORY AND THE STRENGTH OF POWER IN BILATERAL POWER SITUATIONS

For analysis of the two parties' behavior in bilateral power situations, and in particular for quantitative assessment of the two opposite psychological forces governing each party's degree of compliance, we shall use the Zeuthen-Nash theory of the two-person

bargaining game.[14] Our analysis will be based on the following model.[15]

Just as in the model discussed earlier, *A* wants *B* to perform action *X*. But *B* associates disutility *x* with doing *X*. Nevertheless *B* would perform *X* with probability p_1, i.e., would use the mixed strategy $s(p_1)$, even in the absence of *A*'s intervention. This would happen because if *B* completely refused to do *X* (i.e., if he adopted strategy $s[0]$) he would obtain only the utility payoff u_0—while if he did *X* with probability p_1 (i.e., if he adopted strategy $s[p_1]$) then he would obtain the higher utility payoff u_1, making his total expected utility $u_1 - p_1 x > u_0$.

If *B* completely refused to do *X*, then *A*'s utility level would be u_0^*. If *B* did perform *X* (with probability 1), then *A*'s utility would increase by the amount x^*. Accordingly, if *B* did *X* only with probability p_1 then *A*'s expected utility would be $u_0^* + p_1 x^*$.

Now *A* intervenes and offers *B* a reward *R* if *B* will increase the probability of his doing action *X* from p_1 to some mutually agreed figure p_2 (i.e., if *B* adopts strategy $s[p_2]$). In utility units, this reward *R* would represent a gain *r* for *B*, while providing this reward would cost *A* the amount r^*. Hence, if the two parties can agree on some probability p_2, then *A*'s total expected utility will be

$$u_2^* = u_2^*(p_2) = u_0^* - r^* + p_2 x^*, \quad (3)$$

whereas *B*'s total expected utility will be

$$u_2 = u_2(p_2) = u_1 + r - p_2 x. \quad (4)$$

A also sets up the penalty *T* for *B* if *B* refuses to sufficiently increase the probability of his performing action *X*. In utility units, this penalty *T* would cause a loss *t* to *B*, while enforcing this penalty would cost *A* the amount t^*. Hence, if the two parties could not agree on the value of p_2, *A*'s total expected utility would be

$$u_3^* = u_0^* - t^* + p_1 x^* \quad (5)$$

[13] Only in ultimatum games (cf. Footnote 12 above), including all unilateral power situations, is it generally true that one party can extract any degree of concession or compliance from the other party up to the latter's actual concession limit point.

[14] I have set out my reasons for accepting the Zeuthen-Nash theory, and have discussed the theory in some detail, in Harsanyi (1956, 1961). The original references are Zeuthen (1930) and Nash (1950, 1953). For an excellent introduction to game theory in general, see Luce and Raiffa (1957).

[15] See Footnotes 7 and 8 above.

76   JOHN C. HARSANYI

(assuming that B would still perform X with probability p_1), whereas B's total expected utility would be

$$u_3 = u_1 - t_1 - p_1 x. \qquad (6)$$

More generally, we may assume that in a conflict situation *both* parties would use retaliatory strategies against each other, A using strategy T_A and B using strategy T_B. In such a case t should be redefined as the *total loss* that B would suffer in the conflict situation, including both the damages caused to him by his opponent's retaliatory strategy T_A, and the costs to him of his own retaliatory strategy T_B. Similarly, t^* should be redefined as the *total loss* that A would suffer in the conflict situation. But otherwise our conclusions retain their validity.

Now, what will be the equilibrium value of the probability p_2 which tends to be agreed upon in bargaining between two rational bargainers?

We already know that it must lie between the p_2 values corresponding to the two parties' concession limits. A's concession limit is reached when $u_2^* = u_3^*$. By (3) and (5), the corresponding p_2 value is

$$p_2^A = p_1 + \frac{r^* - t^*}{x^*}. \qquad (7)$$

With $p_2 = p_2^A$, A's total expected utility would be

$$u^*_2(p_2^A) = u_3^* = u_0^* - t^* + p_1 x^* \qquad (8)$$

while B's total expected utility would be

$$u_2(p_2^A) = u_1 + r - \frac{x}{x^*}(r^* - t^*) - p_1 x. \qquad (9)$$

On the other hand, B's concession limit is reached when $u_2 = u_3$. By (4) and (6) the corresponding p_2 value is

$$p_2^B = p_1 + \frac{r + t}{x}. \qquad (10)$$

With $p_2 = p_2^B$, A's total expected utility would be

$$u_2^*(p_2^B) = u_0^* - r^* + \frac{x^*}{x}(r + t) + p_1 x^* \qquad (11)$$

while B's total expected utility would be

$$u_2(p_2^B) = u_3 = u_1 - t - p_1 x. \qquad (12)$$

It is easy to see (Fig. 1) that in the utility plane $\{u^*, u\}$ for the two parties, all possible agreement points $U(p) = |u_2^*(p_2), u_2(p_2)|$ must lie on the straight-line interval connecting

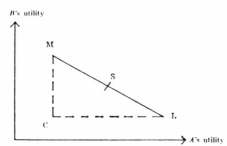

FIG. 1. Zeuthen-Nash utility plane.

the two parties' concession limit points, $L = U(p_2^A) = |u_2^*(p_2^A), u_2(p_2^1)|$ and $M = U(p_2^B) = |u_2^*(p_2^B), u_2(p_2^B)|$. (The two parties' payoffs in the conflict situation are indicated by the conflict point $C = |u_3^*, u_3|$.)

When the locus of all possible agreement points U is a straight line, the Zeuthen-Nash solution takes a particularly simple mathematical form; it is located simply at the midpoint of the distance between the two concession-limit points L and M (i.e., at S).[16] Hence, at the solution point S, A must obtain the expected utility

$$u_4^* = \frac{1}{2}|u_2^*(p_2^A) + u_2^*(p_2^B)| =$$

$$= u_0^* - \frac{r^* + t^*}{2} + \frac{x^*}{2x}(r + t) + p_1 x^* \qquad (13)$$

where the last equality follows from (8) and (11); while B must obtain the expected utility

$$u_4 = \frac{1}{2}|u_2(p_2^A) + u_2(p_2^B)| =$$

$$= u_1 + \frac{r - t}{2} - \frac{x}{2x^*}(r^* - t^*) - p_1 x. \qquad (14)$$

[16] This is obviously true in the special case where the game is perfectly symmetric with respect to the two players. Generally, the result follows from the invariance of the Zeuthen-Nash solution with respect to order-preserving linear transformations.

If we set $u_1{}^* = u_2{}^*(p_2)$ and $u_1 = u_2(p_2)$, by (13) and (3) (or by [14] and [4]) we obtain, as the equilibrium value of p_2 corresponding to the solution point S, the expression

$$p_2 = p_1 + \frac{r+t}{2x} + \frac{r^* - t^*}{2x^*} \quad (15)$$

subject, of course, to the requirement that always

$$p_2 \leqslant 1. \quad (15a)$$

The Zeuthen-Nash theory also tells us that A will choose the reward R he offers B in such a way as to maximize the expression

$$\Delta r = \frac{r}{x} - \frac{r^*}{x^*}$$

which measures, from A's point of view, the value of R as an incentive, less the cost of providing R for B. Moreover, A will select the penalty T in such a way as to maximize the expression

$$\Delta t = \frac{t}{x} - \frac{t^*}{x^*}$$

which again measures, from A's point of view, the value of T as a deterrent, less the cost of administering T to B. This is so because, according to (13), A will maximize his own final utility payoff $u_1{}^*$, by means of maximizing Δr and Δt.

In the more general case where both parties would use retaliatory strategies in the event of a conflict, A (in order to maximize his own final payoff $u_1{}^*$) would again try to select his own retaliatory strategy T_A so as to *maximize* Δt when B's strategy T_B is given. On the other hand, B (in order to maximize his own final payoff u_1) would try to select his own retaliatory strategy T_B so as to *minimize* Δt when A's strategy T_A is given. Hence the equilibrium choice of T_A and T_B will be such as to make Δt take its maximin value.

Now clearly, if B adopts strategy $s[p_2]$ corresponding to the p_2 value defined by (15), then the *amount* of A's power over B with respect to action X will become

$$\Delta p = p_2 - p_1 = \frac{1}{2}\left(\frac{r+t}{x} - \frac{t^* - r^*}{x^*}\right). \quad (16)$$

But of course the value of Δp must be con-

sistent with (15a). Hence (16) is subject to the restriction that

$$\Delta p \leqslant 1 - p_1. \quad (16a)$$

Let X^* denote A's action of *tolerating* B's failure to perform action X on one occasion. (We shall call action X^* the complementary action to action X.) Now suppose that A and B agree that B will perform action X with probability p_2, i.e., that B will *not* perform action X, with probability $(1 - p_2)$. This will mean that A will have to tolerate B's not performing action X, i.e., that A will have to perform action X^*, with probability $(1 - p_2)$. That is, technically, A and B will agree on a *jointly randomized* mixed strategy under which, with probability p_2, B will perform action X while A will *not* perform the complementary action X^*—whereas, with probability $(1 - p_2)$, A will perform action X^* while B will *not* perform action X.

Thus, while A's power over B will primarily consist in A's ability to get B to perform action X with a certain probability p_2; B's power over A will primarily consist in B's ability to get A to perform the complementary action X^* with probability $(1 - p_2)$.

On any given occasion where A performs action X^* (i.e., tolerates B's *not* performing action X), A will lose the utility gain x^* that he would derive from B's performing action X. Therefore A will associate disutility x^* with performing action X^*.

In equation (16), the sum $(r + t)$ is the sum of the *reward* B would obtain for compliance, and of the *penalty* he would suffer for noncompliance, both expressed in utility terms. This sum measures the *difference it would make* for B to have A as his enemy instead of having him as his friend. It represents the total opportunity costs to B of choosing noncompliance leading to the conflict situation instead of choosing compliance, i.e., some strategy $s[p_2]$ acceptable to A. In brief, it represents the *opportunity costs of a conflict*, from B's point of view. In our terminology, it measures the (gross) *absolute strength* of A's power over B. Accordingly, the quotient $(r + t)/x$ measures the *gross relative strength* of A's power over B with respect to action X.

The difference $(t^* - r^*)$ is the difference

between the costs to A of *punishing B* and the costs to A of *rewarding B*, both again expressed in utility terms. This difference measures the difference it would make for A to have B as an enemy instead of having him as a friend. It represents the net opportunity costs to A of choosing the conflict situation rather than performing action X^* with a probability $(1 - p_2)$ acceptable to B, i.e., rather than tolerating B to follow some strategy $s[p_2]$ acceptable to B. (In computing these opportunity costs, r^* has to be deducted from t^*, because in case of a conflict, A of course would save the costs of rewarding B.) In brief, this difference measures the *opportunity costs of a conflict*, this time from A's point of view. In our terminology, it measures the *gross absolute strength* of B's power over A. Moreover, as x^* is the disutility to A of performing action X^*, the quotient $(t^* - r^*)/x^*$ measures the *gross relative strength* of B's power over A with respect to action X^*.

Finally, the difference $[(r + t)/x - (t^* - r^*)/x^*]$ is the difference between the gross relative strength of A's power over B with respect to action X, and the gross relative strength of B's power over A with respect to the complementary action X^*. It may be called the *net strength* of A's power over B with respect to action X. This gives us:

Theorem II. If both parties follow the rationality postulates of the Zeuthen-Nash theory of the two-person bargaining game, then in bilateral power situations the *amount* of A's power over B with respect to some action X tends to be equal to *half* the *net strength* of A's power over B with respect to the same action X—this net strength being defined as the difference between the gross relative strength of A's power over B with respect to action X and the gross relative strength of B's power over A with respect to the complementary action X^*. (But this theorem is subject to the qualification that the amount of A's power over B cannot be so great as to make the probability of B's performing action X become greater than *unity*.)[17]

Of course, in empirical applications the

[17] In other words, Theorem II is subject to conditions (15a) and (16a).

amount-of-power concept in Theorem II (and in Theorem I) must be reinterpreted in terms of empirical *frequencies*, instead of theoretical *probabilities* (see the preceding discussion of this point).

Simon (1957, pp. 66-68) has pointed out that in bilateral power situations—at least, when none of the participants seriously misjudge the situation—it is impossible to disentangle directly by empirical methods what is due to A's power over B, and what is due to B's power over A, so that we cannot measure separately A's power over B and B's power over A. But of course this does not mean that, given a sufficiently rich theoretical framework, we cannot disentangle, and separately measure, these two power relations by theoretical analysis. In effect, our Theorem II does provide us—at least in principle—with separate measures for the gross strength of each of these two power relations, and with a theory about how these two separate measures have to be combined in order to explain the end result.

RELATIONSHIPS OF OUR STRENGTH-OF-POWER MEASURES TO ALTERNATIVE MEASURES FOR SOCIAL POWER

Theorems I (or I') and II describe how the strength-of-power measures described in this paper are related to Dahl's probabilistic measure for the amount of power, in unilateral and in bilateral power situations. As March's probabilistic measure (1957, p. 224) differs from Dahl's only in taking the absolute value of the difference $(p_2 - p_1)$ rather than the difference itself, these conclusions equally apply to March's measure.

The measure for the net strength of A's power over B in bilateral power situations is also related to the field-psychological measure for social power in small groups, proposed by French (1956), French and Raven (1959), and Cartwright (1959).

It was previously argued that B's (as well as A's) behavior must be explained in terms of two opposing psychological forces, one pressing B for more compliance with A's wishes in view of the rewards and penalties set up by A, and one pressing B for less compliance in view of the concessions B expects A to make in enforcing his demand for compliance. Theorem II now suggests that the strength of these two psychological forces can be measured by the *gross relative strength* of A's power over B, and of B's power over A, respectively. According to Theorem II, the strength of the resultant force, the *net strength* of A's power over B, equals the *difference* between the separate strength of the two forces.

Similarly, French (1956, p. 183) defines his measure for social power as "the maximum force which A can induce on B minus the maximum resisting force which B can mobilize in the opposite direction." However, while the *compliance-inducing* force of French's model is closely related to the one of our own model (as both depend on B's incentives to compliance), the *compliance-resisting* force of French's model does not seem to be connected with B's expectation of obtaining concessions as to the degree of compliance that A requires from him, as is the case in our own model. Moreover, it is not clear whether the two opposing psychological forces of French's model are supposed to follow the same quantitative laws as those of our own model. But in any case the relationship between the two models would be worth further investigation.[18]

[18] Cartwright (1959, p. 193) mentions the fact that while he himself defines social power as a *difference* of two opposing forces, Lewin proposed to measure it as a *quotient* of two opposing forces. According to Theorem II, in bilateral power situations the net force that A can exert on B is proportional to the *difference* of two psychological forces. More generally, if a person has both incentives for and incentives against doing a certain action, then the net strength of his incentives will be the difference between the strength of his positive and negative incentives. (For instance, if B's doing X yields him both rewards and penalties, then his net incentive will be the total value of the rewards less the total value of the penalties.) But note that in the former case Theorem II brings in a coefficient $1/2$, which does not occur in the latter case. On the other hand, both in unilateral and in bilateral power situations the gross strength of the force moving B toward compliance is the *quotient* of the strength of his incentives to compliance, and of the disutility to B of performing the required action X. Here the quotient formula arises because the disutility of doing X enters into the definition of B's expected utility as a *multipli-*

Finally, our measure for the net strength of A's power over B in bilateral power situations is also related to the *game-theoretical* measure for power in a committee system proposed by Shapley and Shubik (1954), in that both our and their measures are special cases of the *same* general game-theoretical measure for power in n-person situations.

Our measure for the net strength of power is based on the Zeuthen-Nash theory of the two-person bargaining game. In the following paper I shall discuss how this measure can be generalized for n-person reciprocal power situations, where all n participants mutually possess some power over one another and over the joint policies of their group as a whole. This generalization will be based on my bargaining model for the n-person co-operative game (Harsanyi, 1960; for an earlier version see Harsanyi, 1959), which is itself an n-person generalization of the Zeuthen-Nash theory. This generalized measure for power in n-person situations will be found to contain the Shapley-Shubik measure as a special case.

REFERENCES

Cartwright, D. A field theoretical conception of power. In D. Cartwright (Ed.), *Studies in social power*. Ann Arbor: Univ. of Michigan Press, 1959. Pp. 183-220.

Dahl, R. A. The concept of power. *Behav. Sci.*, 1957, 2, 201-215.

French, J. R. P., Jr. A formal theory of social power. *Psychol. Rev.*, 1956, 63, 181-194.

French, J. R. P., Jr., & Raven, B. The bases of social power. In D. Cartwright (Ed.), *Studies in social power*. Ann Arbor: Univ. of Michigan Press, 1959. Pp. 150-167.

Harsanyi, J. C. Cardinal welfare, individualistic ethics, and interpersonal comparisons of utility. *J. polit. Econ.*, 1955, 63, 309-321.

Harsanyi, J. C. Approaches to the bargaining problem before and after the theory of games: a critical discussion of Zeuthen's, Hicks', and Nash's theories. *Econometrica*, 1956, 24, 144-157.

Harsanyi, J. C. A bargaining model for the cooperative n-person game. In A. W. Tucker and R. D. Luce (Eds.), *Contributions to the theory of games*, IV. Princeton; Princeton Univ. Press, 1959. Pp. 325-355.

Harsanyi, J. C. A simplified bargaining model for the n-person cooperative game. 1960 (hectographed). Available from author on request.

cative factor (it multiplies the probability of B's actually doing X).

Harsanyi, J. C. On the rationality postulates underlying the theory of cooperative games. *J. Conflict Resol.*, 1961, 5, 179-196.

Luce, R. D., & Raiffa, H. *Games and decisions.* New York: Wiley, 1957.

March, J. G. An introduction to the theory and measurement of influence. *Amer. Polit. Sci. Rev.*, 1955, 49, 431-451.

March, J. G. Measurement concepts in the theory of influence. *J. Politics*, 1957, 19, 202-226.

Marschak, J. Rational behavior, uncertain prospects, and measurable utility. *Econometrica*, 1950, 18, 111-141.

Marschak, J. Three lectures on probability in the social sciences. In P. F. Lazarsfeld (Ed.), *Mathematical thinking in the social sciences.* Glencoe: The Free Press, 1954. Pp. 166-215. Reprinted as Cowles Commission Paper, N.S., No. 82.

Nash, J. F., Jr. The bargaining problem. *Econometrica*, 1950, 18, 155-162.

Nash, J. F., Jr. Two-person cooperative games. *Econometrica*, 1953, 21, 128-140.

Schelling, T. C. An essay on bargaining. *Amer. econ. Rev.*, 1956, 46, 281-306.

Shapley, L. S., & Shubik, M. A method for evaluating the distribution of power in a committee system. *Amer. Polit. Sci. Rev.*, 1954, 48, 787-792.

Simon, H. A. *Models of man: social and rational.* New York: Wiley, 1957. Pp. 62-78.

Zeuthen, F. *Problems of monopoly and economic warfare.* London: G. Routledge and Sons, 1930.

(Manuscript received April 17, 1961)

ᕭ

Though it is in the realm of the moral and spiritual that we expect to find the abiding *abstract* truths, there where the masonry of accumulated facts has been transformed into the ideal design, nevertheless it is to the concrete everyday facts, objects of use and beauty and wonder—the inorganic earth substances, and air and fire and water, all the growing things of the earth and all the living creatures, all the people of the earth, and the world of their hands and minds, and the records of all their lives—it is to these that we turn for reassurance of the reality of the world and for support of our endeavors in it. One does well to hold fast to "facts" as firm friends to go by his side in the pursuit of the higher truths.

W. EMBLER, *Language and Truth*

[5]

ECONOMICS AND PUBLIC POLICY: III

Economics, sociology, and the best of all possible worlds

MANCUR OLSON, JR.

Wʜᴀᴛ are the boundaries that separate the social science disciplines from each other? Where (if anywhere) do we draw the line between those problems that call for the expertise of the economist and those that demand the skills of the sociologist, or the psychologist, or the political scientist? This is *not* the kind of methodological question that interests only those scholars who don't want to get on with the job: it is at the center of some debates in Washington about past and prospective decisions on public policy, and has an inescapable intellectual importance as well.

Some of the debates about the roles different social sciences should have in the policy-making process were provoked by two relatively recent innovations in public policy. One of these was the President's directive that the Planning-Programming-Budgeting System, which is an outgrowth of economic analysis, should be used in all departments of the federal government. This prompted disagreement about whether an economic approach is the most appropriate for dealing with the "social" programs of government, or suited to an inevitably political environment. The other innovation was the decision to prepare a trial-run "social report," akin to the Economic Report of the President. This latter innovation is more relevant here, as it raises the question about the relative roles of the different social sciences in a most obvious and ineluctable way.

The "economic" and the "social"

The responsibility for the development of the trial-run social report has been given to the Department of Health, Education and
Welfare. This department obtained the help of a Panel on Social
Indicators, composed of leading social scientists from universities
and research organizations, who work on this Report on a part-time
basis. Daniel Bell, co-Editor of *The Public Interest,* and Alice Rivlin,
Assistant Secretary for Planning and Evaluation, in the Department
of Health, Education and Welfare, are the co-Chairmen of this
panel. I have the immediate responsibility for the effort, and this fact
partly explains the perspective I bring to this subject. On the legislative side, Senator Walter Mondale and ten other senators have introduced a "Full Opportunity and Social Accounting Act"; this bill
would provide for a Council on Social Advisers, which would advise
the President on social policy and issue an annual social report on
the state of the nation. The hearings on this bill have elicited testi-
mony from a wide variety of scholars and public officials.

Inevitably these hearings, and the discussions in the Panel on
Social Indicators, have raised the question of the division of labor
among the social science disciplines, in general, and between economics and sociology, in particular. Several of those who testified on
the Mondale bill wondered whether it might not be better to create
a combined Council of Economic and Social Advisers rather than
two separate councils. And there has been no agreement about how
the "economic" and "social" spheres could be distinguished, so that
there could be a clear allocation of responsibilities between the
Council of Economic Advisers and any new Council of Social Advisers. Proponents of the Mondale bill are especially anxious that
the President get more advice about the problems of the poor and
the disadvantaged. The problems of these groups certainly are "social" problems, and the counsel of the best sociologists, psychologists,
and political scientists should of course be available to the policy-
makers who deal with them. But, if poverty is not an "economic"
problem, then nothing is. Moreover, social programs require scarce
resources and that is what economics is all about. No consensus is
emerging on what the respective roles of the different social sciences
should be.

The debate in Washington about the mix and organization of the
social science input in government obviously reflects the hazy and
diverse definitions of the spheres of the various social sciences in
the universities. Many leading scholars trespass on what are supposed to be the territories of disciplines other than their own. As an
economist with experience of some of the more exotic uses of economic theory, I am naturally best able to cite economists who have

made contributions to other social sciences. There is no doubt in my mind that Kenneth Arrow, Duncan Black, Kenneth Boulding, James Buchanan, Anthony Downs, John Harsanyi, Albert Hirschman, Charles Lindblom, Jerome Rothenberg, Thomas Schelling, and Gordon Tullock have made significant contributions to political science or sociology, and others equally important could be named. It would be possible to compile similarly long lists of scholars in each social science who have made major contributions to other social sciences.

If the problem of distinguishing the spheres of responsibility of the various social sciences has not been solved, and if this problem complicates even current discussions of governmental organization and public policy, then there is the need to give it some careful thought. As we shall see, this problem can be understood by looking at some of the most profound problems and fundamental theories in social science.

The comprehensiveness of theory

The social sciences have not been adequately distinguished from one another largely because it has not usually been understood that the fundamental differences between the social sciences involve not the subjects they study, but rather the preconceptions they have inherited, the methods they use, and the conclusions they reach. To distinguish the defining features of the social science disciplines, we must look at the ways in which scholars in various disciplines work, rather than at the nature of the phenomena they study. For the theories or tools of thought of the social science disciplines are so general that each discipline's theory encompasses objects or problems that convention puts in the reservation of some other discipline. This comprehensiveness, which is manifest most clearly in economics and sociology, is not generally understood.

Thus, the general applicability of economic theory has not usually been understood by laymen, and indeed many of the older generation of economists also interpret economics too narrowly. This is probably due in large part to the special historical circumstances in which economic theory first came to have coherence. The great economists of the eighteenth and nineteenth centuries were often inspired to intellectual innovation by immediate practical problems. They were for the most part caught up in the political controversies of their time and were sometimes passionate ideologues. Most of them, at least in Great Britain, were advocates for the rising middle classes and the mercantile and industrial interests. They were usually utilitarians, democrats, internationalists, and passionate advocates of laissez-faire. Indeed, in nineteenth-century Britain, the word economist was often taken to *mean* an advocate of laissez-faire in general and free trade in particular. The belief that economic theory is applicable only to goods that fetch a price in the markets of "capitalist" economies of the kind the classical economists admired has survived to the present day.

In fact, economic theory not only is, but (if it is to avoid arbitrariness and error) *must be* so general that it also applies to "goods" that are *not* traded in markets—and also to traditional and communistic societies. If an economist is studying the housing market, he cannot ignore the fact that some locations have more prestige than others, are in areas occupied by different races or social groups, are in different political jurisdictions, and have different aesthetic attributes. Obviously any of these factors can affect the satisfaction an owner would get from a house, and the market price of that house, as much as its material characteristics.

Indeed, it is in general *not* possible to give an entirely accurate explanation of economic behavior in a situation unless *all* of the perceived advantages of a given alternative, to the actor being studied or advised, are counted as "returns," and all of the disadvantages of that alternative, as perceived by the relevant actor, as "costs." The economist will frequently—but by no means always—predict that the actor being studied will tend to choose the alternative that promises the largest excess of returns over costs, which is by definition most advantageous in terms of the actor's values.

Of course, the actor may lack the intelligence, information, or detachment needed to choose the alternative that is best in terms of his own preferences. He might be a "satisficer" rather than a maximizer, or operate according to an erroneous traditional rule, or let biases distort his perception of the facts. In such a case the economist can take comfort from the fact that the actor being studied may be in the market for a consultant! In any event, economic theory will have relevance, in a normative, if not always positive, way.

The general relevance of economics

Economic theory is, indeed, relevant whenever actors have determinate wants or objectives and at the same time do not have such an abundance of the means needed to achieve these ends that all of their desires are satiated. The ends in question may be social status or political power, and the means will be anything that is in fact conducive to the attainment of the ends, whether or not these means can bring a price in the market. *Economic (more precisely microeconomic) theory is in a fundamental sense more nearly a theory of rational behavior than a theory of material goods.*

To be sure, economic theory in its most general form can be as vacuous or trivial as it is broad. Many situations are so difficult, or so simple, that no formal method of thinking will be of any practical help. Economics, moreover, has not got very far with the problems of uncertainty, of strategic interaction (in the game theory sense), of acquiring or getting along without information, not to mention other problems we need to understand better before we can have anything like a complete or adequate theory of rational behavior. And where economic theory is not in itself deficient, economists often are: they sometimes lack the fullness of mind, the judgment, and, above all, the imagination needed to apply economic theory to problems outside their traditional purview. In any event, the purpose here is not to glorify or belittle economics, but rather to argue that some of the basic theories of social science, including economic theory, are limited not so much in terms of the objects they can be used to study as in other ways.

The generality of economic theory with respect to the objects of study is illustrated not only by the politically or sociologically relevant work of men such as those named earlier, but also by other recent developments. The output of the United States Department of Defense is not sold for money, yet the economic approach inherent in the Planning-Programming-Budgeting System has proved most helpful there. This system has even shown great promise in departments, such as my own, which deal in such obscure intangibles as health, education, and welfare, and which are relatively far removed from the market place. In the specialty of international relations, too, one finds that insights of economic theory have sometimes been decidedly relevant, as the work of Kenneth Boulding and Thomas Schelling shows, yet these men have dealt with the political-military, rather than the material, wants of nations, and often ignored the market sector in their models. The nations of Eastern Europe have an institutional environment vastly different from that which the classical economists knew or wanted, yet many economists there are beginning to use the same economic theory we know in the West, and sometimes find it helpful in suggesting ways in which their *existing* Marxist-inspired institutions might be made to work more efficiently. (Indeed, economic theory has escaped the original ideological limitations on its generality to such an extent that I have read some interesting work by economists who, as I later learned, were avowed Communists, but whose work was such that, if asked, I would have guessed they were typical Western intellectuals, if not laissez-faire enthusiasts.) Finally, the developing areas of the world, different and diverse as their cultures and conditions may be, have nonetheless proved to be about as amenable to ordinary economic analysis as the Western democracies.

"Better off" and "worse off"

The fact that economic theory has no unique application to material goods, but deals with any objectives that people value in con-

ditions of scarcity, cannot be adequately documented in any brief
discussion. But it may nonetheless be useful to mention one basic
idea that has an important—if in many respects overly simple—
application to politics. This is the notion of "Pareto-optimality,"
which is defined as a situation such that no individual in the group
at issue can be made better off without someone else being made
worse off. This idea is normally used to describe resource allocations
that are efficient and ideal, in the sense that they satisfy individual
wants to the maximum possible degree, given the available resources,
the state of technology, and the distribution of income. If someone
could get more without anyone having less, that would mean a way
had been found to get more output from the available resources.[1]

The generalization to politics comes from the fact that when we
say a Pareto-optimal situation is one in which no one can be made
better off without someone else being made worse off, we need not
define "better off" or "worse off" in terms of material goods alone.
*Indeed, if we consider only these so-called "economic" wants of the
individuals concerned, the whole analysis could be invalid*—for the
only relevant measure of value in this context is that of the individuals concerned, and if one of them values a given degree of social
status or political power more highly at the margin than some
material good, he will be "worse off" if he has to give up that degree
of social status or political power in exchange for the material good.
An attempt to "sub-optimize" by considering only material objectives could be meaningless, for a step that seemed efficient because
it increased the output of material goods might in fact be inefficient
because the social or political goods that had to be sacrificed were
worth more than the material goods gained. There is thus no way
of defining a situation as Pareto-optimal without taking all of the
things people value into account.

When "better off" and "worse off" are understood as they must be,
it becomes clear that Pareto-optimality is a condition of political
equilibrium in democratic societies. (I use the word "equilibrium,"
which is the object of much controversy in political science and sociology, with the same meaning it has in economics.) If there is some
step or combination of steps that will make one or more individuals
better off, without making anyone worse off, there is always the
possibility some political or administrative entrepreneur will respond
to the incentive inherent in the situation and organize a change in
policy. This is, to be sure, only one of a vast variety of necessary
conditions of political equilibrium, and perhaps a rather weak one.
But can we conceive of a complete theory of political change, or of

---

[1] Pareto-optimality means a little more than that aggregate income is a maximum, for the income or value of the goods and services produced depends on
relative prices, which in turn depend on the income distribution in the group.

the politics of consensus, that would leave Pareto-optimality out of account?

Some of the other political insights that can be got from the notion of Pareto-optimality have, however, been explored. The Swedish economist Knut Wicksell pointed out more than a half century ago that optimal measures should be able to command something approaching unanimous support, since by definition there will be some possible distribution of the benefits and costs such that everyone would have an incentive to favor such measures. (This would not be the case under a *complete* unanimity rule, where an individual might withhold his then indispensable vote in an attempt to extort a larger share of the total gains from the measure.) More recently, Professors James Buchanan and Gordon Tullock have, in their important book on *The Calculus of Consent*, argued that reasoning of this sort shows that the majority rule principle is in certain respects arbitrary and unsatisfactory, and that the bicameralism, two-thirds rules, and general checks and balances of the American system have the admittedly unsuspected virtue of preventing passage of many policies that are not toward Pareto-optimality.

A reoccupation with Pareto-optimality can, admittedly, sometimes support a classical-liberal opposition to the coercive redistribution of income. Redistribution cannot be expected to attain anything like unanimous support, yet it may be overwhelmingly important. But there is nothing inherently conservative in the political use of the concept of Pareto-optimality. I have, for example, argued elsewhere that there may sometimes be a tendency toward what has been called public squalor in the midst of private affluence because of the fact that many Pareto-optimal measures for *local* areas may not be able to get majority support in the *national* government. Though the gains from a Pareto-optimal measure are by definition greater than the costs, the number of gainers will be smaller than the number of losers when the benefits are local and the taxes are national. Fortunately, "logrolling" may make it possible for a number of local Pareto-optimal measures to pass as a package. (Logrolling thus does not necessarily deserve its evil popular reputation.) But logrolling requires complex and costly bargains and accordingly often will not occur.

The general relevance of sociology

What I have tried to argue is true of economic theory is quite as true of sociological thought. The perspective of the sociologist has important implications for *all* the other social sciences.

In attempting to illustrate this argument about sociological theory, I am handicapped in three ways: First, as an economist, I don't know the sociological literature as well as I would like to. The argument must therefore be based on what at best is a random sample of that literature. But for all the shortcomings of my knowledge of sociological thought, the major generalizations I will make about this literature will still almost certainly be correct; my sample could hardly be so untypical as to make me wrong about some of the great themes of this major intellectual tradition.

My second handicap stems from the fact that sociological thought is more pluralistic than economic thought: it is not a single, well-defined, almost monolithic entity like economic theory, but rather a collection of diverse and often independent theories. When I refer to "sociological theory," I will be speaking not of sociological thought as a whole, but of one particular sociological theory. That is the one associated with the tradition in which Professor Talcott Parsons has been the dominant contemporary figure. This is unfair to the *many* sociologists who use entirely different conceptions. It will also be unfair to Professor Parsons, whose views should properly be distinguished from those who share only some of this thought.

The third handicap results from the particular nature of Parsonian theory. This theory is not, like economic theory, a logically elaborate but unified hypothetico-deductive system susceptible to succinct (or even mathematical) description. Indeed, it is not "theory" in the sense in which that word is used in some other disciplines. It is rather an uncommonly rich and varied style of thought, replete with special insights, distinctions, and definitions, which makes *any* short summary insufficient and unfair. There is no alternative here, then, to a *Reader's Digest* level of oversimplification; this will naturally prove offensive to the connoisseur of Parsonian sociological literature.

Even the most casual glance at sociological theory of the Parsonian type reveals that it is very general and that it includes the traditional domains of economics and political science, and part of the field of psychology as well. Parsons explicitly makes economic theory, as well as almost every type of systematic study in social science, a special case of his General Theory of Action. This unusual emphasis on generality has been criticized, but I do not think the criticism is justified. Right or wrong, Parsonian theories are general, and have to be.

The necessity of this generality stems largely from the basic role this theory (like many other sociological theories) gives to the process of "socialization." The central preconception of this type of theory is that people do what they are brought up to do. It holds in effect that the hand that rocks the cradle does indeed rule the world. Even when particular individuals fail to want to be true to the values and norms that were inculcated in their childhood, they are still subject to the sentiments society passes on from generation to generation, since societies tend to set up mechanisms of social control, ranging from informal social pressure to the sanctions of the legal system, which enforce the patterns of behavior that they were brought up to believe were right.

The theory at issue holds that through socialization people acquire not only general attitudes relating to society as a whole or its major groupings, but also conceptions of particular "roles," such as husband, wife, businessman, priest, doctor, and soldier. The person who is born in a particular society is educated to expect that people who perform particular roles will act in certain ways—that mothers will care for their children, that doctors will care for the sick, and that businessmen will seek profits. In a well-developed and stable society, there is "institutional integration"—i.e., laws, organizations, and popular attitudes (as well as other mechanisms to ensure conformity) are extensive, elaborate, and in harmony with one another. Mutual role-expectations tend to be consistent. This reduces the amount of stress and alienation and strengthens the tendency to follow the pattern of behavior inculcated by the processes of socialization. There is a pronounced tendency in this tradition to regard extensive and consistent institutionalization as desirable for the health and stability of society, partly on the grounds that it minimizes alienation.

The Parsonian sociologist's emphasis on the socialization of common beliefs and conceptions of roles through families, religions, schools, and other institutions inevitably forces him to encompass many "economic," "political," and "psychological" aspects of reality. For the same processes and institutions that give an individual his social values also inculcate attitudes about economic and political life, and influence his whole personality. The same family that teaches a child social usage passes on a sense of what occupational achievements and political principles are expected. The churches, schools, media of information, and other agencies of socialization are similarly comprehensive. And often the values, ideologies, and religions passed on are themselves so general that they influence diverse aspects of life. It is thus not surprising that probably the most famous work in the sociological tradition at issue—or rather, one of the sources of that tradition—is Max Weber's *Protestant Ethic and the Spirit of Capitalism.* Though much subsequent research has tended to discredit Weber's substantive hypothesis, his heroic attempt to explain the singularity of the early modern European economy in terms of the Calvinistic religious ideas which many Europeans were taught remains a prototypical example of the style of sociology I have described, and of the fact that the sociological perspective is inevitably relevant to economic behavior.

The difference between economics and sociology

It is now possible to see the closest thing there is to a basis for a distinction between economics and sociology in terms of the object

studied. If we define sociology as the discipline that studies the
formation and transmission of wants or beliefs of all kinds, and
economics as the discipline that studies the ways in which people
strive to obtain whatever it is that they want, we would be much
closer to the truth than those who think of sociology as something
such as the study of life in groups and economics as the study of
material gain in the marketplace. The proposed distinction would,
for example, make it clear why both economists and sociologists
should be interested in poverty. The economist is interested in poverty because the poor do not have the resources to meet even their
important needs. If the economist *qua* economist is asked how the
poor are different from us, he says "because they have less money."
But if the sociologist *qua* sociologist is asked how the poor are different from us, he says "because they were brought up in the culture
of poverty."

Still, it won't quite do to say that sociologists specialize in the
study of the formation of wants and economists in the ways to satisfy them. There are a number of reasons for this. One is that they
tend to use different methods, the economists relying on a non-
trivially deductive theory, emphasizing quantification, and using
simultaneous-equation techniques, the Parsonian sociologist using
a less deductive method, relying occasionally on the case study,
and often bringing a fuller knowledge of the history and context of
a problem to bear. There are also differences of preconception, with
some economists almost assuming that rationality is universal in the
human animal, and with some sociologists almost treating rationality as a cultural peculiarity of those with the Protestant or capital-
istic Ethic.

The economist and sociologist also often differ in the substantive
conclusions they draw about the same problem. For example, when
economists are asked to explain the choices about work and saving made by those who receive public assistance, they will often
deplore the traditional 100 per cent tax on any wages or savings
beyond a trivial minimum, and argue that recipients of welfare
checks be allowed to work without sacrificing their claim to virtually all assistance. Some social workers of my acquaintance who have
studied a great deal of Parsonian sociology, on the other hand,
seem to assume that the habits and attitudes people form are more
or less independent of the incentives they face, and that larger
amounts of public assistance to those not working would best provide the basis for the development of middle class values. Another
difference of conclusion typical of the two disciplines is that some
Parsonian sociologists explain the choices a society makes in terms
of what it needs (the "functions" that need to be performed)
or in terms of what the people in it want. The economist, on the
other hand, will not consider as an explanation anything like the

statement that something exists because it has a function in a society, and will emphasize that the relation between wants and social outcomes is complex and even paradoxical (so that, for example, when everyone wants and tries to save more, they may all end up saving less).

What holds a society together?

The differences in method, preconception, and conclusion that distinguish modern economics and Parsonian sociology are perhaps best illustrated by considering the question of what it is that holds societies together or allows them to collapse. The stability of a society is perhaps as central as any concern in sociology. This problem is important in its own right, and draws added interest from the recent race riots and student demonstrations. It is obviously also relevant to any attempt at a social report, for one guide to the health of a society is its degree of unity and the probability that it will hold together.

This is not the place (and I am not the writer) to go into the manifold sociological controversies about the determinants of the stability of societies. But many sociologists, in the tradition considered here, build their explanations of the coherence of societies around the existence of common processes of socialization. They contend that it is mainly the similarity of values, norms, collective attitudes, and role expectations that holds a society together. If people are brought up to want and believe in the same things, they won't need to fight each other. There must in any event be a consensus about the most important things that will keep any divergencies and conflicts within tolerable bounds. Differences in culture, religion, family patterns, or educational systems so great that they inculcate basically different patterns of beliefs and wants are then held to be inimical to the stability of a society.

Economists do not often explicitly consider the question of what holds a whole society together, but they do consider some of the factors that favor the survival of an economic union. And this is enough to reveal that Parsonian sociologists and orthodox economists operate with preconceptions and methods that lead to drastically *opposed* conclusions about the determinants of a society's coherence and unity. The economist who is asked whether a group of nations should form a common market will usually argue that the more diverse the cultures and natural resources of these countries are, the greater the advantage of a common market, other things equal. The more diverse the resources, technologies, and tastes of the nations, the greater the gains from trade among them. Expecting nations that are practically identical to gain vast amounts from a common market is about as realistic as expecting to maximize

motherhood by bringing women together. A rough index of the
gains from trade would be the differences in the relative prices of
different tradable goods in the different countries in the absence
of trade. The larger these differences in relative prices, generally
the greater the gains from selling what has been relatively cheap in
one country in return for something that would be expensive if
produced at home, but which is not expensive in the country with
a comparative advantage in producing it. Many economists would
assume that the greater the gains from trade, and therefore the incentive to trade, the greater will be the interest in preserving the
common market or other institutions that allow the mutually advantageous trade to take place.

If the logic of this argument about economic unions is generalized
and applied to states and societies, it provides a perspective different
from that of most Parsonian sociology (though not altogether different from that of Durkheim's concept of "organic solidarity"). To
see the general applicability of the economic approach, imagine a
society in which everyone was socialized to think that all vacations
should be in August and at the beach. That society would tend to
suffer congestion and conflict at its beach resorts in August, and a
lack of essential services at home for those who couldn't squeeze in
(this is not an altogether unrealistic example: the French have been
concerned about the need for policies to reduce the number of
August vacations). If, on the other hand, some of the people in the
society have been brought up to prefer a skiing vacation, or a
summer cabin in the mountains, there will be less to fight about, and
everyone can get what he wants for less. To take another example,
suppose that a common culture and a common process of socialization mean that in a given culture everyone is brought up to strive to
be a leader. Life in such a society will be a constant struggle for
power and the society may therefore collapse. But if some of the
people in the society should prefer to follow, there would be mutually advantageous relationships between leaders and followers which
they would wish to preserve, along with the society that made these
advantageous relationships possible. The use of the economist's
method and preconceptions therefore seems to suggest that the more
diverse the backgrounds and beliefs of a people, the greater the
incentive they will have to continue their association.

It is in cases such as these, where different disciplinary methods
and preconceptions lead to apparently opposite conclusions, that
the lack of serious, detailed communication between economics and
and the other social sciences is most tragic. A lack of mutual intellectual esteem is often enough evident in the references some
economists and sociologists make to each other's discipline, but this
is no substitute for extended confrontations based on continuing
research. Disciplinary specialization, though obviously beneficial on

balance, is partly responsible. As I see it, there is today some effective censorship of extended interdisciplinary confrontations, not because of any desire to still debate, but because disciplinary parochialism prevents the use of the methods of one social science on the substantive problems that are sometimes supposed to be in the province of another. The absence of constructive communication between economics and sociology is suggested by the ease with which new insights are gained when particular positions of the two disciplines are compared. This can be illustrated with the problem of social cohesion just considered.

Collective and noncollective goods

In order to do this, we will first have to draw a distinction between collective and noncollective (or, as they are more often, but less precisely called, public and private) goods. Leaving some definitional niceties aside, a collective good can be described as a good such that nonpurchasers cannot feasibly be excluded from its consumption. Defense is the classic example of such a good, since it is not practically possible to exclude anyone living in a country from the benefits (or dangers) of the nation's defense system. To a great degree the benefits provided by the police and the system of justice are also collective goods. A constitutional monarch is a particularly neat example of a collective good; the benefits of his reign reach all of his subjects, from those who are more royalist than the King to those who are Republicans.

Noncollective or private goods are, by contrast, goods such that nonpurchasers *can* be kept from consuming them. Thus, if an individual buys bread, or a car, others can be and usually are excluded from the consumption of what he has bought. There is, in other words, no joint or communal consumption of a noncollective good.

Now that the distinction between collective and noncollective goods has been drawn, the opposition between the economic and sociological views can be resolved, and the outlines of an argument that is apparently better than either developed. The conclusion of that argument is that a society will, other things being equal, be more likely to cohere if people are socialized to have diverse wants with respect to private goods and similar wants with respect to collective goods. A "good," in this language, is not of course necessarily a material good, but can be anything that people value. So what has been said means simply that, where individuals have objectives that they can consume or enjoy without others having to participate in this consumption, they will tend to cohere better if they have different tastes and productive capabilities, because this will maximize the gains from exchanges among them; on the other hand, where individuals have objectives such that if they are achieved

ECONOMICS, SOCIOLOGY. . . .   **109**

for some they are automatically also achieved for others, the
greater the similarity in their tastes and situations the easier it will
be for them to agree on a common policy. Thus in a marriage it is
helpful for one spouse to like fat and the other lean, but it is a
danger if they want different numbers of children or different types
of houses. Any gains from a comprehensive Middle Eastern common
market would be increased by the fact that the Israelis and Arabs
have different cultures and skills, but the possibility of a common
regional government with a single established religion would (to
put it mildly) not be increased by the fact that the peoples of the
Middle East have experienced different processes of socialization.

To be sure, many Parsonian sociologists seem to have sensed (as
Durkheim did long ago)[2] that some differences in wants and value
systems could somehow enhance unity, and almost every economist
must have realized (if he had ever considered this question) that in
certain areas divergencies of wants could disrupt a society. A point
as obvious and important as this could hardly be altogether novel.
Still, most discussions of the question of social cohesion are
thoroughly misleading, if not largely wrong, because they do not
make the distinction between collective and noncollective goods
and also make no effort to reconcile the perspectives of economics
and sociology.

The "ideal" society in economics

The divergences in methodology, presupposition, and conclusion
that differentiate modern economics and Parsonian sociology can
also be illustrated by contrasting the "ideal" states of society that are
envisaged by each discipline. The contrasting conceptions of the
"ideal society" held by each of these intellectual traditions have
considerable practical importance, for they help to determine what
advice scholars of different disciplinary backgrounds offer to policy-
makers. They are, moreover, absolutely fundamental to any possible

---

[2] Emile Durkheim distinguished "organic solidarity" resulting from the division
of labor and "mechanical solidarity" due to similar sentiments. Durkheim drew
this distinction in the last century, and did not, of course, know the distinction
between collective and noncollective goods, so his analysis on this point is
accordingly wrong in many respects. Nonetheless, it is far superior to most
modern treatments of the subject. Significantly, Parsons has repeatedly belittled
Durkheim's notion of organic solidarity, subordinated it to an elaborated conception of mechanical solidarity, and failed to develop anything like the needed
distinction between collective and noncollective goods. See Parson's fascinat-
ing but flawed article on "Durkheim's Contribution to the Theory of Integration
of Social Systems," in Kurt H. Wolff, ed., *Essays in Sociology and Philosophy*
(New York: Harper Torchbooks, 1964), pp. 118–153, especially where it distinguishes values, differentiated norms, collective attitudes, and roles. See also
his *Structure of Social Action* (2nd ed.; New York: The Free Press, 1949), pp.
301–342, and Emile Durkheim, *The Division of Labor in Society*, trans. George
Simpson (Glencoe, Ill.: The Free Press, 1947).

"social report," for they provide alternative standards by which to gauge a nation's advance or decline.

My use of the words "ideal society" may, however, create some misunderstandings. Neither economists nor Parsonian sociologists are normally utopians; they do not necessarily believe that their "ideal societies" can be achieved. The purposes these ideal conceptions serve are entirely different from those of, say, the utopian socialists, or of Plato's vision of an ideally just state run by philosopher-kings. They serve, not usually as visions of what we can and should obtain, but rather as intellectual models that can clarify and help to indicate whether a given policy leads in a desirable or undesirable direction. Some misunderstanding may also be caused by the fact that, while the economist's conception of the "ideal society" is at times almost explicit, the particular sociological conception I have in mind receives only tacit recognition. But this difference in the degree of explicitness of the ideal conception does not mean that the one ideal is necessarily more influential or important than the other, so we must strip these two ideal conceptions of their very different clothing and then set them out in a way that will facilitate explicit comparison.

One part of the economic ideal has already been set out in the literature of welfare economics, which describes the necessary conditions for an "efficient" and "optimal" allocation of resources, so there is no need for a rigorous statement of it here. Roughly speaking, a society with given resources and state of technology can be described as efficient if it is "at the frontier of every production possibility function," which means in plainer English that no more of any good can be obtained without giving up some amount of some other good (including leisure and future consumption as goods, to subsume the possibility that more resources would be devoted to production). *Efficiency* says nothing about whether the goods that are produced are those that would provide the most satisfaction, so it is not a sufficient condition for *optimality*. A necessary condition for an optimal allocation of resources is that no reallocation could be made which would make anyone better off without making someone else worse off. The standard of optimality is then the concept of Pareto-optimality mentioned earlier, and Pareto-optimality is not achieved unless the society is *also* efficient.

The society will not, of course, be economically ideal unless the distribution of income is right, and the "just" distribution of income cannot be scientifically determined. The constructs of welfare economics nonetheless can claim general interest, for they describe necessary conditions that would have to prevail if an economy were to be optimal, *whatever* the ideal distribution of income might be. The necessary conditions for Pareto-optimality in a society are stated principally in terms of a series of marginal conditions. These marginal conditions, and the many shortcomings in this sort of analysis, will not be discussed here, since this paragraph is meant to be only impressionistic, and because the welfare economics texts that set out this analysis more carefully are easily accessible.

Welfare economics is static in that it leaves innovation and the advance of technology out of account. Economists have done a great deal of work lately on innovation and on the economics of education and research, but this has not usually been explicitly tied in with welfare economics. In the rough and ready fashion in which we are operating at the moment, this can perhaps be done. In essence, the economically ideal society would maintain a Pareto-optimal allocation of resources at every moment in time *and* at the same time continually change to the best attainable production functions as knowledge advances. The rate of accumulation of productive knowledge and other forms of capital would be the maximum consistent with the society's rate of discount of future versus present consumption. This statement, alas, brushes over a number of unsettled issues (such as the possible Schumpeterian conflict between short-run allocative efficiency and long-run innovation) and many profound complexities (involving particularly what the economists call "optimal growth" theory). But hopefully the subsequent discussion will reveal that these complications are not so important for the very particular purpose of the moment. That purpose is to suggest that most economists have some fairly clear but incomplete models from welfare economics, and some vaguer notions about the importance of rapid innovation, which can be taken to represent something in the nature of a vision of an economically ideal or optimal society. This vision derives from the elemental goal of maximum income, which demands an optimal allocation of resources at each moment in time plus a dynamic technology. This vision is an ideal in the sense that (vexing problems of "second best" solutions notwithstanding) it serves as a standard which economists use to help them judge practical policies.

The "ideal" society in sociology

The school of sociology considered in this paper does not contain any models of "optimality" that parallel the constructs of welfare economics. But there is probably implicit in it a vision of something like an ideal society, which ideal would serve heuristic purposes and influence judgments about public policy. This implicit ideal might be more easily evident in the literature on "mass movements" than in Professor Parsons' own writings, but it is also evident to some degree in his works. The sort of sociological ideal at issue is, moreover, far too complex and comprehensive to be susceptible to brief summary. It is the result not only of extensive theoretical writing, but also of subtle insights that have emerged from many lifetimes of empirical research.

But perhaps the most basic dimension is that ideal can be mentioned, if not precisely defined. That dimension is "alienation." However much they differ in other respects, a whole family of sociological studies unite in treating alienation, or some similar psychological estrangement, as the principal sociological pathology. To say that the minimization of alienation plays a role in many sociological studies not unlike the maximization of satisfaction (or utility) in economics is to enumerate a half-truth—a statement that makes those who believe in the other half angry. Yet it is a half-truth that, because it refers to a part of the truth that has been neglected, should now be emphasized.

Though the minimization of alienation is in a sense the most fundamental variable in this particular sociological ideal, it is not perhaps the most important, or at any event the most often discussed in the theoretical literature. The degree of "integration" of a society is probably even more central, and the ideal is that this degree of integration should be maximized. The degree of integration, or "institutional integration," as it is more carefully called, is important not only because it affects the amount of alienation, but also because it affects in other ways the chances that the society will cohere.

The degree of integration tends to increase with the extent to which a set of individuals forms a "community," and would be nil in a situation in which a set of individuals had no social structure, common values, or institutions. It would be high in a situation in which everyone in a society has tied into the social order by bonds to a wide variety of associations, in which social structure was elaborate, in which common values, norms, and institutions were cherished, where individual roles were well understood, and where mechanisms of social control were well developed. The number and degree of group associations and affiliations, and the degree to which behavior is institutionalized, or organized, structured, and regularized, tends to be a very high, if not indeed at a maximum level, in this ideal society. It is not only the extent of group association and institutionalization that is emphasized, but also its mutual consistency and stability. If the demands or values of different groups or associations with overlapping memberships or objectives are incompatible, and different people have conflicting expectations about what people with particular roles should do, then the degree of integration is limited and the possibility of societal disintegration increased.

It may be possible to give an impression of this ideal type with some examples. Many of the sociologists whom Parsons has influenced give a great deal of emphasis to "voluntary" associations and other "intermediate" groups (organizations smaller than the state).

This is especially true of the literature on the causes of what sociologists call "mass movements," and Professor Parsons has aptly said this literature constitutes a "new pluralism." There are many relevant types of intermediate groups, but perhaps the professional association, the labor union, and the organized pressure group are the leading examples. The professional association is perhaps most important of all. Some of these who share the Parsonian perspective think all types of economic life should be organized the way a profession such as medicine is organized, with a powerful guild organization and a pervasive occupational ethic controlling each industry. To be sure, this idea got most of its strongest support before the Parsonian school began—it was urged by Emile Durkheim, R. H. Tawney, the guild sociologists, some syndicalists, and by some advocates of a corporate or Fascist state. But the systematic conceptions needed to justify a system of economic organization modeled on the professions was developed by Professor Parsons, and he has repeatedly emphasized the functions that professional ethics, institutions, and associations perform.

The labor union and the organized pressure groups have also received special attention. One of the most interesting assertions in this literature is that labor unions, and perhaps even Marxian labor unions, may reduce the chances of a revolution in a modern society, because the labor union, however radical its ideology may initially have been, will provide a source of group participation for many workers, and the sense of belonging or group participation that results may reduce alienation and thereby the desire to overthrow the social order. There is perhaps also a tendency to emphasize the sense of group identity and the feeling of participation fostered by a pressure group rather than its practical impact in the political system. In the sociological conception, it would probably be a necessary condition for an ideal society that there be many groups of the sort we have just discussed.

There will be objections that this ideal is unsatisfactory in its own terms, quite apart from the merits of other types of ideal societies that may be imagined. Many people—probably even some of those who have contributed to the dissemination of this ideal—would say that they personally prefer unstructured and mainly unorganized, if not disorganized, societies. Many of us love ill-defined roles and feel confined by extensive associational networks. A new generation of sociologists, mindful of Marx, emphasizes the inevitability—or even desirability—of social conflict, and thus has only contempt for the Parsonian prediction of consensus. Many people who look at the literature on group participation would agree that more attention ought to be given to the *impact* or share of power that organizational membership can bring, and less to the fact of belonging per se. But the disadvantages of the sociological

ideal described, and the impressionism and injustice of this brief
and selective description of it, are not so important for the special
purpose of the moment, which is to show how economic theory and
a prevalent type of sociological theory can lead to conflicting
conclusions.

Ideals into nightmares

The point is that *the economic and sociological ideals described
are not only different, but polar opposites: if either one were attained, the society would be a nightmare in terms of the other.*
There are no doubt many social arrangements so inept that society
is inside what the economist would call the production possibility
frontier; that is, in a situation where it could get closer to either the
economic or the sociological ideal without getting further from the
other. An example of this would be a society with total anarchy, in
which a step taken to promote integration, such as the establishment of a government that created law and order, would bring
both the economic and the sociological ideals nearer. But these
positions that are inferior by both standards are not very interesting.
The important question is how much of the one ideal to give up in
order to get more of the other when you can't get more of both.
This is an important matter, for in terms of the values of most
people I know (whatever their disciplinary backgrounds), there is
profound merit in both ideals. The economic and sociological ideals,
far from both being destroyed by their contradiction with one another, are in fact expressions of the most fundamental alternatives
human societies face. The fact that most of us want to choose compromise positions between these polar ideals does not negate their
value as intellectual constructs that can give us a clearer understanding of the implications of a marginal move in one direction or
another.

The fundamental character of the conflict between these two
ideals may not, however, be immediately evident, so we must first
show how one ideal prevents the achievement of the other. The
economic ideal required that there be an optimal allocation of
resources at any moment in time and rapid innovation over time.
An optimal allocation of resources requires that a series of marginal
conditions be satisfied throughout the society; the marginal rates of
substitution of any two factors of production must be proportional
to the ratio of their prices and the same in all employments, and
so on. But if there is rapid growth, the demands for different goods,
the methods of production, the location of production, and the
marginal products of particular factors of production will change
incessantly. A Pareto-optimal allocation of resources will therefore
require *constant reallocations of resources.* This will mean that

factors of production, including labor, must frequently move from firm to firm, industry to industry, and place to place.[3] Since methods of production are rapidly changing, the same *combinations* of labor and other resources won't be needed very long: new *groupings* of workers are needed as the economy changes. This means that individual mobility is normally required, and this in turn means that the rewards of the incentive system must be offered on an individual basis.

Rapid change and growth in an economy means great gains in one area and vast losses in another, for incentives are needed to induce the needed mobility of labor and capital, and the changing pattern of incentives means many *nouveaux riches* and *nouveaux pauvres*. Both social and geographical mobility are at a maximum in the economically "ideal" society, and there can be few if any stable group relationships, apart from those in a nuclear family in which *only one* member is in the labor force. There can be no group loyalties or organizational constraints that limit individual mobility in response to changing incentives. There can be no organizations or other mechanisms that give those whose legitimate expectations are frustrated by the pattern of change the power to defend their interests, for this will (except where normally infeasible "lump sum" transfers can be arranged) pervert the pattern of incentives needed to bring about the resource reallocation which is entailed by the economic ideal. No group with a role in the productive process can restrict mobility by regulating entry, giving privilege for seniority, or "featherbedding."

I have elsewhere discussed some aspects of the relationship between rapid economic growth and social and political stability in more detail,[4] so there should be no need to spell out the argument here. It should in any event already be evident that the society that enjoys the benefits of the economic ideal will, because of the magnitude of social and geographic mobility and the dearth of stable group relationships, for that very reason be one in which individuals are constantly uprooted and in which alienation is probably at a maximum. The rapid change will also work against stable institutions and ethical norms. Moreover, the plurality of intermediate organizations, such as professional associations, labor unions, cartels, and lobbying organizations, which the sociological ideal cherishes,

---

[3] It is logically possible that reallocations of resources could be constant, but the rate of reallocation might still be so slow that social costs were small. Only those with a wanderlust, or the young adults who are leaving their parents' homes anyway, would then have to move. Rates of economic growth that are rapid by modern standards could, however, require much faster reallocations than could be handled in this way if the marginal conditions necessary for complete economic efficiency are to be satisfied at all times.
[4] "Rapid Growth as a Destabilizing Force," *Journal of Economic History,* XXIII (December 1963), 529–552.

cannot be allowed, for such organizations, by defending the *group* interests of their clients through the political system, by limiting entry or exit, or by preventing the adoption of new methods of production, would prevent the maximum growth which the economically ideal system will by definition achieve.

It should similarly be obvious that, *when the particular sociological ideal at issue has been achieved, the society will tend to become economically stagnant.* The guild-like institutional integration and regulation that is inherent in the sociological ideal tends to prevent change (just as the medieval guilds did). Without change, there can be no growth, so that the "professionalization" of economic life is one of the surest ways to prevent economic advance. The familiar argument that the Parsonian sociological tradition has a conservative bias turns out to be an heroic understatement when the economic aspect is considered, for the minimization of stress, alienation, and the elaboration and integration of institutions that it involves will tend to prevent economic even more than political change—and opposition even to economic change is indeed conservative! But this ideal must nonetheless not be belittled—its importance is evident whenever we examine the implications of its opposite.

At the most general level, what has been said is that the typical individual's need for some degree of stability in group relationships, and therefore also some institutional stability, can in a wide range of situations work against the maximum attainment of all other individual objectives. To put it another way, the continuous reallocations and rearrangements that are needed to satisfy maximally all of our other individual wants (be they material or not) is not usually consistent with the stable or enduring interpersonal relationships that most people apparently value and need. The ideal situation, interpersonal relationships aside, has been stated, in part explicitly, by economists. A set of ideal arrangements for group interaction, all other things aside, has been described, albeit implicitly, by sociologists. There are many ambiguities and shortcomings in both of these ideals, and even greater failings in my hurried vulgarizations of them, but it surely cannot be denied that it is often important to keep something like both of these polar cases in mind.[5]

These polar cases are not, however, always kept in mind in

---

[5] It might be supposed that even the desire for stable interpersonal relationships can be subsumed under the economic mode of analysis, thereby allowing a clear delineation of a single, comprehensive ideal. The society must "trade off" stable group relationships with the other things it wants, and accordingly needs some conception of an "ideal compromise." Unfortunately, the economist's tools of thought are not well adapted to dealing with situations in which different individuals' wants are highly interdependent (as they are when they cherish given group relationships) and economists have not usually studied this aspect of reality. Thus, in practice, there is still the need to keep both ideals in mind.

scholarly discussions, for each of them is monopolized by a different discipline. This has greatly hindered intellectual advance in the study of such topics as the labor union or foreign aid. It has also made it more difficult to develop methods for helping the country answer questions such as "what is the socially optimal rate of migration of Negroes from the rural South to the urban North?" It also presents a special challenge for a social report, since a social report which keeps only one or the other of these ideals in mind could mislead a nation about some of its profound problems. *The choice of a position along the continuum between the economic and the sociological ideals must be made by the political system.* But scholars fail to do their duty if they do not help a society understand the implications of alternative choices.

Social reality as a whole

All of this argument brings us back to the original thesis: it is futile to attempt to determine the division of labor between social science disciplines in terms of the objects they are supposed to consider. Reality cannot be divided into departments the way universities are, and no logically defensible division of subject matters is possible. The various disciplines are, however, distinguished by their prejudices and their methods. Economics, sociology, psychology, and political science must therefore be whatever economists, sociologists, psychologists, or political scientists do, or rather what they do best. But that can't be definitely determined before each discipline has tried to solve whatever problem is at issue. Therefore we should hope for a great deal of disciplinary overlap so that every problem that might benefit will, if the available resources permit, get the attention of scholars with different attitudes and methodologies.

If the spheres of the separate social sciences cannot properly be defined in terms of the nature of the reality studied, we can also conclude that a government should not in general seek advice about one segment of reality from only one discipline, and advice about some other segment of reality only from another discipline. We should not be surprised that the economic approach embodied in the Planning-Programming-Budgeting System can improve social programs. We should not be surprised when sociologists, psychologists, and political scientists contribute to the study of poverty, or business organization, or labor unions. Above all, we should conceive of any social report in multidisciplinary terms: all of the social science disciplines must be exploited if such a report is to achieve its full potential.

The division of emphasis between the Economic Report and a social report might pragmatically be determined in keeping with the Council of Economic Advisers' traditional and proper preoccupation with "macroeconomic" questions—the problems of recession and inflation, or the fluctuation of the market sector as a whole. "Micro-economic" questions—those that relate to particular sectors and groups—and "social" problems have not been given much attention in the Economic Report, or in any major government document. There is accordingly a need for the systematic public assessment of these problems, and this need suggests that a multidisciplinary social report could be quite useful.

A final conclusion is that the need for interdisciplinary communication and collaboration is even more urgent than it is usually said to be. If the argument of this article is correct, such communication and collaboration is essential to assure that all competing explanations of a particular phenomena are debated and compared, and to assure that society makes an informed compromise between the polarized ideals cherished by different disciplines. Yet interdisciplinary undertakings become steadily more difficult, as the scholarly market grows larger and the house of intellect expands. The very advance of scholarship can make it more difficult to see not only social science, but also social reality, as a whole.

[6]

ECONOMIC THEORY AND SOCIOLOGY: A CRITIQUE OF P. M. BLAU'S 'EXCHANGE AND POWER IN SOCIAL LIFE'

ANTHONY HEATH

Abstract In *Exchange and Power in Social Life* Blau uses the concept of exchange to develop the basis for a theory of social association. To show that his approach can provide predictions he uses aggregate supply and demand curves to analyse the exchange of advice for compliance within a work group, and from this derives predictions about status differentiation. However, his use of aggregate supply and demand curves requires, first, that what is being exchanged should be additive; second, that actors should evaluate exchanges by universalistic criteria; and, third, that they should act atomistically. The third assumption seems implausible within a work group, but, if it is valid, it follows that predictions *cannot* be made about status. This is because status differentiation can be said to occur only when there is *both* social distance *and* differential esteem between actors, and because differential esteem is likely to arise only within solidary groups.

IN THIS paper I am setting out to examine Blau's use of economic theory in his book *Exchange and Power in Social Life*.[1] In this book Blau is attempting to lay the foundations of a theory of social association, and the concept which he makes central is that of social exchange. He uses the term 'social exchange' to refer to voluntary actions of individuals that are motivated by the returns they are expected to bring,[2] and in analysing these exchange transactions he leans heavily on the marginal analysis of economics.

As well as providing a conceptual framework, Blau tries to show that his approach can be used to give specific predictions, and in chapter seven he attempts 'to explore whether the economic principles of marginal analysis, appropriately adapted to social exchange, can help clarify the changes and adjustments of group structure that occur in the course of social interaction and social differentiation' (p. 168). In this chapter Blau deals successively with indifference curves, bilateral monopoly, and aggregate supply and demand curves. He applies these concepts to the analysis of consultations within a work group and this leads him to propositions about changes in the volume of consultation and in the degree of status differentiation in the work group. For example, he predicts that 'changes in the number of experts in a work group will affect the volume of consultation if the task is relatively easy but not, or much less, if it is very difficult' (p. 169). My main concern is with how far Blau has been able to adapt, or could potentially adapt, these concepts to the explanation of social behaviour and, in particular, with how far his predictions about changes in the degree of status differentiation are valid. I will therefore begin with an examination of his use of indifference curves and then turn to bilateral monopoly and aggregate supply and demand curves. Finally, I will examine the predictions about status differentiation.

Indifference Curves

Indifference curves[3] are a geometrical device used by economists to present information about individuals' preferences for differing combinations of commodities. Thus we may ask a consumer to rank different combinations of, say, shirts and handkerchiefs in an order of preference, and those combinations which have the same rank in the preference ordering may be plotted on a graph to give an indifference curve. For example, in Fig. 1 we measure the number of shirts

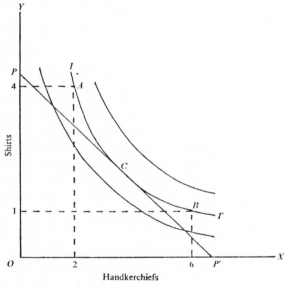

Fig. 1

on the vertical axis and the number of handkerchiefs on the horizontal axis, and the curve II' shows a set of combinations of shirts and handkerchiefs which have the same rank in the consumer's ordering. Since points A and B both lie on this curve, we can infer that the consumer has told us that he is indifferent between the two combinations which they represent (namely four shirts and two handkerchiefs, which is the combination given by point A, and one shirt and six handkerchiefs, which is the combination given by point B).

Similarly, Blau could use indifference curves to present information about individuals' preference rankings of combinations of work done for themselves and status[4] acquired by helping others with their work. However, Blau makes two, relatively minor, mistakes in his presentation of indifference curves:

(1) He says that: 'Any point on an indifference curve indicates that the individual is indifferent to whether he possesses the specified amount of the first or the specified amount of the second commodity, that is, that the two have the same value for him' (p. 171). However, indifference curves (as used in economics) do not show the amounts of two *separate* commodities between which the individual is indifferent, but the *combinations* between which he is indifferent.

(2) Blau measures utility on both axes of his indifference map, whereas indifference maps in economics have the quantities of the commodities represented on the axes and give information on utility only indirectly, through the ordering of the combinations, and not directly through the measurement of the utility derived from the particular combinations. Indeed, one of the objects of using indifference maps is to avoid the direct measurement of utility and to deal with a preference ranking instead.

Blau himself corrects the first error, for he subsequently talks of combinations, and, as to the second error, we can measure work and status on the two axes instead of utility without affecting his argument. This however does not avoid problems of measurement, for status is likely to be as difficult to measure as economists found utility was, and we shall have to return to this problem later.

In drawing hypothetical indifference maps, such as that in Fig. 1, certain assumptions are commonly made about individuals' behaviour. The assumptions are the following:

(1) *Nonsatiety:* the individual is not oversupplied with either commodity.

(2) *Transitivity:* if the consumer is indifferent between combinations A and B, and between combinations B and C, he is indifferent between A and C.

(3) *Diminishing marginal rate of substitution:* the more the individual has of one commodity, the more he is prepared to give up of that commodity in exchange for a given amount of the other.

This third assumption represents what Blau terms the principle of eventually diminishing marginal utility, and he sees it as the basic principle underlying marginal analysis, and exchange generally. Moreover, it can be shown that, given this assumption and those of nonsatiety and transitivity, it follows that indifference curves will be convex to the origin, will not intersect each other, and that a curve lying above and to the right of another will be preferred.

It seems to me that Blau may reasonably make these assumptions for behaviour in the area with which he is concerned in chapter seven (namely, that of work groups). However, he is not primarily concerned simply in mapping individuals' preferences but, as with price theory in economics, in making certain predictions about the allocation of scarce resources. Thus in economics we may examine how

276   ANTHONY HEATH

an individual allocates his available money resources between two commodities, and how this allocation changes if relative prices of the two commodities are altered or if his available money is increased or decreased. For example, in terms of Fig. 1, we may assume that the individual has a given amount of money which he is to spend all on shirts, all on handkerchiefs, or all on some combination of the two commodities. The amounts which he can buy will depend on their prices, and we therefore construct a 'budget constraint line' which shows the combinations the individual can buy given his budget and the prices. Thus in Fig. 1 the budget constraint line *PP′* shows that the individual could spend all his money on shirts and obtain *OP* shirts, or all his money on handkerchiefs and obtain *OP′* hand-kerchiefs, or all his money on any combination lying on the line *PP′*.

The budget constraint line will be a straight line sloping downwards from left to right if the prices of the two commodities are fixed and do not change with the amounts of the two goods that are bought; with the information given by this line and the individual's indifference map we may predict the combination of the two goods that he will buy. In Fig. 1 this is the combination given by point *C*, which is the point where the budget constraint line is tangential to an indifference curve. The individual cannot move to a higher indifference curve, because of his budget constraint line, and if he were to move to a different point within the area *OPP′*, he would put himself on a lower indifference curve.

Similarly, if indifference curve analysis is to be applied to social exchanges, then we must have some constraint comparable to the budget constraint of economics. The one that Blau uses is time, and we can thus draw a time constraint

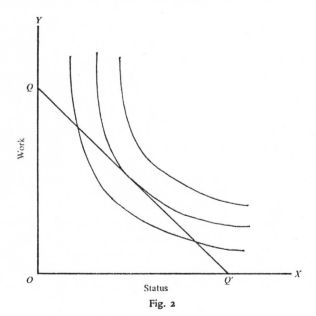

Fig. 2

line QQ′ on the indifference map shown in Fig. 2. This indifference map shows the individual's preferences for combinations of work done for himself and status acquired by helping others, and the time constraint line thus shows that the individual can spend all his time on his own work and complete OQ work, or all his time on helping others and obtain OQ′ status, or all his time on obtaining any combination lying on the line QQ′.

This need for a constraint line makes clear certain limitations on the use of the model. First, it requires that the individual should not be oversupplied with, in this case, time; that is to say, time must be a scarce resource. Second, it requires that the individual be free to allocate his time between the different possible uses. Clearly, neither of these assumptions need be universally true; for example, this particular model would not be adequate for analysing choices between mutually exclusive alternatives, such as occupations. At most, however, this simply restricts the application of the model. It does not prevent its valid use in some areas of social life[5] at least, and nor does it prevent the use of the principle of the diminishing marginal rate of substitution in other areas.

Bilateral Monopoly

More important difficulties arise, however, when Blau tries to use indifference curves to analyse exchange transactions. For the analysis Blau uses a 'box' diagram (Fig. 3). He measures problem-solving ability on the vertical axes and what I will, for the present, term resources of willing compliance on the horizontal axes. The indifference maps of two different individuals are then represented on the diagram:

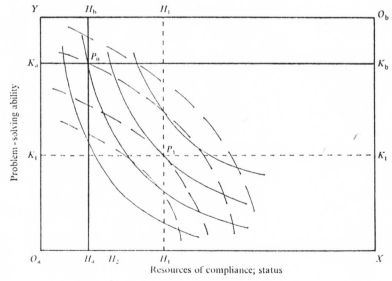

Fig. 3

in the quadrant on the axes O_aX and O_aY an expert's map is shown, and in the quadrant on the axes O_bX and O_bY a non-expert's. Blau then writes:

O_aY (or O_bX) is the total problem-solving ability available in the pair, with O_aK_a representing the greater ability of the expert and O_bK_b the lesser one of the colleague at the initial point P_0, before any consultation takes place (p. 173).

Next Blau turns to status and compliance and writes:

. . . the assumption is made that the expert's superior status makes him less inclined to subordinate himself to the other for any conceivable benefit than the other is to subordinate himself to the expert, which means that the expert has, in effect, less resources of willing compliance (O_aH_a) than his colleague (O_bH_b) (p. 174).

Finally Blau argues that each individual can move to a higher indifference curve than the ones they were on at the initial point P_0 if they exchange work for acts of compliance.

A number of major difficulties arise here. First, there are inconsistencies in the assumption which Blau is making about the relationship between status and resources of compliance. To begin with, he measures resources of willing compliance along the horizontal axes, and he seems to add that an act of compliance lowers the performer's status and raises the recipient's. Thus he writes:

Consultations would be reflected by movements from the initial point P_0 toward the bottom, showing that the expert applies some of his time and ability to the problems of the colleague, and toward the right, showing that the expert's status is raised by the compliance with which the colleague reciprocates for the advice (p. 174).

How, then, are we to interpret an exchange which moves the two individuals from P_0 to P_1? Since Blau measures resources of willing compliance along the horizontal axes, the expert has now increased his resources of compliance by H_aH_1, but, as Blau now argues, the movement from H_a to H_1 also indicates an increase in status. Thus the expert increases *both* his own status *and* his resources of willing compliance, although, according to Blau, it was the expert's superior status which gave him *lesser* resources of willing compliance in the first place.

In other words, Blau began by arguing that a man's resources of willing compliance were *inversely* proportional to his status but then goes on, in his use of the box diagram, to imply that the expert receives compliance in return for advice and that this increases both his status and his resources of willing compliance. The most natural solution to this inconsistency seems to me to be to assume that the expert had originally large resources of compliance (commensurate with his status), and to represent his lack of willingness to express compliance by drawing steeply sloping indifference curves. In other words, let us assume that the expert has large resources of ability and of compliance, and a low marginal rate of substitution of compliance for work.

Intuitively this would seem to be a reasonable assumption, for an act of compliance performed by an expert seems likely to have a much bigger effect on another's status[6] than would an act performed by a non-expert, and hence the expert would have much greater ability to raise another's status than would a non-expert. Moreover, this has the consequence that relatively little exchange will take place between the expert and the non-expert and relatively much exchange between those of more equal status and expertise, and this is indeed what Blau found in his study of welfare agencies.[7]

Blau, therefore, is inconsistent in the way that he relates status to resources of willing compliance, and the natural solution seems to be to deal with resources of potential compliance (which we should take to represent the individual's ability to raise another's status), rather than with his resources of willing compliance, and, further, to assume that resources of potential compliance are directly proportional to status. We may then take Blau's argument to be that a movement from P_0 to P_1 indicates that the non-expert performs an act of compliance such that the expert's status and resources of potential compliance are raised by $H_a H_1$ and his own reduced by $H_b H_1$.

Now this raises a number of empirical questions about the relationship between status and compliance, and I shall return to these later,[3] but one particular difficulty is that by using the box diagram Blau must assume that a given act of compliance will bring about quantitatively identical (although asymmetric) changes in both the expert's and the non-expert's status. That is, $H_a H_1$ must be equal to $H_b H_1$ (and whether we measure resources of willing compliance, resources of potential compliance or level of status on the horizontal axes, Blau must still be assuming quantitatively identical changes in both the expert's and the non-expert's stocks, and all three possible cases seem implausible). The problem seems to be that Blau is assuming isomorphism between the mathematical operations that can be performed on the numbers representing level of status or resources of compliance and the empirical processes that occur in practice. This is a problem which does not arise in economics to the same extent, for in economics we are much of the time dealing with stocks of commodities or money, and processes *do* occur with these which are isomorphic with some mathematical operation. Thus we can be sure that if A gives B, say, £10, his stock of money is reduced by £10 and B's increased by £10, but we cannot be sure if A expresses compliance to B, B's status will increase by any given amount or A's fall by a similar amount. Here, it seems to me, is a crucial difference between the subject-matter of economics and sociology, and it is likely to be one which will in many cases make economic analysis invalid when applied to social behaviour.

In examining this question of isomorphism further, we must distinguish between the empirical processes that we observe and the mathematical operations that we can perform on our measures of social phenomena. I will therefore examine the three types of measure which are commonly in use (namely ordinal, interval and ratio measures), the operations that can be performed with them, and their relationship to the empirical phenomena being measured. I will then return to consider the implications of this for Blau's analysis.

(i) *Ordinal Scales*[9]: Measurement constitutes the assignment of numerals to aspects of objects or events. For example, we may be interested in people's prestige or in objects' weight and we could rank people or objects in a hierarchy according to their prestige and weight. As well as ordering people according to their prestige we could assign numbers to their prestige, and our rule would be that where someone had greater prestige than another, the number assigned to his prestige must be greater than that assigned to the other's.

It can be seen that there will be an isomorphism between the position of the number in the set of numbers assigned and the position of the person's prestige, both in terms of greater and less. Measurement, moreover, is possible only where *some* isomorphism of this kind exists. It will be, however, only a partial isomorphism; only some of the properties of the number system will be isomorphic with the properties of the aspect of the phenomena with which we are concerned. Thus in mineralogy hardness is defined by reference to the scratch test: a mineral x is called harder than another mineral, y, if a sharp point of x scratches a smooth surface of y. But no known empirical operation can be performed which gives meaning to the notion that one mineral is twice as hard as another, and hence the isomorphism between the hardness of the minerals and the properties of the number system is limited to their ordering in terms of greater and less.

If, then, we are able to only rank objects according to whether they are greater or less in terms of the relevant aspect, we can construct only an ordinal scale and hence we cannot legitimately perform the mathematical operations of, for example, addition and subtraction on the numbers assigned. To perform these operations there must be corresponding empirical operations that can be performed on the objects and we must have information about these empirical operations.

(ii) *Interval Scales*: In assigning numbers for an interval scale any rule may be followed provided that it *both* preserves the ordering of the objects with respect to the magnitude of some aspect *and* preserves the *relative differences* between the magnitudes. Thus the fahrenheit and centigrade scales of temperature are both interval scales. For example, if we take objects having the temperatures 20°C, 30°C, and 40°C, we can not only say that the third object has a higher temperature than the second, and the second than the first, but we can also say that the difference between the first and the second temperature is the same as the difference between the second and third. If we now convert these temperatures from the centigrade to the fahrenheit scales we obtain the temperatures 68°F, 86°F, and 104°F and we can see that the relative differences are preserved: the difference between the second and the third temperature is still the same as the difference between the first and second.

Again, our ability to construct an interval scale depends on the existence of empirical operations which give meaning to the notion that there are invariant relative differences between the magnitudes of some aspect. Thus Coleman has devised an interval measure of prestige which depends on the assumption that

ECONOMIC THEORY AND SOCIOLOGY 281

people's choices among different groups depends on the *average* prestige of the members of each.[10] It can be seen that this assumption requires that people's behaviour depends on the relative differences between others' prestige, and if, but only if, this assumption is empirically valid, Coleman would be able to construct his scale.

The construction of an interval scale, then, depends on the existence of certain empirical operations, and it conveys information about these operations. There is more information than is conveyed by the ordinal scale, but it still does not permit us to say, for example, that the magnitude of one object as regards some quality is twice that of another. This is because the zero point on the scale is a matter of convention or convenience, and this in turn derives from the fact that we cannot attach meaning to the notion of a 'true' zero. This can be clearly seen with the arbitrary origins of the centigrade and fahrenheit scales of temperature.

(iii) *Ratio Scales:* Where, however, a 'true' zero can be assigned, we can talk of a ratio scale. This again will depend on the empirical properties of what we are observing and on our means of observation. In the case of temperature an absolute zero can be assigned by using the empirical law that, within the range between the melting point and freezing point of mercury, the temperature of a body of gas under constant pressure is a mathematical function of its volume. We can now extrapolate beyond the range of the mercury thermometer by using a 'gas thermometer'; that is, we measure the temperature of a substance by measuring the volume which a certain standard body of gas assumes under a specified pressure when brought in contact with the substance. The temperature, then, is defined by the formula $T = f(v)$ when it lies outside the range of the mercury thermometer and we can now extrapolate to zero volume and hence zero temperature. Given an absolute zero we can now talk about the magnitude of some quality of an object being twice that of another object's, and thus our rule in constructing a ratio scale must be that it preserves invariant the ratio of the magnitudes.

Our ability to construct a ratio scale, then, depends on our ability to assign an absolute zero to the scale, and if we can assign only an arbitrary zero, then we will have at best an interval scale. However, the fact of having a ratio scale does not necessarily permit us to perform on the objects themselves the operations of addition and subtraction; we can, it is true, say that one object is twice another as regards some aspect, if we have been able to construct a ratio scale, but to be able to perform the operation of addition we must be able to *combine* the objects in some way such that the magnitudes of the relevant aspects when they are combined is the sum of their magnitudes before they were combined. Thus we can add lengths in that we can place two objects end to end and in that their length when combined in this way is the sum of their previous lengths. In this sense there is an isomorphism between the mathematical operation of addition and the empirical operation of combination. However, there is no method of combining objects such that their temperature when combined is the sum of their temperatures before they were combined, and we therefore cannot say that temperature is 'additive'. Nevertheless, having a ratio scale does enable us to test whether some property *is* additive or not.

It can be seen that this question of isomorphism has important consequences for Blau. First of all, in the diagram for exchange in bilateral monopoly, Blau claims that O_aY represents the total problem-solving ability available in the pair, and that this total is the sum of the two individuals' problem-solving ability. Now suppose that by the term 'problem-solving ability' we mean the individual's ability to solve problems of increasing difficulty, and suppose that we have been able to construct ratio scales which measure the difficulty of the problems. Intuitively, it seems unlikely that we can get the two individuals to work together (that is, to combine) in some way so that they can now together do problems the difficulty of which is, as measured by the ratio scale, the sum of the difficulty of the hardest problems they could do when apart. In fact, it is quite likely that they will be able to solve only those problems which are no harder than those the expert could do when on his own.

Alternatively, by problem-solving ability we might simply mean the number of problems that an individual can solve in a given time. If we do not allow the individuals to cooperate, then the total number of problems they can get through will indeed be the sum of the numbers they can get through singly. There are, however, two difficulties to this solution. First, cooperation is bound to take place when consultation occurs, and in this case the total number completed is likely to be more than the sum of the numbers they do individually. Second, consultation may in fact occur when a non-expert has a problem which he finds too difficult, rather than when he has too many, and in this case the measure is likely to be inappropriate.

A second alternative would be to measure not problem-solving ability but time spent on work. Clearly, if the expert spends an hour helping someone else, that is one hour less spent on his own work and one hour more spent on the other's, and the total amount of time available for the pair is the sum of the amounts they have available individually.[11]

There is no such obvious solution, however, to the problem of the measurement of status or of resources of compliance. True, Blau does not say that he is summing the two individuals' resources of compliance, but as we have already seen he does imply that an act of compliance lowers the performer's status by as much as it raises the recipient's. It can be seen that to verify this proposition we must at least have an interval scale for measuring status, but that the construction of an interval scale in no way presupposes the truth of the proposition. It can also be seen that, if we are able to construct only an ordinal scale, we shall be able to test merely the weaker proposition that an act of compliance lowers the performer's status and raises the recipient's; we shall be unable to say whether the magnitude of the changes is the same.

There are, moreover, good reasons to suppose that the stronger statement would not be verified. Thus Blau himself makes a distinction between status that is securely based and that which is not and suggests that the latter is much more vulnerable. This suggests that a man of given, but insecure, status would lose far more by performing an act of compliance than would another man of the same, but more secure, status. Similarly, the man to whom he deferred might gain relatively little status, if his status were already secure. Intuitively this seems plausible, and we may interpret it as follows: in a period of group formation the members' relative status would be uncertain and acts of compliance at this initial stage would be of considerable importance in establishing the status hierarchy. Similarly, a new member entering an established group would have uncertain status, and while his status was uncertain acts of compliance expressed by, or towards, him would have relatively more effect on his status than they would have on the other group members' status.

If this, or some similar, process in fact occurs, then it follows that, in terms of the box diagram in Fig. 3, the following would occur: an exchange of advice for compliance between the expert and the non-expert (whom we shall assume to have insecure status) would lead to the non-expert's status falling by H_bH_1 but the expert's rising by only H_aH_2. If the expert had performed K_aK_1 work for the non-expert, then, it follows, the former would now be at point K_1H_2 (that is, on a *lower* indifference curve) while the latter would be at the point K_1H_1, and hence Blau would be unable to use the diagram in the way he wishes.

A number of difficulties, then, arise in Blau's use of the box diagram to analyse exchange in bilateral monopoly. First, he made inconsistent assumptions about the relationship between status and resources of compliance; this was resolved by assuming that status was directly proportional to resources of potential compliance, although it still leaves some empirical questions unanswered. Second, Blau assumed that problem-solving ability was additive, and this seems intuitively implausible; again, however, the difficulty can be avoided by measuring time spent on work, rather than problem-solving ability, on the vertical axes of the box diagram. Third, Blau has to assume that an act of compliance lowers the performer's status and resources of compliance by as much as it raises the recipient's. This seems implausible, particularly in view of Blau's own distinction between secure and insecure status and, if incorrect, invalidates the use of the box diagram.[12]

This last point would seem to have serious consequences for Blau's analogy between status and capital, which he develops at some length elsewhere in *Exchange and Power*.[13] Thus it would follow that there is not a fixed quantity of status which can be distributed in the way that money can. As I suggested earlier, we can be sure that if A gives B £10 his stock of money will be reduced by £10 and B's increased by £10, but we cannot be sure that, if A expresses compliance to B, B's status will increase by some given amount and A's fall by an identical amount.

Aggregate Supply and Demand Curves

The problems which arise with the box diagram do not, however, invalidate Blau's analysis of price changes, although the question of additivity will clearly remain crucial. First of all, Blau argues that consulting relations in a work group do not exist in isolation and that exchange processes proliferate from bilateral monopolies into wider circles. In his analysis of price changes, therefore, Blau uses aggregate supply and demand curves, and it is for this reason that his failure with the box diagram does not invalidate the general argument.

To obtain the aggregate curves Blau sums the individual supply and demand curves, and these in turn can be derived from the individual indifference maps. Ignoring for the moment the relationship between compliance and status, we will be doing no violence to Blau's argument if we use merely his assumption that assistance with work is repaid in the form of acts of compliance. We can now draw indifference maps of each individual's preferences for combinations of spending time on his own work (or receiving advice) and receiving compliance (or performing acts of compliance). We can then draw a series of time constraint lines which will show the actual combination preferred at each price for advice in terms of compliance. That is to say, if the price in terms of compliance falls, then the expert receives less compliance through spending all his time on advising others than he did before and this therefore means that there must be a new time constraint line. From the combinations preferred at different prices we can now draw the individual's demand or supply curve. This will show on the vertical axis the price in terms of compliance, and on the horizontal axis the number of hours spent on assistance (or spent receiving assistance).

The individual curves are now summed by summing the amounts of advice supplied or demanded at each price. It can be seen that it is essential for this operation that advice should be additive, and it is for this reason that I suggest that advice should be measured in time units. The price for advice in terms of compliance which will actually occur is now given by the inter-section of the demand and supply curves. If subsequently some novices enter the group, thus adding their demand for advice to the existing one, we would have a new demand curve above, and to the right of, the previous one and hence a higher price.

Blau then goes on to analyse the effect of the elasticity of the demand and supply curves on price changes, and hence (he claims) on the status structure of the group, and on the volume of consultation. However, before considering the relationship between compliance and status, I want to examine whether price changes will occur in the way Blau suggests.

There are, I think, two important questions here. First, we must consider whether a common price will exist in the group and whether what goes on in any given exchange relationship will be affected by what goes on elsewhere. In other words, we must question whether proliferation of exchanges occurs in the way that Blau

ECONOMIC THEORY AND SOCIOLOGY 285

assumes it does. Second, we must consider whether the normative framework underlying exchange relationships produces price changes of the kind predicted. In other words, are the norms of economic and social exchanges the same?

At a number of places in *Exchange and Power* Blau points out the differences between economic and social exchanges. In particular, he argues that economic exchanges are *extrinsic*, in that the commodities are detachable from the exchange relationship, whereas social exchanges are more *intrinsic*, in that they cannot be detached to the same extent from the relationship. This difference, he suggests, follows from the trust and the personal obligations which occur in social exchanges, and it is a special case, he says, of Parsons' distinction between universalism and particularism. In other words, economic exchanges tend to take place within an impersonal context and according to universalistic standards, whereas social exchanges take place within a more personal context and with more particularistic standards.

Blau, therefore, seems to see exchanges as lying on a continuum ranging from the extrinsic exchange of economics to the intrinsic exchange of the love relationship. Moreover, he is certainly aware of the importance of particularism in social exchanges, for he writes:

Deep intrinsic attachments fundamentally alter the social transactions in interpersonal relations. The basic difference is between associations that are considered ends-in-themselves by participants and those they consider means for some further ends (p. 35).

Now it can be seen that where exchange relationships are seen as ends in themselves and are judged according to particularistic standards, changes in other exchange relationships are unlikely to affect them. It is only where the relationship is seen primarily as a means to an end that universalistic standards will occur and will form a basis for comparison with other exchanges.

The use of aggregate supply and demand curves, therefore, is likely to be valid only in the degree to which exchanges approximate to the extrinsic pole of the continuum. That is to say, we must make some assumptions about the *orientations* of the individuals (whether they are oriented to the relationship as a means to an end or as an end in itself) in analysing price changes. Now in his discussion of consultation in a work group Blau did assume that what is salient to the members is status (or, perhaps better, compliance) and work, and insofar as this assumption is correct we shall have no quarrel with him on this score, for compliance and work do seem to be relatively extrinsic benefits. If, however, individuals were more interested in friendship, then Blau's model would not suffice.[14]

Considerable further restrictions, then, are placed upon Blau's model. We have already seen that the problem of additivity is likely to restrict its applications, and so is the need for a constraint line. Now we see that it will apply only where a certain type of orientation on the part of the actors predominates. Moreover, as Blau himself argues, this orientation is more typical of economic exchanges than social ones, for in social ones there is a greater element of particularism. This does not mean that the model can be applied to no area of social life but that, at best, it will apply only to exchanges towards the extrinsic pole of the continuum. It still remains to be shown, therefore, whether Blau's general characterisation of behaviour as exchange can yield predictions. What Blau is really doing is saying that some exchanges occur in social life that resemble those of economic behaviour, and hence that economic models can possibly be applied to them.

Moreover, the predominance of extrinsic exchanges may be a necessary and not a sufficient condition for the changes in price which Blau predicts. For example, norms and group processes may affect even extrinsic exchanges, and, as Blau himself suggests, there may be a norm of fair exchange. Blau, however, argues that there may often be a difference between the fair rate of exchange and what he calls the going rate of exchange (which he sees as being governed by the aggregate supply and demand curves); but this does not seem altogether likely. If the non-experts have a standard of what constitutes a fair rate of exchange of help for compliance, they may in fact refuse to pay more and may combine to bring sanctions to bear on the experts if they demand more. This seems to be the case, indeed, in the labour market; thus it is often not accepted as legitimate that employers should reduce wages if the demand for labour falls and, consequently, if employers try to impose what workers regard as unfair wage rates, strikes will be likely.[15]

Similarly with social behaviour; in a work group the non-experts are likely to combine (either as a group on their own, or together with experts) so as to enforce their norms of fair exchanges and this will be reflected in the *group*'s demand curve for advice. In other words, summing the individual demand schedules requires the implicit assumption that individuals act atomistically and it ignores the emergent processes that occur within a solidary group. There may be a difference between the fair rate which is set by the group and the rate which would be predicted on the basis of summing the individual demand curves, and the important question is which is the better predictor of what actually happens. That is to say, does the assumption that individuals act atomistically give a better prediction than the assumption that they act, in some respects, as a cohesive group? Again, this is not a question which can be settled *a priori*, but an empirical one. Nevertheless, the literature on group norms in industry suggests strongly that consideration of these group processes will have to be included in the model.[16]

Moreover, when we allow that group action may emerge on the basis of common interests, many possibilities arise as regards exchange rates. Starting from the position of a single solidary group containing both experts and non-experts and with a norm of fair exchange, the following alternatives at least would seem possible consequences of the addition of some novices to the group:

(1) The norm might be retained and assistance refused to the new members.

(2) The norm might be maintained and the group (including the new members)

might combine against the superiors in order to reduce the pressure of work (and thus enabling the experts to meet the norm).

(3) The norm might be broken and experts and non-experts might break into separate, and opposing, strata.

(4) The norm might be broken and a new norm instituted at a higher price.

The fourth alternative seems likeliest to occur when ties between exchange partners are relatively weak and hence norms are not strongly maintained and/or when there is a history of frequent changes in demand and supply. Neither of these conditions, however, are by any means sufficient conditions for the occurrence of the fourth alternative; for example, even where ties are originally weak, the introduction of novices may lead to the emergence of group action and the development of solidary ties. Similarly, if there is a core of permanent group members, then these may form more of a solidary group and enforce a group norm to which the more transient members may pay little attention.

The use of aggregate supply and demand curves to analyse price changes, then, seems to require, first, that individuals should be oriented to exchange transactions as means to ends and evaluate them according to universalistic criteria and, second, that there should be relatively loose ties (i.e. atomism) between exchange partners or else a normative framework which supports price changes.[17] Where, on the other hand, there are strong group ties, group action is likely to occur and this is likely to differ from that predicted by the aggregation of individual demands. This group action may take the form of cohesive action against the other partner (whether individual or group) in the exchange, or it may take the form of cohesive action to enforce the norms of exchange between partners *within* the group. An example of the first case would be union–employer bargaining; here theories of supply and demand based on aggregation would clearly not be useful and, perhaps, game theory would be more appropriate. In the second case, on the other hand, we would not have bargaining between exchange partners but normative regulation of the transaction, and this might be expected where there were strong group ties or where the exchange was seen as a means to collective goals. Thus in a work group consultation between expert and non-expert might be seen as a protection against interference from the supervisor, and we might consequently expect normative regulation of the exchange.

The type of model which will be appropriate for analysing exchanges will, therefore, depend on the type of social relationships which hold. As we have seen, there seem to be four possibilities:

(1) The participants are relatively atomistic (i.e. have loose group ties) and see the exchange in universalistic terms. Analysis based on aggregate supply and demand curves is most likely to be appropriate here.

(2) The participants form relatively cohesive, but opposed, groups and again see the exchange in universalistic terms. A bargaining model is most likely to be appropriate here.

(3) The participants form a single cohesive group, and again see the exchange in universalistic terms. Normative regulation seems most likely here.
(4) The participants form a single cohesive group and see the exchange in particularistic terms. Normative regulation or simply altruism is likely here.

Nevertheless, even where the aggregation model does not apply, it may have considerable heuristic value. For example, Blau emphasizes the importance of elasticity in price changes and he argues that, where supply (or demand) is inelastic, shifts in the demand (or supply) curve will have relatively large effects on prices and small effects on the volume of consultation. Inelastic supply or demand is likely to occur, Blau suggests, where there is strong pressure for work, considerable difficulty in acquiring expertise and few alternative people who could give advice. Now if there were a cohesive group including both experts and non-experts, a norm of fair exchange and conditions such as those just described, and if there were now a shift in the demand curve following the introduction of new members, we would have a situation where the normative framework and pressure of work imposed incompatible demands on the experts. In such a case we would predict innovating group action of one of the four kinds described above. Where, however, there was a much more elastic supply curve, we would predict that innovating group action of this kind would not occur.

Predictions about Status Differentiation

We have seen that an aggregation model for price changes may be appropriate only under certain restricted conditions. Blau's main objective, however, seems to be not simply the formulation of predictions about changes in the volume of consultation or in the price of advice in terms of compliance, but the formulation of predictions about the consequent changes in status differentiation and group structure. I will attempt to deal now with the problems involved in this.

Blau begins with the assumption that, if the non-expert has no other service which he can offer in return, he will repay the expert with compliance. He seems to assume, further, that a man to whom compliance is owed thereby receives status and that social distance consequently occurs between the two. Now Blau could define status and social distance in terms of compliance, so that these propositions become true by definition. In fact, however, it seems to me that both Blau's, and normal sociological, usage implies distinctions between these terms and that Blau is hence making some empirical propositions.

First, Blau does not make the distinction between a service and compliance altogether clear. In point of fact, I would suggest, there is no clear-cut distinction between performing a service for someone and complying with his requests. Thus a worker provides labour services to his employer, and these services take the form of compliance with the employer's requests *within a certain defined area*. Now services may vary according to the discretion left to the employee in carrying out the request and according to the extent of the area over which the employer's requests are legitimate. Thus a doctor has great discretion; a skilled worker less. Both have more discretion and a much narrower area of compliance than does an unskilled labourer. Nevertheless, there are almost always *some* constraints on the requests which a man can legitimately make to another; these constraints may be implicit or explicit, but at no stage does there seem to be a clear break between a service and compliance.

Nevertheless, it is open to Blau to classify services according to degree of discretion and area over which requests are valid, and to use the term compliance for those services where there is little discretion left to the performer and a wide area of request. In addition, Blau could say that the one man had power, in the defined area, over the other and that the latter was thus subordinate to him in that area. Thus insofar as the worker is bound to comply with his employer's requests while at work, he is subordinate to his employer. This, however, has no necessary or logical connection either with subordination outside that area or with social esteem. It seems likely that there *is* a casual connection between subordination in one area and social distance in others (measuring social distance by the degree of constraint in social interaction), but I would suggest that the existence of social distance between two individuals or groups is *not* a cause of the expression of esteem by the one towards the other.[18]

I have used the degree of social distance, then, to refer to the degree of constraint arising in social interaction, and this I want to distinguish from esteem, by which I refer to the estimations which people have of each other's moral worth. It seems to me, further, that we talk of a man having high status within a group only if there is both a degree of social distance between him and those of lower status and if the latter hold him in high esteem.

As the area of subordination increases (and amount of discretion decreases), then, the amount of social distance increases, but to say that there is also an increase in status differentiation we need to know about the esteem in which the subordinate holds the superior. Two further empirical propositions suggest themselves, moreover. First, where there is mutual, equal esteem, there will tend to be no social distance between the actors and, where there is differential esteem, there will tend to be social distance. In other words, social distance may be a consequence of either compliance or of differential esteem. Blau, on the other hand, requires that differential esteem too should be a consequence of compliance, and there is considerable doubt as to whether this proposition holds.

Where, therefore, changes in the price of advice in terms of compliance (as defined above) occur, we can say that there are, by definition, changes in power and we can probably infer that there will be changes in social distance and, again by definition, in group structure. It is less likely that there will be changes in differential esteem and hence, as a combined result, changes in status differentiation. These, however, are questions which require empirical verification; only the relationships between compliance and power and between status and social distance and esteem are matters of definition.

Nevertheless, I would suggest that esteem is most likely to enter into transactions that occur within cohesive groups. Here, for example, advice may be repaid not by compliance but by esteem[19] and hence status differentiation might arise. Within cohesive groups, however, we would expect normative regulation of exchanges involving esteem too, and we might also find a greater degree of particularism, which might perhaps be reflected in more diffuse transactions. There would thus be no *a priori* grounds for supposing that a model based on aggregate supply and demand curves for advice and esteem would be appropriate here either.

Summary and Conclusions

The central concern of this paper, then, has been Blau's treatment of indifference curves, bilateral monopoly, and aggregate supply and demand curves in the analysis of social behaviour and, in particular, his attempt to derive predictions about status differentiation. With indifference curves the problem arose that a constraint line is necessary, hence perhaps limiting the application of Blau's approach to fairly narrow areas of behaviour. Blau's use of the box diagram to analyse bilateral monopoly, on the other hand, involved serious questions of validity. On the vertical axes he measured problem-solving ability and on the horizontal axes both (apparently) status and resources of willing compliance. This raised the problem of the isomorphism between the mathematical operations that can be performed on the number system and the empirical operations that can be performed on the phenomena being observed. In particular, Blau seemed to assume that problem-solving ability was additive, and that one man's status would rise by as much as another's fell following an act of compliance by the latter. The problems here, we saw, stemmed not from difficulties in measurement but in doubts about the empirical processes that actually occur.

This led to the important point that aggregate supply and demand curves could be constructed only where what was being summed had the property of additivity. In addition, aggregation required the assumption that individuals acted atomistically and on the basis of universalistic standards. These conditions, it was suggested, were not likely to be met in a large part of social behaviour; in many areas group action or action on the basis of particularistic standards was likely to make aggregation invalid.

In addition, even where aggregation was valid, it was unlikely that predictions about status differentiation could be made. Relationships where individuals acted atomistically and on the basis of universalistic values were likely to involve the exchange of services. Where a service involved complying with another's requests over a potentially wide area and where little discretion was left to the performer, social distance was likely, it was suggested, to occur between the two members of the exchange relationship. Status differentiation, however, is usually taken to involve differential esteem as well as social distance, and there was no *a priori* reason to suppose that esteem would arise in such exchange relationships. Rather, it was suggested, esteem would be likely to arise within cohesive groups.

Notes

1. I am grateful to John Goldthorpe and David Newbery for their valuable comments on this paper.
2. See P. M. Blau, *Exchange and Power in Social Life*, New York: Wiley, 1964, p. 91. It is not altogether clear how Blau intends the word 'motivated' in this definition to be interpreted, for on p. 6 he writes: 'Social exchange, as here conceived, is limited to actions that are *contingent* on rewarding reactions from others'. He also writes, on p. 91, about the *implicit* calculations underlying exchange transactions. [My emphasis in both cases.] At its broadest then, Blau's conception of social exchange includes all actions which can be shown to be (statistically) dependent on another's reaction, regardless of whether calculation about rewards takes place.
3. The discussion of indifference curves leans heavily on that in W. J. Baumol, *Economic Theory and Operations Analysis* (2nd edition), Englewood Cliffs, New Jersey: Prentice-Hall, 1965, pp. 183–195.
4. Whether status is in fact acquired by helping others with their work involves a number of questions, which I will deal with later in this paper, but even if status is not acquired by helping with work we could still draw an indifference map showing the individual's preferences for combinations of work and status. In his example of an indifference map in *Exchange and Power*, p. 172, Blau in fact deals with sociability and with status acquired from helping others, but, for the sake of consistency, I have dealt with work and status as it is with these that Blau is concerned in his later discussions of bilateral monopoly and of aggregate supply and demand curves. This change does not alter Blau's argument substantively.
5. Throughout this paper I have used the term 'social life' to refer to all areas of behaviour other than those that form the subject-matter of economics.
6. Following the discussion of status and compliance later on in this paper, it is probably better to say that an act of *deference* performed by an expert is likely to have a bigger effect on another's *esteem* than would an act performed by a non-expert, rather than to talk of the effect of a man's act of compliance on another's status.
7. P. M. Blau, *The Dynamics of Bureaucracy*, Chicago: University of Chicago Press, 1955, pp. 106–110.
8. See the discussions later on in this paper about secure and insecure status and about the relationship between compliance, social distance, esteem and status.
9. The discussion of ordinal, interval and ratio scales and of additivity leans heavily on the discussion in S. S. Stevens, 'Mathematics, Measurement, and Psychophysics' in S. S. Stevens (ed.), *Handbook of Experimental Psychology*, New York: Wiley, 1951, pp. 1–49, and in C. G. Hempel, 'Fundamentals of Concept Formation in Empirical Science' in *International Encyclopaedia of Unified Science*, Vol. II, No. 7, Chicago: University of Chicago Press, 1952.
10. J. S. Coleman, *Introduction to Mathematical Sociology*, New York: Free Press of Glencoe, 1964, pp. 90–2.
11. Similarly, in the field of economic anthropology, it has been pointed out that time is the most adequately measurable item available to the economic anthropologist who is studying non-monetary economic systems. See C. S. Belshaw, *Changing Melanesia: Social Economics of Culture Contact*, Melbourne: Oxford University Press, 1954, pp. 149–150 and R. F.

Salisbury, *From Stone to Steel: Economic Consequences of a Technological Change in New Guinea*, Melbourne: Melbourne University Press, 1962, p. 144. However, the problem with using time as a measure of work done is that the participants in an exchange transaction may be oriented not to the amount of time spent but to the value of what was, or could have been, done in that time.

12. It is probably true that, holding security of status (or, better, esteem) constant, higher status gives higher resources of compliance (or, better, higher resources of deference), and that, *ceteris paribus*, an act of deference lowers the performer's esteem and raises the recipient's. However, it still cannot follow *a priori* that there will be a one-to-one relationship in the changes in the performer's and the recipient's esteem, and this is the crucial point.

13. Analogies between status and capital, and between power and capital, are developed in Blau, *Exchange and Power*, ch. 5.

14. In *op. cit.*, p. 190 Blau argues that he might be making the wrong assumptions about what is exchanged and that he might need to include more, or different, variables, but that this does not necessarily invalidate his model. This is true, but the point that I wish to emphasize is that the model depends on the exchange of extrinsic benefits and that it will not therefore be sufficient to assume that individuals are interested in friendship rather than status, since friendship is *intrinsic* to the relationship.

15. For a discussion of the importance of conceptions of equity in labour relations see H. A. Turner, G. Clack, and G. Roberts, *Labour Relations in the Motor Industry: A Study of Industrial Unrest and an International Comparison*, London: Allen and Unwin, 1967.

16. See, for example, F. J. Roethlisberger and W. J. Dickson, *Management and the Worker*, Cambridge, Mass.: Harvard University Press 1939.

17. I would further suggest that a normative framework which would support price changes would be likely only where there were relatively weak ties between participants.

18. This is not to say that a subordinate (in the sense of one who expresses compliance to another) will not esteem the superordinate for reasons external to the exchange, although we might also suppose that where such esteem occurs the nature of the exchange will be modified.

19. Compliance and esteem need not, of course, be mutually exclusive; for example, where we have leadership we are likely to find both. The point which I wish to make, however, is that there is no logical reason to suppose that the two will accompany each other and that they are likely, on the whole, to arise within different types of social relationship.

Biographical note: ANTHONY HEATH, born 1942, Somerset; studied at Trinity College, Cambridge (Classics and Economics). Fellow and Lecturer in Sociology at Churchill College, Cambridge, 1967. Currently engaged in research on exchange theories in sociology.

[7]

COLLECTIVE ACTION AS AN AGREEABLE n-PRISONERS' DILEMMA

by Russell Hardin[1]

Research Institute on Communist Affairs, Columbia University

The problem of collective action to produce a group collective good is analyzed as the game of Individual vs. Collective and then as an *n*-person game to show that, under the constraints of Mancur Olson's analysis, it is an *n*-prisoners' dilemma in the cases of latent and intermediate groups. The usual analysis according to which noncooperation is considered the rational strategy for classical 2-prisoners' dilemma is logically similar to Olson's analysis, which suggests that rational members of a latent group should not contribute toward the purchase of the group collective good. However, in the game analysis it is clear that the latent and intermediate groups are not logically different, but rather are distinguishable only statistically. Some prisoners' dilemma experimental results are used to suggest how the difference might arise and how the vast prisoners' dilemma literature can be related to the problem of collective action.

The game of collective action is then analyzed not from the view of strategies but of outcomes. There is presented a theorem which states that the outcome in which all player-members of a group pay and all benefit is a Condorcet choice from the set of realizable outcomes for the game. Hence the cooperative outcome in such a game would prevail in election against all other outcomes.

∽

IN *The Logic of Collective Action,* Mancur Olson (1968) has proposed a mathematical explanation for the notable failure of the memberships of large interest groups to work together to provide themselves with their mutually desired collective goods. He concludes that the success of a group in providing itself with a collective good depends on the logical structure of the group.

> In a small group in which a member gets such a large fraction of the total benefit that he would be better off if he paid the entire cost himself, rather than go without the good, there is some presumption that the collective good will be provided. In a group in which no member got such a large benefit from the collective good that he had an interest in providing it even if he had to pay all the cost, but in which the individual was still so important in terms of the whole group that his contribution or lack of contribution to the group objective had a noticeable effect on the costs or benefits of others in the group, the result is indeterminate. By contrast, in a large group in which no single individual's contribution makes a perceptible difference to the group as a whole ... it is certain that a collective good will *not* be provided unless there is coercion or some outside inducements. ... (p. 44)

[1] I am pleased to thank Hayward R. Alker, Jr., Joan Rothchild, and Jean-Roger Vergnaud for the help and advice they gave in the preparation of this paper.

These three sorts of group can be distinguished as the privileged group (i.e., the group in which at least one member could justify his full payment for the provision of the good on the basis of his sufficiently great return), the intermediate group, and the latent group.

Common sense and experience seem to confirm Olson's conclusions, although they seem to suggest a logic counter to our expectations. They suggest that "rational, self-interested individuals will not act to achieve their common or group interests" (Olson, 1968, p. 2). To clarify the logic of collective action, therefore, Olson gives a mathematical demonstration, which can be easily summarized.

The advantage (A_i) which accrues to an individual member (i) of a group as the result of his contribution to the purchase of the group collective good is given by:

$$A_i = V_i - C,$$

where V_i is the value to i of his share of the total collective good provided to the group at cost C to i. Clearly, if A_i is to be positive, then V_i must be greater than C. But this implies that i will contribute toward the

172

purchase of the group collective good on his own rational incentive only if his share of that part of the good purchased at his cost is worth more to him than it cost him (Olson, 1968, pp. 22–25). Hence, the collective good will be provided in a privileged group, where this condition is met, but not in a latent group, where it is not met.

COLLECTIVE ACTION AND PRISONERS' DILEMMA

As with the prisoners' dilemma, we have for the latent group a result that tells us that individual effort to achieve individual interests will preclude their achievement, because if the collective good is not provided, the individual member fails to receive a benefit that would have exceeded his cost in helping purchase that good for the whole group. It would be useful to perform a game theory analysis of collective action to demonstrate that the logic underlying it is the same as that of the prisoners' dilemma. First, however, since Olson's analysis was accomplished from the perspective of an individual in the group, let us consider a particular instance of collective action in the game of Individual vs. Collective.

Individual vs. collective

Let us construct a game matrix in which the row entries will be the payoffs for Individual, and the column entries will be the per capita payoffs for Collective, where Collective will be the group less Individual. The payoffs will be calculated by the prescription for rational behavior: that is, the payoffs will be benefits less costs. The group will comprise ten members whose common interest is the provision of a collective good of value twice its cost. There are two possible results of having one member of the group decline to pay his share: either the total benefit will be proportionately reduced, or the costs to the members of the group will be proportionately increased. Let us assume the former, but either choice would yield the same analysis. For the sake of simplicity, assume also that there are no initial costs in providing the collec-

MATRIX 1
INDIVIDUAL VS. COLLECTIVE
Collective

		Pay	Not Pay
Individual	Pay	1, 1	−0, 8, 0.2
	Not Pay	1.8, 0.8	0, 0

tive good and no differential costs as payments and resultant benefits rise, that is, assume exactly two units of the collective good will be provided for each unit paid by any member of the group.[2]

If all members of the group pay 1 unit (for a total cost of 10 units), the benefit to each member will be 2 units (for a collective good of 20). The individual payoffs will be benefit less cost, or 1 unit. In the matrix, the first row gives the payoffs to Individual if he contributes his share; the first column gives the per capita payoffs to the remaining members of the group, i.e., to Collective, if they pay. The second row gives the payoffs to Individual if he does not pay, and the second column gives those for Collective if it does not pay. The various payoffs are readily calculated, e.g., if Individual does not pay but Collective does, the total cost will be 9 units, the total benefit will be 18 units, and and the per capita benefit will be 1.8 units (for Individual cannot be excluded from the provision of the collective good); consequently, Individual's payoff for this condition will be his benefit less his cost for a pleasant 1.8 units. From the payoffs for the game in Matrix 1, one can see that it is evidently in Individual's advantage to choose the strategy of not paying toward the purchase of the collective good.

Since it is individuals who decide on actions, and since each member of the group sees the game matrix from the vantage point of Individual, we can assume that Collective's

[2] Within a broad range, this assumption entails only that the payoffs in the upper right and lower left cells in Matrix 1 will contain payoffs only slightly higher or lower than might have been the case for a real world problem. Consequently, the logical dynamics of the game are unaffected by the assumption.

474 RUSSELL HARDIN

strategy will finally be whatever Individual's strategy is, irrespective of what Collective's payoffs suggest. The dynamic under which Individual performs is clearly the same as that for the prisoners' dilemma: his strategy of not paying dominates his strategy of paying. For no matter what Collective does, Individual's payoff is greater if he does not pay. This can be seen more clearly perhaps in Matrix 1a, which displays only the payoffs to Individual for each of his choices. As in prisoners' dilemma, not paying is invariably more lucrative than paying.

The payoffs to the two players in a game of prisoners' dilemma are shown in Matrix 2, and Row's payoffs only are shown in Matrix 2a. In this classic game, the delight of game theoreticians, Row and Column will both profit (1 unit each) if both cooperate, and both will lose (1 unit each) if both defect. But as is clear in Matrix 2a, Row is wise to defect no matter what Column does. The Matrices 1a and 2a are strategically equivalent; the preference orderings of the payoffs to Individual and to Row are identical as shown by the arrows in Fig. 1.

n-prisoners' dilemma

For the theorist of *n*-person games, a more cogent analysis of the problem of collective action defined by the game of individual vs. Collective would require a 10-

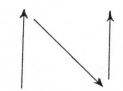

FIG. 1. Preference Ordering for Row and Individual.

dimensional matrix pitting the payoffs of each individual against all others. The payoffs can easily be calculated. The cell defined by all players paying would be $(1, 1, 1, 1, 1, 1, 1, 1, 1, 1)$, and that defined by all players not paying would be $(0, \cdots, 0)$. Every other cell would have payoffs whose sum would be equal to the number (m) of players paying in that cell; each player would receive a payoff of $2m/10 - 1$ if he paid, or $2m/10$ if he did not pay. Anyone able to visualize a 10-dimensional matrix can readily see that each player's dominant strategy is not to pay, because it yields the best payoff for whatever the other players do. The rest of us can easily enough calculate that whereas the payoff to player i is $2m/10 - 1$ with m players including himself paying, the payoff to i with $m - 1$ players not including himself paying would be the preferred $2(m - 1)/10$ (in the latter case i's payoff is 0.8 units greater than in the former). Hence, for each player i, the strategy of not paying dominates the strategy of paying. But playing dominant strategies yields all players the poor payoff $(0, \cdots, 0)$, and this solution is the only equilibrium for the game.

The game now defined is simply the 10-prisoners' dilemma, to which any solution algorithm generalized from the 2-prisoners' dilemma can be applied. To generalize the game further, n prisoners can be substituted for 10, and a ratio r of benefits to costs (with cost being 1 unit to each player) for the ratio of 2 assumed in Individual vs. Collective. The result is analogous, with the choice of not paying always yielding a payoff $(n - r)/n$ units higher than the choice of

MATRIX 1a
INDIVIDUAL'S PAYOFFS

Individual			
	Pay	1	−0.8
	Not Pay	1.8	0

MATRIX 2
PRISONERS' DILEMMA
Column

Row		Cooperate	Defect
	Cooperate	1, 1	−2, 2
	Defect	2, −2	−1, −1

MATRIX 2a
ROW'S PAYOFFS

Row			
	Cooperate	2	−2
	Defect	1	−1

paying (the bonus increases as n increases); and if all pay, all receive payoffs of $(r - 1)$. Olson's privileged group would be the case in which r is greater than n in some player's perception (if costs are a matter of binary choice between paying a fixed sum for all players who pay, or paying nothing).

In this game there is only one (strongly stable) equilibrium (at the payoff of zero to every player, i.e., all players not paying); but this equilibrium solution is not Pareto-optimal. Moving from the equilibrium to the payoff of r to every player (i.e., all players paying) would improve the payoff to every player. Among the 78 strategically nonequivalent 2×2 games in the scheme of Rapoport and Guyer (1966), prisoners' dilemma is unique in its class. It is the only game defined by the condition that it has a single strongly stable equilibrium which, however, is Pareto-nonoptimal. Hence, the generalized game of collective action defined above is logically similar to prisoners' dilemma. (It should be clear that the reason for the equivalence of prisoners' dilemma and the game of collective action for a large, i.e., latent, group is precisely the condition that in such a group a player's contribution to the purchase of the collective good is of only marginal utility to himself. Hence, his payoff is increased by almost the amount he does not pay when he does not pay.)

Empirical consequences

The significance of this result is that any analysis which prescribes a solution for prisoners' dilemma must prescribe a similar solution for the game of collective action. That means that the vast body of experimental and theoretical work on prisoners' dilemma is relevant to the study of collective action in general (and conversely that the growing body of work on collective action can be applied to the study of the prisoners' dilemma). In particular, any analysis of prisoners' dilemma which yielded the conclusion that the mutual loss payoff was not rational would, by implication, contravene

Olson's (1968, p. 44) claim that, for logical reasons, in a latent group "it is certain that a collective good will *not* be provided unless there is coercion or some outside inducements." Considering the fact that there are arguments that the rational solution to prisoners' dilemma is the payoff which results from mutual cooperation, before turning to the rationale of group success, we should perhaps reconsider why it might be that, empirically, latent groups do generally seem to fail. Let us view the 10-prisoners' dilemma defined above in the light of some 2-prisoners' dilemma experimental results.

Some experimental data suggest that about one-half of bona fide players cooperate with and one-half exploit a noncontingent, 100 percent cooperative adversary-partner in 2-prisoners' dilemma (Rapoport, 1968). In the 10-prisoners' dilemma described above, let us assume that this result would mean that 5 of the players would not pay even if the other 5 did pay. In this circumstance, the benefit to each player would be 1 unit, and the cost to each of the 5 payers would be 1 unit: hence, the payoff to the payers would be zero. Consequently, even an analysis which prescribed cooperation, or paying, as the rational strategy under the assumption of all players rational would allow nonpayment as a rational strategy to players in a real world game in which habitual nonpayers drained off any positive payoff to the payers. Assuming the validity of the generalization from the prisoners' dilemma experimental data, in real world games in which the law of large numbers applies and in which the perceived benefits of the collective good are not more than twice the costs, one can expect no provision of the collective good for reasons different from Olson's logic. In the intermediate group (where the statistics of large numbers do not apply), even with benefits considerably less than twice the costs, there is some statistical chance that a collective good will be provided. In either case, the prospects for success decline as the ratio (or perceived ratio) of benefits to costs decreases, and as

476   RUSSELL HARDIN

the differential perception of that ratio increases while the average perceived ratio remains constant.

As Olson (1968, p. 24) notes, the issue is not so much what an adversary-member's payoff will be, but rather whether anyone will choose to play the game at all. In the 10-prisoners' dilemma analysis here, by a different logic, it follows that one of the basic tenets of game theory is in one sense not useful in real world application. Ordinarily, in game theoretical analyses the actual values of payoffs are not important; the only consideration is the rank ordering of payoffs. But clearly, the normal inducement to play a real world game is the expectation of positive payoffs. Hence, a rational player in the game of collective action does not refuse to pay merely because his strategy of not paying is dominant and yields a higher payoff; rather he refuses to pay because enough others in the group do not pay that he would suffer a net cost if he did. Consequently, it would be irrational for him to play the game, and not playing means not paying. (However, this reasoning cannot be considered to give a proof that collective action will fail. That remains an empirical matter.)

THE CONDORCET CHOICE SOLUTION OF THE GAME OF COLLECTIVE ACTION

The usual analysis of prisoners' dilemma prescribes a strategy: the dominating strategy which in the 10-person game of collective action discussed above would be not to pay. Because the general employment of that strategy produces an undesirable outcome, and because many (roughly half) of the subjects in some 2-prisoners' dilemma experiments have not employed that strategy, it would be useful to analyze the outcomes (as opposed to the strategies) of the larger game of collective action. The matrix for the 10-person binary choice game has 2^{10} or 1024 cells, each of which is a uniquely defined potential outcome of the game. Instead of considering the strategies of the players, let us view the game as though the 10 players were collectively choosing among the 1024 outcomes. With a simple notation these 1024 outcomes can be represented as 20 classes of outcomes. We can readily ascertain which among these classes are realizable outcomes, and can determine whether any among the realizable outcomes is a Condorcet choice. It will be a simple matter to demonstrate that in any game of collective action with n players and a ratio r, $r > 1$, of benefits to payments there is a Condorcet choice among the realizable outcomes, and it is the outcome defined by all players paying and all receiving payoffs of $r - 1$ units.

$2n$ classes of outcomes

In the 10-person game of collective action, the possible outcomes in the view of an Individual in the game are as in Matrix 3. The entries in the top row are Individual's payoffs when all ten players pay, nine players including Individual pay, etc. Those in the bottom row are Individual's payoffs when he does not pay, ranging from the case in which all nine other players pay to the case in which no one pays. The upper left payoff results from only one outcome of the game: all pay. The upper row payoff of 0, however, results from 126 different outcomes of the game: all the possible combinations in which Individual and four other players pay while five players do not pay.

It will be useful to represent these classes of outcomes more generally. Let N_k represent any outcome in which exactly k players, including Individual, do not pay. And let P_k represent any outcome in which exactly k players, including Individual, pay. Matrix 3 can be rewritten as Matrix 3a. It is now a simple matter to rank order the outcomes ac-

MATRIX 3

| Pay | 1.0 | 0.8 | 0.6 | 0.4 | 0.2 | 0 | −0.2 | −0.4 | −0.6 | −0.8 |
| Not Pay | 1.8 | 1.6 | 1.4 | 1.2 | 1.0 | 0.8 | 0.6 | 0.4 | 0.2 | 0 |

MATRIX 3a

| Pay | P_{10} | P_9 | P_8 | P_7 | P_6 | P_5 | P_4 | P_3 | P_2 | P_1 |
| Not Pay | N_1 | N_2 | N_3 | N_4 | N_5 | N_6 | N_7 | N_8 | N_9 | N_{10} |

TABLE 1

Payoff Class	Number of Outcomes in this Class
N_1	1
N_2	9
N_3	36
N_4	84
P_{10}, N_5	1,126
P_9, N_6	9,126
P_8, N_7	36,84
P_7, N_8	84,36
P_6, N_9	126,9
P_5, N_{10}	126,1
P_4	84
P_3	36
P_2	9
P_1	1
	Total 1024

TABLE 2

N_1
N_2
N_3
N_4
P_{10}, N_5
P_9
P_8
P_7
P_6
P_5, N_{10}

cording to Individual's preference; the position of an outcome P or N is determined by the payoff to Individual associated with it. Table 1 presents Individual's preference ordering and gives the total number of outcomes in the full 10-dimensional game matrix associated with each payoff class.

Clearly, Individual can guarantee himself his minimax payoff (N_{10} at the lower right in Matrix 3a). Those outcomes P_4, P_3, P_2, and P_1 which fall below the minimax line in Table 1, therefore, are outcomes which he can unilaterally prevent by not paying. Similarly, however, every other player in the game can prevent his own P_4, P_3, P_2, and P_1 outcomes, so that the complementary outcomes N_6, N_7, N_8, and N_9 of opposing players will be prevented (for instance, an N_9 can occur only if some player is willing to pay when no one else does, thus putting himself into a P_1 outcome). Hence, none of these outcomes is realizable, i.e., they would require that some player willingly recline below his minimax, as few of us are wont to do.[3] The only outcomes which can obtain in a play of the game are those of Table 2. It is from this set of realizable outcomes that the players must seek an

agreeable outcome. If one of these outcomes is a Condorcet choice for the set, it is the prominently rational outcome of the game.

Condorcet choice

We can define strong and weak Condorcet choices.[4] Let C be the collective (i.e., the group) of n members choosing among outcomes in the matrix of an n-person collective action game, and let j and k be outcomes from the set M of realizable outcomes in the game matrix (in the 10-prisoners' dilemma matrix there are 1024 cells, of which 639 are realizable outcomes). Let c_{jk} be the number of those in C who prefer outcome j to outcome k, and let c'_{jk} be the number of those in C who are indifferent to whether outcome j or outcome k obtains. Clearly, $c_{jk} + c_{kj} + c'_{jk} = n$.

Definition: j is a strong Condorcet choice if it is preferred by a majority in C to every k ($\neq j$) in M. Reduced to symbolic brevity, this condition is

$$c_{jk} > n/2 \text{ for all } k \neq j.$$

Definition: j is a weak Condorcet choice if it is not a strong Condorcet choice but if, for each $k \neq j$, more of those in C prefer j to k than k to j. This condition is simply

$$c_{jk} > c_{kj} \text{ for all } k \neq j.$$

It should be clear that there can be at most one Condorcet choice.

---

[3] The use of this term conforms with Howard (1967, p. 21), in whose metagame theory an outcome is metarational for all players if every player's payoff in that outcome is at least equal to his minimax payoff. Hence, the only realizable outcomes are those which are metarational for all players.

---

[4] Named for the eighteenth century French economist and intellectual in general, the Marquis de Condorcet, who studied the problem of electoral majorities, believed in man's capacity for unlimited progress, and chose to poison himself rather than meet the guillotine during the Terror.

478   RUSSELL HARDIN

From the definition of the game of collective action for n players the following theorem for the existence of a Condorcet choice among the set of realizable outcomes can be derived.

Theorem: For an n-person game of collective action, P_n is a Condorcet choice from the set of realizable outcomes for the game; it is a strong Condorcet choice except in a game in which n is even and $r = 2$, in which case P_n is a weak Condorcet choice from the set of realizable outcomes.

The proof of this theorem, which is not difficult but is tedious, is left to the appendix. However, it will be instructive to see that it holds for the case of 10-prisoners' dilemma. We need only to compare the outcome P_{10} to each of the other realizable outcomes listed in Table 2 to show that P_{10} is preferred to each of these others. Given an outcome of the class N_1, nine players will prefer P_{10}. Similarly, given an outcome of the class N_2, N_3, or N_4, eight, seven, or six players, respectively, will prefer P_{10}. And nine, eight, seven, or six players will prefer P_{10} to any outcome of the class P_9, P_8, P_7, or P_6, respectively. Finally, given an outcome of the class N_5, the five players whose outcomes are of the class P_5 will prefer outcome P_{10}; and the five players whose outcomes are of the class N_5 will be indifferent to the choice between N_5 and P_{10}. Consequently, a clear majority of the players will prefer P_{10} to any outcome except N_5, in which case all of those with a preference will prefer P_{10}. It follows that P_{10} is a weak Condorcet choice. It is weak because the game has an even number of players and a ratio of benefits to contributions of 2.[5]

Degeneracy—back to the prisoners' dilemma

At the limits of the preceding analysis there occur several classes of degenerate

games of collective action. These result when $r = 1$ or $n = 2$.

In the degenerate case of $r = 1$, the realizable outcomes are P_n and N_n, and all players are indifferent as to which of these obtains. For all cases of $r < 1$, the only realizable outcome is N_n. The game will not be played.

In the degenerate case of $n = 2$ there are five possibilities: $r < 1$, $r = 1$, $1 < r < 2$, $r = 2$, $r > 2$. The first two of these are degenerate in r. In the case of $r = 2$, all outcomes are realizable and the outcome of both pay is a weak Condorcet choice. If $r > 2$, each player's return from his own contribution is greater than his contribution, so presumably both will pay and reap appropriate benefits (recall that in general $r > n$ implies that the group is a privileged group in Olson's terms). The interesting cases remain. They are those for $1 < r < 2$. They are represented in Matrix 4.

The payoffs in the games of Matrix 4 are related according to the preference ordering (if $1 < r < 2$):

$$r/2 > (r - 1) > 0 > (r/2 - 1).$$

This condition meets the definition of the symmetric 2-prisoners' dilemma game. For example, Rapoport and Chammah (1965, pp. 33–34) define the symmetric prisoners' dilemma by the condition that the payoffs (as given in Matrix 5) satisfy the relation:

$$T > R > P > S,$$

in which the letters didactically stand for Temptation (to defect), Reward (for cooperating), Punishment (for defecting), and Sucker's payoff (for cooperating). Note that the preference ordering for row is as in Figure

---

[5] It was noted above that prisoners' dilemma is the only one of the Rapoport-Guyer games with a strongly stable equilibrium that is not Pareto-optimal. This statement can be made stronger. Every outcome in the 2-prisoners' dilemma is Pareto-optimal except the outcome of mutual loss.

In a game of collective action this stronger statement also usually holds. However, if r divides n, then any outcome defined by $N_{n/r}$ for n/r of the players is not Pareto-optimal. (This is because $n - n/r$ of the players would benefit in a shift from this outcome to P_n, and the other n/r players would be indifferent to the shift.) All other outcomes in any game of collective action are Pareto-optimal except the single dismal solution N_n.

MATRIX 4

$r-1, r-1$	$(r/2-1), r/2$
$r/2, (r/2-1)$	$0, 0$

MATRIX 5

R, R	S, T
T, S	P, P

1. From the preference ordering and Matrix 4, it can be seen that only the outcomes $(r-1, r-1)$ and $(0,0)$ are realizable, and that of these $(r-1, r-1)$ is a strong Condorcet choice.

CONCLUSION

It has been shown that the problem of collective action can be represented as a game with a strategic structure similar to that of prisoners' dilemma. The logic which prescribes that a member of a group should not contribute toward the purchase of his group collective interest is the same as that which prescribes that a player in a game of prisoners' dilemma should defect (i.e., should not cooperate). However, from the set of all realizable outcomes in a game of collective action in which the ratio of benefits to contributions exceeds 1, the outcome in which all contribute is a Condorcet choice. The existence of a Condorcet choice, which is by definition unique, implies that a real world group could decide in favor of the Condorcet choice over every other realizable outcome. Consequently, it is rational in a world in which distrust seems endemic to use sanctions to enforce all members of an interest group to contribute toward the purchase of the group interest (Olson, 1968, p. 51). In a world not quite Hobbesian a threat of all against all might, ironically, help overcome distrust.

However, the threat of all against all is not a logical necessity; rather, it is only a potentially useful device, given human psychology. For, there is debate in the literature on the prisoners' dilemma as to whether the cooperative or the noncooperative outcome is rational or logically determinate. Therefore, it can hardly be granted that, as

Olson contends, in the absence of sanctions in a latent group "it is certain that a collective good will *not* be provided," whereas in an intermediate group the result is merely indeterminate. The clarity of the analogy between the logic of collective action and the strategic structure of the prisoners' dilemma game makes it seem likely (as suggested above) that the differences in the statistics of success for the intermediate and latent groups is a function of statistics on, for example, the social distribution of distrust; but in any case it is not a derivation from the logic inherent in the group interactions.

APPENDIX: PROOF OF THEOREM

Assume a group of m player-members in a game of collective action as defined with a ratio r of benefits to payments. When an outcome of class P_k obtains for k players, its complementary outcome of class N_{m-k} obtains for the other players. Let (P_k, N_{m-k}) represent the k outcome set for the game: it is the set of all outcomes which are of class P_k for k players and of class N_{m-k} for $(m-k)$ players. (The total number of outcomes represented by this set is $m!/k!(m-k)!$. For instance, when $k = m$, all players are in the single outcome of class P_m.) Finally, let c_{mk} represent the number of players who prefer outcome P_m to an outcome of the set k.

In order to demonstrate that P_m is a Condorcet choice among the set of realizable outcomes of the m-person game of collective action, we need only show that, for each $k < m$,

(1a) $c_{mk} > m/2$, or

(1b) $c_{mk} > c_{km}$, or

(1c)   the outcomes in set k are not realizable.

Let us note two general conditions before proving the theorem. The condition which renders an outcome not realizable is that in that outcome some player receives a payoff less than his minimax, i.e., less than zero. If p_k represents the payoff to a player in an outcome of class P_k, and n_{m-k} the payoff to a

480   RUSSELL HARDIN

player in the complementary outcome of class N_{m-k}, then

(2) $p_k = kr/m - 1$, and

(3) $n_{m-k} = kr/m$.

By definition it follows that:

Condition 1. The outcomes of the k outcome set are not realizable if $p_k < 0$.

The payoff at P_m is $(r - 1)$. At P_k, $k < m$, the payoff is $p_k < (r - 1)$. It follows that:

Condition 2. The k players in an outcome of class P_k, $k < m$, prefer outcome P_m to P_k.

Proof of the theorem

To prove the theorem, we must show that requirement (1) is met for three possible values of k: (I) $k > m/2$; (II) $k < m/2$; and (III) $k = m/2$.

Region (I)

$$k > m/2$$

By Condition 2, P_m is preferred to P_k by k players, so that $c_{mk} > m/2$. Requirement (1a) is met.

Region (II)

(4) $k < m/2$

There are three regions in the value of the payoff to the players not paying: (a) $kr/m < (r - 1)$; (b) $kr/m = (r - 1)$; and (c) $kr/m > (r - 1)$. We must show that requirement (1) is met in each of these regions.

$$kr/m < (r - 1) \qquad\text{(a)}$$

In this region, it is clear from (2) and (3) that all players prefer P_m to the set (P_k, N_{m-k}). Hence, requirement (1a) is met.

$$kr/m = (r - 1) \qquad\text{(b)}$$

It follows that

$$kr = mr - m, \text{ or}$$

(5) $(m - k)r = m$.

But from (4), we have

(6) $m > 2k$

From (5) and (6) we have

$$(2k - k)r < m, \text{ or}$$

(7) $kr/m < 1$.

But the payoff to those who pay is, according to (2),

$$p_k = kr/m - 1.$$

From (7) it follows that

$$p_k < 1 - 1, \text{ or}$$

$$p_k < 0.$$

From Condition 1 it follows that the outcomes of the k outcome set are not realizable. Hence, requirement (1c) is met.

$$kr/m > (r - 1). \qquad\text{(c)}$$

By an argument almost identical to that for the condition of (b) above, we have

$$kr > mr - m, \text{ or}$$

$$(m - k)r < m.$$

From (6) it follows that

$$kr < m, \text{ or}$$

$$kr/m < 1.$$

This is the same as (7); from the argument above it follows that requirement (1c) is met.

Region (III)

$$k = m/2.$$

It follows from (2) and (3) that

(8) $p_k = r/2 - 1$, and

(9) $n_{m-k} = r/2$.

As in (II), there are three possibilities: (a) $r/2 < r - 1$; (b) $r/2 = r - 1$; and (c) $r/2 > r - 1$.

$$r/2 < r - 1. \qquad\text{(a)}$$

In this region, it is clear from (8) and (9) that all players prefer outcome P_m to the set (P_k, N_{m-k}). Hence, requirement (1a) is met.

(10) $r/2 = r - 1.$ (b)

From Condition 2 it follows that $m/2$ players prefer P_m to the set (P_k, N_{m-k}); and from (9) it follows that the other $m/2$ players are indifferent in the choice between P_m and this set. Hence, $c_{mk} = m/2$, $c_{km} = 0$, so that $c_{mk} > c_{km}$. Requirement (1b) is met.

$$r/2 > r - 1.   \text{(c)}$$

It follows that

$$r/2 < 1.$$

Hence, from (8) we have

$$p_k < 1 - 1, \quad \text{or}$$

$$p_k < 0.$$

From Condition 1 it follows that the outcomes of the k outcome set are not realizable. Hence, requirement (1c) is met.

Requirement (1) is met for all values of r and m, so that there exists a Condorcet choice among the set of realizable outcomes in a game of collective action. Moreover, in almost every case, either (a) or (c) of requirement (1) is met; for all these cases, P_m is therefore a strong Condorcet choice. The only exception to this is case (IIIb), in which requirement (1b) is met; in this case, m is divisible by 2, and from (10) it can be seen that $r = 2$. Consequently, P_m is a weak Condorcet choice among the realizable outcomes in a game of collective action in which there is an even number of players and $r = 2$. The theorem is proved.

REFERENCES

Howard, N. A Method for metagame analysis of political problems. Mimeographed working paper, Management Science Center, University of Pennsylvania, 1967.

Olson, M., Jr. *The Logic of collective action.* New York: Schocken, 1968 (first published, 1965).

Rapoport, A. Editorial comments. *J. conflict Resolut.*, 1968, 12, 222-23.

Rapoport, A., & Chammah, A. M. *Prisoner's dilemma.* Ann Arbor, Mich.: Univ. of Michigan Press, 1965.

Rapoport, A., & Guyer, M. J. A taxonomy of 2 × 2 games. *General Systems*, 1966, 11, 203-14.

(Manuscript received April 27, 1970)

There's always something
one's ignorant of
About anyone, however well
one knows them;
And that may be something of
the greatest importance.
                          T. S. ELIOT

Part II
Theoretical Critique and Development

[8]

Social Theory, Social Research, and a Theory of Action[1]

James S. Coleman
University of Chicago

After an extraordinarily promising beginning in 1937 with *The Structure of Social Action,* Talcott Parsons abandoned his attempt to ground social theory in a theory of purposive action. The functionalism that resulted moved in one direction, while social research has progressively moved in an individual-behavioristic direction, resulting in an ever-widening divergence between research and theory. This paper describes paths in research and in theory development that will reconstitute relevance of each for the other. The essential elements are two. The first is use of a theory of purposive action as a foundation for social theory; this entails acceptance of a form of methodological individualism and rejection of holism. The second is a focus in social research and theory on the movement from the level of individual actions to macrosocial functioning, that is, the level of system behavior.

THE PROMISE AND LOSS OF A THEORY OF ACTION

In 1937, in *The Structure of Social Action,* Talcott Parsons sketched an initial attempt to construct what he described as a voluntaristic theory of action, extending the model of rationality used by economists and systematizing the historians' conception of purposive action. Parsons thus introduced into American sociology the theory of action underlying much of the work in European social thought. In doing so, he was making a natural extension of the orientation shared by three of the four theorists whose work he examined: Max Weber, Alfred Marshall, and Vilfredo Pareto. This orientation, a form of methodological individualism, is one that grounds social theory in a theory of individual action.

The same orientation was shared by social and political philosophers of the 17th, 18th, and 19th centuries such as Hobbes, Smith, Locke, Rous-

[1] I am grateful to Douglas Anderton, Gary Becker, Daniel Bell, Thomas Coleman, Yong-Hak Kim, Michael Hechter, Barbara Heyns, Edward Laumann, Robert Merton, Alan Sica, and Zdzislawa Walaszek for helpful comments on an earlier draft. Requests for reprints should be sent to James S. Coleman, Department of Sociology, University of Chicago, Chicago, Illinois 60637.

American Journal of Sociology

seau, and Mill.[2] A single theory of action, differing only in details, was
shared by all these theorists: individuals were seen as purposeful and goal
directed, guided by interests (or "values," depending on the theorist) and
by the rewards and constraints imposed by the social environment.

Why was a theory of action fundamental to the work of these and other
theorists, when in fact each was concerned with macrosocial phenomena,
with the functioning of political and economic systems, with large-scale
social change? It was fundamental because it allowed connecting intentions of persons with macrosocial consequences. Thus the functioning of
society as well as the engine of social change could be grounded in the
purposive actions of individuals, taken in particular institutional and
structural settings that shaped the incentives and thus the action. Social
theory with this kind of grounding made possible a connection between
the individual and society, and it even made possible a conception of how
social systems might be shaped by human will.[3] Perhaps most important,
it made possible a link between positive social theory and normative
social philosophy, by connecting individual interests with their realization or lack of realization.[4]

But Parsons's 1937 program of theory construction did not work out.
The extraordinarily ambitious and integrative program that he outlined
was not pursued systematically in his further work. In his subsequent
theoretical treatises, *Toward a General Theory of Action* (1951), *The Social System* (1951), *Working Papers in the Theory of Action* (1953), and
part II of the introduction to *Theories of Society* (1961), Parsons progressively abandoned a theory of action (despite the titles of two of these
works) and chose instead to characterize the equilibrium states and
"phases" of social systems. Possibly because he was unable to derive, in a
theoretical fashion, systemic action from the combination of individual
actions, he made a conceptual leap to the systemic level and subsequently

[2] Although Marx, from a continental philosophical tradition, did not fully share this
orientation, he did so in part. For a discussion of the issue of methodological individualism in Marx's work, see Elster (1985, pp. 5–18).

[3] Some social theorists accept or reject this approach because of an optimistic belief
that individuals *can* shape the functioning of social systems or a pessimistic view that
they cannot but are merely products of their environments. But the theoretical stance
is logically independent of the answer to this question. A theoretical position of
methodological individualism is fully compatible with recognition of the constraints on
action that social structure creates.

[4] A good example of the way positive theory and normative social philosophy can
interact is provided by the Spring 1985 issue of *Social Philosophy and Policy*, devoted
to "ethics and economics." In that issue, philosophers and economists examine—with
a common conceptual framework—the moral standing of the market and other economic institutions. Such an interaction based on a conceptual framework from contemporary sociological theory is difficult to visualize—largely, I suggest, because the
conceptual frameworks of sociology are not grounded in a theory of action.

Theory of Action

concerned himself with ways of classifying social equilibria. By so doing (and in the absence of serious contemporary contenders for social theory at that level of generality), he broke the links with earlier social theorists, with political philosophy, with political economy, with legal theory, and he ushered in a period of simple functionalism in sociological theory. It was a kind of social theory that could account for any institution and any social configuration by showing its functions, but it had no place for individuals, except as deviants from norms, and no place for social change except by theoretical fiat, as in the AGIL scheme. It provided no possibility for the normative evaluation of social institutions or social systems, for it never descended to the level of individuals, whose satisfaction (or dissatisfaction) provides our soundest basis for evaluating social configurations.

Modifications to functional analysis toward "structural-functional" analysis were made by other theorists, in particular Robert Merton in his *Social Theory and Social Structure* (1949). In showing that a social form may have positive functions ("eufunctions") for some actors and dysfunctions for others, Merton refocused attention on *actors,* and in showing that the form's continuation was contingent on actions of those actors for whom it had positive functions, he reintroduced purposive action. But these modifications removed the theoretical uniqueness of functional analysis—its homeostatic principle, explaining a social configuration not by proximate causes but by its consequences—leaving a theoretical approach that in its logical properties was not different from others. The effect on the discipline was not to reintroduce the theory of action that Parsons had discarded but to move away from functional explanation via final causes toward explanation by (proximate) causes, that is, toward causal analyses.

There were also direct challenges to Parsons's functionalism. The strongest was that by George Homans, best exemplified by the title of one paper, "Bringing Men Back In." Homans (1958) did introduce actors and a theory of action, perhaps a more explicit purposive action theory than had been set forth in sociology before. But this never moved beyond the social-psychological or small-groups level, and its effect was soon dissipated by his move from purposive action to a reductionism that was little different from the operant conditioning that B. F. Skinner demonstrated with pigeons. As did Parsons, Homans saw the essential problem for sociological theory as the refining of the theory of action. Parsons, failing to find a solution, moved to the macrosocial level and discarded the microfoundation. Homans moved in the other direction, away from goal-directed action, to reductionist behaviorism. Merton reshaped Parsons's functional theory away from final causes but did not bring back in an explicit microfoundation.

1311

American Journal of Sociology

Subsequent challenges to functionalism (the principal one being "conflict theory") have acquiesced in remaining at the collective or systemic level, thus failing to provide a theory grounded in purposive action of individuals. The program outlined by Parsons in 1937, despite the promise it held, remains unfulfilled.

It is useful to explicate my premises here. Implicit in the rejection of functionalism as a theory of social organization and the acceptance of a theory of purposive action as a grounding for social theory is a simultaneous rejection and acceptance of purpose. Purpose is rejected at the level of the system, but not at the level of its component actors. A theory of action as a basis for social theory is indeed a functional theory at the level of the actor: the actor is regarded as acting purposively. Actions are "caused" by their (anticipated) consequences.

Purposive action of individuals can be taken as a starting point by sociologists, who can assume well-organized individuals, though not by psychologists, for whom the individual's psychological organization is centrally problematic. But just as psychologists would lose their problem if they assumed individuals to be internally well organized, sociologists lose their problem when they assume purposes and goal-directed action of societies as units. It may well be that, for some investigations, corporate bodies such as formal organizations are usefully regarded as purposive actors, though in other research and theory in sociology, the coherence of their action would itself be taken as problematic.

The appropriate theoretical strategy for sociology, if I am correct, is not to discard notions of purpose, goal-directedness, and homeostasis (as is true in causal analyses that remain at the social system level), but to limit their employment to the level of *actors* in the social system—not positing them for the system itself. The action, or behavior, of the system composed of actors is an emergent consequence of the interdependent actions of the actors who make up the system.

The rule, in its most simple form, is as follows. Purpose and goal-directedness are useful in theory construction, but not if they characterize the entity or system whose behavior is to be explained. They must instead characterize elements of the system, which in the case of sociology can be regarded as actors in the system, either persons or corporate actors. The central theoretical problems then come to be two: how the purposive actions of the actors combine to bring about system-level behavior, and how those purposive actions are in turn shaped by constraints that result from the behavior of the system. The two problems when taken together provide the elusive result that functional analysis seeks: to characterize the ongoing and sometimes self-equilibrating functioning of a social system.

An especially unfortunate consequence of the loss of a theory of action

Theory of Action

was loss of contact with that one discipline that arguably should have the strongest intellectual links to social theory: common or constitutional law. One might even argue that law, as a set of rules having a high degree of internal consistency, as well as principles behind those rules, has as strong a claim to constitute social theory as does any alternative body of principles offered up by sociologists. All case law is based inherently on a theory of action. For example, modern Western law, both continental law and English common law, is based on the conception of purposive individuals with rights and interests, who are responsible for their actions.[5] In central Europe in the Middle Ages, this was not the underlying theory of action: guilds, households, and other social units were the responsible, purposive, interested actors with rights; the law had little to do with the individual person per se. Similarly in the case of the informal law governing relations between nomadic tribes or clans: the common prescription, "an eye for an eye and a tooth for a tooth," refers not to individual retribution but to clan retribution visited on any member of the offending clan.

Because the theory of action underlying modern economic theory and that underlying Western legal theory have much in common, they have a meeting ground (especially in the area of rights, but also in such branches of law as agency and contracts). Such economic theorists as Joseph Schumpeter or Friedrich Hayek can move easily between economic theory and legal philosophy, with each infusing the other. Richard Posner's book *The Economic Analysis of Law* (1977) is also able to have a strong impact on legal theory. The failure to provide a theory of action as a common basis for discourse prevents social theory from having a similarly fruitful interaction with legal theory.[6]

THE WATERSHED IN EMPIRICAL RESEARCH AND THE GROWTH OF INDIVIDUALISTIC BEHAVIORISM

Concurrently with the emerging dominance in sociology of functional theory at the level of the collectivity came a movement of empirical research that led in precisely the opposite direction. The 1940s constituted

[5] One implication of this is that the law has special difficulties with corporate action, especially in cases of criminal law where the corporation is held to "have committed a crime." Where does responsibility or liability lie? Only with the corporation per se, or with some members? If the latter, which ones? Why? For an examination of these issues see Hopt and Teubner (1985); Coleman (1985); Stone (1975). It is clear that, if organization theory in sociology were grounded in a theory of action (i.e., were a theory in which rights, interests, and responsibilities played an important part), it could make strong contributions to the evolution of legal precedent in this area.

[6] There are beginnings of such interaction. Scheppele (in press) does just this for the law's treatment of information.

American Journal of Sociology

a kind of watershed in empirical research in sociology. Before the watershed, community studies of the *Middletown* variety constituted the dominant empirical mode; after the watershed, survey research was dominant. The watershed was brought into existence in part by new empirical methods; some of the early postwatershed studies were Stouffer's (with others) *The American Soldier* (1949) and Lazarsfeld's (with Berelson and Gaudet) *The People's Choice* (1944) and (with Stanton) *Radio Research, 1941* (1941). The first cases following the watershed contained elements of the prewatershed focus. For example, the samples for Lazarsfeld's early survey research at Columbia were nearly always localized in communities, and some attempts were made (not always successfully) to introduce community structure into the analysis. In the American Soldier studies, social structure entered into the survey design through the organizational structure of the military service. In a few cases, this research lent itself to theoretical developments, as in the work on reference groups by Merton and Kitt (1950) based on the American Soldier analysis, but this was not common.

Although the empirical, statistical survey research was highly individualistic, it lacked one element that could bring about a connection with social theory grounded in a theory of action. The element that was absent was an explicit purposive or intentional orientation. The descriptive community studies that in American sociology preceded this watershed had necessarily incorporated a purposive orientation. This was a natural part of describing how the social conditions affected various persons' orientations to action and how these orientations to action, given the existing structure of relations, combined to produce the system of action that resulted in community action.

But the statistical association basis for inference in survey analysis seemed to have little natural affinity for the intentions or purposes of individuals. Lazarsfeld, one of its pioneers, was very interested in a theory of action.[7] However, it was his paper on the logic of causal inference in survey research (Kendall and Lazarsfeld 1950) that influenced further work in the discipline, not his paper titled "The Art of Asking Why" (1935) or his work on reason analysis. Succeeding work based on survey data has increasingly led toward "causal explanation of behavior," with the causes either social characteristics of the individual or characteristics of the individual's environment, and without recourse to an intervening action orientation on the part of the actor. Purpose or intention in

[7] See, e.g., his "Historical Notes on the Empirical Study of Action" (1972) and his paper with Oberschall on Max Weber's empirical work (1965). Much of Lazarsfeld's work on decision making in voting and consumer behavior expressed this action orientation.

Theory of Action

this work has not vanished altogether, but has been relegated to post hoc accounts that can provide an intuitively appealing set of reasons why the causal structure takes the form it does.

In such an analysis, success of the explanation is ordinarily measured by the amount of variation in behavior "accounted for" by these characteristics. Thus, for example, in causal modeling of individual status attainment or of school achievement, those variables that appear in the causal model are social or environmental factors that taken together account for variations in attainment or achievement, and a successful analysis is one in which a large fraction of the variance in attainment or achievement is explained.

A second important element in the replacement of community studies by survey research—almost unnoticed, it seems, by the discipline—was a shift in the unit of analysis (the unit about which empirical statements were made) from the community to the individual. In much of the work following this change, the focus shifted from social processes within the community shaping the system's behavior to psychological or demographic processes shaping individual behavior. Indeed, as survey research secured its dominance, its practitioners moved more forthrightly toward a focus on individual behavior. Dense community or organizational samples were replaced by national samples, snowball sampling died in its infancy,[8] and the struggling effort to use survey research to make statements about communities, organizations, or social subsystems was overwhelmed by the greater statistical rigor of characterizing "populations" and analyzing behavior of individuals as "independently drawn" members of the population.

Thus one could say that as social theory was moving to a functionalism that remained at the collectivity level, the main body of empirical re-

---

[8] I gave a seminar in 1956 at the University of Chicago on these methods. Leo Goodman heard it, became interested, and wrote a paper (1961) on statistical inference in snowball samples, but the statistical development died there. More generally, there was a variety of early attempts at modifying the new statistical tools for the analysis of functioning social systems. Some of these on the part of sociologists at Columbia at the time took two forms. One, which is hard to generalize from specific cases, is the use of survey data to characterize social subsystems and is exemplified by *The Adolescent Society* and *Union Democracy* (see esp. app. 1). A second comprised attempts to develop more formal techniques of analysis. It is exemplified by a paper of mine appropriately titled "Relational Analysis: The Study of Social Organization with Survey Methods" (1958). It is an interesting footnote in the sociology of knowledge that none of the social and intellectual forces impinging on the discipline was conducive to the development of these analytical tools. My own efforts in this direction were diverted in 1965 by the demands of government for policy research, which resulted in *Equality of Educational Opportunity*.

American Journal of Sociology

search was abandoning analysis of the functioning of collectivities to concentrate on analysis of the behavior of individuals.

On two grounds, then, the empirical research that became the dominant mode in sociology came to be of limited usefulness for social theory. First, it was lacking a theory of action, replacing "action" with "behavior" and eliminating any recourse to purpose or intention in its causal explanations; second, it focused on explaining the behavior of individuals per se, seldom moving up to the level of a community or other social systems.

One may ask just why there came to be such a radical shift toward a focus on individual behavior in a discipline whose subject matter, after all, is the social system. Part of the answer lies in the invention of techniques. The statistical tools of survey design and analysis began in the 1940s to make possible quantitatively precise statements about samples of independent individuals and the populations (again of independent individuals) they represent, as well as analysis of factors affecting individual behavior. There was no comparable development of tools for analysis of the behavior of interacting systems of individuals or for capturing the interdependencies of individual actions as they combine to produce a system-level outcome. The far greater complexity required of tools for these purposes constituted a serious impediment to their development and continues to do so (though some methods such as those generally labeled "network analysis" move in that direction). The end result is extraordinarily elaborated methods for analysis of the behavior of a set of independent entities (most often individuals), with little development of methods for characterizing systemic action resulting from the interdependent actions of members of the system.

This technical development of survey methods for studying individual behavior (and the subsequent development of computers for data processing) helped bring social research and the tradition of demographic research closer together. The influence of the demographic tradition led research even further in the direction of studying individuals, as can be seen most strikingly in research on social stratification.[9]

However, the technical developments and developments in the discipline provide only a part of the explanation of the shift to a focus on individual behavior. Another part derives from a change in the structure of society itself. That change is one that has brought about a change in the very relation of social research to society.

---

[9] Demography is an area in which the micro-to-macro movement can in many cases be carried out purely by aggregation of individual behavior. Only in a few areas, such as the two-sex problem (which has never been solved), do demographers need to have a device more complicated than simple aggregation to move from micro to macro levels.

Theory of Action

CHANGES IN SOCIETY AND CHANGES IN THE RELATION OF SOCIAL RESEARCH TO ACTION[10]

In the middle of this century, while Parsons was turning away from his attempt to build social theory on the basis of a theory of action and empirical research was discovering the techniques of survey research and statistical analysis, there were changes in American society with important implications for social research. These changes (which followed somewhat later in Europe) were ones that shifted the nation from a set of local communities, largely internally focused, to a place in which the focus was no longer local, but national. Manufacture changed in many product areas; instead of local firms selling to local markets, national firms sold to national markets. Concurrently there was an emergence of national media of communication. The national magazines were an important medium, gaining their growth in the 1930s. Radio was a second medium of importance. Through their advertising, these media helped create national markets that facilitated national manufacture. Also, they themselves had national markets, focusing the attention of the population as a whole on common objects.

One consequence of this change was the emergence of a new set of sociological problems. These were problems related to the national markets and national audiences—in short, problems of market research and audience research.

The research problems generated by these social changes differed in an important way from the research problems before this watershed. They were problems of particular actors in society, and the results were of direct interest to those actors, who were prepared to act on them. The earlier research, initiated by disinterested investigators or by philanthropic sponsors, was designed sometimes purely as a "contribution to knowledge," with no action implications but more often with an implicit theory of the relation of research to action, that of the exposé. This implicit theory was based on the premise that exposure of a particular social ill or social problem would set in motion the forces for its elimination. *Middletown,* or the Yankee City studies of Lloyd Warner, or Zorbaugh's *Gold Coast and the Slum* all had this implicit premise, a premise that remained the impetus behind such works as Lynd's *Knowledge for What?* (1939), written as a critique of the postwatershed applied social research.

The new applied research was initiated by corporate actors holding a different premise: that research focusing directly on problems of interest to them would provide information relevant to their actions. This change initiated a new component of macrosocial organization supplied by social

[10] I have discussed these changes in greater detail elsewhere (Coleman 1978, 1980*b*).

American Journal of Sociology

research itself—systematic means of information feedback to large corpo-rate actors in society—and a new relation of social research to action.

The principal locus of the early postwatershed research focused on individual behavior was in these areas of market research and audience research. This was most evident in Lazarsfeld's work, but it can also be seen in the growth of programs in mass communications research in a number of universities in the 1940s and 1950s.

Yet this was only the first stage of the transformation. The change in American society in the structure of interaction from personal and local to impersonal and national induced another change by the 1960s: a change in the structure of responsibility from private and local to public and national. The changed structure of communication increasingly gener-ated claims on the national government and an assumption by the na-tional government of responsibilities that would never have arisen before the changed structure of interaction. Certain of these responsibilities, such as Social Security and emergency work programs, arose in the 1930s, early in the shift from local to national interaction. A later spurt came with the "Great Society" legislation of Lyndon Johnson, beginning in 1964: the Civil Rights Act of 1964, the Elementary and Secondary Education Act of 1965, the Office of Economic Opportunity, the Head-start program, Medicare, and a number of other innovations. With these policies came a new kind of social research: social policy research. This has come to take a number of forms, some with names that were un-known in 1960: large-scale social experimentation, process evaluation, summative evaluation, planned variations, intervention research, and national longitudinal studies.

The end result of these changes is that much if not most applied social research (not only in American society, for these changes have occurred also in Europe) has come to be research directed to problems of policy, that is, designed to inform the actions of large corporate actors, most often government but also business corporations, trade unions, and vari-ous voluntary associations.

This changed relation of social research to social action raises two issues, one an issue for social theory and the other a normative issue. The issue for social theory involves incorporating information into a theory of action involving corporate actors at the societal level and persons who are their clients. Purposive action requires information, and in a social struc-ture in which information is valuable (i.e., a scarce commodity), its pos-session can affect the distribution of power. Social policy research will ordinarily be initiated by the largest corporate actors and be designed to provide information that will allow them better to pursue their interests. In the asymmetric structure of society that has emerged in this century, natural social processes will result (given the problems of paying the cost

Theory of Action

of a public good) in an asymmetry of information, leading to increased asymmetries of power between corporate actors and persons.[11]

This points directly to the normative issue, for it raises questions about the distribution of information rights in society and the way this distribution affects the interests of persons. These questions have been addressed already in legislation (e.g., in the United States, the Freedom of Information Act of 1974), but they have not been incorporated into a normative theory of the initiation of policy research, its design, and its dissemination. If a society's political system is based on a principle of democracy, this principle provides the value premise for a normative theory of the distribution of information rights in policy research.

When such a theory is more fully developed, it can provide the basis not only for legal theory about information rights but also for the conduct of social policy research. Thus sociology finds itself in a reflexive position: social theory could guide the role in society of social policy research. There have been a few contributions that could aid such theory, perhaps the most notable a new book by Duncan MacRae, Jr., titled *Policy Indicators: Links between Social Science and Public Debate* (1985). Yet if I am correct, social theory will be in no position to accept this positive-cum-normative challenge until it rediscovers a theory of action that it has abandoned.

What I have been describing in this and the preceding section is a complex array of changes in the structure of society, in social research, and in the relations between them, changes that can be captured by an appropriate orientation to social theory. The changes that I have described are as follows:

1. Society has become more individualistic, with individuals pursuing paths disconnected from family and community.

2. The mainstream of social research has shifted from explaining the functioning of social systems (e.g., communities) to accounting for individual behavior. Properties of social systems have largely been relegated to the status of factors affecting individual behavior and are seldom the focus of investigation. This shift toward explaining individual behavior was in part of direct consequence of the change in social structure, in part an indirect consequence, through a new research technology that it encouraged, survey research.

3. Simultaneously with this shift in focus from the social system to the individual, the dominant mode of explanation in social research shifted away from one in which purposive action of individuals, taken in combination and subject to various constraints, explained the functioning of social systems. This was replaced by a form of behaviorism, in which

[11] For further discussion, see Coleman (1982); Habermas (1971).

American Journal of Sociology

various factors external to the individual's consciousness are introduced to account for variations in individual behavior. This change followed naturally from the shift in focus to individual behavior because purposive explanation becomes trivial at the level of individual action ("He carried out action x in order to achieve goal y") unless psychological complexity is introduced, thereby changing the problem from one in sociology to one in psychology.[12]

4. The shift toward individualism was accompanied by a growing structural asymmetry in Western society, with large corporate actors (corporations, government) on one side and individuals (not communities, not neighborhoods, not families) on the other, linked together by mass media rather than direct communication.

5. In this social structure, a new kind of social research has arisen, as part of the articulation between corporate actors and persons, first in the form of market research and then in the form of social policy research. With this move, social research has come for the first time directly into the functioning of society—no longer standing outside it but instead modifying the articulation between corporate actors and persons—primarily as the agent of corporate actors. As such, it becomes not only part of sociology but also properly an object of social theory, as part of the larger task of social theory to characterize this articulation between actors of different types and very different size and power.

But this task can be accomplished only by a social theory that has two properties. First, it explicitly recognizes that social action requires not only a verb, "to act," but also a noun as subject, the actor. Second, it is able to make satisfactorily the transition from the micro level to the macro level, from the purposive action of individual actors to the functioning of a system of action. It is to a discussion of this second task that I now turn.

THE MICRO-TO-MACRO PROBLEM

The program that the Parsons of 1937 had was presumably based on a diagnosis of what was lacking in order to move beyond the theorists whose work he described. He saw the theory of action itself as the point at which major modification was necessary and developed an elaborate description of the necessary modifications (1937, pp. 77–82). Later he attempted to use psychoanalytic theory to develop a theory of personality that would constitute his "theory of action." But what neither Parsons nor

---

[12] By "psychological complexity" here I mean to include work that ranges from the kind of complexity that Freud introduced to the kind that Kahneman and Tversky (1979) introduce, so long as it continues to view the individual as purposive or goal seeking.

Theory of Action

others engaged in similar attempts seem to have realized is that the major theoretical obstacle to social theory built on a theory of action is not the proper refinement of the action theory itself, but the means by which purposive actions of individuals *combine* to produce a social outcome. Insofar as Parsons did attempt to move explicitly from the individual level to the social level, it was through a personality-culture leap, disregarding the very structural configurations that are the essential element in determining the social outcome of a combination of individual actions (see, e.g., Parsons, Bales, and Shils 1953, chaps. 1, 2).

This micro-to-macro problem is sometimes called by European sociologists the problem of transformation. In economics, it is (misleadingly) termed the problem of aggregation; in political science, a major instance of it is the problem of social choice. It is the process through which individual preferences become collective choices; the process through which dissatisfaction becomes revolution; through which simultaneous fear in members of a crowd turns into a mass panic; through which preferences, holdings of private goods, and the possibility of exchange create market prices and a redistribution of goods; through which individuals' task performance in an organization creates a social product; through which the reduction of usefulness of children to parents leads families to disintegrate; through which interest cleavages lead (or fail to lead) to overt social conflict.

One way to see the role of the micro-to-macro problem in social theory is to examine different types of relations in sociology. The characteristic problem in sociology is that of accounting for some aspect of the functioning of a social system. Put in causal diagram form, it can be seen as the effect of one macro-level variable on another, such as the effect of religious doctrine on the economic system (e.g., Max Weber's general thesis in *The Protestant Ethic and the Spirit of Capitalism*). It can be diagramed as shown in figure 1.

(Protestant)	(Capitalist)
religious	economic
doctrine	system

FIG. 1.—Macro-level relation: methodological holism

Some social theory and some social research are based entirely on relations of this sort. They exhibit a methodological holism that contrasts to the methodological individualism that grounds sociology in a theory of action.

One of the most serious defects of a program of theory building and research based on such macro-level relations is data inadequacy: At a

American Journal of Sociology

macrosocial level, there is ordinarily too little variation, either in a single social system over time or among different social systems, to test the relation empirically.[13] Another defect is that, unless the theory is functionalist, and the system itself is treated as homeostatic (a solution that eliminates the possibility of immanent change), there is no explanation or understanding of why one relation holds rather than another. A third defect is that such an approach must assume the existence of a social system as a starting point. It can never address questions like the Hobbesian problem of order.

A second theoretical approach to the central problems of sociology is not to remain at the macrosocial level but to move down to the level of individual actions and back up again. This approach, methodological individualism, can be diagramed as shown in figure 2.

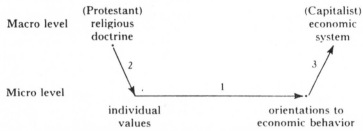

FIG. 2.—Macro-micro-macro relations: methodological individualism

In the context of this diagram, it is possible to see the Parsonian program and the source of its failure. Parsons recognized that the theorists whose work he examined were concerned with relations at the level of the social system (as in fig. 1), that they moved down to the individual level to study these relations (as in fig. 2),[14] and that at the individual level (type-1 relation in fig. 2) they shared roughly the same theory of action. Parsons proposed to develop a general social theory by refining that theory of action on which the relations of type 1 are based.

But it is the type-3 relation that has proved the main intellectual hurdle both for empirical research and for theory that treats macro-level rela-

[13] This defect is exhibited even in the domain of economic activity, where fluctuations occur much more rapidly than do changes in other aspects of social functioning. The business cycle analysis of the 1930s and 1940s, which attempted to correlate changes in macro-level variables and thus predict changes in some macro-level variables on the basis of changes in others, proved unfruitful. Although there are continued attempts in economics to carry out such analysis, its usefulness has not been demonstrated.

[14] His inclusion of Durkheim seems incorrect here, since Durkheim's work takes the form of fig. 1, involving only macro-level relations, or macro-to-micro relations like that of the relation labeled 2 in fig. 2.

Theory of Action

tions via methodological individualism. For example, in Max Weber's analysis of Protestantism and capitalism, he shows through illustration the effect of Protestant doctrine on individual values (type-2 relation) and, again through illustration, the effect of these values on individual orientations to economic behavior. What he fails to show is how these individual orientations combined to produce the structure of economic organization that we call capitalism (if in fact they did in combination produce this effect).[15] For Marx similarly, the heart of his theory is contained in a type-2 relation, where the macro-level variable is the means of production and the micro-level variable is individual consciousness of economic and social interests (a relation that is expressed in his statement, "it is his social existence that determines his consciousness"). He is at his weakest in showing how the common interests thus generated are transformed into class-conscious social action, that is, a relation of type 3.

All historical research on macrosocial systems must move back and forth between macro and micro levels to show how the macro-level changes occurred. But there are characteristic shortcuts that some historians have used to bypass the sociological problems involved. One is the "great man theory of history," in which macrosocial changes result from the actions of a single person. A second is the "conspiracy theory of history," in which macrosocial outcomes are the intentional result of calculations on the part of some subset of actors, rather than the emergent (and often unintended) consequence of interactions among actors with numerous differing purposes. (Here, the very phrase "unintended consequences" aids in reminding that Mertonian modifications of functionalism went in the same direction proposed here, but without letting the second shoe drop by bringing actors and a theory of action explicitly back into social theory.)

If the micro-to-macro problem, the type-3 relation of figure 2, is to be seriously addressed in social theory, what must first be recognized is that it is not a single problem but several problems. A start toward addressing these problems is to recognize that interests or goals of actors may stand in different relations to one another. These different relations bring about

---

[15] It is of course not always the case that type-3 relations are ignored. An instructive case in point is Merton's "Puritanism, Pietism, and Science," in which the thesis parallels that of Weber, except that science replaces capitalism (Merton 1949). Though Merton regards his critical empirical test as a comparison of the *numbers* of Protestants and Catholics engaged or educated in science, he (almost incidentally) shows how the concentration of Puritans generated *institutions* that furthered scientific activity (the Royal Society in England, Puritan academies). It is such evidence that moves toward showing the development of the system of science, for that system depends as much on the institutions as on the bodies that occupy them. It was evidence of this sort that Weber failed to introduce in *The Protestant Ethic*.

American Journal of Sociology

actions that result in different social processes, and different kinds of social institutions result. To give an idea of just what I mean, I will list some of these different relations, processes, and institutions.[16]

A first configuration is that of independent actors, each with differing private interests or goals and each with resources that can aid others' realization of interests. The actions that purposive actors will engage in when this configuration of interests and resources exists is social exchange, and when a number of these exchange processes are interdependent, we describe the whole set as a market institution.[17] Economic markets for exchange of private goods are the most evident example, but there are many others: courtship and marriage markets (see Waller [1938] for a description of such markets and Becker [1981] for work toward a theory of marriage markets), labor markets, the market in which contributions are exchanged for status in an academic discipline, the market for admissions to universities (see Roth [1984] for a description of the institution through which the matching market for medical residencies occurs). The paradigmatic micro-to-macro theoretical work is in economics in general equilibrium theory, which shows how individual holdings and preferences combine in a setting of competitive exchange to produce equilibrium prices and distribution of goods. Little work has been done toward examining effects of the social and institutional structures within which markets operate, though experimental work by Plott and Smith (1978) has made a start. It may also be that work in network theory (see Laumann 1986) will provide contributions to this field.

More generally, this configuration of interests and resources relating two or more actors and leading to social exchange exists in a wide variety of contexts other than markets and is a component of many institutions (e.g., Peter Blau's [1964] examination of informal exchange within formal organizations or Homans's [1958] classic paper on social exchange in small groups).

A second configuration is distinguishable from the first by use of two terms, market and hierarchy. In contrast to the market as a set of relations among independent actors, a hierarchy is a set of relations in which one actor's actions are carried out under the control of another and to advance the other's interests. The resulting relation can be described as

---

[16] There are other ways of characterizing the types of micro-macro problems than the way I propose here. Gary Becker, in a comment on an earlier draft, argues for a major distinction between social phenomena that involve purposive action by individuals separately (including both markets and principal-agent relations) and those that have some public goods component, introducing free rider problems and problems of social choice.

[17] Here I neglect for simplicity the fact that some means of insuring performance in exchange is necessary, as well as other particularities of market institutions.

Theory of Action

an authority relation, and the institutions consisting of a number of interdependent authority relations we call formal organizations or authority structures. They can ordinarily be seen as brought into existence through exchange processes in which one actor, as entrepreneur or principal, engages in a series of exchanges designed to bring about a coherent product, gaining through these exchanges (as in a labor market) the control of others' actions.[18] The resulting institutions contain characteristic problems. One, which has been described as the agency problem, is the problem for the superordinate or principal of devising a structure of incentives for the agent that will best realize the principal's interests. Complementary to this is the agent's problem of realization of interests, for the agent too has interests.[19]

Other characteristic problems in formal organizations, still within a theory of action framework, are those of managerial decision making, involving coordination and other questions of organization. A considerable portion of the existing literature in organization theory addresses these problems. Yet, as with agency theory, it is not these managerial actions alone but their interactions with the purposive actions of subordinates that create the systemic action of the organization.

A somewhat different kind of authority system is one that can be seen as coming into existence, in an action theory framework, through a social contract among a set of independent actors, each of whom sees a benefit in giving up certain rights to a central authority. This is the classic perspective of contractarian political philosophers toward the Hobbesian problem of order. It is appropriately used not only for societal systems but also for various voluntary associations, such as trade unions, professional associations, and clubs.

This origin for authority systems generates characteristic theoretical problems. Because the origin is in a set of independent actors, one problem is that of constitution formation by these independent actors, including the allocation of rights and obligations among members. A second may be described as the free rider problem, in which the very commonness of interests means that others' actions contribute toward the common goal just as do one's own, and thus it may be in one's interest not to contribute to the common good. The classic work on this problem is

---

[18] A major normative difference between the "individualist" political philosophers such as Hobbes and Locke and the "collectivist" political philosophers is that the latter regard such exchanges as illegitimate, except when the principal is the collectivity as a whole, i.e., the state. For a discussion, see MacPherson (1964).

[19] The problems of agency constitute an area where there is a potential for fruitful interaction of sociology with law and with economics. For a review of work on agency in economics, see McDonald (1984). For a treatment of authority that is compatible with this work, see Coleman (1980a).

American Journal of Sociology

Olson's *The Logic of Collective Action* (1965). A third general problem is that of social choice, which is the problem of how to arrive at collective decisions or systemic actions when rights to take corporate action are not vested in a single individual. The classic work here is Arrow's *Social Choice and Individual Values* (1970). These are problems that occupy large portions of political science as a discipline; a considerable amount of formal theoretical work has been done on them under the general rubric of "public choice" (see, e.g., papers in the journal *Public Choice*).

Still a third origin of authority systems stems from the overthrow of an existing authority system via revolution. A central problem in revolutionary theory from the perspective of purposive actors is the conditions under which some subordinates in an authority system will revolt, including the organizational problems posed by the free rider problem (the fact that a potential supporter of the revolution may experience the fruits of its success regardless of participation). Although revolutionary theory is in its infancy, a number of investigators have furthered its development. Their contributions range from historical work on societal revolutions such as that of Tilly (1975) through work on contemporary social movements such as that of Leites and Wolf (1970), Oberschall (1973), and Popkin (1979), to work by psychologists on the restriction of attention that arises in small decision-making groups (e.g., groups of terrorists).

Another broad problem in the theory of revolutions concerns the course that revolutions take from the beginning until a new stable authority system is established. This may be seen as a special case of the dynamics of conflict within a social system, but the tasks that this problem poses for a social theory that has its foundations in a theory of action involve detailed empirical study as well as theory development.

A third configuration, in addition to that of independent actors in exchange relations (in markets or otherwise) and authority structures, is that of common interests within a set of independent actors. These common interests can, as described in the case of constitution formation earlier, create a setting for free rider behavior. They can also, however, lead to the development of social norms. Most social theory not based on methodological individualism assumes the existence of social norms, and most theory that is based on methodological individualism disregards their existence altogether. The central theoretical problem is to characterize the process through which individuals' actions lead norms (with sanctions) to come into existence. This is one of the least well developed areas of work; Ullmann-Margalit (1977) has done some initial work in the area, and current work of my own (1986) is in this direction.

In addition to these broad classes of configurations of actors' interests and resources leading to what may be referred to as markets, authority systems, and systems of norms, there are various others that play a part

Theory of Action

not only in the creation of stable structures that we call institutions, but also in dynamic processes or transient states. The placement of trust by one actor in another is one such relation, which allows the flow of influence. Communication structures that permit or restrict the flow of information are another. Two processes that are central to the field of demography come under this general heading, population reproduction and geographic migration.

In sketching these various configurations, processes, and institutions, I do not claim comprehensiveness. Rather, I have attempted to indicate some of the directions that a social theory based on a theory of purposive action must take—and in some cases is already taking—in order to make the micro-to-macro transition that Parsons failed to carry out after his 1937 beginning. Work that contributes to this may include qualitative and historical work, quantitative research, and formal models.[20] The central criterion for evaluating its contribution is whether it contributes to knowledge of relations as shown in figure 2 above, and in particular to the most elusive of these three relations, the micro-to-macro relation shown as type 3.

EMPIRICAL RESEARCH AND A THEORY OF ACTION

In the empirical research in sociology before the watershed that I described as occurring in the United States in the 1940s (and in some of the research since then), a commonsense theory of purposive action was pervasive. The prototypical research in American sociology was a community study based on ethnographic data, and in description of the functioning of a community, the reasons behind various actors' actions constituted much of the explanation of what went on. An example is provided in the following quotation from *Middletown,* which is used as part of an examination of the importance of dress among young people in high school: "Since one of the chief criteria for eligibility for membership in the exclusive girls' clubs is the ability to attract boys, a plainly dressed girl feels the double force of this taboo by failing to receive a 'bid' which she might otherwise get. 'We have to have boys for the Christmas dances, so we take in the girls who can bring the boys,' explained a senior member of the most exclusive high school girls' club" (Lynd and Lynd 1929, p. 163).

However, in the postwatershed research, largely statistical and largely confined to explaining individual behavior, causal explanation based on statistical evidence has replaced purposive explanation. One way of describing this change is to say that statistical association between variables

[20] An example of qualitative work that has begun this is Michael Hechter's *The Microfoundations of Macrosociology* (1983).

American Journal of Sociology

has largely replaced meaningful connection between events as the basic tool of description and analysis. The "meaningful connection" was ordinarily provided by the intentions or purposes of an actor or combination of actors.[21]

A frequent virtue of the research based on meaningful connections was its richness of description, which provides an understanding of the course of social action. A frequent defect was an inability to go beyond system description, in order to pose and answer analytical questions.

In the context of the kind of causal explanation that has come to pervade quantitative research in sociology, with behavior "affected by" various individual characteristics and social conditions, it seems strange indeed to conceive of examining those same research problems as involving purposive action. In fact, when it is individual action rather than systemic action that is to be explained, the traditional commonsense use of purpose has two serious defects in explaining action, no matter how sophisticated the "reason analysis" (a mode of explanation developed in the 1940s and 1950s, in which survey respondents were asked their reasons for taking an action and these reasons entered the analysis). First, it includes only those elements of which the actor is aware, and second, the actor's explanation must be seen itself as a social action directed toward a goal in the context of which the reason or purpose was stated.

Yet there is another quite different mode of introducing a theory of action into the analysis of individual behavior. In analysis of individual-level survey data, economists study a number of the same individual-level problems examined by sociologists. They do so through statistical analysis of a kind that differs somewhat from that of sociologists analyzing the same or comparable data.

For example, a sociologist setting out to study the participation of women in the labor force through statistical analysis will introduce various possible "determinants" of labor force participation, such as age, marital status, number and ages of children, and husband's income. The explanation will consist of the relative effects of each of these factors on labor force participation.

An economist setting out to study the same phenomenon will begin differently, by assuming that each woman has a utility function and that she will act to maximize that utility (see, e.g., Heckman 1974; Mincer 1974).[22] If her time in the household is of greater value than the wage she

---

[21] In some cases, the meaningful connection was provided by other content, such as the objective relatedness of the events themselves. But a textual analysis of one of the prewatershed community studies will show that subjective states of the actors often supplied the meaning that made it possible to connect events that would otherwise be unrelated.

[22] Sometimes it is the household that is regarded as having the utility function.

Theory of Action

would earn in the labor force, she will not enter the labor force; otherwise she will seek a job—a special case of taking the action that maximizes utility.

In this model of action, there are various "arguments" to the utility function, and here some of the same variables that would be introduced by the sociologist enter. As a result, the econometric analysis carried out by the economist may end up looking similar to the regression analysis carried out by the sociologist. The interpretations, however, are very different. In the sociologist's analysis, the variables "affect labor force participation," whereas in the economist's analysis, the variables affect the value of the woman's time in the household, and her participation depends on her comparison of that value with what she can earn on the labor market.

There has been no careful evaluation of the virtues and faults of these two approaches to the empirical analysis of action. It is safe to say, however, that there are merits in both approaches: the more open-ended approach that remains agnostic about the mechanism through which a variable affects behavior and the more theoretically structured model that specifies how a variable affects action. But there are additional virtues in the economist's approach from the point of view of social theory. By containing a purposive (utility maximization) theory of action, it has greater power to predict how action will change as conditions change (e.g., how a woman's labor force activity will change as the value of her time outside the labor force changes). In addition, it has the merit of compatibility with the conceptual foundations that underlie much of social thought since the 17th-century natural rights political philosophers.

Yet neither of the approaches I have outlined goes beyond a type-1 relation to address the micro-to-macro problem. The question arises whether systematic quantitative research based on individual-level data can be relevant not merely for explanation of individual behavior but also for explanation of social outcomes, that is, for relations of type 3. A start toward answering this can be made by comparing Featherman and Hauser's *Opportunity and Change* (1978) with *Inequality* (1972) by Jencks et al. The problem posed by Featherman and Hauser was an *individual-level* problem of status attainment: What are the determinants of an individual's occupational status attainment? The question posed by Jencks and his colleagues was the *societal-level* problem: Does an increase in the educational level of society reduce income inequality? It was this difference in the question posed, not a question about individual status attainment but a question about societal inequality, which attracted the attention of those outside the social sciences to the Jencks book, whereas interest in the Featherman and Hauser book was largely confined to stratification theorists within sociology. Both books concerned the rela-

American Journal of Sociology

tion of education to occupational outcomes, but their questions were on quite different levels. The Jencks book constituted something of a milestone in quantitative social research based on survey data, precisely because it posed a societal-level question (effect of the educational level of society on income inequality) rather than an individual-level type-1 or type-2 question.

Yet the research methods that are common in quantitative sociology led both sets of investigators to individual-level analyses that were very similar in character. Although Jencks and his colleagues posed a societal-level question about education and income, they answered an individual-level type-1 question: What is the effect of change in an individual's education on that individual's income (in effect holding constant all other individuals' education)? But this answer gives no information on another question that is necessary for answering the societal-level question, How does a change in an individual's education affect his income *when the education of all others in his labor market context changes as well?*[23] Only with the answer to this latter question, a contextual one, can we begin to address the societal problem.[24]

This example illustrates the kinds of steps necessary to examine a type-3 relation. The movement from micro to macro level in this case involves a potentially strong interdependence between one person's education and that of others in the same context, interdependence that can be described as a competitive effect. To carry out an analysis of the type-3 micro-to-macro relation involves specifying the kind of interdependence that may exist, modeling it (more precisely than I have done here), and then setting up an analysis that tests this model. In this case, it is possible to begin such an examination by quantitative analysis of individual behavior of a sort that is familiar to the sociologist. An analysis of the effect of education on income requires inclusion of a contextual term, the education of others in the same context (i.e., the same competitive market). A zero coefficient for the contextual term implies that the individual-level rela-

[23] Economists call this a general equilibrium problem, in contrast to a partial equilibrium problem. In a market, the partial equilibrium problem is based on the question of how a supplier changes the level of production as the price changes or how a consumer changes the level of demand as the price changes. These are type-1 problems. Economists then typically divide type-3 problems into two parts: creating aggregate demand and supply curves for the market; then putting these together to determine what is the price and quantity equilibrium (the general equilibrium) when these two parts function as the components of a market.

[24] The difference between the individual-level question and the societal-level question is closely related to the difference posited by economists between the private rate of return to education and the public rate of return, for when the education of all changes—unless the higher education brings higher productivity—no person's income could change because total national productivity would not change.

Theory of Action

tion between education and income carries forward to the societal-level
(or at least the market-level) outcome, and simple aggregation of individual-level results will suffice. This would imply a social rate of return to
education equal to the individual rate. A nonzero coefficient implies that
the type-3 relation is more complicated, and simple aggregation will not
suffice.[25] (A negative coefficient equal in size [but of opposite sign] to the
coefficient on individual education implies that the societal rate of return
is zero.) An explicit model by which this interdependence leads to a social
outcome becomes necessary.

Competition, of course, is only one form of interdependence between
individual actions. In attitude or value change, for example, the model
linking individual action to behavior of the system would not be one
involving competition, but it might involve trust or social influence. Thus
a macro-level change that (through a type-2 relation) produces direct
change in individual values can, through amplification, have a much
greater ultimate effect.[26] The type-3 relation shows the process through
which the amplification occurs. A failure to develop such models and test
them may be in part responsible for the inability of sociologists to find
such things as effects of mass media on social norms—since a social norm
is a macro-level variable that depends on, but is not the same thing as,
individual values.

What I have done here in describing what is necessary to study type-3
relations with quantitative data is merely to sketch the outlines of a
research program. Such a program involves extensive changes in the
philosophy, design, and analysis of quantitative research based on individual-level data, but these changes are necessary if such data are to be
used to study the behavior of social systems rather than merely that of
individuals.

---

[25] A simple geometric model of this aspect of the labor market could be constructed
with average educational level on the horizontal axis and price paid for education (i.e.,
salary per unit of education) on the vertical. The partial equilibrium line representing
demand for education by employers would be downwardly sloping to the right, and
the supply of education by employees would be upwardly sloping to the right. The
general equilibrium would be at the intersection of these curves. The displacement of
this equilibrium price as the average level of education changes is given by the regression coefficient in a regression of average real income on average education across
isolated labor markets. In this case the lack of isolation of labor markets within a
society might make an analysis of the sort described infeasible. In other situations,
however, where the context is that of a school and the problems concern student
outcomes (i.e., the price paid in grades for a given increment in absolute achievement), analysis of similar problems is feasible.

[26] The use of survey research to study such interdependence was begun in research like
Katz and Lazarsfeld's *Personal Influence* (1955) and Coleman, Katz, and Menzel's
Medical Innovation (1966), but in the absence of an explicit conception of how individ-
ual change may be related to social change, this was not pursued in any extensive way.

American Journal of Sociology

Yet it is possible to move with empirical research a step beyond the examination of isolated micro-to-macro relations, toward studying a system of action. That is what social historians and ethnographers have traditionally done using qualitative data (for a still-instructive example at the level of a neighborhood social system, see Whyte's *Street Corner Society* [1943]). This research is ordinarily descriptive in character without theoretical aspirations, though it may well provide insights for theory construction.

To carry out analysis of systemic action with quantitative data, however, requires a formal theoretical model that relates individual actions to systemic functioning.[27] Some research of this sort has been carried out on community functioning (see Marsden 1981; Marsden and Laumann 1977; Pappi and Kappelhoff 1984), but little more than beginnings have been made. Here, it can reasonably be said, is where a most promising research-and-theory frontier lies for sociology.

The deficiencies in social research that I have described are not merely impediments to the development of social theory. These deficiencies are in part responsible for quite serious biases in the way certain problems in society—absent believable input from sociologists—are formulated and addressed. For example, commonsense and simple paradigms from psychology lead to the prescription to schoolteachers to "individualize instruction" and attend to "individual needs" of children. The absence of theory and research by sociologists showing the way that interdependent individual actions lead to the social structure and culture of the classroom—and these in turn shape motivation, effort, and learning—allows such misleading prescriptions to go unchallenged. Or the simple perfect-market paradigms from economics lead to prescriptions in economic policy for unlimited free trade. Only "economic consequences" are taken into account, and consequences for social institutions are ignored. When these concerns are reintroduced by practicing politicians, it is without intellectual guidance from social theory and research.

CONCLUSION

The promise that Talcott Parsons held out in 1937 of a voluntaristic theory of action has remained unrealized, and since then social theory and social research have moved along diverging paths. Yet this divergence is largely a result of a failure to analyze the structure that social theory based on a theory of action must have. When the sources of this divergence are exposed, as I have done here, the directions for productive theory construction and for research that can contribute to theory (and

[27] For work toward the development of such a model see Coleman (1986).

Theory of Action

thus increase the usefulness of the sociological enterprise for society) become evident. I have attempted in the final two sections of the paper to indicate what those directions are.

REFERENCES

Arrow, Kenneth. 1970. *Social Choice and Individual Values*. 2d ed. New Haven, Conn.: Yale University Press.
Becker, Gary S. 1981. *A Treatise on the Family*. Cambridge, Mass.: Harvard University Press.
Blau, Peter. 1964. *Power and Exchange in Social Life*. New York: Wiley.
Blau, Peter, and O. D. Duncan. 1967. *The American Occupational Structure*. New York: Wiley.
Coleman, James S. 1958. "Relational Analysis: The Study of Social Organization with Survey Methods." *Human Organization* 17 (4): 28–36.
———. 1961. *The Adolescent Society*. New York: Free Press.
———. 1978. "Sociological Analysis and Social Policy." In *A History of Sociological Analysis*, edited by T. Bottomore and P. Nisbet. New York: Basic.
———. 1980a. "Authority Systems." *Public Opinion Quarterly* 44:143–63.
———. 1980b. "The Structure of Society and the Nature of Social Research." *Knowledge: Creation, Diffusion, Utilization* 1 (3): 333–50.
———. 1982. *The Asymmetric Society*. Syracuse, N.Y.: Syracuse University Press.
———. 1985. "Responsibility in Corporate Action: A Sociologist's View." Pp. 69–91 in *Corporate Governance and Directors' Liabilities*, edited by Klaus J. Hopt and Gunther Teubner. Berlin: de Gruyter.
———. 1986. *Individual Interests and Collective Action*. Cambridge: Cambridge University Press.
Coleman, James S., Elihu Katz, and Herbert Menzel. 1966. *Medical Innovation*. Indianapolis: Bobbs-Merrill.
Coleman, James S., et al. 1966. *Equality of Educational Opportunity*. Washington, D.C.: Government Printing Office.
Elster, Jon. 1985. *Making Sense of Marx*. Cambridge: Cambridge University Press.
Featherman, David L., and Robert M. Hauser. 1978. *Opportunity and Change*. New York: Academic Press.
Goodman, Leo A. 1961. "Snowball Sampling." *Annals of Mathematical Statistics* 32:148–70.
Habermas, Jürgen. 1971. *Toward a Rational Society*. London: Heinemann.
Hechter, Michael. 1983. *The Microfoundations of Macrosociology*. Philadelphia: Temple University Press.
Heckman, James J. 1974. "Effects of Child-Care Programs on Women's Work Effort." *Journal of Political Economy* 82, pt. 2:S136–S163.
Homans, George. 1958. "Social Behavior as Exchange." *American Journal of Sociology* 63:597–606.
Hopt, Klaus J., and Gunther Teubner, eds. 1985. *Corporate Governance and Directors' Liabilities*. Berlin: de Gruyter.
Jencks, Christopher, et al. 1972. *Inequality*. New York: Basic.
Kahneman, D., and A. Tversky. 1979. "Prospect Theory: An Analysis of Decision under Risk." *Econometrica* 47:263–91.
Katz, Elihu, and Paul F. Lazarsfeld. 1955. *Personal Influence*. Glencoe, Ill.: Free Press.
Kendall, Patricia L., and Paul F. Lazarsfeld. 1950. "Problems of Survey Analysis." In *Continuities in Social Research*, edited by Robert K. Merton and Paul F. Lazarsfeld. Glencoe, Ill.: Free Press.

American Journal of Sociology

Laumann, Edward. 1986. "Social Network Theory." In *Approaches to Social Theory*, edited by S. Lindenberg, J. Coleman, and S. Nowak. New York: Russell Sage.

Lazarsfeld, Paul F. 1935. "The Art of Asking Why." *National Marketing Review* 1:32–43.

———. 1972. "Historical Notes on the Empirical Study of Action." In *Qualitative Analysis: Historical and Critical Essays*. Boston: Allyn & Bacon.

Lazarsfeld, Paul F., Bernard Berelson, and Hazel Gaudel. 1944. *The People's Choice*. New York: Duell, Sloan, & Pierce.

Lazarsfeld, Paul F., and Anthony R. Oberschall. 1965. "Max Weber and Empirical Social Research." *American Sociological Review* 30:185–92.

Lazarsfeld, Paul F., and Frank N. Stanton, eds. 1941. *Radio Research, 1941*. New York: Duell, Sloan, & Pierce.

Leites, Nathan, and Charles Wolf, Jr. 1970. *Rebellion and Authority*. Santa Monica, Calif.: Rand.

Lipset, Seymour, Martin Trow, and James Coleman. 1956. *Union Democracy*. Glencoe, Ill.: Free Press.

Lynd, Robert. 1939. *Knowledge for What?* Princeton, N.J.: Princeton University Press.

Lynd, Robert, and Helen Lynd. 1929. *Middletown*. New York: Harcourt Brace.

McDonald, Glenn. 1984. "New Directions in the Economic Theory of Agency." *Canadian Journal of Economics* 17:415.

MacPherson, C. B. 1964. *The Political Theory of Possessive Individualism*. Oxford: Oxford University Press.

MacRae, Duncan, Jr. 1985. *Policy Indicators: Links between Social Science and Public Debate*. Chapel Hill: University of North Carolina Press.

Marsden, Peter V. 1981. "Introducing Influence Processes into a System of Collective Decisions." *American Journal of Sociology* 86:1203–35.

Marsden, Peter V., and Edward O. Laumann. 1977. "Collective Action in a Community Elite: Exchange, Influence Resources and Issue Resolution." In *Power, Paradigms and Community Research*, edited by R. J. Liebert and A. W. Imershein. Beverly Hills, Calif.: Sage.

Merton, Robert K. 1949. *Social Theory and Social Structure*. Glencoe, Ill.: Free Press.

Merton, Robert K., and Alice S. Kitt. 1950. "Contributions to the Theory of Reference Group Behavior." In *Continuities in Social Research*, edited by Robert K. Merton and Paul F. Lazarsfeld. Glencoe, Ill.: Free Press.

Mincer, Jacob. 1974. *Schooling, Experience, and Earnings*. New York: Columbia University Press.

Oberschall, Anthony. 1973. *Social Conflict and Social Movements*. Englewood Cliffs, N.J.: Prentice-Hall.

Olson, Mancur. 1965. *The Logic of Collective Action*. Cambridge, Mass.: Harvard University Press.

Pappi, Franz, and Peter Kappelhoff. 1984. "Abhängigkeit, Tausch und Kollektive Entscheidung in einer Gemeindelite." *Zeitschrift für Soziologie* 13 (2): 87–117.

Parsons, Talcott. 1937. *The Structure of Social Action*. New York: McGraw-Hill.

———. *The Social System*. 1951. Glencoe, Ill.: Free Press.

Parsons, Talcott, Robert F. Bales, and Edward A. Shils. 1953. *Working Papers in the Theory of Action*. Glencoe, Ill.: Free Press.

Parsons, Talcott, and Edward Shils, eds. 1951. *Toward a General Theory of Action*. Cambridge, Mass.: Harvard University Press.

Parsons, T., E. Shils, K. Naegele, and J. Pitts. 1961. *Theories of Society*. Glencoe, Ill.: Free Press.

Plott, Charles R., and Vernon Smith. 1978. "An Experimental Examination of Two Exchange Institutions." *Review of Economic Studies* 45 (February): 133–53.

Theory of Action

Popkin, Samuel L. 1979. *The Rational Peasant*. Berkeley and Los Angeles: University of California Press.

Posner, Richard A. 1977. *The Economic Analysis of Law*. 2d ed. Boston: Little, Brown.

Roth, Alvin. 1984. "The Evolution of the Labor Market for Medical Interns and Residents: A Case Study in Game Theory." *Journal of Political Economy* 92:991–1016.

Scheppele, Kim. In press. *Legal Secrets: Common Law Rules and the Social Distribution of Knowledge*. Chicago: University of Chicago Press.

Stone, Christopher. 1975. *Where the Law Ends*. New York: Harper & Row.

Stouffer, Samuel A., Arthur A. Lumsdaine, Marion Harper Lumsdaine, Robin M. Williams, Jr., M. Brewster Smith, Irving L. Janis, Shirley A. Star, and Leonard S. Cottrell, Jr. 1949. *The American Soldier*. Princeton, N.J.: Princeton University Press.

Tilly, Charles, Louise Tilly, and Richard Tilly. 1975. *The Rebellious Century, 1830–1930*. Cambridge, Mass.: Harvard University Press.

Ullmann-Margalit, Edna. 1977. *The Emergence of Norms*. Oxford: Clarendon.

Waller, Willard. 1938. *The Family: A Dynamic Interpretation*. New York: Cordon.

Whyte, W. F. 1943. *Street Corner Society*. Chicago: University of Chicago Press.

[9]

A Reconsideration of the Rationality Postulate:

'Right Hemisphere Thinking' in Economics

By Edward E. Williams and M. Chapman Findlay 3d *

ABSTRACT. The cardinal postulate of *neoclassical economics* is that individuals and entrepreneurs seek to *maximize* their unique positions in the world. Yet behind this postulate is an even more fundamental premise: that men are *rational* and can discern their own best interests. From Adam Smith on, it has been accepted that reasonable men act to maximize their own pecuniary advantage and in most economic models even the potential for irrationality is ignored. Nevertheless, it is becoming increasingly obvious from the research conclusions of other disciplines (*psychology, philosophy, political science,* and *sociology* in particular) that the simplistic notion of *"economic man,"* posited so often in the economics literature, is more fancy than fact. There is an implicit recognition that the neoclassical assumptions may not be correct in the developing area of *economic behaviorism*. The economic behaviorists, however, adopt a more general definition of rationality, substituting what might be called a "modified rationality postulate" for the global rationality assumed in neoclassical theory. As a result, their conclusions do not differ greatly from those of the neoclassicists. Fortunately, ideas are now crystallizing in psychology which may enable us to shed light on decisions which previously would have had to be classified as non-rational, irrational, or unexplainable. Some of those ideas are explored.

I

INTRODUCTION

Man has been called a rational being, but rationality is a matter of choice—and the alternative his nature offers him is: rational being or suicidal animal. . . . All that which is proper to the life of a rational being is the good; all that which destroys it is the evil. . . . By the grace of reality and the nature of life, man—every man—is an end in himself, he exists for his own sake, and the achievement of his own happiness is his highest moral purpose.

JOHN GALT

* [Edward E. Williams, Ph.D., is professor of administrative science, Jesse H. Jones Graduate School of Administration, Rice University, P.O. Box 1892, Houston, Texas 77001; M. Chapman Findlay 3d, Ph.D., is professor of finance, the University of Southern California, Los Angeles, Calif. 90007. The authors express their appreciation to M. Clark and several referees for comments and suggestions.

American Journal of Economics and Sociology, Vol. 40, No. 1 (January, 1981).
0002-9246/81/010017-20$00.75/0

18   *American Journal of Economics and Sociology*

PERHAPS ONE OF THE REASONS Englishmen and Americans have excelled in economics is because the discipline is founded on the rational man premise. Neoclassical arguments in particular strike a responsive chord in the hearts of most Americans who readily discern the philosophical, social, and political implications. Americans and economics literally belong together like "love and marriage" (to cite another Victorian couplet), and the more positivist the reasoning, the more accepted the argument. The English have a less strong commitment to neoclassical theories, but the methodology of economics in the United Kingdom (and the accepted postulate of rationality) is quite similar to its counterpart in the United States.

The rational man postulate has never been universally accepted by social scientists, and there appears to be a small but growing number of methodologists and philosophers who deeply question the premise. In a recent article in this *Journal*, Zinam states:

'Economic man' behavior and maximization are plausible and applicable only under very strictly defined special conditions of predominantly free competitive markets operating in an economy which is an approximation to *laissez-faire*. Even under these conditions the motivation of entrepreneurs, as revealed in the works of Sombart, Max Weber, Schumpeter and some others "include the desire for power, prestige, independence and security as well as the desire to maximize gain and utility" (1).

He cites extensively the work of A. O. Lovejoy who argues that "man's 'reason' has, at most, a secondary and very small influence upon his conduct and . . . irrational or nonrational feelings and desires are the real efficient causes of all or nearly all of men's actions" and Kenneth Boulding who for years has "forcefully exposed . . . the limitations of 'economic man'" (2). To this could be added the thinking of William Barrett who has examined the philosophical underpinnings of rationalism and argues that it is essentially anti-intellectual in character:

It may seem strange, particularly to American readers, that rationalism has been made so much of a target throughout this book . . . But the essence of the existential protest is that rationalism can pervade a whole civilization, to the point where the individuals in that civilization do less and less thinking, and perhaps wind up doing none at all (3).

To Barrett the problem lies in the methodological processes which provide the foundation of Anglo-American philosophy:

Anglo-American philosophy is dominated by an altogether different and alien mode of thought—variously called analytic philosophy, Logical

Rationality   19

Positivism, or sometimes merely "scientific philosophy" . . . it takes as its central fact what is undoubtedly the central fact distinguishing our civilization from all others—science; but it goes on from this to take science as the ultimate ruler of human life, which it never has been and psychologically never can be. Positivist man is a curious creature who dwells in the tiny island of light composed of what he finds scientifically "meaningful," while the whole surrounding area in which ordinary men live from day to day and have their dealings with other men is consigned to the outer darkness of the "meaningless" (4).

The positivist, scientific (scientistic?) bent of Anglo-American philosophy is no less evident in Anglo-American economics, and the inappropriate application of what is thought to be the 'scientific method' to social phenomena is a subject of increasing concern to the authors and others (5). In the present endeavor, our interest focuses on economic assumptions. If it turns out that man has the capacity to act quite inconsistently over time, it may well be that positivist approaches can never explain human behavior. This is particularly true if these approaches presuppose a human decision-making apparatus that exists only in the imagination.

II

THE RATIONALITY OF MAN POSTULATE

IS MAN RATIONAL? Few Americans ever think about the subject. Even most non-"mainstream" economists who are uneasy with both the methods and the conclusions of neoclassicism unhesitatingly adopt assumptions about human behavior that are increasingly questioned elsewhere and in other disciplines. Undoubtedly, the popularity of the rational man assumption "continues to dominate the thinking of most economists because of its great simplicity and convincing *a priori* reasonableness" (6). Nevertheless, the anti-rational position has received both theoretical and empirical support from a number of psychologists and sociologists who have found that, at both the individual and societal level, needs are far more complex than those simple requirements postulated by economic models (7).

These efforts identify the need for achievement (n achievement), the need for affiliation (n affiliation), and the need for power (n power) as the real motives determining human behavior. One writer has attempted to portray the summary of these needs in a so-called "money motive" but he does not redeem the pecuniarily "rational man" so often contemplated in economic models (8).

20   *American Journal of Economics and Sociology*

McClelland *et al.* found that high achievers are not much influenced by money rewards as a score keeping device; while low achievers, on the other hand, *are* motivated by money and can be encouraged to work harder for financial incentives (9). The general consensus among psychologists seems to be that "money matters" but the way it matters is very different from that typically postulated in economics.

Skinner has synthesized the thinking of behaviorists on the subject with the argument that men do not have the freedom to choose that they think they do (10). In essence, "behavior is controlled by forces in the environment outside of the self" (11) and the invisible hand is more often than not palsied by a number of factors not the least important of which might be the way one was reared as a small child (12).

III

NON-RATIONALITY IN ECONOMIC THOUGHT

OF COURSE, not all economists have been unaware that factors other than material well-being affect economic decision-making. Schumpeter argued frequently that other motives (such as the desire to found a private dynasty, or the will to conquer in competitive battle, or the sheer joy of creation) could rule the judgments of the entrepreneur.

Nevertheless, true to his profession, Schumpeter was very much a rationalist. It was his view that ultimately all human endeavors—art, science, religion, the process of invention, and even business management—would be reduced to a completely rationalized social order. He felt, however, that, in the process, the creative entrepreneur would be destroyed. (Bad managerial anal types driving out good entrepreneurial types—a sort of psychological Gresham's law).

Keynes agreed that things other than the economic might be important determinants of economic behavior (*e.g.*, animal spirits), but he was more sanguine about the prospects of human development. David McCord Wright, while supposedly castigating the Keynesian theory of investment, actually lends support to the view (held by Keynes) that irrational (non-economic) motives frequently dominate investment decisions. His famous brewer's paradox is well worth reconsidering:

Is it true that investment in the real world will be made only on a rising demand? To show how mistaken the idea is, when stated as a universal principle, let us ask ourselves under what circumstances a brewer, say, might build a new brewery even though the volume of total beer sales, or the price of beer, or both, were falling. There are

## Rationality 	21

three cases: the better beer, the cheaper beer, and what I have called the 'bullheaded brewer.' If a man invents a new kind of beer which he thinks is going to attract sales from other brands, it may pay him to build a new brewery even though general beer sales are falling. And the shot in the arm given by his new construction *could* raise not only general beer sales but employment in other lines as well. Next, if a man gets hold of a new and much cheaper method of brewing, it may pay to build a new brewery even though beer sales and prices are falling. For though prices are declining, say two percent, if costs are reduced twenty percent, a substantial profit margin remains. Finally, a businessman may simply feel that he is smarter than the market and he (the 'bull-headed brewer') may go ahead and build though things are still depressed. And it is again undeniable that his courage and the stimulus of the construction he is carrying through may start the economy once more expanding (13).

What Wright is trying to do, of course, is analyze how people actually make investment decisions in the real world. He calls attention to the fact that "men do not behave entirely according to rational consideration" (14). Yet, the positivists would argue that such a man as the "bullheaded brewer" could not last for long. Social Darwinists to a man, they maintain that anything less than being a risk-averse, profit maximizer seals the doom of any market participant (15).

Although one may find it difficult to assert that man is an irrational animal, it appears that economic theory cannot afford to overlook alternative explanations of behavior. If, indeed, people have needs beyond simple life support satisfaction (air, water, food, shelter, etc.), models that completely ignore those needs (or assume them away) will be less valuable. If many people, for example, like to gamble, and the only game in town is the stock market, perhaps that institution will more readily resemble a casino than an efficient market place where many buyers and sellers come together to make rational choices. If the need to achieve, or the need to affiliate, or the need for power overshadows the need for simple consumption, it may be the case that entrepreneurs (and large corporations for that matter) do not seek to maximize profits (or seek the highest returns consistent with a given level of risk). In complex organizations, it may not even be possible to ascertain just *whose* needs are being satisfied. Thus, investment may take place for "bullheaded" reasons, and the Darwinian "gambler's ruin" argument may not guarantee the extinction of those who behave in this fashion. Since it is clear that the rationality of man postulate simply does not square with the facts in many situations, perhaps other basic assumptions must be made to explain economic phenomena.

IV

THE MODIFIED RATIONALITY POSTULATE

IN RESPONSE to the discomforting conclusions of an overwhelming number of psychologists (which have developed coterminously with the thinking of such existentialist philosophers as Sartre, Camus, and de Beauvoir), certain economists have abandoned the global rationality presumed by neoclassical theory. These researchers have granted that man operates in a sphere of "bounded rationality" due to his limited ability to process information. The recognition that man may not be smart enough to be rational prompted Herbert Simon to advance down the path that eventually won him the Nobel Prize in Economics (16). Emphasizing the procedural aspects of choice (made both by individuals and organizations), Simon and his followers have examined both normative (*e.g.*, operations research, management science, and artificial intelligence) and positive (*e.g.*, cognitive psychology and simulation) aspects of procedural rationality.

Although the economic behaviorists are prepared to agree that man (and the world) is much more complicated than neoclassical models posit, they reject the nihilism inherent in the notion that man (and the world) is irrational. A recent set of papers in honor of Simon demonstrates that the conclusions of the behavioral economists still closely resemble those of their neoclassical brethren even though their methods differ. Nelson and Winter, for example, contend that "firms cannot optimize in any meaningful sense because their decision problems are too complicated for them to comprehend fully. But over time the decision rules that are used will adapt, and those adapted will be sensible and plausible for the environment in which they are used" (17). Lucas, another example, argues that individuals with the greatest managerial talent will wind up managing the largest firms (18). Still another, Wachter and Williamson, maintains that bounded rationality should not be mistaken for irrationality among economic agents (19). Rather, individuals operate as effectively as they can and "the evolution of economic institutions can be understood in large measure as a sequence of developments which serve to economize on the limited human information-processing capabilities" (20). Simon himself be-

Rationality 23

lieves that:

> . . . evidence suggests that, for humans, accumulated experience is indeed a very large component of high-level skill. . . . This accumulation of experience may allow people to behave in ways that are very nearly optimal in situations to which their experience is pertinent, but will be of little help when genuinely novel situations are presented. That conclusion is consistent with our general belief that the limits of human rationality become particularly important in explaining behavior under uncertainty—where we translate 'uncertainty' here to mean any kind of significant novelty (21).

Hence, man may have a tremendous capacity for behaving inconsistently (irrationally?) when confronted with decision-making in the real uncertain world.

Nevertheless, Simon would demur from describing human behavior as irrational; and, to a large degree, the matter is definitional. In the Ely lecture at the 1977 American Economic Association meetings, he argued that "almost all human behavior has a large rational component, but only in terms of the broader every day sense of rationality, not the economists' more specialized sense of maximization" (22). Thus, when sociologists and political scientists postulate rationality, they are not making the strong assumptions normally made by economists. Simon cites the so-called "social exchange" theories of Homans as an example (23). Under social exchange, when two or more individuals interact, each anticipates deriving satisfaction. One is willing to "give up" something valuable to others in order to get something of value to himself. Nevertheless, "the man of social exchange theory is a rational man, even if he is never asked to equate things at the margin" (24). Simon goes on to mention Freud's theory of psychoanalysis which explains mental illness in terms of the function the disease performs for the patient (25). Unfortunately, such a generalized definition of rationality makes even madmen rational!

V
BOUNDED RATIONALITY, AMBIGUITY, AND THE ENGINEERING OF CHOICE

IN A VERY COMPLEX ARTICLE concerned with both the consequences of an uncertain future and the uncertainty of future preferences, March attempts to hold together the bounded rationality concept (26). Recognizing that individual preferences often appear to be "fuzzy and inconsistent" and that they seem to change over time (at least in part as a consequence of actions taken), he points out that the "theoretical puzzlement" which prevailed earlier regarding the simplicity of decision behavior has now been extended to decision inconsistencies and instabilities and the extent to which "individuals and organizations do things without apparent reason." As a result, there has been "an examination of the extent to which theories of choice might subordinate the idea of rationality altogether to less intentional concepts of the causal determinants of action."

Among these less intentional concepts are ideas of limited rationality, contextual rationality, game rationality, and process rationality, which are all theories of "intelligent individuals making calculations of the consequences of actions for objectives, and acting sensibly to achieve those objectives." Other, very different, rationality *is not intentional.* Yet, "there is intelligence in the suspension of calculation." Following Simon's lead in observing that there are limits placed on rationality due to properties of the human organism (and, hence, human decision-making is more intelligent than it may appear on the surface), March observes, "when we start to discover intelligence in decision-making where goals are unstable, ill-defined, or apparently irrelevant, we are led to asking some different kinds of questions about our normative conceptions of choice and walk close not only to some issues in economics but also to some classical and modern questions in literature and ethics, particularly the role of clear prior purpose in the ordering of human affairs" (27). Thus, despite the fact that in standard prescriptive theories of choice tastes are said to be absolute, relevant, stable, consistent, precise, and exogenous,

Individuals commonly find it possible to express both a taste for something and a recognition that the taste is something that is repugnant to moral standards they accept. Choices are often made without respect to tastes. Human decision makers routinely ignore their own, fully conscious, preferences in making decisions. They follow rules, traditions, hunches, and the advice or actions of others. Tastes change over time in such a way that predicting future tastes is often difficult. Tastes are inconsistent . . . it is often also true that actions and experiences with their consequences affect tastes. Tastes are determined partly endogenously (28).

Only by "suitably manipulating" the concept of tastes can classical theories of choice as "explanations" of behavior be saved, but "probably only at the cost of stretching a good idea into a doubtful ideology." Of course, one can say that deviations from the prescriptive theories stem from stupidity and are errors that can be corrected (the

Rationality 25

usual argument of operations and management analysis). However, ". . . goal ambiguity, like limited rationality, is not necessarily a fault in human choice to be corrected but often a form of intelligence to be refined by the technology of choice rather than ignored by it."

March is not sanguine about the time it will take the "engineering of choice" to accept and refine the "intelligence of ambiguity" (it took twenty years to develop and get a hearing for the notions of bounded rationality and conflicts of interest in the economics literature). However, he does feel the reconstruction involved is not extraordinary. Finally, despite the immense philosophic complexity of the subject (and the phenomena in question), March remains true to the modified rationality postulate. Like the other behavioral economists who continue to believe in calculation and who continue to reach neoclassical conclusions, March is prepared to let his "engineering instincts . . . sacrifice purity to secure tractability" while he accepts "a theory built on a romantic view of human destiny" (29).

VI

RIGHT HEMISPHERE DECISION MAKING

THE ARGUMENTS in the previous two sections pose quite a dilemma for the economic theorist. On the one hand, it is possible to accept March's "romantic view" and let our engineering instincts sacrifice purity to secure tractability. This has been done to a very large extent throughout economics, and we have a large variety of tractable models which do not really explain observed economic behavior, or at least they explain only very poorly. On the other hand, we can resign ourselves to an existential acceptance that man has the ability to be very irrational and adopt the nihilistic view that his behavior is simply beyond explanation. Neither of these views is very palatable, although most of us would probably opt for the former position if we only had two choices. Some theory is better than no theory at all. Nevertheless, it may be possible for a *relevant* theory to be constructed that can indeed explain supposed irrationality even though its precise tractability may be limited. Such a theory actually presses on from March's position, but it requires the introduction of some psychophysical concepts that may be alien to the average economist.

The human brain is a complex organ about which more and more is becoming known. It has been posited for some time, for example, that the brain appears to be functionally (at least in a predominant sense) bihemispheric. For most people (nearly all right-handers and many left-handers) the left cerebral hemisphere seems to process language and certain nonlinguistic (*e.g.,* symbolic and mathematical) information, and it apparently processes data in characteristic ways. Such information is analyzed, linearly arranged, temporally ordered and presented as propositions. Until the 1950s, most neurophysiologists focused their attention on the left hemisphere since it was assumed that it was our capacity for language and reason which distinguished us from the lower species. Thus, the left side of the brain became known as the "major" or "dominant" hemisphere while the right was considered the "minor" or "subordinate" side. Over the past two decades, however, research on the distribution of various mental functions has shown that the right hemisphere may dominate on many types of tasks (30). This has become particularly important in light of the changing attitudes of psychologists regarding intelligence. Whereas language and mathematical skills were once regarded as the *only* measures of intelligence, it is now recognized by many that there is another form of intelligence associated with numerous nonverbal cognitive skills.

The recognition of the potential of right hemispheric dominance in the performance of numerous activities has led to an emphasis on specialization rather than "dominance" per se. This has made it possible for psychologists to dichotomize between the functioning of the two sides of the brain without pejorative references to the "minor side." Nebes summarizes the position of many researchers about hemispheric specialization as follows:

This distinction between the left and right hemispheres has been described as: symbolic versus visual-spatial, associative versus apperceptive, propositional versus appositional, and analytic versus gestalt. All of these dichotomies suggest that the organization and processing of data by the right hemisphere is in terms of complex wholes, the minor hemisphere having a predisposition for perceiving the total rather than the parts. By contrast, the left hemisphere is seen to analyze input sequentially, abstracting out the relevant details and associating these with verbal symbols (31).

Thus, it may be that the right hemisphere simply does different things than the left. These activities are no less important to the overall functioning of the human being than those concentrated in the left hemisphere. It may be argued, in fact, that the two are quite complementary.

Rationality 27

VII

CULTURAL BIAS AND "RIGHT HEMISPHERE THINKING"

ONE MUST BE CAREFUL in distinguishing between the seeming specializations of the two hemispheres. Except for commissurotomized patients (those with the so-called "split brain"), neural cross-connections insure a mutual feedback mechanism between the two hemispheres. This means that both sides of the brain operate in performing most tasks. Nevertheless, because of cultural biases, we may have a tendency to overlook the important features of a kind of thinking we shall call (in the tradition of current knowledge of the brain—one of the frontiers of contemporary research) "right hemisphere thinking" (32). It seems clear that many of us still define intelligence in terms of one's ability to manipulate language and mathematics (college entrance examinations are certainly left hemisphere biased), and most academic disciplines depend almost exclusively on sequential processes to arrive at a given "body of knowledge." Our human decision-making paradigms also postulate a calculating mind operating to solve problems step-by-step. In fact, our entire concept of rationality is tied to the notion that the human brain does (or should) operate like a computer in following a strict, logical path in its approach to decision-making. When it does not (and it frequently appears not to), we feel we have somehow uncovered "aberrant" or at least "unexplainable" behavior.

The normative and positive aspects of right hemisphere thinking are important. Much of the prior discussion in this paper has been directed to the latter. We observe numerous instances where supposedly "irrational" behavior takes place. Yet a clear understanding of right hemisphere thinking may demonstrate that "bullheaded brewers" are not irrational at all; they are merely exercising a different kind of intelligence. On a normative plane, moreover, it may well be the case that this kind of intelligence is vitally important to human progress. Hoover tells us:

When the paradigm being dissected by the logical, scientific method finally fails to explain observations, the creative portion of our intelligence must jump outside the failed "reality." Which is not to say that a new paradigm is any more true than the older idea; it merely explains observations a bit better for the time being. . . . But the important thing here is that the new really doesn't come about rationally, since rationality only can operate within the old rules. As does a computer, the human mind in its logical mode must follow the rules of logic. To go outside them would be "irrational" (33).

Despite the fact that for most people the two hemispheres perform jointly, some individuals seem to operate better than others in left or right hemisphere modes. Not surprisingly, most Englishmen and Americans (and perhaps all occidentals) probably have far better developed left hemisphere skills than right. Undoubtedly, the advent of the computer has accentuated this tendency, but as we found earlier patterns in Anglo-American thought are fundamentally left hemisphere oriented. This does not mean that there are not *some* (perhaps many) individuals in our culture who have well developed right hemisphere abilities. It also does not mean that Western civilization has always evidenced its left hemisphere bias.

Indeed, in a highly provocative volume, Julian Jaynes (34) argues that human consciousness only began about three thousand years ago, that prior to that time men truly had a "bicameral mind" that literally heard voices of gods (emanating from the brain's right hemisphere), and that only catastrophe and cataclysm forced Western man to *learn* consciousness (35). Human history and culture played the key role in the origin of consciousness, according to Jaynes, with neuro-anatomical and chemical explanations being of no value (36). Jaynes' origin of consciousness corresponds with the development of modern problem solving Western man and all his left hemisphere biases. That such a man *had* to evolve to survive speaks strongly for the importance of logical sequential reasoning processes. It should not overshadow, however, the importance of the right hemisphere which, as we have seen, may provide man with an even richer thought perspective than Yahweh talking to Moses (37).

VIII

THE DEVELOPMENT OF LATERAL THINKING

CLOSELY ALIGNED with the process of right hemisphere functioning is the concept of lateral thinking. Vertical thinking bears a similar relationship to left hemisphere processes (38). The contrast between lateral and vertical thought is drawn by de Bono:

Lateral thinking is quite distinct from vertical thinking which is the traditional type of thinking. In vertical thinking one moves forward by sequential steps each of which must be justified. The distinction between the two sorts of thinking is sharp. For instance in lateral thinking one uses information not for its own sake but its effect. In lateral thinking one may have to be wrong at some stage in order to achieve a correct solution; in vertical thinking (logic or mathematics) this

Rationality   29

would be impossible. In lateral thinking one may deliberately seek out irrelevant information; in vertical thinking one selects out only what is relevant.

With vertical thinking one may reach a conclusion by a valid series of steps. Because of the soundness of the steps one is arrogantly certain of the correctness of the conclusion. But no matter how correct the path may be the starting point was a matter of perceptual choice which fashioned the basic concepts used. For instance, perceptual choice tends to create sharp divisions and use extreme polarization. Vertical thinking would then work on the concepts produced in this manner. Lateral thinking is needed to handle the perceptual choice which is itself beyond the reach of vertical thinking. Lateral thinking would also temper the arrogance of any rigid conclusion no matter how soundly it appeared to have been worked out (39).

Several distinctions may be made between vertical and lateral thinking (40): 1) Vertical thinking is selective; lateral thinking is generative. 2) Vertical thinking moves only if there is a direction in which to move; lateral thinking moves in order to generate a direction. 3) Vertical thinking is analytical; lateral thinking is provocative. 4) Vertical thinking is sequential; lateral thinking can make jumps. 5) With vertical thinking one has to be correct at every step; with lateral thinking one does not. 6) With vertical thinking one uses the negative in order to block off certain pathways; with lateral thinking there is no negative. 7) With vertical thinking one concentrates and excludes what is irrelevant; with lateral thinking one welcomes chance intrusions. 8) With vertical thinking categories, classifications and labels are fixed; with lateral thinking they are not. 9) Vertical thinking follows the most likely paths; lateral thinking explores the least likely. 10) Vertical thinking is a finite process; lateral thinking is a probabilistic one.

Can lateral thinking be taught? Apparently. In fact, de Bono devotes much of his volume to demonstrating methods of exercising right hemisphere processes. Should lateral thinking become a substitute for vertical? Not at all. The two are entirely complementary. As Jaynes has argued, man had to become conscious to survive. The development of vertical thinking accompanied the dawn of consciousness. On the other hand, man does not live by logic alone. Totally new ideas do not appear to be generated easily by left hemisphere processes. On strictly neuro-anatomical grounds, "it is evident that the right cerebral hemisphere makes an important contribution to human performance, having functions complementary to those of the left

30   *American Journal of Economics and Sociology*

hemisphere. The right side of the brain probably processes information differently from the left, relying more on imagery than on language, and being more synthetic and holistic than analytic and sequential in handling data. It is certainly important in perceiving spatial relationships. It also probably provides the neural basis for our ability to take the fragmentary sensory information we receive and construct from it a coherent concept of the spatial organization of the outside world—a sort of cognitive spatial map by which we plan our actions" (41).

IX

RIGHT HEMISPHERE THINKING IN ECONOMICS

THE PROCESSES DE BONO DESCRIBES seem to be implicit in the decision-making of a number of economic agents. Bullheaded brewers, many inventors and perhaps most entrepreneurs appear to have one thing in common: They do not make choices in the sequential, logical, left hemisphere fashion. Are they irrational? To an extent the question is definitional. The extreme left hemisphere bias of our culture would call them such. As we have seen above, however, these economic agents may really be exemplifying another form of intelligence that is vitally important to human survival. That we are beginning to recognize motivational factors that may not be of left hemisphere origin is certainly a step in the right direction (pardon the pun) (42). That we can model and describe these processes is another matter. It may well be that we simply cannot employ left hemisphere tools to understand how the right hemisphere works, March's romantic view of human destiny notwithstanding (43).

Economics is in a quandary today both methodologically and in its ability to describe what is going on in the world. The Keynesian explanations can only feebly account for a situation where recession is accompanied by double digit levels of inflation. Hence, many are calling for a retreat to the methods and prescriptions of classical economics (witness the increasing number of economists who now consider themselves to be "neoclassicists"). Yet, it was the failure of laissez-faire and the methods of classicism that produced the Keynesian revolution in the first place. Interestingly, a fairly strong case can be made that Keynes himself did not hesitate to adopt a right hemisphere posture, and much of his thinking from 1925 on made strong use of lateral procedures (44). Neoclassical economics rests on the

Rationality 31

identical foundation of rationality that supported classical theory. It ignores whim, caprice, fancy and a host of other non-rational elements of human behavior. It requires strict adherence to logical processes in its methodology. As such, one may suspect that it will provide no better explanations than did its ancestor. It is sad to see the economics profession trying to resurrect the old order when Keynes pointed the way *methodologically* fifty years ago. Indeed, it may well turn out that both Freud and Keynes (certainly the greatest thinkers in their respective disciplines in the first half of the 20th century) will ultimately be remembered more for their willingness to defy the accepted rationality in their individual ideas than for pointing out the irrationality of man in their theories.

X

CONCLUSIONS

WE FIND that the standard forms of economic analysis may not take us far in laying bare the workings of "animal spirits," "entrepreneurial energies," and "non-economic motivational forces." Yet these clearly important aspects of economic behavior may be approached from a right hemispheric perspective. If we take a holistic, systemic view of economic entities and institutions, we might be better able to appreciate (if not explain) the *results* of how they function (even though we might not be able to describe sequentially the processes at work). Thus, although it may be conceptually incorrect to derive demand curves from utility functions for all individuals, we may still be able to predict how a consumer will behave under given environmental conditions. Although we may not be able to posit profit maximization as the key postulate in the theory of the firm, we may be able to discern patterns of decisions that reflect multi-motivational characteristics. Although we may not be able to describe the U.S. economy at a point in time with one hundred and eleven simultaneously solving equations, we may be able to get a feel for its overall thrust over time. Those who have a deep left hemisphere bias will not be satisfied with the generality and lack of tractability of "right hemisphere economic tools," but the nature of the beast may leave us little choice if we really want to appreciate the whole economic animal. Our current problems require a major breakthrough in thought comparable to that of the *General Theory*. Solutions are not likely to come from patching up the Keynesian system with "logical extensions" or from a retreat to the thoughts of the past. A wholesale revision of ideas that only lateral processes can produce is necessary. Of course, this does not mean we should stop doing research that presumes order, sequence, and precisely logical decisions. The left hemisphere has not diminished in importance because we have discovered the right. That everyone should be involved in research that by assumption *precludes* the introduction of right hemisphere thinking, however, is not only intellectually arrogant; in the long-run, such exclusiveness will simply not be productive.

Human emotion is phylogenetically a high development from simpler processes, and reason is another one; human mentality is an unsurveyable complex dynamism of their interactions with each other, and with several further specialized forms of cerebral activity, implicating the whole organic substructure (45).

1. Oleg Zinam, "The Roles of Equilibrium, Optimality, Maximization, and Discontent in Decision-Making Process," *American Journal of Economics and Sociology,* April, 1979, pp. 170–71. Indirect quotation from Allan G. Gruchy, "The Neoinstitutional Paradigm and the Limits of Keynesian Economics," *Proceedings* of the Inaugural Convention of the Eastern Economic Association, Albany, New York, October 25–27, 1974, p. 81.

2. Zinam, *op. cit.,* p. 170. Quotations from Arthur O. Lovejoy, *Reflections on Human Nature* (Baltimore: The Johns Hopkins Press, 1961), p. 64. Also, see Robert L. Heilbroner, "Kenneth E. Boulding, Collected Papers: A Review Article," *Journal of Economic Issues,* March 1975, p. 75.

3. William Barrett, *Irrational Man* (Garden City: Doubleday, 1958), pp. 238–39.

4. *Ibid.,* pp. 18–19.

5. See M. C. Findlay 3d and E. E. Williams, "Owners' Surplus, the Marginal Efficiency of Capital, and Market Equilibrium," *Journal of Business Finance and Accounting,* Spring, 1979, pp. 17–36; M. C. Findlay and E. E. Williams, "A Positivist Evaluation of the New Finance," *Financial Management,* forthcoming; M. C. Findlay and E. E. Williams, "Toward a Post-Keynesian Theory of Finance," Rice University Working Paper, 1979; M. C. Findlay and E. E. Williams, "The Neoclassical Fantasy and Accounting Theory," Rice University Working Paper, 1979; Dudley Dillard, "Revolutions in Economic Theory," *Southern Economic Journal,* April, 1978, pp. 705–24; and R. B. Ekelund, "Review of *Essays on Hayek,*" *Southern Economic Journal,* April, 1978, pp. 1019–21.

6. David C. McClelland, *The Achieving Society* (revised ed.), New York: Irvington Publishers, Inc. 1976), p. 8.

7. See Sandor Farenczi, *First Contributions to Psycho-Analysis* (London: Hogarth, 1952); A. H. Maslow, *Motivation and Personality* (New York: Harper & Row, 1954); R. A. Dahl, "The Concept of Power," *Behavioral Science,* June, 1957, pp. 201–15; Douglas McGregor, *The Human Side of Enterprise* (New York: McGraw-Hill, 1960); E. H. Erikson, *Childhood and Society* (revised ed., New York: W. W. Norton, 1963); B. F. Skinner, *Beyond Freedom and Dignity* (New York: Knopf, 1971); R. E. Boyatzis, *A Two-Factor Theory of Affiliation Motivation,* unpublished doctoral dissertation, Harvard University, 1972; D. G. Winter *The Power Motive* (New York: The Free Press, 1973); David C. McClelland, *Power: The Inner Experience* (New York: Irvington Publishers, Inc., 1975); David C. McClelland, *The Achieving Society, op. cit.;* David C. McClelland, J. W. Atkinson, R. A. Clark, and E. L. Lowell, *The Achievement Motive* (revised ed., New York: Irvington Publishers, Inc., 1976).

Rationality   33

8. Thomas Wiseman, *The Money Motive* (New York: Random House, 1974).

9. David C. McClelland, *et al., op. cit.*

10. B. F. Skinner, *op. cit.*

11. David C. McClelland, *Power: The Inner Experience, op. cit.,* p. 20.

12. Nevertheless, motives play a crucial role. McClelland has been the leader in forcing a reinterpretation of Social Darwinism in light of motivation. He argues, "For a century we have been dominated by Social Darwinism by the implicit or explicit notion that man is a creature of his environment, whether natural or social. Marx thought so in advocating economic determinism, in arguing that a man's psychology is shaped in the last analysis by the conditions under which he must work. Even Freud thought so in teaching that civilization was a reaction of man's primitive urges to the repressive force of social institutions beginning with the family. Practically all social scientists have in the past several generations begun with society and tried to create man in its image. Even Toynbee's theory of history is essentially one of environmental challenges, though he recognizes that states of mind can create internal challenges. If our study of the role of achievement motivation in society does nothing else, perhaps it will serve to redress the balance a little, to see man as a *creator* of his environment, as well as a creature of it. Much of what the Social Darwinists have taught must be thought through again in terms of a new dimension—*i.e.*, the motives of the men affected by an environmental change or a social institution." David C. McClelland, *The Achieving Society, op. cit.,* pp. 391–2.

13. David McCord Wright, "Mr. Keynes and the Day of Judgment," *Science,* November 21, 1958, pp. 1258–62. Reprinted in Henry Hazlitt, *The Critics of Keynesian Economics* (New Rochelle: Arlington House, 1977), pp. 414–27.

14. David C. McClelland, *The Achieving Society, op. cit.,* p. 13.

15. The authors, in another context, were criticized by a number of neo-classicists for even suggesting that risk seekers might exist. See M. C. Findlay and E. E. Williams, "A Note on Risk Seeker Portfolio Selection and Lender Constraints," *Southern Economic Journal,* January 1976, pp. 515–20.

16. Among Simon's early works in the area are the following: Herbert A. Simon, "A Behavioral Model of Rational Choice," *Quarterly Journal of Economics,* February 1955, pp. 99–118; Herbert A. Simon, "Rational Choice and the Structure of the Environment," *Psychological Review,* March 1956, pp. 129–38; and Herbert A. Simon, *Models of Man* (New York: Wiley, 1957).

17. Richard R. Nelson and Sidney G. Winter, "Forces Generating and Limiting Concentraton under Schumpeterian Competition," *Bell Journal of Economics,* Autumn 1978, pp. 524–48. Quote from Edward C. Prescott, "Papers in Honor of Herbert A. Simon: An Introduction," *Bell Journal of Economics,* Autumn 1978, p. 492.

18. Robert E. Lucas, "On the Size Distribution of Business Firms," *Bell Journal of Economics,* Autumn 1978, pp. 508–23.

19. Michael L. Wachter and Oliver E. Williamson, "Obligational Markets and the Mechanics of Inflation," *Bell Journal of Economics,* Autumn 1978, pp. 549–71.

20. Edward C. Prescott, *op. cit.,* p. 492.

21. Herbert A. Simon, "On How to Decide What to Do," *Bell Journal of Economics,* Autumn 1978, p. 503.

22. Herbert A. Simon, "Rationality as Process and as Product of Thought," *American Economic Review,* May 1978, p. 2.

23. See George Homans, *Social Behavior: Its Elementary Forms* (New York: Harcourt, Brace, Jovanovich, 1974).

24. Herbert A. Simon, "Rationality as Process and as Product of Thought," *op. cit.,* p. 3.

25. Sigmund Freud, "Five Lectures on Psychoanalysis" (originally "The Origin and Development of Psychoanalysis," 1910) in *The Complete Psychological Works of Sigmund Freud,* Vol. 11 (London: Hogarth, 1957).

26. J. G. March, "Bounded Rationality, Ambiguity, and the Engineering of Choice," *Bell Journal of Economics,* Autumn 1978, pp. 587–608.

27. *Ibid.,* pp. 590–95.

34   *American Journal of Economics and Sociology*

28. *Ibid.*, p. 596.

29. *Ibid.*, pp. 597–605.

30. Although the brain may be bihemispheric, neural cross-connections make it difficult to study "sound individuals" to test for hemispheric specialization. Thus, the findings of the past twenty years have come essentially from studies of unilaterally (one side) brain damaged patients and of patients who have undergone a commissurotomy (a surgical sectioning of the corpus callosum—the massive commissure connecting the right and left cerebral cortices and the anterior commissure of the forebrain) to control *grand mal* epilepsy. More recently, procedures have been developed to test for hemispheric dominance among normal subjects, and the results of previous investigations are being confirmed on these individuals (with certain exceptions, noted below). Summaries of conclusions reached by researchers of brain damaged patients may be found in Stephen D. Krashen, "Cerebral Asymmetry," in Haiganoosh Whitaker and Harry A. Whitaker, *Studies in Neurolinguistics.* Vol. 2 (New York: Academic Press, 1976), pp. 157–91; Stephen D. Krashen, "The Left Hemisphere," in M. C. Wittrock, *et al., The Human Brain* (Englewood Cliffs, N.J.: Prentice-Hall, 1977), pp. 107–30; and Robert D. Nebes, "Man's So-called Minor Hemisphere," in M. C. Wittrock, *op. cit.*, pp. 97–106. Split brain results are copiously catalogued in M. S. Gazzaniga, "The Split Brain in Man," *Scientific American*, Vol. 217, 1967, pp. 24–29; M. S. Gazzaniga, *The Bisected Brain* (New York: Appleton-Century-Crofts, 1970); and M. S. Gazzaniga, "Review of the Split Brain," in M. C. Wittrock, *op. cit.*, pp. 89–96. Behavioral studies of "normals" are recited extensively in Jerre Levy, "Psychobiological Implications of Bilateral Asymmetry," in Stuart J. Dimond and J. Graham Beaumont, *Hemisphere Function in the Human Brain* (New York: John Wiley & Sons, 1974), pp. 121–83.

31. Robert D. Nebes, *op. cit.*, p. 102.

32. Indeed, not all researchers have given up their old prejudices. "Even today, some neurophysiologists cling to the view that the right hemisphere is a mere unconscious automation, while we *live* in our left hemisphere" (Nebes, *op. cit.*, p. 98).

33. Thomas Hoover, "Zen, Technology, and the Split Brain," *Omni*, October 1978, p. 124.

34. Julian Jaynes, *The Origin of Consciousness in the Breakdown of the Bicameral Mind* (Boston: Houghton Mifflin Company, 1976).

35. By Jaynes' analysis, Eastern man may still have a bicameral mind. See Hoover, *op. cit.*, for a popular discussion of Eastern thought processes and attitudes.

36. He maintains, "We can only know in the nervous system what we have known in behavior first. Even if we had a complete wiring diagram of the nervous system, we still would not be able to answer our basic question. Though we knew the connections of every tickling thread of every single axon and dendrite in every species that ever existed, together with all its neurotransmitters and how they varied in its billions of synapses of every brain that ever existed, we could still never—not ever—from a knowledge of the brain alone know if that brain contained a consciousness like our own." *Ibid.*, p. 18.

37. Jaynes provides an insightful commentary on the history of thought in psychology with this observation: "It is an interesting exercise to sit down and try to be conscious of what it means to say that consciousness does not exist. History has not recorded whether or not this feat was attempted by the early behaviorists. But it has recorded everywhere and in large the enormous influence which the doctrine that consciousness does not exist has had on psychology in this century. . . . And this is behaviorism. Its roots rummage far back into the musty history of thought, to the so-called Epicureans of the 18th century and before, to attempts to generalize tropisms from plants to animals to man, to movements called Objectivism, or more particularly, Actionism. For it was Knight Dunlap's attempt to teach the latter to an excellent but aweless animal psychologist, John B. Watson, that resulted in a new word, Behaviorism. At first, it was very similar to the helpless spectator theory we have already examined. Con-

sciousness just was not important to animals. But after a World War and a little invigorating opposition, behaviorism charged out into the intellectual arena with the snorting assertion that consciousness is nothing at all. . . . What a startling doctrine! But the really surprising thing is that, starting off almost as a flying whim, it grew into a movement that occupied center stage in psychology from about 1920 to 1960." *Ibid.*, pp. 13–11.

38. A point on nomenclature: The term right hemisphere thinking is used synonymously with lateral thinking by some writers who also frequently designate left hemisphere thought as vertical thinking.

39. Edward de Bono, *Lateral Thinking* (New York: Harper & Row, 1976), p. 12.

40. *Ibid.*, pp. 39–45.

41. Robert D. Nebes, *op. cit.*, p. 104.

42. It is not clear whether McClelland's "needs" (n achievement, n affiliation, n power) emanate from the left or right hemisphere. Many of their characteristics would appear to be right hemisphere directed, however.

43. One should be careful to avoid overstating the case for "right hemisphere thinking." Most neurophysiologists and quite a few psychologists are skeptical to say the least. After setting out the neural basis for the right side providing "a sort of cognitive spatial map by which we plan our actions," Nebes maintains: "What else the minor hemisphere may do is still open to question. Lately, everything from creativity and imagination to the id, ESP, and cosmic consciousness have been suggested to reside in the right hemisphere. Many people are now attempting to superimpose upon the anatomical and functional duality of the brain many of the philosophical and spiritual dualisms which have fascinated man over the centuries. Given the results to date on hemispheric specialization, it seems natural to many researchers in related fields that the scientific and technological aspects of our civilization are products of the left hemisphere, while the mystical and humanistic aspects are products of the right. The right hemisphere has thus been enthusiastically embraced by counterculture groups as their side of the brain. They see in it the antithesis to an upright technological Western society, identifying its synthetic abilities with Eastern mystics' view of the interrelationship of all things (Ornstein, 1971). How well such a grafting of philosophy onto anatomy will stand up is unclear, but certainly right-hemisphere attributes will continue to be explored in the coming years and their role in the various phases of human life examined" (Nebes, *op. cit.*, p. 104–5). Some of the more outrageous claims seem to have prompted an empirical challenge from certain quarters (particularly medical researchers). A recent paper, for example, questions the correlation between interhemispheric asymmetries of ongoing brain electrical activity (EEG) and differences between cognitive tasks, arguing " . . . it has never been established that asymmetries or other EEG features are directly related to cognitive activities" (See A. S. Gevins, *et al.*, "Electroencephalogram Correlates of Higher Cortical Functions," *Science*, February 16, 1979, pp. 665–8). Nevertheless, there is considerable evidence that "the lateralization problem impinges upon the entire spectrum of brain-behavioral research from the synapse to the sentence" (S. Harnard, *et al.*, eds., *Lateralization in the Nervous System*, New York: Academic Press, 1977), and even findings in chemistry research are tending to support the lateralization hypothesis (see A. Oke, *et al.*, "Lateralization of Norepinephrine in Human Thalmus," *Science*, June 28, 1978, pp. 1411–3 and R. G. Robinson, "Differential Behavioral and Biochemical Effects of Right and Left Hemisphere Cerebral Infarction in the Rat," *Science*, August 17, 1979, pp. 707–10).

44. Keynes was frequently accused of "shifting ground" and reversing his position on economic matters. Harrod tells us, ". . . this may be the appropriate place to consider the failing for which he has been most widely criticized—that of inconsistency. It must be placed on record that this charge has been brought not merely by a rabble of detractors, but by many men of judgment, who were in a good position to know. The evidence is both extensive and weighty" (R. F. Harrod, *The Life of John Maynard Keynes*, Harmondsworth, Middlesex, England:

36   *American Journal of Economics and Sociology*

Penguin Books, Ltd., 1972). But what his critics fail to realize is that it took
just this sort of intellectual inquiry, free from the constraints of being logically
consistent, that enabled Keynes to produce both the *Treatise* and the *General
Theory*.

45. Susanne K. Langer, *Mind: An Essay on Human Feeling* (Baltimore: The
Johns Hopkins University Press, 1975), Vol. 1, p. 23.

Some Firms Are Larger Than Most Countries

A RANKING of the world's largest economic units into the 100 largest
lists 39 industrial corporations along with 61 countries, according to
a Conference Board analysis. Or, put another way, the ranking shows
that the 39 corporations—based in the United States, Great Britain,
France, Italy, the Netherlands, West Germany, Switzerland and Japan
—are larger as economic units than the majority of the world's countries.

Based on 1978 data (latest year for which official information is
available), the analysis shows that 18 of the corporations are based
in the U.S. and 21 in foreign countries (1). Countries are ranked
according to gross national product; companies are ranked according
to annual sales.

General Motors heads the corporate list. It is listed as the world's
23rd largest economic unit with 1978 sales of $63.2 billion. Exxon is
24th with sales of $60.3 billion in 1978. Rounding out the top ten
companies are Royal Dutch/Shell, 30th, ($44.0 billion); Ford, 31st,
($42.8 billion); Mobil, 38th, ($34.7 billion); Texaco, 42nd, ($28.6 bil-
lion); British Petroleum, 43rd, ($27.4 billion); Standard Oil of Cali-
fornia, 47th, ($23.2 billion); National Iranian Oil, 49th, ($22.8 billion)
and IBM, 52nd, ($21.1 billion).

John Hein, director of international economics at the Conference
Board and author of the analysis, points out: "When final results for
1979 arrive, the rankings are, of course, bound to change, especially
for the international oil companies. With 1979 sales of $84.4 billion,
Exxon already has emerged as the world's largest corporation and
would move into 16th place, surpassing East Germany and Iran."

The top economic units in the world are, in order, the United States
with a 1978 GNP of $2,106.9 billion; the Soviet Union ($1,046.6
billion); Japan ($727.9 billion); Germany (Federal Rep.) ($513.1
billion); France ($411.3 billion); China (324.0 billion); United King-
dom ($254.2 billion); Italy ($210.7 billion); Canada ($196.6 billion)
and Brazil ($148.9 billion).

[From JOSEPH L. NAAR for the Conference Board.]

1. *Across the Board* (New York: The Conference Board, May, 1980).

[10]

MARXISM, FUNCTIONALISM, AND GAME THEORY

The Case for Methodological Individualism

JON ELSTER

How should Marxist social analysis relate to bourgeois social science? The obvious answer is: retain and develop what is valuable, criticize and reject what is worthless. Marxist social science has followed the opposite course, however. By assimilating the principles of functionalist sociology, reinforced by the Hegelian tradition, Marxist social analysis has acquired an apparently powerful theory that in fact encourages lazy and frictionless thinking. By contrast, virtually all Marxists have rejected rational-choice theory in general and game theory in particular. Yet game theory is invaluable to any analysis of the historical process that centers on exploitation, struggle, alliances, and revolution.

This issue is related to the conflict over methodological individualism, rejected by many Marxists who wrongly link it with individualism in the ethical or political sense. By methodological individualism I mean the doctrine that all social phenomena (their structure and their change) are in principle explicable only in terms of individuals — their properties, goals, and beliefs. This doctrine is not incompatible with any of the following true statements. (a) Individuals often have goals that involve the welfare of other individuals. (b) They often have beliefs about supra-individual entities that are not reducible to beliefs about individuals. "The capitalists fear the working class" cannot be reduced to the feelings of capitalists concerning individual workers. By contrast, "The capitalists' profit is threatened by the working class" can be reduced to a complex statement about the consequences of the actions taken by individual workers.[1] (c) Many properties of individuals, such as "powerful," are irreducibly relational, so that accurate description of one individual may require reference to other individuals.[2]

Department of History, University of Oslo.

454

The insistence on methodological individualism leads to a search for microfoundations of Marxist social theory. The need for such foundations is by
now widely, but far from universally, appreciated by writers on Marxist economic theory.[3] The Marxist theory of the state or of ideologies is, by contrast, in a lamentable state. In particular, Marxists have not taken up the challenge of showing how ideological hegemony is created and entrenched at the
level of the individual. What microeconomics is for Marxist economic theory,
social psychology should be for the Marxist theory of ideology.[4] Without a
firm knowledge about the mechanisms that operate at the individual level, the
grand Marxist claims about macrostructures and long-term change are con-
demned to remain at the level of speculation.

The Poverty of Functionalist Marxism

Functional analysis[5] in sociology has a long history. The origin of functionalist explanation is probably the Christian theodicies, which reach their summit
in Leibniz: all is for the best in the best of all possible worlds; each apparent
evil has good consequences in the larger view, and is to be explained by these
consequences. The first secular proponent perhaps was Mandeville, whose
slogan "Private Vices, Public Benefits" foreshadows Merton's concept of
latent function. To Mandeville we owe the Weak Functional Paradigm: an
institution or behavioral pattern often has consequences that are (a) beneficial for some dominant economic or political structure; (b) unintended by the
actors; and (c) not recognized by the beneficiaries as owing to that behavior.
This paradigm, which we may also call the invisible-hand paradigm, is ubiquitous in the social sciences. Observe that it provides no explanation of the
institution or behavior that has these consequences. If we use "function" for
consequences that satisfy condition (a) and "latent function" for consequences that satisfy all three conditions, we can go on to state the Main Functional Paradigm: the latent functions (if any) of an institution or behavior
explain the presence of that institution or behavior. Finally, there is the
Strong Functional Paradigm: all institutions or behavioral patterns have a
function that explains their presence.

Leibniz invoked the Strong Paradigm on a cosmic scale; Hegel applied it to
society and history, but without the theological underpinning that alone
could justify it. Althusser sees merit in Hegel's recognition that history is a
"process without a subject," though for Hegel the process still has a goal.
Indeed, this is a characteristic feature of both the main and strong paradigms:
to postulate a purpose without a purposive actor or, in grammatical terms,
a predicate without a subject. (Functionalist thinkers characteristically use
the passive voice.) I shall refer to such processes guided by a purpose without

455

an intentional subject *objective teleology*. They should be distinguished from both *subjective teleology* (intentional acts with an intentional subject) and *teleonomy* (adaptive behavior fashioned by natural selection). The main difference between subjective teleology and teleonomy is that the former, but not the latter, is capable of waiting and of using indirect strategies, of the form "one step backward, two steps forwards."[6] To the extent that the Main Functional Paradigm invokes teleonomy, as in the explanation of market behavior through a natural-selection model of competition between firms, there can be no objection to it. In the many more numerous cases where no analogy with natural selection obtains, latent functions cannot explain their causes.[7] In particular, long-term positive, unintended, and unrecognized consequences of a phenomenon cannot explain it when its short-term consequences are negative.[8]

Turning to examples of functional analysis in non-Marxist social science, consider this statement by Lewis Coser: "Conflict within and between bureaucratic structures provides the means for avoiding the ossification and ritualism which threatens their form of organization."[9] If instead of "provides the means for avoiding," Coser had written "has the consequence of reducing," there could be no methodological quarrel with him. But his phrasing implies objective teleology, a simulation of human intentional adaptation without specification of a simulating mechanism. Alexander J. Field has observed that a similar functional explanation lies behind the Chicago school of "economic interpretation of the law."[10] For a somewhat grotesque example, consider a statement by Richard Posner:

> The economic case for forbidding marital dissolution out of concern for the children of the marriage is weakened if the parents love the child, for then the costs to the child of dissolution will be weighed by the parents in deciding whether to divorce, and they will divorce only if the gains to them from the divorce exceed the costs to the child, in which event the divorce will be welfare maximizing. If, as suggested earlier, love is a factor of growing importance in the production of children, this might help to *explain* why the law is moving toward easier standards for divorce.[11]

Posner and his school actually tend toward the Strong Functional Paradigm, which most sociologists have abandoned for the more subtle Main Paradigm. Merton, the leading exponent of the Main Paradigm, is also an acute critic of the Strong Paradigm.[12] In Radical and Marxist social science, however, both the crude Strong Paradigm and the less crude (but equally fallacious) Main Paradigm are flourishing. Although my main concern is with Marxism, a few comments on the closely related Radical approach may be in order. As exemplified in the work of Michel Foucault and Pierre Bourdieu, this tends to see every minute detail of social action as part of a vast design for oppression.

456

For an example, we may take Bourdieu's assertion that when intellectuals play around with language and even deliberately violate the rules of grammar, this is a strategy designed to exclude the petty-bourgeois would-be intellectuals, who believe that culture can be assimilated by learning rules and who loose their footing when they see that it is rather a matter of knowing when to break them.[13] This sounds like a conspiratorial view, but actually is closer to functionalism, as can be seen from Bourdieu's incessant use of the phrase *"tout se passe comme si."*[14] If everything happens as if intellectuals thought of nothing but retaining their monopoly, then objectively this must be what explains their behavior. This argument is a theoretical analogue of envy — arising when "our factual inability to acquire a good is wrongly interpreted as a positive action against our desire."[15]

Marx recognized the Weak Functional Paradigm, but argued that what Sartre calls "counterfinality" — the systematic production of consequences that are harmful, unintended, and unrecognized — was equally important. In addition one can certainly trace to him the Main Functional Paradigm, and in at least one passage the Strong Paradigm as well. In the *Theories of Surplus-Value,* Marx reconstructs the rational core of an adversary's argument:

> 1 . . . the various functions in bourgeois society mutually presuppose each other;
>
> 2 . . . the contradictions in material production make necessary a superstructure of ideological strata, whose activity — whether good or bad — is good, because it is necessary;
>
> 3 . . . all functions are in the service of the capitalist, and work out to his "benefit";
>
> 4 . . . even the most sublime spiritual productions should merely be granted recognition, and *apologies* for them made to the bourgeoisie, that they are presented as, and falsely proved to be, direct producers of material wealth.[16]

Although the context is ambiguous and the text far from clear, a plausible reading suggests the Strong Paradigm. All activities benefit the capitalist class, and these benefits explain their presence. This conspiratorial world view, in which all apparently innocent activities, from Sunday picnics to health care for the elderly, are explained through their function for capitalism, is not, however, pervasive in Marx's work. Much more deeply entrenched, from the level of the philosophy of history to the details of the class struggle, is the Main Paradigm.

Marx had a theory of history, embedded in a philosophy of history: an empirical theory of the four modes of production based on class division, and a speculative notion that before and after the division there was, and will be, unity. In the latter idea, clearly, there is also present the Hegelian or

457

Leibnizian[17] notion that the division is necessary to bring about the unity, and can be explained through this latent function. Marx's objective teleology is especially prominent in the 1862–63 notebooks, of which the middle third was published as the *Theories of Surplus-Value,* while the remaining parts are only now becoming available.[18] Consider in particular the argument that

> The original unity between the worker and the conditions of production . . . has two main forms. . . . Both are embryonic forms and both are equally unfitted to develop labour as *social* labour and the productive power of social labour. Hence the necessity for the separation, for the rupture, for the antithesis of labour and property . . . The most extreme form of this rupture, and the one in which the productive forces of social labour are also most fully developed, is capital. The original unity can be reestablished only on the material foundations which capital creates and by means of the revolutions which, in the process of this creation, the working class and the whole society undergoes.[19]

Elsewhere Marx states that "insofar as it is the coercion of capital which forces the great mass of society to this [surplus labour] beyond its immediate needs, capital creates culture and exercises an historical and social function."[20] He also quotes one of his favorite verses from Goethe:

> Sollte diese Qual uns quälen,
> Da sie unsre Lust vermehrt,
> Hat nicht Myriaden Seelen
> Timur's Herrschaft aufgezehrt?[21]

It is difficult, although perhaps not impossible, to read these passages otherwise than as statements of an objective teleology. Marx, as all Hegelians, was obsessed with *meaning.* If class society and exploitation are necessary for the creation of communism, this lends them a significance that also has explanatory power. In direct continuation, Marx can also argue that various institutions of the capitalist era can be explained by their functions for capitalism, as in this analysis of social mobility:

> The circumstance that a man without fortune but possessing energy, solidity, ability and business acumen may become a capitalist in this manner [i.e., by receiving credit] and the commercial value of each individual is pretty accurately estimated under the capitalist mode of production – is greatly admired by the apologists of the capitalist system. Although this circumstance continually brings an unwelcome number of new soldiers of fortune into the field and into competition with the already existing individual capitalists, it also reinforces the supremacy of capital itself, expands its base and enables it to recruit ever new forces for itself out of the substratum of society. In a similar way, the circumstance that the Catholic Church in the Middle Ages formed its hierarchy out of the best brains in the land, regardless of their estate, birth or fortune, was one of the principal means of consolidating ecclesiastical rule and suppressing the laity. The more a ruling class is able to assimilate the foremost minds of a ruled class, the more stable and dangerous becomes its rule.[22]

458

By using the word "means" in the penultimate sentence, Marx suggests that the beneficial effects of mobility also explain it. In this case the explanatory assertion, although unsubstantiated, might be true, because the Catholic Church was in fact a corporate body, able to promote its interests by deliberate action. This cannot be true of social mobility under capitalism, however, because the capitalist class is not in this sense a corporate body, shaping and channeling everything for its own benefit. That mobility may have favorable consequences for "capital" is neither here nor there, as capital has no eyes that see or hands that move. Indeed, the German "capital logic" school represents a flagrant violation of the principle of methodological individualism, when it asserts or suggests that the needs of capital somehow bring about their own fulfillment.[23]

There is, however, one way in which the capitalist class may promote its collective interests: through the state. Here we confront the difficulty of specifying the capitalist character of the state in a capitalist society. Marx did not believe that the concrete states of the nineteenth century were a direct outgrowth and instrument of capitalist class rule. On the contrary, he argued that it was in the interest of the capitalist class to have a noncapitalist government — rule by the aristocracy in England, by the Emperor and his bureaucracy in France. It was useful for the English capitalists to let the aristocracy remain in power, so that the political struggle between rulers and ruled would blur the lines of economic struggle between exploiters and exploited.[24] Similarly, capitalism on the European continent could only survive with a state that apparently stood above the classes. In these analyses Marx asserts that the noncapitalist state was beneficial for capitalism. He never states or implies that this benefit was deliberately brought about by the capitalist class, and yet he strongly suggests that it explains the presence of the noncapitalist state:

> The bourgeoisie confesses that its own interests dictate that it should be delivered from the danger of its *own rule;* that in order to restore the tranquillity in the country its bourgeois Parliament must, first of all, be given its quietus; that in order to preserve its social power intact its political power must be broken; that the individual bourgeois can continue to exploit the other classes and enjoy undisturbed property, family, religion and order only on condition that his class be condemned along with the other classes to like political nullity; that in order to save its purse it must forfeit the crown, and the sword that is to safeguard it must at the same time be hung over its own head as the sword of Damocles.[25]

I defy anyone to read this text without understanding it as an *explanation* of the Bonapartist régime. What else is it but a functional explanation? The anticapitalist state is the indirect strategy whereby the capitalists retain their economic dominance: one step backward, two steps forward. But an explanation in terms of latent functions can never invoke strategic considerations of this kind. "Long-term functionalism" suffers from all the defects of ordinary functional explanations, notably the problem of a purpose in search of a purposive actor. Moreover, it is *arbitrary,* because the manipulation of the time dimension nearly always lets us find a way in which a given pattern is good for capitalism; *ambiguous,* because the distinction between the short and the long term may be read either as a distinction between transitional effects and steady-state effects, or as a distinction between two kinds of steady-state effects;[26] and *inconsistent,* because positive long-term effects could never dominate negative short-term effects in the absence of an intentional actor. It is not possible, then, to identify the state in a capitalist society as a capitalist state simply by virtue of its favorable consequences for bourgeois economic dominance.

From Marx I now turn to some recent Marxist writings. Consider first some writings by Marxist historians. In an otherwise important study, John Foster makes the following argument:

> The basic function of feudal social organization was, therefore, to maintain just that balance between population and land which (given technological conditions) would produce the biggest possible feudal surplus. . . . It was enough to ensure that [peasant] marriage and childrearing were strictly tied (by customary practice and religion) to the inheritance of land, and rely on peasant self-interest to do the rest.[27]

By what is the subject of the verbs "ensure" and "rely" in the last sentence? This is clearly a case of objective teleology, of an action in search of an actor.

E. P. Thompson writes that in pre-industrial England there were recurring revolts which, although usually unsuccessful in achieving their immediate objectives, had long-term success in making the propertied classes behave more moderately than they would have otherwise. He also seems to conclude that long-term success provides an (intentional or functional) explanation of the revolts. This, at any rate, is how I interpret his rhetorical question of whether the revolts "would have continued over so many scores, indeed hundreds of years, if they had consistently failed to achieve their objective."[28] If functional, the explanation fails for reasons by now familiar. If intentional, it fails for reasons related to a crucial difference between individual and collective action. If an individual acts in a way that he knows to be in his interest, we may conclude that he acted for the sake of that interest. But when a group of individuals act in a way that is to their collective benefit, we cannot conclude that they did so to bring about that benefit.[29]

The attempt to read meaning into behavior that benefits the actors can take one of three distinct forms. First, the functionalist, discussed above. Second,

460

the consequences can be transformed into motives, as in the example from Thompson. This inference, although not always incorrect, is unwarranted in the cases where the benefits emerge only if the actions are performed by *all* the actors concerned, yet the *individual* has no incentive to perform them. For instance, it is beneficial for the capitalist class as a whole if all capitalists search for labor-saving inventions, for then the aggregate demand for labor and hence the wage rate will fall. And it may well be true that historically there has been a trend to labor-saving inventions. Yet the collective benefits cannot explain the trend, for they could never motivate the individual capitalist who, under conditions of perfect competition, is unable to influence the overall wage level. The trend, if there is one, must be explained by some other mechanism, of which the collective benefits are accidental byproducts. Third, one may invoke a conspiratorial design and seek one unifying but hidden intention behind the structure to be explained. Thus, if a pattern such as social mobility benefits the capitalist class as a whole, but not the "already existing individual capitalists," the conspiratorial explanation postulates a secret executive committee of the bourgeoisie. I do not deny that conspiracies occur, or that their existence may be asserted on indirect evidence. I simply argue the need for evidence — preferably direct or, if this is not available, as in the nature of the case it may not be, indirect — pointing to some hidden coordinating hand. Simply to invoke beneficial consequences supplies no such evidence.

Turning now from Marxist history to Marxist social science proper, we find that functionalism is rampant. Functional explanations pervade the theory of crime and punishment,[30] the analysis of education,[31] the study of racial discrimination,[32] and (most important) the analysis of the capitalist state, a Marxist growth industry during the last decade. Not all Marxist studies fall victim to the functionalist fallacies identified above, but most Marxist authors seem to believe that "everything that happens in a capitalist society necessarily corresponds to the needs of capital accumulation,"[33] so that the "correspondence between the actions (and structure) of the state and the requirements of capital accumulation [is] taken for granted."[34] Alternately, the "assumption is made that the capitalist state is universally functional for reproducing the dominance of the capitalist class."[35] These neo-Marxist works appear to be guided by the following principles. (i) All actions of the state serve the collective interest of the capitalist class. (ii) Any action that would serve the collective interest of the capitalist class is in fact undertaken by the state. (iii) Exceptions to the first principle are explained by "the relative autonomy of the state." (iv) Exceptions to the second principle are explained along the lines of Marx in the *Eighteenth Brumaire:* it is in the political interest of the bourgeoisie that the state should not always act in the

461

economic interest of the bourgeoisie. Needless to say, the effect of the last two clauses is to render the first two virtually vacuous. In a seminal article Michal Kalecki[36] raised some of the issues that came to the forefront in recent debates, particularly concerning the limits of state intervention to save capitalism from itself. To the question of why industrial leaders should oppose government spending to achieve full employment, he offers three answers, the two most important of which are these. First,

> under a *laisser-faire* system the level of employment depends to a great extent on the so-called state of confidence. . . . This gives to the capitalists a powerful indirect control over Government policy: everything which may shake the state of confidence must be carefully avoided because it would cause an economic crisis. But once the Government learns the trick of increasing employment by its own purchases, this powerful controlling device loses its effectiveness. Hence budget deficits necessary to carry out the Government intervention must be regarded as perilous. The social function of the doctrine of "sound finance" is to make the level of employment dependent on the "state of confidence."

Second, Kalecki argues that capitalists not only oppose this way of overcoming the crisis, but actually need the crisis itself:

> [under] a regime of permanent full employment, "the sack" would cease to play its role as a disciplinary measure. The social position of the boss would be undermined and the self-assurance and class consciousness of the working class would grow. Strikes for wage increases and improvements in conditions of work would create political tension. It is true that profits would be higher under a regime of full employment than they are on the average under *laisser-faire;* and even the rise in wage rates resulting from the stronger bargaining power of the workers is less likely to reduce profits than to increase prices, and thus affects adversely only the rentier interests. But "discipline in the factories" and "political stability" are more appreciated by business leaders than profits. Their class instinct tells them that lasting full employment is unsound from their point of view and that unemployment is an integral part of the normal capitalist system.

In conclusion Kalecki states that "one of the important functions of fascism, as typified by the Nazi system, was to remove the capitalist objection to full employment." To the extent that this thesis is only a variation on the inherent dilemma of the capitalist class — *Et propter vitam vivendi perdere causas*[37] — there can be no objection to it. As admirably explained in the work of Amid Bhaduri,[38] the ruling class often faces a change that gives short-term economic profit but has adverse long-term political (and hence economic) effects. But Kalecki never says whether his analysis is intentional or functional, in addition to being causal. He does make the case for a causal relation between unemployment and the interests of capital, but how does the latter explain the former? As any serious historian can imagine, a mass of detailed evidence is required to make an intentional explanation credible — hence the strong temptation to take the functionalist short cut.

462

Many contemporary Marxists think the state has three main functions: repression, legitimation, and creating the conditions for accumulation. Whereas traditional Marxists stress the first function, their modern counterparts assert the importance of the second. Indeed, legitimation is viewed as "symbolic violence" that in modern societies is the functional equivalent of repression. The state exerts its legitimating function through "ideological apparatuses" (e.g., education) and the provision of social welfare. The state's function for capital accumulation is mainly to help the capitalist class overcome the particular interests of individual capitalists. In fact, the state is sometimes said to represent "capital in general," which is (logically) prior to the many individual capitals.[39] This of course is a drastic violation of the tenet of methodological individualism defended here. True, there is often a need for concerted capitalist action, but the need does not create its own fulfillment. The necessary collective action may fail to materialize even if seen as possible and desirable, because of the free-rider problem, and *a fortiori* if the need and possibility go unperceived. Failures of cartelization, of standardization, of wage coordination take place all the time in capitalist societies. Moreover, even when the actions of the state serve the interests of capital against those of individual capitalists, evidence must be given to show that this consequence has explanatory power — i.e., that there exists a mechanism by which state policy is shaped by the collective interest of the capitalist class. The mechanism need not be intentional design[40] — but *some* mechanism must be provided if the explanation is to be taken seriously.

Examples of the Marxist-functionalist analysis of the state abound in the German tradition of Altvater or the French manner of Poulantzas. In the United States Marxist functionalism is best represented by James O'Connor's influential *The Fiscal Crisis of the State,* from which the following passage is taken:

> The need to develop and maintain a "responsible" social order also has led to the creation of agencies and programs designed to control the surplus population politically and to fend off the tendency toward a legitimization crisis. The government attempts to administer and bureaucratize (encapsulate) not only monopoly sector labor-management conflict, but also social-political conflict emerging from competitive sector workers and the surplus population. The specific agencies for regulating the relations between capital and organized labor and unorganized workers are many and varied. . . . Some of these agencies were established primarily to maintain social control of the surplus population (e.g. HEW's Bureau of Family Services); others serve mainly to attempt to maintain harmony between labor and capital within the monopoly sector (e.g., the Bureau of Old Age and Survivors Insurance). In both cases the state must remain independent or "distant" from the particular interests of capital (which are very different from the politically organized interests of capital as the ruling class). The basic problem is to win mass loyalty to insure legitimacy; too intimate a relation between capital and state normally is unacceptable or inadmissible to the ordinary person.[41]

463

Note the implicit three-tier structure of capital interests: (1) the interest of the individual capitalist out to maximize profits come what may; (2) the interest of the capitalist class, which may have to curb the individual's greed; and (3) the interest of Capital, which may have to dissociate itself from class interests to ensure legitimacy. It is not surprising that *any* given state action can be viewed from one of these perspectives. O'Connor's scheme suggests the following methodological principle: if crude class interests will not do the explanatory job, then — but only then — invoke subtle class interests. This makes Marxism invulnerable to empirical disconfirmation, and nullifies its scientific interest.

Obviously, an alternative approach is required. Having given my views elsewhere,[42] let me summarize them briefly. (1) There are three main types of scientific explanation: the *causal,* the *functional,* and the *intentional.* (2) All sciences use causal analysis. The physical sciences use causal analysis exclusively. (3) The biological sciences also use functional analysis, when explaining the structure or behavior of organisms through the benefits for reproduction. This procedure is justified by the theory of natural selection, according to which such beneficial effects tend to maintain their own causes. Intentional analysis, on the other hand, is not justified in biology — because natural selection is basically myopic, opportunistic, and impatient, as opposed to the capacity for strategic and patient action inherent in intentional actors. (4) The social sciences make extensive use of intentional analysis, at the level of individual actions. Functional analysis, however, has no place in the social sciences, because there is no sociological analogy to the theory of natural selection. (5) The proper paradigm for the social sciences is a mixed causal-intentional explanation — *intentional understanding* of the individual *actions,* and *causal explanation* of their *interaction.* (6) Individuals also interact intentionally. And here — in the study of the intentional interaction between intentional individuals — is where game theory comes in. The need for game theory arises as soon as individual actors cease to regard each other as given constraints on their actions, and instead regard each other as intentional beings. In parametric rationality each person looks at himself as a variable and at all others as constants, whereas in strategic rationality all look upon each other as variables. The essence of strategic thought is that no one can regard himself as privileged compared to the others: each has to decide on the assumption that the others are rational to the same extent as himself.

The Uses of Game Theory in Marxist Analysis

The basic premises of rational choice theory[43] are (1) that structural constraints do not completely determine the actions taken by individuals in a

464

society, and (2) that within the feasible set of actions compatible with all the
constraints, individuals choose those they believe will bring the best results. If
the first premise is denied, we are left with some variety of structuralism — an
element of which reasoning is present in Marx, and is most fully developed
in French Structuralism. Although it may occasionally be true that the feasible set shrinks to a single point, a general theory to this effect cannot be
defended — unless by the ptolemaic twist of counting preferences or ideologies among the constraints. True, the ruling class often manipulates the constraints facing the ruled class so as to leave it no choice, but this very manipulation itself presupposes some scope of choice for the rulers. If the second
premise is denied, we are left with some variety of role theory, according to
which individuals behave as they do because they have been socialized to,
rather than because they try to realize some goal: causality vs. intentionality.
Against this I would argue that what people acquire by socialization is not
quasicompulsive tendencies to act in specific ways, but preference structures
that — jointly with the feasible set — bring it about that some specific action
is chosen. If the role theory was correct, it would be impossible to induce
behavior modification by changing the feasible set (e.g., the reward structure), but clearly such manipulation is an omnipresent fact of social life.[44]

Game theory is a recent and increasingly important branch of rational choice
theory, stressing the *interdependence of decisions.* If all violence were structural, class interests purely objective, and class conflict nothing but incompatible class interests, then game theory would have nothing to offer to
Marxism. But because classes crystallize into collective actors that confront
each other over the distribution of income and power, as well as over the
nature of property relations, and as there are also strategic relations between
members of a given class, game theory is needed to explain these complex
interdependencies. In a "game" there are several players or actors. Each actor
must adopt an action or a strategy. When all actors have chosen strategies,
each obtains a reward that depends on the strategies chosen by him *and* by
the others. *The reward of each depends on the choice of all.* The notion of a
reward can be understood narrowly or broadly. In the narrow interpretation
it signifies the material benefit received by each actor. In the broad interpretation, it covers everything in the situation of value to the actor, including
(possibly) the rewards to other actors. *The reward of each depends on the
reward of all.*[45] It is assumed that the actors strive to maximize their reward —
to bring about a situation they prefer to other situations. When an actor
chooses a strategy, he must take account of what the others will do. A strategy that is optimal against one set of strategies on the part of the others is not
necessarily optimal against another set. To arrive at his decision, therefore, he
has to *foresee their decisions,* knowing that they are trying to foresee his. *The*

choice of each depends on the choice of all. The triumph of game theory is its ability to embrace simultaneously the three sets of interdependencies stated in the italicized sentences.[46] Nothing could be further from the truth, then, than the allegation that game theory portrays the individual as an isolated and egoistic atom.

An essential element of the situation is the *information* that the actors possess about each other. In games with perfect information, each individual has complete information about all relevant aspects of the situation. These include the capabilities of the other actors, their preferences, their information, and the payoff structure that maps sets of individual strategies into outcomes. The condition of perfect information is likely to be realized only in small and stable groups, or in groups with a coordinating instance. Also crucial is the notion of an *equilibrium point* — a set of strategies in which the strategy of each actor is optimal vis-à-vis those of the others. It is thanks to this notion that game theory can avoid the infinite regress of "I think that he thinks that I think . . ." which plagued early attempts to understand the logic of interdependency. The notion of a *solution* can be defined through that of an equilibrium point. Informally, the solution to a game is the set of strategies toward which rational actors with perfect information will tacitly converge. If there is only one equilibrium point, it will automatically emerge as the solution — it is the only stable outcome, in the sense that no one gains from defection. If there are several such equilibria, the solution will be the one that is collectively optimal — the equilibrium point preferred by all to all the others. Not all games have solutions in this sense.

A brief typology of games may be useful. One basic distinction is between two-person and n-person games, both of which are important for Marxism. The struggle between capital and labor is a two-person game, the struggle between members of the capitalist class an n-person game. Often, however, complicated n-person games can be reduced without too much loss of generality to simpler two-person games — as games played between "me" and "everybody else."[47] The simplest two-person games are zero-sum games, in which the loss of one player exactly equals the gain of the other. This is the only category of games that always have a solution. The conceptual breakthrough that made proof of this proposition possible was the introduction of *mixed strategies,* i.e., the choice of a strategy according to some (optimal) probability distribution. In poker, for instance, a player may decide to bluff in one half of the cases, a policy implemented by tossing a coin in each case. Here the opponent may calculate how often the player will bluff, but not whether he will do so in any particular case. In variable-sum games not only the distribution of the rewards, but also the size of the total to be distributed,

466

depends on the strategies chosen. These games can be further divided into games of pure cooperation and games of mixed conflict and cooperation (whereas zero-sum games are games of pure conflict). Not all variable-sum games have a solution in the sense indicated above. They can, however, have a solution once we take the step from noncooperative to cooperative games. In cooperative games — which should not be confused with the (noncooperative) games of pure cooperation — there is joint rather than individual choice of strategies. The actors can coordinate their choices so as to avoid certain disastrous combinations of individual strategies. If there is a choice between left-hand and right-hand driving, the actors may agree to toss a coin between both driving on the right and both driving on the left — a *jointly-mixed strategy*. If they toss a coin individually, the chances are 50% thay they will end up on a collision course.

The value of the cooperative approach to game theory is contested because it appears to beg the question by assuming that agreements to cooperate will be enforced. On general grounds of methodological individualism, noncooperative games are prior to cooperative games. Assuming that the actors will arrive at a cooperative solution is much like assuming that a functional need will create its own fulfillment. For this reason, and also because there are so many solution concepts for cooperative games, one will have to tread carefully when explaining the emergence of cooperative behavior in terms of cooperative games. Properly used, however, the method can yield important results, and in any case is fruitful for the purpose of normative analysis. For n-person games, the cooperative approach does not involve universal cooperation, but rather the cooperation of some actors against the others. The theory of coalitions in n-person game theory is an increasingly important branch of game theory for economic, political, and normative analysis.[48] The simplest solution concept for such games is that of the "core" — the set of all reward distributions in which no coalition of individuals can improve their lot by breaking out and acting on their own. Once again, the cooperative approach begs the question by assuming that coalitions can be formed and maintained whenever needed. And, once again, this is more an objection to the analytical-explanatory than to the normative use of the theory.

Turning now from exposition to applications, I discuss in turn the logic of solidarity and cooperation within classes, the problem of worker-capitalist coalitions, and some static and dynamic aspects of the class struggle. These applications all presuppose that we have left behind us — if it ever existed — the capitalism of perfect competition, unorganized capital and unorganized labor. The income distribution that would emerge under perfect competition can serve as a baseline for comparison with the distributions that result when

467

one or both of the main classes behave in an organized and strategic manner. Whether the classes will so behave is itself a question to be decided by game-theoretic analysis. I define class consciousness as the capacity of a class to behave as a collective actor. Operationally, this means the capacity to overcome the free-rider problem. This problem arises within both the capitalist and the working classes. As well explained by Mancur Olson,[49] each worker is tempted by the prospect of a free ride, of benefitting from the strikes fought by the other workers without taking part in the action himself. Similarly, capitalists face the same difficulty with regard to cartelization, wage policy, etc. If, however, we want to penetrate past these generalities to the fine grain of the problem, some distinctions must be made. I assume that each actor within the class has a choice between a *solidary strategy* (S) and an *egoist strategy* (E). In the artificial two-person game between "me" and "everybody else," four possibilities can be distinguished:

A. Universal cooperation: everybody uses S

B. Universal egoism: everybody uses E

C. The free rider: "I" use E, "everybody else" uses S

D. The sucker: "I" use S, "everybody else" uses E.

Every individual in the society will rank these outcomes in a particular order, according to what he − in the role of "I" − would prefer. Excluding ties, there are twenty-four possible rankings of these four alternatives.[50] If we disregard all that rank B before A, as we are permitted to do by the very nature of the problem under discussion, we are left with twelve cases. If we then exclude the "masochistic" cases that have D ranked above A, we are left with eight alternatives. I shall limit myself to four cases that have a central place in the literature on collective action. I shall also limit myself to the hypothesis that each "I" views the situation in the same way. Although mixed cases will be the rule in actual situations, the assumption of homogeneity makes for a more tractable analysis.[51]

The first case is the well-known Prisoners' Dilemma, defined by the ranking CABD and characterized by the following features. (1) Strategy E is dominant, i.e., for each actor it is the best choice regardless of what the others will do. Here, then, we need not impose any stringent information requirement for the solution to be realized. Also, it is not true here that "the choice of each depends on the choice of all." In a sense, therefore, it is a rather trivial game. (2) The solution to the game is universal egoism, which everybody ranks below universal cooperation. Individual rationality leads to collective disaster. (3) Universal cooperation is neither individually stable nor individually accessible: everybody will take the first step away from it, and no one

468

the first step toward it. We can apply this to the workers' predicament. For the individual there is no point in going on strike if his fellow workers do so, for by remaining at work he can derive the benefit from their action *and* be (highly) paid during the strike — and if they do not strike he has nothing to gain and much to lose by unilateral action.

Is there a "way out" of the Prisoners' Dilemma? Can individuals caught in this situation overcome the dilemma and behave cooperatively? No consensus has emerged from the extensive literature, but I believe that in the present context two approaches stand out as the most promising. In the case of working-class cooperation the most plausible explanation is by change of the preference structure. Through continued interaction the workers become both concerned and informed about each other. Concern for others changes the ranking of the alternatives, and information about others enables the actors to realize the solution of the ensuing game. This is the "Assurance Game," defined by the ranking ACBD and possessing the following features. (1) There is no dominant strategy in this game. Egoism is "my" best reply to egoism, solidarity the best reply to solidarity. (2) The optimum of universal cooperation is individually stable, but not individually accessible. (3) Universal egoism and universal solidarity are both, therefore, equilibrium points in the game. Because universal cooperation is preferred by all to universal egoism, the former emerges as the solution to the game. (4) Because there is no dominant strategy, the solution will be realized only if there is perfect information. Imperfect information — about preferences or information — easily leads to uncertainty, suspicion, and play-safe behavior. Amartya Sen has argued that Marx's *Critique of the Gotha Programme* can be interpreted in terms of the Assurance Game.[52] Solidarity can substitute for material incentives. I would tend to believe that quite generally working-class solidarity and collective action can be understood in these terms, although I shall later point to an alternative explanation.

Although the Prisoners' Dilemma and the Assurance Game differ profoundly in their structure, behavior — in cases of incomplete information — may occur *as if* the preferences were a Prisoner's Dilemma when in fact they form an Assurance Game. In tax evasion or suboptimal use of public transportation, for instance, the observed outcome may be the result of lack of information rather than of free-rider egoism. Likewise, the Assurance Game preferences should be distinguished from those of the Categorical Imperative, although behaviorally they may be indistinguishable. The Categorical Imperative is defined by the ranking ADBC, with solidarity as a dominant strategy. The history of the working class shows, in my opinion, that cooperative behavior typically is conditional rather than unconditional — motivated by the concern

469

for doing one's share of a common task rather than by the spirit of sacrifice or disregard for actual consequences characteristic of the Categorical Imperative. Indeed, more harm than good sometimes ensues from heroic individual acts of revolt or disobedience, if the others are not willing to follow suit, because such acts may provide the authorities or the employers the excuse they need to crack down further on the workers. This, I believe, shows that Kant's individualistic ethic is not appropriate for collective action.[53]

The Assurance Game also provides an interpretation of Charles Taylor's notion of *common meaning*, designed to elucidate the meaning of consensus. In his polemic against methodological individualism Taylor asserts there are two forms of meaning that are irreducibly nonsubjective: the intersubjective meanings and the common meanings. Intersubjective meanings are, roughly, rules for social behavior whose negation cannot be generalized without contradiction. Thus promises should be kept because the notion of a society in which promises were never kept is logically contradictory. Common meanings illustrate the Assurance Game. Taylor distinguishes common meanings from shared subjective meanings by saying that "what is required for common meanings is that this shared value be part of the common world, that *this sharing itself be shared.*"[54] The phrase I have italicized amounts to a condition of perfect information. For a consensus to be a living force, it must be known to exist. Everybody acts in a solidary manner because of knowing that the others are going to do so as well. This way of looking at consensus enables us to refute the following claim made by Taylor:

> Common meanings, as well as intersubjective meanings, fall through the net of mainstream social science. They can find no place in its categories. For they are not simply a converging set of subjective reactions, but part of the common world. What the ontology of mainstream social science lacks, is the notion of meaning as not simply for an individual subject; of a subject who can be a "we" as well as an "I".[55]

Game theory provides what Taylor claims is lacking — the notion of a subject that can be a "we" as well as an "I". Through the triple interdependence that game theory analyzes — between rewards, between choices, and between rewards and choices — the individual emerges as a microcosm epitomizing the whole network of social relations. A similar demystification makes good sense of Sartre's notion of the "group," even though he claims it cannot be rendered in the "neo-positivist" language of "analytical reason."[56]

Arthur Stinchcombe analyzes Trotsky's account of the October Revolution in terms that fit this analysis of solidarity. The key idea in Stinchcombe's explanation is the breakdown of authority in the prerevolutionary situation. The old authority breaks down when new social orders become thinkable, i.e., real

470

possibilities. The "Revolution grows by the exploration of these possibilities, and by the communication of there being possibilities to those who would support them, 'if only they knew they were really Bolsheviks'."[57] When the workers and the soldiers, especially, come to believe that change is possible, change becomes possible:

> The fickleness of the masses during a revolution thus takes on a completely different interpretation. Trotsky's sarcasm about spontaneity as an explanation of the movements is essentially an assertion that the explanations of the masses about why they are doing what they are doing are going to be reasonable, but that reasonableness is going to be based on their estimates of the probabilities that (a) this institution or authority will pursue my goals; or (b) this institution or authority is the best I am likely to find, because no alternatives are possible or because the alternatives are in the hand of the enemy. And it is these probabilities that fluctuate wildly during a revolution but are reasonably stable during times of governmental quiescence.[58]

Revolutions succeed when these probabilities cease to fluctuate wildly and settle into some new and stable pattern because uncertainty, suspicion, and play-safe thinking no longer are predominant. Tacit coordination that becomes possible when people come to trust each other is the essential condition for successful collective action. The role of the revolutionary leader is to provide the information that makes this tacit coordination possible, rather than to be a center of command and authority. This view constitutes an alternative to the Leninist theory of revolutionary leadership. Mancur Olson,[59] following Lenin, assumes that the only possible motivational structures are the free-rider egoism of the Prisoners' Dilemma and the unconditional altruism of the Categorical Imperative. Rightly rejecting the latter as wishful thinking, and observing that the former can never bring about collective action, he concludes that strikes or revolutions can only be brought about from above, through discipline verging on coercion. But the conditional altruism of the Assurance Game is also a possible motivational structure, which may lead to collective action by tacit coordination, given information provided by the leaders.

The problem of capitalist class solidarity requires different tools. We can hardly assume that interaction between capitalists will make them care about each other and change their motivations. Nor can we assume that the structure of their coordination problems invariably is that of a Prisoners' Dilemma. As to the last question, we can return to the issue of labor-saving inventions, which illustrates the ranking CADB.[60] This game has the paradoxical feature that the optimum is individually accessible, but not individually stable. When everyone uses E, it is in the interest of each actor to use S, but when everyone uses S, it is in the interest of each to switch to E. The game, in fact, has no solution. If no other capitalists seek labor-saving inventions, wages can be

471

expected to rise, which makes it rational for the individual capitalist to preempt the wage rise by saving on labor — but if all capitalists do this, the individual capitalist has no incentive to do so. Clearly, this inherent contradiction sets up a pressure for concerted action,[61] which may or may not be realized.

I have assumed that for the individual capitalists there are costs associated with the search for labor-saving inventions, as distinct from the search for inventions in general. If we drop this assumption, the resulting interaction structure takes the following form. Each capitalist is indifferent between A and C, but prefers both to B and D, between which he is also indifferent. This, again, offers a crucial scope for the exercise of leadership. The task of the business leaders will be to persuade the individual entrepreneurs to act in a way that is neither harmful nor beneficial from their private viewpoint, but which brings about collective benefits when adopted by all. Leadership, then, is to make use of the "zone of indifference" of the individuals.[62]

These problems are hardly discussed in the literature. By contrast, there are many discussions of capitalist Prisoners' Dilemmas, mainly in the context of cartelization. For each firm the best option is to have a high output at the high prices made possible by the cartel restrictions on the output, but such free-rider behavior will of course make the cartel break up, or its anticipation prevent the cartel from forming. Yet cartels sometimes do form without immediately breaking up. This often happens because of asymmetries among the firms. A large firm will be strongly motivated to adopt the cartel policy even if the others do not follow suit, because it can internalize more of the benefits.[63] Moreover, it will typically possess the economic power to retaliate against firms that do not follow suit. But even in competitive markets with many identical firms, cartelization may occur by voluntary and selfish action. This may be explained by the theory of "supergames," or repeated Prisoners' Dilemmas.[64] When the same actors play a Prisoners' Dilemma over and over again, the possibility of retaliation against free riders may make it rational to cooperate. It is easy to see that this will occur only if the number of iterations is indefinite. If the actors know when the games come to an end, there will be no reason for cooperation in the very last game, because no retaliation can take place afterwards if they defect. But this means that for the purposes of decision the penultimate game can be treated as the last, to which the same reasoning applies, and so on in argument that inexorably zips back to the first game. According to John Bowman, this explains the failure of Roosevelt's National Recovery Act: "Voluntary cooperation in the Prisoners' Dilemma is possible only when the supergame is of indefinite length. The N.R.A. had a terminal date. Thus it was in the best interests of every conditional cooperator to break the code provisions before his competitors did."[65]

472

Explanations in terms of supergames may also apply to working-class cooperation, though less plausibly. I believe anyone familiar with the history
of the working class will agree that solidarity is not merely enlightened long-
term selfishness. Operationally, the issue could be decided by looking at cases
in which the working-class interaction was known to have a terminal date, as in
the National Recovery Act, and see whether this had any stifling effects on
cooperation and solidarity. For solidarity among the workers to emerge, it is
crucial that they interact for some time, because otherwise the mutual concern and knowledge will not have time to be shaped. But there should be no
reason to believe that solidarity requires a cooperation of indefinite length,
if my account is correct. In perfectly competitive capitalism, as I have argued
elsewhere, workers are doubly alienated — from the means of production and
from the products of their labor.[66] Alienation from the means of production
stems from the alienation of the workers from their own history, i.e., from
past generations of workers who produced the means of production currently
used. The alienation from the products stems from their alienation from the
class to which they belong, and permits the capitalist to treat each worker as
if he were "the marginal worker," in the economic sense of that term, and to
pay him according to marginal productivity. Only by overcoming this double
alienation, by taking possession of their past history and by acting jointly as a
class, can the workers achieve class consciousness that goes beyond wage
claims to make a radical rupture with capitalist relations.

What happens if the workers overcome the alienation from their class, but not
that from their history — if they see through the "marginalist illusion," but
not the "presentist illusion"? This partial liberation distinguishes the modern
capitalist societies of the social democratic variety, in which working-class
organizations negotiate with employer associations over the division of the
net product. Because the basic assumption behind this bargaining is that capital, as a "factor of production" on a par with labor, has a right to some part
of the product, the only issue of the class struggle becomes the *size* of that
part, not its existence. Take first the simplest case, in which we disregard the
question of reinvestment out of profits. In this purely static setting, workers
do not ask what use is made of the surplus value extracted from them. If they
could get the whole net product and spend it immediately, they would. But
they cannot. The problem, then, is one of dividing a jointly-made product
between the producers. It is, clearly, a mixed conflict-cooperation game, in
which the strategies determine both the total product and how it is to be
divided. Both parties have threats — strikes and lockouts — that are characteristically double-edged: they enhance the probability of getting a large share
of the total, but reduce the total to be shared. In such bargaining each side
has a lower limit beneath which it cannot go, e.g., subsistence for the workers

473

and a minimal profit for the capitalists. And the sum of these limits is smaller than the total to be shared. In other words, there is a set of possible divisions that are compatible with the last-ditch demands of both classes, and over which the bargaining takes place.

There is no way the two groups can converge tacitly in a pair of demands that exactly exhaust the total product. The game has no noncooperative solution. Considerations other than purely rational calculation must, therefore, decide the outcome. Bargaining theory addresses this problem. Its general assumption is that the actors must form some psychological hypotheses about each other, even if these cannot be rationally justified. Indeed, according to some bargaining models, each actor at each step of the process believes himself to be one step ahead of the other.[67] The mutual inconsistency of these beliefs do not, however, necessarily prevent the sequence of demands and counterdemands from converging toward some division of the product, which is then the outcome of the bargaining process.

Of the many varieties of bargaining theory,[68] one has received general attention and is uniquely interesting from the methodological point of view. This is the Zeuthen-Nash theory, named after the authors who proposed two radically different versions, which John Harsanyi later proved to be mathematically equivalent.[69] The Nash version offers an axiomatic method of finding the normatively justified outcome for two-person cooperative games, whereas the Zeuthen method offers a step-by-step method, taking us through claims and counterclaims to a uniquely determined outcome. Because both versions lead to the same result, we can use cooperative game theory without coming into conflict with methodological individualism. We do not, that is, simply *assume* that the cooperative outcome will be realized simply because there is a *need* for it; rather we exhibit *a causal mechanism whereby it will be achieved.* The Nash solution is determined by assuming that a certain number of conditions are fulfilled. First, it should not make any difference to the outcome whether the rewards are measured on one particular utility scale among the many scales that are positive linear transformations of each other. To explain the last expression, it should suffice to point out that the Celsius and Fahrenheit temperature scales are positive linear transformations of each other, differing only in the choice of zero and in the unit of measurement. Secondly, the outcome should be Pareto-optimal, so that it is impossible to improve the situation of one actor without harming that of another. Thirdly, it should be symmetrical, in the sense that equally powerful actors should get equal rewards. Lastly, it should satisfy the "condition of the independence of irrelevant alternatives," stipulating that adding new alternatives to the bargaining situation can only change the outcome if the new outcome is

474

one of the new options. The addition of a new alternative, that is, can never make a different old alternative emerge as the outcome.

Nash's theorem states there is only one division of the product that satisfies these conditions — viz, the division that maximizes the mathematical product of the rewards. From the way these rewards are measured,[70] a further feature of the solution follows: it typically accords the largest portion of the jointly made product to the most powerful actor. This is the "Matthew effect" in bargaining theory: to him that hath, shall be given. For a poor actor, even a small gain is so important that he can be made to be content with it, whereas the more affluent can say with equanimity, "Take it or leave it." The Matthew effect may itself be seen as a form of exploitation,[71] or at least as contrary to distributive justice, which rather demands that the least advantaged person should be given more.[72] This inequity, however, is secondary, because there is no normative basis for the capitalist class to get anything at all. In any case, the model may be behaviorally attractive even if its normative appeal is weak. Zeuthen's argument showed that it is plausible to believe that this outcome will in fact be the result of bargaining, if at each step the player whose relative loss is smaller makes a concession to the opponent.[73] This approach is important in bargaining cases that involve a once-and-for-all confrontation that does not have consequences beyond the present. If, however, the bargaining parties know they will have to bargain again later, and that the outcome of present bargaining will affect future welfare, it will not do. Wage bargaining, in fact, tends to be regular, institutionalized, sometimes even continuous. Also, the current division of the net product between wages and profit makes a big difference to the future welfare of both classes, because part of the profit is reinvested. The less the capitalist class has left in profits, the smaller the prospects for economic growth and future increase in consumption.

Kelvin Lancaster proposes a model that captures this double time-dependence of bargaining.[74] He views the wage struggle between capital and labor as a "differential game," i.e., as a continuous strategic interaction. The model, and even more the general theory behind it, constitutes an important conceptual breakthrough, with many consequences for the way in which we think about exploitation, power, and capitalism. The theory does for social democracy what Marx did for classical capitalism: it explains how class struggle evolves when the workers overcome the synchronic alienation, but not the diachronic one. Lancaster assumes that workers and capitalists confront each other as organized groups, and that there are no other social classes. He assumes, moreover, that each of the two classes controls an essential economic variable. The workers can, within certain limits,[75] determine the rate of working-class consumption out of the current net product, whereas the capitalists can control the rate of investment out of profits. The assumption regarding the capitalists' control variable is simply part of the definition of capitalism, whereas the assumption regarding the workers' control over the current consumption reflects the development of capitalism since Marx. In modern capitalist economies, especially the social democratic variety prominent in northwestern Europe, the workers have the power — either directly through unions or indirectly through profit taxation — to retain for themselves virtually all of the net product, should they so desire. This statement is not easily substantiated, being counterfactual, yet it is defensible. Under early capitalism, working-class consumption was kept down to subsistence for many reasons, including low productivity, weak working-class organizations, a high degree of capitalist cohesion, rapid population growth, and a state that championed the capitalist class. In modern capitalist economies of the social democratic variety, none of these conditions obtains. True, the capitalist class remains strong, in that it is able to discipline its own members. But its capacity for subjugating the workers has been drastically reduced, for if the workers are denied in direct wage bargaining, they can retaliate with state intervention and heavy taxation on profits.

Yet the workers do not use their power. Lancaster suggests, correctly, that this hesitancy owes to certain strategic facts of the situation and to the interest of both classes in present and future consumption. Hence the workers must leave some profit to the capitalists for reinvestment and increased future consumption. Finn Kydland and Edward Prescott suggest that the workers, therefore, should bind themselves — that the "workers, who control the policy, might rationally choose to have a constitution which limits their power, say, to expropriate the wealth of the capitalist class."[76] This is a new twist on the theme of abdication, performed here by the workers instead of the capitalists, as in Marx's *Eighteenth Brumaire*. Their analysis is incomplete, however, as it does not take the strategic nature of the situation into account, as Lancaster does when he observes that both the workers and the capitalists are in a dilemma. To be precise, we have:

> *The Workers' Dilemma:* If they consume everything now, nothing will be left for investment and future increases in consumption, but if they leave something for profits, they have no guarantee that the capitalists will use this for investment rather than for their own consumption.
>
> *The Capitalists' Dilemma:* If they consume the entire profits now, nothing will be left for investment and future increases in consumption, but if they invest out of profits, they have no guarantee that the workers will not retain for themselves the increase in consumption thereby generated.

476

Observe the assumption that capitalists desire consumption rather than profits. The rate of profit is fixed by the working class, hence it cannot also be
maximized by the capitalists. This argument does not deny the importance of
profit maximization, for if capitalists can do even better than the rate fixed
for them, they will also benefit in consumption terms. Observe, too, that the
model has potential applications in many settings. Consider, for instance, the
relation between a multinational firm that controls the rate of local reinvestment out of locally created profits, and the local government that controls
the tax rate on profits.

A strategy, in the game set up by these dilemmas, is a time profile of values of
the control variable, i.e., a continuous sequence of rates of consumption out
of the net product for the workers, and a sequence of rates of investment out
of profits for the capitalists. A solution, here as in general, consists of two
strategies that are optimal against each other. Lancaster shows that if the
two classes are assumed to maximize their consumption over some finite time
period, the game has a solution. He also shows that the solution is suboptimal, in the sense of implying a smaller total consumption for each class than
would be possible with different time profiles. It is also discontinuous: at one
point in time both classes switch from minimal to maximal consumption. In
my view these results depend too heavily on the specific assumptions of the
model to be of great interest. The importance of the model is above all conceptual. It shows how the workers can hold political power, yet be powerless
if the capitalists retain economic power; how the workers may control consumption, yet be powerless if the capitalists control investment; how the
workers can determine the present, yet be powerless if the capitalists determine the future. The exploitation of the working class, then, does not consist
only in the capitalists' appropriation of surplus-value, but also in the workers'
exclusion from decisive investment choices that shape the future. Or, alternatively, the workers suffer not only exploitation, but also lack of self-
determination.[77] In the capitalist countries where social democracy is most
advanced, one may argue with Ralf Dahrendorf that power rather than wealth
is the crux of the class struggle.[78]

Cooperative n-person game theory has been usefully applied to the study of
exploitation. In John Roemer's *General Theory of Exploitation and Class* it
is shown that the feudal, capitalist, and socialist modes of exploitation can be
characterized by means of notions from this theory.[79] A group of individuals
are said to be exploited if, were they to withdraw from society according to
certain withdrawal rules, they could improve their situation. Different forms
of exploitation correspond to different withdrawal rules. Thus the serfs were
exploited in the feudal sense, because they could have done better for them-

477

selves had they withdrawn from society with their own land. Workers are capitalistically exploited because they could have done better were they to withdraw with their per capita share of society's tangible assets, i.e., capital goods. And under socialism a group is exploited if it could do better were it to withdraw with its per capita share of the intangible assets, i.e., skills and talents. Whereas the last notion is somewhat hazy, the characterizations of feudal and capitalist exploitation are very valuable, as is also the observation that the neoclassical view, that workers are not exploited under capitalism, really amounts to a denial of feudal exploitation in capitalist societies. It is also possible to arrive at specific statements about the intensity of exploitation, by using the framework of cooperative game theory. Consider a case discussed by Lloyd Shapley and Martin Shubik,[80] agricultural production where one capitalist owns the land and the workers own only their labor power. How will the product be divided between landowner and workers if coalitions can be formed between the owner and some of the peasants? Shapley and Shubik show that the outcome is worse for the workers than it is under perfect competition where no coalitions of any kind are allowed. Worker—landowner coalitions conform to a "divide and rule" principle: the workers are weakened by landowner inducements that lead them to betray their class. Even if the workers are too weak to agree on concerted action, they may be strong enough to prevent such partial accomodations with the capitalist. Compared to collective bargaining, individual wage negotiations betray weakness; but opposed to coalition bargaining, they betoken incipient class consciousness. Coalition theory thus embraces simultaneously the problems of class solidarity and of class struggle.

The weakness of game theory, in its present state, is the lack of testable hypotheses. There are many experimental studies of gaming, within the non-cooperative and the cooperative framework, but few applications to non-experimental settings. The value of the theory, therefore, is mainly in illuminating the nature of social interaction and in creating more discriminating categories of sociological analysis. Yet I am confident that this is a transitory situation only, and that game theory will increasingly help us understand social and historical problems. My reasons for this belief are somewhat *a priori*. If one accepts that interaction is of the essence of social life, then I submit that the three, interlocking, sets of interdependencies set out above capture interaction better than does any alternative. Game theory provides solid microfoundations for any study of social structure and social change. Yet the problems of aggregation and statistical analysis still confound us when it comes to complex real life cases. This is not an argument for abandoning the search for microfoundations, but a compelling reason for forging better links between aggregate analysis and the study of individual behavior.

478

For Marxism, game theory is useful as a tool for understanding cases of mixed conflict and cooperation: cooperation in producing as much as possible, conflict over dividing up the product. Game theory can help understand the mechanics of solidarity and class struggle, without assuming that workers and capitalists have a common interest and need for cooperation. They do not. The interest of the working class is to suppress the capitalist class — and itself qua wage-earners — not to cooperate with it. Within the alienated framework of capitalism, however, this interest is easily misperceived. For there is the appearance of a common interest, such that working class action will follow lines like those sketched here. Only through proper analysis of the mechanism of this reformist class struggle can one understand how to transform it into one that aims at abolishing the capitalist system.

NOTES

1. The philosophical point invoked here is that in contexts of belief, desire, etc. it is not in general possible to substitute for each other expressions with the same reference, without change of truth value. We fear an object as described in a certain way, and we may not fear it under a different description.
2. For an analysis of this idea, see my *Logic and Society* (Chichester: Wiley, 1978), 20 ff.
3. A forceful statement of the need for microfoundations is in John Roemer, *Analytical Foundations of Marxian Economic Theory* (Cambridge University Press, 1981), Ch. 1 and *passim*.
4. I argue in more detail for this claim in Ch. V of my *Sour Grapes*, forthcoming from Cambridge University Press.
5. For a fuller statement of my views on functional explanation, see Ch. 2 of my *Explaining Technical Change*, forthcoming from Cambridge University Press; see also my exchange with G.A. Cohen in *Political Studies* XXVIII (1980), my exchange with Arthur Stinchcombe in *Inquiry* 23 (1980), and my review of P. van Parijs, *Evolutionary Explanation in the Social Sciences* (Totowa, NJ: Rowman and Littlefield 1981), forthcoming in *Inquiry*.
6. For a fuller statement, see Ch. I of my *Ulysses and the Sirens* (Cambridge University Press, 1979).
7. Natural selection invokes competition between coexisting individuals. Arthur Stinchcombe (in his contribution to *The Idea of Social Structure: Papers in Honor of Robert K. Merton*, ed. Lewis A. Coser (Harcourt, Brace, Jovanovich, 1975)) points to an analogous model involving selection among successive social states. The model pictures social change as an absorbing Markov process — which for the present purposes may be summarized by saying that institutions undergo continuous change until they arrive in a state in which there is no pressure for further change (the "absorbing state"). This view could be used as a basis for functional explanation, with the modification that it would explain social states in terms of the absence of destabilizing consequences rather than through the presence of stabilizing ones. I would argue, however, that — unlike the biological case — there are no reasons for thinking that this adaptive process would ever catch up with the changing social environment.
8. A radically different account of functional explanation is offered by G.A. Cohen, *Karl Marx's Theory of History* (Oxford University Press, 1978). He argues that functional explanations can be sustained by *consequence laws*, of the form "Whenever x would have favourable consequences for y, then x appears." If a law of this form is established, we may affirm that x is explained by its favorable consequences for y, even if no mechanism is indicated (although Cohen asserts that some mechanism must indeed exist). To the (partially misguided) objections to this idea stated in my review of his book in *Political Studies* (note 5 above), I now would like to add the following. First, x and the y-enhancing effect of x might both be effects of some third factor z, and thus related by spurious correlation. Second, the definition of a consequence law is vitiated by the imprecise way in which the time dimension is brought in. The law could in fact be vacuously confirmed by suitably ignoring short-term in favor of long-term consequences.

479

9. "Social Conflict and the Theory of Social Change," in *Conflict Resolution: Contributions of the Behavioral Sciences*, ed. C.G. Smith (University of Notre Dame Press, 1971), 60.
10. "What's Wrong with the New Institutional Economics" (Mimeograph, Department of Economics, Stanford University, 1979).
11. *Economic Analysis of the Law* (Little, Brown, 1977), 106. Italics added, parentheses deleted.
12. R.K. Merton, *Social Theory and Social Structure*, rev. ed. (Free Press, 1957), 30 ff.
13. P. Bourdieu, *La Distinction* (Paris: Editions de Minuit, 1979), 285. For a critical discussion of this inverted sociodicy, which proceeds from the assumption that all is for the worst in the worst of all possible worlds, see my review in *London Review of Books*, 5–18 November 1981.
14. I counted 15 occurrences of this phrase in *La Distinction*.
15. M. Scheler, *Ressentiment* (Schocken, 1972), 52.
16. *Theories of Surplus-Value*, 3 vols. (Moscow: Progress, 1963–71), 1, 287.
17. "You know my admiration for Leibniz" (Marx to Engels, 10 May 1870). For the structure of Leibniz's philosophy of history, see Ch. VI of my *Leibniz et la Formation de l'Esprit Capitaliste* (Paris: Aubier-Montaigne, 1975).
18. The manuscript consists of 23 notebooks, of which books 6 to 15 were published by Kautsky as *Theories of Surplus-Value*. Books 1 to 5 and 16 to 18 have recently been published in the new *Marx-Engels Gesamt-Ausgabe*, and the remaining will soon be available in the same edition. Just as Marx's *Grundrisse* testify to the influence of Hegel's *Logic*, these manuscripts bear witness to the influence of Hegel's philosophy of history.
19. *Theories of Surplus-Value*, 3, 422–23.
20. *Marx-Engels Gesamt-Ausgabe*, Zweite Abteilung, Band 3, Teil 1 (Berlin: Dietz, 1976), 173.
21. *Ibid.*, 327. The verse is also quoted in Marx's article on "The British Rule in India" (*New York Daily Tribune*, 25 June 1853) and, in a more ironic vein, in *Neue Oder Zeitung*, 20 January 1855.
22. *Capital*, 3 vols. (International Publishers, 1967), 3, 600–1. For the distinction between short-term and long-term functionalism in Marxism, see also Roemer, *Analytical Foundations*, 9.
23. For surveys, see B. Jessop, "Recent Theories of the Capitalist State," *Cambridge Journal of Economics* 1 (1977), 353–74 and the Introduction to J. Holloway and S. Picciotta, eds., *State and Capital* (London: Edward Arnold, 1978). I should mention here that by "corporate body" I mean something different from what is later referred to as a "collective actor". The former refers to a juristic person, or more broadly to any kind of formal organization with a single decision-making center. The latter is defined below as any group of individuals who are able, by solidarity or enlightened self-interest, to overcome the free-rider problem. Another way of overcoming it is to create a corporate body with legal or effective power to keep individual members in line, but in the discussion below I mostly limit myself to cooperation emerging by tacit coordination.
24. *New York Daily Tribune*, 25 August 1852.
25. "The Eighteenth Brumaire of Louis Bonaparte," in Marx and Engels, *Collected Works* (Lawrence and Wishart, 1979), 143.
26. De Tocqueville, in *Democracy in America*, distinguishes both between the transitional effects of democratization and the steady-state effects of democracy; and between the inefficient use of resources and the efficient creation of resources that are both inherent in democracy as a going concern. For details, see Ch. 1 of my *Explaining Technical Change*.
27. *Class Struggle and the Industrial Revolution* (Methuen, 1974), 15. Thus Marxist functionalism explains the institutional arrangements of feudalism in terms of their favorable consequences for the surplus product, whereas non-Marxist functionalists such as D. North and R.P. Thomas (*The Rise of the Western World* (Cambridge University Press, 1973)) explain the same arrangements in terms of their favorable consequences for total product.
28. "The Moral Economy of the English Crowd in the Eighteenth Century," *Past and Present* 50 (1971), 120.
29. For an analysis of this fallacy, see my *Logic and Society*, 118 ff.
30. Stark examples include W.J. Chambliss, "The Political Economy of Crime: A Comparative Study of Nigeria and the USA," in *Critical Criminology*, ed. I. Taylor, et al. (Routledge and Kegan Paul, 1975), and W.J. Chambliss and T.E. Ryther, *Sociology: The Discipline and Its Direction* (McGraw-Hill, 1975), 348. The closely related Radical approach is exemplified by M. Foucault, *Surveiller et Punir* (Paris: Gallimard, 1975), 277 and *passim*.

480

31. S. Bowles and H. Gintis, *Schooling in Capitalist America* (Routledge and Kegan Paul, 1976), e.g., 103, 114, and 130 features many such examples. In the same vein is also M. Levitas, *Marxist Perspectives in the Sociology of Education* (Routledge and Kegan Paul, 1974). A Radical version is that of P. Bourdieu and J.-C. Passeron, *La Reproduction* (Paris: Editions de Minuit, 1970), e.g., 159.

32. H. Bowles and S. Gintis, "The Marxian Theory of Value and Heterogeneous Labour: a Critique and Reformulation," *Cambridge Journal of Economics* 1 (1977), 173–92; J. Roemer, "Divide and Conquer: Microfoundations of a Marxian Theory of Wage Discrimination," *Bell Journal of Economics* 10 (1979), 695–705. The fallacy involved in both these articles is the belief that because internal cleavages in the working class benefit capitalist class domination, they are to be explained in terms of this benefit. This, however, is to confuse what Simmel (*Soziologie* (Berlin: Dunker und Humblot, 1908), 76 ff.) referred to as, respectively, *tertius gaudens* and *divide et impera*. Third parties may benefit from a struggle even when they have not been instrumental in setting it up.

33. As Jessop, "Recent Theories," 364, characterizes the "capital logic" school.

34. Introduction to Holloway and Picciotta, 12, characterizing Yaffe's work.

35. E.O. Wright, *Class, Crisis and the State* (New Left Books, 1978), 231.

36. M. Kalecki, "Political Aspects of Full Employment," in *Selected Essays on the Dynamics of the Capitalist Economy* (Cambridge University Press, 1971), 139–41.

37. "And for the sake of life to sacrifice life's only end" (Juvenal), quoted by Marx in *Neue Oder Zeitung,* 12 June 1855.

38. A. Bhaduri, "A Study in Agricultural Backwardness under Semi-Feudalism," *Economic Journal* 83 (1973), 120–37 and "On the Formation of Usurious Interest Rates in Backward Agriculture," *Cambridge Journal of Economics* 1 (1977), 341–52.

39. R. Rosdolsky, *Zur Entstehungsgeschichte des Marxschen "Kapital"* (Frankfurt: Europäische Verlagsanstalt, 1968, 61–71), refers to the passages (mainly in the *Grundrisse*) where Marx develops the concept of "capital in general."

40. For a survey of alternatives to intentional design, see P. Van Parijs.

41. *The Fiscal Crisis of the State* (St. Martin's, 1973), 69–70. Closely related explanations of the welfare state are given in J. Hirsch, *Staatsapparat und Reproduktion des Kapitals* (Frankfurt: Suhrkamp, 1974), 54 and N. Poulantzas, *Pouvoir Politique et Classes Sociales* (Paris: Maspero, 1968), 310.

42. Van Parijs, passim; also *Ulysses and the Sirens*, Ch. I.

43. A standard treatment is R.D. Luce and H. Raiffa, *Games and Decisions* (Wiley, 1957). Some nonstandard problems are raised in *Ulysses and the Sirens*, especially Ch. 3.

44. For an elaboration of my critique of structuralism and role theory, see *Ulysses and the Sirens*, Ch. III.1 and III.6.

45. This could be part of what Marx meant by his statement in the *Communist Manifesto*: "In place of the old bourgeois society, with its classes and class antagonism, we shall have an association in which the free development for each is the condition for the free development of all." (Another possible reading is indicated in the next note.) If "each" and "all" are transposed in this passage, a more adequate expression occurs. Proper understanding of the philosophical anthropology behind this statement presupposes the idea that even for the single individual, the free development of all faculties is the condition for the free development of each faculty (*The German Ideology*, in Marx and Engels, *Collected Works* (Lawrence and Wishart, 1976), 5, 262). The freely-developed person is both a totality of freely-developed faculties and part of a totality of freely-developed persons. Hypertrophy is atrophy, in the individual and in society.

46. A fourth kind of independence falls outside game theory, however. It can be summed up by saying that the *preferences of each depend on the actions of all,* by socialization and more invidious mechanisms such as conformism, "sour grapes," etc. Game theory takes preferences as given, and has nothing to offer concerning preference formation. The transformation of a Prisoners' Dilemma into an Assurance Game (see below) must be explained by social psychology, not by game theory. We can explain behavior intentionally in terms of preferences, but the latter themselves are to be explained causally.

47. For n-person versions of some of the games discussed here, see A. Sen, "Isolation, Assurance and the Social Rate of Discount," *Quarterly Journal of Economics* 80 (1967) 112–24. For a treatment of heterogeneous preferences in n-person games, see the brilliant framework developed by T.S. Schelling, *Micromotives and Macrobehavior* (Norton, 1978).

48. The most general analysis, permitting overlapping coalitions, is J. Harsanyi, *Rational Behavior and Bargaining Equilibrium in Games and Social Situations* (Cambridge University Press, 1977). The economic theory of the core is made easily accessible by

481

W. Hildebrand and A.P. Kirman, *Introduction to Equilibrium Theory* (Amsterdam: North-Holland, 1976). Applications to ethics include John Roemer, *A General Theory of Exploitation and Class*, forthcoming from Harvard University Press, and Roger Howe and John Roemer, "Rawlsian Justice as the Core of a Game," forthcoming in the *American Economic Review*.

49. *The Logic of Collective Action* (Harvard University Press, 1965), Ch. 4.
50. For a more fine-grained typology, see A. Rapoport, M.J. Guyer, and D.G. Gordon, *The 2x2 Game* (University of Michican Press, 1976). For other discussions of the relation among the preference structures analyzed here, see S.-C. Kolm, "Altruismes et Efficacités," *Social Science Information* 20 (1981), 293–344; and R. van der Veen, "Meta-Rankings and Collective Optimality," *Social Science Information* 20 (1981), 345–74.
51. For a brief discussion of some mixed cases, see my "Introduction" to the articles by Kolm and van der Veen cited in the preceding note. See also Schelling.
52. A. Sen, *On Economic Inequality* (Oxford University Press, 1973), Ch. 4.
53. The point is that acting unilaterally on the Categorical Imperative may be downright unethical. A striking example could be unilateral disarmament, if the situation is such that other countries will rush in to fill the power vacuum. Instead of acting in a way that would lead to good results *if* everyone else did the same, one should act to promote the good on realistic assumptions about what others are likely to do. A little morality, like a little rationality, may be a dangerous thing. There is room and need for a "moral theory of the second best," corresponding to the economic theory of the second best which shows that if out of n conditions for an economic optimum, one is not fulfilled, the optimum may be more closely approached if additional conditions are violated. (R.G. Lipset and K. Lancaster, "The Economic Theory of Second Best," *Review of Economic Studies*, XXIV (1957–8), 133–62.)
54. C. Taylor, "Interpretation and the Sciences of Man," *Review of Metaphysics* 25 (1971), 31.
55. *Ibid.*, 31–32.
56. J.-P. Sartre, *Critique de la Raison Dialectique* (Paris: Gallimard, 1960), 417, 404 ff.
57. A. Stinchcombe, *Theoretical Methods in Social History* (Academic Press, 1978), 54.
58. *Ibid.*, 41.
59. Olson, 106.
60. For details about this game (often called "Chicken" after a well-known ritual of American juvenile culture), see A. Rapoport, *Two-Person Game Theory* (University of Michigan Press, 1966), 140 ff.
61. Luce and Raiffa, 107.
62. I am indebted to Ulf Torgersen for this observation. See also A. Stinchcombe, *Constructing Social Theories* (Harcourt, Brace and World, 1968), 157 for a discussion and some further references.
63. Olson, 29–30.
64. For the general theory of supergames, see M. Taylor, *Anarchy and Cooperation* (Wiley, 1976). For applications to competition and cooperation among firms, see M. Friedman, *Oligopoly and the Theory of Games* (Amsterdam: North-Holland, 1977).
65. "New Deal, Old Game: Competition and Collective Action among American Capitalists, 1925–1934" (unpublished manuscript, University of Chicago, Department of Political Science, 1979).
66. "The Labor Theory of Value," *Marxist Perspectives* 3 (1978), 70–101.
67. A. Coddington, *Theories of the Bargaining Process* (Allen and Unwin, 1968), 58 ff.
68. For surveys, see Coddington, and the articles collected in *Bargaining*, ed. O. Young (University of Illinois Press, 1975).
69. For a full explanation, see Harsanyi.
70. The rewards are measured in cardinal utilities, which are constructed from the individual's preferences over alternatives some of which may be lotteries (Luce and Raiffa, Ch. 2). This lends great importance to the attitude toward risk-taking; and typically the rich will be less risk-averse than the poor.
71. Perhaps Marx had something like this in mind when he wrote that in some forms of international trade, the "richer country exploits the poorer one, even where the latter gains by the exchange" (*Theories of Surplus-Value*, 3, 106).
72. This requirement could be defended either on utilitarian grounds, because the poor generally will get more utility out of a given increase in income, or on the grounds of the "difference principle" (J. Rawls, *A Theory of Justice* (Harvard University Press, 1971)), stating that one should maximize the welfare of the least-advantaged.
73. "Relative loss" means the difference between demand and offer, divided by the demand. "Concession" means making a new demand that gives one's opponent the smallest relative loss.

482

74. K. Lancaster, "The Dynamic Inefficiency of Capitalism," *Journal of Political Economy* 81 (1973), 1092–1109. Further developments of the model include M. Hoel, "Distribution and Growth as a Differential Game Between Workers and Capitalists," *International Economic Review* 19 (1978), 335–50; and, importantly, A. Przeworski and M. Wallerstein, "The Structure of Class Conflict in Advanced Capitalist Societies," Paper Presented at the Annual Meeting of the American Political Science Association, August 1980.

75. These limits are required for the game to have a solution, but they may be arbitrarily close to = and 100% respectively, and hence do not restrict the model in any substantial manner.

76. "Rules Rather than Discretion: The Inconsistency of Optimal Plans," *Journal of Political Economy* 85 (1977), 473–92.

77. L. Kolakowski (*Main Currents of Marxism* (Oxford University Press, 1978), 3 vols., 1, 333) defines exploitation in terms of the "exclusive powers of decision" held by the capitalist. Similarly, E.O. Wright in various works (e.g., *Class Structure and Income Determination* (Academic Press, 1979), 14 ff.) adds authority to surplus extraction as a component of exploitation and class. John Roemer (*A General Theory of Exploitation and Class*) takes the more orthodox line that the lack of power over economic decisions is distinct from exploitation.

78. It should be observed at this point that even the Marxists who accept that authority relations are a component of class restrict themselves to intra-firm relations of command and subordination, whereas Dahrendorf extends the notion to include authority relations in any organization.

79. Roemer also argues, more ambitiously, that exploitation can be *defined* in terms of hypothetical alternatives. In my contribution to a symposium on Roemer's work (forthcoming in *Politics and Society*) I argue that this proposal has counter-intuitive consequences. It remains true that important cases of exploitation can be (nondefinitionally) characterized in the way he proposes.

80. "Ownership and the Production Function," *Quarterly Journal of Economics* 80 (1967), 88–111.

Theory and Society 11 (1982) 453–482
0304–2421/82/0000–0000/$02.75 © 1982 Elsevier Scientific Publishing Company

[11]

REPLY TO ELSTER ON "MARXISM, FUNCTIONALISM, AND GAME THEORY"

G. A. COHEN

Jon Elster and I each worked sympathetically on Marxism for a long time, and each of us independently came to see that Marxism in its traditional form is associated with explanations of a special type, ones in which, to put it roughly, consequences are used to explain causes. In keeping with normal practice, Elster calls such explanations *functional* explanations, and I shall follow suit here.[1] He deplores the association between Marxism and functional explanation, because he thinks there is no scope for functional explanation in social science. It is, he believes, quite proper in biology, because unlike social phenomena, biological ones satisfy the presuppositions that justify its use. Elster therefore concludes that the Marxist theory of society and history should abandon functional explanation. He also thinks that it should, instead, draw for its explanations on the resources of game theory.

I do not think that course is open to historical materialism. I believe that historical materialism's central explanations are unrevisably functional in nature, so that if functional explanation is unacceptable in social theory then historical materialism cannot be reformed and must be rejected. But I do not think functional explanation is unacceptable in social theory. My judgment that historical materialism is indissolubly wedded to functional explanation naturally reflects my conception of the content of historical materialist theory. To display, then, the grounds of that judgment, I shall expound what I think historical materialism says. I shall provide a résumé of the theory that I attribute, on a textual basis, to Marx, and that I explicate and defend in my book *Karl Marx's Theory of History*.[2]

In my book I say, and Marx says, that history is, fundamentally, the growth of human productive power, and that forms of society rise and fall according as they enable and promote, or prevent and discourage, that growth. The canonical text for this interpretation is the famous 1859 "Preface" to *A*

Department of Philosophy, University College, London.

Contribution to the Critique of Political Economy, some sentences of which we shall look at shortly. I argue (in section 3 of Chapter VI) that the Preface makes explicit the standpoint on society and history to be found throughout Marx's mature writings, on any reasonable view of the date at which he attained theoretical maturity. In attending to the "Preface," we are not looking at just one text among many, but at that text which gives the clearest statement of the theory of historical materialism. The presentation of the theory in the "Preface" begins as follows:

> In the social production of their life men enter into definite relations that are indispensable and independent of their will, relations of production which *correspond* to a definite stage of development of their material productive forces. The sum total of these relations constitutes the economic structure of society, the real *basis, on which arises* a legal and political superstructure. . . . (italics added)

These sentences mention three ensembles, the productive forces, the relations of production, and the superstructure, among which certain explanatory connections are asserted. Here I say what I think the ensembles are, and then I describe the explanatory connections among them. (All of what follows is argued for in *KMTH*, but not all of the argument is given in what follows, which may therefore wrongly impress the reader as dogmatic). The productive forces are those facilities and devices used in the process of production: means of production on the one hand, and labor power on the other. Means of production are physical productive resources; e.g., tools, machinery, raw materials, and premises. Labor power includes not only the strength of producers, but also their skills, and the technical knowledge (which they need not understand) they apply when laboring. Marx says, and I agree, that this subjective dimension of the productive forces is more important than the objective or means of production dimension; and within the more important dimension the part most capable of development is knowledge. In its higher stages, then, the development of the productive forces merges with the development of productively useful science.

Note that Marx takes for granted in the "Preface," what elsewhere he asserts outright, that "there is a continual movement of growth in productive forces."[3] I argue (in section 6 of Chapter II of *KMTH*) that the relevant standard for measuring that growth in power is how much (or, rather, how little) labor must be spent with given forces to produce what is required to satisfy the inescapable physical needs of the immediate producers.[4] This criterion of social productivity is less equivocal than others that may come to mind, but the decisive reason for choosing it is not any such "operational" advantage but its theoretical appropriateness: if kinds of economic structure correspond, as the theory says they do, to levels of productive power, then this way of measuring productive power makes the theory's correspondence thesis more plausible.[5] (I do not say that the only explanatory feature of productive power is how much there is of it: qualitative features of productive forces also help to explain the character of economic structures. My claim is that insofar as quantity of productive power is what matters, the key quantity is how much time it takes to reproduce the producers).

We turn to relations of production. They are relations of economic power, of the economic power[6] people enjoy or lack over labor power and means of production. In a capitalist society relations of production include the economic power capitalists have over means of production, the limited but substantial economic power workers (unlike slaves) have over their own labor power, and the lack of economic power workers have over means of production. The sum total of production relations in a given society is said to constitute the economic structure of that society, which is also called – in relation to the superstructure – the basis, or base, or foundation. The economic structure or base therefore consists of relations of production only: it does not include the productive forces. The "Preface" describes the superstructure as legal and political. So it at any rate *includes* the legal and state institutions of society. It is customary to locate other institutions within it too, and it is controversial what its correct demarcation is: my own view is that there are strong textual and systematic reasons for supposing that the superstructure is a lot smaller than many commentators think it is.[7] It is certainly false that every noneconomic social phenomenon is superstructural: artistic creation, for example, is demonstrably not, as such, superstructural for Marx. In these remarks I shall discuss the legal order only, which is uncontroversially a part of the superstructure.

So much for the identity of the three ensembles mentioned in the "Preface". Now relations of production are said to *correspond* to the level of development of the productive forces, and in turn to be a *foundation* on which a superstructure rises. I think these are ways of saying that the level of development of the productive forces explains the nature of the production relations, and that they in turn explain the character of the superstructure co-present with them. But what kind of explanation is ventured here? I argue that in each case what we have is a species of functional explanation.

What sort of explanation is that? It is, very roughly, an explanation in which an event, or whatever else, if there is anything else that can have an effect, is explained in terms of its effect. But now let us be less rough. Suppose we have a cause, e, and its effect, f. Then the form of the explanation is not: e occurred because f occurred – that would make functional explanation the

486

mirror image of ordinary causal explanation, and then functional explanation would have the fatal defect that it represented a later occurrence as explaining an earlier one. Nor should we say that the form of the explanation is "*e* occurred because it caused *f*." Similar constraints on explanation and time order rule that candidate out: by the time *e* has caused *f*, *e* has occurred, so the fact that it caused *f* could not explain its occurrence. The only remaining candidate, which I therefore elect, is: *e* occurred because it *would* cause *f*, or, less tersely but more properly, *e* occurred because the situation was such that an event of type *E* would cause an event of type *F*.[8] So in my view a functional explanation is an explanation in which a dispositional fact explains the occurrence of the event-type mentioned in the antecedent of the hypothetical specifying the disposition. I called the laws justifying functional explanations *consequence laws*. They are of roughly this form: $(E \rightarrow F) \rightarrow E$ (a more precise specification of their form is given in section 4 of Chapter IX of *KMTH*). If this account of what functional explanations are is correct, then the main explanatory theses of historical materialism are functional explanations. For superstructures hold foundations together, and production relations control the development of productive forces: these are undeniable facts, of which Marx was aware. Yet he asserts that the character of the superstructure is explained by the nature of the base, and that the base is explained by the nature of the productive forces. If the intended explanations are functional ones, we have consistency between the effect of *A* on *B* and the explanation of *A* by *B, and I do not know any other way of rendering historical materialism consistent.*

I now expound in greater detail one of the two functional explanatory theses, that which concerns base and superstructure. The base, it will be recalled, is the sum total of production relations, these being relations of economic power over labor power and means of production. The capitalist's control of means of production is an illustration. And the superstructure, we saw, has more than one part, exactly what its parts are is somewhat uncertain, but certainly one *bona fide* part of it is the legal system, which will occupy us here. In a capitalist society capitalists have effective power over means of production. What confers that power on a given capitalist, say an owner of a factory? On what can he rely if others attempt to take control of the factory away from him? An important part of the answer is this: he can rely on the law of the land, which is enforced by the might of the state. It is his legal right that causes him to have his economic power. What he is effectively able to do depends on what he is legally entitled to do. And this is in general true in law-abiding society with respect to all economic powers and all economic agents. We can therefore say: in law-abiding society people have the economic powers they do because they have the legal rights they do.

487

That seems to refute the doctrine of base and superstructure, because here superstructural conditions — what legal rights people have — determine basic ones — what their economic powers are. But although it seems to refute the doctrine of base and superstructure, it cannot be denied. And it would not only seem to refute it, but actually would refute it, were it not possible, *and therefore mandatory* (for historical materialists), to present the doctrine of base and superstructure as an instance of functional explanation. For we can add, to the undeniable truth emphasized above, the thesis that the given capitalist enjoys the stated right because it belongs to a structure of rights, a structure that obtains because it sustains an analogous structure of economic power. The content of the legal system is explained by its function, which is to help sustain an economy of a particular kind. People do usually get their powers from their rights, but in a manner that is not only allowed but demanded by the way historical materialism explains superstructural rights by reference to basic powers. Hence the effect of the law of property on the economy is not, as is often supposed, an embarrassment to historical materialism. It is something that historical materialism is committed to emphasizing, because of the particular way it explains law in terms of economic conditions. Legal structures rise and fall according as they sustain or frustrate forms of economy that, I now add, are favored by the productive forces. The addition implies an explanation why whatever economic structure obtains at a given time does obtain at that time. Once more the explanation is a functional one: the prevailing production relations prevail because they are relations that advance the development of the productive forces. The existing level of productive power determines what relations of production would raise its level, and relations of that type consequently obtain. In other words: if production relations of type R obtain at time t, than that is because R-type relations are suitable to the development of the forces at t, given the level of their development at t.[9]

Now to say that A explains B is not necessarily to indicate *how* A explains B. The child who knows that the match burst into flame because it was struck may not know how the latter event explains the former (because he is ignorant of the relationship between friction and heat, the contribution of oxygen to combustion, and so on).[10] In this sense of "how," we can ask: how does the fact that the economic structure promotes the development of the productive forces (or that the superstructure protects the base) explain the character of the economic structure (or the superstructure)? Consider an analogy: to say, correctly, that the species giraffe developed a long neck because of the utility of that feature in relation to the diet of giraffes (acacia tree leaves) is not to say how the utility of that feature accounted for its emergence or persistence. To that question Lamarck gave an unacceptable answer and Darwin

488

an excellent one. To the corresponding questions within historical materialism no one has given excellent answers. I make some unexcellent attempts in Chapter X of my book. This seems to me an important area of future research for proponents of historical materialism, because the functional construal of the doctrine cannot be avoided.

Let me now summarize my argument for the thesis that the chief explanatory claims of historical materialism are functional in form. Historical materialism's central claims are that

(1) The level of development of the productive forces in a society explains the nature of its economic structure, and

(2) its economic structure explains the nature of its superstructure.

I take (1) and (2) to be functional explanations, because I cannot otherwise reconcile them with two further Marxian theses, namely that

(3) the economic structure of a society promotes the development of its productive forces, and

(4) the superstructure of a society stabilizes its economic structure.

(3) and (4) entail that the economic structure is functional for the development of the productive forces, and that the superstructure is functional for the stability of the economic structure. These claims do not by themselves entail that economic structures and superstructures are *explained* by the stated functions: *A* may be functional for *B* even when it is false that *A* exists, or has the character it does, *because* its existence or character is functional for *B*. But (3) and (4), *in conjunction with (1) and (2)*, do force us to treat historical materialist explanation as functional. No other treatment preserves consistency between the explanatory primacy of the productive forces over the economic structure and the massive control of the latter over the former, or between the explanatory primacy of the economic structure over the superstructure and the latter's regulation of the former. I did not come to associate historical materialism with functional explanation because I thought functional explanation a good thing and I therefore wanted Marxism to have it. I began with a commitment to Marxism, and my attachment to functional explanation arose out of a conceptual analysis of historical materialism. I do not see how historical materialism can avoid it, for better or for worse. Contrast Jon Elster's attitude to Marxism and game theory. He wants Marxism to liaise with game theory because he admires game theory and thinks Marxism can gain much from the match. He wants to put Marxism and game theory together. I would not say that I want to put together Marxism and functional explanation, because I think functional explanation is inherent in Marxism.

489

At the beginning of his article Elster complains that Marxist social analysis has been contaminated by the principles of functionalist sociology. I am sure that claim is both historically and conceptually incorrect. Marxists do not indulge in functional explanation because they are influenced by the bad bourgeois science of functionalist sociology, and it is not open to them to use the better bourgeois science of game theory instead. They indulge in functional explanation because they are committed to historical materialism. Because functional explanation cannot be removed from the center of historical materialism, game theory cannot be installed there in its stead. But it might be thought that game theory could also figure at the center of historical materialism, not as a replacement but as an addition. Yet that, too, I argue, is false. Game theory may be, as Elster says, "tailor-made for Marxist analysis,"[11] but it is irrelevant to historical materialism's central theses, which are propositions (1) and (2). Its relevance, as I now explain, is to theses immediately peripheral to (1) and (2).

Elster makes deft use of game theory in a discussion of the dialectics of class struggle that I greatly admire. And it is not surprising that game theory illuminates class behavior. But Marxism is *fundamentally* concerned not with behavior, but with the forces and relations constraining and directing it. When we turn from the immediacy of class conflict to its long-term outcome game theory provides no assistance, because that outcome, for historical materialism, is governed by a dialectic of forces and relations of production that is background to class behavior, and not explicable in terms of it. Game theory helps to explain the vicissitudes of the struggle, and the strategies pursued in it, but it cannot give a Marxist answer to the question why class wars (as opposed to battles) are settled one way rather than another. The Marxist answer is that the class that rules through a period, or emerges triumphant from epochal conflict, does so because it is the class best suited, most able and disposed, to preside over the development of the productive forces at the given time.[12] That answer may be untenable, but I cannot envisage a game-theoretical alternative to it that would qualify as historical materialist.

Elster says that "game theory is invaluable to any analysis of the historical process that centers on exploitation, struggle, alliances, and revolution." But for Marxian analysis those phenomena are not primary but, as it were, immediately secondary, on the periphery of the center: they are, in the words of the 1859 "Preface," the "forms in which men become conscious of the conflict [between forces and relations of production] and fight it out." To put the point differently, we may say that the items on Elster's list are the actions at the center of the historical process, but for Marxism there are also items more basic than actions at its center.[13] By "revolution" Elster must mean the

490

political phenomenon of transfer of state power, as opposed to the transformation of economic structure political revolution initiates or reflects. Many facts about political revolutions are accessible to game theoretical explanation, but not the world-historical facts that there was a bourgeois revolution and that there will be a proletarian one. Elster urges that game theory bears on strategic questions of great importance to Marxists. I accept that contention, which is amply supported by the excellent illustrations in his article. When faced with a strategic problem, such as how to transform society, we need strategic, not functionalist, thinking. But when Marx called on the workers to revolutionize society he was not asking them to bring about what would explain their doing so: the exhaustion of the progressive capacity of the capitalist order, and the availability of enough productive power to install a socialist one.

The concepts exercised in the previous sentence take us away from game theory to the fundamental context of historical materialism, that of forces and relations of production. There exists a splendid unpublished essay by Jon Elster entitled "Forces and Relations of Production." The essay makes no use of game theory. That is striking confirmation of my view that it is irrelevant to the foundational claims of Marxism: it shows that Elster himself agrees, in practice, with that view. Having constructed a rigorous theory of contradiction between forces and relations of production, Elster says that "the great weakness of the theory is that it is very difficult to link it to action." Now despite my insistence on the centrality in historical materialism of things that are not actions, I do appreciate that actions are prominent proximate causes of social effects. If links with action cannot be forged, if the question *how* the functional explanations of historical materialism explain cannot even in principle be answered, then that would have lethal significance for historical materialism. And this brings me to Elster's critique of functional explanation.

I remarked earlier that even when A is functional for B, A's existence or character need not be *explained* by that fact. Thus to confer credibility on the claim that B functionally explains A one must supply evidence in excess of that needed to show that A *is* functional for B. Elster and I disagree about what sort of further evidence is necessary. He demands that the claim that B functionally explains A be supported by a plausible story that reveals *how B* functionally explains A. I think that is sufficient, but not necessary. For I think one can support the claim that B functionally explains A even when one cannot suggest what the mechanism is, if instead one can point to an appropriately varied range of instances in which, whenever A would be functional for B, A appears.[14] This is an application to functional explanatory claims of a general truth about explanatory claims. There are always two

491

ways of backing them up. Suppose, for example, that Elster and I notice a dead body in the library of the country house the morning after the dinner party, and that we hypothesize that its owner died because of something he ate the night before. Further research can take either of two forms. We might open him up to see whether there are any poisons in him, which would be analogous to what Elster thinks we must do to back up functional explanations, or we might find out what he ate, what other guests ate, and which other guests took ill or died, and that would be analogous to the way I say we can proceed with functional explanations. In my procedure we look for appropriately consonant and discrepant parallel instances. In Elster's we rely on pre-existing knowledge about parallel instances at a more basic causal level and we look for a mechanism in the given case that is consonant with that knowledge.

I can illustrate what is at stake by reference to the case of Lamarck and Darwin. Darwin showed how functional facts about the equipment of organisms contribute to explaining why they have it: the answer lies in the mechanism of chance variation and natural selection. Now I claim, and Elster denies, that, before Darwin thereby advanced the science of natural history, the belief that the useful characters of organisms are there because they are useful was already justified, by the sheer volume of evidence of adaptation. The belief was certainly widely held, by people who had no idea how to elaborate it and by others, such as Lamarck, who had what proved to be an unsatisfactory idea of how to elaborate it. And I contend, and Elster denies, that it was a justified belief. This debate is pursued elsewhere, and I shall not take it further here.[15]

Now because I concede that Marxists have not yet produced good elaborations of their functional explanatory theses, I concede that historical materialism is *at best* in a position like that occupied by natural history before Darwin transformed the subject. But I am not convinced that it has got even that far. For whereas Elster and I disagree strongly about what would confirm functional explanations, we disagree less about whether Marxists have actually produced well-confirmed functional explanations. The essays in Marxist functional explanation which he discusses are sadly representative, and I have no desire to defend them against his criticisms. Here we can make common cause. Many Marxist exercises in functional explanation fail to satisfy even the preliminary requirement of showing that A is functional for B (whether or not it is also *explained* by its function(s)).[16] Take, for example, the claim that the contemporary capitalist state functions to protect and sustain the capitalist system. Legislation and policy in the direct interest of the capitalist class can reasonably be regarded as confirming it. But what about putative counter-

492

examples, such as social welfare provision and legal immunities enjoyed by trade unions? These too might be functional for capitalism in an indirect way, but that is something which needs to be argued with care, not just asserted. But those who propound the general claim about the state rarely trouble to say what sort of evidence would falsify or weaken it, and therefore every action of the state is treated as confirmatory, because there is always some way, legitimate or spurious, in which the action can be made to look functional. Methodological indiscipline is then compounded when, having established to his own satisfaction that state policy is functional, the theorist treats it, without further argument, as also functionally explained. He proceeds from "*A* is functional for *B*" to "*B* functionally explains *A*" without experiencing any need to justify the step, if, indeed, he notices that he has taken a step from one position to a distinct and stronger one.[17]

Most Marxists are methodologically unself-conscious. If they were more sophisticated, they might provide a better defense of the functional explanations they offer. And then, again, they might not. I do not know how to be confident about this, one way or the other. But I maintain my insistence, first, that historical materialism cannot shed its commitment to functional explanation, and, second, that there is nothing inherently suspect in it. Elster's philosophical criticisms of historical materialist functional explanation still strike me as without force, by contrast with his polemic against particular essays in functional explanation. Our philosophical disagreement is pursued in *Political Studies* and *Inquiry*. In fn. 8 of his present contribution Elster offers two new objections to my own theory of functional explanation, both of which are misguided. His first objection is that even when it is true that whenever *A* would have favorable consequences for *B*, *A* appears, *A* might not be explained by its possession of such consequences, because a third factor, *C*, might both cause *A* to have favorable consequences for *B*, and cause *A* to appear, without causing the latter as a result of causing the former. That is so, but it is not an objection to my theory.[18] The form of an ordinary causal law is: whenever *A* occurs, *B* occurs. Once again, this might be caused by a third factor, *C*, so related to *A* and *B* that *A* does not qualify as causing *B*. But there are tests which, when appropriate results are forthcoming, render the hypothesis that there exists such a *C* implausible, and suitably analogous tests may be conducted in the case of consequence laws.[19] Elster's second fresh objection rests on the premise that I do not mention time in my characterization of consequence laws. It is true that I do not mention particular amounts of time when describing the form of such laws in general terms, just as one does not when one describes the form of ordinary causal laws as "whenever *A* occurs, *B* occurs." But causal laws are not therefore "vacuously confirmable," because particular causal laws include appropriate temporal

493

specifications. All that need be said in general terms about consequence laws and time will be found on pp. 260–1 of *KMTH*.

I now take up two issues in the part of Elster's article in which he successfully conjoins Marxism and game theory. In a highly original account of the ideology and practice of social democratic capitalism, Elster sets the stage by describing the dissolution of the marginalist illusion, and the action unfolds along lines scripted by Zeuthen and Nash on the one hand and Lancaster on the other. I have two criticisms of this treatment. The first is that Elster misidentifies the illusion that survives after the marginalist one has been dissolved. He calls it "the presentist illusion" (472), and attributes it to "diachronic alienation" (474). Workers are alienated "from their own history, i.e., from past generations of workers who produced the means of production currently used," and they overcome that alienation "by taking possession of their history" (472). Elster would agree that unrevolutionary workers believe that the capitalist is entitled to a return because he is the morally legitimate owner of the means of production. He thinks the presentist illusion explains why they think the capitalist's ownership is legitimate. But in what does the illusion consist? In a false belief that the means of production were not produced by workers in the past? But workers know better than that. They know, if they reflect on the matter, that means of production were produced by earlier workers, but just as they believe that their own employer is entitled to a return, so, in parallel, they think the employer of earlier workers was; whence, in particular, employers of workers producing means of production came to possess them legitimately and passed them on, directly or indirectly, through market exchange and gift (especially inheritance), to the employers of today. If there exists any kind of presentist illusion, why should workers not project it backwards when they think about their predecessors?

My second criticism of the game theoretical part of Elster's article concerns his remarks on the locus of exploitation. He writes that

> the exploitation of the working class . . . does not consist *only* in the capitalists' appropriation of surplus-value, but also in the workers' exclusion from decisive investment choices that shape the future. (476, my emphasis).

Much the same sentence occurs in an earlier version of Elster's article, except that the word "mainly" occurs where the word "only" appears in this final version. This reply was originally composed in response to that earlier version. Having read my response, Elster changed "mainly" to "only," thereby partly spoiling some criticisms I had made of the original version. I shall nevertheless enter the following paragraph of criticism of his original formulation (the one with "mainly") here, not only out of vanity but also because it still

494

applies, if with reduced force, against his revised formulation, and most importantly because I think it is useful to try to identify rather precisely what exploitation consists in.

I do not doubt that workers are excluded from investment decisions, but I deny that they are thereby *exploited*. If someone robs me of the power to control my own life, he does not *ipso facto* use me unfairly to his own advantage, which is what, very roughly, exploitation is. Authoritarian parents do not, by virtue of being authoritarian, qualify as exploiters of their children, and authoritarian parenthood is a good analogue to the relationship Elster highlights here, which is one of subordination, not exploitation. That subordination is, moreover, a consequence of exploitation in the traditional sense, which is therefore not displaced by (what is anyway wrongly considered) a further form of exploitation. It is because capitalists appropriate surplus value that they are able to decide what to do with it, to consume and invest in whatever proportions they choose. And the exploitation of the worker lies in the appropriation, not in the subsequent disposal over what has been appropriated. Part of what moved Elster to make his (original) statement was the fact, which he emphasizes elsewhere, that only a small proportion of total social product remains for capitalist consumption after workers' income and capitalist investment have absorbed their shares.[20] But because there are relatively few capitalists, that small proportion enables them to enjoy a life of comfort and freedom inaccessible to workers. The difference in *per capita* personal income remains massive, and it matters a great deal to the self-perception and sense of dignity of working people. Working-class existence, even in America, is full of strain unknown to wealthy people. Elster's (original) formulation overlooks that sheer difference in standard of living between the classes remains a major part of the injustice of capitalism.

My present view about the matters in contention between Elster and myself is as follows: (1) Functional explanation lies at the heart of historical materialism. (2) Game theory therefore cannot replace functional explanation within Marxist social analysis. (3) Nor is there a place for game theory at the heart of historical materialism, alongside functional explanation. (4) But game theory is very helpful in relation to claims near, but not quite at, historical materialism's heart. (5) There is no methodological error in historical materialism's functional explanatory theses. (6) But Marxists have not done much to establish that they are true. If Marxian functional explanation remains as wanting in practice (as opposed to high theory) as it has been, the foundational claims of historical materialism might need to be severely modified. Positions of great traditional authority might have to be abandoned. One of Elster's achievements is that he has shown how fruitfully what would remain of the doctrine we have inherited can be enriched and extended.

495

NOTES

1. For reasons given in my "Functional Explanation, Consequence Explanation, and Marxism" (*Inquiry*, 1982) I am not certain that explanations of causes by consequences should be considered functional explanations, but that issue is irrelevant to Elster's article, so I shall here fall in with the standard practice of regarding what I would call *consequence* explanations as functional explanations. Much of this reply has already appeared in the *Inquiry* article mentioned above, and I am grateful to the editor of that journal for allowing it to be reproduced here.
2. G. A. Cohen, *Karl Marx's Theory of History* (Oxford and Princeton, 1978): henceforth referred to as *KMTH*.
3. *The Poverty of Philosophy*, in Marx and Engels, *Collected Works* (Lawrence and Wishart, 1976), Vol. 6, 166.
4. As opposed, for example, to their socially developed needs, reference to which would be inappropriate here (though not, of course, everywhere).
5. For a set of correspondences of relations to forces of production, see *KMTH*, 198.
6. I call such power "economic" in virtue of what it is power over, and irrespective of the means of gaining, sustaining or exercising the power, which need not be economic. See *KMTH*, 223–4.
7. The common practice of overpopulating the superstructure is criticized in my review of Melvin Rader's *Marx's Interpretation of History* (Oxford University Press, 1979) in *Clio*, X, 2 (1981),229–33.
8. Small letters represent phrases denoting particular events, and capital letters represent phrases denoting types of event. Where the letters are the same, the particular event belongs to the type in virtue of the meanings of the phrases denoting them.
9. For a detailed account of the nature of the primacy of the forces, see section 5 of Chapter VI of *KMTH*, which also discusses the transitional case where relations of production fetter the development of the productive forces.
10. In a widely favored idiom, he may not know the *mechanism* linking cause and effect, or, as I prefer to say, he may be unable to *elaborate* the explanation. I use both forms of expression in the sequel.
11. Jon Elster, *Ulysses and the Sirens* (Cambridge University Press, 1979), 34.
12. See *KMTH*, 148–9.
13. Hence to say, as some Marxists do, that "class struggle is the motor of history," is to abandon historical materialism.
14. That is the simplest way of confirming a functional explanation without establishing a mechanism. For more complicated ways, see *KMTH*, Chapter IX, sections 5 and 7.
15. See the exchange between Elster and myself referred to in his fn. 5, especially 126, 133–4, and the *Inquiry* article mentioned in my fn. 1. One result reached in the latter article bears mention here. I show that if Elster is right about what functional explanation is (he says what it is in *Ulysses and the Sirens*), then he is wrong that natural selection is necessary to sustain functional explanations in biology. It follows that he is also wrong in the corresponding claims about sociological functional explanation at 455 and 463.
16. Elster does not always distinguish this criticism from the one I make in the next paragraph: see, for example, his comments (458) on the passage from the *Eighteenth Brumaire*. If he is right, both criticisms apply, but he does not properly separate them.
17. And sometimes it is unclear that a step has been taken from a statement of functionality to a functional explanation, and, therefore, it is correspondingly unclear that a fallacy has been committed. Thus, for example, I do not share Elster's confidence that Marx's use of the word "means" in the quotation from Volume III of *Capital* on p. 457 proves that Marx is offering a functional *explanation*, and I am sure that he is wrong when he claims (456) that Marx subscribed to "the main functional paradigm."
18. It is, indeed, a point I made myself: see *KMTH*, 267ff.
19. See, further, "Functional Explanation."
20. See "Exploring Exploitation," *Journal of Peace Research*, XV, (1978), 12, where he concludes that "in modern capitalist economies the notion of exploitation should be linked to the lack of power over investment decisions rather than to the fact (or to the possibility) of capitalists having a high level of consumption at the expense of workers."

Theory and Society 11 (1982) 483–495
0304–2421/82/0000–0000/$02.75 © 1982 Elsevier Scientific Publishing Company

[12]

METHODOLOGICAL INDIVIDUALISM AND DEDUCTIVE MARXISM

JOHN E. ROEMER

I would like to defend the position of Elster against two sorts of attack: (1) that the key propositions of Marxism are those of historical materialism, whose study is not furthered with the approach of methodological individualism in general and game theory[1] in particular (this is the position of G. A. Cohen in his article in this issue); (2) that the method of methodological individualism is natural only to bourgeois social science and is antithetical to Marxism. Proponents of (2) will claim class analysis and methodological individualism are antithetical, while I will claim that class analysis must have individualist foundations. It is important to distinguish these two positions. Cohen, for example, does not deny the usefulness of game theory for problems immediately at the periphery of the core of Marxism (nor, in particular, for analysis of class struggle), only that Marxism's very central questions are not ones for which this method is useful. Certainly proponents of (2) will also agree with attack (1), but not conversely.

In brief, my argument is, against (1), that the key questions of historical materialism require reference to the specific forms of class struggle, and that an understanding of such struggles is elucidated by game theory; against (2), I argue that class analysis requires microfoundations at the level of the individual to explain why and when classes are the relevant unit of analysis. Two dichotomies that perhaps elucidate the respective roles of functional explanation (à la Cohen) and methodological individualism are: (i) inductive versus deductive method, and (ii) proofs of the existence of equilibrium versus demonstrations of paths of convergence towards equilibrium. Functional explanation is the inductive method: it claims certain correspondences hold on the basis of seemingly irrefutable and repeated historical evidence, in the absence of knowledge of the microfoundations of the correspondence. (I refer here to Cohen's version of functional explanation, to be distinguished from what he calls in his book (1978) functionalism.[2] For Cohen, there is some

Department of Economics, University of California, Davis.

514

micro mechanism that must elaborate the correspondence in question, but
even without knowledge of it, one is entitled to state the correspondence as a
fact based on inductive evidence and perhaps some modicum of common
sense.) Methodological individualism is the deductive method: it attempts to
deduce historical observations from basic postulates on individual behavior
that are sufficiently fundamental to be considered self-evident. (These postulates may be proposed, however, on the basis of prior inductive evidence.)
Concerning the second dichotomy, some of the laws of historical materialism
that Cohen considers central are what I take to be observations about equilibrium situations: if the forces of production are such and such, then corresponding to them in equilibrium will be an economic structure that looks like
thus and so; if the economic structure is such and such, then its corresponding
superstructure will look like thus and so. These laws also contain impossibility
theorems, that is, statements of the form: to a level of development of productive forces that is so high, there cannot possibly correspond an economic
structure of a certain type. Notice these statements are of the existence variety; they do not explain how societies pass from one equilibrium to another
(only that such a transition must take place), nor is there any insight into
what society looks like during the transition. The approach of methodological
individualism and game theory, as explained by Elster, is largely one that is
useful in a dynamic setting. It is concerned with *how one gets* from one situation to another. What alliances form, how do struggles occur, who wins the
battles (if not the war). It is only by knowledge of a mechanism that one can
have a good description of disequilibrium (that is, what transpires in the passage from one equilibrium to another). In this light, Cohen's lack of emphasis
on class struggle in his theory of historical materialism makes sense if he is
concerned mainly with the grand historical correspondences, and if class
struggle is not decisive in equilibrium. For those concerned with explaining
the path of transitions, of convergence to the new equilibrium, I think class
struggle and therefore methodological individualism and game theoretic analysis in particular are key.

An inexact analogy, but one I should give because of my choice of economic
metaphor in (ii) above, concerns the relationship of prices in a market economy to the data describing the underlying economy (resource endowments,
technology, tastes). In the usual neoclassical story, prices in equilibrium are
explained by these underlying "technological" data: in particular, the levels
of prices are explained by their ability, at those levels, to clear markets, given
the supplies and demands that are forthcoming as a consequence of the
endowments, technology, and tastes of economic agents. This is an equilibrium observation: it is a characterization of prices in a tranquil situation,
when they are not changing. When, however, the underlying data change,

515

then prices must change. Perhaps surprisingly, there is no good dynamic theory of how prices change. For such a theory, a detailed description of the behavior of individuals would be needed in a situation out of equilibrium. All the equilibrium theory can state is that when prices settle at a new equilibrium level, they will look like thus and so. We have an equilibrium theory without a dynamic theory of convergence.

The historical work of Brenner[3] exemplifies a Marxist approach in one sense diametrically opposed to Cohen's historical materialism. For Brenner, class struggle is the engine of history, and explains why in some parts of Europe capitalism flourished and in other parts feudalism did. The class capacity of the feudal lords in Eastern Europe and the lack of class capacity of the peasantry explained the second serfdom there, while in Catalonia the internal cohesion of the peasantry explained their ability to smash feudal rule. Similarly, the success of British agricultural capitalism contrasted with France's small peasant landholding is explained by the different class alliances between the peasants and state apparatuses. For Brenner, class capacity has the status of an exogenous parameter; it is taken as given before the story starts, determined, perhaps, by prior history. Presumably the classical historical materialist would claim that different class capacities were themselves determined by different ensembles and levels of productive forces, although Brenner tries to show that class capacity was quite independent of what the technological determinist would have predicted.

My claim is that the inductive historical approach of Brenner, with its emphasis on class capacities and struggle, and the differential success of these struggles, calls for the deductive methods of Elster to provide it with microfoundations. Cohen would not deny this; he would only deny, I assume, that the topic of Brenner's story is central to historical materialism. Brenner's microscopic examination of class capacities and struggle illuminates the path transition took: does it illuminate also the reason that transition was bound to occur (the central question of historical materialism for Cohen), or is that reason deduced rather from the degree of correspondence between forces and relation of production? If we believe Brenner's history then the balance of class forces bears a sufficiently stochastic relationship to the determinist categories of historical materialism that an explanation of transition cannot be made independently of the description of the *path* of the transition. Perhaps one could assert with confidence that give or take one thousand years the transition from feudalism to capitalism had to occur, and no reference to class struggle need be made in explanation; but if one is concerned with history in the small, where relevant neighborhoods of time are one or two centuries, then class struggle (and therefore game theory and methodological individual-

ism) becomes a necessary explanatory variable. One should not define historical materialism's central core so as to exclude concern with events that are
differentiated on a time scale measured in centuries rather than millenia. All
this is not to imply that Brenner's exogenous treatment of the balance of class
forces is satisfactory, but rather that the data of classical historical materialism
seem insufficient to explain that balance (at least in the small).

To the extent that the important claims of historical materialism do not concern the grand equilibria, but are statements about transition, I think the
necessity for methodological individualism becomes paramount: our understanding of historical law is not sufficiently precise that we can assert explanations of transitions independently of having explanations of their paths,
and explanations of paths, I have claimed, requires a micro theory of agent
interaction. For example, according to Cohen, one of the central claims of
historical materialism is what he names the development thesis, that the productive forces tend to develop throughout history, which is a disequilibrium
statement. Cohen's argument for the development thesis suffers from the lack
of microfoundations. That argument is based on the premises:

(c) Men are, in a respect to be specified, somewhat rational.

(d) The historical situation of men is one of scarcity.

(e) Men possess intelligence of a kind and degree which enables them to improve
their situation.[4]

The argument in brief is that, as men are constantly struggling to survive
(because of (d)), and because they possess intelligence ((e)), innovations will
occasionally occur to them that would enable them to meet their needs with
less labor. The rationality of men ((c)) implies they will not reject such innovations. Cohen points out there are two gaps in the argument. The relevant
one here I call the aggregation gap: just because it would be rational for society as a whole to adopt an innovation does not prove it will be adopted, for
that adoption may not be in the interests of the individuals who have the
power to prevent its adoption. As Cohen puts it,

> There is some shadow between what reason suggests and what society does. Further
> considerations are required to show that the shadow is not unduly long. (153)

To bridge the aggregation gap requires, I think, precisely the sort of micro
arguments I have been discussing: how classes and class capacities form, and
how sometimes as a result of class conflict the aggregation gap is bridged.[5] To
point out why such a theory will not be just a trivial one, but must have a
fairly delicate structure, notice there are at least three different types of

517

"game" being played in the historical situations with which historical materialism should deal. In societies characterized as hydraulic despotism, there appears to have been little if any development of the productive forces for hundreds or perhaps thousands of years (the aggregation gap was not bridged). Ruling groups changed, but not ruling classes. The struggle here was between cliques vying for power, but the direct producers did not seem to have the capacity to alter the mode of production, nor even to develop the productive forces. Clearly the structure of the conflict was different in this case from the next two cases. In the transition from feudalism to capitalism, there are three important collective actors: the capitalists (mercantile and industrial), the feudal landed class, and the direct producers. (Of course, we could make a finer partition.) In many situations, the struggle between the two competing ruling classes was a decisive element. This game is to be contrasted with hydraulic despotism, in which ruling cliques fought each other, but not ruling classes, and also with the third case, which is the transition from capitalism to socialism, where there appear to be only two important collective actors, the working class and the capitalist class. Thus in the socialist transition we cannot explain the development of the productive forces by the competition between two surplus appropriating classes, one of which has mastery or capacity to provide better for society. (One case is a two-person game, the other a three-person game.) In the socialist transition, the direct producers for the first time do not simply form an alliance with one ruling class against another, but win themselves. I assume here, what may not be obviously true, that there is a socialist mode of production following from capitalism in which, indeed, the working class is in control of the surplus. But even the answer to the question implied by that skepticism can be elucidated, I think, with game-theoretic formulations of the problem. The advocate of functional explanation might reply that just because the structure of historical conflict appears to have at least three different forms does not imply we should study the problem with conflict models highlighting these differences. Indeed, there may be a general rule obscured by concentrating on the differentiated class conflicts. On the contrary, if there is a general rule, I think it will be more quickly discovered by learning first the specific rules for the different historical transitions, which is to say, by treating seriously the different game structures of the various conflicts, or what I called above the different paths of transition.

I turn now to the second attack methodological individualism will receive, that it is a method inherently antithetical to Marxism. Marxism's method, it is often claimed, is the dialectical analysis of social forces; Marx's key insight was to see the individual was determined by his social milieu, indeed his relation to the means of production; methodological individualism ignores this insight by placing the individual in the center of the story. Classes must be

518

the atoms of the Marxian system, not strategic individuals. The power of the Marxian argument must come, however, not by postulating that classes are the atoms of the system, but by proving that as a *theorem*. One has no choice but to take individuals as given and separate. We observe that individuals frequently act in class units, the problem being to explain this in a deductive way, based on postulates of individual behavior. A huge deficiency of bourgeois history and social science is its inability to understand class behavior and solidarity: as well as observing the importance of such behavior, Marxists are obliged to explain it. Marxism consists of at least these claims:

(1)　that classes act as units in certain historical situations;

(2)　that class position is best defined with reference to a person's relation to the means of production;

(3)　that class struggle is the mechanism of historical change;

(4)　that historical change has a certain pattern (feudalism, capitalism, socialism);

(5)　that capitalism is ethically bad (exploitation).

To argue these points, Marxism requires at least three types of work – history, social science and philosophy. I think the role of history is to formulate inductive laws, with reference to (1)–(4) above. The role of social science is partly inductive, to formulate laws on a somewhat more micro level than history does, but also deductive, to formulate axiomatic theory that can explain the inductive laws. For example, I have referred to proving a theorem that individuals will act as classes in some situations as an example of how (1) can be given such an axiomatic basis. An example of (2) is the work of Wright,[6] who shows by analysis of data that defining class by reference to the relations to the means of production gives more cogent explanations of certain phenomena than defining class with reference to income or status as non-Marxist sociology does. Game theory can be an important tool, as Elster effectively argues, for claim (1) at least. I have argued above it is also useful in (3). It is the role of Marxist philosophy to argue for (5), although that argument must depend on historical work. It is also interesting to note that game theory can be useful (5), in clarifying ethical positions (see the use of cooperative game theory in providing a general taxonomy of ethical positions associated with different conceptions of exploitation in my book[7]).

On this account, what distinguishes Marxist from non-Marxist social science is not the postulate of methodological individualism, but the level of aggregation deduced as applicable in social analysis. In the non-Marxist view history is determined originally by man's struggle against nature, and no further level of aggregation is fruitful. In the Marxist view history may be determined origi-

519

nally by man's struggle against nature, but the struggle against nature leads to the formation of classes that struggle against each other. Indeed, class interests can then affect the struggle against nature. It is in this sense that Marxism performs an aggregation that bourgeois thought does not. The most efficacious lens for analysis may not be the one with the highest magnifying power, and by resolving always to the level of the individual one may lose the pattern.

But why, if class analysis is correct, must one provide a deductive basis for it? Why is not the inductive observation of class struggle sufficient? Why need we explain class behavior by appeal to rules of behavior among more elementary particles? In part, because the question poses itself. In part, because without deductive apparatus, we cannot predict what will happen in new situations that have not been observed. Functional and inductive explanation without a deductive mechanism may be convincing as an account of certain past history, but it can hardly provide good instruction about future developments. (As Elster points out in his description of Marxist theories of the state, anything can be explained by involving either the short-term or long-term interests of particular capitalists or the capitalist class or capital in general.) For example, suppose socialism becomes ubiquitous, and the means of production are controlled by the producers who pay themselves according to their work. Classical Marxism claims that eventually a transformation will occur after which people are paid according to their need. Are we to conclude that a point will be reached after which the forces of production are fettered in their further development by the socialist economic structure, and that tension will be relieved by a change in the economic structure to a communist one, which will enable further development of the productive forces? I find the historical materialist claims useless in understanding this question. I would require a theory of class formation under socialism, an argument on the nature of class struggle during socialism, an argument on how class capacity would develop as the productive forces developed, and so on. If we had a good axiomatic theory of class formation and development of class capacity under capitalism, perhaps a generalization would suggest itself applicable to socialism. I think the inadequacy of the Marxist understanding of developments in twentieth century socialism in large part results from the lack of formulation of a general deductive theory of class, inspired by the inductive observations that constitute historical materialism.

There is a secondary purpose for using deductive models in Marxism: to win over non-Marxists by showing them that Marxism can be formulated as a consistent system, requiring that the choice for or against it must be made on the basis of which world-view better conforms to historical evidence, not on the basis of internal consistency. I do not mean to imply these ideological deci-

520

sions are taken in the pristine vacuum of the library; but if we believe academic Marxism has any role, we must acknowledge the power and importance of rigorous argument in ideological debate. Both world-views, it appears, can be made internally consistent by modern standards of rigor. But I think this pedagogic purpose is secondary. The axiomatic method, and methodological individualism in particular, is useful not mainly as a language to convince skeptics, but as a tool to teach ourselves.

NOTES

1. In this article, I use "methodological individualism" and "game theory" somewhat interchangeably. Game theory is an application of methodological individualism to a setting where individuals cannot treat their environments parametrically but must be strategic. The points against which I wish to defend the use of game theory in Marxism apply more generally to methodological individualism.
2. G.A. Cohen, *Karl Marx's Theory of History: A Defense* (Princeton University Press, 1978).
3. Robert Brenner, "Agrarian Class Structure and Economic Development in Pre-industrial Europe," *Past and Present,* 70(1976), 30–75.
4. These premises, and Cohen's argument, are presented in Cohen, 152–55.
5. Cohen's argument, which I think fails, for bridging the aggregation is presented in an extended footnote beginning on p.154 of his book.
6. Erik O. Wright, *Class Structure and Income Determination* (Academic Press, 1979).
7. John E. Roemer, *A General Theory of Exploitation and Class* (Harvard University Press, 1982).

Acknowledgment

I thank G.A. Cohen for his comments on an earlier draft of this article. Lest my critical stance towards some of his positions be misinterpreted, I wish to acknowledge the influence of his work in shaping my understanding of historical materialism. The superb clarity of his book educates all and crystallizes the opposition.

Theory and Society 11 (1982) 513–520
Elsevier Scientific Publishing Company, Amsterdam – Printed in the Netherlands

[13]

THE CONTRIBUTION OF RATIONAL CHOICE THEORY
TO MACROSOCIOLOGICAL RESEARCH*

Debra Friedman and Michael Hechter

Russell Sage Foundation and University of Arizona

Because it consists of an entire family of specific theories derived from the same first principles, rational choice offers one approach to generate explanations that provide for micro-macro links, and to attack a wide variety of empirical problems in macrosociology. The aims of this paper are (1) to provide a bare skeleton of all rational choice arguments; (2) to demonstrate their applicability to a range of macrosociological concerns by reviewing a sample of both new and classic works; and (3) to discuss the weaknesses of current rational choice theory and the possibilities for its future development.

Until recently, microsociologists and macrosociologists have fundamentally disagreed about the proper level of analysis for sociological inquiry. As members of these two camps increasingly have come to appreciate the theoretical and empirical payoffs of joint venture, however, there is a new call for micro-macro research (Collins 1981; Hechter 1983; Coleman 1986a; Alexander, Giesen, Munch and Smelser 1987). One of the (several) starting points from which it is possible to generate explanations that provide for micro-macro links is rational choice theory.[1] Beyond its reliance on the concept of purposive action (the idea that all action is intentional) and its commitment to methodological individualism (the doctrine that all social phenomena are, in principle, only explicable in terms of the action of individuals)[2], the properties of rational choice theory are poorly appreciated by many sociologists.[3]

Our aims in this paper are threefold: (1) to provide the bare skeleton of all rational choice arguments; (2) to demonstrate their applicability to a range of macrosociological concerns; and (3) to discuss the weaknesses of rational choice and the possibilities for its future development.

A case for rational choice theory could be made on epistemological grounds, but we shall not make it; such philosophical discussions have flowered at least since the time of Thomas Hobbes. Nor will we argue for its merits in accounting for social-psychological and small group processes; in sociology this has been the province of exchange theory (Heath 1976; Emerson 1981; Cook 1987). Nor will we argue for the development of the theory merely for theory's sake; the search for Nash equilibria and for saddle points we leave to others. Instead, we shall argue that rational choice offers an alternative theory to explain, and sometimes to predict, *empirical observations* that have traditionally been of concern to *macrosociologists*. In future contests with other kinds of explanations of these same phenomena, we will be content to let empirical analyses tip the balance in favor of one theory or the other[4].

I. A SKELETAL RATIONAL CHOICE MODEL

What follows is a basic skeleton of all rational choice models, inclusive of the bones found in nearly every rational choice argument, and exclusive of the flesh of any specific rational

---

* A previous version of this paper was presented at the panel on Micro-Macro Linkages at the Annual Meetings of the American Sociological Association, Atlanta, 1988. We are grateful to Mary Brinton, Carol Diem, Douglas Heckathorn, David Jacobs, Edgar Kiser and two anonymous reviewers for their comments on an earlier draft.

[1] The rational choice approach to the micro-macro problem is epistemologically positivistic. Non-positivist attempts to address this problem can be found in Giddens (1979), Habermas (1983), and in some of the essays in Alexander, Giesen, Munch and Smelser (1987).

[2] Some rational choice analyses do not use individuals as the units of analysis, per se, but use states or firms as (corporate) actors. In so doing, theoretically they treat the state or firm as if it were an individual while at the same time appreciating that in actuality states and firms do not act.

[3] For a sample of critical reviews of rational choice written by sociologists, see Oberschall and Leifer (1986), and Hirsch, Michaels, and Friedman (1987).

---

[4] We recognize that paradigms often appear impervious to contravening data. Nonetheless, judging a theory, or set of theories, against the available evidence remains the scientific ideal to which we subscribe.

choice model. For the moment, the work of those who would rearrange the skeletal frame will be set aside. A diagram of the main points of the argument that follows is to be found in Figure 1.

Figure 1 is intended to be a heuristic device to accompany the discussion in the first and second sections of the paper. The solid lines represent the explanatory paths of typical rational choice theories. Some theories, for example, link purposive actors to social outcomes through the mechanism of opportunity costs, while others link purposive actors with social outcomes through the mechanism of institutional constraints, or preferences. The paths are numbered for the purpose of identification. The aggregation mechanism is enclosed in broken lines to indicate that it is often implicit in these theories.

Basic Assumptions

Rational choice models always rely on conceptions of actors as purposive and intentional. These actors are conceived to have given preferences, values or utilities (hereafter termed *preferences* in this essay). They act with the express purpose of attaining ends that are consistent with their hierarchy of preferences. In general, rational choice theory is mute about what these preferences might be and where they come from.[5] In any specific rational choice theory, however, actors' ends

---

[5] The issue of preference-formation is discussed further below.

(and the preferences implied by those ends) must be specified in advance. Without such prespecification of actors' ends, rational choice explanations are liable to be tautological.

Yet individual action is not solely the product of intention. It is also subject to constraints that derive from at least two independent sources. The first set of constraints is due to a scarcity of resources. Differential possession of and access to resources make some ends easy for individuals to attain, some more difficult, and preclude the attainment of others altogether. On account of scarcity, then, the *opportunity costs*—those costs associated with foregoing the next most attractive course of action—will vary considerably for different actors. Hence, actors will not always choose that course of action which satisfies their most valued ends. In seeking to reap maximum benefit, actors keep a wary eye on opportunity costs, for these lower the net benefit of any contemplated action.

Social institutions can be a second source of constraints.[6] The modal individual will find his or her actions checked from birth to death by familial and school rules; laws and ordinances; firm policies; churches, synagogues and mosques; and hospitals and funeral parlors. By restricting the feasible set of courses of action available to individuals, enforceable rules of the game—including norms, laws, agendas, and voting rules—systematically affect social outcomes. These constraints serve to provide sanctions of both a positive and a negative kind that raise or lower the net benefit of any contemplated course of action.

Therefore, within rational choice models, variations in outcomes can be due logically to

---

[6] There is considerable confusion about the relationship between opportunity costs and institutional constraints, especially around the issue of whether institutional constraints are reducible to opportunity costs. We believe that it is useful to maintain an analytic distinction between the two. Institutional constraints are invariant across the individuals subject to them, while opportunity costs often vary considerably for different individuals subject to those same institutional constraints. To cast a ballot in a U.S. presidential election, everyone must register to vote, arrive at a polling place during specified hours, and punch a computer card. These are institutional constraints, and they affect all eligible voters. Yet the opportunity costs associated with casting a ballot—depending on resources such as occupation, access to transportation, literacy, and so on—vary widely.

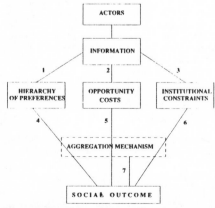

Figure 1. The Various Paths to Social Outcomes in Rational Choice Explanations

variations in preferences, in opportunity costs, and/or in institutional constraints.[7] We will discuss examples of research demonstrating each of these three sources of variation. For example, Thomas Schelling's (1978) model of residential segregation is based on the assumption that individuals have a weak *preference* for living with their own kind (this kind of explanation corresponds to path 4 in Figure 1). This low level preference, he shows, rapidly results in a chain of actions that leads to extreme segregation—a social outcome that is unintended by any of the individual actors who participate in the system. Take away the weak preference assumption and Schelling's predicted outcome disappears. Another example of a model in which variation in social outcomes is attributed to variations in preferences is illustrated in Anthony Downs's (1957:118–25) discussion of the causes of two-party as against multi-party systems. For Downs, the distribution of single-peaked voter preferences across a left/right political dimension is a major determinant of the number of parties in a given society.[8]

Opportunity costs also can be the source of variation in outcomes (path 5). These are not distributed equally, either over every category of actor, or for the same sort of action. Consider the relationship between age and opportunity costs. Older people (especially older women) tend to attend church more frequently than younger people do: the opportunity costs associated with foregoing possible salvation rise as the prospect of death nears (Azzi and Ehrenberg 1975). In general, these costs drop in the post-child-rearing, post-retirement phase of life. Young people engage in crime more often than their elders

(Gottfredson & Hirschi 1986) because, in general, they have less to lose if they are apprehended (that is, they have lower opportunity costs). Finally, it has often been observed that hard science is a young person's game. This is because the opportunity costs associated with retooling each time a technological advance occurs are often prohibitively high.

The third major source of variation in outcomes is due to *institutional constraints* (path 6). It is by now well appreciated that different voting rules—majority, plurality, or unanimity—can influence both the time it takes to arrive at a decision as well as the actual decision itself (Buchanan and Tullock 1962). As any member of an academic department knows, the order of items on an agenda may have implications for which items hold the day (Riker 1986).

Opportunity costs and institutional constraints are more often the cause of variation in rational choice explanations than are preferences. Less is known about preferences—about their origin, persistence, or malleability—than about either opportunity costs or institutional constraints. There are several reasons that the role of preferences tends to be slighted in rational choice models. First, opportunity costs and institutional constraints are more reliably measured than are internal states. Second, while price theory undergirds opportunity cost arguments, and a multitude of empirical generalizations support institutional constraint arguments, no comparable theoretical or empirical structure supports arguments based on preferences. Until we have a robust theory of preference-formation, or a rich body of data, the persuasiveness of explanations based upon preferences will hinge on reader's perceptions of their intuitive appeal.

There are two other elements common to all rational choice models. The first is an *aggregation mechanism* by which the separate individual actions are combined to produce the social outcome. Often rational choice theories read as if there were no aggregation problem.[9] This is because in most of the

---

[7] Even if preferences, opportunity costs and the effects of social institutions all could be exactly specified, some unexpected variation in outcomes might still be noted due principally to the effects of uncertainty, either objective or subjective. One anonymous reviewer suggested that strategic interaction also might be an independent source of variation. For us, however, it is not an independent source but an important subset of the category of social institutions. Strategic interaction describes the action of participants in a game, and a game is a social institution.

[8] The other main determinant is an institutional constraint that Downs called the electoral structure (basically, whether there are single-member districts or proportional representation). It is significant that subsequent rational choice research on the determinants of party systems has focused almost exclusively on the role of institutional factors as against preferences.

[9] In a very limited set of cases (especially in legislatures), an institutional constraint carries with it an aggregation mechanism—thus any kind of voting rule will yield a collective decision. Many of the institutional constraints that macrosociologists are concerned with do not share this feature, however.

original applications the market is taken to be the mechanism that aggregates preferences. In non-market applications there is an assumption, which is frequently hidden, that all actors have similar preference orderings over a given set of choices. The usual defense of this assumption relies on the law of large numbers (Stinchcombe 1968:67–8; Hechter 1987:31–3).

The alternative to making an assumption of homogeneous preference orderings is to specify an aggregation mechanism that reflects the preferences of the constituent actors. It has been difficult to formulate such a mechanism: when actors have heterogeneous preference orderings, no determinate collective outcome may be able to be predicted (Arrow 1951). The most extensive work on this problem has been done as part of the scholarship on voting. The work on the Condorcet paradox is relevant here (for an overview, see Mueller 1979: Ch. 3).

The final element is *information*. Initially, rational choice models assumed that actors had perfect or sufficient information necessary for making purposive choices among alternative courses of action. In much of the most recent work, however, the quantity and quality of available information is taken to be a variable, and a highly significant one at that (Hirshleifer and Riley 1979).

II. EXEMPLARY AND NEW RATIONAL CHOICE EXPLANATIONS OF MACROSOCIOLOGICAL PROBLEMS[10]

If this is the skeleton upon which all rational choice arguments are built, how can such explanations be used to illuminate macrosociological problems? We will illustrate their applicability by discussing examples of research—drawn from both classical or exemplary studies and from new ones—illustrating the various paths represented in Figure 1. Thus far most research has concentrated on the connections between social outcomes and

---

[10] This paper explicitly focuses on the uses of rational choice theory by sociologists and for sociologists. Because the use of rational choice theory in sociology is relatively new, however, work that serves as exemplars in this tradition was generally not done by sociologists. So we draw on the work of economists and political scientists to provide classic or exemplary models of scholarship, but only on the work of sociologists to illustrate the range of new applications to macrosociological phenomena.

preferences (Path 4), opportunity costs (Path 5), or institutional constraints (Path 6). The bulk of our discussion therefore concerns these issues.

The studies that are described in this section constitute the best evidence we can muster to try to convince a skeptic of the merit of this approach. (Those who do not need convincing may wish to proceed directly to Section III.) The rational choice theories that are utilized in these studies compete with established general theories (Marxist or structural theories, for instance) and with a wide variety of inductive theories in accounting for their subject. In attempting to secure a place in macrosociology alongside these other theories, many of these studies analyze classic empirical problems, the outcomes of which are well-known. These are, then, post hoc explanations. Yet in the competitive arena of macrosociological theory it is essential that a general theory be applicable to the historical phenomena that are the staple of this branch of sociology (economic development, voting patterns, protest movements, stratification). When rational choice theories have demonstrated their worth in elucidating these subjects, the case for rational choice as a predictive theory then can be persuasively advanced. Some of this predictive work is already underway, and is also detailed in the following pages.

Examples of Research Investigating Path 4 (Hierarchy of Preferences → Social Outcome)

There are as many hierarchies of preferences as there are actors in the world. On the one hand, this allows for infinite gains from exchange. On the other hand, when a narrow range of ends is considered, large numbers of people may share similar preferences. Whether a given social outcome results from exchange or from commonality, the dynamic element in these kinds of analyses is the content of the preferences held by relevant actors.

a. *The similarity of American political party platforms*. Why do the American Democratic and Republican parties tend to adopt virtually indistinguishable platforms relative to the parties in Western European democracies, which seem to have much more ideologically distinctive political programs? One possible explanation is the lack of sophistication of American voters relative to

RATIONAL CHOICE THEORY   205

their European counterparts. Another ascribes the difference to the lower salience of class identification in the United States as against the European democracies (Campbell et al. 1966).

The exemplary rational choice explanation, as presented by Anthony Downs (1957:Ch. 8), holds voter preferences to be responsible for the type of party system (two- or multi-party system), together with the type of electoral rules (single-member district or proportional representation). In Downs' model, (1) voters support a given party because they expect that enactment of its policies will make them better off; (2) legislators are principally interested in re-election; and (3) parties are teams seeking to control the governing apparatus by winning national elections. Each party wants to garner the maximum number of votes. Using Hotelling's (1929) general theory of optimal location, Downs explains that in a two-party system where all voters vote, each party can attract the maximum number of votes only by appealing to the center of the ideological spectrum. Thus, each party will intentionally alter its platform to attract the median voter.[11] Not only will the parties come to resemble Tweedledum and Tweedledee, but their platforms will be as ambiguous as they can manage.

In contrast, multi-party systems create conditions favorable to one party at each ideological mode (and perhaps to balancing parties between modes). In such systems parties strive to distinguish their party platforms and to maintain the purity of their positions.[12]

b. *The origin of collective action.* In 1973 James S. Coleman published *The Mathematics of Collective Action* (Coleman 1973) in which he proposed a market solution to the problems of coordination and information exchange that occur in every instance of collective action. In any given group, some individuals will prefer to pursue one collective good while others will prefer to pursue another. Yet in most instances, the efforts or resources of those who are less interested are as important to the attainment of the good as are the efforts of those who are most interested. Since all of the actors appreciate that successful collective action (that which they are interested in, as well as that which others are interested in) requires the contributions of a wide range of group members, they sometimes seek to exchange their control over events. Thus, there is a supply of control over a given collective action held by those less interested in the outcome, and a demand for that control emanating from those with significant interest in the outcome. This market solution leads to predictions about the probability of a successful collective action as well as to predictions about the expected value of an event for involved actors. Unlike most treatments of collective action, Coleman's contribution recognizes that most instances of collective action involve collective decision-making processes. (For other papers written from these theoretical premises, see Marsden [1981] and Coleman [1986b].)

What can be taken from these studies as general lessons about the relationship between preferences and outcomes? First, it can be noted that the rational choice perspective directly challenges the sociological tradition on this subject. The effect of preferences on social outcomes long has been a central concern in sociology. The rise of the sample survey—surely a major achievement of modern sociology—was, after all, predicated on the notion that given better information, government officials—as well as the producers of other kinds of goods—would formulate policies—or other products—that were tailored to preferences, as reflected in public

---

[11] Downs presents arguments both for how electoral rules can be determined by voter preferences and for how voter preferences can be determined by electoral rules. On the one hand, if the distribution of voter preferences is normal (that is, unimodal and symmetric), it is likely that no large group will be ignored politically. Thus, single-member districts are preferred, and these, in turn, tend to produce two party systems. If, however, voter preferences are polymodal, lawmakers may choose multi-member districts—that is, proportional representation—in order to allow sizeable extremist groups to have a voice. This tends to produce multi-party systems. On the other hand, Downs also argues that the number of parties is likely to affect the distribution of voter preferences: in a two-party system, voter preferences are likely to converge in the long run, whereas the opposite effect may occur in a multiparty system with proportional representation. The relationship between preferences and number of parties also depends upon assumptions regarding voter turnout. So long as all voters vote, the parties will cater to the median voter regardless of the preference distribution. If some voters abstain, however, then the median voter result is upset if the preferences are asymmetric or multimodal (Mueller 1979:98–105).

[12] For more recent work in this tradition, see Enelow and Hinich (1984).

opinion polls. In contrast, these rational choice studies suggest that preferences rarely, if ever, determine social outcomes in any such simple, intuitive fashion.

Schelling's (1978) study of residential segregation, for example, implies that (1) the preferences that are reflected in social outcomes are likely to be more extreme than those held by the constituent actors. Downs's (1957) analysis implies that, at least in the American political context, (2) a political party that is self-consciously responsive to the preferences of a constituency will produce a vapid set of policies. And from Coleman's (1973) work on collective action comes the counterintuitive finding that (3) in pre-existing groups, successful collective action depends on mobilizing the disinterested, rather than those whose interest is strongest and least ambiguous.

Examples of Research Investigating Path 5
(Opportunity Costs → Social Outcome)

Like preferences, opportunity costs vary across individuals. Nonetheless, individuals sharing social characteristics—age, sex, marital status, income—often have roughly comparable opportunity costs as well. What is common to these explanations is the idea that social outcomes derive from the alternative courses of action available to similarly situated actors.

a. *The failure of class consciousness.* One of the oldest predictions of social science holds that people who occupy structurally similar positions will act collectively to further their common interests. This expectation underlies Thomas Hobbes' explanation for the rise of the state, Adam Smith's account of the existence of protectionist tariffs, and Karl Marx's dictum that advanced capitalist societies would undergo socialist revolutions. Yet there are many instances in which this principle does not hold. For instance, what has kept Marx's prediction from being fulfilled? One possibility is that the failure of socialist revolution is due to 'false consciousness.'[13]

Rational choice theory offers quite a different explanation for the failure of socialist revolutions to occur in advanced capitalist societies. A socialist revolution is in the collective interest of those workers who believe that their welfare will be improved by it. Yet, even though they are potential beneficiaries, rational workers will be unlikely to help bring about a socialist revolution. Since each individual makes only a negligible difference to the likely success of the revolution, the best individual strategy is one that combines non-participation with the (hoped-for) consumption of the fruits of the new order. If, however, most workers follow this individualist logic and actually do not participate in the revolutionary movement, then it is clear that few such social transformations will ever occur.

This explanation for the failure of revolution in capitalist societies is based on a general rational choice theory known as the theory of public goods. As formulated by Mancur Olson (1965), a *public good* is one that, once produced, can be consumed by anyone in the relevant public. The difficulty with public goods is that rational individuals will consume them without contributing to their provision. In other words, rational individuals will act as free riders. So if a given group is composed of a large number of free riders, then a less than desirable amount of the public good will be produced. This kind of logic can account both for the rarity of collective actions in the absence of organizations providing significant private benefits (or what Olson calls selective incentives), and for its likelihood in the presence of such organizations.[14]

b. *Explaining variations in patterns of collective protest.* Working to propose a version of rational choice theory closer to the richness of the empirical evidence on collective action, Karl-Dieter Opp (1986a; 1986b) suggests that the selective incentives needed to induce participation in protest—of both the legal and illegal varieties—are of two types. The first includes external selective incentives, including normative expectations of others, and positive and negative sanctions.[15]

---

[13] It should be noted that (1) some recent Marxist scholarship (Elster 1985; Przeworski 1985) uses rational choice arguments, as well; and (2) many other Marxist scholars rely on structural constraints of all sorts to explain the absence of revolution (even though they do

not place their scholarship in the rational choice tradition).

[14] The best overall summary of the literature in response to Olson is Hardin (1982); see also Oliver, Marwell and Teixeira (1985).

[15] There is some debate in rational choice circles about the consequences of countenancing non-material incen-

RATIONAL CHOICE THEORY 207

In addition, there are internal incentives, including norms of participation, norms about violence, intrinsic value, entertainment value, and catharsis value. Together these go far in explaining participation in anti-nuclear protest activities in the United States and in West Germany by elucidating the relationship between community integration and participation. Opp (1986a; 1986b) tests these hypotheses derived from rational choice theory and holds them to be superior to those derived from other approaches—relative deprivation, resource-mobilization and demographic models—in accounting for observed empirical relationships.

Also dedicated to explaining various instances of collective action is an elaborate rational choice model of social conflict in Anthony Oberschall's 1973 book, *Social Conflicts and Social Movements.* Expanding on the work of Olson (1965), Oberschall (1973) focused on recruitment processes that facilitated movement mobilization and applied these hypotheses to a wide field of collective actions, most notably to the Civil Rights movement.

More recently, Oliver, Marwell and Teixeira (1985) have investigated the effect of group heterogeneity on production functions for collective action. They distinguish two types of production functions—accelerating and decelerating ones—and show that collective actions characterized by accelerating production functions hardly ever succeed in getting off the ground, while those characterized by decelerating production functions are more likely to begin, but yield reduced marginal returns of subsequent contributions.

c. *Rewarding and punishing participants in collective action.* Pamela Oliver and Gerald Marwell, together with their associates, have sought to expand on Olson's theory of collective action in order to bring it more into line with empirical evidence about the probability of collective action. In a series of experiments, Marwell and Ames (1980) have demonstrated that contributions to collective action were far more prevalent than would be

---

tives, particularly admittedly fuzzy ones like norms. Some argue that adding non-material incentives brings these theories dangerously close to the precipice of tautology. Others—like Opp—argue that the most important criterion for a theory is whether it captures social reality and if non-material incentives are a key to participation in protest, then they must have a place in a theory of protest (Klosko, Muller and Opp 1987).

expected on the basis of Olson's theory. In a related article Oliver (1980) has argued that there are positive and negative selective incentives and that these have different implications for producing collective action: rewards are effective in motivating small numbers of participants while punishments are effective only when the situation requires unanimous cooperation.

d. *Political influence and tax rates.* In a study of political influence and tax rates, David Jacobs (1988) traces one implication of the rational choice theory of collective action—namely, that economic concentration should bring forth political influence. When assets are concentrated and large proportions of the productive resources in one economic sector (such as manufacturing) are controlled by a relatively small number of firms, each large firm will have a greater stake in the provision of a public policy that benefits all the firms in that sector. For under these conditions, each firm will be better able to monitor and sanction potential free riders. Jacobs argues that tax rates offer an indicator of political influence. Since firms cannot easily pass the cost of increased taxes on to consumers, when they pay greater taxes it is unlikely that this is due to their expanding political influence. But if effective tax rates diminish in response to an increase in corporate resources, this suggests that the corporations in question have succeeded in translating their resources into political influence. Jacobs finds that the concentration of assets among the largest firms (regardless of their industry) is an important predictor of effective tax rates on manufacturing.

e. *Political regionalism.* Why do the peasants in western France vote for right-wing parties, whereas those in the Mediterranean region vote for left-wing parties? In contrast to prevailing interpretations that emphasize such normative factors as the transmission of traditional party loyalties, collective memories, or religious values, William Brustein (1988a) links specific regional structures to the actors (here, the peasants) who are subject to them. His theory proposes that different modes of production are chiefly responsible for political regionalism in France (see also Brustein 1988b). The mode of production shapes voting behavior both directly and indirectly. Individuals' perceptions of their interests are derived directly from their economic activity and property rights, and are determined indirectly by the dominant structure of the economic activity and property rights they possess. The social outcome of these processes is that particular modes of production of western and Mediterranean France have produced divergent regional constellations of economic interests. Right-wing voting is fostered by a mode of production characterized by a subsistence-oriented economy, medium-to-large sized tenancy or sharecropping, population dispersion, and the presence of social elites. In contrast, left-wing voting is fostered by a mode of production characterized by a market-oriented economy, small-scale owner-cultivation or salaried agricultural labor, population agglomeration, and the absence of social elites.

f. *The solidarity of political parties.* What explains cross-national variations in the solidarity of major political parties? Or variations in solidarity among parties of the same nation? Or variations in party solidarity from one legislative session to another? Whereas many previous attempts to answer these questions emphasized the ideology of party members, in Michael Hechter's book, *Principles of Group Solidarity* (1987), these questions are taken to be an instance of the more general problem of group solidarity.

Roll-call voting provides a means to assess variations in party solidarity. The roll-call vote compels the legislator to make decisions which test his or her compliance with party obligations. Since it is voters rather than the party leaders who can sanction the representative by preventing his or her re-election, differences in party control capacity are apt to be minimal. Thus most of the observed variation in solidarity is not due to the different control capacities of the parties, but rather to differences in members' dependence on their party. The greater the value of party-derived benefits that aid legislators in their quest for re-election and career advancement, the greater their dependence on the party. Conversely, the greater the value of benefits available to them from alternative sources, the lower their dependence on the party. There are many factors which would be expected to influence legislators' dependence on the party. Some of these, such as legislative rules, lead to differences in party solidarity between political systems (or in a single political system, over time), and others (including incumbency, characteristics of the

district, and whether the vote is on a procedural or a substantive issue) contribute to differences in party solidarity within political systems.

g. *The corruption of officials.* Why do the legislative representatives of western European socialist parties so often compromise the interests of their constituents by supporting bourgeois initiatives (Michels [1911] 1962)? Why are narcotics police routinely on the take? And why are prison guards so often corrupted by the prisoners they guard (Sykes 1958)? One kind of explanation suggests that those who are so easily corrupted were morally defective in the first place. Once again, rational choice logic offers a different sort of explanation for the corruptibility of officials.

Consider the case of the prison guards. Whereas the employers (the wardens) direct them to maintain order within the walls, the guards can do this in two quite different ways. Guards can enforce prison regulations to the hilt (as the wardens would like them to do), or they can make deals with their prisoners. Why would they choose the latter strategy over the former? The simple reason is that the net benefit of making deals is likely to exceed that of enforcing the rules because it provides an additional source of income without threatening the loss of guards' jobs. Why then are the guards not punished for this egregious behavior? Only because wardens have no means of monitoring the guards' corruption. This case is a specific instance of a more general phenomenon known as the principal-agent problem (Jensen and Meckling 1976). In a principal-agent relationship agents will act in the principals' interests only when they are sufficiently rewarded or constrained to do so. Hence principals' ability to monitor agents is a key determinant of agents' compliance with principals' demands.

h. *The autonomy of Absolutist kings.* Explanations of the role of Absolutism in the transition from feudalism to capitalism have typically concentrated either on internal political and cultural dynamics of these societies, or on exclusively economic aspects. Seeking to provide a link between these two kinds of arguments, Edgar Kiser (1987) inquires into crown autonomy, state policies, and economic development in Western European Absolutisms. Using principal-agent theory, he argues that variation in autonomy of Absolutist rulers is explained by differences in the relative resources of nobles and

RATIONAL CHOICE THEORY

monarchs and in the control capacities of nobles. These variations lead, in turn, to different state policies, policies which have important ramifications for economic development. In England and France, both countries with ample resources, high crown autonomy generally hindered economic development. In the less advantaged countries of Sweden and Spain, however, high crown autonomy was a necessary but insufficient condition for economic development.

What can be concluded about the effect of opportunity costs on social outcomes from these various studies? The most important insight is that (1) social structural commonality alone is insufficient to produce collective action. Another insight about collective action that can be drawn from Olson's (1965) book, as well as from other studies in the same tradition (Opp 1986a, 1986b; Oliver, Marwell and Texeira 1985) is that (2) in amorphous groups (those without well-defined boundaries), successful collective action depends on mobilizing potential beneficiaries. The experiments of Marwell and Ames (1980) and Oliver's (1980) research implies, further, that (3) rewards and punishments do not follow expected patterns in motivating behavior oriented toward the attainment of a collective good. Brustein's (1988a) study, which explains why the political behavior of peasants is so heterogeneous, provides graphic evidence that (4) many structural categories (e.g. the peasantry) are so broadly defined that they are inadequate to explain political outcomes. The structural parameters that actually will affect outcomes can be determined only by carefully considering the individual's opportunity costs. One lesson inspired by Hechter (1987) is that (5) dependence overcomes ideology. From Jensen and Meckling (1976) we can infer that (6) one cannot automatically rely on wages to produce compliance. Finally, Kiser's (1987) research reminds us that (7) if the economic well-being of a country is of concern, rulers with large amounts of resources at their disposal cannot be left alone to rule.

Examples of Research Illustrating Path 6 (Institutional Constraints → Social Outcome)

A plethora of institutional constraints can alter social outcomes. These range from strategic games circumscribing actors' choices—like Prisoners' Dilemma games—to contractual forms, to stratificational barriers to mobility. What is common to all of these arguments is that the choice set is limited by factors that are beyond the control of the actors themselves.

a. *The superpower arms race.* Since the leaders of both the United States and the U.S.S.R. are well aware that nuclear stockpiling is potentially destructive of the entire world, why do they continue to participate in a nuclear arms race? One popular answer is that key decisions in both countries are made by military-industrial elites whose private interests differ from that of the public, here including the world at large (see Pursell 1972; Sarkesian 1972; and Rosen 1973). Another kind of explanation is that both the American and Soviet economies depend on military expenditures to avoid recessions or depressions and that this functional necessity inevitably leads to an arms race (Boulding 1973; Udis 1973; Leontieff and Duchin 1983).

Quite a different kind of answer is suggested by rational choice logic. The relationship between superpowers may be analyzed as a Prisoner's Dilemma game (Luce and Raiffa 1957). In this kind of game the costs or benefits of each player's strategy—armament or disarmament—depend on the opponent's strategy. The best *joint* solution (meaning the one that is most beneficial to both players simultaneously) is mutual disarmament. Yet the best strategy for each *individual* player is to arm while hoping that the other disarms. Since in rational choice theory self-interest is generally presumed, each player will follow this strategy, and both will end up arming (Brams 1985).

It turns out that this solution will hold even when both leaders prefer to disarm. The reason is that neither can be sure about the other's intentions and actions (witness the emphasis on verification in the arms talks), and lacking any assurance, each seeks to limit losses by arming. The non-cooperative strategy wherein both countries arm—either to maximize their gains or limit their losses—produces an equilibrium wherein neither player has an incentive to deviate unilaterally, for each either would do worse, or would do no better.[16]

b. *The tenacity of gender stratification patterns.* In contrast to traditional Marxian and Weberian accounts of the persistence of stratification patterns, Mary Brinton (1988) seeks to explicate the mechanisms that perpetuate gender stratification. She chooses two industrial societies with different social-institutional patterns, norms, and degrees of gender stratification—Japan and the United States—and argues that distinctive features of the school-labor market configuration in Japan condemn Japanese women to more severe gender stratification than their American counterparts. Although education is essential for status attainment in each society, both the type of education necessary for such attainment and the conditions for entry into these institutions differ in important ways. Employment in high-status firms in Japan is reserved largely for the graduates of universities who receive a general education and, after hiring, are subsequently given considerable on-the-job training. But admission to universities in Japan is determined irrevocably in late adolescence. Youths who fail to earn a place in a Japanese university typically forego this kind of employment forever. In the United States, however, much of the technical training for specific jobs occurs in the educational institutions, entry to which can occur at many different points in a person's life.

In consequence, the Japanese institutional structure gives educators and employers a much greater role in determining who will be favored in human capital investment than in the United States, where self-investment is, to some extent, an alternative route to status

---

[16] Another example of the application of the Prisoners' Dilemma game logic to macrosociological problems is offered by Douglas Heckathorn (in press) who investigates the effects of collective punishments and rewards in inducing compliance with group norms. Using this logic he shows that the effect of control depends upon the attributes of the agent who controls collective incentives (that is, the agent's monitoring ability, vulnerability to revolt, and the strength of the agent's sanctions), as well as the attributes of the group (such as group size, degree of intergroup control, proportion of the group composed of potential violators, and the costliness of normative control and revolt). Collective sanctions are demonstrated to be a potentially unstable means of behavioral control because the same factors that motivate compliance may also motivate rebellion.

attainment. Guidance and sponsorship are more crucial therefore to individual socio-economic success in Japan than in the United States, but since educators and employers are motivated to sponsor individuals who are sure to remain as committed employees in firms across time, and since women are less likely to meet such a qualification than men (due to family responsibilities), then this system imposes greater disadvantages. Additionally, when parents perceive that employers engage in sex discrimination, they will be motivated to invest, psychologically and economically, in the education of sons rather than daughters. In these ways employers and parents unwittingly conspire to perpetuate gender stratification in education and employment.

c. *The production of insurance contracts.* Last, Carol Heimer inquires as to the origins of different kinds of social institutions—in this instance, insurance contracts. She argues (Heimer 1985) that if the reactiveness of risk is a constraint on insurance markets, and if it shifts according to different types of losses, then the contractual arrangements associated with these kinds of losses should vary systematically on this dimension. By effectively transforming reactive risks into fixed ones, such contracts make insurance markets possible. Heimer shows that this is indeed the case by comparing the contractual arrangements in fire and marine insurance, and in fidelity and surety bonding.

What, then, can be learned about the relationship between institutional constraints and social outcomes from these studies? In general, rational choice suggests that the effects of institutions on outcomes can never be taken for granted; the mere existence of an institution (a norm, for example) has no necessary behavioral implications. Institutions affect outcomes not by virtue of custom or of hallowed tradition, but only to the degree that they carry with them the capacity to reward or punish the individuals who are subject to them. Hence the study of institutions necessarily becomes an analysis of the incentive structures that they entail.

In this sense, Prisoners' Dilemma games (Luce and Raiffa 1957; Brams 1985) have been among the most intensively studied of any social institutions. Analyses of these games have a host of implications, two of which are that (1) collective outcomes that benefit the whole are difficult to achieve through individual actions; and (2) prefer-

RATIONAL CHOICE THEORY 211

ences do not determine actions. By treating the gender stratification system as an institution, Brinton (1988) shows that, despite the best of intentions, (3) individuals are responsible for perpetuating societal-level discriminatory practices. Finally, Heimer's (1985) study indicates that (4) certain kinds of collective goods (especially those involving moral hazard) can be provided only in the presence of institutions that enforce stringent controls.

Research Exemplifying the Remaining Paths

Research focusing on the connection between information and constraints (Path 3) generally has considered the role of uncertainty in complicating actors' perceptions of the constraints under which they operate. There is a large corpus of research in economics on this issue, starting with the classic work of Frank Knight (1921). In sociology, uncertainty has been principally the province of those who are interested in the environmental context within which organizations make decisions.

In another kind of application, Friedman (1987) proposes that the rational choice model is appropriate for explaining and predicting collective action only under conditions of objective certainty—that is, when the future can be predicted with some degree of confidence. Under such conditions, individuals can make judgments about the relative benefits of joining a collective action and can act accordingly. Under conditions of objective uncertainty, however, actors are robbed of the implements necessary to make a rational decision—information key among them—and they are thereby motivated to seek the advice and counsel of their fellows. Uncertainty thus provides a special kind of impetus for collective behavior that can be marshalled into collective action. In an application to strikes, Friedman shows that strikes occur predominantly under conditions of objective uncertainty when that uncertainty is combined with certain contractual loss. This explanation offers an alternative to macroeconomic, political, and earlier rational choice accounts of strikes.

There are significant bodies of research investigating paths 2 (Information→ Opportunity Costs) and 7 (Aggregation Mechanism→ Social Outcome), but these address issues rather far removed from the traditional concerns of macrosociologists. These literatures are theoretically relevant, however, and the interested reader can turn to a variety of sources for further discussion.[17]

Payoffs of Rational Choice Applications

In the previous sections a few of the substantive payoffs that rational choice applications already have brought to macrosociology were highlighted. Some of the insights drawn from the individual studies are counterintuitive; some challenge other general theories; and some recall established knowledge. Some are merely provocative. Despite the substantive specificity and diversity of the studies reported, then, they yield general insights that can easily be transformed into propositions and into testable hypotheses with *new* substantive content. In this way each piece of research contributes not only to understanding a given empirical problem, but also to the cumulative body of sociological knowledge. Of course, the adequacy of any explanation can only be determined after weighing the findings of many different empirical studies.

Yet there are also important methodological payoffs. One of our purposes in highlighting these applications is to demonstrate that rational choice offers a very general means of attacking a wide variety of problems in macrosociology. Rational choice has this ability not because it is merely an overarching metatheoretical perspective, but precisely because it consists of an entire family of *more specific* theories derived from the same first principles that can be employed to explain a wide variety of macrosociological phenomena.

The key to this methodological approach is to locate any specific empirical phenomenon as an instance of a more general problem, and then to apply the theory that is appropriate to the analysis of the general problem to the particulars of the specific case. Thus, the failure of socialist revolution in a particular time and place is identified as a (more general) collective action problem and the theory of pubic goods is applied to it. At the

---

[17] See Arrow (1951) for the classic work on the subject of the relationship between aggregation and social outcomes. For a sample of work inspired by Arrow's, see Barry and Hardin (1982). On information, see, for example, Stigler (1961); Simon (1957); and Arrow (1987).

same time, there are many other kinds of empirical phenomena that can be considered to be collective action problems and thereby can be profitably analyzed in an analogous fashion. Hence, the causes and frequency of strikes, wars, rebellions, and nationalist movements are all amenable to treatment as collective action problems.

Similarly, Downs explained the ideological homogeneity of American political parties as a specific instance of an optimal location problem and then applied Hotelling's (1929) general theory of spatial competition to it. Hotelling illustrated his theory by considering how one could locate grocery stores optimally in a given territory, but was imaginative enough to understand that the same principle which could aid investors to select grocery store sites could help account for the behavior of voters. Downs picked up Hotelling's idea twenty-six years later and incorporated it into his general theory of democracy.

So too with the contemporary Soviet-American arms race. This is easily classified as a non-cooperative game for which the Prisoners' Dilemma is the appropriate model. All sorts of bargaining problems are amenable to this kind of analysis, as are some problems of collective action (Hardin 1982). The guards' deviation from the wardens' directives is treated as an instance of a principal-agent problem and agency theory (rudimentary though it may be) is applied to it. Lawyer-client relations, labor-management bargaining outcomes (Friedman 1986), king-ruling class disputes, and owner-management conflicts all provide further empirical grist for this particular theoretical mill.

It should be emphasized that these separate explanations all share a common theoretical maternity. They employ the same first principles—all are based on common meta-theoretical assumptions of methodological individualism and purposive action. In addition to their agreement about how individuals make choices, each explanation also attributes the differences in outcomes to variations in preferences, opportunity costs, and/or institutional constraints.

These claims for rational choice theory are, to some extent, claims for any general theory. Why, then, prefer rational choice? Perhaps the most compelling reason is that it is explicitly concerned with linking micro and macro levels of analysis rather than asserting the analytical supremacy of one or the other

(for a good discussion of the importance of this goal, see Coleman 1986a). Other distinguishing virtues include the increased possibility for fruitful exchange across social (and perhaps even biological) sciences; the large body of formal modelling that undergirds many of the theoretical insights; and rational choice's agnosticism with respect to types of data and techniques of data reduction.

We have argued that the adoption of rational choice theory can improve the quality of empirical analysis in macrosociology. At the present time it cannot be claimed, however, that there is a coherent corpus of research in this tradition. Nevertheless, after considering already completed works, we believe that the outlines of such a research program are beginning to emerge. Yet there is no question that these new studies will have to pay close attention to the limitations of current rational choice explanations. It is to these that we now turn.

III. LIMITATIONS OF CURRENT RATIONAL CHOICE EXPLANATIONS

Despite their ability to explain a variety of empirical phenomena, rational choice models are by no means exempt from criticism. Criticism comes from many different sources. The advocates of interpretive analysis (phenomenologists, hermeneuticists, and neofunctionalists, among others) often argue for a social science that is antipositive; as noted earlier, we shall not deal with their work here. Some Durkheimians, network analysts, Marxists and other structuralists object on principle to *any* approach that is based on methodological individualism. A consideration of this objection is also beyond the scope of this paper. What we discuss here are the criticisms levelled at rational choice either from those who work within the tradition, or from those who explicitly advocate an alternative to it without, however, rejecting methodological individualism out of hand (see Hogarth and Reder [1987] for a state-of-the-art collection of papers critical to various aspects of rational choice).

Most of the critics object to the highly unrealistic behavioral assumptions of rational choice models. Especially in the earliest models, most real-world complexities were suppressed in order to derive determinate solutions. That which could not be modelled was not considered. Thus, heterogeneity of

RATIONAL CHOICE THEORY 213

preferences and interests among groups of actors, strategic interaction (such as sophisticated voting), and the costs of information all were assumed away.

It was no surprise that the inadequacy of these simple models was revealed as empirical tests proceeded. One famous example was that Americans vote in much greater numbers than Downs could account for under any extension of his, or (for that matter) any other plausible rational choice voting model. It was terribly clear to analysts and voters alike that hardly any given individual voters ever would feel themselves to be casting the deciding ballot, which is the only readily allowable motivation in rational choice models of voting. Why then did they bear opportunity costs to take an action that could not materially affect the outcome? Another famous example was that there is far more collective action than Olson—or any other rational choice theorist of collective action—could easily explain. While the lack of selective incentives seemed to provide a powerful explanation for the failure of collective action to occur, collective action sometimes did occur in the absence of sufficient selective incentives. So strikes, riots, anti-apartheid demonstrations in South Africa and in New York City, civil rights marches, and even contributions to public goods in laboratory settings, all took place with a frequency that defied explanation in strict rational choice terms.

Resolving the growing disjuncture between theory and data became a problem of paramount importance. Three tacks to more successfully account for real world phenomena seemed promising. The first was to fiddle with the behavioral assumptions of rational choice theory—especially those of its most testable form, expected utility theory (see Arrow 1987:204–206). The second was to maintain the standard behavioral assumptions of rational choice, but to explore in depth the effects of incomplete information on subsequent action. The third was to elaborate the contribution of structural constraints in determining social outcomes.

Fiddling with the Behavioral Assumptions of Rational Choice Theory

A growing body of research has indicated that there are significant and systematic empirical deviations from the hypotheses of expected utility theory that underlie standard rational choice behavioral assumptions (as conceived of and formalized by von Neumann and Morgenstern 1947; see also Allais and Hagen 1979; Kahneman and Tversky 1979; Machina 1983; and Hogarth and Reder 1987). For economists interested in accounting for market-oriented behavior, these findings are not so troubling, for in the market setting wealth maximization can be realistically substituted for utility maximization: any participant in a perfectly competitive market whose behavior is not motivated by wealth maximization will not long survive. Yet for social scientists interested in accounting for non-market-oriented behavior, these results were both distressing and intriguing.

They were distressing because the kinds of predictions that could be derived from the simplistic assumptions of expected utility theory all became suspect; they were intriguing because some of these findings provided a basis for explanations of empirical findings that otherwise seemed to fly in the face of some of rational choice theory's key predictions.

For example, the work of Tversky and Kahneman (1987), which demonstrates the inconstancy of preferences about risk (the same people are risk-seeking when choosing among losses and risk-averse when choosing among gains), may be used to account for hitherto mystifying behavior about gambling and insurance (see also Brenner 1983: Ch. 1; Einhorn and Hogarth 1985). Thus, what had seemed to be clearly non-rational behavior could, in fact, be accounted for when simplistic assumptions about risk preferences were modified.[18]

While improving the fit of the theory to the data, complicating the behavioral assumptions nonetheless begs a fundamental question. Where do preferences come from? If people are said to act rationally to pursue their most preferred ends, what are these ends and why do individuals hold these ends dear as

---

[18] There is a lively debate between traditional and behavioral economists about the boundaries of rational choice theory (Hogarth and Reder 1987). Are these new explanations consistent with the older versions of rational behavior or do they represent the beginnings of a new paradigm? From the perspective of most sociologists, however, traditional and behavioral economists may be considered to be in the rational choice camp since they both accept the two key assumptions of purposive action and methodological individualism.

against others? As long as the behavior in question is market-oriented behavior, this question can be skirted simply by inserting wealth-maximization for the "most preferred ends" part of the model.[19] With any kind of non-market oriented behavior such a substitution can be made, but only in a post-hoc fashion, and only with considerable qualification. For instance, in Friedman's (1987) model of collective action, it is assumed that people prefer certainty to uncertainty. She can provide a theoretical reason for this particular assumption (e.g. people cannot act rationally under conditions of uncertainty), and can assemble considerable supportive empirical evidence, yet it is quite conceivable that a different logic and a different body of evidence might be mustered to support the opposite claim.

That there is no theory of preference formation has implications not only for the behavior of individuals and groups, but also for social outcomes.[20] The nature of any social outcome clearly depends upon the set of underlying preferences. For instance, if people are wealth-maximizers, they will desire social outcomes that provide for the greatest economic efficiency. Even so, there are a multitude of possible Pareto-efficient equilibria, depending upon the initial distribution of resource endowments across individuals. Other kinds of behavioral assumptions lead to different social outcomes, however. These outcomes might emphasize certainty,

fairness, or justice, as against efficiency. Such outcomes are not at all far-fetched from rational choice premises, for no single individual stands to benefit from efficiency as a state of affairs (because it is a public good), whereas all individuals may well find that fairness is in their own self-interest.

Until the time that significant progress is made toward an understanding of preferences, the scope or power of rational choice analyses is clearly limited. Since preferences are given rather than explained in rational choice analyses, these analyses are far better suited for social phenomena that are the outgrowth of individual preferences that are strong (relative to competing), stable (over time), and uniform (across actors).[21] Hence, social outcomes dependent on preferences that result from fundamental biological drives or from strongly sanctioned social conventions are good candidates for rational choice analyses. Social outcomes dependent on unstable, weak, or variable preferences—consumer behavior,[22] for example—are by this token poor subjects for rational choice analyses.

Elaborating the Role of Information

Yet another way to increase the empirical fit of rational choice models is to appreciate that variable amounts and types of information will have systematic effects on outcomes. These models typically require some assump-

---

[19] Simon (1985) and Arrow (1987) object even to this solution on the grounds that any kind of maximization is impossible due to computational and informational limits.

[20] None of the social sciences has contributed much in the way of a positive theory of preference formation. Pleas for greater attention to this issue have been emanating recently in nearly all of the social science disciplines. A select list would include Scitovsky (1976), Sen (1977), Hirschman (1985) and Arrow (1987) in economics; Douglas and Isherwood (1979) in anthropology; March (1978) and Wildavsky (1987) in political science; Zajonc (1980), Simon (1985) and Ainslie (1986) in psychology; Elster (1983) and Nelson (1986) in philosophy, and Emerson (1987), Friedman (1987) and Etzioni (1986) in sociology. Most of these writers, however, do not claim to be constructing an explanatory theory of preference formation themselves, and the models of the few who do make such a claim are far from elaborated. The most ambitious attempts to address the issue of preference formation theoretically have not come from social scientists at all, but from evolutionary biologists (Alexander 1987; Boyd and Richerson 1985). This is not the place to discuss the merits of these works, however.

[21] We are grateful to Douglas Heckathorn (personal communication) for his suggestions in this regard.

[22] One anonymous reviewer of this paper suggests that consumer behavior is one of the greatest success stories of macroeconomics, for as the price of a good goes up its consumption generally goes down. The ambitions of the economic theory of consumer behavior go considerably beyond the making of price/quantity predictions for the consumption of a single commodity, however, for in this case the critical problem of the substitutability of goods simply does not arise. The theory of consumer behavior seeks to explain nothing less than how individuals allocate their budget given the totality of commodities and other goods available in their environment. Since the proponents of the ordinal theory of utility (most mainstream economists) eschew the possibility of independently measuring individual preferences—let alone satisfaction—apart from actual behavior, they are compelled to assume the constancy of preferences in order to derive any empirical implications at all from their models. Since this assumption is known to be highly unrealistic, models of this kind can have little to say about the empirical determinants of consumer behavior. For a recent assessment of the poverty of current economic approaches to consumer behavior, see Roth (1987).

RATIONAL CHOICE THEORY 215

tion of "sufficient information" in order for individuals to choose successfully among alternatives. This assumption is increasingly regarded as problematic, however. To illustrate, consider a situation in which two people who are subject to the same structural constraints behave differently. We can account for this by saying either that they have different preferences, or that they have different information about the consequences of their actions. To claim that behavior is explicable by reference to different preferences is tautological, and undermines the standard methodology of rational choice. The second explanation is more satisfying: the amount of information that agents have can affect behavior *independently* of constraints or preferences. It may well be that information is the crucial intervening variable in all rational choice explanations.

Indeed, information has become an increasingly key variable in studies of contracting, bargaining, and organization. Both principal agent and transaction-cost models start with the assumption that informational asymmetries are significant. What seems to be missing in these literatures, however, is a theory of optimal information investment.[23] Such a theory would have to answer a host of questions. How much information is it rational to collect and use in making a specific decision? How does the agent decide when to stop searching? How do we understand the case in which two individuals have precisely the same information but draw different conclusions from it? Finally, suppose that the information that is required to make a decision rationally is inherently unavailable (that is, the situation is marked by uncertainty). What then should we expect rational actors to do?

Elaborating the Contribution of Structural Constraints

In addition to modifying behavioral assumptions to increase their verisimilitude, it is also possible to introduce other structural constraints than purely institutional ones explicitly into these models (we refer here to constraints such as those produced by macroeconomic fluctuations, wars, and even the

size of one's generational birth cohort). All structural constraints affect behavior by determining the objective probabilities that an individual's most preferred end can be realized. In this way they act as inducements to the pursuit of one end as against another.

Not a great deal of effort has gone into this area of rational choice analysis (see, however, Easterlin 1981), but sociologists know a great deal about how it is that locations within social structures limit individual choices. One cannot marry an Eskimo if there are none around (Blau 1987:79). Among those who wish to work full-time, everyone would clearly prefer to work in a primary rather than a secondary labor market. That not everyone does is often explicable by race, class, and/or gender position. Much of the new work by sociologists using rational choice theory to understand macrosociological problems falls into this category (Brustein 1988a; Brinton 1988; and Kiser 1987).

Another way to elaborate the role of structural constraints in determining outcomes is to inquire as to the origins of the institutions that produce such constraints. This line of research is just beginning (Coleman 1989; Hechter 1989; Kliemt 1989).

CONCLUSION

Rational choice provides a number of discrete benefits to researchers who work within its confines. Once scholars can identify the appropriate problem to which their research question belongs, they are assured of finding a determinate solution. Armed with a given theory, the investigator knows which facts are critical for the solution and which facts are largely irrelevant. Since this often leads to a demand to collect new kinds of data, rational choice has a built-in tendency to create new research agendas out of old ones. Further, researchers beginning from rational choice premises never need to build their theory anew, starting from first principles and defining and justifying the use of each concept. Not only does this save a good deal of intellectual energy, but it also enables scholars with quite different substantive interests and areas of expertise to communicate with one another. All of these conditions combine to help sustain a research program in which knowledge cumulates relatively efficiently and progress is swift.

---

[23] This must go beyond the limits of Stigler's (1961) search theory, however, for reasons discussed by Arrow (1987:207).

216   SOCIOLOGICAL THEORY

Debates about the merits or demerits of rational choice theories often take on an ideological cast, and sometimes rational choice theories are rejected because they seem to have unpalatable political implications. In this regard we think that it is important to note two characteristics of rational choice theories. First, in these theories, individuals are accorded significantly more respect than in most other sociological models. Rational choice theories of collective action, for instance, take into account contextual constraints on action but also leave room for the informed choices of actors. This is in contrast to those who would argue that participants are merely sheep heeding the call of the shepherd, or individuals who ignore reason when their sensibilities are excited. Second, arguing that individuals will often follow their self-interest in choosing among actions is not the same thing as saying that they ought to do so. While this was the position of Bentham and the utilitarians, positive and normative analyses have no necessary connection.

As rational choice explanations come to include more realistic behavioral assumptions, more knowledge about the effects of social structures, and greater appreciation of the role of information, they cannot fail to provide more satisfactory empirical accounts. Scholarship is required on all of these separate fronts. Sociologists have a comparative advantage in contributing to at least one aspect of this work, namely, to the study of the effects of social structural constraints on social outcomes. Sociologists also know a great deal about how organizations control information. At the same time, cognitive scientists enjoy a comparative advantage in the search for more realistic behavioral assumptions, and indeed much research on this subject is already underway. Together these two strands of research may well contribute to the development of positive theory in social science.

REFERENCES

Ainslie, George. 1986. "Beyond Microeconomics: Conflict Among Interests in a Multiple Self as a Determinant of Value." Pp. 133–76 in Jon Elster, ed., *The Multiple Self*. Cambridge: Cambridge University Press.

Alexander, Jeffrey C., Bernhard Giesen, Richard Munch, and Neil J. Smelser, eds. 1987. *The Micro-Macro Link*. Berkeley: University of California Press.

Alexander, Richard D. 1987. *The Biology of Moral Systems*. New York: Aldine De Gruyter.

Allais, M. and O. Hagen. 1979. *Expected Utility Hypotheses and the Allais Paradox: Contemporary Discussions of Decision under Uncertainty with Allais' Rejoinder*. Dordrecht: D. Reidel.

Arrow, Kenneth J. 1951. *Social Choice and Individual Values*. New Haven: Yale University Press.

Arrow, Kenneth J. 1987. "Rationality of Self and Others in an Economic System." Pp. 201–16 in Robin M. Hogarth and Melvin W. Reder, eds., *Rational Choice: The Contrast between Economics and Psychology*. Chicago: University of Chicago Press.

Azzi, Corry and Ronald Ehrenberg. 1975. "Household Allocation of Time and Church Attendance." *Journal of Political Economy*, 83, 1:27–55.

Barry, Brian and Russell Hardin, Eds. 1982. *Rational Man and Irrational Society?* Beverly Hills, CA.: Sage.

Blau, Peter. 1987. "Contrasting Theoretical Perspectives." Pp. 71–86 in J.C. Alexander, B. Giesen, R. Munch, & N. Smelser, eds., *The Micro-Macro Link*. Berkeley: University of California Press.

Boulding, Kenneth E., ed. 1973. *Peace and the War Industry*. New Haven: Yale University Press.

Boyd, Robert and Peter J. Richerson. 1985. *Culture and the Evolutionary Process*. Chicago: University of Chicago Press.

Brams, Steven. 1985. *Superpower Games*. New Haven: Yale University Press.

Brenner, Reuven. 1983. *History: The Human Gamble*. Chicago: University of Chicago Press.

Brinton, Mary. 1988. "The Social-Institutional Bases of Gender Stratification: Japan as an Illustrative Case." *American Journal of Sociology* 94:330–34.

Brustein, William. 1988a. *Social Origins of Political Regionalism: France 1849–1981*. Berkeley: University of California Press.

Brustein, William. 1988b. "The Political Geography of Belgian Fascism: The Case of Rexism." *American Sociological Review* 53(1):69–80.

Buchanan, James, and Gordon Tullock. 1962. *The Calculus of Consent*. Ann Arbor: University of Michigan Press.

Campbell, Angus, Philip E. Converse, Warren E. Miller, and Donald E. Stokes. 1966. *Elections and the Political Order*. New York: John Wiley and Sons.

Coleman, James S. 1973. *The Mathematics of Collective Action*. Chicago: Aldine.

Coleman, James S. 1986a. "Social Theory, Social Research, and a Theory of Action." *American Journal of Sociology* 86(5):984–1014.

Coleman, James S. 1986b. *Individual Interests and Collective Rationality*. New York: Cambridge University Press.

Coleman, James S. 1989. "The Emergence of Norms." In M. Hechter, K.D. Opp, & R. Wippler, *Social Institutions: Their Emergence Maintenance and Effects*. New York: Aldine de Gruyter.

Collins, Randall. 1981. "On the Microfoundations of Macrosociology." *American Journal of Sociology*, 86, 5:984–1014.

Cook, Karen, ed. 1987. *Social Exchange Theory*. Beverly Hills: Sage Publications.

Douglas, Mary and Baron Isherwood. 1979. *The World of Goods*. New York: W.W. Norton and Company.

Downs, Anthony. 1957. *An Economic Theory of Democracy*. New York: Harper & Row.

Easterlin, Richard A. 1980. *Birth and Fortune: The Impact of Numbers on Personal Welfare*. New York: Basic Books.

RATIONAL CHOICE THEORY

Einhorn, Hillel J. and Robin M. Hogarth. 1985. "Ambiguity and Uncertainty in Probabilistic Inference." *Psychological Review*, 92, 4:433–61.

Elster, Jon. 1983. *Sour Grapes: Studies in the Subversion of Rationality*. Cambridge: Cambridge University Press.

Elster, Jon. 1985. *Making Sense of Marx*. Cambridge: Cambridge University Press.

Emerson, Richard M. 1981. "Social Exchange Theory." Pp. 30–65 in Morris Rosenberg and Ralph H. Turner, eds., *Social Psychology: Sociological Perspectives*. New York: Basic Books.

Emerson, Richard M. 1987. "Toward a Theory of Value in Social Exchange." Pp. 11–46 in Karen S. Cook, ed., *Social Exchange Theory*. Newbury Park, CA: Sage.

Enelow, James and Melvin Hinich. 1984. *The Spatial Theory of Voting*. New York: Cambridge University Press.

Etzioni, Amitai. 1986. "The Case for a Multiple-Utility Conception." *Economics and Philosophy* 2:159–183.

Friedman, Debra. 1986. "The Principal-Agent Problem in Labor-Management Negotiations." Pp. 87–104 in Edward J. Lawler, ed., *Advances in Group Processes*, Vol. 3. Greenwich, CT.: JAI Press.

Friedman, Debra. 1987. "Notes on 'Toward a Theory of Value in Social Exchange.' " Pp. 47–58 in Karen S. Cook, ed., *Social Exchange Theory*. Newbury Park, CA: Sage.

Friedman, Debra. 1987. "Uncertainty and Collective Action." Unpublished paper.

Giddens, Anthony. 1979. *Central Problems in Social Theory: Action, Structure and Contradiction in Social Analysis*. Berkeley: University of California Press.

Gottfredson, Michael and Travis Hirschi. 1986. "The True Value of Lambda Would Appear to be Zero: An Essay on Career Criminals, Criminal Careers, Selective Incapacitation, Cohort Studies, and Related Topics." *Criminology*, 24, 2:213–234.

Habermas, Jurgen. 1983. *The Theory of Communicative Action*. Boston: Beacon Press.

Hardin, Russell. 1982. *Collective Action*. Baltimore: Johns Hopkins University Press (for Resources for the Future).

Heath, Anthony. 1976. *Rational Choice and Social Exchange*. Cambridge: Cambridge University Press.

Hechter. Michael. ed. 1983. *The Microfoundations of Macrosociology*. Philadelphia: Temple University Press.

Hechter, Michael. 1987. *Principles of Group Solidarity*. Berkeley and London: University of California Press.

Hechter, Michael. 1989. "The Emergence of Cooperative Social Institutions." In M. Hechter, K.D. Opp, & R. Wippler, eds., *Social Institutions: Their Emergence, Maintenance and Effects*. New York: Aldine de Gruyter.

Heckathorn, Douglas. In press. "Collective Sanctions and the Creation of Prisoner's Dilemma Norms." *American Journal of Sociology*.

Heimer, Carol A. 1985. *Reactive Risk and Rational Action: Managing Moral Hazard in Insurance Contracts*. Berkeley: University of California Press.

Hirsch, Paul, Stuart Michaels and Ray Friedman. 1987. " 'Dirty Hands' versus 'Clean Models': Is Sociology in Danger of Being Seduced by Economics?" *Theory and Society* 16:317–36.

Hirschman, Albert O. 1985. "Against Parsimony: Three Easy Ways of Complicating Some Categories of Economic Discourse." *Economics and Philosophy* 1(1):7–22.

Hirshleifer, J. and John G. Riley. 1979. "The Analytics of Uncertainty and Information—An Expository Survey." *Journal of Economic Literature*, 27:1375–1421.

Hogarth, Robin M. and Melvin W. Reder, eds. 1987. *Rational Choice: The Contrast between Economics and Psychology*. Chicago: University of Chicago Press.

Hotelling, Harold. 1929. "Stability in Competition." *The Economic Journal* 39, 1:41–57.

Jacobs, David. 1988. "Images of the State and Corporate Economic Power: Aggregate Concentration and Business Tax Rates." *American Journal of Sociology* 93(4):852–81.

Jensen, Michael C. and William H. Meckling. 1976. "Theory of the Firm: Managerial Behavior, Agency Costs and Ownership Structure." *Journal of Financial Economics*, 3, (4):305–360.

Kahneman, Daniel and Amos Tversky. 1979. "Prospect Theory: An Analysis of Decision Under Risk." *Econometrica*, 21:263–91.

Kiser, Edgar. 1987. *Kings and Classes: Crown Autonomy, State Policies and Economic Development in Western European Absolutisms*. PhD Dissertation, Department of Sociology, University of Arizona.

Kliemt, Hartmut. 1989. "The Costs of Organizing Social Cooperation: Some Remarks About the Game of Creating a Game." In M. Hechter, K.D. Opp, & R. Wippler, eds., *Social Institutions: Their Emergence, Maintenance and Effects*. New York: Aldine de Gruyter.

Klosko, George, Edward N. Muller, and Karl-Dieter Opp. 1987. "Rebellious Collective Action Revisited: An Exchange." *American Political Science Review* 81 (2):557–64.

Knight, Frank. 1921. *Risk, Uncertainty, and Profit*. Boston: Houghton Mifflin.

Leontieff, Wassily W. and Faye Duchin. 1983. *Military Spending: Facts and Figures, Worldwide Implications, and Future Outlook*. New York: Oxford University Press.

Luce, R. Duncan and Howard Raiffa. 1957. *Games and Decisions*. New York: John Wiley.

Machina, Mark J. 1983. "Generalized Expected Utility Analysis and the Nature of Observed Violations of the Independence Axiom." Pp. 263–293 in B.P. Stigum and F. Wenstop, eds., *Foundations of Utility and Risk Theory with Applications*. Dordrecht: D. Reidel.

March, James G. 1978. "Bounded Rationality, Ambiguity, and the Engineering of Choice." *The Bell Journal of Economics* 9(2):587–608.

Marsden, Peter. 1981. "Introducing Influence Processes into a System of Collective Decisions." *American Journal of Sociology* 86(6):1203–35.

Marwell, Gerald, and Ruth E. Ames. 1980. "Experiments on the Provision of Public Goods. II. Provision Points, Stakes, Experience, and the Free-Rider Problem." *American Journal of Sociology*, 85, (4):926–937.

Michels, Robert. 1962 (1911). *Political Parties: A Sociological Study of the Oligarchical Tendencies of Modern Democracy*. New York: Free Press.

Mueller, Dennis C. 1979. *Public Choice*. Cambridge: Cambridge University Press.

Nelson, Alan. 1986. "New Individualistic Foundations for Economics." *Nous* 20:469–90.

Oberschall, Anthony. 1973. *Social Conflict and Social Movements.* Englewood Cliffs, N.J.: Prentice-Hall.

Oberschall, Anthony and Eric Leifer. 1986. "Efficiency and Social Institutions: Uses and Misuses of Economic Reasoning in Sociology." *Annual Review of Sociology* 12:233–53.

Oliver, Pamela. 1980. "Rewards and Punishments as Selective Incentives for Collective Action: Theoretical Investigations." *American Journal of Sociology,* 85, (6):1356–1375.

Oliver, Pamela, Gerald Marwell and Ruy Teixeira. 1985. "A Theory of the Critical Mass. I. Interdependence, Group Heterogeneity and the Production of Collective Action. *American Journal of Sociology,* 91, 3:522–56.

Olson, Mancur. 1965. *The Logic of Collective Action.* Cambridge: Harvard University Press.

Opp, Karl-Dieter. 1986a. "Soft Incentives and Collective Action: Participation in the Anti-Nuclear Movement." *British Journal of Political Science,* 16:87–112.

Opp, Karl-Dieter. 1986b. *The Rationality of Political Protest.* Unpublished manuscript.

Pursell, Carroll W., Jr., ed. 1972. *The Military-Industrial Complex.* New York: Harper and Row.

Przeworski, Adam. 1985. *Capitalism and Social Democracy.* Cambridge: Cambridge University Press.

Riker, William H. 1986. *The Art of Political Manipulation.* New Haven: Yale University Press.

Rosen, Steven, ed. 1973. *Testing the Theories of the Military-Industrial Complex.* Lexington, Mass.: D.C. Heath.

Roth, Timothy P. 1987. *The Present State of Consumer Theory.* Lanham, Md.: University Press of America.

Sarkesian, Sam C., ed. 1972. *The Military-Industrial Complex: A Reassessment.* Beverly Hills, Calif.: Sage Publications.

Schelling, Thomas C. 1978. *Micromotives and Macrobehavior.* New York: W.W. Norton.

Scitovsky, Tibor. 1976. *The Joyless Economy: An Inquiry into Human Satisfaction and Consumer Dissatisfaction.* New York: Oxford University Press.

Sen, Amartya K. 1977. "Rational Fools: A Critique of the Behavioral Foundations of Economic Theory." *Philosophy and Public Affairs* 6(4):316–34.

Simon, Herbert A. 1957. *Models of Man.* New York: Wiley.

Simon, Herbert A. 1985. "Human Nature in Politics: The Dialogue of Psychology with Political Science." *American Political Science Review,* 79:293–304.

Stigler, George. 1961. "The Economics of Information." *Journal of Political Economy,* 69:213–25.

Stinchcombe, Arthur. 1968. *Constructing Social Theories.* New York: Harcourt and Brace.

Sykes, Gresham M. 1958. *The Society of Captives.* Princeton: Princeton University Press.

Tversky, Amos and Daniel Kahneman. 1987. "Rational Choice and the Framing of Decisions." Pp. 67–94 in Robin M. Hogarth and Melvin W. Reder, eds., *Rational Choice: The Contrast between Economics and Psychology.* Chicago: University of Chicago Press.

Udis, Bernard, ed. 1973. *The Economic Consequences of Reduced Military Spending.* Lexington, Mass.: D.C. Heath.

von Neumann, John and Oskar Morganstern. 1947. *Theory of Games and Economic Behavior.* Princeton: Princeton University Press.

Wildavsky, Aaron. 1987. "Preferences by Constructing Institutions: A Cultural Theory of Preference Formation." *American Political Science Review* 81(1):3–21.

Zajonc, R.B. 1980. "Feeling and Thinking: Preferences Need No Inferences." *American Psychologist* 35(2):151–75.

[14]

1983 APA Award Addresses

Choices, Values, and Frames

Daniel Kahneman *University of British Columbia*
Amos Tversky *Stanford University*

ABSTRACT: We discuss the cognitive and the psychophysical determinants of choice in risky and riskless contexts. The psychophysics of value induce risk aversion in the domain of gains and risk seeking in the domain of losses. The psychophysics of chance induce overweighting of sure things and of improbable events, relative to events of moderate probability. Decision problems can be described or framed in multiple ways that give rise to different preferences, contrary to the invariance criterion of rational choice. The process of mental accounting, in which people organize the outcomes of transactions, explains some anomalies of consumer behavior. In particular, the acceptability of an option can depend on whether a negative outcome is evaluated as a cost or as an uncompensated loss. The relation between decision values and experience values is discussed.

Making decisions is like speaking prose—people do it all the time, knowingly or unknowingly. It is hardly surprising, then, that the topic of decision making is shared by many disciplines, from mathematics and statistics, through economics and political science, to sociology and psychology. The study of decisions addresses both normative and descriptive questions. The normative analysis is concerned with the nature of rationality and the logic of decision making. The descriptive analysis, in contrast, is concerned with people's beliefs and preferences as they are, not as they should be. The tension between normative and descriptive considerations characterizes much of the study of judgment and choice.

Analyses of decision making commonly distinguish risky and riskless choices. The paradigmatic example of decision under risk is the acceptability of a gamble that yields monetary outcomes with specified probabilities. A typical riskless decision concerns the acceptability of a transaction in which a good or a service is exchanged for money or labor. In the first part of this article we present an analysis of the cognitive and psychophysical factors that determine the value of risky prospects. In the second part we extend this analysis to transactions and trades.

Risky Choice

Risky choices, such as whether or not to take an umbrella and whether or not to go to war, are made without advance knowledge of their consequences. Because the consequences of such actions depend on uncertain events such as the weather or the opponent's resolve, the choice of an act may be construed as the acceptance of a gamble that can yield various outcomes with different probabilities. It is therefore natural that the study of decision making under risk has focused on choices between simple gambles with monetary outcomes and specified probabilities, in the hope that these simple problems will reveal basic attitudes toward risk and value.

We shall sketch an approach to risky choice that derives many of its hypotheses from a psychophysical analysis of responses to money and to probability. The psychophysical approach to decision making can be traced to a remarkable essay that Daniel Bernoulli published in 1738 (Bernoulli 1738/1954) in which he attempted to explain why people are generally averse to risk and why risk aversion decreases with increasing wealth. To illustrate risk aversion and Bernoulli's analysis, consider the choice between a prospect that offers an 85% chance to win $1000 (with a 15% chance to win nothing) and the alternative of receiving $800 for sure. A large majority of people prefer the sure thing over the gamble, although the gamble has higher (mathematical) expectation. The expectation of a monetary gamble is a weighted average, where each possible outcome is weighted by its probability of occurrence. The expectation of the gamble in this example is .85 × $1000 + .15 × $0 = $850, which exceeds the expectation of $800 associated with the sure thing. The preference for the sure gain is an instance of risk aversion. In general, a preference for a sure outcome over a gamble that has higher or equal expectation is called risk averse, and the rejection of a sure thing in favor of a gamble of lower or equal expectation is called risk seeking.

Bernoulli suggested that people do not evaluate prospects by the expectation of their monetary outcomes, but rather by the expectation of the subjective

Copyright 1984 by the American Psychological Association, Inc.
Vol 39 No 4 341-350

value of these outcomes. The subjective value of a gamble is again a weighted average, but now it is the subjective value of each outcome that is weighted by its probability. To explain risk aversion within this framework, Bernoulli proposed that subjective value, or utility, is a concave function of money. In such a function, the difference between the utilities of $200 and $100, for example, is greater than the utility difference between $1,200 and $1,100. It follows from concavity that the subjective value attached to a gain of $800 is more than 80% of the value of a gain of $1,000. Consequently, the concavity of the utility function entails a risk averse preference for a sure gain of $800 over an 80% chance to win $1,000, although the two prospects have the same monetary expectation.

It is customary in decision analysis to describe the outcomes of decisions in terms of total wealth. For example, an offer to bet $20 on the toss of a fair coin is represented as a choice between an individual's current wealth W and an even chance to move to W + $20 or to W − $20. This representation appears psychologically unrealistic: People do not normally think of relatively small outcomes in terms of states of wealth but rather in terms of gains, losses, and neutral outcomes (such as the maintenance of the status quo). If the effective carriers of subjective value are changes of wealth rather than ultimate states of wealth, as we propose, the psychophysical analysis of outcomes should be applied to gains and losses rather than to total assets. This assumption plays a central role in a treatment of risky choice that we called prospect theory (Kahneman & Tversky, 1979). Introspection as well as psychophysical measurements suggest that subjective value is a concave function of the size of a gain. The same generalization applies to losses as well. The difference in subjective value between a loss of $200 and a loss of $100 appears greater than the difference in subjective value between a loss of $1,200 and a loss of $1,100. When the value functions for gains and for losses are pieced together, we obtain an S-shaped function of the type displayed in Figure 1.

This article was originally presented as a Distinguished Scientific Contributions Award address at the meeting of the American Psychological Association, Anaheim, California, August 1983. This work was supported by grant NR 197-058 from the U.S. Office of Naval Research.

Award addresses, submitted by award recipients, are published as received except for minor editorial changes designed to maintain *American Psychologist* format. This reflects a policy of recognizing distinguished award recipients by eliminating the usual editorial review process to provide a forum consistent with that employed in delivering the award address.

Requests for reprints should be sent to Daniel Kahneman, Department of Psychology, The University of British Columbia, Vancouver, BC, Canada.

Figure 1
A Hypothetical Value Function

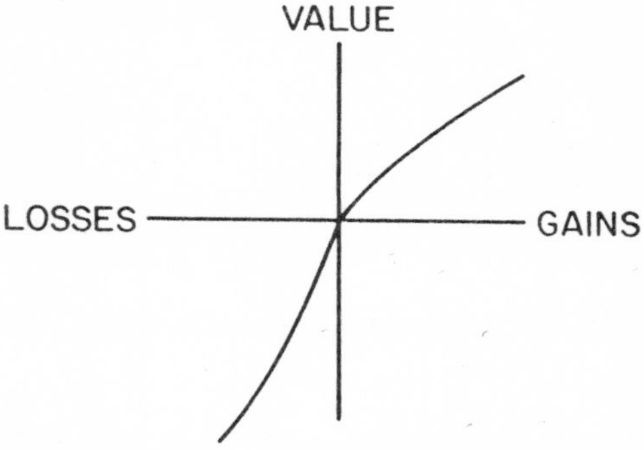

The value function shown in Figure 1 is (a) defined on gains and losses rather than on total wealth, (b) concave in the domain of gains and convex in the domain of losses, and (c) considerably steeper for losses than for gains. The last property, which we label *loss aversion*, expresses the intuition that a loss of $X is more aversive than a gain of $X is attractive. Loss aversion explains people's reluctance to bet on a fair coin for equal stakes: The attractiveness of the possible gain is not nearly sufficient to compensate for the aversiveness of the possible loss. For example, most respondents in a sample of undergraduates refused to stake $10 on the toss of a coin if they stood to win less than $30.

The assumption of risk aversion has played a central role in economic theory. However, just as the concavity of the value of gains entails risk aversion, the convexity of the value of losses entails risk seeking. Indeed, risk seeking in losses is a robust effect, particularly when the probabilities of loss are substantial. Consider, for example, a situation in which an individual is forced to choose between an 85% chance to lose $1,000 (with a 15% chance to lose nothing) and a sure loss of $800. A large majority of people express a preference for the gamble over the sure loss. This is a risk seeking choice because the expectation of the gamble (−$850) is inferior to the expectation of the sure loss (−$800). Risk seeking in the domain of losses has been confirmed by several investigators (Fishburn & Kochenberger, 1979; Hershey & Schoemaker, 1980; Payne, Laughhunn, & Crum, 1980; Slovic, Fischhoff, & Lichtenstein, 1982). It has also been observed with nonmonetary outcomes, such as hours of pain (Eraker & Sox, 1981) and loss of human lives (Fischhoff, 1983; Tversky, 1977; Tversky &

Kahneman, 1981). Is it wrong to be risk averse in the domain of gains and risk seeking in the domain of losses? These preferences conform to compelling intuitions about the subjective value of gains and losses, and the presumption is that people should be entitled to their own values. However, we shall see that an S-shaped value function has implications that are normatively unacceptable.

To address the normative issue we turn from psychology to decision theory. Modern decision theory can be said to begin with the pioneering work of von Neumann and Morgenstern (1947), who laid down several qualitative principles, or axioms, that should govern the preferences of a rational decision maker. Their axioms included transitivity (if A is preferred to B and B is preferred to C, then A is preferred to C), and substitution (if A is preferred to B, then an even chance to get A or C is preferred to an even chance to get B or C), along with other conditions of a more technical nature. The normative and the descriptive status of the axioms of rational choice have been the subject of extensive discussions. In particular, there is convincing evidence that people do not always obey the substitution axiom, and considerable disagreement exists about the normative merit of this axiom (e.g., Allais & Hagen, 1979). However, all analyses of rational choice incorporate two principles: *dominance* and *invariance*. Dominance demands that if prospect A is at least as good as prospect B in every respect and better than B in at least one respect, then A should be preferred to B. Invariance requires that the preference order between prospects should not depend on the manner in which they are described. In particular, two versions of a choice problem that are recognized to be equivalent when shown together should elicit the same preference even when shown separately. We now show that the requirement of invariance, however elementary and innocuous it may seem, cannot generally be satisfied.

Framing of Outcomes

Risky prospects are characterized by their possible outcomes and by the probabilities of these outcomes. The same option, however, can be framed or described in different ways (Tversky & Kahneman, 1981). For example, the possible outcomes of a gamble can be framed either as gains and losses relative to the status quo or as asset positions that incorporate initial wealth. Invariance requires that such changes in the description of outcomes should not alter the preference order. The following pair of problems illustrates a violation of this requirement. The total number of respondents in each problem is denoted by *N*, and the percentage who chose each option is indicated in parentheses.

Problem 1 (*N* = 152): Imagine that the U.S. is preparing for the outbreak of an unusual Asian disease, which is

expected to kill 600 people. Two alternative programs to combat the disease have been proposed. Assume that the exact scientific estimates of the consequences of the programs are as follows:

If Program A is adopted, 200 people will be saved. (72%)

If Program B is adopted, there is a one-third probability that 600 people will be saved and a two-thirds probability that no people will be saved. (28%)

Which of the two programs would you favor?

The formulation of Problem 1 implicitly adopts as a reference point a state of affairs in which the disease is allowed to take its toll of 600 lives. The outcomes of the programs include the reference state and two possible gains, measured by the number of lives saved. As expected, preferences are risk averse: A clear majority of respondents prefer saving 200 lives for sure over a gamble that offers a one-third chance of saving 600 lives. Now consider another problem in which the same cover story is followed by a different description of the prospects associated with the two programs:

Problem 2 (*N* = 155): If Program C is adopted, 400 people will die. (22%)

If Program D is adopted, there is a one-third probability that nobody will die and a two-thirds probability that 600 people will die. (78%)

It is easy to verify that options C and D in Problem 2 are undistinguishable in real terms from options A and B in Problem 1, respectively. The second version, however, assumes a reference state in which no one dies of the disease. The best outcome is the maintenance of this state and the alternatives are losses measured by the number of people that will die of the disease. People who evaluate options in these terms are expected to show a risk seeking preference for the gamble (option D) over the sure loss of 400 lives. Indeed, there is more risk seeking in the second version of the problem than there is risk aversion in the first.

The failure of invariance is both pervasive and robust. It is as common among sophisticated respondents as among naive ones, and it is not eliminated even when the same respondents answer both questions within a few minutes. Respondents confronted with their conflicting answers are typically puzzled. Even after rereading the problems, they still wish to be risk averse in the "lives saved" version; they wish to be risk seeking in the "lives lost" version; and they also wish to obey invariance and give consistent answers in the two versions. In their stubborn appeal, framing effects resemble perceptual illusions more than computational errors.

The following pair of problems elicits preferences that violate the dominance requirement of rational choice.

Problem 3 (*N* = 86): Choose between:

E. 25% chance to win $240 and
   75% chance to lose $760   (0%)

F. 25% chance to win $250 and
   75% chance to lose $750   (100%)

It is easy to see that F dominates E. Indeed, all respondents chose accordingly.

Problem 4 (*N* = 150): Imagine that you face the following pair of concurrent decisions. First examine both decisions, then indicate the options you prefer.

Decision (i) Choose between:
A. a sure gain of $240   (84%)
B. 25% chance to gain $1000 and
   75% chance to gain nothing   (16%)

Decision (ii) Choose between:
C. a sure loss of $750   (13%)
D. 75% chance to lose $1000 and
   25% chance to lose nothing   (87%)

As expected from the previous analysis, a large majority of subjects made a risk averse choice for the sure gain over the positive gamble in the first decision, and an even larger majority of subjects made a risk seeking choice for the gamble over the sure loss in the second decision. In fact, 73% of the respondents chose A and D and only 3% chose B and C. The same pattern of results was observed in a modified version of the problem, with reduced stakes, in which undergraduates selected gambles that they would actually play.

Because the subjects considered the two decisions in Problem 4 simultaneously, they expressed in effect a preference for A and D over B and C. The preferred conjunction, however, is actually dominated by the rejected one. Adding the sure gain of $240 (option A) to option D yields 25% chance to win $240 and 75% to lose $760. This is precisely option E in Problem 3. Similarly, adding the sure loss of $750 (option C) to option B yields a 25% chance to win $250 and 75% chance to lose $750. This is precisely option F in Problem 3. Thus, the susceptibility to framing and the S-shaped value function produce a violation of dominance in a set of concurrent decisions.

The moral of these results is disturbing: Invariance is normatively essential, intuitively compelling, and psychologically unfeasible. Indeed, we conceive only two ways of guaranteeing invariance. The first is to adopt a procedure that will transform equivalent versions of any problem into the same canonical representation. This is the rationale for the standard admonition to students of business, that they should consider each decision problem in terms of total assets rather than in terms of gains or losses (Schlaifer, 1959). Such a representation would avoid the violations of invariance illustrated in the previous problems, but the advice is easier to give than to follow. Except in

the context of possible ruin, it is more natural to consider financial outcomes as gains and losses rather than as states of wealth. Furthermore, a canonical representation of risky prospects requires a compounding of all outcomes of concurrent decisions (e.g., Problem 4) that exceeds the capabilities of intuitive computation even in simple problems. Achieving a canonical representation is even more difficult in other contexts such as safety, health, or quality of life. Should we advise people to evaluate the consequence of a public health policy (e.g., Problems 1 and 2) in terms of overall mortality, mortality due to diseases, or the number of deaths associated with the particular disease under study?

Another approach that could guarantee invariance is the evaluation of options in terms of their actuarial rather than their psychological consequences. The actuarial criterion has some appeal in the context of human lives, but it is clearly inadequate for financial choices, as has been generally recognized at least since Bernoulli, and it is entirely inapplicable to outcomes that lack an objective metric. We conclude that frame invariance cannot be expected to hold and that a sense of confidence in a particular choice does not ensure that the same choice would be made in another frame. It is therefore good practice to test the robustness of preferences by deliberate attempts to frame a decision problem in more than one way (Fischhoff, Slovic, & Lichtenstein, 1980).

The Psychophysics of Chances

Our discussion so far has assumed a Bernoullian expectation rule according to which the value, or utility, of an uncertain prospect is obtained by adding the utilities of the possible outcomes, each weighted by its probability. To examine this assumption, let us again consult psychophysical intuitions. Setting the value of the status quo at zero, imagine a cash gift, say of $300, and assign it a value of one. Now imagine that you are only given a ticket to a lottery that has a single prize of $300. How does the value of the ticket vary as a function of the probability of winning the prize? Barring utility for gambling, the value of such a prospect must vary between zero (when the chance of winning is nil) and one (when winning $300 is a certainty).

Intuition suggests that the value of the ticket is not a linear function of the probability of winning, as entailed by the expectation rule. In particular, an increase from 0% to 5% appears to have a larger effect than an increase from 30% to 35%, which also appears smaller than an increase from 95% to 100%. These considerations suggest a category-boundary effect: A change from impossibility to possibility or from possibility to certainty has a bigger impact than a comparable change in the middle of the scale. This hypothesis is incorporated into the curve displayed in

Figure 2, which plots the weight attached to an event as a function of its stated numerical probability. The most salient feature of Figure 2 is that decision weights are regressive with respect to stated probabilities. Except near the endpoints, an increase of .05 in the probability of winning increases the value of the prospect by less than 5% of the value of the prize. We next investigate the implications of these psychophysical hypotheses for preferences among risky options.

In Figure 2, decision weights are lower than the corresponding probabilities over most of the range. Underweighting of moderate and high probabilities relative to sure things contributes to risk aversion in gains by reducing the attractiveness of positive gambles. The same effect also contributes to risk seeking in losses by attenuating the aversiveness of negative gambles. Low probabilities, however, are overweighted, and very low probabilities are either overweighted quite grossly or neglected altogether, making the decision weights highly unstable in that region. The overweighting of low probabilities reverses the pattern described above: It enhances the value of long shots and amplifies the aversiveness of a small chance of a severe loss. Consequently, people are often risk seeking in dealing with improbable gains and risk averse in dealing with unlikely losses. Thus, the characteristics of decision weights contribute to the attractiveness of both lottery tickets and insurance policies.

The nonlinearity of decision weights inevitably leads to violations of invariance, as illustrated in the following pair of problems:

Problem 5 ($N = 85$): Consider the following two-stage game. In the first stage, there is a 75% chance to end the game without winning anything and a 25% chance to move into the second stage. If you reach the second stage you have a choice between:

A. a sure win of $30   (74%)
B. 80% chance to win $45   (26%)

Your choice must be made before the game starts, i.e., before the outcome of the first stage is known. Please indicate the option you prefer.

Problem 6 ($N = 81$): Which of the following options do you prefer?

C. 25% chance to win $30   (42%)
D. 20% chance to win $45   (58%)

Because there is one chance in four to move into the second stage in Problem 5, prospect A offers a .25 probability of winning $30, and prospect B offers .25 × .80 = .20 probability of winning $45. Problems 5 and 6 are therefore identical in terms of probabilities and outcomes. However, the preferences are not the same in the two versions: A clear majority favors the higher chance to win the smaller amount in Problem

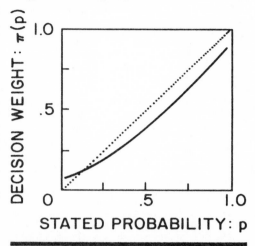

Figure 2
A Hypothetical Weighting Function

5, whereas the majority goes the other way in Problem 6. This violation of invariance has been confirmed with both real and hypothetical monetary payoffs (the present results are with real money), with human lives as outcomes, and with a nonsequential representation of the chance process.

We attribute the failure of invariance to the interaction of two factors: the framing of probabilities and the nonlinearity of decision weights. More specifically, we propose that in Problem 5 people ignore the first phase, which yields the same outcome regardless of the decision that is made, and focus their attention on what happens if they do reach the second stage of the game. In that case, of course, they face a sure gain if they choose option A and an 80% chance of winning if they prefer to gamble. Indeed, people's choices in the sequential version are practically identical to the choices they make between a sure gain of $30 and an 85% chance to win $45. Because a sure thing is overweighted in comparison with events of moderate or high probability (see Figure 2) the option that may lead to a gain of $30 is more attractive in the sequential version. We call this phenomenon the *pseudo-certainty* effect because an event that is actually uncertain is weighted as if it were certain.

A closely related phenomenon can be demonstrated at the low end of the probability range. Suppose you are undecided whether or not to purchase earthquake insurance because the premium is quite high. As you hesitate, your friendly insurance agent comes forth with an alternative offer: "For half the regular premium you can be fully covered if the quake occurs on an odd day of the month. This is a good deal because for half the price you are covered for more than half the days." Why do most people find such probabilistic insurance distinctly unattractive? Figure 2 suggests an answer. Starting anywhere in the region of low probabilities, the impact on the decision weight of a reduction of probability from p to $p/2$ is considerably smaller than the effect of a reduction from $p/2$ to 0. Reducing the risk by half, then, is not worth half the premium.

The aversion to probabilistic insurance is significant for three reasons. First, it undermines the classical explanation of insurance in terms of a concave utility function. According to expected utility theory, probabilistic insurance should be definitely preferred to normal insurance when the latter is just acceptable (see Kahneman & Tversky, 1979). Second, probabilistic insurance represents many forms of protective action, such as having a medical checkup, buying new tires, or installing a burglar alarm system. Such actions typically reduce the probability of some hazard without eliminating it altogether. Third, the acceptability of insurance can be manipulated by the framing of the contingencies. An insurance policy that covers fire but not flood, for example, could be evaluated either as full protection against a specific risk, (e.g., fire) or as a reduction in the overall probability of property loss. Figure 2 suggests that people greatly undervalue a reduction in the probability of a hazard in comparison to the complete elimination of that hazard. Hence, insurance should appear more attractive when it is framed as the elimination of risk than when it is described as a reduction of risk. Indeed, Slovic, Fischhoff, and Lichtenstein (1982) showed that a hypothetical vaccine that reduces the probability of contracting a disease from 20% to 10% is less attractive if it is described as effective in half of the cases than if it is presented as fully effective against one of two exclusive and equally probable virus strains that produce identical symptoms.

Formulation Effects

So far we have discussed framing as a tool to demonstrate failures of invariance. We now turn attention to the processes that control the framing of outcomes and events. The public health problem illustrates a formulation effect in which a change of wording from "lives saved" to "lives lost" induced a marked shift of preference from risk aversion to risk seeking. Evidently, the subjects adopted the descriptions of the outcomes as given in the question and evaluated the outcomes accordingly as gains or losses. Another formulation effect was reported by McNeil, Pauker, Sox, and Tversky (1982). They found that preferences of physicians and patients between hypothetical therapies

for lung cancer varied markedly when their probable outcomes were described in terms of mortality or survival. Surgery, unlike radiation therapy, entails a risk of death during treatment. As a consequence, the surgery option was relatively less attractive when the statistics of treatment outcomes were described in terms of mortality rather than in terms of survival.

A physician, and perhaps a presidential advisor as well, could influence the decision made by the patient or by the President, without distorting or suppressing information, merely by the framing of outcomes and contingencies. Formulation effects can occur fortuitously, without anyone being aware of the impact of the frame on the ultimate decision. They can also be exploited deliberately to manipulate the relative attractiveness of options. For example, Thaler (1980) noted that lobbyists for the credit card industry insisted that any price difference between cash and credit purchases be labeled a cash discount rather than a credit card surcharge. The two labels frame the price difference as a gain or as a loss by implicitly designating either the lower or the higher price as normal. Because losses loom larger than gains, consumers are less likely to accept a surcharge than to forego a discount. As is to be expected, attempts to influence framing are common in the marketplace and in the political arena.

The evaluation of outcomes is susceptible to formulation effects because of the nonlinearity of the value function and the tendency of people to evaluate options in relation to the reference point that is suggested or implied by the statement of the problem. It is worthy of note that in other contexts people automatically transform equivalent messages into the same representation. Studies of language comprehension indicate that people quickly recode much of what they hear into an abstract representation that no longer distinguishes whether the idea was expressed in an active or in a passive form and no longer discriminates what was actually said from what was implied, presupposed, or implicated (Clark & Clark, 1977). Unfortunately, the mental machinery that performs these operations silently and effortlessly is not adequate to perform the task of recoding the two versions of the public health problem or the mortality-survival statistics into a common abstract form.

Transactions and Trades

Our analysis of framing and of value can be extended to choices between multiattribute options, such as the acceptability of a transaction or a trade. We propose that, in order to evaluate a multiattribute option, a person sets up a mental account that specifies the advantages and the disadvantages associated with the option, relative to a multiattribute reference state. The overall value of an option is given by the balance of its advantages and its disadvantages in relation to the reference state. Thus, an option is acceptable if the value of its advantages exceeds the value of its disadvantages. This analysis assumes psychological—but not physical—separability of advantages and disadvantages. The model does not constrain the manner in which separate attributes are combined to form overall measures of advantage and of disadvantage, but it imposes on these measures assumptions of concavity and of loss aversion.

Our analysis of mental accounting owes a large debt to the stimulating work of Richard Thaler (1980, in press), who showed the relevance of this process to consumer behavior. The following problem, based on examples of Savage (1954) and Thaler (1980), introduces some of the rules that govern the construction of mental accounts and illustrates the extension of the concavity of value to the acceptability of transactions.

Problem 7: Imagine that you are about to purchase a jacket for $125 and a calculator for $15. The calculator salesman informs you that the calculator you wish to buy is on sale for $10 at the other branch of the store, located 20 minutes drive away. Would you make a trip to the other store?

This problem is concerned with the acceptability of an option that combines a disadvantage of inconvenience with a financial advantage that can be framed as a *minimal, topical,* or *comprehensive* account. The minimal account includes only the differences between the two options and disregards the features that they share. In the minimal account, the advantage associated with driving to the other store is framed as a gain of $5. A topical account relates the consequences of possible choices to a reference level that is determined by the context within which the decision arises. In the preceding problem, the relevant topic is the purchase of the calculator, and the benefit of the trip is therefore framed as a reduction of the price, from $15 to $10. Because the potential saving is associated only with the calculator, the price of the jacket is not included in the topical account. The price of the jacket, as well as other expenses, could well be included in a more comprehensive account in which the saving would be evaluated in relation to, say, monthly expenses.

The formulation of the preceding problem appears neutral with respect to the adoption of a minimal, topical, or comprehensive account. We suggest, however, that people will spontaneously frame decisions in terms of topical accounts that, in the context of decision making, play a role analogous to that of "good forms" in perception and of basic-level categories in cognition. Topical organization, in conjunction with the concavity of value, entails that the willingness to travel to the other store for a saving of $5 on a calculator should be inversely related to the price of the calculator and should be independent of the price of the jacket. To test this prediction, we constructed another version of the problem in which the prices of the two items were interchanged. The price of the calculator was given as $125 in the first store and $120 in the other branch, and the price of the jacket was set at $15. As predicted, the proportions of respondents who said they would make the trip differed sharply in the two problems. The results showed that 68% of the respondents ($N = 88$) were willing to drive to the other branch to save $5 on a $15 calculator, but only 29% of 93 respondents were willing to make the same trip to save $5 on a $125 calculator. This finding supports the notion of topical organization of accounts, since the two versions are identical both in terms of a minimal and a comprehensive account.

The significance of topical accounts for consumer behavior is confirmed by the observation that the standard deviation of the prices that different stores in a city quote for the same product is roughly proportional to the average price of that product (Pratt, Wise, & Zeckhauser, 1979). Since the dispersion of prices is surely controlled by shoppers' efforts to find the best buy, these results suggest that consumers hardly exert more effort to save $15 on a $150 purchase than to save $5 on a $50 purchase.

The topical organization of mental accounts leads people to evaluate gains and losses in relative rather than in absolute terms, resulting in large variations in the rate at which money is exchanged for other things, such as the number of phone calls made to find a good buy or the willingness to drive a long distance to get one. Most consumers will find it easier to buy a car stereo system or a Persian rug, respectively, in the context of buying a car or a house than separately. These observations, of course, run counter to the standard rational theory of consumer behavior, which assumes invariance and does not recognize the effects of mental accounting.

The following problems illustrate another example of mental accounting in which the posting of a cost to an account is controlled by topical organization:

Problem 8 ($N = 200$): Imagine that you have decided to see a play and paid the admission price of $10 per ticket. As you enter the theater, you discover that you have lost the ticket. The seat was not marked, and the ticket cannot be recovered.

Would you pay $10 for another ticket?
Yes (46%)   No (54%)

Problem 9 ($N = 183$): Imagine that you have decided to see a play where admission is $10 per ticket. As you enter the theater, you discover that you have lost a $10 bill.

Would you still pay $10 for a ticket for the play?
Yes (88%)   No (12%)

The difference between the responses to the two problems is intriguing. Why are so many people unwilling to spend $10 after having lost a ticket, if they would readily spend that sum after losing an equivalent amount of cash? We attribute the difference to the topical organization of mental accounts. Going to the theater is normally viewed as a transaction in which the cost of the ticket is exchanged for the experience of seeing the play. Buying a second ticket increases the cost of seeing the play to a level that many respondents apparently find unacceptable. In contrast, the loss of the cash is not posted to the account of the play, and it affects the purchase of a ticket only by making the individual feel slightly less affluent.

An interesting effect was observed when the two versions of the problem were presented to the same subjects. The willingness to replace a lost ticket increased significantly when that problem followed the lost-cash version. In contrast, the willingness to buy a ticket after losing cash was not affected by prior presentation of the other problem. The juxtaposition of the two problems apparently enabled the subjects to realize that it makes sense to think of the lost ticket as lost cash, but not vice versa.

The normative status of the effects of mental accounting is questionable. Unlike earlier examples, such as the public health problem, in which the two versions differed only in form, it can be argued that the alternative versions of the calculator and ticket problems differ also in substance. In particular, it may be more pleasurable to save $5 on a $15 purchase than on a larger purchase, and it may be more annoying to pay twice for the same ticket than to lose $10 in cash. Regret, frustration, and self-satisfaction can also be affected by framing (Kahneman & Tversky, 1982). If such secondary consequences are considered legitimate, then the observed preferences do not violate the criterion of invariance and cannot readily be ruled out as inconsistent or erroneous. On the other hand, secondary consequences may change upon reflection. The satisfaction of saving $5 on a $15 item can be marred if the consumer discovers that she would not have exerted the same effort to save $10 on a $200 purchase. We do not wish to recommend that any two decision problems that have the same primary consequences should be resolved in the same way. We propose, however, that systematic examination of alternative framings offers a useful reflective device that can help decision makers assess the values that should be attached to the primary and secondary consequences of their choices.

Losses and Costs

Many decision problems take the form of a choice between retaining the status quo and accepting an alternative to it, which is advantageous in some respects and disadvantageous in others. The analysis of value that was applied earlier to unidimensional risky

prospects can be extended to this case by assuming that the status quo defines the reference level for all attributes. The advantages of alternative options will then be evaluated as gains and their disadvantages as losses. Because losses loom larger than gains, the decision maker will be biased in favor of retaining the status quo.

Thaler (1980) coined the term "endowment effect" to describe the reluctance of people to part from assets that belong to their endowment. When it is more painful to give up an asset than it is pleasurable to obtain it, buying prices will be significantly lower than selling prices. That is, the highest price that an individual will pay to acquire an asset will be smaller than the minimal compensation that would induce the same individual to give up that asset, once acquired. Thaler discussed some examples of the endowment effect in the behavior of consumers and entrepreneurs. Several studies have reported substantial discrepancies between buying and selling prices in both hypothetical and real transactions (Gregory, 1983; Hammack & Brown, 1974; Knetsch & Sinden, in press). These results have been presented as challenges to standard economic theory, in which buying and selling prices coincide except for transaction costs and effects of wealth. We also observed reluctance to trade in a study of choices between hypothetical jobs that differed in weekly salary (S) and in the temperature (T) of the workplace. Our respondents were asked to imagine that they held a particular position (S_1, T_1) and were offered the option of moving to a different position (S_2, T_2), which was better in one respect and worse in another. We found that most subjects who were assigned to (S_1, T_1) did not wish to move to (S_2, T_2), and that most subjects who were assigned to the latter position did not wish to move to the former. Evidently, the same difference in pay or in working conditions looms larger as a disadvantage than as an advantage.

In general, loss aversion favors stability over change. Imagine two hedonically identical twins who find two alternative environments equally attractive. Imagine further that by force of circumstance the twins are separated and placed in the two environments. As soon as they adopt their new states as reference points and evaluate the advantages and disadvantages of each other's environments accordingly, the twins will no longer be indifferent between the two states, and both will prefer to stay where they happen to be. Thus, the instability of preferences produces a preference for stability. In addition to favoring stability over change, the combination of adaptation and loss aversion provides limited protection against regret and envy by reducing the attractiveness of foregone alternatives and of others' endowments.

Loss aversion and the consequent endowment effect are unlikely to play a significant role in routine economic exchanges. The owner of a store, for example, does not experience money paid to suppliers as losses and money received from customers as gains. Instead, the merchant adds costs and revenues over some period of time and only evaluates the balance. Matching debits and credits are effectively cancelled prior to evaluation. Payments made by consumers are also not evaluated as losses but as alternative purchases. In accord with standard economic analysis, money is naturally viewed as a proxy for the goods and services that it could buy. This mode of evaluation is made explicit when an individual has in mind a particular alternative, such as "I can either buy a new camera or a new tent." In this analysis, a person will buy a camera if its subjective value exceeds the value of retaining the money it would cost.

There are cases in which a disadvantage can be framed either as a cost or as a loss. In particular, the purchase of insurance can also be framed as a choice between a sure loss and the risk of a greater loss. In such cases the cost–loss discrepancy can lead to failures of invariance. Consider, for example, the choice between a sure loss of $50 and a 25% chance to lose $200. Slovic, Fischhoff, and Lichtenstein (1982) reported that 80% of their subjects expressed a risk-seeking preference for the gamble over the sure loss. However, only 35% of subjects refused to pay $50 for insurance against a 25% risk of losing $200. Similar results were also reported by Schoemaker and Kunreuther (1979) and by Hershey and Schoemaker (1980). We suggest that the same amount of money that was framed as an uncompensated loss in the first problem was framed as the cost of protection in the second. The modal preference was reversed in the two problems because losses are more aversive than costs.

We have observed a similar effect in the positive domain, as illustrated by the following pair of problems:

Problem 10: Would you accept a gamble that offers a 10% chance to win $95 and a 90% chance to lose $5?

Problem 11: Would you pay $5 to participate in a lottery that offers a 10% chance to win $100 and a 90% chance to win nothing?

A total of 132 undergraduates answered the two questions, which were separated by a short filler problem. The order of the questions was reversed for half the respondents. Although it is easily confirmed that the two problems offer objectively identical options, 55 of the respondents expressed different preferences in the two versions. Among them, 42 rejected the gamble in Problem 10 but accepted the equivalent lottery in Problem 11. The effectiveness of this seemingly inconsequential manipulation illustrates both the cost–loss discrepancy and the power of framing. Thinking

of the $5 as a payment makes the venture more acceptable than thinking of the same amount as a loss.

The preceding analysis implies that an individual's subjective state can be improved by framing negative outcomes as costs rather than as losses. The possibility of such psychological manipulations may explain a paradoxical form of behavior that could be labeled the *dead-loss effect*. Thaler (1980) discussed the example of a man who develops tennis elbow soon after paying the membership fee in a tennis club and continues to play in agony to avoid wasting his investment. Assuming that the individual would not play if he had not paid the membership fee, the question arises: How can playing in agony improve the individual's lot? Playing in pain, we suggest, maintains the evaluation of the membership fee as a cost. If the individual were to stop playing, he would be forced to recognize the fee as a dead loss, which may be more aversive than playing in pain.

Concluding Remarks

The concepts of utility and value are commonly used in two distinct senses: (a) *experience value,* the degree of pleasure or pain, satisfaction or anguish in the actual experience of an outcome; and (b) *decision value,* the contribution of an anticipated outcome to the overall attractiveness or aversiveness of an option in a choice. The distinction is rarely explicit in decision theory because it is tacitly assumed that decision values and experience values coincide. This assumption is part of the conception of an idealized decision maker who is able to predict future experiences with perfect accuracy and evaluate options accordingly. For ordinary decision makers, however, the correspondence of decision values between experience values is far from perfect (March, 1978). Some factors that affect experience are not easily anticipated, and some factors that affect decisions do not have a comparable impact on the experience of outcomes.

In contrast to the large amount of research on decision making, there has been relatively little systematic exploration of the psychophysics that relate hedonic experience to objective states. The most basic problem of hedonic psychophysics is the determination of the level of adaptation or aspiration that separates positive from negative outcomes. The hedonic reference point is largely determined by the objective status quo, but it is also affected by expectations and social comparisons. An objective improvement can be experienced as a loss, for example, when an employee receives a smaller raise than everyone else in the office. The experience of pleasure or pain associated with a change of state is also critically dependent on the dynamics of hedonic adaptation. Brickman & Campbell's (1971) concept of the hedonic treadmill suggests the radical hypothesis that rapid adaptation will cause the effects of any objective improvement to be short-lived. The complexity and subtlety of hedonic experience make it difficult for the decision maker to anticipate the actual experience that outcomes will produce. Many a person who ordered a meal when ravenously hungry has admitted to a big mistake when the fifth course arrived on the table. The common mismatch of decision values and experience values introduces an additional element of uncertainty in many decision problems.

The prevalence of framing effects and violations of invariance further complicates the relation between decision values and experience values. The framing of outcomes often induces decision values that have no counterpart in actual experience. For example, the framing of outcomes of therapies for lung cancer in terms of mortality or survival is unlikely to affect experience, although it can have a pronounced influence on choice. In other cases, however, the framing of decisions affects not only decision but experience as well. For example, the framing of an expenditure as an uncompensated loss or as the price of insurance can probably influence the experience of that outcome. In such cases, the evaluation of outcomes in the context of decisions not only anticipates experience but also molds it.

REFERENCES

Allais, M., & Hagen, O. (Eds.). (1979). *Expected utility hypotheses and the Allais paradox.* Hingham, MA: D. Reidel Publishing.

Bernoulli, D. (1954). Exposition of a new theory on the measurement of risk. *Econometrica 22,* 23–36. (Original work published 1738)

Brickman, P., & Campbell, D. T. (1971). Hedonic relativism and planning the good society. In M. H. Appley (Ed.), *Adaptation-level theory: A symposium* (pp. 287–302). New York: Academic Press.

Clark, H. H., & Clark, E. V. (1977). *Psychology and language.* New York: Harcourt Brace Jovanovich.

Erakar, S. E., & Sox, H. C. (1981). Assessment of patients' preferences for therapeutic outcomes. *Medical Decision Making, 1,* 29–39.

Fischhoff, B. (1983). Predicting frames. *Journal of Experimental Psychology: Learning, Memory and Cognition. 9,* 103–116.

Fischhoff, B., Slovic, P., & Lichtenstein, S. (1980). Knowing what you want: Measuring labile values. In T. Wallsten (Ed.), *Cognitive processes in choice and decision behavior* (pp. 117–141). Hillsdale, NJ: Erlbaum.

Fishburn, P. C., & Kochenberger, G. A. (1979). Two-piece von Neumann-Morgenstern utility functions. *Decision Sciences. 10,* 503–518.

Gregory, R. (1983). *Measures of consumer's surplus: Reasons for the disparity in observed values.* Unpublished manuscript, Keene State College, Keene, NH.

Hammack, J., & Brown, G. M., Jr. (1974). *Waterfowl and wetlands: Toward bioeconomic analysis.* Baltimore: Johns Hopkins University Press.

Hershey, J. C., & Schoemaker, P. J. H. (1980). Risk taking and problem context in the domain of losses: An expected-utility analysis. *Journal of Risk and Insurance, 47,* 111–132.

Kahneman, D., & Tversky, A. (1979). Prospect theory: An analysis of decision under risk. *Econometrica, 47,* 263–291.

Kahneman, D., & Tversky, A. (1982). The simulation heuristic. In D. Kahneman, P. Slovic, & A. Tversky (Eds.), *Judgment under uncertainty: Heuristics and biases* (pp. 201–208). New York: Cambridge University Press.

Knetsch, J., & Sinden, J. (in press). Willingness to pay and compensation demanded: Experimental evidence of an unexpected disparity in measures of value. *Quarterly Journal of Economics.*

March, J. G. (1978). Bounded rationality, ambiguity, and the engineering of choice. *Bell Journal of Economics, 9,* 587–608.

McNeil, B., Pauker, S., Sox, H., Jr., & Tversky, A. (1982). On the elicitation of preferences for alternative therapies. *New England Journal of Medicine, 306,* 1259–1262.

Payne, J. W., Laughhunn, D. J., & Crum, R. (1980). Translation of gambles and aspiration level effects in risky choice behavior. *Management Science, 26,* 1039–1060.

Pratt, J. W., Wise, D., & Zeckhauser, R. (1979). Price differences in almost competitive markets. *Quarterly Journal of Economics, 93,* 189–211.

Savage, L. J. (1954). *The foundation of statistics.* New York: Wiley.

Schlaifer, R. (1959). *Probability and statistics for business decisions.* New York: McGraw-Hill.

Schoemaker, P. J. H., & Kunreuther, H. C. (1979). An experimental study of insurance decisions. *Journal of Risk and Insurance, 46,* 603–618.

Slovic, P., Fischhoff, B., & Lichtenstein, S. (1982). Response mode, framing, and information-processing effects in risk assessment. In R. Hogarth (Ed.), *New directions for methodology of social and behavioral science: Question framing and response consistency* (pp. 21–36). San Francisco: Jossey-Bass.

Thaler, R. (1980). Toward a positive theory of consumer choice. *Journal of Economic Behavior and Organization. 1,* 39–60.

Thaler, R. (in press). Using mental accounting in a theory of consumer behavior. *Journal of Marketing.*

Tversky, A. (1977). On the elicitation of preferences: Descriptive and prescriptive considerations. In D. Bell, R. L. Kenney, & H. Raiffa (Eds.), *Conflicting objectives in decisions. International Series on Applied Systems Analysis* (pp. 209–222). New York: Wiley.

Tversky, A., & Kahneman, D. (1981). The framing of decisions and the psychology of choice. *Science, 211,* 453–458.

von Neumann, J., & Morgenstern, O. (1947). *Theory of games and economic behavior* (2nd ed.). Princeton: Princeton University Press.

[15]

A New Model of Rational Choice*

Howard Margolis

Classical economic theory always assumes that the individual will "act in his interest"; but it has never examined carefully the entity to which "his" refers. Often, as when households are taken as the unit for income and consumption, it is implicitly assumed that "the family" or "the household" is this entity whose interest is being maximized. Yet this is without theoretical foundation, merely a convenient but slipshod device. In this case, as in many others (e.g., when a man is willing to contribute much, even his life, to national defense, rather than use a strategy which will push the cost onto others), men act *as if* the "his" referred to some entity larger than themselves. That is, they appear to act in terms, not of their own interest, but of the interests of a collectivity or even of another person. Indeed, if they did not do so, the basis for society could hardly exist.

Yet how can this be reconciled with the narrow premise of individual interest? . . . We could simply solve the problem by fiat, letting "his" refer to whatever entity the individual appeared to act in the interest of. This obviously would make the theory trivially true, and never disconfirmable. A more adequate solution is one which states the conditions under which the entity in whose interests he acts will be something other than himself.[1]

. . . As regards useful acts, one might ask, useful to whom? To the individual who performs them or to society? The two utilities are only too separate and distinct, and it would seem necessary to have had very little experience of the world to maintain that an action that is useful to society is generally useful to the individual who performs it, and vice versa.[2]

Between them, Coleman and Mosca sum up the problem I attack and the nature of the solution I propose. For an empirically tenable theory of social choice, we require a model of individual choice which does not fail catastrophically in the presence of public goods. But the conventional model of choice does so fail, the most familiar illustration being the fact that it cannot even account for the elementary fact that people vote.

*This article summarizes my study, *Selfishness, Altruism and Rationality* (New York: Cambridge University Press, forthcoming). I am indebted to the Andrew Mellon Foundation for research support and to the editors, a reviewer, Jack Hirshleifer, Richard Musgrave, Susan Rose-Ackerman, Jerome Rothenberg, Richard Sclove, T. C. Schelling, and Nicolaus Tideman for comments.

1. James S. Coleman, "Individual Interests and Collective Action," *Papers on Non-Market Decision-making* 1 (1966): 49–63, quotation from p. 55.
2. Gaetano Mosca, *The Ruling Class*, ed. A. Livingstone, trans. H. D. Kahn (New York: McGraw-Hill Book Co., 1937), p. 37.

Ethics 91 (January 1981): 265–279

266   *Ethics   January 1981*

Now the problem in accounting for voting, put in a more general context, is that we must account for the observation that people make contributions to what they perceive as the public interest (as by perceiving and acting upon a duty to vote) in contexts where the return to the individual appears inconsequential and the effect on society is so microscopic as to be invisible. How can this be reconciled with the notion of rational, utility-maximizing individuals which proves so potent in analyzing economic behavior?

Mosca suggests we recognize the hopelessness of supposing that utility to society can be understood as congruent with utility to the individual. And indeed, if individuals are observed to be acting in a manner which seems rational from a social point of view, but not from an individual point of view, then—without prejudice yet to the conventional model of choice—we can say that they are acting as if they had two different utility functions.[3] For on as small a matter as bothering to vote, or as large a matter as risking one's life in time of war, we have no difficulty seeing the behavior as a rational use of resources if the utility function the individual is seeking to maximize concerns group interest, rather than self-interest.

Further, such a presumption would be inconsistent with individual maximizing only if we supposed that utility to society was something determined for the individual, or given to the individual, rather than his own perception of group interest. But if we clearly understand that the group utility the individual seeks to maximize reflects his own perception of group interest, by no means necessarily identical with the perception of some other individual, then the individual is using any resources allocated to group interest to maximize his own group-interested utility function.

So far, though, we have only reformulated the problem. Instead of a puzzle as to how an individual maximizing his own interest could rationally use resources to further group interest, we have the puzzle of what governs the extent to which this individual uses resources to maximize his own self-interest and to what extent he uses resources to maximize his own sense of group interest. How do what we may call his "ultimate preferences" somehow reconcile his group- and self-interested preferences?[4]

3. The notion of a distinction between a person's motivation as a private individual and as a citizen goes all the way back to Plato. For a recent discussion in this journal, see S. G. Salkever, "Who Knows Whether It's Rational to Vote?" *Ethics* 90 (1980): 215–30.

4. Economists use the term "self-interested" in two senses, rarely alerting the reader to a shift in usage. In one sense, it means "narrowly self-interested" or "selfish," at least with respect to individuals outside one's own household. In the other, it means only "personal," allowing for the possibility that personal interests may involve altruism (the individual derives satisfaction from doing good for others). Neither of these uses encompasses what I mean by "group-interested" or "social" motivation, which does not require that the actor benefit in any personal way from his behavior, since he is motivated by what he takes to be the interests of society. Of course it sometimes also happens that self-interest is interpreted so loosely that anything the individual chooses to do is automatically his self-interest. That was what Coleman was talking about. Note that, exactly as in the case of a derivative in calculus,

From this point of view, we are led to ask a question which would otherwise seem entirely bizarre. Imagine that inside Smith there are two individuals—an S-Smith who values only self-interest and a G-Smith who values only group interest. Is it then possible to specify an allocation rule, or a social welfare function, for this two-person "society," with the property that, given this rule, Smith behaves the way we observe real people to behave? The simplest way to do this, I believe, is to use the "inside Smith" metaphor, since, given an allocation between S- and G-Smiths, each can then be allowed to maximize his own preference function exactly as in the conventional model. The critical thing here, as Coleman suggests, will be definition of a viable allocation rule, since until we have an allocation rule, we have a helpful "manner of speaking," but not a model of any real analytical power.

AN ALLOCATION RULE

The allocation rule, or principle, I want to propose says this:

> The larger the share of my resources I have spent unselfishly, the more weight I give to my selfish interests in allocating a marginal bit of resources. On the other hand, the larger the benefit I can confer on the group compared to the benefit from spending a marginal bit of resources on myself, the more I will tend to act unselfishly.

This principle (or pair of principles) does not purport to say how a person ought to behave. Whether the principle is acceptable or unacceptable as a normative precept is irrelevant to the purpose at hand, since we are postulating a principle intended to account for the way that people do behave.

The two components of the principle are independent, one turning on the extent of Smith's participation in socially motivated activity, the other turning on (Smith's judgment of) the value of marginal effort in the pursuit of group (vs. self-) interest. To try to make this clear, I give, first, a verbal description using concrete examples, then an algebraic statement of the model, and finally a short discussion using diagrams.

Suppose that Smith has been contributing to some activity which he takes to be socially valuable, say the Red Cross, a political campaign, an arts organization, or whatever. We make the usual assumption of diminishing marginal utility for all goods. This is not an essential feature of the model, but it is convenient and harmless here. Similarly, we will suppose that, as is very often, though not necessarily, the case either in the model or in the world, Smith's own contribution (to the Red Cross or whatever) is but a microscopic fraction of the whole effort, so that the marginal social value of another dollar will not be perceptibly affected by any contribution of the magnitude that an ordinary citizen such as Smith might make. The ratio of marginal utilities from group- versus self-

---

the ratio between costs and benefits can easily be large, even though, from a social viewpoint, both the spending and the effect of the spending are microscopically small.

268   *Ethics*   *January 1981*

interested spending will then define what we will call the "value ratio" of Smith's spending opportunities.

Suppose now that Smith donates an additional $100 to the activity, but simultaneously receives a $100 increment to his wealth. His participation has changed: both the magnitude of his total contribution and the fraction of his wealth contributed have increased. But there has been no change in his marginal utility from private spending and no perceptible change in the marginal utility from social spending. So participation has changed, but not (perceptibly) Smith's value ratio. Alternatively, an emergency (say a flood in the next county) can create an abrupt shift in Smith's perception of the marginal utility of a contribution, while a fire in Smith's own house would create a corresponding shift for Smith's spending on himself. Now participation has not changed, but (in either version of this illustration) the value ratio has changed.

Ordinarily,these two components will be mixed together, since if we imagine how Smith allocates a fixed bundle of resources, then necessarily a bit more spent on social goals means a bit less spent on private goals. Hence, a shift in participation will ordinarily be accompanied by a shift in the value ratio. But as has just been illustrated, it is easy to define situations in which participation changes but not the value ratio, or the reverse. The two notions are conceptually distinct, and what drives the model is the interaction between these two motives.

Let G and S be Smith's utility from the point of view of perfectly group-interested G-Smith and perfectly self-interested S-Smith, respectively. For any given situation, let G' and S' then be the corresponding marginal utilities of a dollar spent to maximize utility to G-Smith and S-Smith, respectively. So the ratio G'/S' is the value ratio already introduced. For this ratio to be well defined, G- and S-utility must be measured on some common scale. But the internal logic of the model provides for that. For Smith himself is one member of the group; hence G-utility "includes" S-utility. This does not mean that Smith will see value to aiding the blind only if he himself is blind; but the blind who are helped must be part of a larger entity of which Smith feels he is a part. (See the comments later in the article on the question of what defines the "group.")

Now G-utility evaluates Smith's perception of the situation of society as a whole (not excluding Smith, but giving no special weight to Smith), and S-utility evaluates Smith's own situation. Neither depends on any necessary relation to Smith's own resources. It is easiest to see this in connection with public goods, since S-utility will depend substantially on the supply of public goods in Smith's society, which will be essentially independent of Smith's own wealth or spending, and G-utility will ordinarily be almost completely independent of Smith's own wealth or spending. Hence the value ratio, though defined in terms of Smith's own values, is not defined only in terms of Smith's own resources. And there is no necessary connection between the value ratio and Smith's own participation in the provision of goods either to himself or to society at large. Smith's participation, on the other hand, depends only on how large a share of Smith's resources have been devoted to group interest, not at all on his judgment of the value of the spending (or of the value of the resources he has devoted to self-interest). If Smith contributes to a charity he later discovers to be fraudulent, his judgment of the value of his contribution changes drastically, but there is no change in the extent to which he has participated.

Let *g* be the total amount that has been allocated to G-Smith (which by definition will have been spent to maximize G-utility), and let *s* be the total amount that has been allocated to S-Smith (which by definition will have been spent to maximize S-utility). So the ratio g/s, which we will call the "participation ratio," gives the ratio in which Smith has allocated his resources between spending to maximize G- versus S-utility.

Finally, let *W* be the weight that Smith gives to S-utility in choosing whether to allocate a marginal dollar to S-Smith versus G-Smith. (Actually, it is better not to say "Smith gives," but perhaps "the referee inside Smith gives," since we are not postulating a rule that Smith consciously follows but rather an internal mechanism of which Smith may be quite unconscious.)

Summing up, what the allocation principle requires is then:

    1. The larger the value ratio, G'/S', the greater the tendency must be for Smith to allocate a marginal dollar to G- rather than S-Smith.

    2. The weighting function, *W*, must vary positively with the participation ratio, g/s, since the likelihood that Smith will allocate a marginal dollar to S- rather than G-Smith must increase in the participation ratio.

    3. Smith will be in equilibrium when the propensity to favor self-interest just balances the propensity to act in group interest.

Casting this in mathematical terms, all of the discussion of the previous several pages can be summarized very compactly by defining the FS equilibrium condition as follows.

Smith is in equilibrium if and only if

$$W = G'/S' , \tag{1}$$

$$\text{where } W = f(g/s); \ W^\circ \geq 1; \ W' > 0 . \tag{2}$$

In words, what equation (2) says is that, until Smith has spent *something* in group interest (i.e., as long as $g = 0$; hence $g/s = 0$), then $W = W^\circ$. In the simplest case, setting $W^\circ = 1$, he gives no more weight to his self-interest than he does to his perception of group interest. However, any increase in the participation ratio, g/s, increases *W*. In mathematical notation, $W' \equiv dW/d(g/s) > 0$.

So long as the ordinarily reasonable assumption of diminishing marginal utility holds, then if Smith is out of equilibrium with $W > G'/S'$ he will move closer to equilibrium by shifting resources from group interest to self-interest (decreasing g, increasing s); and the reverse holds if he is out of equilibrium with $W < G'/S'$. For shifting resources from g to s decreases g/s, hence decreasing W, and simultaneously increases G'/S'; and the reverse if the shift is from s to g.

Figure 1 illustrates this equilibrium notion. The dashed line slanting upward to the right shows W increasing (eq. [2]) as the share of Smith's income allocated to group interest (g) increases from zero to his whole income, I, along the horizontal axis. The solid line slanting down from the left in figure 1 gives the value ratio, G'/S', which (provided that $S'' < 0$, $G'' \leq 0$) will have a negative slope, as shown, yielding the unique equilibrium allocation at E.

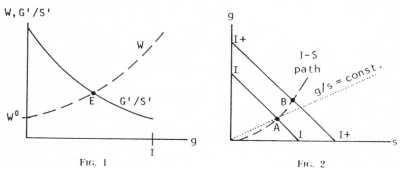

FIG. 1   FIG. 2

Figure 2 then illustrates a fundamental property of Smith's equilibrium income-spending path (the set of equilibrium allocations as Smith's income increases) for the important special case in which Smith is an ordinary citizen in a large society and faces stable spending opportunities. For this case (which has already been mentioned in introducing the model), G' will not be affected by Smith's own allocation, which will be microscopic compared to the spending of all members of society on outlets for group-interested spending.

In figure 2, Smith's allocation to G-Smith (g) is now shown on the vertical axis, and his allocation to S-Smith (s) is shown on the horizontal axis. Together, $g + s = $ Smith's income, I. Possible allocations Smith might make, subject to his income constraint, are given by the $-45°$ line labeled $I-I$. As we move northwest along $I-I$ (equivalent to moving to the right in fig. 1), W increases, while G'/S' decreases. Somewhere along this line there will be a unique equilibrium point (recall fig. 1), such that $W = G'/S'$. In figure 2, this is point A. We now draw a vector (the straight line in fig. 2) from the origin through point A. This will be the locus of all points such that the participation ratio, g/s, hence also W, will be the same as at A. But as we move out along this constant-W vector the value ratio, G'/S', must increase (for S' is decreasing, but G' is remaining constant). So A must be the only point on that line at which Smith could be in equilibrium, as well as the only such point along the income constraint line, I-I. At points along the constant-W line closer to the origin than A, we must find $W > G'/S'$ (G' would be the same as at A, as is W; but S' must be greater, hence the value ratio would be reduced); and the reverse at points on the constant-W line, but further from the origin than A. This means that, if Smith's income is less than I (the income constraint lies closer to the origin than I-I), the equilibrium point must lie southeast of the constant-W line; and for incomes greater than I, the equilibrium point will lie northwest of the constant-W line.

Since this argument can be applied to any equilibrium point, Smith's equilibrium income-spending path must have the upward-bending shape sketched by the curved dashed line in figure 2. For example, at income $I+$, Smith's equilibrium allocation must lie at a point, such as B, northwest of the intersection of the constant-W line and the enlarged income constraint, $I+$-$I+$. At a still higher income level, the new equilibrium would lie northwest of a line drawn from the origin through B. And so on.

So it turns out, given some rather innocuous-seeming assumptions, that the allocation rule implies that spending in group interest will be a superior good; as income increases, the fraction of resources allocated to G-Smith increases, even though (in a sense) Smith is becoming more selfish (W is increasing).

However, one or more of the assumptions on which this result depends (such as "fixed spending opportunities") will be violated in many practical contexts. So while the upward-bending income-spending path illustrated in figure 2 is a very important property of the model, with many empirical implications, other situations arise in which allocations shift even though income has not; where relatively poor individuals are moved to great efforts in what they deem to be group interest; where individuals face unstable spending opportunities, so that the assumption that G' can be taken as constant with respect to Smith's own spending does not hold; and so on. So it is by no means the case that all the behavior implied by the model follows from or is contingent on the validity of the superior good result. Nor, of course, can we realistically suppose that Smith's spending opportunities consist only of the voluntary choice between abstract spending in pure self-interest and in pure group interest. Empirically, mixed goods—opportunities of significant value to both S- and G-Smiths—are very important (Smith may wish sincerely to serve his country; but a couple of years in government might also be good for his career); and coerced spending (taxes), not just voluntary spending, is socially important.

However, for the two-person society "inside Smith," all goods are public goods. For Smith's loaf of bread is simultaneously consumed by both S- and G-Smiths. So goods that in Smith's external society are private, as well as goods which are public, are all public goods "inside Smith."

We require some equivalent of Samuelson's omniscient referee to manage a Samuelsonian "pseudomarket" inside Smith.[5] But here the problem of preference revelation that plagues the standard analysis of public goods is mooted by the fact that the only entity that must know G-and S-Smiths' true preferences is also inside Smith. We need postulate no new metaphorical entity here, since we have implicitly supposed some equivalent of a referee inside Smith to apply the allocation rule. Further, once the logic of the model leads us to this "inside Smith" pseudomarket we have a context which proves to be sufficient to define the allocation scheme in terms of goods which are public goods as well as private goods in the real society outside Smith and also mixed goods, coerced goods, and the various combinations among these.

Having come this far, we can then hardly avoid noticing that we have inside Smith a G-Smith which seems to have properties rather like those of Freud's superego, an S-Smith which looks rather like Freud's id, and a third entity which mediates between these two and appears to have the integrating function which is so essential to the Freudian notion of the ego. I certainly do not want to claim that the structure described here is what Freud had in mind, or that it is what he should have had in mind. However, given the explicitly speculative tone of Freud's own treatment of this trichotomy, I doubt that it can be fairly argued that the scheme here is fatally inconsistent with Freud's insight on this matter. Having been led to Freud by this aspect of the model, I was struck especially by the following remark: "Man is not only far more immoral than he believes but also far more moral than he knows. . . . Human nature has a far greater extent, both for good and for evil, than it thinks it has—i.e., than its ego is aware of through conscious perception."[6]

Summing this up: the Samuelson pseudomarket analysis (showing how efficient allocations would be made if, contrary to fact, there could be an omniscient referee for society) finds a kind of real existence in this model, made necessary by the internal logic of the model and made possible by the fact that the revelation of preferences problem can hardly arise if the revelation goes no further than to some other entity inside Smith. This scheme allows the model to handle cases of mixed motivation in the use of resources (self-interest and group interest are both involved). It also allows the model to handle allocations (between g and s) of coerced spending, mainly taxes for public goods. Both are obviously very important empirically. In turn, this leads to a trichotomous structure inside Smith which looks rather like the kind of structure that Freud intuited.

The final issue I want to mention, before turning to a sketch of results, concerns the Darwinian roots of the model. A century ago, Darwin himself recognized that competition among individuals within a breeding

---

5. P. A. Samuelson, "Pure Theory of Public Expenditure and Taxation," in *Public Economics*, ed. J. Margolis and H. Guitton (New York: St. Martin's Press, 1969), pp. 98–123.

6. Sigmund Freud, *The Ego and the Id*, trans. Joan Riviere (New York: W. W. Norton & Co., 1963), p. 52. The second half of the quotation is Freud's footnote to the first.

group would reward self-interest, whereas competition between breeding groups would reward group interest. Hence the possibility arises that some structure of preferences would develop which constituted a compromise between the rival advantages of group interest and self-interest. It turns out, in fact, that a reasonably simple line of argument in these terms leads to just the equilibrium conditions given by equations (1) and (2).

This is a delicate topic, given the distaste many people have for Darwinian explanations in the social sciences and the tendency among social scientists toward overestimation of the degree to which the "selfish gene" argument has undercut (among population biologists and allied specialties) the respectability of any argument which invokes group selection. The essential point is to realize that the selfish gene argument turns on an application of Occam's razor, not a proof; and which way that razor cuts depends a good deal on whether we are studying human beings or something else. For even adherents of the selfish gene view are driven, in the context of human behavior, to invoke a good deal of argument which is tantamount to "as if" group selection.

In any case, unless we dogmatically rule out a measure of (real or "as if") group selection, we can develop the model given here on a Darwinian basis, and this proves to be very fruitful. For example, the model would become very clumsy if we felt bound to stay with the traditional view of economics which takes it as self-evident that a model of rational choice derives its equilibrium allocations from a total utility function. For there is no neat utility function that (without imposing empirically unreasonable restrictions on the scope of the model) would yield equation (1) as its first-order condition.[7] But from the Darwinian viewpoint, there is no reason to expect that any such function should be other than a clumsy artifact. The allocation rule arises as a resolution of conflicting selection pressures. Seen in that light, the notion of two distinct utility functions is perfectly natural, and it is the conventional supposition that Smith is really maximizing a single utility function that seems artificial and puzzling.

Similarly, the "inside Smith" allocation scheme is likely to appear bizarre from a conventional viewpoint, but if indeed, as the Darwinian view suggests, there are distinct S- and G-preferences, then the scheme is, mathematically, the most efficient solution to the allocation problem for mixed goods. And although it is rather surprising to think of natural selection as accounting for so sophisticated a scheme, it is hardly implausibly sophisticated compared to other elegant adaptations throughout the living world. So on a variety of matters, like the two examples just

7. For the case of fixed spending opportunities, we can use a version of the function discussed in G. C. Archibald and D. Donaldson, "Notes on Economic Equality," *Journal of Public Economics* 12 (1979): 202–15. However, if spending opportunities shift, the utility function (if you wish to call something so unstable a utility function) must change. I am indebted to an anonymous reviewer for this reference.

mentioned, the Darwinian viewpoint proves to be an important part of the theory.

But what can be done with the theory?

SKETCH OF RESULTS

The simplest situations are those in which we can suppose that a one-time allocation is made for the whole spending period (say the year) between G- and S-spending, such that Smith is in equilibrium (eq. [1] holds), given his spending opportunities and his income. The higher his income, the more of his self-interested wants can be satisfied for a given fraction of income assigned to S-Smith. On the other hand, as an ordinary member of a large society—the situation to which such "static" analysis is mainly relevant—spending by Smith will have no perceptible effect on aggregate spending opportunities in group interest. So in this static context, S' declines with any increase in resources allocated to S-Smith, but G' is essentially constant. Hence, on the argument already given in connection with figure 2, an increase in income implies that Smith's participation ratio, g/s, must increase, and we get the rising income-spending path discussed earlier. As income grows the share of income allocated to group interest grows, even though the weight (W) given to self-interest is also growing. There is a good deal of empirical evidence to support this basic inference of the model, and indeed something close to this is built into the way that words such as "noble" and "peasant" are used in most languages. But bear in mind that G-Smith acts according to his own perception of social values, which may be very different from that of G-Jones.

This, in turn, brings us to questions of the nature of the "group" whose group interest G-Smith acts to advance. My study says very little about that; and in terms of the Darwinian argument mentioned earlier, it is not a salient problem. For a very long time, the group to which a human being belonged was obvious. But as human societies come to be organized on a larger scale, the problem of group identity becomes more and more complicated. In the modern world, it is very complicated indeed, involving a very rich mixing of affiliations based on locality, kinship, common traditions, religion, cooperative interactions, and so on. So if we wish to move ahead with work using this model, we will be quickly drawn into what are generally recognized as the central issues of sociology. But I will argue that we are not talking here about a *weakness* of the model. For in contrast to the conventional model, it is here possible to begin to address the crucial sociological puzzle of the nature and determinants of group identity within the rational choice framework. So I would hope that one of the virtues of the model is that it provides a potential link across the economic and sociological modes of analysis.

A crude but, I think, useful first cut, sufficient to let us get on with a beginning discussion of empirical applications, is to suppose just two levels of loyalty: say, national and local. In other words, we will set aside the undoubted fact Smith is likely to have sub- (and even trans-) national loyalties of many kinds (local, professional, religious, and so on). G-Smith, we will suppose, will never willfully use his resources to advance local interests at the expense of national interests; however, among alternative ways to contribute to national interest, he will particularly favor those uses of resources which favor local interests.

Now in a perfectly homogeneous world in which there also was perfect information, this interpretation of group interest would not have strong implications. For cases in which local interests served to discriminate among equally attractive ways to advance national interests could be regarded as empirically not very important. But in a heterogeneous world with vastly imperfect information, there is no reason for G-Smith to believe that all local interests (his and Jones's and Green's) are equally important to the national interest. And imperfect information leaves G-Smith quite uncertain about just how effective various ways of using resources in group interest might be. However, Smith will naturally be much better informed on his own local interests than on those of Jones or Green.

Further, it would be irrational for Smith to use up a substantial share of G-resources trying to improve his assessment of outlets for G-resources, for the same reasons that it would be irrational for S-Smith to use a substantial fraction of S-resources to improve his assessment of the best way to use his S-resources. G-Smith, like S-Smith (and like "economic man" in the conventional model, since the conventional analysis ordinarily treats Smith as if he were just S-Smith), will be one of Herbert Simon's "satisficers," and not because he is irrational after all. Rather, taking a reasonably realistic view of his information-processing capabilities and the costs of acquiring information, the most rational realistic course available to him involves just the behavior Simon describes as limited rationality, with its emphasis on limited search of alternatives, rules of thumb, and so on.[8] G-Smith will be led to use his G-resources on a reasonable-looking "portfolio" of group-interested activities.

This view has many consequences for such things as the nature of voluntary organizations, the role of self-interested incentives in channeling group-interested allocations (by securing some participation by S- as well as G-Smith) and occasionally the reverse, the evolution of state-supported expenditures, the role then played by private good works and charity in a system in which most such activity has become a government enterprise, the role of ideology as an integrator of diverse group interests, and so on. (Each of these matters is discussed in more or less detail in the full study referred to on the first page.)

All of this, thus far, has been in the "static" context of a one-time allocation between G-spending and S-spending. However, while there is a wide and important class of situations in which the static assumption is a reasonable simplifying assumption, there is obviously also a wide and

8. Herbert Simon, *Models of Man* (New York: John Wiley & Sons, 1957).

276   *Ethics   January 1981*

important class of situations in which it is empirically untenable. Many things can happen which change the value ratio (G'/S') of equation (1) for particular individuals or even for the members of society generally, and hence prompt a reallocation between S-Smith and G-Smith to reestablish equilibrium.

The main examples of the former concern individuals in the society who in one way or another (most obviously by being elected or appointed to office) come to control substantial resources beyond their own. In such situations, the value of G' for their own resources increases, since their own resources can be used as levers to move much larger bundles of resources. The effect on political leaders will be particularly striking, since their leverage is so great that it is no longer realistic, even in a large society, to treat the value of G' for resources used in a certain way as essentially constant. Further, where large and visible social effects turn on a leader's choice, and substantial resources for gathering and analyzing information are at the leader's disposal, the situation is very different from that of Citizen Smith choosing whether to donate to the March of Dimes or to the Muscular Dystrophy Fund. On the other hand, for Citizen Smith, G-Smith gives no special weight to Smith's private needs. But for President Smith, who may reasonably regard the personal well-being and freedom from merely material concerns of the president as a socially important matter, G-Smith will presumably assign some special value to Smith. From a leadership role, Smith may be in a position to influence the information available to more ordinary citizens and so be able to shape their tastes and beliefs. Obviously G'/S' is likely to be large compared to that of a private citizen, hence also the equilibrium value of W. The reader will be able to add to this list.

Consequently, and in a variety of ways, the behavior of political leaders (and indeed other figures who find themselves with special powers, even on as humble a level as a local school board member, e.g.) will be more complicated, appear to be more contradictory, than could be expected either in terms of the conventional model or in terms of a merely static analysis using the model proposed here.

There are also important situations, as mentioned, in which G'/S' shifts for the society as a whole, notably in the context of crises of all kinds, such as declarations of war and natural disasters. Such crises (or the later stages of such crises) will often also affect incomes in the society. It is straightforward, within the framework of the model, to deduce the kinds of situation in which crisis leads to widespread self-sacrifice (a "rush to the colors") and when it leads to panic and extremes of selfishness. Curious analogues turn up between such major events and matters on a local level, such as the feasibility of keeping a beach or neighborhood clean by voluntary action. And some useful insight, I think, can be gained into the conditions under which Mancur Olson's shrewd analysis of the "logic of collective action" in terms of self-interest governs outcomes and when (as in the political salience in recent years of civil rights, the environment, abortion, and so on) socially important forces are moved far beyond any reasonable allowance for self-interest.[9]

CONCEPTUAL RESULTS

By conceptual results, the most interesting of which I will describe next, I mean using the new model to sort out certain technical puzzles that arise inside the conventional theory.

In particular, the conventional theory has never been able to produce a definition of demand for public goods which is consistent with the elementary empirical observation that citizens have preferences about public goods which are inexplicable in terms of self-interest. The exact nature of the dilemma cannot be described short of a more technical presentation than would be appropriate here. But the problem turns on the fact that the utility function used by Samuelson in his justly celebrated 1954 paper (which is to say, the conventional utility function of economics, expanded to include public as well as private goods) allows Smith to consider only his own bundle of private goods plus the bundle of public goods available to all.[10] There is no place in the analysis for Smith's consideration of the effect of a given choice about public goods on the bundles of private goods available to others. What this means is that the cost (i.e., private goods forgone) to anyone but Smith of a given choice of public goods is not counted in Smith's preferences. But empirically, it is obvious that people do have preferences about budgets for public goods which turn on social judgments of costs and benefits to society as a whole (how much defense is enough and so on), not merely on how much an incremental aircraft carrier, for example, is personally worth to Smith.

The closest those working within the conventional theory have come to resolving this very fundamental problem is to specify certain restrictive forms of citizen preference: for example, the condition called "nonpaternalism," which specifies that the individual's preferences with respect to private goods for Jones are never inconsistent with Jones's own preference.[11] So if Jones is an alcoholic, Smith might be willing to be taxed to help pay for appropriate medical care for Jones, but only if that is how Jones would spend the money were it given directly to him. The possibility that Smith would be willing to contribute to drying out Jones, but not

9. Mancur Olson, *The Logic of Collective Action* (Cambridge, Mass.: Harvard University Press, 1965).

10. P. A. Samuelson, "The Pure Theory of Public Expenditure," *Review of Economics and Statistics* 36 (1954): 386–89. An enormous amount of work over the past twenty-five years is heavily in debt to this short paper, including of course the work presented here. Samuelson's "pseudomarket" paper, cited earlier, is a discussion of this 1954 paper.

11. Musgrave's invention of the category of "merit goods" provides a way of handling outside the formal theory any social spending that cannot be accounted for otherwise. For practical work on policy analysis, the merit-good notion is useful and indeed essential. But the fact that this extratheoretical device is needed says something significant about the state of the formal theory (see R. A. Musgrave, *The Theory of Public Finance* [New York: McGraw-Hill Book Co., 1959], pp. 13 ff.).

278   *Ethics*   *January 1981*

willing to give the money directly to Jones to spend as he pleases, is ruled out as paternalistic. Obviously, real individuals are commonly paternalistic, so that a formulation restricted to nonpaternalistic preferences does not work empirically. Similar problems arise with other suggestions within the conventional framework. But under the model proposed here, it turns out that well-defined demand curves exist for public goods. These demand curves reduce to the standard demand curves for the special case of self-interested behavior. But in the general case, they allow for (and in fact the model here implies) the kind of preferences we actually observe in human beings.

An interesting application in this context is to what are called "demand-revealing" (DR) mechanisms, which have been proposed as providing the basis for a solution to the "free-rider" problem of social choice.[12] Here simple and uncontroversial calculations show that in an American election, supposing that DR were in use, a voter willing to spend even a penny to increase the effect of his vote (for under DR a voter is charged a special incentive tax based on the effect of his vote on the outcome) could increase the effect several hundred times over, as compared to the effect of a citizen whose vote reflects only his self-interest. But the implausibility of supposing that a citizen would take the trouble to vote, but not be willing to spend the penny, turns out to imply that in fact the DR mechanisms would not lead to the efficient social outcomes claimed for them. The heart of the difficulty is simply that citizens' preference for public goods cannot (i.e., not without implying behavior which is empirically absurd) be treated as if only self-interest were involved. This conventional assumption works tolerably well in the context of private goods, for reasons that Wicksteed described very eloquently seventy years ago.[13] But it fails catastrophically in the context of public goods.

It is a striking illustration of the blinders imposed by the conventional theory that the very simple DR calculations just described, and the gross consequences that follow, were never worked out by economists despite the great attention given to demand-revealing mechanisms in recent years.

A well-known economist, Jack Hirshleifer, recently commented: "Economic study of market interactions may yield satisfactory results while postulating pure egoistic men, acting within an unexplained social environment of regulatory law. But as the power of economic analysis

12. Nicolaus Tideman and Gordon Tullock, "A New and Superior Process for Making Social Choices," *Journal of Political Economy* 84 (1976): 1145–59; Theodore Groves and John Ledyard, "Optimal Allocation of Public Goods: A Solution to the 'Free Rider' Problem," *Econometrica* 45 (1977): 783–809. I give a comparison of the two mechanisms, together with the calculations referred to here, in "Relation between the Groves/Ledyard and Tideman/Tullock DR Mechanisms," mimeographed (May 1980). A large DR literature has developed, including at least two books and at least two special issues of journals.

13. P. Wicksteed, *The Common Sense of Political Economy* (London: Routledge & Kegan Paul, 1933). The citation is to Lionel Robbins's edition, which is still in print and contains a valuable introduction by Robbins. The original edition was published in 1910.

comes to be employed outside the traditional market context, for example in the area of public choice, the egoistic model of man . . . will not suffice."[14] To which I would only add: and neither will some routine extension of the egoistic model. For if that were all that is required it would have been done long ago.

14. Jack Hirshleifer, "Privacy: Its Origins, Function, and Future," Working Paper no. 166 (Los Angeles: University of California, Los Angeles, November 1979), p. 20.

[16]

REASON AND RATIONALITY*

ARTHUR L. STINCHCOMBE

Northwestern University

INTRODUCTION

The central dependent variable in this paper is a specified ideal long-run relationship between what Max Weber called "substantive rationality" and what he called "formal rationality." By formal rationality he meant standardized methods of calculation on which routines can be based, such as "a bachelor's degree should involve passing 120 semester hours of courses," or "profits are maximized when marginal costs are equated with marginal revenue," or "iterated proportional fitting of a cross tabulation approaches the maximum likelihood estimates of the cell frequencies under loglinear models with any of several sampling schemes," or "contracts in which one of the parties receives no 'consideration,' no benefit from the transaction, cannot be enforced."

By substantive rationality we mean going behind such formal methods to the substance of the matter, as in the process by which instruction received in England or France is translated into American semester hours by rough theories of international equivalency, or by which the back list of a publisher, the inventory of books, is judged to represent a certain flow of marginal revenue based on the experience of the industry, or even more basically that money returns are a good approximation to marginal revenue, or by the principles of asymptotic efficiency which make maximum likelihood estimates of appropriate statistics a good thing, or by the hypothesis in legal reasoning that if a contract lays costs on one of the parties but gives them no benefits it is likely to be based on coercion, fraud, or illegal trading and that contracts so based are a bad thing.

The basic reason we are interested in the relationship between these two things is that for reliable social organization of calculation, one needs routines and procedures that can be judged quickly by external features, can be taught to ordinary men and women, and the like. The social extension of modes of reasoning by institutions depends on the formality of reasoning. But in general formal reasoning is vulnerable to variations in the situation—for example, social surveys are never carried out by any of the sampling schemes that justify iterative proportional fitting, so loglinear parameters do not ever have the standard errors estimated for them in sociology—and to variations in the objectives, so that few of us value the production of our books as exactly equal to the discounted stream of sales, because it still gives us a thrill to see them checked out of a library 20 years after they are out of print. So formal rationality is only as good as its grounding in substantive rationality. Only if semester hours are in fact equal (which we teachers all know they are not from differences between our own courses and differences of students within them) is a bachelor's degree a reliable measure of educated competence.

So what we want of our institutions of reason is a proper balance between efficient formal approximations that can have a reliable social effect, and substantive good sense to know their limits and to improve them. I should emphasize that substantive rationality is vulnerable, and often inferior to formal rational rationality, as in the example of "clinical judgement" in medical investigations.

The big predictor in whether a medical procedure appears in the literature as a success or as a failure is whether or not there was a control group (Gilbert, Light and Mosteller 1975; Gilbert, McPeek and Mosteller 1977). By basing their medical results on clinical substantive judgement rather than on a formal experimental control, physicians regularly deceive themselves.

Anyhow, what one wants to preserve from a policy point of view is a correct relation between socially instituted formal methods of calculation and substantive good sense. The paper below can be seen as an argument about what that dependent variable looks like in reality, how one recognizes high values of it in social life, and about what its main causes are. The ideal type of a rationalized institution, that

* Andrew Abbott and Kim Scheppele provided me with detailed and astringent critiques of a previous version of this paper. I have not changed the essential argument in response to their astringency, but I believe I have removed a large number of unclear patches from it, sometimes so as to sharpen the disagreements between us. I measure the quality of comments on drafts by the number and importance of changes induced in the paper (this "quality" is of course a joint product of my receptivity and the inherent quality of the critiques). By that measure these critiques were intelligent and relevant, and I greatly appreciate them. This paper was presented in Paris at the Maison des Sciences de l'Homme in a conference organized by Jon Elster and Pierre Bourdieu on rationality and norms.

is the outcome of the first half of the paper, is a combination of an analysis of what the variable looks like in social life, and an analysis of its causes. For example, when I argue (following Parsons 1939) that no serious institution of reason can do without protections from its judges' rationality, it is on the one hand an indicator of where in society we may have found a system that balances the institutional efficiency of formal rationality with substantive good sense. On the other hand it is, of course, an analysis of the causes of disinterested reasoning, of that socially precarious pattern of preferring the right answer over the wrong one merely because it is right. One of the causes of that precarious pattern is socially instituted protections of decision processes from corruption by passions or interests. It is a sign by which we can recognize normative elements in the use of reasoning in social life, and a cause of the solidity of norms that lead us to prefer good reasoning to bad.

The remainder of the essay after the development of the ideal type is about the variety of relations that the normative use of rational faculties have with he theory of utility maximization that we have lately come to understand as rationality. One part of the argument here is that normative behavior can very often be analyzed in terms of what has come to be called the theory of agency in economics, but with more of less fictional, socially established, utilities of the principals. The central contribution to this extension of the theory of agency is an unpublished paper by Carol Heimer (1986). It involves an analysis of what we mean by "taking responsibility," as in the sentence, "I'll take responsibility for the seminar series this year."

Another part of the argument is that the definition of the improvement of bodies of reason is a derivative of the proper balance of substantive and formal rationality. Only if a body of reasoning is routinized is it self-reproducing. Only if grounded in new conquests of substantive understanding of reality is it improving. So if we get the causes of the dependent variable of the paper, the balance of formal and substantive rationality, we will also have the causes of the evolution of bodies of reason, namely the causes of reliable reproduction and those of the preservation of favorable changes.

Another bit of the argument is that formal reasoning would not in general be socially viable, would not produce the social advantages of reliability and calculability that Weber emphasized so much, unless it were truly better. Unless the law of contract in fact allows people to enforce their voluntary agreements but is not easily available for coerced or fraudulent

agreements, it will not provide the calculability needed for capitalism because people will avoid it. So the formal rule about consideration has to be applied with some discretion, so that it achieves the ends of the law of contract, or people will try to invent other ways of making voluntary agreements work, and to exclude coerced and fraudulent agreements. Similarly the formal rationality of an American university registrar is only socially viable if there are very few ways to get a semester hour's credit without reading a book. A theory of why people go through ritual motions of reasoning—a theory of what social incentives there are to get a semester hour of credit regardless of the substance of the course, for example—without not suffice to explain why education has come to be a central institution in the American labor market and marriage market. Only by noting that there is some rational substance in most of those semester hours of credit can we understand the economic and social functions of semester hours of credit.

I would add as a preliminary *caveat* that there are many forms of substantive rationality that are not embedded in formal structures for getting an authoritative rational answer. There are other ways of getting authority for an answer than reason.

Bargaining is one. What makes a bargain authoritative is its being agreed to by the parties. People bargaining give many reasons, but the reasons are to persuade, not to give authority. For example in April of 1986 there was a lot of bargaining about the limits of the right to strike or to lockout in public employment in Norway. It took the form of applying for "dispensations" from the effects of the strike or the lockout. The public airline might apply for a dispensation from a strike of a union which includes controllers at airports, and whether or not that dispensation is granted is a bargain over whether *that* degree of damage to the public is part of the right to strike. Both the labor union and the management bargainers have to agree to a dispensation. People gave many arguments, as well as threats of binding arbitration if the dispensation were not granted, consultations of public opinion polls, offers to restrict the work in such a way as to minimize the revenues of the other party to the strike, and so on. Some combination of reason and perceived bargaining advantage was no doubt involved in the agreements that were reached by granting or not granting the dispensation. But what made the grant authoritative was the agreement of labor and management that the dispensation should be granted, not that the reasoning behind the application was unchallenged.

Similarly people in legislatures make arguments about legislation, of very varying quality.

REASON AND RATIONALITY

But once the vote has been taken, the quality of the arguments does not affect the validity of the legislation. It may possibly make it more or less likely that the legislation will be reconsidered by the legislature at another time, or that it will be struck down by the Supreme Court. But although we all believe that much better legislation comes about in legislatures with quite free debate, what makes legislation authoritative is not the reasoning but the votes.

Bargaining systems and legislatures then have substantive reasoning involved in them, but not routinized formal reasoning, and are no doubt the better for it. But they are not institutions of reason in the sense of this paper, and should be distinguished from institutions such as science, appellate court legal reasoning, or auditing financial accounts, which satisfy the criteria for institutions of reason developed in the first half of this paper. Not all socially significant reasoning is institutionalized so that reasons are the source of authority, and such reasoning is excluded from consideration in this paper.

Reasoning in Normative Systems and in Rational Action

In this paper I want to use the word "reason" and its relatives to refer to *norms governing a body of thought recognized as authoritative* in a culture, so that reason is characteristic of science, of the law, or of accounting practice. I want to use the term "rationality" and its relatives to refer to *individual behavior that maximizes benefits or minimizes costs* in achieving some goals of individuals or of groups such as households or firms, so that rationality is characteristic of the ideal-typical economic man, of the person who obeys maximizing rules of strategy given in game theory, or of machiavellian use of the law or of accounting practice for one's own ends.

Reason then is a normative concept in the sense that following the rules of, say, legal reasoning from precedent results in an authoritative judgement about what law applies to a particular case, whether following such rules maximizes anything for the individual judge or not. Rationality is normative only in the sense that one can derive a correct course of action *given* a set of goals; in some sense the normative element inheres in the set of goals, not in the derivation from them of the profit or utility maximizing course of conduct, as Parsons argued in *The Structure of Social Action* (1937).

By reason then I mean a socially established method of calculating what should be authoritative in a particular case. For example, when an appellate court in the United States makes a ruling on a particular case and explains it, this provides an authoritative paradigm for reasoning

about similar cases. The paradigm may tell, for example, what "facts" must be established for there to be an "invasion of privacy," or what warnings must be given to a prisoner for police conduct to be acceptable "due process of law." The point here is that the judgement of the appellate court is stated in general form by the court itself, rather than just being an administrative decision about a particular case; it is "formally rational" in the sense of following a set of norms about reason, rather than a "substantively rational" judgement about the particular case. This general form of the reasoning given allows other lawyers, including in particular lower court judges, to apply the paradigm laid down as authoritative in deciding whether some other particular breach of good taste by a newspaper is an invasion of privacy in the eyes of the law. A city attorney can use it in deciding, for example, what routine procedures should be instituted in police departments so that their convictions will stand up in court.

Such a standard method of calculation of authoritative normative judgements then is the application of "legal reasoning," and the development of such paradigms, and the social systems for creating and interpreting paradigms, constitutes the "rationalization" of law.

Similarly when a referee of an academic paper makes a recommendation against publication, he or she is ordinarily required to give reasons why it is unacceptable (see generally on referees Zuckerman and Merton 1971). These reasons must be couched in terms acceptable in the discipline, so that the availability of reagents of standard purity from chemical supply houses rules out challenges that the authors did not specify purification procedures, or the asymptotic efficiency of maximum likelihood estimates makes such estimates routinely acceptable in disciplines that usually use large samples, challengeable in disciplines that often work with small samples. But these "terms acceptable in the discipline" form a more or less coherent set of principles of reasoning, so that a referee's report recommending rejection will ordinarily contain a rationale of why the scientific results reported in *this* particular paper may be faulty, given the standards of evidence and reasoning accepted as authoritative in the discipline. That is, the referee is applying a standard method of calculation, a paradigm of reasoning, in coming to his or her judgement, and any sign that that judgement is "rational" from the point of view of the individual interests of the referee is ordinarily taken as a mark against it.

When scientific procedures in a laboratory for testing drugs fall below a minimum professional level (the minimum here seems to be pretty low), the FDA can inform drug manufacturers that reports from that laboratory will be examined with special care, and drive the laboratory out of business (Braithwaite 1984, p. 86). The willingness to apply sanctions of such severity shows that the methods of calculation involved are authoritative (e.g. that one should not substitute new animals for those that died after being administered the drug, and try again for a better result), and can be used to specify delicts.

Similarly the rules of accounting practice specify how inventories should be evaluated. In the book industry much of the inventory will never be sold for the current market price; some convention must be adopted that does not count capital value as accruing at the nominal price when the books are produced, and there is some dispute between the tax authorities and the industry about what that convention should be (Coser Kadushin and Powell 1982, p. 370–71). But when an auditor comes into a firm he or she is supposed to apply a convention that will protect potential investors or creditors as well as satisfy the tax authorities. The reasoning of the auditor is normative in the sense that one looks askance at auditors who provide reports on corporations based on their own self interest, or the self interest of the present officers of the corporation.

It may be useful to contrast the use of "normative" in phrases like "the standards of legal reason are normative" from other uses of that word. The general meaning of normative is that some social process, which may, for example, be quite unorganized "public opinion" or quite organized "due process of law," recognizes some decisions or actions or symbolic products as better. A theory of the normative order is, so to speak, a generative grammar of judgements of "better." The simplest such grammar is perhaps the stratification grammar suggested by Bourdieu (1984), perhaps with roots in Veblen (1899): "better" consists of those symbols by which people with more resources urge that they are more distinguished than those with less, so the dimensions of better, the dimensions of the normative, are dimensions which describe what people with more resources can do that people with less cannot. Normative judgments then are simply judgements with an invidious purpose, used to distinguish the rich, the wise, and the well born from their inferiors. The difficulty with such a theory was crisply formulated by Paul Veyne, "one is not ostentatious unless one feels superior (Veyne, 1976; p. 232)." A symbol cannot be convincing as a sign of distinction unless it adds something, unless it makes the greater amount of resources into meaningful superiority".

A second proposal is that of Jaeger and Selznick (1964), based in part on Dewey (1958), that what is better in a cultural sense is that set of things that people actually experience as giving meaning to their lives, that bring order, that symbolize values, that turn the flow of events into memorable experiences. But it is hard to apply that criterion here to recognize a reasoned judgement as better, because while some reasoning may improve our appreciation of values and may turn the flow of events into meaningful experiences, others such as the proper valuation of inventories so that inflation of their value does not appear as profit are merely technically better for recognized human purposes.

We are arguing for a sense of "normative" which implies that the people or organizations involved have a hierarchy of standards. They recognize rules or principles by which, in particular cases, "better" judgements or outcomes can be judged. In particular, for a normative system to be a system of "reason" as we are using it here, standards that rank highly in the system must require that reasons developed according to accepted paradigms are an essential component of judging some decision as "better" than alternative decisions. People may, for example, get carried away by an elegant model of neighborhood segregation by Schelling (1971, 1978), but when reasoning shows that the model bears no sustainable relation to empirical reality (Taub, Taylor, and Dunham 1984, p. 142–166) the superiority of the norm of empirical reasoning in social science outweighs the aesthetic norm of elegant simplicity and the feeling of understanding the sources of evil in a good world, that we get from Schelling and that the Jaeger and Selznick theory of the normative in culture would lead us to predict should receive the judgment of "better." That is, what makes the norms of rationality normative is that when people agree that they are participating in a science, they agree that a particular set of norms of reasoning will be taken as authoritative, unless and until that body of norms of reasoning is improved by the application of more general and higher ranking principles of reasoning.

Of course reason in the sense defined above is useful to individuals trying to be rational in several ways. In the first place, some types of reason are authoritative because they are thought to give the right answer. A rational actor might want the right answer about whether, for example, a ship of a given design loaded in a particular way might have its center of bouyancy below its center of gravity and consequently turn turtle. A naval engineer working for a classification society is normatively required to be able to give the right answer to such a question, whether it is in his or her own interest or not, and so his behavior manifests institutionalized reason. But insurance companies insist on an opinion from a classification society because they want that right answer, because if ships turn turtle insurors lose money (Heimer 1985a).

Further the paradigm of rational action is itself sometimes a paradigm which is socially established as normative. For example, in deciding what to do with an inventory, a rational actor would rationally want to know what it was worth on the market, and older accounting conventions which gave systematically wrong answers in times of inflation were bad for rational action of the inventory holder. But an auditor is obliged to protect investors and creditors in part by making sure that the accounting conventions of a corporation are correctly evaluating the inventory, in the sense that in an emergency it could be sold for somewhere near what is evaluated at in the accounts. So it is the responsibility of auditors (and others who specialize in the paradigm of accounting) to propose new accounting conventions when inflation systematically gives the wrong answer about the value of inventories. The paradigm of rational action in a market then is binding on auditors in a normative sense, in the sense that a really good auditor will look for assets overevaluated by the accounting conventions of a firm.

So just as rationality may make use of socially established paradigms of reasonable calculation for achieving private ends, so some socially established paradigms of reason have sections which are adopted from the theory of rational action. The crucial difference between an auditor's use of the theory of rational action and the firm's is that the auditor is required to follow the rules in order to make an authoritative judgment of the creditworthiness (and other financial characteristics) of a particular firm, rather than to choose his or her own most rational course of action. And while a firm which overvalues its inventory and so does not sell when it should is acting irrationally, its irrationality is not by the same token socially irresponsible, a violation of institutional responsibilities to calculate correctly according to a body of norms. In fact the management of the firm is not responsible for knowing all the conventions of good accounting.

What has been implicit in the distinction above is that the explanation of the incidence of reason in social life will not, in general, be the same as the explanation of rationality. For example, the function of legal reasoning, of enabling citizens (or at least other lawyers) to predict what the courts will do in the future, to predict the terms on which violence and coercion will be available in civil society, is not the same as the functions that one might expect to be served by rationality in the application of

coercion, as we have known at least since Hobbes.

The purpose of this essay taken as a whole is to point to differences in the motives of behavior, in the effectiveness of action, in the possibilities of development to higher levels of the use of the faculties of rationality, that we have when we are explaining the incidence or consequences of reason rather than the incidence of, or the systemic consequences of, rationality.

The rest of the essay has four sections. The second section after this introduction treats the preconditions of reason as an institutionalized normative order governing some subpart of social life. In some ways this is a brief explication of what Max Weber means by the "rationalization" of social institutions in Western society (for a good short definition of what he means, see the discussion of "intellectualization" in Weber 1919, p. 139; see also Kalberg 1980). The third section deals with the problem of the rationality of judges, and how that can interfere with the institutionalization of reason; the problem of a person being a judge in his or her own case is the core of this section. The fourth section elaborates the point made briefly above, that reason in institutions often has to take account of the rationality of individuals, so that authoritative normative reasoning about rationality is a part of what reason is. The fifth section discusses the functions of reason for rationality, in particular its sociological function of providing social predictability rather than its function of being in fact the most rational method of calculation for individuals.

An Ideal Type of Socially
Institutionalized Reason

The purpose of this section is to outline the elements that we find in fully developed institutions which enjoin the use of standards of reasoning in an area of social life. If we imagine our dependent variable as the degree to which paradigms of calculation of normative results that are reproducible by the use of a cognitive process are pervasive in an area of social life, and the degree to which the different outcomes of the application of reason in that area of social life can be reduced to a few "reasoned" paradigms well understood by practitioners in that area, we can search for arrangements of social life that would produce such a social pattern. The main source for building such an ideal type of "rationalization" is Max Weber's work on the rationalization of Western culture, especially in his sociology of law (Weber 1921–22: especially 785–808), but also in his famous ideal type of bureaucracy and scattered in his treatment of rationalization of other institutions.

The first obvious requirement for such a social institution to function is that there be a supply of practitioners who know the system of reason. Weber observed (Weber 1921–22, pp. 785–792, 802–805) that the rationalization of a body of culture depended on future practitioners being taught in schools rather than in apprenticeships. The existence of schools secures two important features of an institution of reason: that there will be teachers (and textbooks written by teachers) who will rationalize (in the sense of "systematizing," of reducing the body of practice to the fewest possible paradigms of reasoning) the body of culture, and that the learner can learn in a way dictated by the structure of the body of culture rather than in a way dictated by the flow of work or what sort of culture is necessary to complete a given task as a whole, as an apprentice necessarily learns.

The segregation of schools from work allows enough detachment to the teacher so that he or she can attend to the "impractical" matter of fitting the body of culture into paradigms, either by inductive methods as in studying cases in American law schools or by more deductive methods as in "continental" law schools. The same segregation allows students to learn the "impractical" paradigms without their work suffering because they do not yet know enough about the details to complete any job of work. Of course, as Weber points out in his discussion of rationalization in schools of theology, such rationalization can be entirely formulaic, and impractical in the sense that it could never be applied (1921–22, pp. 809–838).

Institutions based on reason are of course often in fact created to give advantages to the practitioners of a given variety of reason, rather than to perfect the exercise of reason. Medicine and law try to create monopolies for people officially certified as practitioners of reason in their fields, and many of the people so certified are not very good at reason, nor at all interested in extending the discipline to new areas or in developing techniques that will be more effective but will make their skills archaic. Institutions of reason, like other institutions that purportedly serve higher values, depend as little as they can on the altruism of their members.

Such a temple built on a sewer will, of course, show signs of its lack of a thoroughly sacred character. Medical practitioners will keep secrets about other physicians' malpractice so that physicians will be less vulnerable to lawsuits. Lawyers will oppose no-fault divorces because these use smaller amounts of lawyers' services. Colleges devoted to teaching will hire people with research degrees because these look good to accrediting agencies, and then make no provision in teaching loads or facilities to make research possible. The politics of the professions

can at most produce an institution guided by reason part of the time, because the same rational motives it "makes use of" by creating career incentives for the use of reason are also often served by the corruption of the institution.

The learning of apprentices is in general organized in a fashion that will allow them to complete simple jobs, then later to complete complex jobs. The basic principles to which practice can be reduced do not necessarily come arranged from simple to complex in the same order as the jobs that constitute a work flow are organized from simple to complex. A particular law case may, for example, embody some principles from the law of evidence, some from the law of contracts, and some from the law relating to monopoly. The paradigms of such subfields may be learned separately in law school. But the process of using the power of discovery in an anti-trust case against IBM to get evidence of the use of contracts to monopolize a market may be extremely complex, while the same mixture of bodies of law might be relatively simple, and much of the work turned over to paralegals, when one is merely trying to collect damages *after* an anti-trust finding has been established in a different proceeding.

The basic idea then is that the existence of schools that teach a large share of what needs to be known to practice in an area of social life facilitates the rationalization of the body of culture pertaining to it by producing specialists in rationalization, the teachers. It also facilitates rationalization by producing learners for whom rationalization promotes efficiency, students, rather than learners for whom rationalization distracts from mastery of enough different components of the culture to get some useful work done, apprentices. A powerful indicator of such rationalization is the appearance of textbooks designed for use in schools, rationalized into an orderly presentation; then behind these an indicator of the depth of rationalization is the appearance of technical monographs or scholarly papers which the writers of textbooks read.

In addition to having teacher rationalizers and student users of rationalized culture, the body of culture has to be inherently rationalizable. One of the difficulties with charismatic authority from this point of view is that the arbitrary will of a person endowed with the gift of grace cannot be reproduced by a paradigm (though it can perhaps be functionally replaced by the arbitrary will of a substitute). Part of the reason that succession crises tend to lead toward rationalization is that they bring up the question of reproducibility of the authority, and so can lead to the production of paradigms.

In general a principle like "the greater glory of monarch" is not as reducible to rationalized

REASON AND RATIONALITY

paradigms as "due process of law" or "maximum likelihood estimation." For another example, the physics of pitch and of the temporal periodicity of rhythm are rationalizable, and can form the basis of a notation for music. But the feeling of wanting to dance to certain types of music cannot easily be reduced to a paradigm or a notation, nor can the feeling of sadness induced by a dirge, nor the feeling of listening to one's own kind of music when one hears the music one heard all through childhood. Musicology is much more likely to become a scholarly profession than is virtuoso performance for that reason (this may be why Max Weber's essay on the rationalization of music is often taken as essentially irrelevant by people who like music).

The rationalizability of a body of culture depends then on having at its core principles which are inherently rationalizable; a complex subfield of culture like music which has some rationalizable and some unrationalizable elements will result only in a partially rationalized system, even under the influence of music teachers and music schools.

The most difficult conceptual job here is to distinguish rationalization which gets at the core of an area of culture (I imagine the rationalization of physics to be at the high extreme here) from rationalization which is "scholasticism," which rationalizes an irrelevant part of the culture because that is all that can be rationalized and leaves the core unrationalized (number mysticism or numerology would be an extreme of scholasticism). When one gets schools and students studying subjects which have an irrational principle (in the sense of not being reducible to a paradigm) at their core, the same process that produces reason in inherently paradigmatic bodies of culture produces scholasticism, produces mechanical prayer wheels that increase one's productivity at praying, or the fluffy critics' language to describe the experience of listening to music. It takes a great gift in writing, like George Bernard Shaw's, to make music criticism sound sensible (of course, whether or not it correctly represents the music, as well as being good reading, is a matter that we can hardly judge now).

I suppose the decisive criterion to distinguish such bodies of rationalized non-paradigmatic culture is that different experts tend not to come to the same judgements after applying their methods of calculation to produce an authoritative judgement. The reliability or reproducibility of the judgements of experts (in the mass of cases—of course there are unrationalized areas of the law or of a science like physics as well as of aesthetic experience—the question is the correlation among experts judgements over a large mass of cases, not whether or not there are disagreements) is a central operative criterion.

But for an area of social life to be rationalized, institutionalized reason not only has to exist—it also has to be used to resolve particular cases. Here the crucial social criterion is whether the person (or committee or whatever) who makes a judgement in an individual case can be required to give an explanation to other experts justifying that decision. Thus when a scientist announces that he or she (tentatively) believes a certain thing in a scientific paper, an explanation of the reasoning and evidence leading to that belief is required. When a referee recommends that the paper be rejected, he or she is ordinarily required to give a reason, which in its turn involves showing that in some respect the reasoning and evidence of the author were not adequate to the purpose. Similarly appellate courts give "opinions" explaining the legal reasoning behind their judgements; auditors can be required by a firm to give an explanation of their different evaluations of the state of the firm's finances than the firm itself has arrived at; a physician's diagnosis can be compared with an autopsy report or with a second opinion (though in less rationalized areas of medicine such as psychiatry the institution of a second opinion is not as well developed, and of course the autopsy report is not ordinarily a useful check on the diagnosis of a psychiatrist).

The expectation in a rationalized area of culture then is that a skilled practitioner can produce the elements of the paradigm he or she has used to make a judgement, and that these elements can be judged by other skilled practitioners and used in a calculation that ought to produce the same result. The criterion of reliability or reproducibility then is socially institutionalized when an area of social life is rationalized, as well as being a criterion a sociologist can use to tell whether a bit of culture is really rationalized. This social institutionalization of reproducibility criteria provides a mechanism for ensuring discipline in the application of the paradigm. And the most sensitive indicator of whether reproducibility or reliability is socially instituted is whether or not a judge of a particular case is normally required (or can be required if there is a question) to produce his or her reasons.

The normal form of the rule about producing reasons is that they should be routinely produced whenever there would be any reason to question them. Thus the requirement is universal in scientific papers, because there would be no reason to publish the paper unless there were some question about what to believe, but explanation of the evidence is not at all universal in textbooks. The requirement to explain in rationalized legal systems applies to appellate judgements (the appeal shows that there was some uncertainty about the application of the paradigm) but not always to lower court judgements. The requirement in auditing does not ordinarily apply if the auditor approves the accounts as kept by the firm, but only if the auditor finds an error or evidence of dishonesty.

A second opinion or an autopsy may not be required in medicine when there is not much doubt about the judgement of the physician or when there is little risk if the physician is wrong: autopsy reports when these are routinized ordinarily show that physicians are wrong about the cause of death in more than a third of the cases—the reason medicine is not pervaded with the sense of uncertainty about physicians' judgements is presumably that in most cases, even if they had known the correct diagnosis, there wouldn't have been anything they could have done to prevent the death (Geller 1983, p. 125–27).

Reason is a weak cause of people's behavior, and can only work reliably when the strong causes, personal interests and passions or "rationality" in the now conventional sense, are segregated from institutional decisions. If therefore an institution is going to reliably produce decisions guided by principles in the paradigms embedded in the institution, it has to have arrangements not only to make the paradigm available to practitioners, but also to prevent personal interests and passions from interfering. Unless such provisions to prevent "conflicts of interest" are present, the sociologist can assume that an institution is not very serious about institutionalizing reason; unless it has protected reason from corruption by the judges' personally oriented rationality. Weber analyzes this most completely in his ideal type of bureaucracy.

When Weber specifies that "rational-legal" administration requires full time officials recruited from schools rather than from aristocratic families, having a career involving promotions in the bureaucracy and lasting until retirement, having bureaucratic property separated from their own property and the office separated from the home, he is describing a set of provisions to keep the personal and family interests of officials from interfering with the reasoned judgement of cases (Weber 1921–22, p. 956–989). These are extensive provisions that all tend toward a bureaucrat never being judge in his or her own case.

Similar normative arrangements try to ensure that judges in law courts withdraw when they have an interest in the case, that scholars' papers are not refereed by colleagues who have collaborated with the author (or either married or divorced the author), that physicians do not treat close relatives, especially if they are beneficiaries of the relatives' insurance policies,

or that accountants employed by a firm cannot serve as auditors.

Finally, reason has to have materials to work on, a flow of evidence regularly provided by social institutions that tend to make that information accurate. Auditors are nearly helpless without accounting departments within the firm trained in accounting practice. Scientists without laboratories and papers without citations are both indications that a finding is not backed up by the routine information collecting structures that make science reliable. The trial court is a core method of establishing facts relevant to legal cases, and is backed up by laws or regulations about discovery (requiring the opponent in a legal case to provide the evidence that shows legally relevant facts), about compulsory process for witnesses, about delays to prepare a defense, about availability of counsel, and so on. Weber uses the criterion that the administration keeps files about its cases in his ideal type of bureaucracy.

Social structures that make information available to decision makers and that protect the quality of information reaching those decision makers are essential to the operation of reason as a social institution.

Thus we can construct an ideal type description of institutionalized reason with the following elements:

1. People are trained as practitioners in an area in schools in which both the role of teacher and the role of student are differentiated from the roles in the practical work of the institution; in the highest development the role of teacher itself carries an obligation to contribute to the rationalization of the body of culture by writing textbooks or technical monographs and papers, and students learn the paradigms separately from practice rather than only by doing progressively more complex jobs.

2. The body of culture itself has at its core cultural principles that can be reduced to paradigms, structures of rules of rational calculation which produce a capacity of different experts to come to the same judgement in a large number of cases.

3. Judges of particular cases in the institutionalized area are required, at least in problematic cases, to give reasons which can be examined by other experts to justify their decisions. In general standardized reasoning is used to try to persuade other experts, so that concerted social action (e.g. incorporating scholarly findings in textbooks, routinized warnings about their rights to arrestees being questioned) is ordinarily preceded by institutionalized exchanges of reasons: debates or litigation or refereed publications.

4. There are structural provisions that have the purpose of keeping the personal interests of

REASON AND RATIONALITY 159

the judge in a given case separate from the process of judgement, a set of norms of "disinterestedness" so that reason can prevail over both rationality and passion.

5. There are regular routines for information collection before judgement, in which information is protected from corruption and degradation, examined for veracity and relevance, and entered into a regular information storage system so that it will be available for the application of reason to it. This information collection is socially established rather than being at the discretion of the reasoning person. For example, a scientist cannot publish a paper without doing the experiment even if he or she knows how it will come out.

Like all ideal types, this one describes the high end of a variable; reason is the more institutionalized, the more all five characteristics given above describe practice in an area of social life.

But one can make distinctions along the dimension of "degree of institutionalization of reason" at various points. For example, the evaluation of art works for their authenticity, aesthetic value, and economic value is more of a rationalized body of social practices than is the aesthetic response of members of the general population who might, like Dwight D. Eisenhower, say, "I don't know much about art, but I know what I like." But it is by no means as rationalized as, say, nuclear physics or pure mathematics, which show all the above five characteristics to a very high degree.

The Rationality of Judges

It is now time to consider the implications of all the above considerations on "conflicts of interest" for the problem of the rationality of judges. It is clear that many of the same "faculties" are assumed for judges as are necessary to the model of people as rational actors: judges have to receive and assess information, to calculate according to paradigms that have a high probability of giving the right answer, to modify the paradigms when evidence or reasoning shows that the paradigm as previously used sometimes gives the wrong answer, sometimes to put oneself in the place of other rational actors (e.g. firms being audited) to see what would be rational for them, and the like. But equally obviously the institutions of reason depend on judges in courts or referees of scientific journals or auditors of firms *not* pursuing their own interests, not seeking bribes, not doing as little work as possible to make a decision, not plagiarizing papers submitted to journals, not modifying their decisions out of fear or favor.

Further the maintenance of the institutions that prevent conflicts of interest in judges themselves require an amount of rational care. Judges in law courts are themselves supposed to declare themselves unable to hear a case when their interests would lead them to be prejudiced, and judges are supposed to monitor each other to see that this norm is followed. The requirements here are very often called "professional ethics" or the "responsibilities of office." As Parsons pointed out long ago, the requirements of professional ethics are, in some sense, rational for a professional, because one's professional fate often depends on a reputation among one's colleagues as a person to be trusted (Parsons 1939).

But the principles by which the institutions are constructed which make it rational to maintain a professional reputation for ethical behavior are perhaps best summed up in Weber's phrase, the "ethic of responsibility," though it is the power of institutionalized reason rather than the power of violence of the state that has to be applied in a way balanced among ends (Weber 1921, e.g. at p. 127). By the ethic of responsibility one means roughly that one is required to use the faculties that would otherwise make one selfishly rational to adjust one's own professional response, or an institution's response, to a situation so that some value is served. To put it another way, what an ethic of responsibility means is that one should be rational on behalf of others or on behalf of a value, rather than on behalf of one's own utilities and purposes. Weber's point was especially that since political action involves coercion, all responsible choices in politics have to take account of the costs of using coercion as part of the process of choice. The use of socially institutionalized reason is coercive on people's motives and beliefs in much the way that physical force is, and necessarily involves some making of choices for others that involves them in costs and opportunities forgone.

So from the point of view of the rationality of judges, the key thing we need to do is to explain what is going on in the exercise of "rationality on behalf of" people or values.

Presumably a set of values embedded in an institution, say the set of ideals that make up the notion of "justice" in the legal system, or of "financial soundness" in the accounting profession, or of "scientific creativity" in scholarship, has to be thought of as a utility function of the institution. Or rather perhaps a "stylized utility function," a set of tradeoffs between objectives and principles and costs that represent approximately what the institution is all about. This institutionalized utility function is, from the point of view of the individual, an intellectual notion. It embodies such principles in the law as "in construing a contract, the central question is what the contracting parties intended, but one should not be too interested in idiosyncratic intentions of particular parties, but rather than customary understandings of intentions in the line of business of the parties," or in science such principles as "theories in a science should be compatible with the experimental results, but fundamental theoretical innovations often have this or that difficulty at first in explaining particular results and one should extend an appropriate degree of latitude to reasoning on fundamental questions."

These are not politically determined *rules* of an institution, but principles defended in collegial settings within the institution, and *sometimes manifested* in attempts to write rules on particular subjects or opinions on particular decisions. One expects that different members of the institution will have somewhat different weights for the values in tradeoffs (e.g. different relative evaluations of teaching versus research in science, or of enforcing the customary practices in contracts versus codification and uniformity of the law in the legal profession). But within the range of responsible interpretations of the institutional utility function, practitioners are supposed to act in their institutional roles as rational actors trying to maximize the institutional utility function as if it were their own. (I do not mean here literally "maximize," as by taking derivatives and the like. Instead I mean the sort of behavior humans actually do, which economists and game theorists approximate by models of rational action. Since the choices we are concerned with involve several values or dimensions of utility and multiple sources of causal uncertainty [it is all this complexity that makes managing them a profession requiring training], the behavior is ordinarily quite far from the model. The model will be at most a predictor of the central tendency. In what follows "maximize" and its relatives should be read in this loose sense, as no more than what economists and game theorists mean by it when they are trying to predict or explain real behavior.)

In particular, the profit maximization of a corporation is such a conventionalized utility function. It forms the basis of a corporation-specific institution of reason, with its arrangements for giving reasons for decisions (in terms of profit maximization), protecting against the corrupt rationality of the institution's members on their own behalf by auditing practices, procedures internal to the corporation for bringing evidence to bear on decisions, and all the other features of an institutionalized rationality that we have defined as "reason."

The utility function set up in such a conventional fashion in a corporation usually is not, even in its "official" form, a simple profit maximizing rule. For example a life insurance company is supposed to have a different tradeoff between income versus risk, and between capital appreciation versus maximum current return, than does a uranium prospecting company or a wildcat oil driller. All profit maximizing rules actually involve an implicit choice for the firm of the tradeoff between risk and profit, and a choice of the shape of the prospective income stream over time. These choices can, of course, be controlled by portfolio methods in corporations that engage in many businesses, but even then each investment in the portfolio has to be held to its income, risk, and time stream tradeoffs in order for the portfolio to have the aggregate features chosen.

This means that even the profit-maximizing rule of a corporation is actually a complex utility function involving tradeoffs among at least three values. The actual utility function that shapes the reasoning about firm decisions often has other utilities in it, such as reputation (crucial for professional firms), craftsmanship, commitment to a historical industry (e.g. Ford's commitment to the American car market for a long period in which they had to spend profits earned abroad to sustain American losses), satisfying regulatory authorities, safety (for example, unless deep sea diving firms treat safety as a more or less ultimate value, they have difficulty hiring experienced divers), or developing new products (a general feature of firms in the chemical industry, for example).

The point then is not that institutions of reason never maximize the same things people do, such as profits. Instead the contrast is that institutions of reason, even when maximizing something that an individual entrepreneur might maximize, do so by controlling and limiting the rationality of their component individuals. A main implication of this essay is that, as a primitive institution of reason, a corporation will tend to look in certain respects like the institutions of justice or the institutions of science, though these maximize other conventionalized utilities than profits. In other respects, of course, corporations look quite different from the law or from science.

In particular institutions of reason, will tend to have roles making important institutional decisions which are organized as *fiduciary* roles, roles whose defining features have much to do with *responsibility* for the general structure relating the institution's conventionalized utility function to the rationalized procedures that make up its formal organization. Such responsible roles are, then, in particular responsible for *creating* the formal procedures, formal job descriptions, and the like, that constitute the institution as a formal organization. Such a structure describes well the internal organization of the corporation.

Of course such "responsibility" to an institutionalized utility function may not in fact produce the utilities for individuals it is supposed to. For example, if "responsible" military reason, as exemplified in the higher staff colleges of a country's armed services and carried into reality by the generals trained there, creates a national security utility function that makes an international arms race an equilibrium outcome, every nation's security may in fact be decreased. Responsibly extending such a utility function into space may (or, of course, may not) destabilize the balance of terror that keeps the peace, and may wipe out all the people who might otherwise have had different utilities. In modern states not too many individuals find it rational in their personal best interests to go to war, but a well developed tradition of rationality built up in a staff college may make it institutionally reasonable and responsible for millions to go to war. Part of the problem here is that not all people's individual interests may get into the utility function that institutions become committed to. Part of the problem is that specialized rationalities may not be able to handle reasonably utilities outside their purview. (See Weber 1922, p. 171, on why pacifist movements very often fail.)

To some degree acting as a fiduciary on behalf of individuals (on behalf of beneficiaries of a trust, or on behalf of stockholders in a corporation entrusting investments to a board of directors, etc.) is much the same sort of thing. When for example an inheritance is administered by a trustee on behalf of a minor child, the trustee is supposed to create a fictional utility function for the child—"what the child would choose if he or she were an adult." Fiduciary institutions will develop rules deriving from an institutionalized notion of what such a utility function ought to look like, and courts will try to enforce vague tradeoffs by a "reasonable man rule." What shows that a trustee is not acting "as an agent" on behalf of a "principal" is that the child does not get to correct the trustee when he or she does not agree with the trustee's interpretation of the utility function, while presumably a principal does.

There is then continuous variation between this notional utility function of an abstract beneficiary of a trust and the imposed utility function of principals who impart (with sanctions of their own choosing) information to an agent about what their individual utility functions actually are.

The more the rational faculty of people adapting action to a situation is governed by an institutionalized definition of what utility function ought to be maximized, the more we have to deal with "reason" rather than "rationality." And the more this is true, the more what is demanded of the actor in an institutionalized role is "responsibility," pursuing institutionalized utility functions rationally in changing situations, rather than the "rationality" that is assumed about the agent in the economic theory of the principal-agent relationship. Thus a physician may refuse to accept the wishes of the parents (who are paying) that a defective baby should not be given expensive life support (which the parents will have to pay for although they opposed it). The partiality of the institutionalization of a utility function for the clients is indicated by the fact that the physician will follow the parents wishes during the first trimester of pregnancy, and that it is only after the child is potentially viable that a fictionalized utility function of the child spends the parents' money.

The question of the definition and social supports of "responsibility" in general is beyond the scope of this essay (see Heimer 1986).

But from the point of view of this paper, what this conception of responsibility implies is that much of the substantive content of reason in the socially institutionalized sense is the same sort of calculation that is involved in the theory of rationality. Insofar as people are being responsible members of an institution embodying reason, what they are quite often doing is to behave as if they were rational individuals, but trying to maximize someone else's utility function. The function may be that which some sort of abstract someone else (an ideal system of justice, the advance of science, or a conventionalized idea of what the utility function of a minor child who was an adult would look like) is imagined to have by an institution responsible for the values. But that means they have to be prevented by the institution from being rational on their own behalf, so that they can be rational on behalf of such an institutionalized fiction.

Normative Rationality in Institutions of Reason

If we now imagine the history of a body of doctrine embedded in an institution we have just described, it will be a process of depositing precedents by a long line of people professionally concerned with trying to embody rational decision-making in a set of institutional practices. Each improvement of institutional regulations will be, at least in apparent intention, for example, a development of a more complex notion of what is needed to maximize the long run welfare of minor beneficiaries of trusts, or what is needed to maximize the long run degree of support for scientific creativity in the structure of careers in universities, or whatnot.

We can think of such a history as an evolutionary process, in which, by and large, a more nuanced and rational way of maximizing the long run welfare of minor children or of scientific creativity will tend to win out. It will win out because the principles of reason are institutionalized over a long period of time, and people keep on applying their rational faculties to improving the rationality of that fictional child or improving the fictional utility function of the advance of science. The individuals who have, during this evolutionary process, applied their rational faculties to a particular maximization problem in a particular situation may not have been able to maximize the whole utility function over the whole set of aspects of the situation, but may have improved it somewhat for that particular situation.

What this means in its turn is that there may be an "institutional wisdom," a rationality at a deeper level than is routinely understood consciously by the practitioners, so that by following the tradition of the institution people do better, behave more rationally, than they would do with their unaided rational faculties.

Where there are subtle problems in particular kinds of contracts, such as the problem of "moral hazard" in insurance contracts, then one may find a model of what is rational in the institutions of insurance that is as good as the rational model even an expert in rationality can construct *ab novo*. An empirical investigation of how the institutions of insurance deal with varying problems of moral hazard, such as that carried out in Carol A. Heimer's *Reactive Risk and Rational Action* (1985b), may be more illuminating about what is rational from the point of view of an individual insurer than the advice the insurer might get from Kenneth Arrow (1971). Of course, then again, it may not.

The tradition of the American or English law review article is to apply this insight to the codification of law, and thereby to its improvement. The notion is that if one can find the deep structure behind the individual opinions on appellate decisions, the argument of the review article will be more reasonable as a paradigm of calculation on how to achieve the ends in view in a given area of law, and consequently will be more rational for individuals to know whenever they want to use the law for their own purposes. Similarly Paul Lazarsfeld's mode of developing the methodology of quantitative social science, by picking out pieces of quantitative analysis he thought good and trying to give a systematic account of the reasoning behind what they had done, takes advantage of the rationality of individuals in their particular situations to construct a better "model of a social scientist acting rationally."

The evolutionary drift is, in general, governed by the institutionalized utility function it is supposed to serve. After the "liberal revolution" in English law, the revolution often associated with the name of Jeremy Bentham, the evolutionary drift of master-servant law in both England and the United States was in the direction of destroying all non-market protections of workers (Kim Scheppele pointed this out in a critique of a previous version of this paper; she mentioned specifically the fellow-servant rule, which largely exempted employers from liability for industrial accidents). The time span between the big change in philosophy (marked, say, by the new poor laws or by the repeal of the statute of artificers) and the development of a thoroughly bourgeois master-servant common law should be measured in decades or half centuries, perhaps the ordinary pace of social evolutionary processes.

The tendency of British trade unions to think that all law and all formal regulation will be to the disadvantage of the working class (and the lesser version of this belief in the United States), and the lowered assent to efficiency-improving innovations that it has carried with it, may be the indirect outcome of that persistent anti proletarian evolution which rationalized Benthamite thought in 19th century labor law.

The only thing that can be expected to improve over time in an institution of reason is the intellectual technology for refining and achieving institutionalized utilities or values. Those purposes tend to be refined, the tradeoffs between them made subtler, their adaptation to a changing world made more rapid, by being embedded in an institution of reason. This fine tuning may, of course, be quite socially irrational if, for example, creating agile institutions for destroying protections of workers intensifies class conflict. As Andrew Abbott put it in a critique of an earlier draft, "There is . . . a 'politics' of who is the client hidden behind your evolutionist view."

The prediction of evolutionary improvement of the reasonableness of institutions of reason is derived from the ideal type. One of the most common ways for the ideal type to fail to be fulfilled in reality is for individual rewards to become tied to particular actions in the institutions. The special concern of foreign language departments in universities a few years ago to preserve language requirements for scientific degrees, the drift of obstetric practice away from vaginal deliveries toward higher-fee caesarean, the careful preservation of impossibly complex land transfer procedures in English law (Andrew Abbott pointed out this example in the critique mentioned above), all show that reason often has a hard time winning out over the interests of institutional practitioners. Other people's inter-

REASON AND RATIONALITY   163

ests may be rationalized away without much delay, as in the case of non-market protections of workers mentioned above, but solicitors' interests are very resistant to rationalization.

The same interrelationship between reason and rationality that explains evolutionary improvement in institutionalized reason means that development of the theory of rationality may itself make substantial contributions to institutional development. For example, the development of formal risk analysis in actuarial science and in economic theory has contributed to the specification of what a life insurance company should look like (specifications in turn to be embedded in regulations requiring life insurance companies to look like that). This improves the ability of buyers of insurance to cover the risks they want to insure against as much as they want to, for the premium they are willing to pay, by guaranteeing the amount of risk reduction the contract formally promises through reserve requirements imposed on insurance companies (Hansmann 1985, p. 133–138). In the old days before such regulations, the only way to get insurance companies to keep enough reserves so they could actually pay off was to organize a mutual—once the state figured out what an insurance company had to do to be safe, and demanded it of all insurance companies, then one could buy as good insurance from a stock company as from a mutual, and evolutionary pressures started which increased the proportion of all insurance provided by stock companies.

That is, because many of the substantive purposes of bodies of reason require the application of that reason to maximizing the welfare of clients, or maximizing an institutionalized system of tradeoffs which might be called the institution's utility function, institutions have a built in interest in developments in the formal theory of rationality. For example, when new optimizing techniques are developed in statistics for unusual situations ("robust" statistics), they spread quickly in the relevant scientific community, and are demanded in situations where before other, more vulnerable, methods gave the same results. When economically more rational methods of cash management are developed, auditors start to look askance at companies that keep too large balances in too highly liquid (and hence low return) accounts. And in general the innovations of economics spread out imperially to the institutions of reason, as maximizing principles designed to explain the behavior of rational actors become institutionalized principles of how reason should be applied. This makes economics a broadly "applied" discipline, because its micro theory promptly becomes institutionalized in many places in social life.

Institutionalization of new varieties of reason

of course often leads to fake rationality. People use the newest statistical procedures when they have not yet learned to manage them. For example, I recall Jöreskog (1973) using LISREL in an early example in a data set that caused him to overestimate the measurement error of a verbal test, hence overestimate its effect, and consequently to show that mathematical ability decreased achievement in science—almost any standard psychometric method of estimating the measurement error of the verbal test (including looking it up in a reference on psychometric tests) would have given better results than this "provably statistically best" technique. Computer simulations of infantry and armored tactics are usually constructed in imaginary perfectly flat fields, and so greatly underestimate the value of shovels as defensive weapons, and hence greatly overestimate the value of armor and mobile artillery (Stockfisch 1973). Cost-benefit techniques are generally alleged to underestimate the effects of a program on utilities that are hard to measure (though convincing examples are hard to come by). The general point is that fashions in rational technique can spread faster than their value justifies, and value choices can be concealed in the choice of technique not understood by the people or organizations whose utilities are supposedly being maximized by rational means.

In spite of all the reservations above, I am arguing something stronger than an evolutionary pressure on formal rationality. If reasons must be given and defended, if self-interested behavior of institutional officials is seen as a force that has to be protected against, and all the rest, then good reasons will tend to dominate in the long run over bad reasons—that is my argument. For example: the evolution of course content (as part of the substantively rational institution of science) will be faster than the evolution of the course numbering system (as a part of formal rationality); course content will evolve in the same direction in different countries, while course numbering systems will differ radically between countries; in rationalized legal systems procedural rights essential to the achievement of justice will tend to be instituted more readily (and will die out more slowly) than procedures that make people consult lawyers over simple land transfers; if the extra caesareans actually kill more mothers and babies than retaining more vaginal births would, the institution of medicine will eventually work out tighter decision principles on when caesareans are indicated, when vaginal births are indicated. In short, I am arguing for a reserved and somewhat cynical polyanna view of the institutions of reason, insofar as the institution fits the ideal type developed above. The "insofar" in the previous sentence is central to the argument of this paper.

Reason as a Social Basis for Rationality

Max Weber emphasizes the importance of the predictability of the law for capitalism (Weber 1921–22, p. 333–337). Capitalism involves coordinated activity, and the mechanisms of coordination are political creations like money, sales and labor contracts, penal law for thefts, organizational charters for corporations, and so on. Weber's argument is that such market coordination (''the peaceful pursuit of market advantage,'' in Weber's phrase) can only take place if these political instrumentalities of market exchange are available to participants in the market on predictable terms. Only if the political system is predictable (at least in respect to these central mechanisms of exchange) is the rational calculation of the meaning of contracts, charters of incorporation, and the like, possible. Weber studies the rationalization of law because, he argues, rationalization is the central process that increases predictability of the law.

Paul Starr (1982, pp. 112–144) makes a rather similar point about medicine, that the establishment of the cultural authority of medicine involved the institutionalization of many of the features of the ideal type of reason as outlined above, and that the consequence of this was a sense among the public of the predictability of what sort of medicine one was going to get if one went to a physician. To establish the right to a monopoly over medical practice, medicine had to establish that the service one got from a certified physician was reliably better than one would get elsewhere. This required, in Magali Sarfatti Larson's wonderful phrase, ''the production of standardized producers'' of professional services (1977, pp. 14–18). But that standardization in its turn required the rationalization of medicine, and in particular its rationalization as a ''science'' which could claim cultural authority from its method, and its rationalization as a subject for a school, which could transfer that cultural authority to practicing clinicians.

In both these cases there are actually two aspects to the use that non-practitioners make of the fact that a body of culture has been rationalized. The first has to do with the fact that any paradigm with non-random rules of calculation of authoritative outcomes is *predictable*. The printing of the marriage service in the Book of Common Prayer makes the content of the ceremony predictable, without presumably making it any more effective in achieving the ends of the parties to the marriage; the printed version is an authoritative paradigm without any pre-

tence to a rationalization which might establish that this was a *better* marriage ceremony.

The second has to do with the presumption that the long term evolution of repeated applications of reason to institutional practice will have made, for example, the standard form of the contract efficient for the usual ends of capitalist contracting parties, or will have produced the best standardized producer of medical services that could reasonably be produced with the current knowledge of bacteriology, oncology, and anesthesiology.

The first of these features of the activities of the institutions of reason ensures that the parties to various interactions know what to calculate about in maximizing their own ends. They provide secure inputs of knowledge of what will happen under this and that condition for the calculations of actors in the market, without the parties having to invent complicated structures of hostages, reserves of resources in escrow, and the like, that would otherwise be required to make contracts certain. It ''reduces transaction costs'' to have such paradigms institutionalized elsewhere.

In the extreme, the paradigms of reasoned action may be so thoroughly embedded in the structure of the offer the institution makes that clients need not (and sometimes cannot) calculate about it at all. For example, by offering health insurance in group plans only if all the employees of a company are required to be covered, insurance companies prevent ''adverse selection,'' namely people buying insurance only if they know they are in bad health and likely to need it. Except when people try to buy the same insurance individually, and discover they must pay twice as much, they do not ever calculate the advantages of buying insurance with a contract that prevents adverse selection from operating. If the health insurance company does not offer individual insurance (as many do not) the client cannot calculate even from market information the advantages of a contract that prevents adverse selection.

The second feature, that institutionalized reason has been repeatedly applied to improve institutional practice, secures the quality of the service being rendered by the institution. The clients need not develop the competence to make rational choices for themselves, because lawyers', physicians', scientists', or auditors' skills will make a better choice than they could themselves. One need not worry because one knows how the courts will interpret a standard contract, but one also need not worry because the standard contract will provide for most of the contingencies that need to be provided for in ordinary business relations, without having to hire a master of contract law to advise one on constructing such a contract. One can consult standard statistics textbooks so that one's computations will give the same result as is common in one's discipline, but also do so rather than going back to read R. A. Fisher on why maximum likelihood is in general a best estimate, because one can have (more or less) faith that the writers of statistics textbooks will have examined Fisher's reasoning, and will have picked out the best statistic. One reduces computation costs for oneself by using institutionalized computations, because one has some faith that those institutionalized computations will be as good as one could do for oneself.

Of course the institution can create a situation in which "the good is the enemy of the best," because for example cookbook techniques in a scientific discipline are accepted by referees who were trained to use them, preventing especially sophisticated practitioners from using techniques more appropriate to the particular problem being addressed. One may have to write a general article justifying a method before one can use the method in a particular substantive work, because one needs a citation to show that it is part of the paradigm. I have enough examples of this that I could write a long, tedious and tendentious paragraph here on the subject.

Thus rationalized institutions, the embodiment of reason in social life, improve the rationality of individuals. They do so first by regularizing social and political life, that principal source of uncertainty in attempts to apply rationality to one's personal goals. And they do so secondly by enabling one to construct one's rationality out of pieces of reasoning which someone better at it than the client has already "suboptimized," in the sense of perfecting the reasoning in that piece so that for most purposes of most clients, there will be no better solution of a legal, medical, scientific, or auditing problem.

Conclusion

The achievement of civilization could be formulated as the successful detachment of the faculties that make people rational from the limiting context of personal goals, so that they can be applied to the improvement of social life. The result of such provision of an "irrational" context for the faculties of rationality is an improvement in rationality through the institutionalization of reason. The institutionalization of reason in various fields makes people individually more rational. If Weber was right, the rationalization of law makes the free market possible; at least it is clear that it makes it a lot easier, reduces transaction costs, and generally lubricates the wheels of capitalism. Rational actor models become reasonable models of

individual action especially in societies in which a lot of people's rational faculties are applied to the maximization of goals not their own.

But the case is more complicated still, for much of the content of rationalized institutions, those institutions which have to be defended against corruption, against the individual rationalities of the judges, consists of models for maximization. This is perhaps most obvious if we examine who mostly uses the latest advances of economics to maximize economic goals—it is usually corporate entities run by people who are, as best we as stockholders can secure it, maximizing on behalf of someone else. Corporate policy is more shaped by the normative content of economic science than is the policy of individuals. But it is also true that judges try to set up the rules for interpreting contracts so as not to interfere with their understanding of what rational actors will be trying to achieve with the law of contracts; the science that goes into auditing (including the special branches like actuarial science that goes into auditing insurance companies) is a science of what a corporation ought to be doing in order for a rational person to want to invest in it. So the body of institutionalized reason includes as a large part of its substantive content the norms of rationality in the narrow sense, a body of doctrine about how best to maximize returns or minimize costs.

In order to embody rationality and reason in institutions protected from too much rationality of their institutional practitioners, one has to construct institutions with due care that the utilities and rationalities of the judges can be achieved without undermining reason in social life. Such protections in fact require intelligent attention by the judges themselves. This is most obvious when a judge personally has to declare that he or she is too much an interested party in a case to render an unbiased judgement, and so should be disqualified. But the vigorous debates about, for example, what "academic freedom" ought to consist of, how it should be defended, which parts should be part of the contract of employment of professors as construed by the courts and which merely parts of the grievance procedure within universities, and the like, show that a good deal of intellectual effort has to go into keeping the institutions of reason in good shape. One needs judges who are not only disinterested in particular cases, but also are disinterested developers of better institutions of reason itself (cf. Oakeschott 1962, p. 100–106, for the argument that rationality works mainly by improving a traditional line of conduct, i.e. by improving "reason" as defined here).

Such institutions of reason render social life more predictable. Since it is in social life that most valuable things are created, this means that most sources of most valuable things will be more amenable to rational self interested calculation in societies that are more rationalized. But the institutions of reason would not govern so much of social life unless they were seen not only as predictable, but also as better. And they will be seen as better only if people do not have the daily experience of knowing better than the institutions they have to deal with. Unless the teacher actually knows more about the subject than the student, academic authority is unstable. Unless medicine has better answers on the average than chiropractic, it will not be likely to gain a monopoly of delivery of medical services (insurance companies would presumably usually rather pay the lower fees of chiropractors, if they could convince their clients that the services were as effective — but in fact insurors generally refuse to pay chiropractic fees, because the reasoning behind their expertise does not enjoy cultural authority). And in general unless rationalized institutions give, on the average, better answers than the unaided reason of individuals, they will not prosper and grow.

The social matrix of individual rationality then is institutionalized reason, and people are more rational than they used to be because they live in a more rationalized society.

REFERENCES

Arrow, Kenneth. 1971. *Essays in the Theory of Risk Bearing.* Chicago: Markham.

Bourdieu, Pierre. 1984. *Distinction: A Social Critique of the Judgement of Taste.* Cambridge, MA: Harvard.

Braithwaite, John. 1984. *Corporate Crime in the Pharmaceutical Industry.* London: Routledge and Keegan Paul.

Coser, Lewis A., Charles Kadushin and Walter W. Powell. 1982. *Books: The Culture and Commerce of Publishing.* New York: Basic Books.

Dewey, John. 1958. *Art as Experience.* New York: Capricorn Books.

Geller, Stephen. 1983. "Autopsy." *Science American* 248:124–136.

Gilbert, J.P., R.J. Light and F. Mosteller. 1975. "Assessing Social Innovation: An Empirical Base for Policy." In *Evaluation and Experiment,* edited by C. A. Bennett and A. A. Lumsdaine. New York: Academic Press.

Gilbert, J.P., B. McPeek and F. Mosteller. 1977. "Progress in Surgery and Anesthesia: Benefits and Risks in Innovative Therapy." In *Costs, Risks and Benefits of Surgery,* edited by J. P. Bunker, B. A. Barnes and F. Mosteller. New York: Oxford University Press.

Hansmann, Henry. 1985. "The Organization of Insurance Companies: Mutual versus Stock." *Journal of Law, Economics and Organization* 1:125–153.

Heimer, Carol A. 1985a. "Allocating Information Costs in a Negotiated Information Order: Interorganizational Constraints on Decision Making in Norwegian Oil Insurance." *Administrative Science Quarterly* 30:395–417.

————. 1985b. *Reactive Risk and Rational Action.* Berkeley: University of California Press.

————. 1986. "On Taking Responsibility." Northwestern University: Unpublished.

Jaeger, Gertrude and Philip Selznick. 1964. "A Normative Theory of Culture." *American Sociological Review* 29:653–669.

Jöreskog, K.G. 1973. "A General Method for Estimating a Linear Structural Equation System." Pp. 85–112 in *Structural Equation Models in the Social Sciences,* edited by Arthur S. Goldberger and Otis Dudley Duncan. New York: Seminar Press.

Kalberg, S. 1980. "Max Weber's Types of Rationality: Cornerstones for the Analysis of Rationalization Processes in History." *American Journal of Sociology* 85:1145–1179.

Larson, Magali Sarfatti. 1977. *The Rise of Professionalism: A Sociological Analysis.* Berkeley: University of California Press.

Oakeschott, Michael. 1962. "Rational Conduct." Pp. 80–110 in *Rationalism in Politics and Other Essays,* by Michael Oakeschott. London: Methuen.

Parsons, Talcott. (1937) 1949. *The Structure of Social Action.* New York: Free Press.

————. (1939) 1954. "The Professions and Social Structure." Pp. 34–49 in *Essays in Sociology,* by Talcott Parsons. New York: Free Press.

Schelling, Thomas, 1971. "Dynamic Models of Segregation." *Journal of Mathematical Sociology* 1:143–186.

————. 1978. "Micromotives and Macrobehavior. New York: W.W. Norton.

Starr, Paul. 1982. *The Social Transformation of American Medicine.* New York: Basic Books.

Stockfisch, Jacob A. 1973. *Plowshares into Swords: Managing the American Defense Establishment.* New York: Mason and Lipscomb.

Taub, Richard P., D. Garth Taylor, and Jan D. Dunham. 1984. *Paths of Neighborhood Change: Race and Crime in Urban America.* Chicago: University of Chicago Press.

Veblen, Thorstein. (1899) 1934. *The Theory of the Leisure Class.* New York: Random House Modern Library.

Veyne, Paul. 1976. *Le pain et le cirque: Sociologie historique d'un pluralisme politique.* Paris: Editions de Seuil.

Weber, Max. (1919) 1946. "Science as a Vocation." Pp. 129–156 in *From Max Weber: Essays in Sociology,* edited by Hans H. Gerth and C. Wright Mills. New York: Oxford University Press.

————. (1921) 1946. "Politics as a Vocation." Pp. 77–128 in *From Max Weber: Essays in Sociology,* edited by Hans H. Gerth and C. Wright Mills. New York: Oxford University Press.

————. (1921–1922) 1968. *Economy and Society,* edited by Gunther Roth and Claus Wittich. New York: Bedminster Press.

————. (1922) 1946. "Structures of Power." Pp. 159–179 in *From Max Weber: Essays in Sociology,* edited by Hans H. Gerth and C. Wright Mills. New York: Oxford University Press.

Zuckerman, Harriet and Robert K. Merton. 1971. "Patterns of Evaluations in Science: Institutionalization, Structure, and Functions of the Referee System." *Minerva* 9:66–100.

[17]

THE MANY FACES OF POWER AND LIBERTY: REVEALED PREFERENCE, AUTONOMY, AND TELEOLOGICAL EXPLANATION*

PETER ABELL

Abstract Concepts of bargaining power, influence, and manipulation are introduced and related to three different ways of operationalization—namely from decision-making, non-decision-making, and studying information flows. The concept of autonomy is introduced and briefly studied in the context of causal and teleological accounts of 'power play'.

Introduction

In recent years, both within the framework of general sociological theory and in the more restrictive context of organization theory, we have witnessed a resurgence of interest in the concept of 'power' and its many close relatives like influence, persuasion, manipulation, inducement, and so on. This is in part, I suspect, a reaction to functionalism which, at least in the hands of its most distinguished proponent, largely relegated issues of conflict resolution—and thus at least one conception of power—to a special case of the consensus-model of social systems (Parsons, 1967; 1963*a*, *b*). Despite, however, the increased attention the concepts have attracted, many of the old conceptual hazards remain and the seemingly intractable problems of locating operational definitions which capture the concepts in anything like their full complexity, have not been solved. Furthermore, with one or two notable exceptions, most attempts, both conceptual and operational, to use the concept are afflicted with the endemic sociological disease, namely a failure to situate the concepts in models which reflect actual social process. It is relatively easy to detail fine conceptual distinctions, but unless we can project these into models of social process which generate reasonably general explanations of social phenomena they are only of marginal interest to the sociologist.

In this paper I want to consider in detail a number of particularly thorny issues which seem to me to surround the concept of power: namely, the relative role that, on the one hand, *revealed preferences* (i.e. in decision-making), and on the other, *individual autonomy* might reasonably be permitted to play in the formulation of models designed to reflect the processes in which 'power', 'influence', and 'manipulation' serve an *explanatory* purpose. My presentation derives directly from the model of *Organisations as Bargaining and Influence Systems* (Abell, 1975) though I

*Accepted: 18.5.76

4   PETER ABELL

trust what I have to say will be of wider interest than merely to students of organizational process.

The immediate stimulus for the paper, however, has been my reading of Steven Lukes' most important and stimulating book *Power: A Radical View* (Lukes, 1974) which seems to me to raise a number of issues in a most delightful and challenging way. He contrasts three viewpoints on the conceptualization and measurement of power: firstly, the decision-making approach, perhaps most closely associated with the name of Dahl (1957, 1958); secondly, an approach usually associated with Peter Bachrach and Morton S. Baratz (1962, 1963), which centres attention upon 'non-decision-making'; and, thirdly, the viewpoint, which most pleases Lukes himself, whereby the concept of latent interest is involved in the definition of power. Thus, A's power over B becomes the extent to which A can 'affect' B in a manner contrary to B's *interests*. This latter orientation has, of course, a long history and is in some way central to the Marxist 'theory' of conflict and false consciousness. Although I do not intend to give an overview of the limitations and achievements of the three viewpoints, I will in several respects contrast them in confronting my central questions, namely the role of 'revealed preferences' and 'autonomy' in the structure of explanations from power.

An additional, but subsidiary, purpose to this paper is to try to kindle an awareness of some aspects of what we might term the 'sociology of freedom or liberty'; a neglected, not to say forgotten, sociological category. This neglect is, of course, not surprising since, as usually construed, the sociological enterprise involves a search for 'patterns', 'determinants', 'causes', and so on—ideas that do not lie at all easily with the concepts of individual or group liberty. Despite centuries-old exhortations to find 'freedom in necessity' and heroic efforts (Parsons, 1937) to preserve the voluntaristic basis of social action in the thought of our founding fathers, Durkheim's conception of a social fact as 'ways of acting, thinking, and feeling external to the individual and endowed with the power of coercion by reason of which they control him' has taken its toll. And if we are to believe Peter Berger (1963) then 'freedom is not empirically available'. More precisely, 'while freedom may be experienced by us as a certainty along with other empirical certainties, it is not open to demonstration by any scientific methods'. Be this as it may, there seems to be some robust sense in the assertion that A's power over B may be equated with A's ability to reduce B's freedom or liberty. Thus, on this count, there seems to be a reciprocal relationship between power and liberty which would inevitably lead to the conclusion that, if what Berger says of freedom is correct, it must likewise be so of the concept of power. It is part of the burden of this paper to show that Berger is not in fact correct.

Preliminary definitions

I will limit my analysis to the power interactions (relationship) between two actors only—A and B. In this respect I follow many others, finding it convenient

THE MANY FACES OF POWER AND LIBERTY 5

for expository purposes, though I recognize that the extension to the many actor case introduces a number of additional conceptualizations.[1]

Most authors, at least since the time of Weber, accept as a starting point (or, as some would say, as a sensitizing-definition) that: A has power over B to the extent that A's action/behaviour[2] (to include his forbearance and lack of behaviour[3]) 'affects' B's action/behaviour (again to include forbearance and lack of behaviour) in such a manner that had it not been for A's action/behaviour, B would have acted/behaved otherwise. I do not pretend this, as it stands, is at all adequate as a definition but it does catch at least one possible intuitive notion of the concept of power.

The above very simple 'definition' seems to invite evidence concerning the following:

(P1) A's action—let us say x;
(P2) B's action—let us say y;
(P3) The way B would have acted had it not been for A's action (x). Let us say ȳ.[4]

We will see how evidence is obtained on these matters, using the three different approaches to power outlined by Lukes. In so doing, however, I will draw a tripartite conceptual distinction between 'power', 'influence', and 'manipulation'.

When considering the 'power' relationship between A and B, there are two major 'problems' (i.e. 'why' questions) which arise and potentially link A to B:

(i) why has B changed his 'state of mind'?
(ii) why has B, despite his 'opposition' to A, not changed his state of mind, but changed his action.[5]

It is clear that an answer to (ii) can be provided in terms of evidence of the sort P1, 2, and 3, but, furthermore, (i) can also be answered in an entirely parallel manner in terms of:

(P*1) A's action (e.g. communication of beliefs);
(P*2) B's 'state of mind';
(P*3) B's 'state of mind' had it not been for A's action.

Questions (i) and (ii) effectively distinguish between a pair of social processes which link A to B. Firstly, the process whereby A changes (modifies) B's mind (attitude, sentiments, knowledge, etc.) and secondly, where A modifies B's action (without changing his state of mind). This is rather loosely expressed but if one, for the moment, reads state of mind as 'convictions' then the intent of the distinction is, I think, clear.

The English language provides a plethora of words to cover the possible nuances in such processes. However, I wish to argue for a tripartite conceptual distinction which will, in my opinion, suffice to *model* these complex processes—they are:

(i) the process of social *influence*, whereby A changes B's state of mind (and concomitant action) but in so doing increases (or maintains[6]) B's 'autonomy';

6   PETER ABELL

(ii) the process of *manipulation*, whereby A changes B's state of mind (and concomitant action) but in so doing decreases B's 'autonomy';
(iii) the process of *power*, whereby A changes B's action (obtains his compliance)
through the agency of sanctions[7] even in the face of B's opposition (i.e. an
opposed state of mind).

Roughly speaking, by degree of autonomy I mean an actor's range of feasible
alternatives (see below). In practice, it is difficult to conceptualize and operationalize
this idea whilst avoiding circularity, but it is nevertheless essential if we are to draw
what I believe to be a vital distinction between influence and manipulation. An
alternative formulation might appear to be one whereby we speak in terms of B's
increased or decreased basis for 'rational deliberation' (in decision-making) which,
in turn, might derive from the concept of objective or latent interest as specified by
Lukes in his third.dimension of power (Lukes, 1974, p. 34). Whichever formulation
we adopt however, what is clear, is that we need, in addition to P^*1, 2, and 3, a
fourth criterion enabling us to draw the distinction between what I have, admittedly
rather arbitrarily, termed 'influence' and 'manipulation'. So, provisionally, we may
add alongside P^*1, 2, and 3:

(P^*4) an 'estimate' of whether B's change of action (concomitant upon a change
of mind) is associated with an increase or decrease in his 'autonomy'.

It might be argued that to draw a distinction between manipulation and influence
is an unnecessary multiplication of categories. Why should we want to separate the
two, especially when they may both have the same behavioural consequences?
Clearly the issue revolves around the concept of autonomy which to the present
remains rather opaque; but who would want to deny the importance of differentiating between, on the one hand, those processes that cripple man's very existence
as a consequence of his slavish subservience to ideas that limit his perspectives and
potential development, and, on the other hand, processes that liberate him by
awakening his awareness of new possibilities and previously unrecognized hori-
zons? Much, thus hinges on the concept of autonomy—we need ways of conceptualizing and operationalizing it—but rather than considering the problems in an
entirely abstract manner, I will situate my analyses in the context of the different
approaches to the measurement of 'power'.

Before I continue the analysis, however, I should like to make a general aside
concerning the distinction between 'manipulation' and 'influence'. What I am
driving at is a way of demarcating processes of what some would term rational as
opposed to irrational persuasion. Analysis of this distinction has, in my opinion,
become a matter of extreme urgency with recent developments in political
economy. With the increasing realization, for example, that 'consumer sovereign-
ity' can no longer be accepted as an uncontroversial assumption (e.g. Galbraith,
1974) comes the necessity of analysing those processes that shape consumer preferences. Galbraith, for instance, wishes to invert the traditionally assumed consumer/

producer relationship by suggesting the monopolistic and oligopolistic producer has the 'power' to fashion preferences. If this is so, are we not entitled to ask whether the fashioning is a case of manipulation or influence in the sense in which I am using the terms. In a number of ways theory and practice require us to develop ideas about the processes which shape people's political, social, and economic preferences. Gone are the days when we can uncritically accept a set of preferences and search for the most appropriate allocation of resources to maximize their satisfaction. Is it too much to hope that, with theories (and thus with adequate conceptualization) of the generation of preferences that we might reasonably hope to see a 'rapprochement' between economic and social theory?

Power, influence, and manipulation in decision-making

Following closely behind the reputational technique,[8] the analysis of decision-making has most frequently been used to elucidate the concept of 'interpersonal power' (Dahl, 1957). The basic idea underlying the analysis is one which considers individuals with competing preferences, bargaining to a collective outcome; and the relative success of an individual in getting his preferences embodied in an outcome is supposedly indicative of his 'power'. Most investigators have, in practice, reduced the complexity of the bargaining process to a simple win-lose, zero-sum situation, but this is not in any way conceptually necessary to the model. The literature has not, however, drawn the types of distinctions I am arguing for; in particular, the preferences of the actors party to the decision-making are taken as *given* and in this respect the models reflect practice in welfare economics. If by dint of this assumption economic theory should gain the label 'bourgeois', then accordingly the conventional decision-making models of power should likewise earn the same title. However, in the presentation that follows I have attempted to remedy the situation by seeking ways of modelling the formation of preferences.

Let us assume that A and B face a set (population) of decisions which they have to 'make' or 'take'—$D—\{d_i\}i, = 1, 2 \ldots n$.[9] How could we conceptualize and measure the concepts of 'power', 'influence', and 'manipulation' from A's and B's decision-making? First, let us get an intuitive idea of the distinction between the concepts in the spirit of the 'definitions' I gave earlier. Let us assume (i) that both A and B come to the decision-making with initial preferred outcomes (IPOs) for each of the decisions,[10] (ii) that A and B make these preferred outcomes known to each other.

If the IPOs of A and B are identical over set D, then A and B are in a *consensual posture*. (We can then ask for an explanation of why this should be so—I will return to this below.) But, for the moment, let us assume that A and B have (at least over some decisions) different IPOs. Now, putting it rather informally to start with, I will say that A has *influence* over (or manipulates) B to the extent that A can change B's IPOs, and vice versa (without the application of sanctions).

Let us assume, over set D, A's IPOs are X_{Ai} and B's are X_{Bi}. Then let us allow that the influence or manipulation process, as outlined above, can take place both ways, i.e. A can 'change B's mind' and vice versa. So, let A's and B's 'influenced'/'manipulated' MPOs (modified preferred outcomes) be given by Y_{Ai} and Y_{Bi} respectively.

Then we postulate:

$$Y_{Ai} = f(X_{Ai}, X_{Bi}, U_{Ai}) \qquad \text{(a)}$$
$$\text{and} \qquad Y_{Bi} = f(X_{Bi}, X_{Ai}, U_{Bi}) \qquad \text{(b)} \qquad \Big\} \text{ (1)}$$

$i = 1, 2 \ldots, n$. U_A and U_B have the standard interpretation representing 'other factors' impinging on A and B respectively. In the context of each functional statement in (1) we are first interested in the variation in the MPOs accountable for by the actors' own IPOs and then how much residual variation is accounted for by the other actors' IPOs. So, for (1)(a) if we postulate, for the sake of argument, a linear relationship[11] between Y_A and X_B we obtain:

$$Y_{Ai} = \propto + I_{AA} X_{Ai} + U'_{Ai} \qquad (2)$$

$i = 1, 2 \ldots, n$.
Where, I_{AA} is, if you will, the 'degree of conviction' of A. Then we postulate a linear relationship between the rsidual U'_A and X_B

$$U'_{Ai} = \propto' + I_{AB} X_{Bi} + U''_{Ai} \qquad (3)$$

$i = 1, 2 \ldots, n$.
Where, I_{AB} is B's influence/manipulation of A.

Similar reasoning gives:

$$Y_{Bi} = \propto'' + I_{BB} X_{Bi} + U'_{Bi}$$
$$\text{and} \qquad U'_{Bi} = \propto''' + I_{BA} X_{Ai} + U''_{Bi} \qquad \Big\} \text{ (4)}$$

$i = 1, 2 \ldots, n$.
Thus with sample data on A's and B's IPOs and MPOs, we can, in principle, obtain estimates of I_{AA}, I_{BB}, I_{AB}, and I_{BA}. The coefficients I_{BA} and I_{BA} do not, however, as they stand distinguish between processes of manipulation and influence—we will return to this problem below.

Let us now turn to our third concept, namely 'power', and see how it is embodied in the decision-making approach. If we assume that A and B are not consensual (as a consequence of their mutual influencing or manipulation) over the set D then they will have to bargain over the disputed decisions to a set of *collective outcomes*—O_i. Then let:

$$O_i = f(Y_{Ai}, Y_{Bi}, U_i) \qquad (5)$$

$i = 1, 2 \ldots, n$.
Once again, for the sake of expository convenience, assuming the adequacy of a linear additive specification we obtain:

$$O_i = C + \beta_{OA} Y_{Ai} + \beta_{OB} Y_{Bi} + U_i \qquad (6)$$

$i = 1, 2 \ldots, n$.
Then, estimates of β_{OA} and β_{OB}, i.e. the marginal propensities to get outcomes

in accord with one's (modified) preferred outcomes is a convenient measure of A's and B's relative *bargaining power over decision outcomes*.[12] If one then wishes to move to a measure of A's power over B (or vice versa), it is necessary to enquire into the degree to which the stream of outcomes O_i 'affect' the behaviour/action of A and B. I have explored elsewhere, via the concept of *control-loss*, situations where the outcomes do not 'affect' the behaviour of A and B, as intended (Abell, 1975) but here, for the sake of clarity, I will assume that outcomes do 'affect' behaviour as intended.

So, we might now ask how these simple models are supposed to satisfy the evidental requirements P1, 2, and 3 and P*1, 2, and 3. Consider, first of all, A's attempt to get his MPOs embodied in the outcomes O_i (reflected in (6)). This we must assume constitutes evidence for P1; B's compliance with the outcomes (assuming $Y_{Ai} \neq Y_{Bi}$[13]) is evidence for both P2 and the counterfactual P3—the evidence for this latter component of the explanation being provided indirectly by the assumption that B, because of his differing preferences, would in the absence of A's activity have behaved differently. In this context it is most easy to construe O_i as a stream of commands constraining B's (and of course possibly A's) behaviour. The decision-making approach to power is thus, based upon a series of assumptions:

(i) that both A and B have clearly articulated preferences;
(ii) that they are more or less successful in getting these preferences embodied in outcomes;[14]
(iii) that the outcomes constrain A's and B's subsequent behaviour.

It might quite rightly be referred to as a *kinematic* rather than a *dynamic* model since, as it stands, it does not enquire into why it should be that one party is 'willing' to comply with or 'unable' to resist the outcomes when they do not embody his preferred line of action; merely that they do. An answer to such queries is, of course, normally provided in terms of the relative distribution of sanctions (positive and negative) available to the parties—more of which later.

A similar line of reasoning to the above applies to the influence/manipulation process P*1, 2, and 3. So far, however, I have made no attempt to distinguish between influence and manipulation, since the equations (3) and (4) are, as they stand, not able to do this—they only chart changes in A's and B's preferences (changes of mind) and we need additional evidence enabling us to say whether, in changing their preferences, they are more or less autonomous, i.e. evidence for P*4. It is important, however, to recognize that the 'shifts' in preferences X to Y must be out of conviction or 'genuine', not as a consequence of imposed sanctions or threats. Influence and manipulation are, as I use them, sanction-free.

To ask whether an individual is more *autonomous* in one 'mental state' rather than another is clearly a highly complex matter, not least because one would have to understand the—as far as I am aware not understood, but no doubt highly complex —interaction between the conscious and unconscious emotional and cognitive

states of the individual in question to answer the question definitively. But what
we can perhaps provisionally say is that an individual is more autonomous to the
degree that:

(i) he recognizes a greater[15] range of *physically* possible alternatives open to him
(i.e. loosely 'ends'). These may not be socially realizable, of course, due to the
power of his adversaries;

(ii) he recognizes a greater range of feasible means physically open to him which
will realize one or more of his ends;

(iii) he understands (ie. can critically evaluate) the implications of selecting certain
ends or means.

We might wish, in a general way to refer to these conditions as indicative of greater
choice[16] or even *freedom for*.[17]

Let us examine these ideas in the context of B's shift in IPO to an MPO. Clearly
(i) is satisfied if we assume that *both* preferences (and their concomitant action) are
now open to him. In practice, principles (ii) and (iii) may, I think, be provisionally
lumped together. Although the empirical problems of guaranteeing that they are
satisfied are immense and I do not pretend that I can more than touch upon them
here—it seems to me that their fulfilment can, in principle, be studied in terms of
the direct or indirect *information provision* by A. If we can establish that A (intentionally or otherwise) is providing information for B which (in the process of
shifting his preferences) *does not decrease* any one of: B's (i) range, (ii) means, and
(iii) understanding of implications, then I would wish to regard the shift as a case
of influence. If, on the other hand, there is a diminution of any one of these 'free-
doms' then we should regard the shift as manipulative. I would thus wish to attempt
an operational definition of the principles of autonomy in terms of information
provision. Although this formulation raises almost as many problems as it solves[18]
it has the distinct advantage that it ties my formulation to two of the most empirically fruitful approaches to the study of 'power' which see, on the one hand, information as a *strategic resource* (Pettigrew, 1974) and, on the other, as a bounded
meaning system (Pondy, 1975). It should be noted that in adopting this sort of
operational formulation we are forced to accept that A might (intentionally or
otherwise) be keeping 'information' to himself that would, if it were given to B,
further change his preference. Thus A may be influencing B less than he might
(perhaps because it is in his interests to do so). Some might be tempted to call this
manipulation but on my usage it is rather a case of, shall we say, less than possible
influence. B is still more autonomous in adopting Y (rather than X) but not as
autonomous as he might be (vis-à-vis A). If we believe this to be the case then we
must presumably ascribe to the truth of a counterfactual—'if A were to provide
this further information then B would not have adopted *either* X *or* Y'. We
may be able to study evidence for such a statement by comparative method (see
below).

There are, finally, a number of points which need emphasising about the decision-making approach. In deriving a measure from the full set of decisions we are, as it were, *aggregating* over the entire set. A's power, for instance, is his marginal propensity to bring collective outcomes in line with his own MPOs *over set D*. Thus, the measure points to a generalized capacity of A. We could, of course, data permitting, find more particular estimates by breaking out sub-sets of set D (by decision-type, for instance). But even then there is some implied generalized capacity—albeit of a more restricted scope.[19] Colloquially, however, we are prone to use the terms 'influence' and 'power' both in a generalized and a very specific manner. In this latter respect, we say: A influenced B over one particular issue. The model I have outlined could, in principle, give a probability measure for such individual events, but one would require a suitable sample of events to establish frequency estimates of the probability numbers. I will return to these issues below, but we might observe that some have argued that the concepts of power and influence are only of any relevance in a generalized capacity (Parsons, 1963). Thus, it is argued, we would not want to employ the concepts at all, unless they explain some general pattern, for surely as sociologists it is to patterns that we look. I believe this argument to be essentially correct but I will show below that we can render the concept of influence and power issue specific (other than in a probabilistic sense), though I still believe this of little *sociological* interest.

The 'non-decision-making' approach

A number of cogent criticisms can be made against sole reliance upon decision-making as a basis for conceptualizing and measuring power. The one that has caused the greatest stir is due to Bachrach and Baratz (1962, 1970) and delights under the title of 'non-decision-making'. The burden of their extremely penetrating argument is to the effect that the decision-making approach may (will?) give biased estimates of A's and B's power. Although it is not entirely clear whether Bachrach and Baratz want to imply biases in A's and B's *absolute* or *relative* 'power' I will assume that they are concerned with possible biases in A's power relative to B and vice versa. They believe that the decision-making fails to secure information whereby:

a person or group—consciously or unconsciously—creates or reinforces barriers to the public airing of policy conflicts,

or in a more recent formulation:

Power is also (i.e. in addition to decision-making) exercised when A devotes his energies to creating or reinforcing social and political values and institutional practices that limit the scope of the political process to public consideration of only those issues which are comparatively innocuous to A.

Thus, part of A's power, for instance, is his ability to create and maintain barriers to a full consideration of *all* decisions by B. In the most extreme case he selects those decisions which B may 'consider', keeping others to himself. A failure to incorporate this sort of social process into any operational model, will, it is argued, give unrealistic results and in Lukes' terms miss an essential 'dimension of power'. Bachrach and Baratz consequently implore us to consider the set of *potential decisions* that B could in practice, be involved in, as well as those he actually is involved in. It is easy to see that a failure to do this will almost invariably overestimate B's power in relation to A.

All this seems reasonably straightforward; however, in other places Bachrach and Baratz use a rather different argument (although they appear to regard it as identical), namely that part of A's power is his ability, in one way or another to 'curtail' what another actor 'feels' he wants out of a decision (or set of decisions). That is, in the terms of our foregoing analysis, to shape an actor's preferred outcomes. This line of argument I hope I have shown, can be accommodated within the 'decision-making approach' as either manipulation or influence, and we need, therefore, give it no further attention.

Returning, therefore, to what we might term the 'potential decision-making'[20] argument, let us note first of all, that if we are sufficiently liberal in our interpretaon of P1, 2, and 3 we can interpret the situation as follows:

P1 A's action X . . . 'A keeps the decision to himself';

P2 B's action Y . . . 'B does *not* get involved in the decision';

P3 The way B would have acted had it not been for A's action . . . 'B would have got involved in the decision'.

So, at first appearances, the non-decision-making (potential decision-making) thesis has the essential ingredients of our sensitising definition. This easy translation unfortunately clouds a number of rather complex issues—in particular on how to adduce evidence for the truth of the counterfactual P3.

As before it will be convenient to limit our attention to the two actor case facing a set of *potential* decisions. We will, furthermore, assume A is B's superordinate and is able to limit B's access to decision-making. Clearly, A's and B's access to the set of decisions in question may in turn be limited by other actors and their preferences may also be influenced or manipulated by these other actors. Thus, we encounter the *nested contingency* of power systems (bargaining-zones in terms of Abell, 1975). The important point being that we are concerned here with A's power vis-à-vis B and vice versa, *within a given power-system* (bargaining-zone).

We assume that A keeps a sub-set of the potential decisions to himself and this is indicative of his non-decision-making 'power' in relation to B.[21] It is important, I think, to draw a distinction between two rather different interpretations of A's retention of decision-making 'power'. On the first interpretation A 'makes the decision himself' (i.e. they embody his IPOs—although these may, needless to say, have been manipulated or influenced). The decision—outcomes we must assume— then carry implications for B's behaviour and it is perhaps easiest to think of them as commands or rules concerned to 'affect' or guide B's behaviour. On the second interpretation—which is a rather more subtle and challenging version of the argument—it is not so much that A takes the decisions himself (i.e. by excluding B) but rather, A prevents certain potential decisions becoming 'current'. So, in one way or another, A prevents B from either participating in or even having the opportunity *to respond to any appropriate potential outcomes.*

Let us consider the first interpretation; it is clear that we are merely dealing with a centralized decision-making mechanism and conceptually nothing of a very profound nature is involved. If B agrees with the outcome (i.e. they embody what his own preferences would have been had he been involved in the decision); then according to the decision-making approach no power is involved. B could have been manipulated or influenced by A into this posture—but that is conceptually handled within the decision-making approach and likewise calls for nothing new. If B 'disagrees' with the outcomes and once again they are supposed to dictate his behaviour, then he is accordingly potentially subject to A's power. Of course he may be able to evade the intention of these outcomes, then he has 'power' also. It is possible to formalize these matters (Abell, 1975) entirely within the framework of the decision-making approach in terms of the concepts of *control-loss*.[22] But once again there are no grounds, on this count, for claiming any conceptual distinctiveness for a non-decision-making approach to the measurement of power.

Finally, it should be noted that the truth of the counterfactual is *inferred* from the fact that B's preferred outcome is different from A's so we are willing to say, had it not been for A's 'command' B would not have done what he did do.

It seems to me that the best way of conceptualizing the second above-mentioned interpretation is in terms of A's ability to effectively *reduce the range of options open to B*. We have already encountered the concept of influence whereby A brings B's preference into line with his own preferences. Here we have a situation where B cannot form preferences as the grounds for his so doing are systematically denied to him by A. It appears conceptually to make little difference whether this is because he—(i) is not given 'information' about a potential decision, or (ii) because he 'cannot' formulate certain potential preferences about decisions in which he is directly involved. *The important point about all these situations is that we have a situation where A 'affects' B's behaviour without B's overt opposition.* They seem to be adequately captured by our concept of manipulation.[23]

Power, influence, manipulation, and latent interests

The third 'dimension' of power recognized by Lukes involves the concept of interests. He says:

A exerts power over B when A affects B in a manner contrary to B's interests.

Lukes admits that 'interests' are 'irreducibly evaluative'; be this as it may, the essential difference between this third viewpoint and the previous two is the explicit introduction of B's *interests* rather than his preferences as revealed in decision *or* potential decision-making. Of course, if B's interests are fully expressed in his revealed preferences then the distinction falls away. However, if this is not the case, then the baseline with which B's actual action should be compared is not his revealed preferences but his interests. It seems most convenient to contrast this formulation with our concepts of manipulation and influence. For, presumably Lukes would want to explain an occurrence of B not acting in accord with interests in terms of A preventing B from realizing what his latent or real interests are. Thus B's action might be quite rational in his own terms but this is only because A has, in some way, denied him realization of his true interests. So, the counterfactual takes the form—if it had not been for A doing so and so, B would have acted in a manner in accord with his 'true' interests.

Clearly then Lukes is in a position close to our concepts of influence and manipulation—but how close? My preference was to adopt B's *autonomy* as the operative concept in P*4, Lukes appears to prefer interests. We can perhaps find common ground with Lukes here in the proposal that manipulation rather than influence is the significant concept. For, adapting my concept of influence slightly, one would suspect Lukes would endorse the statement whereby 'influence' is a 'mind changing' process that makes B aware (or more aware) of his interests. So I am arguing that B is manipulated to the degree that A reduces his autonomy, whereas Lukes is (implicitly) arguing that distortions of interests is the operative concept.

Is there any significance in this difference? I think there is, but in order to make clear what is involved we need to enquire a little more deeply into the explanatory role of counterfactuals.

The problem of counterfactuals and explanatory form

To summarise: we have seen that a statement concerning the power or influence of A over B or manipulation of A by B involves evidence of four types specified in P1, 2, 3, and P*1, 2, 3, and 4.

It is in the sense of (P3) that a statement about the 'power' one actor has over another entails a counterfactual. For, according to our previous deliberations a necessary (though not sufficient) condition for the truth of the statement that A exerts power over B with respect to the action instanced in (P1) and (P2), is that we must know (or infer) the *truth* of a subjective conditional—if A had not done x then B would not have done y (would have done ȳ). It is this requirement that generates much of the operational difficulty about the concept of power and its close relatives. It is helpful to note that P1, 2, and 3 also provide the elements of an *explanation* of B's behaviour corresponding to the question—'Why did (does) B do y?'. In answer we might say 'Because A did x', it being implied that 'B did y *because* A did x'. (In what follows I shall initially concentrate upon the concept of power, though much of what I say applies to the other two central concepts also. Furthermore, for convenience, I will assume 'not having done (doing) y' is equivalent to 'doing

THE MANY FACES OF POWER AND LIBERTY   15

not y' which is strictly incorrect but to draw on a deeper logic of action, at this stage, would take us too far afield.)

Now such colloquial explanations blur a basic distinction: is B's behaviour to be construed as *teleologically or causally determined*?

I wish to argue that our attitude to the evidential requirements of 'explanations from power' depends very centrally upon whether we take a teleological or causal viewpoint of such explanations. Furthermore, that an adequate analysis of the concepts of manipulation, latent interest and autonomy are also dependent on this distinction.

Consider first the case where we wish to interpret the explanation of B's behaviour in causal terms. This being the case we are searching for a *causal law* connecting A's and B's behaviour. Presumably the explanation would then depend upon the hypothesized truth of a universal proposition (law) of the form:

$$\text{(A) (B) } [Ax \Leftrightarrow By]$$

(for all A and B, if and only if A does x, then B does y.)[24]

The universal proposition will, of course, be circumscribed by a set of appropriate initial conditions describing the individuals of type A and B and perhaps some common circumstances. The explanation of B's action would then be of the classical covering-law (hypothetico-deductive) variety. Putting the relationship between A and B in this way highlights its empirical requirements; in order to 'test' an explanation based upon a causal-generalization one would need observations where (*ceteris paribus*) of the four logically possible combinations we only observe situations where:

 (i) A's exhibit action x and B's exhibit action y;

(ii) A's do not exhibit action x and B's do not exhibit action y.

The role of the subjunctive conditional—if A had not done x then B would not have done y—takes on the stature of a counterfactual in any causal (hypothetico-deductive) explanation. For from the 'truth' of the 'law': 'if and only if A does x then B does y' we may deduce the truth of the subjunctive conditional, if and only if A had done x then would B have done (do) y. The interesting twist with (causal) explanations from power is that the counter-factual is naturally expressed in double negative form: 'if it had *not* been for A doing x, then B would *not* have done y'. But, of course:

$$\text{(A) (B) } [Ax \Leftrightarrow By] \Rightarrow \text{(A) (B) } [A\bar{x} \Leftrightarrow B\bar{y}]$$

is a tautology and so, *if* it is deemed legitimate to construe explanations from power as causal, then the issues surrounding the use of the counterfactual are no more controversial than those associated with the logic of causal explanations in any form of enquiry.

All this might seem rather laboured, but it seems necessary in the light of the remarks common to a number of scholars, claiming that studies of power raise special methodological difficulties whilst at the same time implicitly accepting a causal account of power relationships. For example, Lukes in praising Crenson's book (1971) claims that it is 'a real theoretical advance in the empirical study of power relations' as 'it explicitly attempts to find a way to explain things that do not happen'. I believe Crenson's book does raise a number of interesting methodological issues but not quite in the sense in which Lukes wishes to claim. Crenson's concern, working in the non-decision-making framework, is to explain why the issue of air pollution is 'raised' in some North American cities and not in others. He wishes to 'explain' the *lack* of interest in some cities in terms of the 'power' of large corporations in these cities. Despite Lukes' claims, I believe Crenson's methodology is entirely traditional for, in effect, he 'explains' what 'does not happen' by the use of simple and well established comparative methods: cities (presumably as far as possible matched on all relevant criteria[25]) are compared and it is found that those which are rather tardy in adopting pollution control are, for various historical reasons, by and large dominated by specific corporations, whereas those that are not polluted are free of such corporations. Such a research strategy is entirely in accord with the spirit of the methodology of causal explanations outlined above. *Indeed such explanations account for what 'did (does not) happen' in the sense of all suitably elaborated causal explanations.* The point is that a variance is generated across cities (some do have controls, others do not) which is 'causally' accounted for. All the other examples that Lukes cites are of the same logical structure and consequently, despite his protestations, do not, as far as I can see, take us into controversial logical terrain. However, there is a situation of special interest; suppose we believe in the '*truth*' *of the general causal explanation but because it is universally operative across the full population (i.e. over all known actors of type B) we can find no cases of B that did not (have not done) y.* Here we have a situation where there is no variance to explain—the causally operative 'power relation' is keeping, as it were, everybody, in line. I believe it is this sort of situation which provides us with rather unique challenges and as such deserves a name, I will (following Gramsci) call it *hegemonic control.*

It seems, therefore, that with the sole but extremely important exception of those situations where there is no variance (across relevant units) and where we take a *causal* interpretation of 'power relations', explaining what does not happen is quite a routine sociological practice. There is, however, one slight complication and this concerns *overdetermined* causal systems (Abell, 1971).

If the causal law in question takes the form:

$$\text{(A) (B) } [Ax \Rightarrow By]$$

then A's action is only a sufficient (not necessary) condition for B's action. Such a law is compatible with observations of 'B doing y' but 'A not having done x'. The law guarantees the truth of the subjunctive conditional—'if A had done x then B would have done y' but not, 'if A had not done x then B would not have done y'. So in contrast to the situation where the law is in 'necessary and sufficient'

THE MANY FACES OF POWER AND LIBERTY 17

form the first counterfactual does not logically imply the second one in the double negative form. That is:

$$(A) \ (B) \ [Ax \Rightarrow By] \Rightarrow (A) \ (B) \ [A\bar{x} \Rightarrow B\bar{y}]$$

is not tautologous. Overdetermination is usually handled by supposing that a set of alternatives are severally sufficient and collectively necessary and sufficient for the given event.

So,

$$(B) \ (A) \ (A') \dots (A^N) \ [(Ax \lor A'x' \dots \lor A^Nx^N) \Leftrightarrow By]$$

Then we may say that if it had *not* been for A doing x, or A' doing x' ... or A^N doing x^N then B would not have done y.

The role of teleology in explanations from power

I have already remarked upon a natural tendency to interpret explanations from power in causal terms. Lukes, for instance, seems to do this—sometimes explicitly, other times implicitly—and most of the available operational models are more or less based upon a causal interpretation.[26] Since colloquially we think of 'power' as a 'force' which changes people's action, such an interpretation is perhaps quite excusable. However, I believe causal accounts as outlined in the previous section, are not always adequate.

Let us now, therefore, turn to a *teleological* interpretation of A's power over B; once more we can fruitfully consider the issues involved by thinking in terms of an explanation of B's *action*. I will assume that teleological explanations take the form such that B's action (i.e. his doing y) can be explained in terms of a *practical syllogism* (Von-Wright, 1971) as follows:

(i) 'B intends (wants) I' (the intentional premise);
(ii) 'B believes in a situation he perceives as S, *only* by doing y will he bring about I' (the cognitive premises),

therefore:

(iii) 'B does y'[27]

The most significant feature about this explanatory form is its independence of the hypothesized truth of any universal proposition, analogous to the causal 'law' above. The reason being that the proposition 'B does y' (i.e. B acts y) cannot be false whilst the conjoin of propositions 'B intends I' and 'B believes (in situation S) that by doing y he will bring about I' is true; for to say that B *does* y (in situation he perceives as S) implies that he intends to do y. His action, in short, is teleological, or self-directed. Thus the relationship between the premises and conclusion of the above 'explanation' is not of a causal variety.[28] The explanatory form provides a general teleological explanation of B's *action* whereas 'explanation from power' must, in addition, make provision for some specific content to the proposition 'B intends I' which relates B's action y to A's action x.[29] This can be accomplished in

18   PETER ABELL

a variety of ways but let us, without loss of generality, concentrate upon one rather simple wording 'B intends (wants) to secure some reward which A has at his disposal'. So we now have an explanation of B's action y of the form:

(i) B intends (wants) to secure reward W from A;
(ii) B believes that (in virtue of A's action) *only* if he does y will he secure reward W.

Therefore:

(iii) B does y.[30]

Thus, in explaining B's action in teleological terms we need evidence of:

(i) B's intention;
(ii) his beliefs concerning A's 'possession of W';
(iii) his belief that action will secure him the reward W in situation S;
(iv) his belief that x is signal for the truth of (iii).

These evidential requirements are entirely in line with P1, 2, and 3 except that it is now made explicit that it is B's belief—which may of course be false—that x is indicative of A's willingness to behave in a particular way. This rather crude formulation can be much refined, and provides a general framework for the analysis of the logic of social interaction. I will not, however, pursue the details any further here as they will be covered at length in Abell (forthcoming).

The centrally important feature of teleological explanations becomes dramatically evident when we recall that to test the 'truth' of a causal explanation we need to generate a variance across a set of actors. In particular, we need to locate some actors of the appropriate type that do not 'do y'. The query we left unresolved above was, what would happen if A was 'all powerful' across all actors of type B—for then there is no way of generating variance and thus testing a causal model—a condition I described as hegemonic control. *With a teleological explanation, however, it would be sufficient to test the scope of A's power by providing valid teleological explanations of the above type for each of the subjugated individuals. Thus teleological explanations provide a methodology for the study of lack of variance.* Admittedly, there may be rather acute problems in ascertaining the 'truth' about people's intentions, beliefs, and so on, *nevertheless we do not have to resort to the comparative method.*

It is also worth noting, in passing, that since teleological accounts do not depend upon generalizations they likewise do not, when used in the context of 'power', entail what I earlier termed a *generalized capacity* interpretation. Teleological explanations are not incompatible with a generalized capacity of A, but by their very nature they can provide an account of the 'power' in one decision or issue.

There are a number of points I should like to emphasise about a teleological explanation of A's power over B. First, it is often natural to interpret the first premise (i.e. the intentional premise) of the explanation in terms of the sanctions that A controls (using the term in the broadest possible sense). Thus linking our analysis with another well established approach to the measurement of power.[31] Secondly, the power of A over B is clearly not to be confused with A's ability to physically force B to comply with his wishes. For the essence of B's behaviour is one of choice where he selects to receive rewards W.[32] This could, of course, include the avoidance of anticipated negative sanctions which are 'threatened' by A. Thus, on this interpretation, explanations from power are compatible with the voluntaristic bases of social action.[33] Central to this sort of teleological account of power relations is the exchange of sanctions (however tenuous these may be) and the idea that B is guiding his own action accordingly. He can, of course, be wrong about (a) A's willingness to reward/threaten him, (b) the truth of the proposition that the situations are adequately described as S and, (c) that in those situations doing y will lead to his being rewarded. Nevertheless, the explanation of his action will still be valid. (Whether or not, in the absence of the truth, of (a) we would wish to call this an 'explanation from power' is a moot point.)

The truth of the counterfactual is inferred from the fact that B *himself* gives A's possession of W etc., as the 'reason' (necessary and sufficient) for his action, thus we are accordingly entitled to assent to the truth of the proposition that 'if it had not been for A's possession of W then B would not have done y'. If we know the explanation is valid then we know the truth of the counterfactual. Furthermore, though I have chosen to analyse 'power' relationships in terms of sanctions W, it is clear that an entirely parallel argument could be produced where B's action is teleologically dependent upon some feature in his environment which is controlled by A (see note 4).

So far, the aforegoing analysis has not explicitly brought into play the distinction between power, on the one hand, and manipulation/influence on the other. Are the distinctions between causal and teleological explanation of any use here?

If A 'changes B's mind' in the spirit of P*1, 2, and 3, then we may interpret this (from a teleological point of view) in a number of ways. Firstly, A may change B's intentional premise. Secondly, he may change B's cognitive premise in one or both of two ways. Firstly, by changing his belief that his action y will secure his objectives (intentions); secondly, by changing his belief that the circumstances he is in are adequately described as S. There thus seem to be three rather distinct ways in which A can 'change B's mind'. It will not have escaped the reader's notice that, as expressed, they appear to bear a close relationship to our three principles of autonomy mentioned above. I will examine each of them in turn, and sketch how they are intrinsically intertwined in our three central concepts.[34]

We are concerned, first of all, to explain (and in explaining to categorize) B's change in preference (objective).[35] The type of explanation we give will place the change as a case of A's power, manipulation, or influence. In the teleological framework, if we seek an answer to the question, why did B change his preference, if B's answer is, as we have analysed, in terms of sanctions that A, directly or indirectly, holds (note 29), then B has chosen to trade his *real* preference for a change in the distribution of sanctions. In this case A would not be able to control B's action if he did not control the sanctions. Needless to say the sanctions may be extremely diverse in nature.[36] If B's answer to the question as to his change in preferences does *not* involve sanctions (or conditions) that A controls then the change is a case of influence or manipulation. In both cases he will adopt his preference in terms of its own merits, expressive or instrumental; in the latter case his preference should be derivable from 'deeper' intentions (objectives) and becomes a 'means'. B has still 'chosen' between alternatives and his *range* has accordingly been increased. It is, therefore, to his cognitive premise that we must look for the differentiation between manipulation and influence. If, in the process of changing B's preferences, A intentionally or otherwise controls B's access to relevant information, such that he either (a) reduces B's understanding of his situation (S) (including implications of adopting one course of action rather than another) or, (b) reduces the perception of means open to him then A is *manipulating* B. If, however, no such reductions take place, then we must call this *influence*. A similar line of reasoning would apply to the more restrictive empirical situation of hegemonic control. Here there is no shift in preferences—everybody has the same preferences. But as we have seen we can explain this lack of variance in teleological terms. In this case we would have to show that A's information control in the sense of (a) and (b) above was sufficient to induce B to adopt certain objectives. We do this *not* by specifying an alternative objective, this must be an open question that is essentially conjectural and perhaps, therefore, subject to the contemporary emphasis on action research and/or praxis. The essential point is that the content of the counterfactual is open—B would have done 'something' else.[37]

I have argued for the rather difficult concept of autonomy as a base line (P*4) in differentiating between manipulation and influence; though I am not so sanguine as to believe that I have more than scratched the surface of the problems associated with establishing a 'sociology of freedom' but it remains finally to compare my concept of 'autonomy' with the Marxian/Lukesian concept of 'interest' as a baseline in the study of 'power'.

The Marxian/Lukesian view is disarmingly straightforward; it implies that in deciding when a shift in B's preferences, induced by A, is to be regarded as a case of A's manipulation, or influence, we merely have to ask whether the shift takes B nearer or further from his latent interests. Thus, when neither of the preferences reveal B's interests per se then we have to impose some external criterion. It cannot, by definition, be available to B, for if it were, he would clearly adopt it. The possible authoritarian implications of this viewpoint are well known and the implied justifications in over-riding preferences of those suffering from 'false consciousness' have disturbed many of a liberal frame of mind.

It seems to me that in adopting the base line 'individual autonomy' one begins to overcome these difficulties for in describing B as manipulated we do not have to take recourse in an external criterion involving his *objective interests*. Is this correct —can we specify the conditions for B's autonomy independently of B's *latent*

THE MANY FACES OF POWER AND LIBERTY 21

interests? I think we can, but to make this evident would involve a much deeper analysis of autonomy than I have space for here.

Notes

1. I have begun a discussion of these problems in Abell (1975) and they are further analysed in Abell (forthcoming). Problems also arise when we wish to consider A and B as collectivities which are not entirely consensual.

2. Although the distinction between behaviour and action has played such a central role in sociological meta-theory, it has rarely been given any detailed consideration in the context of power and influence relations. Since I am concerned with 'states of mind' and therefore more often than not with 'meaningful' behaviour, I will refer to 'action' in what follows.

3. I am using the word forebearance to mean inaction.

4. It may well be, of course, that there are very many factors 'intervening' between x and y. Thus we should not construe the power relationship between A and B as exclusively tied to a face to face sort of interaction. Indeed, if we can establish 'causal' chains of the form $x \rightarrow x_1 \rightarrow x_2 \rightarrow x_3 \rightarrow y$ then it may be that B is unaware of x, but nevertheless we would still want to say A has power over B to the extent that x ultimately determines x_3.

5. I do not pretend that the phrase 'state of mind' is at all clear. I hope what is involved will be more evident later on in the paper. For the moment it may be interpreted as B's preferences or objectives. Under (ii) we are implying that B behaves in a manner contrary to his preferences. Clearly, in one sense, B 'decides' to do this (i.e. changes his mind) but the point is he does not do this out of 'conviction', but because of some sort of sanction that (he believes) A controls.

6. We allow that A influences B by maintaining B's more autonomous state of mind in the face of other 'actors' attempting to manipulate him.

7. The distinction I am drawing, then, is one between situations where 'B does y' because it is instrumental in terms of some sanction (positive or negative) and where 'B does y' because of its intrinsic merit to him. It does not, of course, take much thought to realize that the dividing line between the two is not always as clear-cut as one would like. For example, when B follows a moral or ethical injunction promulgated by A, is this to be regarded as working through B's 'conviction' that the injunction is right (a case of influence or manipulation) or in order to avoid feelings of 'guilt' (a negative sanction)? Nevertheless, however difficult the divide may be to draw, it appears we need to do so. It should also be emphasized that the sanction involved must be so from B's point of view (see below).

8. By reputational technique I mean the method of asking suitably placed respondents to estimate various power-holders' degree of power. The technique has been much criticized, but has the advantage of being easy and cheap to use and in situations where it is cross-validated with more soundly based techniques can still be very useful (see Abell, 1975). I have not included a detailed consideration of the technique in this paper as it is not conceptually based.

9. For the sake of expository convenience I will assume that the decisions are serially independent in the sense that the outcome of one does not constrain or determine the outcome of others. This is patently an oversimplification, however; the introduction of decision dependence would complicate the presentation without adding to the basic conceptual issues I wish to discuss.

10. We might ask for an explanation of the variation in these preferences this would merely take us a stage back in the analysis—in the language of Abell (1975) into a different bargaining zone.

11. The argument is in no way dependent upon such a specification.

12. In practice we may wish to know how β_{OA} and β_{OB} depart from unity, not zero, as a value of unity means, in effect, perfect agreement between the outcomes and preferences (assuming they are on the same scale). The models presented in Abell (1975) are rather more complex than those presented here containing measures of *subjective salience* of each actor in each term in equation (6).

13. If preferences are identical over all decisions there is no need for power in the system.

14. One side might of course not attempt this in an active way recognizing the other's power. We must assume that the preferences involved are A's and B's 'real' preferences not necessarily those explicitly stated in the bargaining process or to the investigator. This poses a series of empirical problems, but I do not want to pursue them here. Furthermore, the model only touches on the diversity of methods that the parties can use to communicate their preferences and 'get their own way'—the content of P1 may well be highly complex.

15. A might be *maintaining*, rather than increasing B's range in the face of others who are potentially manipulating him.

16. I am trying to use the word *choose* to contrast with determination.

17. The formulation seems to come close to Berlin's (1969) classic statement.

18. Much clearly revolves on the word information and even if I were able, space precludes a detailed analysis. What is clear, however, is that it is not necessarily the 'amount' of information that matters—one can clearly manipulate by swamping somebody with information.

19. See Abell (1975) and forthcoming.

20. There are rather difficult problems in deciding what a potential decision is as Bachrach and Baratz recognize.

21. We must assume that if it were the case that the 'non-decisions' were 'given' to B he would have a preference which would be contrary to A's. Thus, Bachrach and Baratz (1970, p. 44) —'A non-decision, as we define it, is a decision that results in suppression or thwarting of a latent or manifest challenge to the values or interest of the decision maker.'

22. The idea of control-loss was first introduced by Williamson (1967).

23. It should be noted that the concept of manipulation as I have used it does not necessarily imply an intention to do so on A's behalf. It might be, therefore, useful to distinguish between intentional and inadvertent manipulation.

24. I will initially centre the argument upon propositions in the necessary and sufficient form ($\Leftrightarrow$) rather than just sufficient form—thus ruling out multiple causation. It should not be assumed incidentally that the author believes that causal explanation is unproblematic in the affairs of men.

25. That is, the initial conditions in the above presentation.

26. Dahl, for instance, not surprisingly seems to operate with an implicit causality. Indeed, since most empirical studies of power relations derive from North America, the positivist concept of power is more or less explicit in them.

27. I have again ruled out overdetermination of B's behaviour by making the doing of y a necessary and sufficient condition for I. I do this merely for ease of presentation.

28. For the relationship between the premises and conclusion to be causal it is necessary that all four combinations of truth and falsity of the premises and conclusions to be *logically* possible. From our above argument this is clearly not possible.

29. We may or may not wish to construe A's action x as teleological in terms of controlling B. Also we should recall the point I made in Note (4). x may well be remote from A's immediate action and, in fact, B may not even recognize that x is controlled by A.

30. What I said in Note (29) applies here also it may be that B wants W without realizing that it is A that controls W, etc. We could thus reformulate the analysis without specific mention of B's *recognition* of A's role in the relationship.

31. The so-called control of resources approach.

32. It may of course be instrumental to a 'deeper lying' objective of B. If this is the case then one should in principle be able to give a higher order teleological explanation starting from this objective and concluding in a statement about W.

33. The dividing line between 'force' and 'power' may in practice be rather difficult to draw; there is clearly a grey area of habitually induced behaviour lying between very clear poles. I do not, however, in an exploratory paper of this sort wish to get involved in this particular debate. The question naturally arises, though, as to whether in the teleological account (explanation), 'W' can be regarded as a 'cause' of B's action. Clearly in one sense of the word 'W' determines B's action, it is also logically possible for him not to have *chosen* to 'do y' in the presence of W, and W is temporarily prior to y. The relationship, therefore, accords with some of the standard (Humean) canons of causality. However, there is no need to link W to y in terms of a universal generalization (Law) and thus, in order to establish the 'truth' of the link, to resort to comparative method. I prefer, as a consequence, to refer to W as a 'teleological patterning factor' (see Abell, forthcoming).

34. The issues deserve a lengthy consideration, but I will only pen an outline here. Clearly there are a number of ways that an individual can be manipulated because of his emotional proclivities. I will not consider these. I admit I am in fact taking an 'over-cognitive' viewpoint.

35. We will assume that B's preferences in decision-making (and for that matter, non-decision-making) derive from his objectives. This idea is central to the concept of belief/value system which centres on the idea that there is in some sense of the word an internal logic to such systems such that preferences in 'one-off' decisions can be deductively unpacked from deep-lying beliefs/values. We know this is an over-optimistic interpretation of how individuals hold beliefs (pace cognitive consistency theories), but it would take me too far afield to introduce any complications of this sort here.

36. In fact what is and what is not regarded as a *sanction* may itself be subject to 'power play'. Thus, part of A's 'power' over B may be attributable to A's ability to implant the idea that certain rewards, etc., are worthwhile in B's mind. Thus the legitimization of sanctions is an important aspect of influence or manipulation. (I will expand these issues in Abell (forthcoming)). Furthermore, it is also possible that A and B's interpretation of sanctions are different. Our analysis rests rather heavily on B's interpretation of the sanctions involved. Clearly since I have chosen to make the provision of information a characteristic of influence and manipulation processes we must not interpret sources of information as sanctions. Nor should information flow be interpreted in purely quantitative terms—A can manipulate B by outfacing him with an abundance of information.

37. The analyst may be able, because of his understanding of B, to show that A, by virtue of additional information he controls, could increase B's autonomy if he made it available to him.

References

ABELL, PETER (1971). *Model Building in Sociology*, London: Weidenfeld and Nicholson.

—— (1975). *Organisations as Bargaining and Influence Systems*, London: Heinemann.

—— (forthcoming): *Organisations as Bargaining and Influence Systems*, Vol. II, London: Heinemann.

BACHRACH, PETER, and BARATZ, MORTON S. (1962). 'The Two Faces of Power', *American Political Science Review*, 56, pp. 947–52.

—— and —— (1970). *Power and Poverty: Theory and Practice*, New York: Oxford University Press.

BERGER, PETER (1963). *Invitation to Sociology: A Humanistic Perspective*, London: Penguin Books.

24   PETER ABELL

BERLIN, SIR ISAIAH (1969). *Four Essays on Liberty*, London: Oxford University Press.

CRENSON, MATHEW A. (1971). *The Un-Politics of Air Pollution: A Study of Non-Decision-Making in The Cities*, London: John Hopkins Press.

DAHL, ROBERT (1957). 'The Concept of Power', *Behavioural Science*, **2**, pp. 201–5.

—— (1958). 'A Critique of the Ruling Elite Model', *American Political Science Review*, **52**, pp. 463–9.

GALBRAITH, J. KENNETH (1974). *Economics and The Public Purpose*, London: Penguin Books.

HARSANYI, JOHN C. (1962). 'Measurement of Social Power, Opportunity Costs and the Theory of Two-Person Bargaining Games', *Behavioural Science*, **7**, pp. 27–52.

LUKES, STEVEN (1974). *Power: A Radical View*, London: Macmillan.

PARSONS, TALCOTT (1957). 'The Distribution of Power in American Society', *World Politics*, **10**, pp. 123–43.

—— (1963a). 'On the Concept of Influence', *Public Opinion Quarterly*, 27, pp. 37–62.

—— (1963b). 'On the Concept of Political Power', *Proceedings of the American Philosophical Society*, **107**, pp. 232–62.

—— (1937). *The Structure of Social Action*, New York: Free Press.

PETTIGREW, ANDREW (1972). *The Politics of Organisational Decision-Making*, London: Tavistock.

PONDY, LEWIS (1975). 'The Other Hand Clapping an Information-Processing Approach to Organisational Power'. Mimeo, University of Illinois.

VON WRIGHT, GEORGE H. (1971). *Explanation and Understanding*, London: Routledge and Kegan Paul.

WILLIAMSON, O. E. (1967). *The Economics of Discretionary Behaviour: Managerial Objectives in the Theory of the Firm*, Chicago: Markham.

Biographical note: PETER ABELL, B.Sc., Ph.D.; 1967–71, Lecturer, Senior Lecturer, Department of Sociology, Essex; 1971–6, Reader (Director of Research) Industrial Sociology Unit, Imperial College; 1976–, Professor of Sociology, University of Birmingham; author of books on Model-building, Inward Investment, and Organizational Theory.

Acknowledgement

I should like to thank the following friends and colleagues for their helpful comments on an earlier version of this paper: Kerry Thomas, Sandra Dawson, Robin Cohen, Peter Lassman, Ricardo Peccèi, Norman Stockman, and Ann Westenholz.

Part III
Applications:
Theoretical and Empirical

[18]

Journal of Mathematical Sociology, 1986, Vol. 12(1) pp. 35–48
0022-250X/1201-0035 $20.00/0

A MODEL OF RELATIVE DEPRIVATION

KENJI KOSAKA

*Kwansei Gakuin University
Nishinomiya, Japan*

July 1985

. . . it was precisely in those parts of France where there had been most improvement that popular discontent ran highest. This may seem illogical — but history is full of such paradoxes.

A. de Tocqueville

1. INTRODUCTION

The notion of "relative deprivation" as well as of "reference group", seems to be widely accepted among sociologists and social psychologists as one of significant concepts. Although the notion itself dates back to Tocqueville (1856) and Durkheim (1893), *The American Soldier* (1941) played a pioneering role in the studies of relative deprivation since it coined the term as a key concept to give a consistent interpretation for seemingly paradoxical phenomena of material plenty and individual dissatisfaction. There have been quite a number of studies since then which attempted to either clarify or apply the concept (Merton and Kitt, 1950; Pettigrew, 1964; Gurr, 1968; Runciman, 1966; Soranaka, 1970; Suls and Miller, 1977 to mention some). However, there have been only few efforts (Davis, 1959; Boudon, 1982) to represent formally the mechanisms or processes where relative deprivation is generated.

The present paper is an extension of Boudon's essay, which seems to be more in line with the method of generating process than Davis's earlier work.[1] Boudon attempts to formalize "the logic of frustration" within a game-theoretic framework as *a* case of what he calls perverse effects or unintended consequences of social action. Individuals behave more or less rationally trying to maximize their subjective expected utility;[2] but as a consequence of aggregation of individual behavior, the end-result might be frustrating to them. Some of the individual actors may be, of course, satisfied with it; but some may not.

Boudon constructs a simple model to capture such a situation, thereby to see implications of the phenomena generated by the model. Boudon's model is, however, half-way done in the sense that he does not go far beyond a mere illustration of the phenomena with some numerical examples.

In the following, we aim firstly to follow Boudon's discussion and go a step further to see more precisely the implications of Boudon's model; secondly to see how well it captures various empirical episodes; and finally to modify a model from a non-stratified to a stratified society model, again according to Boudon's suggestion.

2. BOUDON'S PRESENTATION OF THE LOGIC OF RELATIVE DEPRIVATION

He considers the following betting situation, which we express in axiomatic forms.

Ax. 1   There is a group or a society of N players.

Ax. 2   Players are offered binary choices.

   Move 1: Stake C_1 for a possible win of B_1

   Move 2: Stake C_2 for a win of B_2.

   where $B_1 > C_1, B_2 > C_2, B_1 > B_2, C_1 > C_2, B_1 > 0, C_1 > 0, B_2 \geqslant 0$, and $C_2 \geqslant 0$.

Ax. 3   The numbers of winners of lots B_1 and B_2 are n_1 and n_2, respectively. We assume that $n_1 + n_2 = N$. That is, every player is entitled to gain at least B_2 as long as he participated in a game by betting either C_1 or C_2.

Ax. 4   Players are advised to stake C_1 rather C_2 if the expected net profit of betting C_1 exceeds that of betting C_2. This is the axiom of rational behavior.

If more than n_1 players bet C_1, some of them surely fail to gain B_1 even though it seemed more profitable to stake C_1 from the behavioral principle of rationality. They are put into a position of "relative depriva-

A MODEL OF RELATIVE DEPRIVATION 37

tion'' as defined by Runciman (1966: 10), since (i) they are deprived of B_1; (ii) they know that there are some others who adopted the same type of behavior (Move 1) on the same behavioral principle (Axiom 4) *and* succeeded in obtaining B_1; (iii) they also want B_1 and (iv) they see that they are entitled to gain B_1 by the equal probability to all players who adopted Move 1. With the above in mind, we could have the following definition.

Definition.   The rate of relative deprivation is given by the proportions of individuals who find themselves in the position of acquiring at the high price C_1 the lot of least value B_2.

Here those who stake C_1 for B_1 are regarded as referent persons. Those who are relatively deprived are actually more deprived than those who gain B_2 by betting C_2, since the net profit of the former $(B_2 - C_1)$ is less than that of the latter $(B_2 - C_2)$.

Suppose that $(x_1 - 1)$ other players $(n_1 \leqslant x_1 \leqslant N)$ stake C_1. The expectation of net profit of a player also betting C_1, denoted by $E_1(x_1)$, would be:

$$E_1(x_1) = (B_1 - C_1)\frac{n_1}{x_1} + (B_2 - C_1)\frac{x_1 - n_1}{x_1}$$

$$= (B_1 - B_2)\frac{n_1}{x_1} + B_2 - C_1 \tag{1}$$

On the other hand, the expectation of net profit E_2 of a player betting C_2 when $(x_1 - 1)$ other players stake C_1 is,

$$E_2 = B_2 - C_2 \tag{2}$$

Thus when $(x_1 - 1)$ other players stake C_1, a player is advised to stake C_1 rather than C_2 if

$$E_1(x_1) \geqslant E_2$$

or

$$(B_1 - B_2)\frac{n_1}{x_1} + B_2 - C_1 \geqslant B_2 - C_2 \tag{3}$$

More simply,

$$\frac{B_1 - B_2}{C_1 - C_2} \geqslant \frac{x_1}{n_1} \tag{4}$$

Boudon stops here, and then goes on to explain the logic of relative deprivation only by using numerical examples. In the following, we carry on a line of his effort to express the logic in formal terms.

Let us allow all of the players to be informed of how many players are betting C_1 at every moment of a going session of a betting game. It does mean that each player is in a position which allows him to decide, independently and without communication with others, whether Equation (4) holds or not when he also stakes C_1^2. Then eventually at the end of a going session of a game, the number of players who stake C_1 will reach the critical point or an equilibrium point x_1^*, which is given by:

$$x_1^* = \left(\frac{B_1 - B_2}{C_1 - C_2} \right) n_1 \qquad (5)$$

We introduce more definitions and notations as follows. In general,

$$P = B - C$$

which reads "the (net) profit is equal to benefit minus cost" as is usually claimed in social exchange theory (Homans, 1974). For our binary choices then,

$$P_1 = B_1 - C_1$$
$$P_2 = B_2 - C_2$$

By denoting $B = B_1 - B_2$, $C = C_1 - C_2$, $P = P_1 - P_2$, we could define a meaningful quantity R as follows:

$$R = \frac{P}{C}$$

which is interpreted as the marginal rate of return (or profit) relative to investment (the risked quantity C). Then Equation (5) can be expressed as:

$$x_1^* = (R + 1)n_1 \qquad (5)'$$

However, since x_1^* can not be greater than N, Equation (5)' holds as long as $x_1^* \leqslant N$, that is

$$(R + 1)n_1 \leqslant N \quad \text{or} \quad \frac{n_1}{N} \leqslant \frac{1}{R + 1}$$

If $(R + 1)n_1 > N$, that is, $\dfrac{n_1}{N} > \dfrac{1}{R + 1}$,

$$x_1^* = N \qquad (5)''$$

We shall be interested, next, in the rate of relative deprivation, which we express from our earlier definition as follows.

A MODEL OF RELATIVE DEPRIVATION 39

$$S = \frac{x_1 - n_1}{N} \qquad (6)$$

The rate of relative deprivation simply represents the proportion of those who failed to gain B_1 while betting C_1.

From (5)′, if $\dfrac{n_1}{N} \leqslant \dfrac{1}{R+1}$,

$$S = \frac{(R+1)n_1 - n_1}{N} = R\left(\frac{n_1}{N}\right) \qquad (6)′$$

We have here a family of linear functions as the slope varies.

From (5)″, if $\dfrac{n_1}{N} > \dfrac{1}{R+1}$,

$$S = \frac{N - n_1}{N} = 1 - \frac{n_1}{N} \qquad (6)″$$

Here S is a function of only n_1/N, which does not involve R or any other parameters. We are able now to examine the behavior of n_1/N and/or R.

3. ANALYSIS

Let us see how the rate of relative deprivation behaves as the marginal rate of return varies.

R = 0

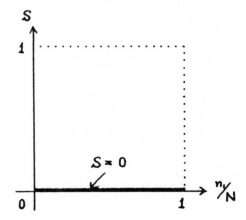

FIGURE 1.   The rate of relative deprivation when R = 0.

This is a trivial case. There exists no difference in net outcome between choosing Move 1 and Move 2. In this case, nobody feels deprived for all n_1/N.

R = 1

The rate of relative deprivation gets to the highest (S = .5) when a half of the total number of players are allowed to be winners. The rate of relative deprivation decreases as n_1/N moves toward extremes in either direction.

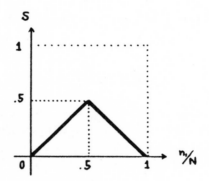

FIGURE 2.   The rate of relative deprivation when R - 1.

If $n_1/N \leqslant 1/2$, $S = n_1/N$.
If $n_1/N > 1/2$, $S = 1 - n_1/N$.

R = 2

If $n_1/N \leqslant 1/3$, $S = 2(n_1/N)$.
If $n_1/N > 1/3$, $S = 1 - n_1/N$.

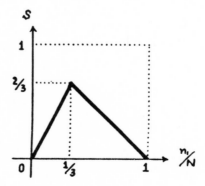

FIGURE 3.   The rate of relative deprivation when R - 2.

A MODEL OF RELATIVE DEPRIVATION 41

In summary,

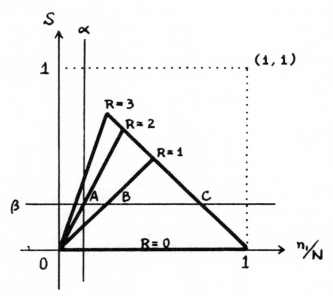

FIGURE 4. The rate of relative deprivation when R varies.

Several implications can be derived from observing Figure 4.

1) For a certain level of R, the rate of relative deprivation increases up to a "critical point," then decreases as n_1/N increases.

2) A "critical point" occurs at the level where the number of players (x_i') staking C_1 for B_1 reaches the total number of players in a group or a society. In other words, once everyone adopts Move 1, the rate of relative deprivation decreases, as the number of possible winners of lot B_1 increases. Below the level of a critical point, however, improvement of objective conditions would not contribute to lessening the rate of relative deprivation; it would rather increase the rate of relative deprivation.

3) As the marginal rate of return as measured by R increases, the possible maximum rate of relative deprivation also increases.

4) The possible maximum rate of relative deprivation occurs at smaller number of winners of lot B_1, as R increases.

5) For a fixed level of n_1/N ($\leqslant 1/2$), the rate of relative deprivation grows as R ($\geqslant 1$) increases. See line α in Figure 4. For any level of n_1/N ($> 1/2$), the rate of relative deprivation remains the same for all R.

6) We could think of situations of the same level of relative deprivation, according to different combinations of R and n_1/N. A, B, and C
on line β belong to the same level of deprivation rate. See line β in Figure
4. As Boudon (1982: 120) suggests, "equivalent levels of frustration are
obtained by distributing important lots (i.e., lots with greater R)
parsimoniously or less important lots (i.e., lots with smaller R)
generously."

4. DISCUSSION

Since we have not set up an appropriate data yet, we can not go further
to test our model. But we could go back to previous studies of relative
deprivation to see if our model provides a different interpretation of
given empirical data.

Let us take up the original work of *The American Soldier* for a
moment. One of the empirical findings which is relevant to studies of
relative deprivation is this:

> For a given rank, longevity, and educational level, the less the
> promotion opportunity afforded by a branch or combination of
> branches, the more favorable the opinion tends to be toward
> promotion opportunity. (Vol. I: 256)

"The less, the more" type of statement seems to suggest that there
exists a linear, positive or negative according to how to set up X-axis
and Y-axis, relationship between the level of relative deprivation and
the level of objective material conditions. As far as the authors of *The
American Soldier* are concerned, they do not seem to pay any attention
to extreme cases of, say, promotion opportunities. If we strictly stay
with a linear relationship type of proposition, it should be that a very
high rate of relative deprivation corresponds to the extremely high rate
of promotion opportunity, or inversely, a very low rate of relative
deprivation corresponds to the extremely low chances of promotion.

As we have already seen in Figure 4, our model gives a different
picture; different for the cases where n_1/N exceeds the critical point.
Our model predicts that the rate of relative deprivation will decrease
rather than increase to zero beyond the critical point as n_1/N goes
toward unity.

It should be noted that chances of promotion in the Air Corps were
reported to range from 47% up to 56% (according to different levels
of education and/or longevity), while chances of promotion in the

Military Police were 17% up to 34% at the highest (also according to different levels of education and/or longevity). Our present model predicts that the rate of relative deprivation might have been lessened among the Air Corps if chances of promotion had been far greater, say, 70% or 80%.

Merton and Kitt also suspect the validity of the linear relationship suggested by the authors of *The American Soldier*, although just in passing. In their footnote, Merton and Kitt pointed out (1950: 53-54):

> . . . it is scarcely probable that this relationship between actual mobility rates and individual satisfaction with mobility chances holds throughout the entire range of variation. If promotion rates were reduced to practically zero in some of these groups, would one then find an even more "favorable opinion" of promotion chances? Presumably, the relationship is curvilinear, and this requires the sociologist to work out toward the conditions under which the observed linear relation fails to obtain.

Presumably, what they suggest by "the curvilinear relationship" is this: toward the extreme low level of promotion rates, the rate of relative deprivation will rise, or at least will not decrease monotonically. Although we do not know precisely what kind of curve they had in mind for the extreme high level of promotion rates, they had certainly a picture quite different from that of our model. Since the data available in *The American Solder* are limited, we unfortunately cannot tell which of the above conjectures is most plausible and which is not until we obtain more data.

5. A MODIFIED MODEL

Boudon suggests several possible directions for modification of the model (1982: 121-123). One of the interesting possibilities is to assume a stratified society where players are differentiated in terms of resources available for betting; hence differentiated are the players' attitudes with regard to risk. In the following, we set up a modified model of a betting game in such a stratified society.

Assumption: A society consists of two classes, say, the rich and the poor. The probability of the poor making a high bet is less than that of the rich, since the risk of losing is all the greater for the poor because of a paucity of resources.

Additional Notation and Definitions:

N_r: the number of the rich
N_p: the number of the poor

$$(N = N_r + N_p)$$

$x_1^*(r)$: the number of the rich who stake C_1
$x_1^*(p)$: the number of the poor who stake C_1
r: the maximum risk for the poor $(0 \leqslant r < 1)$

Let r be defined as follows.

$$r = \frac{\hat{x}_1^* - n_1}{\hat{x}_1^*}$$

or

$$\hat{x}_1^* = \frac{n_1}{1 - r} \tag{8}$$

We use $\hat{x}_1^*$ instead of x_1^* because $\hat{x}_1^*$ is the equilibrium number of players betting C_1 only in the image of players who assume population homogeneity. Namely, we are assuming that the members of each of the two classes reckon that those of the other class will behave as they do. From the rich's point of view*, the number of those who would stake C_1 will be:

$$\hat{x}_1^* = (R + 1)n_1 \qquad \text{(from (5))}$$

Then the number of the rich who stake C_1 will be:

$$x_1^*(r) = \hat{x}_1^*\left(\frac{N_r}{N}\right) = \frac{N_r}{N} \cdot (R + 1)n_1 \tag{9}$$

From the poor's point of view, the number of those who would stake C_1 will be:

$$\hat{x}_1^* = \frac{n_1}{1 - r} \qquad \text{(from (8))}$$

Then the number of the poor who stake C_1 will be:

$$x_1^*(p) = \hat{x}_1^*\left(\frac{N_p}{N}\right) = \frac{N_p}{N} \cdot \frac{n_1}{1 - r} \tag{10}$$

---

* N.B. For the following discussion, we assume

$$x_1^*(r) < N_r$$
$$x_1^*(p) < N_p$$

A MODEL OF RELATIVE DEPRIVATION 45

Thus, the total number of those who stake C_1 is:

$$\left[\frac{N_r}{N} \cdot (R + 1)n_1\right] + \left[\frac{N_p}{N} \cdot \frac{n_1}{1 - r}\right] = \frac{n_1[N_r(R + 1)(1 - r) + N_p]}{N(1 - r)}$$

(11)

The rate of relative deprivation under a modified model is given by:

$$S = \frac{\left[\frac{N_r}{N}(R + 1)n_1\right] + \left[\frac{N_p}{N} \frac{n_1}{1 - r}\right] - n_1}{N}$$

$$= \frac{n_1[(1 - r)(N_r(R + 1) - N) + N_p]}{N^2(1 - r)}$$

$$= \frac{n_1[v(N_r(R + 1) - N) + N_p]}{N^2 v}$$

(12)

$$v = 1 - r$$
$$0 < v \leqslant 1 \text{ since } 0 \leqslant r < 1$$

Denote:

S_{m1}: the rate of relative deprivation under the earlier model (m1), i.e., a non-stratified system model

S_{m2}: the rate of relative deprivation under a modified model(m2), i.e., a stratified system model

We shall be interested in the difference $(S_{m1} - S_{m2})$, that is, the difference of the rate of relative deprivation between a non-stratified system model and a stratified system model.

$$D = S_{m1} - S_{m2}$$

$$= R\left(\frac{n_1}{N}\right) - \frac{n_1[v(N_r(R + 1) - N) + (N - N_r)]}{N^2 v}$$

$$= \frac{n_1(N - N_r)(vR + v - 1)}{N^2 v}$$

(13)

$D > 0$ if $(vR + v - 1) > 0$
$D \leqslant 0$ if $(vR + v - 1) \leqslant 0$

Since R is greater than unity and r is no greater than 0.5 in ordinary cases, $(vR + v - 1) > 0$ holds (see Figure 5); hence D turns out to be positive. In other words, under a stratified system, the rate of relative deprivation is attenuated. When the poor tempt to retain from making a high bet, the overall rate of deprivation decreases.

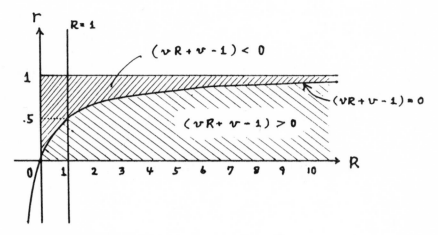

FIGURE 5.   The curve of $(vR + v - 1) = 0$ or $r = 1 - \dfrac{1}{R+1}$

In the following, we use techniques of differential calculus by regarding all the relevant variables as continuous, thereby to examine the influences of parameters upon the behavior of S_{m2} and D.

1) $\dfrac{\partial S_{m2}}{\partial n_1} = \dfrac{N(1-v) + N_r(vR + v - 1)}{N^2 v} > 0$ if $(vR + v - 1) > 0$

S_{m2} increases as the number of possible winners of B_1 increases, if $(vR + v - 1) > 0$ which is the case in ordinary cases.

2) $\dfrac{\partial S_{m2}}{\partial v} = - \dfrac{n_1(N - N_r)}{N^2 v^2} < 0$

As the poor become more conservative (risk aversive), the overall rate of relative deprivation decreases.

3) $\dfrac{\partial S_{m2}}{\partial R} = \dfrac{n_1 N_r}{N^2} > 0$

The overall rate of relative deprivation increases as the marginal rate of return increases.

4) $\dfrac{\partial S_{m2}}{\partial N_r} = \dfrac{n_1(vR + v - 1)}{N^2 v} \begin{array}{l} > 0 \\ \leqslant 0 \end{array}$ 　　　　$\begin{array}{l} \text{if } (vR + v - 1) > 0 \\ \text{if } (vR + v - 1) \leqslant 0. \end{array}$

As the proportion of the rich increases, the overall rate of relative deprivation also increases if $(vR + v - 1) > 0$.

A MODEL OF RELATIVE DEPRIVATION   47

5) $\dfrac{\partial D}{\partial n_1} = \dfrac{(N - N_r)(vR + v - 1)}{N^2 v}$ $\begin{array}{l} > 0 \\ \leqslant 0 \end{array}$ $\begin{array}{l} \text{if } (vR + v - 1) > 0 \\ \text{if } (vR + v - 1) \leqslant 0 \end{array}$

The differences in the rate of relative deprivation between a non-stratified system and a stratified system increases as the number of possible winners of B_1 increases if $(vR + v - 1) > 0$.

6) $\dfrac{\partial D}{\partial v} = \dfrac{n_1(N - N_r)}{N^2 v^2} > 0$

The difference in the rate of relative deprivation between a non-stratified system and a stratified system increases as the maximum risk for the poor decreases; that is, the poor become more conservative or risk aversive.

7) $\dfrac{\partial D}{\partial R} = \dfrac{n_1(N - N_r)}{N^2 v} > 0$

The difference in the rate of relative deprivation between a non-stratified system and a stratified system increases as the marginal rate of return increases.

8) $\dfrac{\partial D}{\partial N_r} = - \dfrac{n_1(vR + v - 1)}{N^2 v}$ $\begin{array}{l} < 0 \\ \geqslant 0 \end{array}$ $\begin{array}{l} \text{if } (vR + v - 1) > 0 \\ \text{if } (vR + v - 1) \leqslant 0 \end{array}$

The difference in the rate of relative deprivation between a non-stratified system and a stratified system decreases as the proportion of the rich increases if $(vR + v - 1) > 0$.

The above analyses are to see how S_{m2} and D are effected by each one of the parameters n_1, r, R and N_r with other three parameters being constant. The effects are caused by the behavior of a segment of the population we called the poor, who are inclined to avert risks to more or lesser degree. This behavior of the poor leads us to another important implication. From Equation (10), it is seen that the number of the poor who stake C_1 will decrease as the maximum risk for the poor decreases. Hence the probability is that the absolute number of the poor who win B_1 will decrease as r decreases. Therefore, as Boudon (1982: 122) puts it, "stratification has the effect of determining effects of self-reproduction of classes: the rich are the beneficiaries of the relatively more intense withdrawal of the poor" as well as the effect of attenuating the overall rate of relative deprivation.

48   KENJI KOSAKA

NOTES

1) See Boudon (1979) and Fararo (1969) for a significance of the method of generating process for the development of sociological theories.

2) See Simon (1983) and Coleman (1973) for various meanings of 'rationality' of human behavior or social action under different conditions.

3) This assumption creates the difficulty of the model with respect to the knowledge conditions of players. Strictly speaking, some recursive or dynamic processes have to be introduced to get an equilibrium.

REFERENCES

Boudon, R. 1979. Generating models as a research strategy. In R.K. Merton, J.S. Coleman and P.H. Rossi (eds.) *Qualitative and Quantative Social Research*. NY: The Free Press.

Boudon, R. 1982. *The Unintended Consequences of Social Action*. The Macmillan Press.

Coleman, J.S. 1973. *The Mathematics of Collective Action*. Chicago: Aldine Publishing Company.

Davis, J.A. 1979. A formal interpretation of the theory of relative deprivation. *Sociometry* 22, 280-296.

Durkheim, E. 1983. *De la division du travail social*. Paris: Alcan.

Fararo, T.J. 1969. The nature of mathematical sociology. *Social Research* 36, 75-92.

Gurr, T. 1968. Psychological factors in civil violence. *World Politics* 20, 245-278.

Homans, G.C. 1974. *Social Behavior*. Revised edition. NY: Harcourt Brace Jovanovich.

Merton, R.K. and A.S. Kitt. 1950. Contributions to the theory of reference group behavior. In R.K. Merton and P.F. Lazarsfeld (ed.), *Continuities in Social Research*. Illinois: The Free Press, Glencoe.

Pettigrew, T. 1964. *A Profile of the Negro American*. D. Van Nostrand.

Runciman, W.G. 1966. *Relative Deprivation and Social Justice*. London: Routledge and Kegan Paul.

Simon, H.A. 1983. *Reason in Human Affairs*. CA: Stanford University Press.

Soranaka, S. 1970. Relative deprivation and social movements. *Behavioral Science Research* 7, 1-16. (In Japanese.)

Stouffer, S.A. *et al.* 1949. *The American Soldier*. Princeton University Press.

Stouffer, S.A. 1950. Some afterthoughts of a contributor to THE AMERICAN SOLDIER. In R.K. Merton and P.F. Lazarsfeld (eds.), *Continuities in Social Research*. Illionois: The Free Press.

Suls, J.M. and R.L. Miller. 1977. *Social Comparison Processes*. Washington: Hemisphere Publishing Co.

Tocqueville, A. de. 1856. *L'Ancien régime et la revolution*.

[19]

The Evolution of Cooperation

Robert Axelrod and William D. Hamilton

The theory of evolution is based on the struggle for life and the survival of the fittest. Yet cooperation is common between members of the same species and even between members of different species. Before about 1960, accounts of the evolutionary process largely dismissed cooperative phenomena as not requiring special attention. This position followed from a misreading of theory that assigned most adaptation to selection at the level of populations or whole species. As a result of such misreading, cooperation was always considered adaptive. Recent reviews of the evolutionary process, however, have shown no sound basis for a pervasive group-benefit view of selection; at the level of a species or a population, the processes of selection are weak. The original individualistic emphasis of Darwin's theory is more valid (1, 2).

To account for the manifest existence of cooperation and related group behavior, such as altruism and restraint in competition, evolutionary theory has recently acquired two kinds of extension. These extensions are, broadly, genetical kinship theory (3) and reciprocation theory (4, 5). Most of the recent activity, both in field work and in further developments of theory, has been on the side of kinship. Formal approaches have varied, but kinship theory has increasingly taken a gene's-eye view of natural selection (6). A gene, in effect, looks beyond its mortal bearer to interests of the potentially immortal set of its replicas existing in other related individuals. If interactants are sufficiently closely related, al-

Dr. Axelrod is a professor of political science and research scientist at the Institute of Public Policy Studies, University of Michigan, Ann Arbor 48109. Dr. Hamilton is a professor of evolutionary biology in the Museum of Zoology and the Division of Biological Sciences, University of Michigan.

truism can benefit reproduction of the set, despite losses to the individual altruist. In accord with this theory's predictions, apart from the human species, almost all clear cases of altruism, and most observed cooperation, occur in contexts of high relatedness, usually between immediate family members. The evolution of the suicidal barbed sting of the honeybee worker could be taken as paradigm for this line of theory (7).

Conspicuous examples of cooperation (although almost never of ultimate self-sacrifice) also occur where relatedness is low or absent. Mutualistic symbioses offer striking examples such as these: the fungus and alga that compose a lichen; the ants and ant-acacias, where the trees house and feed the ants which, in turn, protect the trees (8); and the fig wasps and fig tree, where wasps, which are obligate parasites of fig flowers, serve as the tree's sole means of pollination and seed set (9). Usually the course of cooperation in such symbioses is smooth, but sometimes the partners show signs of antagonism, either spontaneous or elicited by particular treatments (10). Although kinship may be involved, as will be discussed later, symbioses mainly illustrate the other recent extension of evolutionary theory, the theory of reciprocation.

Cooperation per se has received comparatively little attention from biologists since the pioneer account of Trivers (5); but an associated issue, concerning restraint in conflict situations, has been developed theoretically. In this connection, a new concept, that of an evolutionarily stable strategy, has been formally developed (6, 11). Cooperation in the more normal sense has remained clouded by certain difficulties, particularly those concerning initiation of cooperation from a previously asocial state (12) and its stable maintenance once established. A formal theory of cooperation is increasingly needed. The renewed emphasis on individualism has focused on the frequent ease of cheating in reciprocatory arrangements. This makes the stability of even mutualistic symbioses appear more questionable than under the old view of adaptation for species benefit. At the same time other cases that once appeared firmly in the domain of kinship theory now begin to reveal relatednesses of interactants that are too low for much nepotistic altruism to be expected. This applies both to cooperative breeding in birds (13) and to cooperative acts more generally in primate groups (14). Here either the appearances of cooperation are deceptive—they are cases of part-kin altruism and part cheat-

ing—or a larger part of the behavior is attributable to stable reciprocity. Previous accounts that already invoke reciprocity, however, underemphasize the stringency of its conditions (15).

Our contribution in this area is new in three ways.

1) In a biological context, our model is novel in its probabilistic treatment of the possibility that two individuals may interact again. This allows us to shed new

light on certain specific biological processes such as aging and territoriality.

2) Our analysis of the evolution of cooperation considers not just the final stability of a given strategy, but also the initial viability of a strategy in an environment dominated by noncooperating individuals, as well as the robustness of a strategy in a variegated environment composed of other individuals using a variety of more or less sophisticated strategies. This allows a richer understanding of the full chronology of the evolution of cooperation than has previously been possible.

3) Our applications include behavioral interaction at the microbial level. This leads us to some speculative suggestions of rationales able to account for the existence of both chronic and acute phases in many diseases, and for a certain class of chromosomal nondisjunction, exemplified by Down's syndrome.

Strategies in the Prisoner's Dilemma

Many of the benefits sought by living things are disproportionally available to cooperating groups. While there are considerable differences in what is meant by the terms "benefits" and "sought," this statement, insofar as it is true, lays down a fundamental basis for all social life. The problem is that while an individual can benefit from mutual cooperation, each one can also do even better by exploiting the cooperative efforts of others. Over a period of time, the same individuals may interact again, allowing for complex patterns of strategic interactions. Game theory in general, and the

Prisoner's Dilemma game in particular, allow a formalization of the strategic possibilities inherent in such situations.

The Prisoner's Dilemma game is an elegant embodiment of the problem of achieving mutual cooperation (16), and therefore provides the basis for our analysis. To keep the analysis tractable, we focus on the two-player version of the game, which describes situations that involve interactions between pairs of

Summary. Cooperation in organisms, whether bacteria or primates, has been a difficulty for evolutionary theory since Darwin. On the assumption that interactions between pairs of individuals occur on a probabilistic basis, a model is developed based on the concept of an evolutionarily stable strategy in the context of the Prisoner's Dilemma game. Deductions from the model, and the results of a computer tournament show how cooperation based on reciprocity can get started in an asocial world, can thrive while interacting with a wide range of other strategies, and can resist invasion once fully established. Potential applications include specific aspects of territoriality, mating, and disease.

individuals. In the Prisoner's Dilemma game, two individuals can each either cooperate or defect. The payoff to a player is in terms of the effect on its fitness (survival and fecundity). No matter what the other does, the selfish choice of defection yields a higher payoff than cooperation. But if both defect, both do worse than if both had cooperated.

Figure 1 shows the payoff matrix of the Prisoner's Dilemma. If the other player cooperates, there is a choice between cooperation which yields R (the reward for mutual cooperation) or defection which yields T (the temptation to defect). By assumption, $T > R$, so that it pays to defect if the other player cooperates. On the other hand, if the other player defects, there is a choice between cooperation which yields S (the sucker's payoff) or defection which yields P (the punishment for mutual defection). By assumption $P > S$, so it pays to defect if the other player defects. Thus, no matter what the other player does, it pays to defect. But, if both defect, both get P rather than the larger value of R that they both could have gotten had both cooperated. Hence the dilemma (17).

With two individuals destined never to meet again, the only strategy that can be called a solution to the game is to defect always despite the seemingly paradoxical outcome that both do worse than they could have had they cooperated.

Apart from being the solution in game theory, defection is also the solution in biological evolution (18). It is the outcome of inevitable evolutionary trends through mutation and natural selection: if the payoffs are in terms of fitness, and

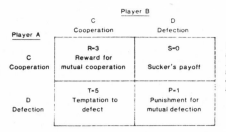

Fig. 1. The Prisoner's Dilemma game. The payoff to player A is shown with illustrative numerical values. The game is defined by $T > R > P > S$ and $R > (S + T)/2$.

the interactions between pairs of individuals are random and not repeated, then any population with a mixture of heritable strategies evolves to a state where all individuals are defectors. Moreover, no single differing mutant strategy can do better than others when the population is using this strategy. In these respects the strategy of defection is stable.

This concept of stability is essential to the discussion of what follows and it is useful to state it more formally. A strategy is evolutionarily stable if a population of individuals using that strategy cannot be invaded by a rare mutant adopting a different strategy [11]. In the case of the Prisoner's Dilemma played only once, no strategy can invade the strategy of pure defection. This is because no other strategy can do better with the defecting individuals than the P achieved by the defecting players who interact with each other. So in the single-shot Prisoner's Dilemma, to defect always is an evolutionarily stable strategy.

In many biological settings, the same two individuals may meet more than once. If an individual can recognize a previous interactant and remember some aspects of the prior outcomes, then the strategic situation becomes an iterated Prisoner's Dilemma with a much richer set of possibilities. A strategy would take the form of a decision rule which determined the probability of cooperation or defection as a function of the history of the interaction so far. But if there is a known number of interactions between a pair of individuals, to defect always is still evolutionarily stable and is still the only strategy which is. The reason is that defection on the last interaction would be optimal for both sides, and consequently so would defection on the next-to-last interaction, and so on back to the first interaction.

Our model is based on the more realistic assumption that the number of interactions is not fixed in advance. Instead, there is some probability, w, that after the current interaction the same two

individuals will meet again. Factors that affect the magnitude of this probability of meeting again include the average lifespan, relative mobility, and health of the individuals. For any value of w, the strategy of unconditional defection (ALL D) is evolutionarily stable: if everyone is using this strategy, no mutant strategy can invade the population. But other strategies may be evolutionarily stable as well. In fact, when w is sufficiently great, there is no single best strategy regardless of the behavior of the others in the population [19]. Just because there is no single best strategy, it does not follow that analysis is hopeless. On the contrary, we demonstrate not only the stability of a given strategy, but also its robustness and initial viability.

Before turning to the development of the theory, let us consider the range of biological reality that is encompassed by the game theoretic approach. To start with, an organism does not need a brain to employ a strategy. Bacteria, for example, have a basic capacity to play games in that (i) bacteria are highly responsive to selected aspects of their environment, especially their chemical environment; (ii) this implies that they can respond differentially to what other organisms around them are doing; (iii) these conditional strategies of behavior can certainly be inherited; and (iv) the behavior of a bacterium can affect the fitness of other organisms around it, just as the behavior of other organisms can affect the fitness of a bacterium.

While the strategies can easily include differential responsiveness to recent changes in the environment or to cumulative averages over time, in other ways their range of responsiveness is limited. Bacteria cannot "remember" or "interpret" a complex past sequence of changes, and they probably cannot distinguish alternative origins of adverse or beneficial changes. Some bacteria, for example, produce their own antibiotics, bacteriocins; those are harmless to bacteria of the producing strain, but destruc-

tive to others. A bacterium might easily have production of its own bacteriocin dependent on the perceived presence of like hostile products in its environment, but it could not aim the toxin produced toward an offending initiator. From existing evidence, so far from an individual level, discrimination seems to be by species rather even than variety. For example, a *Rhizobium* strain may occur in nodules which it causes on the roots of many species of leguminous plants, but it may fix nitrogen for the benefit of the plant in only a few of these species [20]. Thus, in many legumes the *Rhizobium* seems to be a pure parasite. In the light of theory to follow, it would be interesting to know whether these parasitized legumes are perhaps less beneficial to free living *Rhizobium* in the surrounding soil than are those in which the full symbiosis is established. But the main point of concern here is that such discrimination by a *Rhizobium* seems not to be known even at the level of varieties within a species.

As one moves up the evolutionary ladder in neural complexity, game-playing behavior becomes richer. The intelligence of primates, including humans, allows a number of relevant improvements: a more complex memory, more complex processing of information to determine the next action as a function of the interaction so far, a better estimate of the probability of future interaction with the same individual, and a better ability to distinguish between different individuals. The discrimination of others may be among the most important of abilities because it allows one to handle interactions with many individuals without having to treat them all the same, thus making possible the rewarding of cooperation from one individual and the punishing of defection from another.

The model of the iterated Prisoner's Dilemma is much less restricted than it may at first appear. Not only can it apply to interactions between two bacteria or interactions between two primates, but it can also apply to the interactions between a colony of bacteria and, say, a primate serving as a host. There is no assumption of commensurability of payoffs between the two sides. Provided that the payoffs to each side satisfy the inequalities that define the Prisoner's, Dilemma (Fig. 1), the results of the analysis will be applicable.

The model does assume that the choices are made simultaneously and with discrete time intervals. For most analytic purposes, this is equivalent to a continuous interaction over time, with

the time period of the model corresponding to the minimum time between a
change in behavior by one side and a
response by the other. And while the
model treats the choices as simultaneous, it would make little difference if
they were treated as sequential (21).

Turning to the development of the
theory, the evolution of cooperation can
be conceptualized in terms of three separate questions:

1) *Robustness*. What type of strategy
can thrive in a variegated environment
composed of others using a wide variety
of more or less sophisticated strategies?

2) *Stability*. Under what conditions
can such a strategy, once fully established, resist invasion by mutant strategies?

3) *Initial viability*. Even if a strategy is
robust and stable, how can it ever get a
foothold in an environment which is predominantly noncooperative?

Robustness

To see what type of strategy can thrive
in a variegated environment of more or
less sophisticated strategies, one of us
(R.A.) conducted a computer tournament for the Prisoner's Dilemma. The
strategies were submitted by game theorists in economics, sociology, political
science, and mathematics (22). The rules
implied the payoff matrix shown in Fig. 1
and a game length of 200 moves. The 14
entries and a totally random strategy
were paired with each other in a round
robin tournament. Some of the strategies
were quite intricate. An example is one
which on each move models the behavior of the other player as a Markov
process, and then uses Bayesian inference to select what seems the best
choice for the long run. However, the
result of the tournament was that the
highest average score was attained by
the simplest of all strategies submitted:
TIT FOR TAT. This strategy is simply
one of cooperating on the first move and
then doing whatever the other player did
on the preceding move. Thus TIT FOR
TAT is a strategy of cooperation based
on reciprocity.

The results of the first round were then
circulated and entries for a second round
were solicited. This time there were 62
entries from six countries (23). Most of
the contestants were computer hob-
byists, but there were also professors of
evolutionary biology, physics, and computer science, as well as the five disciplines represented in the first round. TIT
FOR TAT was again submitted by the

winner of the first round, Professor Anatol Rapoport of the Institute for Advanced Study (Vienna). It won again. An
analysis of the 3 million choices which
were made in the second round identified
the impressive robustness of TIT FOR
TAT as dependent on three features: it
was never the first to defect, it was
provocable into retaliation by a defection
of the other, and it was forgiving after
just one act of retaliation (24).

The robustness of TIT FOR TAT was
also manifest in an ecological analysis of
a whole series of future tournaments.
The ecological approach takes as given
the varieties which are present and investigates how they do over time when
interacting with each other. This analysis
was based on what would happen if each
of the strategies in the second round
were submitted to a hypothetical next
round in proportion to its success in the
previous round. The process was then
repeated to generate the time path of the
distribution of strategies. The results
showed that, as the less successful rules
were displaced, TIT FOR TAT continued to do well with the rules which
initially scored near the top. In the long
run, TIT FOR TAT displaced all the
other rules and went to fixation (24).
This provides further evidence that TIT
FOR TAT's cooperation based on reciprocity is a robust strategy that can
thrive in a variegated environment.

Stability

Once a strategy has gone to fixation,
the question of evolutionary stability
deals with whether it can resist invasion
by a mutant strategy. In fact, we will
now show that once TIT FOR TAT is
established, it can resist invasion by any
possible mutant strategy provided that
the individuals who interact have a sufficiently large probability, w, of meeting
again. The proof is described in the next
two paragraphs.

As a first step in the proof we note that
since TIT FOR TAT "remembers" only
one move back, one C by the other
player in any round is sufficient to reset
the situation as it was at the beginning of
the game. Likewise, one D sets the situation to what it was at the second round
after a D was played in the first. Since
there is a fixed chance, w, of the interaction not ending at any given move, a
strategy cannot be maximal in playing
with TIT FOR TAT unless it does the
same thing both at the first occurrence of
a given state and at each resetting to that
state. Thus, if a rule is maximal and

begins with C, the second round has the
same state as the first, and thus a maximal rule will continue with C and hence
always cooperate with TIT FOR TAT.
But such a rule will not do better than
TIT FOR TAT does with another TIT
FOR TAT, and hence it cannot invade.
If, on the other hand, a rule begins with
D, then this first D induces a switch in
the state of TIT FOR TAT and there are
two possibilities for continuation that
could be maximal. If D follows the first
D, then this being maximal at the start
implies that it is everywhere maximal to
follow D with D, making the strategy
equivalent to ALL D. If C follows the
initial D, the game is then reset as for the
first move; so it must be maximal to
repeat the sequence of DC indefinitely.
These points show that the task of
searching a seemingly infinite array of
rules of behavior for one potentially
capable of invading TIT FOR TAT is
really easier than it seemed: if neither
ALL D nor alternation of D and C can
invade TIT FOR TAT, then no strategy
can.

To see when these strategies can invade, we note that the probability that
the nth interaction actually occurs is
w^{n-1}. Therefore, the expression for the
total payoff is easily found by applying
the weights $1, w, w^2 \ldots$ to the payoff
sequence and summing the resultant series. When TIT FOR TAT plays another
TIT FOR TAT, it gets a payoff of R each
move for a total of $R + wR + w^2R$
$\ldots$, which is $R/(1 - w)$. ALL D playing with TIT FOR TAT gets T on the first
move and P thereafter, so it cannot invade TIT FOR TAT if

$$R/(1 - w) \geq T + wP/(1 - w)$$

Similarly when alternation of D and C
plays TIT FOR TAT, it gets a payoff of

$$T = wS + w^2T + s^3S \ldots$$
$$= (T + wS)/(1 - w^2)$$

Alternation of D and C thus cannot invade TIT FOR TAT if

$$R/(1 - w) \geq (T + wS)/(1 - w^2)$$

Hence, with reference to the magnitude
of w, we find that neither of these two
strategies (and hence no strategy at all)
can invade TIT FOR TAT if and only if
both

$$w \geq (T - R)/(T - P) \text{ and}$$
$$w \geq (T - R)/(R - S) \qquad (1)$$

This demonstrates that TIT FOR TAT is
evolutionarily stable if and only if the
interactions between the individuals
have a sufficiently large probability of
continuing (19).

Initial Viability

TIT FOR TAT is not the only strategy that can be evolutionarily stable. In fact, ALL D is evolutionarily stable no matter what is the probability of interaction continuing. This raises the problem of how an evolutionary trend to cooperative behavior could ever have started in the first place.

Genetic kinship theory suggests a plausible escape from the equilibrium of ALL D. Close relatedness of interactants permits true altruism—sacrifice of fitness by one individual for the benefit of another. True altruism can evolve when the conditions of cost, benefit, and relatedness yield net gains for the altruism-causing genes that are resident in the related individuals (*25*). Not defecting in a single-move Prisoner's Dilemma is altruism of a kind (the individual is foregoing proceeds that might have been taken) and so can evolve if the two interactants are sufficiently related (*18*). In effect, recalculation of the payoff matrix in such a way that an individual has a part interest in the partner's gain (that is, reckoning payoffs in terms of inclusive fitness) can often eliminate the inequalities $T > R$ and $P > S$, in which case cooperation becomes unconditionally favored (*18, 26*). Thus it is possible to imagine that the benefits of cooperation in Prisoner's Dilemma–like situations can begin to be harvested by groups of closely related individuals. Obviously, as regards pairs, a parent and its offspring or a pair of siblings would be especially promising, and in fact many examples of cooperation or restraint of selfishness in such pairs are known.

Once the genes for cooperation exist, selection will promote strategies that base cooperative behavior on cues in the environment (*4*). Such factors as promiscuous fatherhood (*27*) and events at ill-defined group margins will always lead to uncertain relatedness among potential interactants. The recognition of any improved correlates of relatedness and use of these cues to determine cooperative behavior will always permit advance in inclusive fitness (*4*). When a cooperative choice has been made, one cue to relatedness is simply the fact of reciprocation of the cooperation. Thus modifiers for more selfish behavior after a negative response from the other are advantageous whenever the degree of relatedness is low or in doubt. As such, conditionality is acquired, and cooperation can spread into circumstances of less and less relatedness. Finally, when the probability of two individuals meeting each other again is sufficiently high,

cooperation based on reciprocity can thrive and be evolutionarily stable in a population with no relatedness at all.

A case of cooperation that fits this scenario, at least on first evidence, has been discovered in the spawning relationships in a sea bass (*28*). The fish, which are hermaphroditic, form pairs and roughly may be said to take turns at being the high investment partner (laying eggs) and low investment partner (providing sperm to fertilize eggs). Up to ten spawnings occur in a day and only a few eggs are provided each time. Pairs tend to break up if sex roles are not divided evenly. The system appears to allow the evolution of much economy in the size of testes, but Fischer (*28*) has suggested that the testis condition may have evolved when the species was more sparse and inclined to inbreed. Inbreeding would imply relatedness in the pairs and this initially may have transferred the system to attractance of tit-for-tat cooperation—that is, to cooperation unneedful of relatedness.

Another mechanism that can get cooperation started when virtually everyone is using ALL D is clustering. Suppose that a small group of individuals is using a strategy such as TIT FOR TAT and that a certain proportion, p, of the interactions of members of this cluster are with other members of the cluster. Then the average score attained by the members of the cluster in playing the TIT FOR TAT strategy is

$$p[R/(1 - w)] +$$
$$(1 - p)[S + wP/(1 - w)]$$

If the members of the cluster provide a negligible proportion of the interactions for the other individuals, then the score attained by those using ALL D is still $P/(1 - w)$. When p and w are large enough, a cluster of TIT FOR TAT individuals can then become initially viable in an environment composed overwhelmingly of ALL D (*19*).

Clustering is often associated with kinship, and the two mechanisms can reinforce each other in promoting the initial viability of reciprocal cooperation. However, it is possible for clustering to be effective without kinship (*3*).

We have seen that TIT FOR TAT can intrude in a cluster on a population of ALL D, even though ALL D is evolutionarily stable. This is possible because a cluster of TIT FOR TAT's gives each member a nontrivial probability of meeting another individual who will reciprocate the cooperation. While this suggests a mechanism for the initiation of cooperation, it also raises the question about whether the reverse could happen once a

strategy like TIT FOR TAT became established itself. Actually, there is an interesting asymmetry here. Let us define a nice strategy as one, such as TIT FOR TAT, which will never be the first to defect. Obviously, when two nice strategies interact, they both receive R each move, which is the highest average score an individual can get when interacting with another individual using the same strategy. Therefore, if a strategy is nice and is evolutionarily stable, it cannot be intruded upon by a cluster. This is because the score achieved by the strategy that comes in a cluster is a weighted average of how it does with others of its kind and with the predominant strategy. Each of these components is less than or equal to the score achieved by the predominant, nice, evolutionarily stable strategy, and therefore the strategy arriving in a cluster cannot intrude on the nice, evolutionarily stable strategy (*19*). This means that when w is large enough to make TIT FOR TAT an evolutionarily stable strategy it can resist intrusion by any cluster of any other strategy. The gear wheels of social evolution have a ratchet.

The chronological story that emerges from this analysis is the following. ALL D is the primeval state and is evolutionarily stable. This means that it can resist the invasion of any strategy that has virtually all of its interactions with ALL D. But cooperation based on reciprocity can gain a foothold through two different mechanisms. First, there can be kinship between mutant strategies, giving the genes of the mutants some stake in each other's success, thereby altering the effective payoff matrix of the interaction when viewed from the perspective of the gene rather than the individual. A second mechanism to overcome total defection is for the mutant strategies to arrive in a cluster so that they provide a nontrivial proportion of the interactions each has, even if they are so few as to provide a negligible proportion of the interactions which the ALL D individuals have. Then the tournament approach demonstrates that once a variety of strategies is present, TIT FOR TAT is an extremely robust one. It does well in a wide range of circumstances and gradually displaces all other strategies in a simulation of a great variety of more or less sophisticated decision rules. And if the probability that interaction between two individuals will continue is great enough, then TIT FOR TAT is itself evolutionarily stable. Moreover, its stability is especially secure because it can resist the intrusion of whole clusters of mutant strategies. Thus cooperation based on reciprocity can get

started in a predominantly noncooperative world, can thrive in a variegated
environment, and can defend itself once
fully established.

Applications

A variety of specific biological applications of our approach follows from two
of the requirements for the evolution of
cooperation. The basic idea is that an
individual must not be able to get away
with defecting without the other individuals being able to retaliate effectively
(29). The response requires that the defecting individual not be lost in an anonymous sea of others. Higher organisms
avoid this problem by their well-developed ability to recognize many different
individuals of their species, but lower
organisms must rely on mechanisms that
drastically limit the number of different
individuals or colonies with which they
can interact effectively. The other important requirement to make retaliation
effective is that the probability, w, of the
same two individuals' meeting again
must be sufficiently high.

When an organism is not able to recognize the individual with which it had a
prior interaction, a substitute mechanism
is to make sure that all of one's interactions are with the same interactant. This
can be done by maintaining continuous
contact with the other. This method is
applied in most interspecies mutualism,
whether a hermit crab and his sea-anem-
one partner, a cicada and the varied
microorganismic colonies housed in its
body, or a tree and its mycorrhizal fungi.

The ability of such partners to respond
specifically to defection is not known but
seems possible. A host insect that carries
symbionts often carries several kinds
(for example, yeasts and bacteria). Differences in the roles of these are almost
wholly obscure (30). Perhaps roles are
actually the same, and being host to
more than one increases the security of
retaliation against a particular exploitative colony. Where host and colony are
not permanently paired, a method for
immediate drastic retaliation is sometimes apparent instead. This is so with
fig wasps. By nature of their remarkable
role in pollination, female fig wasps
serve the fig tree as a motile aerial male
gamete. Through the extreme protogyny
and simultaneity in flowering, fig wasps
cannot remain with a single tree. It turns
out in many cases that if a fig wasp
entering a young fig does not pollinate
enough flowers for seeds and instead
lays eggs in almost all, the tree cuts
off the developing fig at an early stage.

All progeny of the wasp then perish.

Another mechanism to avoid the need
for recognition is to guarantee the
uniqueness of the pairing of interactants
by employing a fixed place of meeting.
Consider, for example, cleaner mutualisms in which a small fish or a crustacean
removes and eats ectoparasites from the
body (or even from the inside of the
mouth) of a larger fish which is its potential predator. These aquatic cleaner mutualisms occur in coastal and reef situations where animals live in fixed home
ranges or territories (4, 5). They seem to
be unknown in the free-mixing circumstances of the open sea.

Other mutualisms are also characteristic of situations where continued association is likely, and normally they involve
quasi-permanent pairing of individuals or
of endogamous or asexual stocks, or of
individuals with such stocks (7, 31). Conversely, conditions of free-mixing and
transitory pairing conditions where recognition is impossible are much more
likely to result in exploitation—parasitism, disease, and the like. Thus, whereas
ant colonies participate in many symbioses and are sometimes largely dependent on them, honeybee colonies, which
are much less permanent in place of
abode, have no known symbionts but
many parasites (32). The small fresh-
water animal *Chlorohydra viridissima*
has a permanent stable association with
green algae that are always naturally
found in its tissues and are very difficult
to remove. In this species the alga is
transmitted to new generations by way
of the egg. *Hydra vulgaris* and *H. atten-
uata* also associate with algae but do not
have egg transmission. In these species it
is said that "infection is preceded by
enfeeblement of the animals and is accompanied by pathological symptoms indicating a definite parasitism by the
plant" (33). Again, it is seen that imper-
manence of association tends to destabilize symbiosis.

In species with a limited ability to
discriminate between other members of
the same species, reciprocal cooperation
can be stable with the aid of a mechanism that reduces the amount of discrimination necessary. Philopatry in general and territoriality in particular can
serve this purpose. The phrase *stable
territories* means that there are two quite
different kinds of interaction: those in
neighboring territories where the probability of interaction is high, and strang-
ers whose probability of future interaction is low. In the case of male territorial
birds, songs are used to allow neighbors
to recognize each other. Consistent with
our theory, such male territorial birds

show much more aggressive reactions
when the song of an unfamiliar male
rather than a neighbor is reproduced
nearby (34).

Reciprocal cooperation can be stable
with a larger range of individuals if discrimination can cover a wide variety of
others with less reliance on supplemen-
tary cues such as location. In humans
this ability is well developed, and is
largely based on the recognition of faces.
The extent to which this function has
become specialized is revealed by a
brain disorder called prosopagnosia. A
normal person can name someone from
facial features alone, even if the features
have changed substantially over the
years. People with prosopagnosia are not
able to make this association, but have
few other neurological symptoms other
than a loss of some part of the visual
field. The lesions responsible for prosopagnosia occur in an identifiable part of
the brain: the underside of both occipital
lobes, extending forward to the inner
surface of the temporal lobes. This local-
ization of cause, and specificity of effect,
indicates that the recognition of individual faces has been an important enough
task for a significant portion of the
brain's resources to be devoted to it (35).

Just as the ability to recognize the
other interactant is invaluable in extending the range of stable cooperation, the
ability to monitor cues for the likelihood
of continued interaction is helpful as an
indication of when reciprocal cooperation is or is not stable. In particular,
when the value of w falls below the
threshold for stability given in condition
(1), it will no longer pay to reciprocate
the other's cooperation. Illness in one
partner leading to reduced viability
would be one detectable sign of declining
w. Both animals in a partnership would
then be expected to become less cooperative. Aging of a partner would be very
like disease in this respect, resulting in
an incentive to defect so as to take a one-
time gain when the probability of future
interaction becomes small enough.

These mechanisms could operate even
at the microbial level. Any symbiont that
still has a transmission "horizontally"
(that is, infective) as well as vertically
(that is, transovarial, or more rarely
through sperm, or both) would be expected to shift from mutualism to parasitism when the probability of continued
interaction with the host lessened. In the
more parasitic phase it could exploit the
host more severely by producing more
infective propagules. This phase would
be expected when the host is severely
injured, contracted some other wholly
parasitic infection that threatened death,

or when it manifested signs of age. In fact, bacteria that are normal and seemingly harmless or even beneficial in the gut can be found contributing to sepsis in the body when the gut is perforated (implying a severe wound) (36). And normal inhabitants of the body surface (like *Candida albicans*) can become invasive and dangerous in either sick or elderly persons.

It is possible also that this argument has some bearing on the etiology of cancer, insofar as it turns out to be due to viruses potentially latent in the genome (37). Cancers do tend to have their onset at ages when the chances of vertical transmission are rapidly declining (38). One oncogenic virus, that of Burkitt's lymphoma, does not have vertical transmission but may have alternatives of slow or fast production of infectious propagules. The slow form appears as a chronic mononucleosis, the fast as an acute mononucleosis or as a lymphoma (39). The point of interest is that, as some evidence suggests, lymphoma can be triggered by the host's contracting malaria. The lymphoma grows extremely fast and so can probably compete with malaria for transmission (possibly by mosquitoes) before death results. Considering other cases of simultaneous infection by two or more species of pathogen, or by two strains of the same one, our theory may have relevance more generally to whether a disease will follow a slow, joint-optimal exploitation course ("chronic" for the host) or a rapid severe exploitation ("acute" for the host). With single infection the slow course would be expected. With double infection, crash exploitation might, as dictated by implied payoff functions, begin immediately, or have onset later at an appropriate stage of senescence (40).

Our model (with symmetry of the two parties) could also be tentatively applied to the increase with maternal age of chromosomal nondisjunction during ovum formation (oogenesis) (41). This effect leads to various conditions of severely handicapped offspring. Down's syndrome (caused by an extra copy of chromosome 21) being the most familiar example. It depends almost entirely on failure of the normal separation of the paired chromosomes in the mother, and this suggests the possible connection with our story. Cell divisions of oogenesis, but not usually of spermatogenesis, are characteristically unsymmetrical, with rejection (as a so-called polar body) of chromosomes that go to the unlucky pole of the cell. It seems possible that, while homologous chromosomes gener-

ally stand to gain by steadily cooperating in a diploid organism, the situation in oogenesis is a Prisoner's Dilemma: a chromosome which can be "first to defect" can get itself into the egg nucleus rather than the polar body. We may hypothesize that such an action triggers similar attempts by the homolog in subsequent meioses, and when both members of a homologous pair try it at once, an extra chromosome in the offspring could be the occasional result. The fitness of the bearers of extra chromosomes is generally extremely low, but a chromosome which lets itself be sent to the polar body makes a fitness contribution of zero. Thus $P > S$ holds. For the model to work, an incident of "defection" in one developing egg would have to be perceptible by others still waiting. That this would occur is pure speculation, as is the feasibility of self-promoting behavior by chromosomes during a gametic cell division. But the effects do not seem inconceivable: a bacterium, after all, with its single chromosome, can do complex conditional things. Given such effects, our model would explain the much greater incidence of abnormal chromosome increase in eggs (and not sperm) with parental age.

Conclusion

Darwin's emphasis on individual advantage has been formalized in terms of game theory. This establishes conditions under which cooperation based on reciprocity can evolve.

References and Notes

1. G. C. Williams, *Adaptations and Natural Selection* (Princeton Univ. Press, Princeton, 1966); W. D. Hamilton, in *Biosocial Anthropology*, R. Fox, Ed. (Malaby, London, 1975), p. 133.
2. For the best recent case for effective selection at group levels and for altruism based on genetic correction of non-kin interactants see D. S. Wilson, *Natural Selection of Populations and Communities* (Benjamin/Cummings, Menlo Park, Calif., 1979).
3. W. D. Hamilton, *J. Theoret. Biol.* 7, 1 (1964).
4. R. Trivers, *Q. Rev. Biol.* 46, 35 (1971).
5. For additions to the theory of biological cooperation see I. D. Chase [*Am. Nat.* 115, 827 (1980)], R. M. Fagen [*ibid.*, p. 858 (1980)], and S. A. Boorman and P. R. Levitt [*The Genetics of Altruism* (Academic Press, New York, 1980)].
6. R. Dawkins, *The Selfish Gene* (Oxford Univ. Press, Oxford, 1976).
7. W. D. Hamilton, *Annu. Rev. Ecol. Syst.* 3, 193 (1972).
8. D. H. Janzen, *Evolution* 20, 249 (1966).
9. J. T. Wiebes, *Gard. Bull. (Singapore)* 29, 207 (1976); D. H. Janzen, *Annu. Rev. Ecol. Syst.* 10, 31 (1979).
10. M. Caullery, *Parasitism and Symbiosis* (Sidgwick and Jackson, London, 1952). This gives examples of antagonism in orchid-fungus and lichen symbioses. For the example of wasp-ant symbiosis, see (7).
11. J. Maynard Smith and G. R. Price. *Nature (London)* 246, 15 (1973); J. Maynard Smith and G. A. Parker, *Anim. Behav.* 24, 159 (1976); G. A. Parker, *Nature (London)* 274, 849 (1978).
12. J. Elster, *Ulysses and the Sirens* (Cambridge Univ. Press, London, 1979).
13. S. T. Emlen, in *Behavioral Ecology: An Evolu-*

tionary Approach, J. Krebs and N. Davies, Eds. (Blackwell, Oxford, 1978), p. 245; P. B. Stacey. *Behav. Ecol. Sociobiol.* 6, 53 (1979).
14. A. H. Harcourt, *Z. Tierpsychol.* 48, 401 (1978); C. Packer, *Anim. Behav.* 27, 1 (1979); R. W. Wrangham, *Soc. Sci. Info.* 18, 335 (1979).
15. J. D. Ligon and S. H. Ligon, *Nature (London)* 276, 496 (1978).
16. A. Rapoport and A. M. Chammah, *Prisoner's Dilemma* (Univ. of Michigan Press, Ann Arbor, 1965). There are many other patterns of interaction which allow gains for cooperation. See for example the model of intraspecific combat in J. Maynard Smith and G. R. Price, in (11).
17. The condition that $R > (S + T)/2$ is also part of the definition to rule out the possibility that alternating exploitation could be better for both than mutual cooperation.
18. W. D. Hamilton, in *Man and Beast: Comparative Social Behavior* (Smithsonian Press, Washington, 1971), p. 57. R. M. Fagen [in (5)] shows some conditions for single encounters where defection is not the solution.
19. For a formal proof, see R. Axelrod, *Am. Political Sci. Rev.*, in press. For related results on the potential stability of cooperative behavior see R. D. Luce and H. Raiffa, *Games and Decisions* (Wiley, New York, 1957), p. 102; M. Taylor, *Anarchy and Cooperation* (Wiley, New York, 1976); M. Kurz, in *Economic Progress, Private Values and Public Policy*, B. Balassa and R. Nelson, Eds. (North-Holland, Amsterdam, 1977), p. 177.
20. M. Alexander, *Microbial Ecology* (Wiley, New York, 1971).
21. In either case, cooperation on a tit-for-tat basis is evolutionarily stable if and only if w is sufficiently high. In the case of sequential moves, suppose there is a fixed chance, p, that a given interactant of the pair will be the next one to need help. The critical value of w can be shown to be the minimum of the two side's value of A $p(A + B)$ where A is the cost of giving assistance, and B is the benefit of assistance when received. See also P. R. Thompson, *Soc. Sci. Info.* 19, 341 (1980).
22. R. Axelrod, *J. Conflict Resolution* 24, 3 (1980).
23. In the second round, the length of the games was uncertain, with an expected probability of 200 moves. This was achieved by setting the probability that a given move would not be the last at $w = .99654$. As in the first round, each pair was matched in five games (24).
24. R. Axelrod, *J. Conflict Resolution* 24, 379 (1980).
25. R. A. Fisher, *The Genetical Theory of Natural Selection* (Oxford Univ. Press, Oxford, 1930); J. B. S. Haldane, *Nature (London) New Biol.* 18, 34 (1955); W. D. Hamilton, *Am. Nat.* 97, 354 (1963).
26. M. J. Wade and F. Breden, *Behav. Ecol. Sociobiol.*, in press.
27. R. D. Alexander, *Annu. Rev. Ecol. Syst.* 5, 325 (1974).
28. E. Fischer, *Anim. Behav.* 28, 620 (1980); E. G. Leigh, Jr., *Proc. Natl. Acad. Sci. U.S.A.* 74, 4542 (1977).
29. For economic theory on this point see G. Akerlof, *Q. J. Econ.* 84, 488 (1970); M. R. Darby and E. Karni, *J. Law Econ.* 16, 67 (1973); O. E. Williamson, *Markets and Hierarchies* (Free Press, New York, 1975).
30. P. Buchner, *Endosymbiosis of Animals with Plant Microorganisms* (Interscience, New York, 1965).
31. W. D. Hamilton, in *Diversity of Insect Faunas*, L. A. Mound and N. Waloff, Eds. (Blackwell, Oxford, 1978).
32. E. O. Wilson, *The Insect Societies* (Bellknap, Cambridge, Mass., 1971); M. Treisman, *Anim. Behav.* 28, 311 (1980).
33. C. M. Yonge [*Nature (London)* 134, 12 (1979)] gives other examples of invertebrates with unicellular algae.
34. E. O. Wilson, *Sociobiology* (Harvard Univ. Press, Cambridge, Mass., 1975), p. 273.
35. N. Geschwind, *Sci. Am.* 241, (No. 3), 180 (1979).
36. D. C. Savage, in *Microbial Ecology of the Gut*, R. T. J. Clarke and T. Bauchop, Eds. (Academic Press, New York, 1977), p. 300.
37. J. T. Manning, *J. Theoret. Biol.* 55, 397 (1975); M. J. Orlove, *ibid.* 65, 605 (1977).
38. W. D. Hamilton, *ibid.* 12, 12 (1966).
39. W. Henle, G. Henle, E. T. Lenette, *Sci. Am.* 241 (No. 1), 48 (1979).
40. See also I. Eshel, *Theoret. Pop. Biol.* 11, 410 (1977) for a related possible implication of multiclonal infection.
41. C. Stern, *Principles of Human Genetics* (Freeman, San Francisco, 1973).
42. For helpful suggestions we thank Robert Boyd. Michael Cohen, and David Sloan Wilson.

[20]

Political Studies (1987), XXXV, 173–188

Exploitation, Extortion and Oppression

ALAN CARLING

School of Interdisciplinary Human Studies, University of Bradford

Exploitation, extortion and oppression describe unjust social arrangements that ought to be changed. The concept of exploitation is particularly associated with Marx's critique of capitalism, and the term 'extortion' sometimes designates the injustice of feudalism. The distinctions between these concepts can be clarified using the framework of rational-choice theory. Oppression is a situation of unfair exclusion (from resources, or utilities more generally). Exploitation is the unfair use by one person of the excluded situation of another. Extortion involves the deliberate creation of an exploiting situation. The relation of these phenomena to coercion is a logical one only in the case of extortion: coercion being necessary to extortion.

Introduction

There is a revival of Marxist theory now in full swing which comes from unexpected quarters of scholarship and geography—analytical philosophy and mathematical economics in Northern Europe and North America. The new approach has some claim to be considered a novel paradigm for Marxist theory as a whole, which deserves the title 'Rational-choice Marxism'. Its leading emphases include a restatement of technological determinism; a jaundiced attitude towards the labour theory of value; an aversion to recent sociology of the Althusserian type; a willingness to discover a moral dimension in Marx's thought; a general inclination towards methodological individualism and the acceptance in some form or other of the concept of 'human nature'.

It should go without saying that each one of these emphases is highly contro-versial within the received Marxist tradition, and many critics might be prone to conclude that the new paradigm (if such it is) is a paradigm for something other than Marxism. The concern here is not to review this development, nor to examine its credentials in Marx or in fact.[1] Instead, the article concentrates on a concept—'exploitation'—and some cognate concepts—extortion, oppression and coercion—which are clearly important in the classical corpus of Marxism and have received fresh significance recently through the works of the Cali-fornian economist J. E. Roemer, and other prominent exponents of the revival such as J. Elster and G. A. Cohen.[2]

[1] I attempt both examinations in 'Rational-choice Marxism', *New Left Review*, 160 (Nov./Dec. 1986), 24–62.

[2] The major works are J. E. Roemer, *A General Theory of Exploitation and Class* (Cambridge, Mass., Harvard University Press, 1982); J. Elster, *Making Sense of Marx* (Cambridge, Cambridge University Press, 1985); G. A. Cohen, *Karl Marx's Theory of History: A Defence* (Oxford, Oxford University Press, 1978) and E. O. Wright, *Classes* (London, Verso, 1985). Relevant collections include J. R. Pennock and J. W. Chapman (eds), *Nomos XXVI* (New York, New York University

0032-3217/87/02/0173-16/$03.00 © 1987 *Political Studies*

The treatment pursued in this article will be at a more abstract (and hence potentially more general) level than that adopted by Marx in his critique of capitalism, in which the concept of 'exploitation' is tied closely to the labour theory of value. According to this theory, exploitation is intrinsic to capitalism because wage labourers yield a substantial proportion of their working effort to capitalists for no return. Exploitation thus construed is one kind of unequal exchange, to be set alongside extortion, theft, blackmail, hijack, daylight robbery and more savoury varieties such as donation and H. Steiner's 'benefit' (as in 'benefit performance').[3] Marx's treatment of capitalism will be taken as a motivating example for the analysis of some of these phenomena, without considering in this context whether or not Marx was right to lean as he did on the labour theory of value.[4]

A fundamental distinction has to be recognized between the situation in which an actor is placed by the (perhaps rational) choices of others, and the (perhaps rational) choices made by the actor herself or himself, which in turn help to create the situation in which other actors choose. It is clearly possible to envisage a concatenation of such actions and reactions of almost endless complexity. What is commonly called 'society' is composed of complex chains of this kind involving large numbers of actors, but the distinctions recognized in the use of terms such as exploitation, extortion and oppression often relate to basic variations among the simplest of these chains. In particular, one must be alive to the number of actors involved, and the number of steps in the chain, where a step is, roughly, an action (or a choice) by one actor which creates a situation for another actor [though actors can also be in situations which are not the result of action (or deliberate action) by some other actor]. Thus, theft (which is a case of oppression) and donation are two-person one-step transactions. Extortion and exploitation are both two-person two-step transactions. Further distinctions are obviously necessary to discriminate cases with the same number of persons and steps. The distinctions most relevant to the intuitions which seem to underlie the use of the relevant terms are

1. the actors' payoffs at each step;
2. the causal and intentional relations between the different steps (wherever there is more than one step);
3. an independent criterion of 'fairness', which applies separately to the situation in which actors find themselves and the outcome of the action they take in the given situation;
4. the relation of the whole transaction to coercion, itself conceived as a two-person, two-step transaction.

The following discussion will illuminate these rather formal considerations.

Press, 1983); T. Ball and J. Farr (eds), *After Marx* (Cambridge, Cambridge University Press, 1984) and especially J. E. Roemer (ed.), *Analytical Marxism* (Cambridge, Cambridge University Press, 1986). I would like to thank G. A. Cohen, J. Elster, N. Geras, P. Halfpenny, M. Taylor, P. Van Parijs and my colleague G. Macdonald for their partly futile attempts to impose some discipline on an earlier version of this paper.

[3] H. Steiner, 'A liberal theory of exploitation', *Ethics*, 94 (January 1984), 225–41.

[4] I support the neo-Ricardian line that he was wrong. See 'Value and strategy', *Science and Society*, XLVIII: 2 (1984), 129–60 and 'Observations on the labour theory of value', *Science and Society*, XLVIII: 4 (1984–5), 407–18.

Exploitation and Extortion

Exploitation seems to be distinct from donation because donation is fair and voluntary. J. Elster has argued that there is a further distinction to be made among varieties of unfair unequal exchange 'between an unjust distribution resulting from voluntary transactions and the production of injustice by force'.[5] The former is exploitation, which is unfair and voluntary; the latter counts as extortion, which is unfair and involuntary. It is exploitation compounded by intimidation.

In the Marxist tradition, this distinction is sometimes introduced to capture the difference between capitalist *exploitation*, arising from free market transactions, and feudal *extortion*, resting on coercive 'extra-economic pressure'.[6] But Elster chooses to illustrate the distinction from a rather different field:

> Women are exploited by their employers if they get more rapid promotion
> by sexual favours, but are victims of extortion if they have to give them
> favours in order to obtain even the normal promotion.[7]

This example is interesting mainly for the light its form throws on Elster's distinction between exploitation and extortion, in which rôle it is indispensable. But the interpretation of form will always depend on content and participants in public discussion have found the content of this example offensive. I can readily appreciate this reaction, which demands an initial response. We can notice first that employees are made gender specific ('women') whereas employers are not ('them'), but we may infer that the employers in question are indeed men. If the expression is indirect, the inferred mapping of gender onto

---

[5] J. Elster, 'Roemer versus Roemer: a comment on "New Directions in the Marxian Theory of Exploitation and Class"', *Politics and Society*, 11 (1982), 363–73, p. 365. The untroubled reference throughout this paper to the unfairness of exploitation reflects a firm judgement on one side of the long-running debate about 'Marx and Justice'. The best appraisal of this debate is given by N. Geras, 'The controversy about Marx and justice', *New Left Review*, no. 150 (1985), 47–88.

[6] The canonical reference is this: 'The direct producer, according to our assumption, is to be found . . . in possession of his own means of production . . . He conducts his agricultural activity and the rural home industries connected with it independently . . . Under such conditions the surplus-labour can only be extorted from [the small peasants] by other than economic pressure, whatever the form may be'. K. Marx, *Capital, III* (London, Lawrence and Wishart, 1974), p. 790. The restriction of the term exploitation to capitalism is by no means a universal convention either in Marx or his recent revivalists. For Marx compare 'the [higher] exploitation of labour, because of the use of slaves, coolies etc' and the contention that 'the agricultural economies of antiquity' do not correspond to the 'really capitalist mode of exploitation', which implies that they are modes of exploitation, but not really capitalist ones (*Capital*, III, pp. 238 and 787). Roemer discusses 'feudal exploitation' at some length (*A General Theory of Exploitation and Class*, pp. 199 ff.) and Cohen goes so far as to regard the 'exploitation of the feudal serf' as the 'paradigm of exploitation' in 'The labour theory of value and the concept of exploitation', in I. Steedman *et al.* (eds), *The Value Controversy* (London, Verso, 1981), p. 221.). Elster himself has now qualified to the point of rejection the claim recorded above that exploitation is restricted to capitalist market relations (*Making Sense of Marx*, p. 168). However, he does not go on to offer any general reformulation of the distinction between exploitation and other varieties of unequal exchange, since he now regards 'this terminological issue [as] less important than the substantive [historical] one'. On the other hand, his discussion of the substantive issue still relies on the distinction between 'extraction of surplus labour through extra-economic coercion and exploitation in the market' which originally motivated the use of the term extortion. The effect of this is not to solve the problem so much as shift it from the definition of exploitation to the definition of coercion (on which, see n. 16 below).

[7] J. Elster, 'Roemer versus Roemer', p. 365.

employment status is certainly realistic, just as the situation described is more common than many men might like to admit. But sociological realism is hardly a conclusive defence, since the casual statement of an odious reality might appear to reproduce that reality, and it remains to set the example in a more critical context required by feminism. Here, the sexual activity described is clearly instrumental, and it might be that such an attitude towards sexual activity, or the conduct of sexual activity in such a vein, is itself 'typically male'. Indeed, it may be that non-instrumental sexual activity has a transcendent quality which altogether escapes the utilitarian framework of rational-choice theory, and is belittled by the attempt at incorporation within it—a finding tending to indict rational-choice theory for its contribution to the male-streaming of thought. The strongest argument would be that a radical loss of the sense of self is involved; with a consequent loss of definition of the unit to which the individualism inherent in the theory assigns utility. Alternatively, and returning within the rational-choice framework, it may be that non-instrumental sexual activity is a public good, whereas the example plainly makes the payoffs to the woman and the man mutually independent, divisible private goods. Again, though the action of the man is subject to condemnation by the use of the terms exploitation and extortion, the preferable alternative for the woman is not made quite explicit in the example. We shall also see that there is an unacknowledged asymmetry between the man and the woman, as 'proposer' and 'disposer', which conforms to a rather uncritical stereotype of the respective gender rôles. A serious question therefore arises as to whether one should pursue a discussion of the example within a rational-choice framework, or abandon it, accepting that there are some areas of social life in principle beyond the scope of rational-choice theory. My reluctance to take the latter course is reinforced by the conviction that some of the central insights of second-wave feminism are naturally construed within the rational-choice framework, but the question is neither closed nor settled.[8]

Elster introduced the example primarily to distinguish coercive extortion from non-coercive exploitation. Unfortunately, it can be shown that both cases involve an identical relation to coercion, according to the following account of coercion also given by Elster.

> The common feature of . . . cases [of coercion] is that an agent A performs an action X that has the intended and actual consequence of making another person B perform an action Y that differs from the action Z that B would have performed had A indeed pursued his 'normal' course of action W. We must stipulate that B prefers the counterfactual situation in which A does W and he does Z to the actual one in which A does X and he does Y. We need not add, however, that A prefers the actual situation to the counterfactual one, although standardly this will be the case.[9]

In the case of sexual harrassment at work, A stands for the boss, while B is

---

[8] Some of the foregoing points were made by participants in the 1985 PSA Conference in Manchester, and by J. Hearn of Bradford University. I am grateful to them, and hope they recognize my expression of their objections. A tentative formulation of feminist positions in terms of rational-choice theory is attempted in the closing sections of 'rational-choice Marxism'.

[9] J. Elster, 'Exploitation, freedom and justice', *Nomos XXVI*, p. 285. The definition is repeated verbatim in *Making Sense of Marx*, p. 212.

the employee. To further relate the general model of coercion to the example requires the careful consideration of a certain asymmetry between A and B, and the quality of their actions. A is principally a meta-actor. What A does is not so much choose from among the first-order alternatives available to him (to give rapid promotion, normal promotion, or zero promotion) as to choose to create a situation in which B will subsequently exercise choice. This distinction is important even though the presumption may also exist that A will himself respond to B's first-order choice with a specific first-order choice, and that the attractiveness of some such joint outcome is the motive governing A's second-order action aimed at changing B's schedule of alternatives. Specifically, the full set of outcomes available in the example are the six possible combinations of one choice by A from among the three promotion options and one choice by B from her two responses (sex/no sex). But A's initial action will lie in either restricting or extending the outcomes available to B rather than in choosing a specific course of action himself. In the first instance, A does not choose: he offers a deal. The problem now is to relate both the first-order choices and the deals on offer to the actions Elster labelled W, X, Y, Z in his general characterization of coercion. Y and Z are straightforward enough. Z is the 'normal' first-order choice of the employee (no sex) and Y is the non-normal choice (sex). A's purpose is to induce a switch of B's behaviour from the normal to the non-normal course of action. For this ploy to work, we have to assume that B's descending order of preference over outcomes in the case alleged to be exploitation is given by (R, S), (N, S^*), (N, S) where R and N are rapid and normal promotion and S and S^* are sex and no sex respectively. In the case alleged to be extortion, the equivalent ordering is (N, S), (O, S^*), (O, S), where O stands for zero promotion. It is implicit (i) that the boss is somewhat repulsive to B (who would not be, who made this kind of offer?), (ii) that B is nevertheless sufficiently ambitious to choose promotion before chastity whenever these options are the only two on offer. We note that B's ranking of the five outcomes considered thus far is also consistent between the two cases [that is, (R, S), (N, S^*), (N, S), (O, S^*), (O, S)]. (O, S)—zero promotion with sex—is the worst-ranked outcome for B, and will not be considered further. The last of the six outcomes—rapid promotion without sex (R, S^*)—will play a crucial rôle in the subsequent discussion.

Turning to A's preference ordering, the examples are constructed to suggest that the employer is largely indifferent between the first-order choices it is in his power to make (whether to give zero, normal or rapid promotion). But A is not at all indifferent to the choice B makes, since A would always prefer sex to no sex. Indeed, the extraction of this benefit is the purpose of the whole exercise from A's point of view. This 'B-directedness' of A is a further source of asymmetry within the example. It is out of the general run of two-person games in which both players' payoffs from outcomes depend on the choices both players make.

If the normal course of action for B is always no sex and the non-normal action is sex, so that $Z = S^*$ and $Y = S$, it remains to identify A's normal and non-normal actions W and X. Since A appears in the character of a dealer, his normal action W must be the offer of the normal deal. What Elster seems to have in mind is a normal deal which will not countenance rapid promotion (and may not countenance zero promotion either). With these restrictions, the normal outcome seems to be normal promotion without sex. This is of course the 'usual situation' and coincides with B's highest preference among the set of outcomes the normal deal makes available.[10]

What is now said to distinguish the cases of exploitation and extortion from the perspective of the normal deal is that A acts exploitatively by adding the supernormal deal 'rapid promotion with sex' whereas A acts extortionately by excluding the normal deal (normal promotion without sex). Both of these actions X are second-order actions like W and are unlike the actions Y and Z performed by B. Both X-actions (exactions?) intend the same result (the same switch in B's behaviour from no sex to sex) but exploitation supposedly attempts it by offering more whereas extortion attempts it by offering less. Exploitation involves a voluntary and non-coerced response to an inducement. Extortion involves a non-voluntary and coerced response to a threat.

But this distinction does not in fact apply to the case in point. There are two aspects of the envisaged departure from the normal deal which Elster has elided. The first concerns the level of promotion, in which the possibility of a supernormal utility is held out to B. The second is the attachment of strings to promotion, regardless of the level of promotion at which attachment takes place. Both of these departures are certainly non-normal. The difficulty is that while the two varieties of harrassment are distinguished in terms of the first variety of non-normality, they are not distinguished in terms of the second. And it is distinction on the second criterion of non-normality which is relevant to Elster's attempt to divide coercive extortion from voluntary exploitation.

What A is extorting or exploiting is always B's dependence on A for promotion (correlative to A's power to grant promotion). In the case alleged to be extortion, A is making use of B's dependence for normal promotion. In the case alleged to be exploitation, A is making similar use of B's dependence for rapid promotion. A cannot be making use of a power to offer normal promotion when it is rapid promotion that he is offering. At either level of promotion, A attaches the same string (sex), which aims to increase his benefit to B's disadvantage but without going so far as to eliminate B's incentive to cooperate altogether. What raises the spectre of exploitation or extortion is this adverse use of power.

But it follows from this that the relevant comparison of outcomes involves a normal course of action not making such adverse use of power. The relevant normal course of action for A in the case in which normal promotion is denied is to offer 'normal promotion without sex'. This is uncontroversial. But in the other case, the relevant normal course of action is no longer the offer of 'normal promotion without sex' but the implied offer of 'rapid promotion without sex'. It is the power to offer rapid promotion which is here abused. Unstrung rapid promotion is therefore the normal course of action despite the fact that rapid promotion is non-normal on the first criterion of non-normality.

---

[10] If normal promotion is the only option A countenances, then (N, S^*) will be the outcome. If A has a maginal preference for N above both R and O (a preference for 'doing the usual and/or proper thing') and refuses to contemplate the benefits derivable from B's choice of S, then N and S^* are dominant strategies, with the normal outcome (N, S^*). However, we can sense the loosening role of 'temptation' in A's contemplation of sex, his beginning to countenance the strategies R and O and his overriding of his earlier preference for the proper course of action. Neither his perception of the situation nor his preferences are as stable as B's.

But since *B* prefers unstrung to hamstrung rapid promotion (on the principle that *B* prefers no sex to sex, other things being equal), *B* is equally coerced in the case alleged to be voluntary exploitation as in the case alleged to be non-voluntary extortion. The offer of rapid promotion with sex must be understood as the denial of rapid promotion without sex. The two cases share the payoff structure given in Figure 1, in which the relevant preference orderings for *B* in the two cases have been superimposed on each other to exhibit their formal identity.

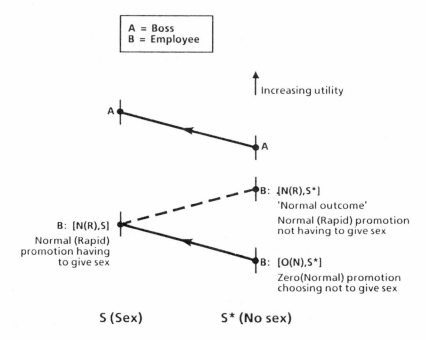

Coercion: W = Inclusion of 'Normal outcome', Y = S
X = Exclusion of 'Normal outcome', Z = S*

Figure 1. Harrassment at work.

Elster has therefore failed to illuminate how coercion might distinguish exploitation from extortion.[11] In particular, he has failed to put forward an example which intuitively involves exploitation, and yet in which the exploitation arises from a genuine improvement rather than a latent deterioration of the

[11] G. Macdonald has suggested that Elster's definition of coercion is too narrow, since one might be coerced by the exclusion of a non-preferable alternative (e.g. the grievance the employee might feel if the boss made sex a condition of promotion when the employee preferred sex in any case). This criticism is distinct from the criticism of the intentional condition in Elster's definition I advance below. It amounts to the contention that coercion can exist even if Y = Z.

choice set available to the victim of exploitation. The difference between exploitation and extortion must be sought elsewhere.

If we have rejected the connotation of 'normal promotion' which entails something like normalization in the mathematical sense (that is, a benchmark for the level of B's utility established by the 'normal outcome'), it is worth attending to the more conventional normative connotation which may have helped to cloud the comparison of the two cases. Both cases certainly involve A (if not B) in improper actions, but the character of the impropriety seems to differ. In particular, it may be important that normal promotion is a right whereas rapid promotion is not. A's special iniquity in denying normal promotion consists not of using a threat to gain an advantage but in violating a right that B has. In denying rapid promotion A merely refuses to exercise a discretion—an act that hardly seems culpable at all. Indeed, whereas A infringed his duty by denying normal promotion, he has a positive duty in the other case to deny B a promotion more rapid than her qualities of work merit. More generally, the supposed difference now relates only to what might be called the moral sociology of the situation (the ascription of rights and duties) and not the political economy (the description of the payoffs and power relations established between A and B).

It seems, therefore, that Elster's illustration is mistaken and that the fault lies in at least one of the following areas:

1. the choice of example to illustrate the distinction between feudalism and capitalism;
2. the contention that feudalism is coercive whereas capitalism is not;
3. the definition introduced for coercion.

I will argue that Elster is certainly mistaken in the first two areas, and faces some difficulties in the third.

Capitalism and Feudalism

In his path-breaking work on exploitation, J. E. Roemer has insisted that a charge of exploitation in the status quo can only be judged in relation to some counterfactual alternative scheme (alternative social arrangement, alternative course of action) under which the payoffs specifying the distribution of benefits and burdens among people will change. In particular, the putative exploiter must be worse off, and the putative exploited better off under the counterfactual alternative than under the status quo. What kind of exploitation exists (and whether it exists) comes to depend on the precise alternative against which the status quo is being evaluated.[12] Thus the female employee in Elster's example is exploited/extorted in the status quo with respect to a counterfactual alternative under which the employer no longer imposes a link between sexual

[12] These are the two major conditions in J. Roemer's general definition of exploitation (*A General Theory of Exploitation and Class*, Part III). In the book and subsequent articles, Roemer considers a variety of candidates for a third necessary condition in the definition of exploitation, but the problem remains a troublesome one. The problem can be motivated by observing that all payoff structures like those of Figures 1 and 2 satisfy the two major conditions, so we are seeking to discriminate further among cases with similar payoff structures. I analyse Roemer's suggestions in greater detail in 'Rational-choice Marxism'.

activity and promotion. Under this alternative, the employee could choose 'no sex' without her promotion prospects suffering adversely. In the application of this frame of reference to either capitalism or feudalism, the relevant counter-factual alternatives will involve social arrangements not requiring the performance of surplus labour. Such possibilities include a self-sufficient peasant economy without taxes or feudal dues, a free market society with an equal endowment of property to all, or a society with collective property embodying the basic principle of distribution Marx called 'socialist' in his *Critique of the Gotha Programme*.[13]

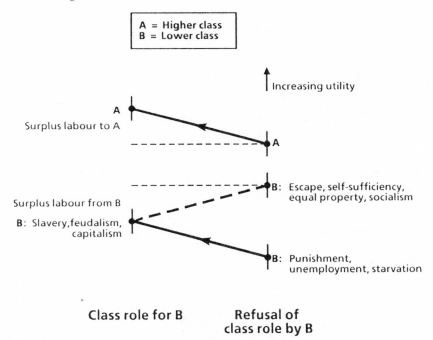

Figure 2. Modes of production.

As is evident from Figure 2, both feudalism and capitalism evaluated against some such alternative will share the payoff structure of Figure 1. Indeed, if we define class societies in terms of the expropriation of surplus labour, all class societies will appear in the same way, regardless of the historical form in which

[13] That a free market society with an equal property endowment to all will involve everyone performing equal labour is proved in Roemer, *General Theory of Exploitation and Class*, Part I.

The basic socialist principle in *Critique of the Gotha Programme* is 'to each according to contribution'. Marx qualified this basic principle to allow for the support of the young, the old, the sick, public investment and other deserving causes. These transfers establish examples of fair, but presumably involuntary, unequal exchanges which could be called taxation or appropriation, completing the quartet already containing donation, exploitation and extortion (in Elster's opening definitions of the latter terms).

surplus labour is 'siphoned off' (surplus value/money profit, labour services, material surplus of slave labour etc.). If Elster's illustration is thus faithful at least to the basic payoff structures of the world historical cases, it remains to be seen whether the attempt to distinguish exploitation and extortion via coercion which fails for the illustration fails also in the intended demarcation of non-coercive capitalism from coercive feudalism. Recall that the employer coerced his employee by denying her first preference (promotion, no sex) and that, on Elster's account, coercion is in general the wilful denial of another's preference in order that they behave in some way differently. Note also that an idea of power (strictly a power relation) is implicit in this conception, since the denial of the preference must be effective. Colloquially, the denial of the preferred alternative is 'within the power' of the denying person with respect to the denied person. As far as régimes of production are concerned, the relevant denial (and therefore locus of coercion) is the denial of the alternative under which no surplus labour is performed. Without this denial the payoff structures imply that rational feudal serfs, slaves or wage labourers would all migrate rapidly to self-sufficiency, equal property or socialism (whichever is currently on offer). Without coercion, the status quo is liable to prove unstable.[14]

If, contrary to Elster's claim, feudalism, capitalism and other class régimes of production necessarily involve coercion, there may nevertheless remain important distinctions concerning the way in which, or the bodies by which, coercion is exercised. In feudalism, for example, the feudal lord intimidates his own peasantry. It may be possible to assume (with maximum charity to the intentional conditions in Elster's definition of coercion) that the lord intimidates the peasant in order to extract surplus labour rather than because he thinks, for example, that intimidation of the peasantry is his duty to his own noble heritage or just treatment for a lower form of human life. On this account, feudal lords are coercers because they are self-conscious extractors of labour services, just as Elster's employer coerces as a self-conscious extractor of sexual services.

The crucial departure between feudalism and capitalism can then be summed up in the idea of the 'separation of the political from the economic'. This means that the agent of intimidation (the state) becomes distinct from the agent that receives the surplus labour (the capitalist). But this separation tends to falsify the condition Elster requires for coercion to have taken place. That is, the capitalist state does not uphold rights to unequal property in order that surplus labour is performed for private owners. If anything, it stabilizes property rights in order that tax revenue be forthcoming (in the monetarized extension precisely of its 'feudal' rôle). It is even clearer that capitalists do not uphold property rights in order that surplus labour be performed, since they do not uphold property rights at all, though they do benefit greatly from property rights being upheld. Even more daunting is the consideration that self-consciousness about labour extraction would always require consciousness of labour extraction. According to Marx, capitalist social relations systematically

---

[14] Instability is possible rather than certain in these circumstances because the status quo may be preserved by ideology rather than power (e.g. a belief among those who carry the burdens that the burdens are legitimate). But it is probably rare historically for benefiters from the burdens of others to have trusted this mechanism alone (cf. medieval monasticism).

mask the necessary awareness. No one can be a self-conscious extractor of surplus value who does not understand and accept the labour theory of value. Only Marxist capitalists or moles in the Civil Service could ever be self-conscious enough to be coercers! It seems therefore that there may be no coercion under capitalism (since Elster's intentional conditions fail), and that a distinction between coercive feudalism and non-coercive capitalism may be available (although not along either of the lines Elster himself seemed to attempt in the example of sexual harrassment.)

But a moment's reflection suggests that this is an unacceptable conclusion. It is unacceptable because nothing has changed in the transition from feudalism to capitalism from the point of view of the person at the receiving end. One wants to say that in either case the serf or the wage-labourer is coerced (at least has a preferable alternative denied), and that as a result of coercion gives something for nothing (surplus labour). The only difference is that under capitalism (but not feudalism) the person (or institution) who does the coercing is not the same person (or institution) who does the gaining for no return.[15]

This point raises a difficulty for the definition of coercion. One solution would be to define coercion solely in terms of an intention to deny a preferable alternative rather than via the denial of a preferable alternative governed by some specific ulterior motive (for example, the intention that the coerced agent perform the action Y in Elster's definition). But this solution will violate the ordinary language sense that one is not merely restricted by coercion but coerced into something else.[16] It seems a better solution to recognize a possible variation in the scope of the intentions which may govern the coercion. Thus, the action that feudal coercion intends to secure in the peasant is both non-appropriation of property in the means of production and the performance of surplus labour, whereas capitalist coercion (or rather, coercion by the state in a capitalist society) has the more limited intention of securing non-appropriation of property (by anyone, but especially the wage-labourer). In this case, there is a relevant 'actual and intended consequence' of state coercion (Y: the non-

[15] Formulae which express the virtual integration of the state with capital ('but a managing committee', 'fusion into a single mechanism', etc.) will make capitalism look more straightforwardly crooked (so to speak).

[16] 'Coerce: Forcibly constrain or impel [person] into quiet, obedience or any course' (OED). Coercion is thus a two-step transaction: Step 1 is 'forcible constraint' and Step 2 is 'any course'. In his most recent discussion of coercion as it applies to capitalism, Elster resorts to a new distinction between coercion and force, in which those subject to force (rather than coercion) have options apart from compliance so unfavourable that they effectively have no choice but to comply. A person is forced rather than coerced if the action Y in the definition at coercion is the only one left to them. Force thus appears as a limiting case of coercion in which the coercive act leaves the victim no alternative—a limit at which a two-step transaction becomes a one-step one. This also connects with the implication of physical sanctions in the use of the term 'force' since physical restrictions are the most restrictive a person can suffer. The OED offers little help in this area. It has 'force: 1. Use violence to, ravish. 2. Constrain, compel', and if synonyms are substituted in the definition of coercion, one rapidly reaches either 'coerce: Forcibly force or force [person] into etc.' or 'coerce: Constrainingly constrain or constrain [person] into etc.'! I should add that Elster abstains on the question whether the capitalist labour contract is in general coerced or forced (beyond recording that Marx probably thought it forced but not coerced (which is an inconsistent position by my construal)) and that there are plenty of hints of the general tendency in Elster's recent work to abandon the search for definitions of any of the fundamental terms of the theory. Certainty of definition is no doubt elusive, but I am not sure if this renders it 'chimerical' (*Making Sense of Marx*, p. 216).

appropriation of private property in the means of production) and a relevant actual but unintended consequence of Y (employment for wages).

It then seems to be in line with ordinary usage to reinstate the distinction between capitalist exploitation and feudal extortion and simultaneously register the significance of the 'separation of the political and the economic' as follows: The capitalist exploits the worker because the capitalist exploits the situation in which the worker is placed by the coercion of the state. The feudal lord extorts the feudal serf because the lord himself creates the situation (exercises the coercion) which he subsequently exploits. The formula seems to capture an appropriate sense in which extortion is a more wilful and culpable act than exploitation. The argument further suggests that exploitation always involves making adverse use of a person's situation, however caused, so that it is only by a conventional abbreviation that one person is said to exploit another person.

Take, for example, a case in which I am at the bottom of a deep, dark hole and someone offers to throw me a rope for a million pounds. For this to be exploitation, does it matter how I got there? I may have created the situation inadvertently by my own actions: stumbling down the hole while preoccupied with thinking out the distinction between exploitation and extortion. It may have been an act of God, which caught me in an earthquake. It may have been an unintended consequence of ancient mining operations which made the ground subside at just the moment I walked over it. I may have wanted to commit suicide, failed and had second thoughts. A third party may have thrown me down the hole in a fit of pique.

Neither the causal nor the intentional sequence seems necessary to the finding of exploitation.[17] Only in the case in which the person offering me the rope is the same person who threw me down the hole (having the subsequent offer in mind) does something else seem to be involved. This is, precisely, where exploitation gives way to extortion.

To sum up: both exploitation and extortion count as two-step phenomena, unlike a one-step unfair unequal exchange such as theft.

In the first step there is the denial of the preferable alternative to the victim. The second step involves the choice victims make in the situation in which the first step has placed them. It is this choice which benefits the exploiter/extorter. From the point of view of the victim, the first step is involuntary and the second is voluntary. Exploitation and extortion thus share the same recipe of voluntary and involuntary transactions. Elster was wrong to divide them according to voluntariness. It is the existence of intentional and causal relations between step 1 and step 2 that make the difference.

The wage labourer is coerced by the state and exploited by the capitalist. Although state coercion is the empirical reality of capitalism (and very likely explains its stability) coercion by a third party is not generally necessary to exploitation. Exploitation can arise from a situation which is caused by the exploited, by accident, by natural law or even by the exploiter, so long as exploitation was not the motive governing the exploiter's action against the exploited. All of these are two-person cases. This conclusion is contrary to Steiner's 'liberal theory of exploitation' in which 'rights violation—paradigmatically theft—is a bilateral relation [whereas] an exploitation is essentially

---

[17] I am grateful to G. Macdonald for making me aware of this point.

a trilateral one'.[18] He is led to this view in the belief that two-person unequal exchanges are essentially exhausted by theft and gift—the cases in which a one-way transmission of a good respectively does and does not violate the sender's right. His error is to generalize from this observation in the wrong direction—to three-person one-step transactions rather than two-person two-step transactions.

Extortion is the two-person case of unfair unequal exchange in which the coercer intends to benefit from the coercion, and does so.[19] Feudalism is extortionate so long as feudal lords intend the consequence that the peasantry work part of the time for nothing when the lords deny the peasants access to unencumbered land or free cities. Both cases of office harrassment are extortionate if the exclusion of the employee's higher preference is relevantly deliberate.[20]

Exploitation and Oppression

It has been maintained throughout that exploitation and extortion are unfair. But where, precisely, does the unfairness come in? Given that exploitation and extortion are two-step phenomena, the possible answers are: Step 1, Step 2 or both. Unfairness at Step 1 involves the unfairness of the denial of the preferable alternative. The unfairness of the denial makes the situation of the denied person unfair. Unfairness at Step 2 involves the unfair utilization of another person's situation, regardless of whether that person's situation is unfair in itself. Unfairness at both steps adds insult to injury.

With these possibilities in mind, it seems most appropriate to call the unfair denial of a (presumptively preferable) alternative *oppression*. To be oppressed is to have one's best options unfairly excluded. Unjust imprisonment is perhaps the ideal typical example of oppression. The next question is the relation between oppression, so defined, and exploitation.[21]

It is first of all clear that oppression is not sufficient for exploitation. Unfair exclusion can simply stop at unfair exclusion. Private owners with means of production can retire hurt and sit on their hands, as they are doing a great deal

---

[18] H. Steiner, 'A liberal theory of exploitation', p. 233.

[19] '*A* may coerce *B* just to flex his muscles' (Elster, *Making Sense of Marx*, p. 212).

[20] It may be a further element in the intuition distinguishing the two cases that while the denial of normal promotion without sex must be fully deliberate (because normal promotion is within the normal cognizance of the employer), the denial of rapid promotion without sex may only be implicit when the offer of rapid promotion with sex is explicit. But the sharp-witted employee can expose what is implied, and even turn it to her own advantage: 'If you can give me rapid promotion if I sleep with you, you can give it to me if I don't. In fact, you'd better give me rapid promotion now anyway, since otherwise I will publicize your conduct'. Such cases of blackmail deserve separate study.

[21] The question also arises of the relation between oppression, coercion and force, given the above definitions of the terms. The main point is that since oppression is a one-step phenomenon and coercion is only a one-step phenomenon in the limiting case of force, coercion and oppression are unlikely to be related intimately. In addition, oppression is unfair whereas coercion and even force may not be. Thus just imprisonment is coercive (probably forced) but not oppressive, and it may be that oppression does not involve coercion if we allow any examples of unfair denial not caused by deliberate human action (e.g. the effects of bureaucratic inertia in the provision of some entitlement or the possible unfairness of a handicap which precludes certain kinds of social satisfaction).

these days. This is just to say that oppression is a one-step while exploitation is a two-step transaction. But is oppression necessary to exploitation? Although it is necessary to exploitation that a preferable alternative be denied, this exclusion might not be unfair in itself: it might not constitute oppression. Consider the following example.

Many countries require a licence which acknowledges some competence to drive a motor vehicle. Such a licence is a paradigm of exclusionary social closure—a legal monopoly of a good creating an exclusive caste of eligibility. F. Parkin calls the general phenomenon of this example 'credentialism'.[22] But the principle behind the driving licence hardly seems controversial, except to a loony libertarian. It is an exclusion but not an oppression. Suppose however that I do not have a licence, and I need a motor vehicle to take a dying relative to hospital. If I am charged exorbitantly by a cartel of motorists, then they are clearly exploiting me (exploiting the situation in which my non-possession of a licence places me). So exploitation need not rest on oppression. It is now possible to elaborate the cases:

Among one-step transactions, there is fair and unfair exclusion of a preferable alternative. The latter is called oppression.
Among two-step transactions there are:
  Case (1) Unfair use of a fair exclusion.
  Case (2) Fair use of an unfair exclusion.
  Case (3) Unfair use of an unfair exclusion.

Case (1) covers the driving licence example and cases (2) and (3) evidently involve oppression. At first sight, case (2) seems rather incoherent since the unfairness of the original exclusion must presumably contaminate the fairness of its use. Case (2) therefore means that any unfairness in the use relates only to the unfairness of the original exclusion.[23] The major interest involves the distinction between cases (1) and (3).

I have argued above that the proper distinction between exploitation and extortion involves intentional and causal relations rather than the moral considerations which Elster's original illustration seemed to suggest. The discussion has nevertheless reached the point at which Elster's moral distinction has resurfaced in the distinction between cases (1) and (3). It might be deemed exploitative for the boss to use the incentive of rapid promotion, even though

---

[22] F. Parkin, *Marxism and Class Theory: A Bourgeois Critique* (London, Tavistock, 1979) develops a very interesting general theory of social division from Weberian insights. In the present context, the problems with his approach are (i) his definitional connection of exclusion with exploitation, bypassing the moral conditions for exploitation: (ii) his view of exploitation as a one-step phenomenon; (iii) his alignment of exclusion with power, in the sense of a domination relation between social groups. I have argued that power is implicit, but that it has a more strategic, interactive rôle than the sociological conception of a fixed relation between groups sometimes suggests.

[23] Examples of case (2) seem rather hard to come by. Suppose a person is unfairly convicted of a crime, but confined to prison with a relentlessly liberal régime administered by the prisoners themselves. If the other prisoners ask the victim to help in the collective housekeeping, they are certainly using the unfair exclusion, since the victim would not be helping the collective régime in a prison unless he or she were confined there. The victim's situation is unfair, but is it also unfair for the other prisoners to make the subsequent demand? Does the injustice of the sentence justify total non-cooperation, or is it possible to hold the two aspects of the victims situation in separate moral compartments? I do not feel confidence in either general judgement.

the exclusion of rapid promotion was fair. It might be deemed extortionate to use the incentive of normal promotion, since the exclusion of normal promotion was unfair in itself, regardless of any unfair use of this exclusion the boss subsequently attempted to make. In one interpretation of Elster's illustration, another difference between exploitation and extortion therefore seems to arise because extortion rests on oppression whereas exploitation does not. Is this line of thought the source of a useful distinction between feudalism and capitalism at the level of rights?

Feudalism, Capitalism and Rights

By analogy with the case of office harrassment, capitalism would be exploitative (but not extortionate) so long as workers' rights are not infringed in the denial of what is necessary to their highest preference—namely, equal access to property in the means of production. Although this does not quite establish the capitalist's right to unequal property in the means of production (it may still be wrong to steal from a thief), it certainly creates a rather large dent in the moral case for socialism. It seems, in other words, that if workers have the right to establish a socialist distribution of property, capitalism is extortionate; if it is only exploitative, they do not. If it is thus possible to be a socialist in good faith only on condition that capitalism is not a system of exploitation, it seems that something had better give.

Suspending the question of terminology for a moment, it is clear that Marx thought capitalist property involved the unfair use of an unfair exclusion. Indeed, he spent most of his life trying to prove that capitalism fitted in with case (3) and nowhere else. He argued against treating capitalism under case (2) that capitalist market relations violated even the norms of right which they announced for themselves (fair exchange). As is well known, this argument turns on the relations between surplus value and profit, justly called 'The Fundamental Marxian Theorem'.[24]

What requires greater emphasis is the argument he used against the inclusion of capitalism within case (1). First, Marx was at pains to show how capitalism came into the world bathed in blood. Property-rights libertarians concede the possible injustice of this initial property distribution, even if they tend to concede the radical political implications of this possibility *sotto voce*.[25] But Marx sought to show that a system of capitalist private property was oppressive in principle, even if it originated from a system of justly acquired non-capitalist private property. This is the moral implication of 'capital as dead labour'. That is, despite its form of existence in a seamless legal garment of private ownership, Marx was concerned to argue that the value-substance of capitalist property is iteratively transformed in the circuit of capital until 'there is not a single atom of its value that does not owe its existence to unpaid labour'.[26] The labour theory of value thus gave a moral unity to a dual indictment of capitalism. According to Marx, capitalism is exploitative because of surplus value. It is oppressive from the same cause. Profit and property are theft.

[24] M. Morishima, *Marx's Economics* (Cambridge, Cambridge University Press, 1973).
[25] See Elster, 'Exploitation, freedom and justice', p. 300, commenting on Nozick.
[26] K. Marx, cited in Elster, 'Exploitation, freedom and justice', p. 291.

I would therefore retain the time-honoured description of capitalism as a system of exploitation, extending the scope of the concept to cover cases (1) and (3), while preserving a distinction between exploitation without oppression [case (1)] and exploitation with oppression [case (3)]. This stipulation also satisfies the emphasis in the ordinary meaning of 'exploitation' on an unfair utilization by the exploiter. It is emphasis on the iniquity of step 2 that seems to mark out exploitation as a concept.

Where does this leave extortion? Extortion always seems to involve coercion. But does extortion always involve oppression? In the case of office harrassment in which rapid promotion is offered, the implicit denial of rapid promotion without sex is not oppressive since rapid promotion is unfair. The corresponding denial of normal promotion in the other case is however oppressive, since normal promotion is fair. Just like exploitation, it seems that extortion can occur with and without oppression. Extortion is only distinguished from exploitation by the causal and intentional relations between an act of coercion and the act of extraction.

With this taxonomy, it would follow from the labour theory of value that the state oppresses workers if workers have rights in the unequal property their unpaid labour creates. The state would not exploit or extort workers unless the state unfairly exacted some benefit from the workers it oppressed (or merely coerced). Capitalists certainly exploit workers, according to the labour theory of value (so long as the theory is fleshed out with some ideals governing the rights and unrights of labour and capital).[27] Do capitalists oppress workers as well? They do if they unfairly help to create the situation which makes workers vulnerable to exploitation. But the labour theory of value makes unfair the payment of wages so low that workers cannot accumulate their own property. The circuit of capital alternates oppression with exploitation. The state and capital therefore form a conspiracy of oppression.[28] But capitalists do not extort, since the necessary intentional connection between the act of oppression and the act of exploitation would require their appreciation of a labour theory of value which does not occur to them.

These proposals seem to be most in keeping both with colloquial usage and the intentions of classical Marxism. But they do not settle the substantive issues on the analysis of capitalism. If, as I believe, the labour theory of value is misguided, Marxists must ask themselves again whether capitalism is oppressive as well as whether it is exploitative.[29] They must also ask who (or what) is oppressing or exploiting whom.

[27] Marx's principal *Critique of the Gotha Programme* is to suggest that workers do not have a right to the full proceeds of their labour under socialism. But this is fully compatible with the operative value in his critique of capitalism: the absence of the right to any product of the unpaid labour of others which results from the ownership of means of production.

[28] I mean conspiracy in the convenient sense of the English Law which requires no concerted action or specific common purpose among the conspirators. A full characterization of the tripartite relations between state, capitalists and workers would require a more detailed analysis of taxation.

[29] cf. '. . . capitalism is just if and only if capitalists have the right to own the means of production they do, for it is their ownership of means of production that enables them to make profit out of labour, and if that ownership is legitimate, then so too is making profit out of labour. The key question, then, is whether capitalist private property is morally defensible'. G. A. Cohen, 'Freedom, justice and capitalism', *New Left Review*, No. 126 (1981), p. 15. The possibility of exploitation without oppression makes it invalid to infer the legitimacy of profit from the legitimacy of property, even if profit is the causal consequence of the use of property.

[21]

Journal of Public Economics 15 (1981) 295–310. North-Holland Publishing Company

ECONOMISTS FREE RIDE, DOES ANYONE ELSE?

Experiments on the provision of public goods, IV

Gerald MARWELL and Ruth E. AMES*

University of Wisconsin, Madison, WI 53706, USA

Received August 1980, revised version received January 1981

Eleven closely related experiments testing the free rider hypothesis under different conditions, and sampling various subpopulations, are reported. Results question the empirical validity and generality of a strong version of the hypothesis. Some reasons for its failure are discussed.

1. Introduction

The free rider hypothesis [Hardin (1968), Olson (1968)] has been one of the most widely accepted propositions in the literature on the provision of public goods by groups. This acceptance, however, has been based primarily on the strength of the theoretical argument, and the citation of commonplace example, rather than rigorous empirical test. In this paper we report on a series of experiments expressly designed to test the hypothesis and related aspects of the theory. Some of these experiments have been extensively reported in the sociological literature [Marwell and Ames (1979, 1980) contain experiments 1, 2, 5, 6; Alfano and Marwell (1980) reports on experiment 11]. Others will be reported here for the first time. Our objective is to review and consider the sum of our findings.

The experiments reported here add substantially to a small, but quickly growing experimental literature whose general trend has been to question the power of the free rider hypothesis for predicting behavior in collective action situations. A large portion of this work has been done by psychologists and has recently been reviewed by Dawes (1980) and Edney (1980). Almost all of this work, however, has dealt with free riding in small groups. Similarly, the few articles by economists and sociologists which have appeared in the literature also tend to deal with relatively small numbers of subjects in

*This research was supported by National Science Foundation grants No. GS-3742 and No. GS-43507. A version was presented at the Public Choice Association meeting in March, 1980. We would like to thank Geraldine Alfano and John Fleishman for their advice on and participation in this work. We also thank Gene Smolensky, Michael Rothschild, Lee Hanson and Arthur Goldberger for their patience.

0047-2727/81/0000-0000/$02.50 © North-Holland Publishing Company relatively small groups [Bohm (1972), Brubaker (1975), Sweeney (1973), Smith (1978), Schneider and Pommerehne (1979)]. These latter works also tend to use very complex experimental designs, running individual subjects through multiple trials, each of which involves a somewhat different experimental condition.

In the research reported below standard social psychological experimental procedures are employed. Care is taken to have subjects understand the task and the situation. Subjects are not used in more than one condition so that there is no contamination from order effects, etc. Equally important, the number of experiments and subjects involved serves to replicate and give weight to our conclusions.

In our experiments 'free riding' refers to the absence of contribution. towards the provision of a public good by an individual, even though he or she will not be excluded from benefiting from that good. The free rider hypothesis is based on the assertion that under such conditions it is irrational for an individual to voluntarily contribute. Following Brubaker (1975), however, we will consider two versions of the group-level implication of this assertion: the 'weak' version of the free-rider hypothesis, which states that the voluntary provision of public goods by groups will be sub-optimal; and the 'strong' version, which argues that (virtually) no public goods at all will be provided through voluntary means.

2. The research paradigm

To test the free rider hypothesis, and related aspects of the theory, we created a highly controlled, very abstract, experimental situation. The original experiments were designed to maximize the probability of free riding by minimizing the possible effects of normative and other pressures for contributing towards the public good. Although aspects of the paradigm changed for different experiments, it is useful to begin by describing the simplest version that we used. All experiments in the program may be seen as variants of this situation.

2.1. Dependent variable: Investment in the public good

The central ingredient in the research paradigm was the operationalization of our dependent variable — investment in a public good. For this purpose, subjects were provided with a given amount of resources, in the form of tokens, which they had to invest in one of two 'exchanges': The 'group exchange' or the 'individual exchange'. The group exchange was our operationalization of a public good, while the individual exchange was a private good. Tokens invested in the individual exchange earned a set amount, regardless of the behaviour of other group members or anything else. In a typical experiment this might be one cent per token. The individual exchange was thus like a bank in assuring a specific return on investment. The return was 'excludable' in neither affecting, nor being affected by, returns to other group members.

The group exchange, on the other hand, paid its cash earnings to *all* members of the group by a pre-set formula, regardless of who invested. The subject received a *share* of the return on his own investment in the group exchange (if any), and also the same share of the return on the investment of each of the other group members. Thus, the group exchange provided a joint, nonrival, nonexcludable, or *public* form of payoff. What made the group exchange a public *good* when compared with the individual exchange, was that it was possible to have the group exchange return substantially *more* than the fixed amount set for the individual exchange. For example, in several experiments reported below the group exchange returned 2.2 cents to the group for every token invested by any group member. Under these circumstances, all members of the group would be better off if all the group's resources were invested in the group exchange than if all were invested in the individual exchange. On the other hand, each individual would be best off if s/he invested in the individual exchange while everyone else invested in the group exchange. This is the incentive to 'free ride' on the investments of others in the public good.

Subjects were allowed to divide their investment between the two exchanges in any way they wished. The investment decision they made comprised the measure of the dependent variable.

2.2. Procedures

In general, all contact with the subjects of these experiments was by telephone and mail. The subjects were first reached by telephone and asked if they were interested in participating in an experiment concerning investment decisions. If they wished to participate they were sent a packet of instructions. The instructions gave a complete, and (in all but one particular) honest description of the nature of the study, the investment decision to be made, and all other factors that might be relevant to that decision. Our intention was to have the subject act with 'full information'. The instructions were carefully designed, with cartoons and tables, and were repetitive, so that we might make as clear as possible a mildly complex situation.

A few days after the mailing an experimenter called the subject and went over each point in the instructions, testing and reviewing until the subject fully understood the situation and the decision to be made. The subject was then given one or two days to decide on an investment, and was again called by the experimenter. At this point the subject reported the investment decision, answered several questions checking for understanding of the situation, and verbally explained the reasons for his or her behavior. Finally, subjects responded to a mailed questionnaire regarding certain background and personality characteristics and their reactions to the experiment.

3. Consensual validation of the operationalization

Largely because neither of us is a trained economist, we felt somewhat insecure in defending our operationalization of economic theory, and in asserting the predictions of theory for behavior in our experimental situation. In response to these problems we decided to validate our approach by consulting with acknowledged experts in this area. Some of our consultation, of course, was of the usual kind, and helped us in refining our hypotheses, methods and procedures. In addition, however, we pursued a more systematic method of validation which can be usefully summarized.

Using our own knowledge of the literature, advice from our consulting economists, and excluding all those experts with whom we had previously discussed this project, we selected six economists and one sociologist prominent in this area.[1] Each expert was sent a version of our experimental situation (see experiment 3, below) along with a questionnaire. He was asked to indicate what he thought relevant *theory* would predict about our subjects' investment behavior, and also whether he personally agreed with the prediction from theory. If he did not agree with the theory (as he saw it), he was asked to indicate the bases on which he disagreed.

One economist declined to answer our questions, arguing that economic theory made no relevant predictions. A second economist had major qualms about making predictions, since he felt the situation was too 'rich' for a pure test of relevant theories. Nevertheless, he did make predictions, and we will include them below. The six panel members who did make predictions all felt that either 'economic theory' or 'game theory', or both, were relevant to this situation.

Five of the six respondents agreed that theory clearly supported the *strong* free rider hypothesis. Four stated that theory predicted that group members would invest no tokens at all, while the fifth estimated investments of less than 5% of the tokens in the group exchange. The sixth respondent said the typical individual would invest 30% of his or her tokens, but added that this prediction came from a combination of theory *and* his reading of previous, vaguely related, empirical research. In general, then, we consider our description of the theoretical predictions for our operations to be strongly supported.

We should add, however, that four of the experts felt that the subjects would actually invest *more* than the theory predicted, and suggested 25%, 25%, '5 to 15%' and '10 to 20%' of available tokens as typical investments. In all, the average prediction by our experts was approximately 20% of

[1] Names available on request, but we'd prefer you didn't ask.

resources, with a range from 0 to 30%. The major reasons given for these 'non-theory' predictions were that people either liked taking risks and were willing to pay for them, or were altruistic (equated to some extent with being 'silly' or 'irrational'). It should be remembered, however, that even these somewhat higher predictions envision behavior that is primarily free riding, with only small amounts of investment resulting from 'irrationality'.

4. Experiment 1: The basic experiment

In the simplest version of our experiments all subjects were presented with a single set of conditions, and their behavior compared with predictions from theory. Subjects were sixteen male and sixteen female high school juniors and seniors selected from a list of such students for Madison, Wisconsin. In this study, as in the other studies reported below, about 40% of all students asked to participate in the research declined. Nevertheless, differences on a series of background factors among those who participated and those who did not were negligible, and the sample is much less of a 'convenience' sample than is usually found in experimental work. For an extended discussion of sampling and other methodological issues, see Marwell and Ames (1979).

Subjects were told that they belonged to a group of eighty high school students 'like themselves', all of whom were making a similar economic decision. Each was provided with 225 tokens which he or she could invest in either the group or the individual exchange. The individual exchange returned one cent for each token invested. The group exchange paid in accordance with the schedule contained in table 1. This table was actually mailed to every subject. Returns were given in a table, and were not continuous, because pretesting indicated that subjects were better able to understand the structure of payoffs under these conditions. In addition, pretests indicated that subjects did not make the fine predictions of others' investments that would be required for them to calculate whether an additional investment on their part would 'put the group over' the border of specific intervals. Payoffs for the group exchange averaged 2.2 cents per token.

Results

Investment in the public good by members of the group certainly did not fit a strong version of the free rider problem. The mean investment was 93.8 tokens or 42% of available resources. Although this is clearly sub-optimal, it is just as clearly not zero, or insignificant. Considering the explicitly depersonalized, profit-oriented, full information nature of the experiment, the strong free rider proposition did not appear to predict behavior accurately.

Table 1

Payoffs from group exchange, study 1 and comparable condition in study 3.

If the total tokens invested in the group exchange by all group members is between	Study 1		Study 3	
	Total money earned by the group is	How much money you get (1.25 cent of each group dollar)	Total money earned by the group is	How much money you get (1.25 cent of each group dollar)
0 and 1999 tokens	$000.00	$0.00	$000.00	$0.00
2000 and 3999	044.00	0.55	014.00	0.18
4000 and 5999	088.00	1.10	032.00	0.40
6000 and 7999	132.00	1.65	054.00	0.68
8000 and 9999	176.00	2.20	320.00	4.00
10000 and 11999	220.00	2.75	350.00	4.38
12000 and 13999	264.00	3.30	390.00	4.88
14000 and 15999	308.00	3.85	420.00	5.25
16000 and 17999	352.00	4.40	440.00	5.50
18000	396.00	4.95	450.00	5.63

The weak version, of course, fared better. However, its requirements are not very stringent.

5. Experiment 2: Skewed resources and interest

At the same time as we ran experiment 1, ninety-six subjects were examined under somewhat different, more complex conditions. Since variations in these conditions did *not* produce significant variations in investment we will not describe them in detail. It should be sufficient to indicate that the key independent variables were the perceived distribution of resources within the group, and the perceived distribution of interest. In some conditions a number of subjects were given 165 tokens to invest, while others received 405 tokens each. The subjects were aware of this skewed distribution of resources. Under other conditions some subjects received 2.25% of returns to the group from the group exchange, while other subjects received 0.92%. Again, subjects were aware of this skewed distribution of interest. Finally, under some conditions both interest and resources were skewed.

Along with the conditions reported above as experiment 1, these conditions constituted a multifactor, fully crossed experimental design, whose independent variables had little consistent effect on investment. What is important to report, however, is that for these 96 additional subjects mean investment in the public good was even *higher* than for the subjects reported on under experiment 1. For the 96 additional subjects mean investment was 119.8 tokens, or 53% of available resources. If all 128 subjects (including those from experiment 1) are considered as participating in a single experiment, the mean investment was 113 tokens, or 50% of the possible maximum.

In all, these results certainly reinforce our earlier conclusions.

6. Experiment 3: Provision point

One characteristic of some public goods that was not considered in the experiments reported above, but which many sociologists, at least, consider crucial, is the fact that they are 'lumpy'. Small amounts of the good are worth little or nothing. Only when some specified provision point is passed is the good valuable. For example, 49% of the workforce joining a union might just as well be 4.9% — in neither case does the union get bargaining power, recognition, or a contract.

Experiment 3 was identical to experiments 1 and 2 (combined) in design, with one fundamental exception — the payoff schedule for the group exchange was altered. The right-hand side of table 1 presents the new schedule, as given to the participants. The key difference here was the presence of a 'provision point'. For the first 8000 tokens invested *by the group* in the group exchange (i.e. up to 44% of the group's available resources) returns to investment were near zero. If more than 8000 tokens were invested however, the group exchange returned approximately 3.8 cents for *every* token invested, including the first 8000.

Results

Again, the results strongly support the previous findings. Over all treatments, an average of 112.8 tokens were invested in the public good by individuals as compared with 113 in experiments 1 and 2. This again comprised 51% of the available resources. Differences among treatments were not significant. Consistency with the previous studies was remarkable.

7. Experiment 4: Small groups

Experiment 4 was identical to experiment 3 in every way except one — subjects were informed that their groups contained four rather than 80 persons. Under these conditions some subjects perceive that they are in a position to profit even if they provide the public good all by themselves. They have sufficient interest that they should not free ride.[2] Of course, it was partly to see if these subjects would provide the good that these conditions were examined in the first place.

Results

As expected, subjects with sufficient interest in the public good to profit from any investment they made in the group exchange invested at particularly high levels — an average of 87% of their available resources. More important for this paper, the remaining subjects invested an average of 124 tokens, approximately 60% of their available resources. For this group the strong free rider hypothesis was once again not supported. Subjects invested at high levels. Only the weak free rider hypothesis received any support.

8. Experiment 5: Experienced subjects

One threat to the generalizability of the above experiments is the fact that each subject confronted his or her investment decision only once. Since subjects were in a highly abstract, 'unrealistic' situation, their initial decisions might have reflected a lack of understanding — or lack of full information.

---

[2]Because of the provision point, and the fact that many of the subjects did not have sufficient resources to reach that point, investment was *not* always their dominant strategy.

Experiment 5 therefore replicated the procedures of experiment 1, with the key exception that all 32 subjects were experienced. Each had previously participated in either experiment 1 or experiment 2. In addition, all payoffs were doubled, partly to meet some of the effects of inflation on the value of the decision, and generally to increase the importance of the decision. Thus, for example, returns from the individual exchange were now 2 cents per token.

Results

The most important result from this experiment is the full replication of findings from experiment 1. Subjects invested an average of 106 tokens in the group exchange, or 47% of their available resources. Comparing these subjects with those in experiment 1 reveals no significant difference in mean investment. In general, subjects tended to invest in much the same way they invested the first time, the correlation between first and second investment being 0.42.

9. Experiment 6: High stakes

The departure from theoretical expectations found in the previous experiments might also arise from the fact that subjects were deciding about relatively small amounts of money. With such 'low' stakes they might have been willing to gamble, or be altruistic. Thus, experiment 6 was designed to completely replicate experiment 1, except that the stakes were raised substantially — by a factor of five. Every token invested in the individual exchange returned five cents. Group returns were similarly affected, and it appeared to subjects that up to $1,980 could now be earned by the group. This meant that the maximum any of the subjects under these conditions could earn was $33.25 — if he or she free rode while everyone else invested in the public good. This was certainly a meaningful amount for the typical high school student.

Results

Results from this study are somewhat complex because of a problem that developed with new experimenters. For the only time in the research program, results systematically differed (although not extremely) depending on which individual experimenter conducted the interviews. For a full analysis of the results the reader is referred to the original report [Marwell and Ames (1980)].

Taken generally, however, the results indicate that there *might* be some reduction in contribution to the group exchange when stakes are raised. Depending on which analytic strategy is pursued, the mean level of investment is between 63 and 78 tokens, or 28% and 35% of available resources. The latter, higher estimate, is probably more accurate, as it reflects the responses of subjects interviewed by more experienced interviewers. In either case, however, subjects under high stakes conditions clearly invest in the group exchange at a level much higher than would be predicted from a strong version of the free rider hypothesis. A subject who invests even 70 tokens in the group exchange is giving up a certain $3.50 to help the other members of his or her group, without knowing whether any of them will reciprocate. We should understand that at some level of stakes it becomes improbable that people would invest in a public good of our kind — who would risk a certain $100,000 to earn a possible but not very probable, $220,000? But the free-rider proposition is supposed to apply whenever people are making 'rational' choices about amounts of money they find meaningul, not only when the stakes are enormous.[3]

10. Experiments 7, 8 and 9: Feedback

One of our long-held expectations was that the free rider problem might be more severe under conditions where individuals get little or no information about the intentions of other group members than where some information was available. In particular, we realized that in the real world people rarely make all-or-nothing decisions at a single point of time. For example, potential contributors to the United Fund are constantly informed of the Fund's progress so that they can evaluate whether others are contributing or not. If others are contributing we might be more willing to contribute our share as well. If not, we might be more inclined to join them in free riding.

In experiments 7, 8 and 9 we gave our subjects a chance to gather information on each other's behavior. The experiments were identical to experiment 1, except that there were two opportunities to invest. In experiment 7, subjects could make an initial investment of some, none, or all of their tokens in the group or the individual exchange, thus to some extent informing each other of their 'intentions'. After information about the group's response to this initial phase was broadcast, each subject could distribute the tokens he or she hadn't yet invested. In experiments 8 and 9 tokens invested in the group exchange at time 1 remained in the group exchange at time 2, but additional tokens could be moved from the individual to the group exchange after feedback. In all three experiments subjects were arbitrarily assigned to groups of 4, whose behavior determined the feedback those subjects would get about other group members' behavior. Of course, subjects

---

[3]It is interesting to note that despite the greater range of possible investment with higher stakes, subjects in experiments 1 and 6 had comparable variances in investment. The respective standard deviations were 67 and 72 tokens.

were still told that the whole group determined the payoffs, and had no reason to think otherwise. However, feedback varied over subjects. Experiments 7 and 8 each used 32 high school aged students as subjects, while experiment 9 studied 32 college volunteers.

Results

No significant differences from previous studies were found in these studies. Subjects in experiment 7 invested 46% of their available tokens in the group exchange, while subjects in experiments 8 and 9 invested 50% and 49% of their tokens, respectively. The previous results were replicated once again.

11. Experiment 10: Manipulated feedback

Our last experiment with feedback involved manipulating what the subjects were told prior to the second stage of investment. Sixteen randomly selected college subjects were told that their group of eighty (including themselves) had invested 7% of its total resources in the group exchange at time 1. Another sixteen were given a more moderate level of investment, 48% of the group's tokens. A third group was given the high figure of 88%. Procedures were otherwise identical to experiment 7.

Results

Once again, the treatment made little difference. The low, medium, and high feedback groups invested 43%, 50% and 44% of their tokens, respectively. None of these figures is much different from those previously reported.

12. Experiment 11: Non-divisibility

The next-to-last experiment to be reported in this series required a somewhat different methodology. Our objective was to see whether subjects dealing with a non-divisible public good would behave similarly to those in our previous experiments. We defined a non-divisible good as one which must be consumed collectively. It cannot be divided up, taken home, and consumed privately [Head (1962)]. A park or a bridge is of this nature. Our previous experiments involved a good — the higher payoff from the group exchange — that was divisible, like an increase in wages won by a union, or a cartel's forced increase in prices.

Making this comparison, however, required that we study *real* groups with members who might reasonably conceive of themselves as consuming something collectively. At the same time, our procedures require that our

306   *G. Marwell and R.E. Ames, Free rider hypothesis*

subjects neither know one another nor interact. To deal with these contradictory demands we studied a sample of incoming freshman in the summer before they arrived at the University of Wisconsin. The subjects were told that they had been assigned to a specific dormitory floor and that they and the other prospective floor residents were the group being studied. The group that was offered a divisible good was then given the standard instructions used in experiment 1. The subjects in the non-divisible treatment were given identical instructions, with one exception: they were told that all earnings from the group exchange had to be spent on a *group* project. They could choose anything they wanted on which to spend the money, such as a party, or a hi-fi for their floor, so long as there was something purchased collectively.

Since the payoff structures for the two groups were formally identical, we expected that the non-divisible group would be less inclined to invest in the group exchange. We reasoned that demanding collective consumption meant that individuals could not maximize the use of their individual shares according to their individual tastes, thus reducing the utility of the returns from the group exchange.

Results

Results were exactly the opposite of our expectations. Members of the non-divisible group invested almost twice the amount invested by subjects given our standard experimental treatment. This is particularly noteworthy because the control group once again replicated our basic finding — they invested 43% of their resources in the public good. Therefore the investment of 84% of all tokens in the group exchange by the subjects in the non-divisible condition is remarkable.

13. Experiment 12: Economics graduate students

The last experiment we report is identical to our first with two exceptions: most importantly, the subjects were thirty-two first-semester graduate students in economics at the University of Wisconsin; in addition, the value of all tokens was doubled (as in study 5). Interestingly, when questioned later, only two of the graduate students could specifically identify the theory on which this study was based. As first-year students they had yet to reap the full benefits of the remarkable education assuredly to be theirs.

Results

At last, a result that is really different. Economics graduate students contributed only an average of 20% of their resources to the group exchange. They were much more likely to free ride than any of our other groups of subjects. The differences between them and the subjects in experiment 1 is significant at the 0.05 level, (*F*-test). The previous results do not replicate. One could argue that for this group the strong free rider hypothesis receives some support.

14. Summary and conclusions

For ease of reference, table 2 presents the mean investment behavior of subjects in all twelve experiments.

Table 2

Summary of results: Experiments 1–11.

Experiment	Mean % of resources invested
1. Basic experiment	42%
2. Skewed resources and/or interest	53%
Experiments 1 and 2, combined	51%
3. Provision point	51%
4. Small groups with provision point (except those with sufficient interest to provide the good themselves)	60%
5. Experienced subjects	47%
6. High stakes	
Experienced interviewers	35%
All interviews	28%
7. Feedback, no changing initial investment	46%
8. Feedback, could change investment in individual account	50%
9. Feedback, could change investment in individual account — college students	49%
10. Manipulated feedback	
Low	43%
Medium	50%
High	44%
11. Non-divisibility	
Divisible (control)	43%
Non-divisible	84%
12. Economics graduate students	20%

Summarizing most of the results seems ridiculously easy: over and over again, in replication after replication, regardless of changes in a score of situational variables or subject characteristics, the strong version of the free rider hypothesis is contradicted by the evidence. People voluntarily contribute substantial portions of their resources — usually an average of between 40 and 60 percent — to the provision of a public good. This despite the fact that the conditions of the experiment are expressly designed to maximize the probability of individualized, self-interested behavior. Free riding does exist — subjects do not provide the optimum amount of the public good, and tend to reserve a meaningful fraction of their resources. The 'weak' free rider hypothesis is supported. Nevertheless, the amount of contribution to the public good is not easily understood in terms of current theory. As the analyses of our expert economists demonstrate, the basic thrust of individual decision theory argues for the strong version of the free rider hypothesis.

Of course, any set of experimental results must be treated with some skepticism. Problems about generalizing from a single, unrealistic situation, and a rather restricted sample, are intrinsic to the method. A variety of questions might be asked about specific decisions regarding how much money was involved, where different control conditions were set, etc. For economists, the key problem may be the non-iterative nature of the situation. Subjects do not engage in this decision over and over again, learning the risks and payoffs through experience, and eventually settling on an experientially informed stable pattern of behavior. Regardless of how well the instructions are understood the subjects are relatively naive, even in experiments 7, 8 and 9 where they are making the decision for the second time. It is still only the second time. Despite all of these caveats, however, our findings are real, unusually well replicated, and constitute a challenge to the generality and utility of the strong free rider hypothesis.

We do not have a clear basis on which to suggest some alternative theoretical approach that might account for these results. In doing these experiments, however, we collected a wide range of additional information regarding the backgrounds, perceptions, expectations and explanations for behavior of our subjects. With a single exception, perusal of this information failed to suggest any systematic differences among those who did and those who did not invest substantially in the public good. The exception, however, may be instructive.

Two questions we asked of subjects concerned 'fairness' in this investment situation. One asked what they thought a fair investment in the group exchange would be. The other asked whether they were 'concerned with fairness' in making their own investment decision. There was surprising unanimity of thought regarding what was considered fair. Using all subjects except the economics graduate students and those subjects in study 4 with sufficient interest in the group exchange to provide the good by themselves, we found that more than three out of four thought that 'about half' or more of a person's resources should be contributed, and more than one out of four thought people who were fair would contribute *all* of their tokens. These constitute major investments, and also relate to the levels of investment actually found. The correlation between investment and definitions of fairness, however, is not very high — only 0.23. Much higher is the correlation between investment and whether or not the individual indicated he or she was 'concerned with fairness' when investing — 0.47. However, as shown in table 3, both of these significant zero-order relationships are reduced to near zero in a regression which also contains an interaction term. It is the interaction term which remains substantial and significant, indicating that those who *both* considered fairness when deciding how to behave, *and* defined higher levels of contribution as fair, were the ones who contributed the most.

Comparisons with the economics graduate students is very difficult. More than one-third of the economists either refused to answer the question regarding what is fair, or gave very complex, uncodable responses. It seems

Table 3

'Fairness' and percent of resources invested in the group exchange.

Independent variables	Regression coefficients (standard errors in parentheses)	
	Additive model	Interactive model
Constant	−17.67	16.56
	(5.69)	(11.72)
What's fair?	6.43[a]	−3.14
	(1.18)	(3.10)
Concerned with fairness?	17.78[a]	2.45
	(1.54)	(4.85)
Interaction		4.27[a]
		(1.28)
R^2	0.516	0.532
F	83.11	60.53
N	462	462

[a]Significant at 0.001 level.

that the meaning of 'fairness' in this context was somewhat alien for this group. Those who did respond were much more likely to say that little or no contribution was 'fair'. In addition, the economics graduate students were about half as likely as other subjects to indicate that they were 'concerned with fairness' in making their investment decision.

Perhaps these results make sense. Economists may be selected for their work by virtue of their preoccupation with the 'rational' allocation of money and goods. Or they may start behaving according to the general tenets of the theories they study. Confronted with a situation where others may not behave rationally, they nevertheless behave the way good economic theory predicts. Note as well the very similar responses of our 'famous' economists.

Of course, we might also turn the causal order around and gain insight into the deficiencies of the theory of collective action. We may do well to pay more attention to questions of fairness and equity, as they affect behavior in collective action situations. Such variables are difficult to include in formal theories, as they are often perceived quite differently by different actors. Nevertheless, their empirical power may be more important than their heuristic drawbacks.

References

Alfano, G. and G. Marwell, 1981, Experiments on the provision of public goods III: Non-divisibility and free riding in 'real' groups, Social Psychology Quarterly 43, 300–309.

Bohm, P., 1972, Estimating demands for a public good: An experiment, European Economic Review 3, 111–130.

Brubaker, E.R., 1975, Free ride, free revelation, or golden rule? Journal of Law and Economics 18, 147–161.

Dawes, R.M., 1980, Social dilemmas, American Psychological Review 31, 169–193.

Edney, J.J., 1980, The commons problem: Alternative perspectives, American Psychologist 35, 131–150.

Hardin, G., 1968, The tragedy of the commons, Science 162, 1243–1248.

Head, J.G., 1962, Public goods and public policy, Public Finance 17, 197–219.

Marwell, G. and R.E. Ames, 1979, Experiments on the provision of public goods I: Resources, interest, group size, and the free rider problem, American Journal of Sociology 84, 1335–1360.

Marwell, G. and R.E. Ames, 1980, Experiments on the provision of public goods II: Provision points, stakes, experience and the free rider problem, American Journal of Sociology 85, 926–937.

Olson, M. Jr., 1968, The logic of collective action: Public goods and the theory of groups (Schocken Books, New York).

Samuelson, P.A., 1954, The pure theory of public expenditure, Review of Economics and Statistics 36, 387–390.

Schneider, F. and W.W. Pommerehne, 1979, On the rationality of free-riding: An experiment, Zurich, mimeo.

Smith, V., 1978, Incentive compatible experimental processes for the provision of public goods, in: Research in experimental economics (J.A.I., Greenwich).

Sweeney, J., 1973, An experimental investigation of the free rider problem, Social Science Research 2, 277–292.

[22]

THE PARADOX OF GROUP SIZE IN COLLECTIVE ACTION: A THEORY OF THE CRITICAL MASS. II.*

PAMELA E. OLIVER   GERALD MARWELL
University of Wisconsin

Many sociologists incorrectly believe that larger groups are less likely to support collective action than smaller ones. The effect of group size, in fact, depends on costs. If the costs of collective goods rise with the number who share in them, larger groups act less frequently than smaller ones. If the costs vary little with group size, larger groups should exhibit more collective action than smaller ones because larger groups have more resources and are more likely to have a critical mass of highly interested and resourceful actors. The positive effects of group size increase with group heterogeneity and nonrandom social ties. Paradoxically, when groups are heterogeneous, fewer contributors may be needed to provide a good to larger groups, making collective action less complex and less expensive.

Empirical researchers have often found that the size of a group is the best predictor of its level of collective action. Spilerman (1970, p. 654) summarized his analysis of the black riots of the 1960s: "[T]he larger the Negro population, the greater the likelihood of the disorder. Nothing else appears to matter." Scott and El-Assal (1969) found that size of student body was the only significant predictor of demonstrations and other disturbances on college campuses. Interpreting their results, Marwell (1970) argued that the simplest theory would assume that

> a given proportion of students [at all schools] are ready to stage a demonstration in response to certain types of events but . . . this proportion is small. Given that a demonstration is a collective event, it takes some minimum number of such students to get a demonstration off the ground. The larger the university, the greater the chance it has to get a minimum number. (p. 916)

Very large constituencies such as Afro-Americans or women have given rise to much larger social movements in the United States than small constituencies like Armenian-Americans or paraplegics. These empirical findings make a great deal of sense, since larger groups have more resources and more people who might contribute them for collective action.

Nevertheless, many believe on theoretical grounds that it is more difficult for larger groups to sustain voluntary collective action. The major source of this belief is Mancur Olson's *Logic of Collective Action* (1965). Hardin describes Olson's "central conclusion" as "large groups will fail; small groups may succeed (1982, p. 38)."[1]

When theory conflicts with empirical research, the problem usually lies with the theory. Hardin calls Olson's "group size" assertion "the most controversial issue in the contemporary literature on collective action." As he and others have shown, Olson's argument, which seems so plausible at first, does not stand up to close technical analysis. We begin by reviewing the key issue in this dispute, effects of jointness of supply on the size argument.[2] This review suggests a paradox to which we next turn: providing a collective good to a larger interest group may require *fewer* individual contributors. The final section discusses the implications of this paradox by considering it in relation to the social processes underlying the organization of collective action and the conceptualization of the "group" in collective action theory.

Many sociologists have believed that instrumentalist assumptions must be abandoned to account for the obvious inconsistencies between the real world and Olson's "group size" argument, but our analysis of the paradox of group size stays within the instrumentalist framework. We assume that decisions are made

---

* Direct all correspondence to Pamela E. Oliver, Department of Sociology, University of Wisconsin-Madison, Madison, WI 53706.

This research was supported by National Science Foundation Grant Number SES-8408131.

---

[1] In the social psychological literature, "diffusion of responsibility" findings also suggest that the presence of others reduces an individual's propensity to assist someone in need (Piliavin, et al. 1981, pp. 120–32; Latane and Nida 1981).

[2] In an earlier draft, we presented a much more abbreviated review of the literature in this area, and found that reviewers and colleagues who were obviously well-read sociologists nevertheless thought that we were misunderstanding Olson. Thus, we feel it is appropriate to provide a thorough treatment of this issue in a sociological journal, even though the relevant arguments have been published by scholars in other disciplines.

consciously with attention to costs and benefits, and that resources are limited. This is a correct, although partial, description of the behavior of people who care about some collective good, have limited resources, and want to "spend wisely" in pursuit of the good. We do not say that people always act out of instrumentalist motives; rather, we show what the consequences will be when they do. We assume that each person can be described by a relatively fixed "potential contribution level." It does not matter to our analysis what individual motives generate these levels, or whether they are the same or different for different people. Solidarity, altruism, or personal morality may all affect the potential contribution level, as may "external" factors such as the intensity of a propaganda campaign or a conversion process.[3]

JOINTNESS OF SUPPLY AND THE GROUP SIZE ARGUMENT

A *public good* is defined by its nonexcludability: if any one group member consumes it, it cannot feasibly be withheld from other group members (Olson 1965, p. 14). Here, a "group" is all individuals in a relevant population who have a positive interest in the good.[4] Anyone who wants to enjoy a public good must be prepared to provide it to everyone in the group.

For Olson, groups come in three theoretically different sizes: *small* or *privileged*, in which some individual may have enough interest in the collective good to provide some level of it himself; *moderate*, in which no individual can provide a significant portion of the good himself, but some individuals can make a "noticeable" difference in the level of provision of the collective good, i.e., affect it enough that it seems to have increased a small amount; and *large*, in which no individual can make even a noticeable difference (p. 44). Although he seems to *define* a large group as one in which no contribution is noticeable (e.g., p. 45), Olson notes that this would be tautological (pp. 48–9n), and recasts his position as "the (surely reasonable) empirical hypothesis that the total costs of the collective goods wanted by large groups are large enough to exceed the value of the small fraction of the total benefit that an individual in a large group would get" (p. 49n). Hence, Olson argues, no rational individual in a

large group would ever contribute towards the provision of a public good.

Although this may seem a reasonable empirical hypothesis, it has been well established that Olson's group size argument is either tautological or wrong. Although a variety of critical issues have been raised (Chamberlin 1974; Frohlich and Oppenheimer 1970; McGuire 1974; Oliver 1980), jointness of supply is most important. (See Hardin 1982, pp. 38–49 for a very thorough treatment of this issue.)

A good with *jointness of supply* costs the same no matter how many people "enjoy" it.[5] The classic jointly supplied good is a bridge, which has a fixed cost regardless of how many people use it. The cost of defending a border is roughly the same regardless of how many people are protected within that border. A special interest tax loophole may involve the same lobbying costs whether it benefits one company or a thousand. Jointness of supply can be a matter of degree. A classic private good has zero jointness of supply and a cost which is proportional to the number who enjoy it. A good with pure jointness of supply has all fixed costs and no proportional costs. Between these extremes lie economies of scale, costs that rise less than proportionately with the number who enjoy a good.

Olson discusses jointness of supply in a footnote:

> at least one type of collective good considered here exhibits no jointness whatever, and few if any would have the degree of jointness needed to qualify as pure public goods. Nonetheless, most of the collective goods to be studied here do display a large measure of jointness (p. 14n)

Despite this, Olson never discusses how jointness of supply would affect his group size argument.

To appreciate the significance of jointness of supply for the group size argument, it is crucial to recognize that the relevant cost for collective action is that borne by the collective actors. Even though a tax loophole that applies to many will cost taxpayers more than one that applies to few, what matters is how much the *lobbying* will cost. The cost of cleaning up pollution is roughly proportional to the number of polluters, but the cost of obtaining laws requiring polluters to clean up their own messes is not. Government policy as a public good usually has high jointness of supply. An interest group or social movement campaigns for legislation of benefit to them, but their costs are unaffected by the

---

[3] We are not claiming that this is the *best* way to capture such feelings, simple that they *can* be incorporated into an instrumentalist model.

[4] This definition of "group," which is fairly standard in economics, is different from that most common in sociology, and is closer to the idea of an "interest group" or "beneficiary constituency" (McCarthy and Zald 1977).

---

[5] See Samuelson (1954) and Head (1974) for general treatments of public goods.

THE PARADOX OF GROUP SIZE IN COLLECTIVE ACTION 3

existence of others who would also be benefited by the legislation.

Zero Jointness of Supply: Group Size Has Negative Effect

Olson's group size argument is clearly correct *only* when the good has zero jointness of supply, i.e., when the cost of providing the good is proportional to the number who share in it. Consider an example loosely drawn from our experience. Imagine that wiring arrangements and university regulations require that all terminals for a departmental computer be placed in public access space and be available to all members of the department. If 50 percent of the department's members want to work at a time, 5 terminals are necessary to provide perfect computer access in a 10-person department, and 50 terminals are necessary for a 100-person department. Suppose individual faculty members are encouraged to buy terminals for the department from their research grants. One terminal is $\frac{1}{10}$ of the number necessary in the smaller department, but only $\frac{1}{100}$ of the number necessary for the larger department. The individual who buys a terminal raises her own ability to work on the computer whenever she wants to by .1 in the smaller group (since all 10 members have equal access to the terminal), but by only .01 in the larger group, where all 100 members have equal access. If a terminal costs $500, an expected-value maximizer would have to value computer access at more than $5000 to be willing to buy a terminal for the small department, which is bad enough, but would have to value access at $50,000 to be willing to buy a terminal for the larger community. Every increase in group size would lower the expected value of a contribution of a given size or, alternately, raise the price of a given level of provision of the good in terms of individual benefit.

If the cost of a nonexcludable good increases proportionately (or more) with the number who enjoy it, larger groups are much less likely to be provided with the good than smaller groups. This is clearly the situation Olson has in mind in his analysis, and there is nothing wrong with his logic. The trouble is that few collective goods meet this condition. Most goods with no jointness of supply are also quite excludable. We had to invent a nonexcludability constraint in our example. Olson's major example is a group of businesses joining together to restrict production in a perfectly competitive market. This is hardly the kind of "collective action" that interests sociologists and political scientists.

Pure Jointness of Supply: Positive Effect of Group Size

The opposite result obtains when goods have pure, or complete, jointness of supply. Then, larger interest groups are much more likely to have a "critical mass" (Oliver, Marwell, and Teixeira 1985) of people willing to provide the collective good. For any individual deciding whether to contribute to a collective good with pure jointness of supply, it is irrelevant how many others might share in the good. Individuals will provide the good if their own benefit from the good outweighs its cost. We may use another example from our own experience. In the course of this research, we had to purchase a simulation compiler. The license for the compiler is for the whole computer, but we could have placed the compiler in a public access file or in a private file available only to ourselves. Obviously, the fact that others can use the compiler is totally irrelevant to the benefits we obtain from it, so we opted for public access. Because this good has pure jointness of supply, we had absolutely no reason to withhold it from others.

In general, the irrelevance of group size for individuals' decisions when there is pure jointness of supply translates into a positive effect of group size on (1) the probability that *someone* in a group will provide the good, and (2) the total amount of contributions from the group. The only exception to this rule is the extreme (but common) case in which the cost of a collective good is so high relative to the interest and resource distributions of those interested in it that no one in the group is willing or able to provide the good. In this case, group size is irrelevant to the outcome. *There really is a dilemma of collective action for public goods, but the dilemma adheres to the high cost of providing them, not to the number who share in them.*

To illustrate this point, let us look at a case at the opposite extreme. When the cost of the collective good is very low relative to the group's interest, the group's size will have little effect on the probability that *somebody* in the interest group will contribute. But group size will have a positive effect on the total number of contributors and the total amount of their contribution. Consider the problem of providing the collective good of calling the power company to report an outage. Making a phone call entails some cost and will benefit others who have not called. There are doubtless many free riders, and even a "diffusion of responsibility" effect of people assuming that someone else is making a call that they would be perfectly willing to make. Nevertheless, someone nearly always calls, whether the affected group is big

4

or small. In fact, there are almost always quite a few calls made about any particular outage, and the number of calls is usually greater the more people are affected. Although a higher *proportion* of smaller affected populations may call, there is a greater total number of calls, that is, more overall collective *action*, in a larger group.

What about intermediate goods, whose cost is low enough that someone might be willing and able to pay for them, but high enough that this willingness and ability is a relatively rare trait? Continuing with computer examples, consider the problem of paying the fairly large cost of linking a computer installation to a world-wide communication system such as BITNET. Users at each installation vary in their interest (e.g., how much they collaborate with people in other countries) and in their resources (e.g., discretionary grant or overhead funds). Only a few users combine high interest in BITNET with large discretionary funds. For the sake of a model, we assume that the whole fee must be paid out of one user's fund, that only a small proportion of all computer users combine high interest with large funds, and that users are randomly distributed across installations.

We can model this as a large population from which samples of various sizes are drawn. Imagine, for example, a distribution of interest (collaboration) and resources (grants) such that the probability is .01 (i.e., 1 in 100) that an individual from that distribution would be willing and able to provide the collective good (pay the fee). The probability that a sample (installation) of size n will have at least 1 person who exceeds a threshold with probability p is $1 - q^n$, where $q = (1-p)$, while the expected number who will exceed that threshold is np. If the installation size is 10, the expected number of purchasers when p is .01 is .1, and the probability that someone will purchase BITNET rounds off to about .1. That is, only 10 percent of installations of size 10 would be expected to connect to BITNET. If the installation size is 100, the number who can be expected to contribute is 1, and the probability that at least one will do so is about .6, so that 60 percent of all installations of size 100 would be on BITNET. But if the installation size is 1,000, the expected number of users who have both interest and funds is 10, and it is virtually certain that there will be at least one person who will pay for the connection.

Interactions: Group Size and Economies of Scale

Most real cases lie between the extremes of pure and no jointness of supply. They exhibit partial jointness of supply, or economies of scale, in which the cost of the collective good rises less

than proportionately with the number who enjoy it. In these intermediate cases, the amount of collective action as a function of group size depends on the interaction between the cost function for the collective good and the distribution of potential contribution levels among members of the group.

These interactions are always specific to a particular case, but we can identify the two important principles that govern them. First, the more the cost function for the collective good approximates jointness of supply, the more likely group size is to have a positive effect on the provision of the good. Secondly, the more heterogeneous and positively skewed the distribution of potential contribution sizes, the more likely group size will have a positive effect on the provision of the good.

These two relations interact. Group size has a positive effect whenever the interest and resource distributions are skewed enough relative to the steepness of the cost function that the effect of enlarging the pool of potential contributors compensates for increased costs. If costs increase only slightly with group size, almost any heterogeneity in contribution levels is enough to make larger groups more successful than smaller ones. If costs increase substantially with group size, however, then larger groups will be less successful unless they are very heterogeneous.[6]

THE PARADOX OF GROUP SIZE AND THE NUMBER OF CONTRIBUTORS

In general, the complex interactions described above are a difficult basis on which to build useful substantive principles. However, they have allowed us to recognize at least one important paradoxical relation that has not previously been appreciated. *When groups are heterogeneous, a larger interest group can have a smaller "critical mass."* That is, when a good has high jointness of supply, it may be provided by fewer people in a larger group than in a smaller group.

There are precursors of this result in the literature. Both Olson, briefly (1965, p. 29), and Hardin, much more extensively (1982, pp. 67–89), argue that group heterogeneity has a positive effect on the prospects for collective action. Hardin gives several examples to show

---

[6] Using simulations, we have explored these numerical relations extensively. However, we do not think that numerical examples would do much to clarify the substantive meaning of this result. The principles are as we state them in the text, but real world situations differ greatly in the actual forms of the two functions and, thus, differ greatly in the outcome predicted by their interaction.

THE PARADOX OF GROUP SIZE IN COLLECTIVE ACTION 5

that the especially interested and resourceful members of an interest group may provide collective goods that benefit many others. He proves that what he calls the "efficacious subgroup" (what we call the critical mass) will be smaller in a more heterogeneous group. We go one step farther and demonstrate that, if groups are heterogeneous, the critical mass will be smaller in a larger interest group.

We may illustrate the paradox with an example. Suppose the users of a computer facility are asked to chip in to buy a $125 software package that will be publicly available. For the moment, ignore the social process problem of coordinating contributions. It happens that the average person is willing to contribute $5. If the group is homogeneous, it takes 25 people to provide the good, a result that is invariant with group size.

In contrast, consider three installations with 100, 1,000, and 10,000 users, in which the distribution of resources among users is *heterogeneous*. Table 1 shows the proportions and actual numbers of users within each of these installations (groups) expected to have each whole number of resource units for two arbitrary distributions. The first is a normal distribution (which is, of course, symmetric), and the second is a moderately skewed lognormal distribution; both have a mean of $5 and a standard deviation of $1.

The data in Table 1 show that, regardless of group size, the simple fact of heterogeneity (around the same mean) reduces the minimum size of the critical mass. Even in the symmetric distribution, the smallest heterogeneous group (100), contains a minimum critical mass of size 20 (1 person contributing $8, 6 contributing $7, and 13 contributing $6), 5 less than the 25 contributors needed under homogeneity. This

Table 1. Computation of Critical Mass for Two Distributions (Normal and Lognormal with Mean 5 and Standard Deviation 1) and Three Group Sizes (100, 1,000, and 10,000)

A. Expected Numbers of Individuals Willing to Make Each Size Contribution. Rounded to Integers.

Value	Prob.	Normal E(100)	Normal E(1,000)	Normal E(10,000)	Prob.	Lognormal E(100)	Lognormal E(1,000)	Lognormal E(10,000)
0	.0000	0	0	0	.0000	0	0	0
1	.0002	0	0	2	.0046	0	5	46
2	.0060	1	6	60	.0747	7	75	747
3	.0606	6	61	606	.1877	19	188	1,877
4	.2417	24	242	2,417	.2197	22	220	2,197
5	.3829	38	383	3,829	.1821	18	182	1,821
6	.2417	24	242	2,417	.1273	13	127	1,273
7	.0606	6	61	606	.0815	8	81	815
8	.0060	1	6	60	.0497	5	50	497
9	.0002	0	0	2	.0296	3	30	296
10	.0000	0	0	0	.0175	2	17	175
11					.0103	1	10	103
12					.0061	1	6	61
13					.0036	0	4	36
14					.0022	0	2	22
15					.0013	0	1	13
16					.0008	0	1	8
17					.0005	0	1	5
18					.0003	0	0	3
19					.0002	0	0	2
20					.0001	0	0	1
21					.00008	0	0	1
22					.00005	0	0	1
23					.00003	0	0	0
24					.00002	0	0	0
25					.00001	0	0	0

B. Computation of Size of Critical Mass.

Distribution	Group Size	Size of Critical Mass	Detail
Normal	100	20	1 @ 8; 6 @ 7; 12 @ 6; 1 @ 3.
Normal	1,000	17	6 @ 8; 11 @ 7.
Normal	10,000	16	2 @ 9; 13 @ 8; 1 @ 3.
Lognormal	100	15	1 @ 12; 1 @ 11; 2 @ 10; 3 @ 9; 5 @ 8; 2 @ 7; 1 @ 1.
Lognormal	1,000	9	1 @ 17; 1 @ 16; 1 @ 15; 2 @ 14; 3 @ 13; 1 @ 10.
Lognormal	10,000	7	1 @ 22; 1 @ 21; 1 @ 20; 2 @ 19; 1 @ 18; 1 @ 6.

minimum number declines slightly with the group size: to 17 for the installation with 1,000 users, and to 16 for the largest group of 10,000 members.

This pattern is more pronounced when the resource distribution is more skewed. For the moderately skewed distribution in this example, the minimum number of contributors is 15 for the smallest group, 9 for the medium-sized group, and 7 for the largest group. Extremely skewed distributions, in which some members might be willing and able to contribute 100 times more than the mean of all others, would show even more pronounced effects, so that one or two people might be able to provide the good for the whole group.

It should be clear that this pattern is not dependent on any particular distribution, but rather may arise whenever a group is heterogeneous in the sizes of its members' potential contributions. The mechanism causing the paradox is really very simple: the expected number of individuals willing and able to give at any specific contribution level will always be higher for a larger group. Since collective goods with pure jointness of supply have a fixed cost that does not vary with the size of the group enjoying the good, the greater expected number of large contributors in a larger group means that, in general, fewer people will be needed to achieve a given *total contribution* size than in a small group.

GROUP SIZE AND THE SOCIAL PROCESSES FOR COLLECTIVE ACTION

Olson is right: there are many public goods which will never be provided by individuals acting in independent isolation. However, Olson argues that, even if we allow for social processes, the group size effect would obtain, since such social processes, as well as feelings of group solidarity, are more likely to overcome the collective dilemma in "moderate" sized groups than in large ones (p. 48). This argument is seriously flawed by a floating conception of what the "group" is. When a good has jointness of supply, it is irrelevant to those who contribute how many others there are "out there" in the interest group who might benefit. When a "social" solution to the collective dilemma is required, what matters is the relationship among the possible contributors in the critical mass, not the relationship among everyone in the interest group. Paradoxically, the size of the critical mass will be smaller when the size of the interest group is larger, and social processes may be *more* beneficial in larger interest groups.

Because larger interest groups have more total resources, they are generally more likely to have the *possibility* for a successful collective action.

Especially when goods have high and "lumpy" costs (i.e. where a large minimum amount is needed to provide any of the goods such as a bridge), smaller interest groups may be simply unable to supply enough resources, no matter how well they organize. Where a larger group might need to mobilize only 5 percent of its potentially available resources to provide a good, the smaller group might require 100 percent of its resources, or more.

There are doubtless some small interest groups with the kind of social structure that would permit them to mobilize 100 percent of their members to action, and it is likely to be very exciting when it happens. But it is probably more common to see a critical mass coalesce within a larger interest group. There are costs to organizing and coordinating contributions by a number of people, and those costs are usually higher the more contributors there are involved. Thus, it will generally be much easier and cheaper to organize a collective action involving a small number of contributors from within a large interest group than one involving a larger number of contributors from within a small interest group.

Of course, it may be especially difficult and costly for the small number of potential contributors in a very large interest group to find one another and coordinate their actions. If society were organized randomly, this would always be a serious problem for collective actors. If social ties were distributed randomly across a large city, it would be unlikely that the five people who would be willing to contribute $1 million each to a geology museum, or the ten people who would be willing to devote six months of their lives to organizing a nuclear freeze campaign, would ever meet. In fact, the real world surely contains many "interests" whose distributions are essentially random, and about which collective action is very unlikely. But randomness is *not* the rule. Especially wealthy people know most of the other especially wealthy people. Potential political activists associate themselves with events and organizations expressing their political concerns. City residents who would be most harmed by a proposed expressway live near each other, in its path.

The problem of collective action is not whether it is possible to mobilize every single person who would be benefited by a collective good. It is not whether it is possible to mobilize everyone who would be willing to be mobilized. It is not even whether all the members of some organization or social network can be mobilized. Rather, the issue is whether there is some social mechanism that connects enough people who have the appropriate interests and resources so that they can act. It is whether there is an

THE PARADOX OF GROUP SIZE IN COLLECTIVE ACTION 7

organization or social network that has a *subset* of individuals who are interested and resourceful enough to provide the good when they act in concert, and whether they have sufficient social organization among themselves to act together.

In one sense, our argument is that Olson's "large group" problem is resolved by the "small group" solution. Olson is right in saying that collective action almost never takes the form of small, unnoticeable contributions from thousands or millions of isolated individuals. If everybody's interest or resources are equally small, collective action will generally not happen, no matter how big or small the interest group. Collective action arises around those interests for which there are a group of especially interested and resourceful individuals who are socially connected to one another. (For a much fuller analysis of the effects of social ties within groups, see Marwell, Oliver, and Prahl, forthcoming.)

The small number of wealthy people are able to act collectively to get what they want not because there are few of them, but because they are wealthy. Resources and interests being equal, movements on behalf of very large constituencies often are more successful than movements on behalf of tiny minorities. Large interest groups do sustain more collective action then smaller ones, when costs are equal and the individuals in the groups have comparable interest and resource levels. Resources and social organization are the problem, *not* group size. If a group is heterogeneous enough that it contains a critical mass who can make large contributions, and if those members are socially connected to one another so that they can act in concert, collective action *is* possible and *more* likely in larger groups.

Our theoretical analysis is consistent with much recent empirical scholarship on social movements. It is never the case that all women (Freeman 1983), all blacks (Morris 1981, 1984), everyone opposed to the reopening of the Three Mile Island reactor (Walsh and Warland 1983), everyone for a clean environment (Mitchell 1979), or all northern whites concerned about voting rights in the South (McAdam 1986) are mobilized, nor is the existence of a large mass of "free riders" any particular hindrance to the mobilization or success of a movement. In fact, public opinion polls identifying large pools of nonactivist adherents to a cause tend to help the cause, not hurt it. What matters for successful mobilization is that there be enough people who *are* willing to participate and who are also reachable through social-influence networks. Empirical accounts of actual social movements and movement organizations show over and over that most of the

action originates from a relatively small number of extremely active participants.

The "free rider" dilemma, correctly analyzed, is the problem of not being able to make a big enough difference in the outcome to compensate for the costs one bears. Thus understood, the theory of collective action does not predict that collective action will *never* occur, but rather that it will not take the form of small isolated contributions. Instead, the theory of collective action explains why most action comes from a relatively small number of participants who make such big contributions to the cause that they know (or think they know) they can "make a difference." In social movements, these contributions are usually time and energy, not money.

Theory and empirical research also agree in tending to discount the causal significance of the size of the aggrieved population as a direct determinant of collective action. Current research stresses the importance of social networks and organizational resources among some interested subset of the population, coupled with "political opportunities" created through party politics (e.g. McAdam 1982; Jenkins 1983). Full-time professional activists (McCarthy and Zald 1973, 1977) are also seen as important, although less so than several years ago.

Let us not, however, conclude that the masses are irrelevant for collective action. We have shown theoretically that larger groups *should be* more likely to give rise to collective action than smaller ones (given the jointness of supply of so many collective goods), and it is empirically true that very large social movements tend to arise from very large mass bases. However, undifferentiated impoverished masses do not usually support social movements. What seems to be critical is the presence of a *minority of the aggrieved population* who are well educated or especially politically conscious, who have high discretionary time, or who are economically independent of the oppressors.[7] Larger populations are likely to have larger numbers of these "unusual" members, and the size of their potential contributions is likely to be larger.

The more obvious effect of interest-group size is also important: larger populations generally have more total resources than smaller ones. This has frequently been ignored by those who are theoretically sophisticated, because it is understood that those resources do not automat-

---

[7] Perhaps we should cite Lenin on this point, as well as the social movements literature. We should stress that we are emphasizing the theoretical importance of differentiation *within* the aggrieved population, which is very different from an "external resources" argument, which has fared badly empirically (e.g. McAdam 1982; Jenkins and Eckert 1986).

8   AMERICAN SOCIOLOGICAL REVIEW

ically or easily become contributions. But one thing the small critical mass of large contributors can do is invest time, energy, and money in organizing and coordinating events that draw in and make use of small contributions. The critical mass can use preexisting organizations and networks to create the social conditions under which small contributors will participate in a march or demonstration. They can pay the overhead for large mass mailings to solicit small monetary contributions under circumstances that make the donors' costs low relative to their psychic "benefits" (see Oliver and Furman forthcoming for more discussion). The larger the total size of the interest group, the larger the potential gain from either of these strategies.

As a final note, it is important that our argument not be read only as a critique of Olson. Instead, we have tried to constructively describe *how* group size affects the prospects for collective action. Of course, the kind of cost/benefit considerations we analyze are not all that are involved in collective action. But if we understand how the cost structure of a good, and the distribution of resources and interest across the pool of people interested in that good, interact with the size of the group to produce structural constraints on the possibilities for action, we can use this information as a baseline for investigating the effects of other factors on the prospects for collective action. The time is long past for sociologists to stop debating whether free riding does or does not occur (sometimes it does and sometimes it does not) and get on with specifying the conditions that favor or hinder collective action.

REFERENCES

Chamberlin, John, 1974. "Provision of Collective Goods as a Function of Group Size." *American Political Science Review* 68:707–16.

Freeman, Jo. 1975. *The Politics of Women's Liberation.* New York: Longman.

Frohlich, Norman and Joe A. Oppenheimer. 1970. "I Get By With A Little Help From My Friends." *World Politics* 23:104–20.

Hardin, Russell. 1982. *Collective Action.* Baltimore: Johns Hopkins University Press.

Head, John G. 1974. *Public Goods and Public Welfare.* Durham, NC: Duke University Press.

Jenkins, J. Craig. 1987. "Interpreting the Stormy Sixties: Three Theories in Search of a Political Age." *Research in Political Sociology* 3:269–303.

Jenkins, J. Craig and Craig M. Eckert. 1986. "Channeling Black Insurgency: Elite Patronage and Professional Social Movement Organizations in the Development of the Black Movement." *American Sociological Review* 51:812–29.

Latane, Bibb and Steve Nida. 1981. "Ten Years of Research on Group Size and Helping." *Psychological Bulletin* 89:308–24.

Marwell, Gerald. 1970. "Comment on Scott and El-Assal." *American Sociological Review* 35:916.

Marwell, Gerald, and Pamela E. Oliver, and Ralph Prahl. Forthcoming. "A Theory of the Critical Mass. III. Social Networks and Collective Action." *American Journal of Sociology.*

McAdam, Doug. 1982. *Political Process and the Development of Black Insurgency, 1930–1970.* Chicago: University of Chicago Press.

———. 1986. "Recruitment to High-Risk Activism: The Case of Freedom Summer." *American Journal of Sociology* 92:64–90.

McCarthy, John and Mayer Zald. 1973. *The Trend of Social Movements in America: Professionalization and Resource Mobilization.* Morristown, NJ: General Learning Press.

———. 1977. "Resource Mobilization in Social Movements: A Partial Theory." *American Journal of Sociology* 82:1212–39.

McGuire, Martin C. 1974. "Group Size, Group Homogeneity, and the Aggregate Provision of a Pure Public Good Under Cournot Behavior." *Public Choice* 18:107–26.

Mitchell, Robert Cameron. 1979. "National Environmental Lobbies and the Apparent Illogic of Collective Action." Pp. 87–121 in *Collective Decision Making: Applications from Public Choice Theory,* edited by Clifford S. Russell. Baltimore: Johns Hopkins University Press for Resources for the Future.

Morris, Aldon. 1981. "Black Southern Student Sit-In Movement: An Analysis of Internal Organization. *American Sociological Review* 46 (December):744–67.

———. 1984. *The Origins of the Civil Rights Movement: Black Communities Organizing for Change.* New York: The Free Press.

Oliver, Pamela. 1980. "Rewards and Punishments as Selective Incentives for Collective Action: Theoretical Investigations." *American Journal of Sociology* 85:1356–75.

Oliver, Pamela and Mark Furman. Forthcoming. "Contradictions Between National and Local Organizational Strength: The Case of the John Birch Society." In *Organizing For Change,* edited by Bert Klandermans. Greenwich, CT: JAI Press.

Oliver, Pamela, Gerald Marwell, and Ruy Teixeira. 1985. "A Theory of the Critical Mass. I. Interdependence, Group Heterogeneity, and the Production of Collective Goods." *American Journal of Sociology* 91:522–56.

Olson, Mancur. 1965. *The Logic of Collective Action.* Cambridge, MA: Harvard University Press.

Piliavin, Jane Allyn, John Dovidia, Sam Gaertner, and Russell Clark, III. 1981. *Emergency Intervention.* New York: Academic Press.

Samuelson, Paul A. 1954. "The Pure Theory of Public Expenditure." *Review of Economics and Statistics* 36:387–89.

Scott, J.W. and M. El-Assal. 1969. "Multiversity, University Size, University Quality and Student Protest—An Empirical Study." *American Sociological Review* 34:702–9.

Spilerman, Seymour. 1970. "The Causes of Racial Disturbances: A Comparison of Alternative Explanations." *American Sociological Review* 35:627–49.

Walsh, Edward and Rex Warland. 1983. "Social Movement Involvement in the Wake of a Nuclear Accident: Activists and Free Riders in the TMI Area." *American Sociological Review* 48:764–80.

[23]

Collective Sanctions and the Creation of Prisoner's Dilemma Norms[1]

Douglas D. Heckathorn
University of Missouri—Kansas City

Social psychologists, sociologists, and economists have all proposed theories of norm emergence. In general, they view norm emergence as depending on three factors: (i) actors' preferences regarding their own behavior (*inclinations*); (ii) actors' preferences regarding the behavior of others (*regulatory interests*); and (iii) measures for enforcing norms (*enforcement resources*), such as access to sanctions and information. Whereas most studies of norm emergence have focused on inclinations or enforcement resources, this article analyzes the role of regulatory interests in norm emergence. Specifically, it analyzes systems of *collective sanctions* in which, when an individual violates or complies with a rule, not merely the individual but other members of that person's group as well are collectively punished or rewarded by an external agent. These collective sanctions give individuals an incentive to regulate one another's behavior. This paper demonstrates that when a group is subjected to collective sanctions, a variety of responses may be rational: the group may either create a secondary sanctioning system to enforce the agent's dictates, or it may revolt against the agent to destroy its sanctioning capacity. According to the proposed theoretic model, the optimal response depends quite sensitively on the group's size, internal cohesion, and related factors.

Many social groups are subject to collective sanctions, including both *collective punishment* (e.g., the military practice of punishing all recruits in a barracks for the violation of a single recruit) and *collective rewards* (e.g., bonuses for especially productive work groups). These incentives sometimes encourage group members to monitor and regulate one another's behavior and, in so doing, to create norms and enforce their compliance. Yet collective incentives can have exactly the opposite effect:

[1] An earlier version of this paper was presented at the annual meeting of the Public Choice Society, March 27–29, 1987, Tucson, Arizona. I thank Roger Carlson, James S. Coleman, Susan LoBello, Scott McNall, and two anonymous reviewers for their valuable advice and comments on this paper. Requests for reprints should be sent to Douglas D. Heckathorn, Department of Sociology, University of Missouri—Kansas City, 5100 Rockhill Road, Kansas City, Missouri 64110.

a group threatened by collective punishment, for example, could react not by complying but by attacking the agent that issues that threat. This paper analyzes collective incentive systems as N-person Prisoner's Dilemmas (PD), in which players face a threefold choice. First, they can comply with the imposed PD by participating in the creation and enforcement of conformity norms that require others to cooperate. Second, they can ignore defections and subject themselves and other group members to the threat of sanctions. Third, rather than merely play out their roles in the imposed PD game, they can seek to *destroy* that imposed PD game by attacking or escaping the agent that threatens collective punishment or withholds collective rewards. I present a stochastic rational choice model to account for this threefold choice. Collective sanctions, I show, are a potentially unstable means of behavioral control in that many of the same factors that motivate compliance may also motivate rebellion.

An explicit system of collective sanctions (CS) exists as a prominent feature of traditional societies wherein kinship governs relations among persons. As Barkun (1968, p. 20) observes, "Primitive law has long been known to be weak in concepts of individual responsibility. A law-breaking individual transforms his group into a law-breaking group, for in his dealings with others he never stands alone." For example, according to Karsden (1967, p. 311), among the Jibaros of eastern Ecuador, "The members of the same family are regarded as, so to speak, organically coherent with each other, so that one part stands for all and all for one. . . . For the deed of one member the rest are held equally responsible." Similar systems of shared responsibility have been found among the Ashanti of eastern Africa (Hoebel 1968, p. 231), the Bankutu and Fang (Driberg 1970, p. 167), in 11th-century Ireland (Cherry 1890, p. 29), and in 19th-century Albania (Hasluck 1967, p. 387).

Corporate responsibility is by no means limited to tribal societies, as the case of traditional China shows. Meijer (1971, p. 8) states, "A father would be punished if his son committed robbery, while rebellion of a son against the Emperor spelled disaster for the whole family. . . . All male members of the family over 16 years would suffer capital punishment; the other members would be given away as slaves. The property would be confiscated." According to Chen (1973, p. 10), capital punishment was sometimes inflicted more broadly: the "culprit is cut in two at the waist; his father, mother, wife, children, brothers, and sisters, all without distinction between young and old, are publicly executed."

The ambivalent effect to be expected from such a policy is clear. On the one hand, Chinese families had enhanced incentives to prevent their members from committing crimes. On the other hand, once a grievous crime had been committed, the family's incentive was to throw their lot in

Collective Sanctions

with the culprit, assisting him to avoid detection, fleeing with him, or joining in his rebellion.

Systems of corporate responsibility as stern as that of traditional China are exceptional, though not unique. For example, Hoebel (1968, p. 86) discusses a case among the Copper Eskimos where village members decide to exterminate a family to forestall a blood feud. The well-known use of reprisals against civilians by Nazi armies of occupation to avenge attacks on Nazi soldiers provides a more recent example. It has also been claimed (Chowdhury 1972, p. 104) that the Pakistani army employed similar tactics when seeking to suppress the rebellion in East Pakistan that eventually gave rise to Bangladesh. Allegedly, resisting villages were set on fire, and anyone who fled the flames was shot. In essence, then, everyone in a village was held responsible for a sniper's actions. Rather than suppress resistance, the probable effect of this tactic was to fuel support for the rebellion.

In whatever social context, any CS system entails the presence of an *agent* to which the group is responsible, an agent that is the source of either collectively administered punishments or rewards. Four types of agents are possible. First, the agent may be the *state* in its judicial role, as in traditional China. Second, the agent may be *supernatural*. For example, the Ashanti (Hoebel 1968, p. 232) believed that certain acts were so offensive to their tribal spirits that, if those acts remained unavenged, the entire tribe would be punished with plagues and crop failures.

Third, the agent may be a subgovernmental *organization*. Many instances of CS in modern societies employ an agent of this type. For example, in juvenile detention facilities, correctional officers frequently punish an entire group of inmates for the offenses of a few. If two youths get into a shoving match, for example, their entire block loses recreational privileges for that day—two hours' access to television and pool tables. As one correctional officer said to me, "That policy makes habitual culprits very unpopular with their peers." The implication is that the policy succeeds in evoking the creation of exogenous complicance norms. Similar CS systems operate in adult prisons (see Irwin 1980). Serious violations lead to "lock downs," in which prisoners are denied most privileges and remain in their cells throughout the day, and cells are subjected to thorough searches that deprive prisoners of the contraband they have accumulated. A more extreme application of CS occurred in Stalinist prisons (Dallin and Nicolaevsky 1947), where prisoner compounds earned points through work and conformity to prison rules, and allocations of food, medicine, and other essentials of life depended on the points earned by the group. For example, after an unsuccessful escape attempt, Pyotr Yakir (1972, p. 100) was told, "Do you realize that because of your escape our colony's dropped from first place down to twenty-ninth in the competition. . . ? If I let you go into the compound now, the lads will tear you apart."

The use of collective punishment in U.S. military boot camps (Gilham 1982) provides a third example of organizational CS. Gilham reports that recruits whose violations have frequently provoked the punishment of their peers are sometimes beaten in an institution known as the "blanket party." The remarkable speed with which exogenous (i.e., external agent–motivated) compliance norms emerge in this setting is indicative of the potential effectiveness of CS as a technique of control. Additional and more mundane examples of organizational CS include profit-sharing plans employed by many corporations and rewards directed to especially productive work groups. Democratically organized producer cooperatives constitute a special example of organizational CS in that the agent is the group itself in its role as a collective decision-making body.

Fourth, the agent of collective responsibility may be *normative*. Here, collective incentives are administered not by the agent of a spiritual, governmental, or organizational entity but by a more diffuse agent. For example, in contemporary Japan and India, an individual's life chances, including marital and employment prospects, are importantly affected by family reputation. A person whose criminality, alcoholism, or other deficiencies bring shame on his family causes his family to lose esteem in the community and thereby punishes the family collectively. In contrast, a person whose conspicuously praiseworthy accomplishments bring honor to the family enhances the life prospects of other family members, thereby collectively rewarding them. Similarly, in certain West African tribes, tendencies toward theft are believed to be hereditary. Consequently, a known thief brings suspicion on his entire family and makes them less attractive marital partners; so too, in certain cultures, insanity is considered hereditary.

When CS is normative, or otherwise, the effects on compliance are potentially ambivalent. On the one hand, families are given enhanced incentives to control their members. Yet the potential also exists for the culprit's group becoming trapped in the deviant role, thereby enhancing rather than reducing deviance.

A unique feature of CS systems, as opposed to other enforcement systems, should also be noted. It concerns the relationship between monitoring by the agent (formal monitoring) and monitoring by group members (informal monitoring). Generally, informal monitoring is much more effective than formal monitoring (Hechter 1984, p. 175). Individuals generally know more about the behavior of their peers than does any external agent, except for supernatural agents, which are usually assumed to be omniscient (see Brams 1983). Consequently, when CS-based control suc-

Collective Sanctions

ceeds in creating compliance norms, the agent can potentially exercise extraordinarily thorough control over group behavior. For, then, formal monitoring is supplemented by the more effective informal monitoring system.

COLLECTIVE SANCTIONS AND PRISONER'S DILEMMA NORMS

The Prisoner's Dilemma has become the paradigm for cases where collectively irrational outcomes result from individually rational actions (Rapoport and Chammah 1965; Rapoport 1983). Social situations of this type are common and include the production of public and semipublic goods (Hardin 1982; Komorita 1976), constitutional contracts (Buchanan 1975; Taylor 1982; Heckathorn and Maser 1987*a*), and social norms that prohibit exploitative or predatory behavior (Ullmann-Margalit 1977). In these systems, universal cooperation is preferred to universal defection. Yet the common interest in cooperation (e.g., cooperation to produce a public good) coexists with individual interests in defection (e.g., the temptation to free ride by allowing others to bear the costs of producing public goods).

The initial studies of the PD focused primarily on the one-shot game and emphasized the *fragility* of cooperation in these systems. Numerous small-group experiments (Rapoport 1983) explored the problems of sustaining cooperation. For example, they showed that in the absence of preplay communication, defection is highly probable. Similarly, following the publication of Mancur Olson's (1965) *The Logic of Collective Action* and the restatement of his argument in game-theoretic terms (Hardin 1971), a voluminous literature has arisen documenting the obstacles to cooperation in the N-person PD as groups increase in size. In the one-shot game, the means available with which to suppress defection and ensure cooperation are quite limited. As a result, the solutions to the dilemma frequently invoked centralized authority, analogous to Hobbes's sovereign.

Recently, the focus of analysis has shifted away from the one-shot game to the iterated game and other sequential games (Axelrod 1986; Schotter 1981; Opp 1982; Coleman 1986), and that in turn has yielded a growing emphasis on the *robustness* of cooperation in the PD. Even in the absence of centralized authority, social groups ranging from oligopolies with price-leader systems to informal groups with norms prohibiting theft frequently succeed in establishing stable patterns of cooperation despite PD-type incentives to defect. In the real world, cooperation is neither rare nor fragile. Sustained patterns of cooperation frequently arise even under what might appear to be exceedingly inhospitable circumstances. For example, Axelrod (1984) showed that the informal truces soldiers arrived

American Journal of Sociology

at during World War I's trench warfare can be fruitfully viewed as involving cooperation in an iterated PD situation. In such cases, no centralized authority is required to ensure cooperation.

The robustness of cooperation in the iterated PD results from the availability of *normative* mechanisms for enforcing cooperation without resort to centralized authority. These regimes of *decentralized* control generally involve the emergence of systems of reciprocity wherein cooperation is conditional on others' cooperation. Cooperation tends to be stable in groups of moderate size and reasonable cohesion since the short-term gains from defection are outweighed by the long-term costs of disrupting an established pattern of cooperation.

This paper focuses on the emergence of PD norms of a highly particular sort, termed *collective sanction* (CS) norms. All norms may be seen as having a motivational basis in what are here termed "regulatory interests." The CS norms are norms whose regulatory interests derive significantly from collective sanctions, either collective punishment or collective reward. These include cases where collective sanctions reinforce regulatory interests in a preexisting PD, cases where no regulatory interests would have existed in the absence of collective sanctions, and cases where collective sanctions reverse the polarity of regulatory interests. I analyze situations where PDs are *created* as an instrument of behavioral control or *destroyed* in opposition to that control. More specifically, I show first that when an agent employs collective incentives such as collective punishments to control a group, that has the effect of thrusting the group into an iterated PD game. Members then face a threefold choice. As in any PD, they can either cooperate in the imposed PD by complying to avoid sanctions for themselves and others or defect in the imposed PD by ignoring the threat of sanctions in subsequent iterations of the PD game. Members also have an additional option that does not exist in the classical PD: to attack the imposed PD, seeking to destroy the agent's ability to impose collective punishment or withhold collective rewards. Hence, members of the group may refuse merely to play in the game served up to them by the agent controlling collective sanctions. Instead, they may act directly against the agent to deprive it of control of collective sanctions and thereby change the game that they play.

The CS norms are of special theoretic interest for several reasons. First, they are ideally suited to observing norm emergence outside the small-group laboratory. Whereas many norms, such as those prohibiting theft, have ancient histories, CS norms emerge in a pristine, less complicated form, so the process of norm emergence and enforcement can be observed from the very beginning. In contrast, in the case of other norms, ascertaining whether behavioral conformity results from internalization of the norm, deterrence, or mere habit is frequently impossible. Second, CS

Collective Sanctions

norms provide a link between the macro- and microsocial levels and between formal and informal social control. They constitute a hybrid the study of which may help to illuminate that link. Finally, CS norms have been created in a diverse range of contexts, depending on the nature of the agent and the group subject to the agent's sanctions. Separate literatures have arisen specific to each context. For example, there have been extensive discussions of systems of corporate responsibility in tribal societies (Driberg 1970), schools (Slavin 1983; Bronfenbrenner 1970), revolution and counterrevolution (Rapoport 1984), and prisons (Irwin 1980). Analysis of CS norms can help to integrate these literatures theoretically.

CREATION OF A PRISONER'S DILEMMA THROUGH COLLECTIVE SANCTIONS

The PD arises from a conflict between each actor's preferences regarding his or her own behavior (the actor's *inclinations*) and preferences regarding the behavior of others (*regulatory interests*). Whereas strictly personal behavior is motivated by inclinations, when viewed from a rational-choice perspective, the creation and enforcement of norms are motivated by regulatory interests. Consequently, the analysis of norms requires an examination of the origins of regulatory interests. In other words, the question must be asked, Why do people prefer to control one another?

Many regulatory interests derive from fundamental preferences, such as the desire for physical safety, on which Hobbes focused. He made much of the point that even the strongest person can be killed if caught unawares by someone much weaker. Therefore, even the strongest possess an interest in regulating indiscriminate violence.

Other regulatory interests may derive from collective sanctions. These give social actors a stake in regulating one another's behavior so as to prevent others from triggering collective punishment or the withholding of collective rewards. By way of illustration, consider figure 1's two-player collective-punishment system. Figure 1*A* depicts the system *before* the institution of collective sanctions. Each player chooses between strategy 1 and 2, where the former awards a utility of 6 and the latter a utility of 13. Therefore, each player prefers strategy 2 to strategy 1; that is, they are both inclined toward strategy 2. Furthermore, this game contains no interdependence or conflict of interest between the players because the utility awarded to each is not affected by the other's choice. The players possess no regulatory interests.

The introduction of collective sanctions by an external agent that seeks to control behavior in the game may profoundly alter this situation. That is illustrated by figures 1*B* and 1*C*, which depict alternative systems *after* the imposition of collective sanctions that vary in the magnitudes of their

American Journal of Sociology

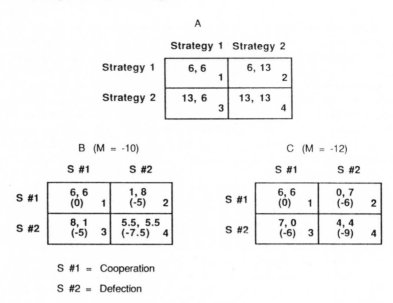

S #1 = Cooperation

S #2 = Defection

FIG. 1.—Creation of an exogenous Prisoner's Dilemma through collective sanctions. *A*, Game where strategy 1 awards each player 6 units of utility, and strategy 2 awards each player a utility of 13. This game's equilibrium is for each player to choose strategy 2. *B*, *C*, Game as modified by collective sanctions, where the probability of detection of each violation is 1/2 and the disutility of punishment is 10 in fig. *B* and 12 in fig. *C*. The number in parentheses in each cell is the expected utility of punishment: 0 for zero violations, −5 or −6 for one violation, and −7.5 or −9 for two violations. Note that both games are Prisoner's Dilemmas since each player's order of preference is: unilateral defection (cell 3 for row, cell 2 for column); cooperation (cell 1); mutual defection (cell 4); and finally unilateral cooperation (cell 2 for row, cell 3 for column).

disutility. The collective sanction is milder in figure 1*B*, where the disutility of punishment is 10, and more extreme in figure 1*C*, where the disutility of punishment is 12. In each figure, it is assumed that if *either* player took action 2, this would constitute a violation for which *both* would be punished if the violation were detected. For example, if the probability of detection of each violation is 0.5, then if both choose strategy 2 and the detections of violations are independent, the probability of detection is 0.75. Thus, if the disutility of punishment is 10, as in figure 1*B*, the cost to each actor of a single violation is 5, and the cost of two violations is 7.5. As a result, each actor acquires a regulatory interest, a preference that the other *not* choose strategy 2. The game resulting from that sanction is a PD since each player's order of preference from best to worst is: unilateral

Collective Sanctions

defection (choosing strategy 2 when the other chooses strategy 1), cooperation (both choose strategy 1), mutual defection (both choose strategy 2), and finally unilateral cooperation (choosing strategy 1 when the other chooses 2). In addition, the players prefer cooperation to a mixture of unilateral defection and unilateral cooperation (e.g., in fig. 1B's game, $6 > [8 + 1]/2$).

The creation of regulatory interests through collective sanctions sets the stage for a secondary "enforcement game" (that may or may not also constitute a PD game), in which each player makes the threefold choice: to participate in creating compliance norms to prevent others from violating the agent's dictates, that is, *compliance;* to ignore the agent, that is, *passivity;* or to seek to destroy the agent's capacity to administer sanctions, that is, *revolt.* This paper focuses on play in this secondary enforcement game.

Given the range of choices available to a group subject to CS, the mere creation of a PD situation through collective sanctions obviously does not suffice to create compliance norms. First, the group must possess internal sanctioning resources that are ample enough to allow it to create and enforce norms. That is, the group cannot be wholly atomized. Furthermore, the group must possess whatever additional internal sanctioning resources are required to resolve a second-order free-rider problem. That is, the benefits of cooperation in a PD are often attainable only through the costly process of creating an enforcement system. Therefore, individuals can potentially benefit from second-order free riding, in which they allow others to bear the costs of creating and maintaining that enforcement system (see Oliver 1980; Oliver and Marwell 1988; Yamagishi 1986). Consequently, sustained cooperation in a PD may require a dual level enforcement system: a primary enforcement system consisting of norms that sanction free riding and one that Axelrod (1986, p. 1100) terms "metanorms," that is, norms that mandate active participation in the norm enforcement system. (For an analysis of the second-order free-rider problem in CS systems, see Heckathorn [1988].)

This paper focuses not on the mechanisms by which enforcement systems are created but rather on structural factors that either inhibit or facilitate the creation of such systems. Consider by way of illustration the contrast between the games depicted in figures 1B and 1C. In the latter game, the disutility of punishment is increased from 10 to 12. That has two theoretically significant effects. First, it reduces inclinations to defect. Each individual's gain from unilateral defection declines 50%, from $8 - 6 = 2$ to $7 - 6 = 1$. All else equal, a weaker enforcement system therefore would suffice to deter defections. Second, the increase in the strength of collective punishment bolsters regulatory interests, for example, the cost of a single defection increases from 5 to 6, and the cost of

American Journal of Sociology

two defections increases from 7.5 to 9. Thus, individuals' incentives to bear the costs of participating in the creation of an enforcement system are enhanced, thereby facilitating the resolution of the second-order enforcement problem. Consequently, all else equal, a weaker secondary enforcement system would suffice to resolve the second-order free-riding problem. These conclusions, it should be noted, remain valid whether one adopts what Yamagishi (1986, p. 111) terms the "instrumental cooperation" approach of Olson (1965), the "elementary cooperation" approach of Brubaker (1975), or Yamagishi's own synthetic "structural goal/expectation" approach. For whether cooperation results from the creation of a sanctioning system to deter defections or the creation of mutual trust through reciprocity, cooperation is facilitated either by weaker inclinations to defect or stronger regulatory interests.

In sum, strengthening collective sanctions may facilitate creation of compliance norms in two analytically distinct ways. It both reduces inclinations to defect and strengthens regulatory interests. Therefore, whereas comparatively mild collective sanctions may suffice to create CS norms in groups that are abundantly endowed with internal enforcement resources, stronger collective sanctions may be required in groups that are more atomized. It might seem, therefore, that from the agent's standpoint the optimal strategy is to maximize the severity of collective sanctions to ensure that an ample motivational basis exists to support the creation of compliance norms. However, as is shown below, such may not necessarily be the case. For, while more extreme sanctions strengthen incentives to create compliance norms, they also increase incentives to revolt.

A FORMAL MODEL OF COLLECTIVE SANCTION SYSTEMS

The dynamics of CS systems are relatively complex. In some cases, they induce the rapid creation and enforcement of compliance norms, as in the U.S. boot camps described by Gilham (1982). Here, the actors comply with the agent's dictates. In other cases, collective sanctions backfire, provoking revolt rather than compliance, as in Bangladesh. Finally, actors may remain passive, neither revolting nor participating in the creation of compliance norms. For example, a group may become discouraged and eventually abandon its efforts to earn collective rewards, or it may become resigned to the inevitability of collective punishment.

This section presents a mathematical model for CS systems that employs a rational-choice approach (Hechter 1983) to explain that threefold choice. Consistent with social exchange theory (Blau 1964; Emerson 1976), individuals are seen as striving to maximize anticipated utility within informational and institutional constraints.

Collective Sanctions

Payoffs from Passivity versus Compliance

In a CS system, the payoff from remaining passive depends in part on the probability that sanctions will be administered if actors neither revolt nor comply. In the absence of control, let an actor i's probability of *violation* be V_i, and the probability of that violation's *detection* be D_i. The probability of i's committing a detected violation and thereby triggering *sanctions* S_i is then $V_i \times D_i$; that is,

$$S_i = V_i \times D_i. \tag{1}$$

Thus, administration of sanctions requires the conjunction of two events, a violation, V, and detection of that violation, D.

In a system of collective sanctions, all members of a group are responsible for the offenses of any other member. Sanctions are avoided only if all group members conform, committing no violations, or apparently conform, committing no detected violations. Therefore, the probability of the group's being sanctioned is the probability that one or more members will trigger sanctions. In a group of N members, the probability that at least one actor will cause the group to be sanctioned, S, is

$$S = 1 - (1 - S_1) \times (1 - S_2) \times (1 - S_3) \times \ldots \times (1 - S_N), \tag{2}$$

or, equivalently, in expanded form,

$$S = 1 - (1 - V_1 \times D_1) \times (1 - V_2 \times D_2) \times \ldots \times (1 - V_N \times D_N). \tag{3}$$

In a homogeneous group (i.e., a group where violations and detection probabilities are independent and uniform across all actors, such that for any actors i and j, $V_i = V_j$, and $D_i = D_j$), equation (3) reduces to

$$S = 1 - (1 - V \times D)^N. \tag{4}$$

Though this homogeneity assumption may appear implausible, equation (4) is also subject to an alternative interpretation, where $(1 - V \times D)$ is the geometric mean of actors' probabilities of apparently conforming to the agent's dictates. This in turn is a function of the *proportion* of violators in the group, V, and the *proportion* of violations that would be detected, D. Then S expresses, as before, the probability of the group's being sanctioned.

Compliance in a CS system yields benefits deriving from the reductions in the probability of group sanctions brought about by normative control. Let C_{ij} be the control of actor i by actor(s) j, defined as the *proportional reduction* in actor i's violation probability (V_i) brought about because of j's control. Here, i and j may represent either individual actors or sets of actors. Three distinct cases can be distinguished. First, if i and j are individuals, C_{ij} serves as an indicator of interpersonal power. Second, if j

American Journal of Sociology

is an individual and i is the rest of the group, C_{ij} represents individual actor j's control over the other group members. This latter term is significant in assessing the *marginal gain* available to actor j from participating in the creation and maintenance of a secondary sanctioning system. Hence, it affects the actor's incentive to comply by participating in sanctioning rather than to engage in second-order free riding by remaining passive. Third, if i is an individual and j the rest of the group, C_{ij} serves as an indicator of the group's behavioral control over i. That is significant in assessing the group's degree of normative control over individuals, which is the fundamental focus of this paper.

More formally, where V_i is i's probability of violation before j's control attempt and C_{ij} is j's control over i, then i's violation probability subsequent to control V_i' is

$$V_i' = V_i \times (1 - C_{ij}). \tag{5}$$

For example, if i's violation probability is X, and j's degree of control is 3/4, i's violation probability is reduced to $X \times (1 - 3/4) = X/4$.

The degree of control among actors (C) can be expected to vary as a function of the sanctions controlled by each, the capability of each to monitor the other's behavior, and related factors. In groups that are highly cohesive, actors' abilities to influence one another's behavior are great, and the mean value of C approaches one; whereas in atomized groups actors' abilities to influence one another are limited, and the mean value of C approaches zero. That reduction in violative acts, in turn, diminishes the probability of sanctions, making punishment less probable or reward more probable. Expressed formally, the probability of sanctions subsequent to control, S', is given by substituting V' for V in equation (4); that is,

$$S' = 1 - [1 - (V' \times D)]^N, \tag{6}$$

or equivalently, in expanded form,

$$S' = 1 - \{1 - [V \times (1 - C) \times D]\}^N. \tag{7}$$

As specified by this expression, the probability of sanctions after control diminishes to zero if control is total, that is, if $C = 1$, $S' = 0$. Where group members can totally control one another, they can then suppress all violations and eliminate the possibility of sanctions. However, in groups where control is imperfect (i.e., $C < 1$), the reduction in violations is less, so the probability of sanctions is correspondingly greater.

The payoff to an actor from participating in the creation of a collective sanction–based, normative-control system depends on three factors: (i) the reduction in the probability of sanctions brought about by control, that is, $S - S'$; (ii) the magnitude of the sanctions, M; and finally (iii) the

Collective Sanctions

costs of control, CC, including the direct and indirect costs of normative control attempts[2] (where the latter may in the iterated game include the cost to the actor of the loss of opportunities to defect if the actor's control attempts provoke efforts by others to prevent his defection). In a collec-

[2] The cost of control (CC) may be seen as having two distinguishable components. First, exercising control over other people requires monitoring performance and access to sanctions that can reward compliance or punish noncompliance. These require consumption of valued resources, including opportunity costs. Such costs may be termed the *resource costs of control* (RCC). Second, if the controlling actor has a preexisting nonzero regulatory interest (i.e., a regulatory interest before any changes wrought by the imposition of collective sanctions), that change in the target actor's behavior affects the controlling actor. For example, the controlling actor gains if control suppresses behavior for which he possesses a prohibitory interest (i.e., a negative regulatory interest) and loses if control suppresses behavior for which he possesses a promotional interest (i.e., a positive regulatory interest). In addition, these costs are *contingent* on the efficacy of behavioral control since the controlling actor's utility is affected only to the extent that the other's behavior is actually altered. These may be termed the *contingent costs of control* (CCC). The ultimate cost of control, CC, is, therefore, the sum of the resource and contingent costs of control, i.e.,

$$CC = RCC + CCC. \tag{a}$$

The contingent costs depend on two factors: first, as noted above, the actor's preexisting *regulatory interests* (RI); second, the actor's ability to affect the target's behavior, which, in turn, depends on the actor's degree of control (C) and the target's violative propensities (V). These functional interdependencies can be more formally stated as follows. Recall from eq. (5) that, when control is exercised, the target's probability of violation is changed from V to $V' = V \times (1 - C)$. Assuming von Neumann–Morgenstern utilities, the expected utility of that change is $RI \times (V' - V)$. Equivalently, the *cost* of that change is $-RI \times (V' - V)$. Thus, the expression for the contingent costs of control (CCC) is

$$CCC = -RI \times (V' - V). \tag{b}$$

Therefore, substituting eq. (b) into eq. (a) above, the expression for the ultimate costs of control, CC, can be expanded as follows:

$$CC = RCC - RI \times (V' - V), \tag{c}$$

or, in expanded form from eq. (5),

$$CC = RCC - RI \times [V \times (1 - C) - V]. \tag{d}$$

By algebraic manipulation, this expression reduces to

$$CC = RCC + RI \times V \times C. \tag{e}$$

In this expression, a positive relationship exists between the costs of control, CC, and both the resource costs of control, RCC, and regulatory interests, RI. Its relation to V and C can be either positive or negative, depending on the polarity of RI. This equation has significant implications for understanding the relationship between preexisting regulatory interests and CS-based control. For example, the positive relationship between RI and CC suggests that, when regulatory interests are negative, as in the case where the initial game corresponds to a PD, CS-based control is facilitated because the costs of intragroup control are reduced. The agent's collective sanctions then serve to reinforce the preexisting common interest in deterring defection. In

547

American Journal of Sociology

tive punishment system, the expression for the expected net utility[3] from compliance versus passivity, that is, the *gain from compliance, Gc,* is

$$Gc = M \times (S' - S) - CC. \tag{8}$$

Equivalently, in expanded form,

---

contrast, when actors' regulatory interests are positive, CS-based control becomes more problematic. For compliance requires actors to suppress behaviors that they would instead prefer to promote. These points are further discussed under hypothesis 2 below. To facilitate the exposition and presentation of the formal model of CS systems, in the balance of this paper it will be assumed, unless otherwise stated, that actors lack initial regulatory interests (i.e., $RI = 0$) and hence that the cost of control consists solely of resource costs (i.e., $CC = RCC$).

[3] The expression for gain from compliance over passivity (Gc) can be derived more rigorously using von Neumann–Morgenstern expected utilities. The expected utility from passivity is a function of two factors. First, it depends on the actor's decision to cooperate or defect in the original game (e.g., to select strategy 1 or 2 in fig. 1's game). Let Us be that utility, i.e., the utility awarded by cooperation or defection. Second, it depends on the magnitude and probability of sanctions from the agent. The actor receives punishment M with probability S and escapes punishment with probability $1 - S$. Hence, the expected utility from passivity, Up, is

$$Up = [(Us + M) \times S] + [Us \times (1 - S)]. \tag{f}$$

The actor's utility from compliance, Uc, can be derived in a similar manner by substituting the probability of sanctions subsequent to compliance (S') for that probability before compliance (S) in the above expression and deducting the cost of control, CC; i.e.,

$$Uc = [(Us + M - CC) \times S'] + [(Us - CC) \times (1 - S')]. \tag{g}$$

The gain from compliance over passivity (Gc) is the difference between these two utilities; i.e.,

$$Gc = Uc - Up, \tag{h}$$

or, equivalently, in expanded form from eqq. (f) and (g) above,

$$Gc = [(Us + M - CC) \times S' + (Us - CC) \times (1 - S')]$$
$$- [(Us + M) \times S + Us \times (1 - S)]. \tag{i}$$

By algebraic manipulation, this expression reduces to

$$Gc = M \times (S' - S) - CC, \tag{j}$$

which is identical with eq. (8)'s expression for Gc. Note that the actor's utility from either cooperating or defecting in the original game (Us) *cancels out* of the expression for gain from conformity (Gc). This result, a theorem of collective sanctions, states that the actor's inclinations to cooperate or defect in the original game are irrelevant to the decision to comply or remain passive in the secondary exogenous normative control game on which this paper focuses. It is important to note, however, that this result does *not* imply that the structure of the initial game is irrelevant to the gain from compliance in the subsequent CS game. For recall, as was shown in n. 2, that an actor's regulatory interests (RI) affect the costs of control (CC), which in turn affect gain from compliance, Gc. Thus, an actor's gains from compliance are determined not by his inclinations in the original game but only by his regulatory interests.

Collective Sanctions

$$Gc = M \times \{(1 - V \times D)^N - [1 - V \times (1 - C) \times D]^N\} - CC. (9)$$

A rational actor chooses compliance over passivity if the gain from compliance, Gc, is positive. In addition, the stronger the incentive to comply, the more stable the CS system can be expected to be. This leads to several conclusions about the conditions under which CS serves as a potentially effective system of social control. Partial differentiation of equation (9) reveals that the gains from compliance over passivity, Gc, are: HYPOTHESIS 1. Positively related to the strength of the agent's sanction, M, (i.e., $dGc/dM > 0$); HYPOTHESIS 2. Negatively related to the cost of control, CC (i.e., $dGc/dCC < 0$); and HYPOTHESIS 3. Positively related to the degree of intragroup control, C (i.e., $dGc/dC > 0$). According to the first hypothesis, CS-based control fails if the agent's sanctions are too weak. For example, an agent who promises rewards counted in pennies will be ignored unless the costs of compliance are small, whereas an agent who threatens death or other grave consequences makes passivity untenable. However, as will be shown below, an agent who employs strong sanctions enhances not only incentives to choose compliance over passivity but also incentives to revolt. Thus, from the agent's standpoint, strong sanctions—particularly strong punishments—may be counterproductive.

According to the second hypothesis, CS-based control fails if the cost of intragroup control, CC, is too high. For example, CS control may fail in geographically dispersed groups where monitoring costs are high. A further implication is that CS-based control is facilitated if it reinforces preexisting regulatory interests in the group, for compliance then serves not only the agent but also the regulatory interests of group members. The effect is to reduce the cost of intragroup control (see n. 2). For example, if the preexisting situation corresponds to a PD, the regulatory interest of group members is the preference that others cooperate rather than defect. The group may then welcome the intervention of an agent that employs collective sanctions to promote cooperation. (For an analysis of the "demand for intervention" in PD situations where internal sanctioning resources are inadequate, see Heckathorn and Maser [1987b].)

Furthermore, hypotheses 2 and 3 suggest that CS is most effective when applied to socially cohesive groups. The frequency and intensity of interactions in cohesive groups create opportunities for informal monitoring and the exercise of influence, thereby enhancing intragroup control, C, and reducing the costs of that control, CC. In such groups, the "weight of the future" (Axelrod 1984) looms heavily since players anticipate much future interaction.

In contrast, in a highly atomized system, CS is less effective as a control technique. For example, in a study of the conditions under which

American Journal of Sociology

cooperative incentives in the classroom increase student achievement, Slavin (1983, p. 441) found that such incentives alone "are not sufficient to increase student achievement . . . the performance of each group member must be clearly visible and quantifiable to the other group members." Similarly, this hypothesis is consistent with the observation that familial CS is most prevalent in traditional societies where kinship governs most social relations, and hence the degree of control exercised by the family is great. In modern, more atomized societies, the significance of kinship is less, and familial CS is correspondingly less prevalent.

A second setting in which the theoretic requirements for CS are present, even in otherwise quite atomized contemporary societies, is in custodial and quasi-custodial settings, for example, prisons, juvenile group homes, mental hospitals, military boot camps, and schools. As was seen above, these are indeed settings in which CS continues to be routinely applied, frequently with great success.

Whereas the first three hypotheses express simple unidirectional (i.e., monotonic) relationships, the relationship between gain from compliance over passivity and other system parameters is more complex. For example, figure 2 depicts the relationship between Gc and group size for an illustrative CS system. As is apparent on inspection, compliance gains are greatest for a group of about five members, and incentives to conform are weaker in both larger and smaller groups. In systems of more than 11 or fewer than two members, the gains from compliance are negative, indicating that rational actors would choose passivity over compliance. Clearly, group size is a potent determinant of the effectiveness of CS-based social control.

An effective system of CS requires a *minimum* group size because, if the group is too small, the probability of sanctions even in the absence of control becomes so remote, so insignificant, that its further reduction does not justify the costs entailed in exercising control, CC.

A CS system breaks down in the sense that gains from compliance over passivity become negative above a *maximum* group size for somewhat similar theoretic reasons. If control is imperfect ($C < 1$), at least some violative inclinations are present ($V > 0$), and detection capabilities exist ($D > 0$); then as N becomes indefinitely large, S' approaches one. Sanctions become inevitable as group size is increased. Therefore, a point necessarily exists at which sanctions have become so highly probable that the control attempt's costs (CC) fail to justify any scant reduction in the probability of punishment ($S - S'$) it produces. Thus, exercising intragroup control becomes no longer rational.

The implication is that effective CS systems are necessarily limited in size. However, the extent of that limitation depends on a number of factors, three of which are readily apparent from hypotheses 1–3. Max-

Collective Sanctions

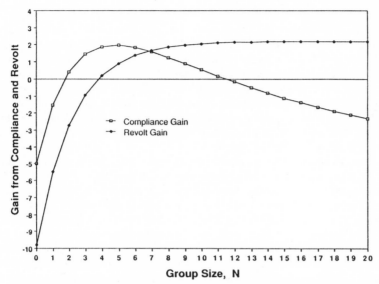

FIG. 2.—Gains from compliance (*Gc*) and revolt (*Gr*) as a function of system size (*N*) in a representative collective sanction system with a magnitude of punishment, $M = -12$; proportion of violators, $V = 0.4$; intragroup control, $C = 0.8$; costs of control, $CC = 5$; detection of violations, $D = 0.9$; vulnerability of the agent, $VA = 0.6$; and revolt cost, $R = 5$. Note that whereas the gain from revolt is a monotonically increasing function of size, the gain from compliance is positive only in groups of 2–11 members. Revolt is preferred to compliance in groups of seven or more members.

imum, stable CS system size is positively related to the strength of the agent's sanction, M, and to the degree of intragroup control, C, and negatively related to the costs of that control, CC.[4]

Furthermore, maximum effective CS system size is negatively related

[4] The optimum size for a CS system, *Nopt*, defined as the size that maximizes the group members' incentives to choose conformity over passivity (i.e., max[*Gc*]) can be computed as follows: First, differentiate *Gc* (eq. [9]) with respect to *N*, yielding *dGc/dN*; i.e.,

$$\frac{dGc}{dN} = M \times \{(1 - V \times D)^N \times \log (1 - V \times D) - [1 - V \times (1 - C) \times D]^N$$

$$\times \log[1 - V \times (1 - C) \times D]\}. \qquad (k)$$

This gives the slope of the *Gc* curve. Then, set *dGc/dN* equal to zero, since *Gc* is maximal when the slope of that curve is zero (horizontal). Finally, solve for *N*. This procedure yields the expression for optimum group size, *Nopt*:

$$Nopt = \frac{\log\{\log(1 - V \times D) / \log[1 - V \times (1 - C) \times D]\}.}{\log\{[1 - V \times (1 - C) \times D] / (1 - V \times D)\}} \qquad (l)$$

American Journal of Sociology

to the propensity for violation in the group, V, and the detection capability, D. The dynamics involved are intuitively clear. For example, the greater the propensities for violations in a group, the earlier will come the point at which the capacity to contain violations normatively is overtaxed by an increase in the group's size. Similarly, the greater the capability of the agent to detect violations, the earlier will come the point at which the capacity of normative control to protect the group from sanctions becomes overtaxed by an increase in the group's size. Thus, ironically, too much strict monitoring may prove counterproductive for the agent. This point is further discussed below.

The relations between maximum effective CS system size and other system parameters can be summarized as follows: HYPOTHESIS 4. The maximum CS system size for which group members possess incentives to choose compliance over passivity is positively related to sanction strength, M, and the degree of intragroup control, C, and negatively related to the costs of control, CC, violative propensities, V, and the agent's detection capabilities, D. This hypothesis that effective CS systems are bounded in size is consistent with the empirical observation that such groups are seldom large. For example, they frequently consist of nuclear or coresidential extended families, as in traditional China, or custodial groups, as in prisons and boot camps. An important further reason for the characteristically small size of effective CS systems, is that the degree of intragroup control (C) generally declines as group size increases (i.e., dC/dN is generally negative). That, in turn (consistent with hypothesis 3 above), reduces CS system effectiveness as size increases. Hence, two independent mechanisms serve to limit the size of groups in which CS serves as an effective means of behavioral control.

To be sure, not all effective CS-based control systems are small; some have members numbering in the thousands. Yet even these apparently anomalous systems are explicable by the dynamics I have just described. For example, the segmentary lineage system of the Nuer (Howell 1954) encompasses hundreds of thousands of people in a hierarchical system of six distinct levels (Scott 1976, p. 608). The lowest level consists of homesteads made up of the huts of close kinsmen who are collectively responsible for their actions toward members of other homesteads in their hamlet. Members of a hamlet are in turn jointly responsible for their behavior toward members of other hamlets in the village. Similarly, villagers are responsible for their behavior toward residents of other villages in their district. Districts in turn combine to form tertiary tribal segments; these

---

For example, when (1) is applied to fig. 2's CS system, where $V = .4$, $C = .8$, and $D = .9$, $Nopt = 4.81$. Partial differentiation of this expression shows that $Nopt$ is a decreasing function of V and D and an increasing function of C.

Collective Sanctions

then combine to form the tribe's two primary segments. The advantage of such a structure is that it reduces the number of collectively responsible entities at each hierarchical level. For example, a district-level dispute occurs not among hundreds of persons but rather among the handful of villages composing the district.

Other sizable yet effective CS-based control groups employ additional means to contain the potentially destructive effects of size. For example, collectivist organizations (Rothschild-Whitt 1979) are highly selective in recruitment, requiring not only technical competence but also compatibility with the goals of the organization and successful completion of a probationary period of employment, all measures that can be understood as efforts to reduce violative propensities in the group. In addition, collectivist organizations place great explicit emphasis on social cohesion and other symbolic rewards mediated by the group while downplaying material rewards, all of which appear as efforts to enhance intragroup control.

The Mondragon system of producer cooperatives (Johnson and Whyte 1977) also manifests a clear recognition of the potentially disruptive effects of excessive size. Growth occurs not through the enlargement of existing cooperatives but through the creation of new cooperatives through a process resembling fission. That is, successful cooperatives do not necessarily grow larger; they give rise to new independent cooperatives. In addition, these producer cooperatives are quite selective in recruitment. Let us now turn to a consideration of the third alternative choice that is available to a member of a CS system: revolt.

Payoffs from Revolt

Like compliance, revolt against the agent in a CS system involves both prospective benefits and costs. The benefits stem from the ability of a successful revolt to reduce the probability that the agent will be able to administer punishment. Whether those benefits will be realized depends on the vulnerability of the agent, VA, defined as the probability of the revolt's success. If the revolt fails (an event with probability $1 - VA$), the agent retains the ability to administer sanctions. So in essence revolt changes the probability of sanctions from S to $1 - VA$, and that may benefit group members if S exceeds $1 - VA$. However, revolt also entails costs, R, including costs of resources expended during the revolt and the costs of harsher sanctions that the agent makes contingent on revolt (of course, these latter costs are discounted depending on the agent's vulnerability).[5] In sum, revolt changes the probability of sanctions (M) from S to

[5] The cost of revolt (R) can be seen as having two distinguishable components. First, there are noncontingent costs intrinsic to revolt, e.g., the opportunity and other *resource costs of revolt* (RCR) entailed in revolt. Second, revolt may involve contingent

American Journal of Sociology

$1 - VA$ at the cost of R, so in a collective punishment system the *gain from revolt over passivity,*[6] *Gr,* is $M \times (1 - VA - S)$, less R; that is,

$$Gr = M \times (1 - VA - S) - R. \tag{10}$$

---

costs, such as harsher sanctions imposed by the agent if the revolt fails. Where H is the greater disutility of these harsher sanctions, and $1 - VA$ the probability of the revolt's failure, the expected disutility of this increase in the magnitude of punishment is $H \times (1 - VA)$. The cost of revolt is then the sum of its noncontingent and contingent costs; i.e.,

$$R = RCR + H \times (1 - VA). \tag{m}$$

Note that the effect of these contingent costs is to establish an interdependence between the agent's vulnerability and the cost of revolt. For example, if an agent employs the threat of harsher sanctions to deter revolt, and if that agent then becomes more vulnerable, the effect is to reduce the cost of revolt against that agent (i.e., if $H > 0$ and VA increases, then R decreases). It should also be noted that a second-order freerider problem may arise with respect to participation in revolts. That is, individuals can potentially benefit from a revolt without bearing the costs of participating. However, a consideration of that issue would exceed the scope of this paper.

[6] The expression for gain from revolt over passivity (Gr) can be derived using von Neumann–Morgenstern expected utilities. The expected utility from revolt, Ur, depends on several factors. First, it depends on the utility (Us) awarded by the player's cooperation or defection in the original game, e.g., the utility awarded by strategy 1 or strategy 2 in fig. 1's game. Second, it depends on the costs of revolt, R. Third, it depends on whether the revolt succeeds in terminating the agent's ability to administer sanctions. If the revolt succeeds (an outcome with probability VA), the actor escapes sanctions but bears the costs of revolt, R, yielding the payoff $Us - R$. If the revolt fails (an outcome with probability $1 - VA$), the actor is sanctioned and bears the costs of revolt including (see n. 4) the possibility of harsher sanctions, yielding the payoff $Us + M - R$. Hence, the expected utility of revolt is

$$Ur = [(Us + M - R) \times (1 - VA)] + [(Us - R) \times VA]. \tag{n}$$

The gain from revolt over passivity (Gr) is the difference between the utility from revolt and the utility from passivity; i.e.,

$$Gr = Ur - Up, \tag{o}$$

or, equivalently, when expanded using eqq. (n) and (f),

$$Gr = [(Us + M - R) \times (1 - VA) + (Us - R) \times VA]$$
$$- [(Us + M) \times S + Us \times (1 - S)]. \tag{p}$$

Algebraic manipulation allows this expression to be reduced to

$$Gr = M \times (1 - VA - S) - R, \tag{q}$$

which is identical with eq. (10)'s expression for Gr. Observe that the actor's utility from the original game (Us) drops out of the expression for gain from revolt. This second theorem of collective sanctions is somewhat counterintuitive. For it states that the structure of the initial game, including the actors' inclinations and regulatory interests, is wholly irrelevant to their choice between revolt and passivity in CS systems. Thus, the proposed theory predicts that the potential for revolt exists even in systems where the prexisting game corresponds to a PD and the agent's sanctions are intended to reinforce cooperation in that PD.

Collective Sanctions

Equivalently, when expanded and rearranged,

$$Gr = M \times [(1 - V \times D)^N - VA] - R. \tag{11}$$

This equation leads to a number of hypotheses about the conditions under which revolt will occur in CS systems: HYPOTHESIS 5. The greater the strength of the agent's sanction, M, the greater the incentive for group members to choose revolt over passivity. This deduction stems from the positive linear relationship specified in equation (11) between M and Gr. It suggests that when agents employ stronger sanctions they risk revolt by making passivity an increasingly untenable option. For example, if stronger punishment is threatened, that enhances incentives for members to incur the risks and costs of revolt, or to escape.

HYPOTHESIS 6. The greater the vulnerability of the agent, VA, the greater the incentive for group members to choose revolt over passivity, Gr. This hypothesis stems from the negative relationship specified between VA and Gr in equation (11) (recall that M is assumed to be negative), and it is also reinforced by the negative relationship between VA and R (see n. 5). One reason why exogenous norm creation appears so effective in U.S. boot camps may be that the agent is immensely powerful compared with the group being controlled. That is, no company of new recruits could successfully revolt against the U.S. military. Similarly, this result is consistent with social psychological theories of revolutionary coalition formation and experimental results that indicate that the anticipated probability of success is a determinant of revolution (Michener and Lawler 1971; Schellenberg 1982).

HYPOTHESIS 7. The greater the costs of revolt, R, the weaker are the incentives, Gr, for group members to choose revolt over passivity. This conclusion comes from the negative relationship indicated in equation (11) between R and Gr. From a rational-choice perspective, it is obvious that the costliness of revolt would be negatively related to the incentives to rebel.

HYPOTHESIS 8. The larger the group, N, the greater are the incentives for group members to choose revolt over passivity, Gr. The positive relation between N and Gr specified by equation (11) is nonlinear but consistently positive, that is, dGr/dN is positive. See, for example, figure 2's depiction of this relationship. In essence, this relationship exists because, all else equal, the larger the group, the greater is the probability of sanctions, S, and hence the stronger is the incentive to terminate sanctions by revolt.[7]

[7] Since Gr is an increasing function of N, there may exist a value of N at which Gr becomes positive, indicating that the utility of revolt exceeds the utility of passivity. This "revolt point" (RP) can be computed by setting $Gr = 0$ (eq. [11]) and solving for N. This procedure yields the expression

American Journal of Sociology

Two additional hypotheses derive from this same mechanism: HY-POTHESIS 9.   The greater the violative propensities in the group, V, the greater the incentive to choose revolt over passivity, Gr. HYPOTHESIS 10.   The greater the detection capabilities of the agent, D, the greater the incentive to choose revolt over passivity, Gr. These hypotheses suggest that the prospects for revolt are maximal when an agent with efficient monitoring capacities faces a group with many prospective violators. In essence, the high probability of sanctions under such circumstances strengthens incentives to terminate sanctions through revolt. Similarly, measures that reduce the prospects for sanctions correspondingly diminish incentives to revolt and contribute to a CS-system stability. For example, in traditional China, with its system of familial CS, the option existed for a family to pay the emperor for permission to expel a family member formally. The rationale for the payment was to compensate the emperor in advance for the person's misdeeds. The effect was to free the family from any responsibility for those misdeeds. Thus, families could protect themselves from sanctions by ridding themselves of potential violators.

THE DILEMMA OF CS-BASED CONTROL

Controlling a group through collective incentives is rather like walking a tightrope. For the same factors that encourage members to choose compliance over passivity may also induce them to revolt. For example, hypotheses 1 and 5 state that stronger sanctions enhance incentives for both compliance and revolt. That obviously complicates the agent's choice of sanction strength.

The ultimate stability of a CS system depends on the strength of group members' incentives to choose compliance over the best available alternative, revolt or passivity, whichever is the preferred. This set of relationships is depicted in figure 3, which relates the formal model's basic elements: (i) the eight system parameters, C, N, D, V, M, CC, R, and VA and (ii) gains from compliance and revolt over passivity, Gc and Gr, respectively. The complexity of the dilemma facing agents that employ collective incentives is illustrated by the positive connections relating four

$$RP = \frac{\log(VA - R/M)}{\log(1 - V \times D)} \tag{r}$$

Partial differentiation of this expression reveals that the revolt point is an increasing function of the cost to the group of revolt, R, and a decreasing function of sanction strength, M; violation probability, V; detection capability, D; and the agent's vulnerability, VA.

Collective Sanctions

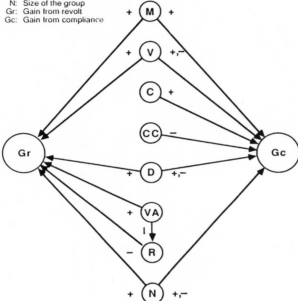

KEY

M: Magnitude of punishment
V: Proportion of violators in the group
C: Degree of intragroup control
CC: Cost of control
D: Proportion of violators detected
VA: Vulnerability of the agent
R: Cost of the revolt
N: Size of the group
Gr: Gain from revolt
Gc: Gain from compliance

FIG. 3.—Summary of relationships in a CS system. The small circles represent the eight defining parameters of a CS system, and the larger circles represent gains from conformity and revolt. Arrows represent functional relationships, which are either positive (i.e., monotonically increasing), negative (i.e., monotonically decreasing), or mixed (i.e., neither consistently increasing nor decreasing). Note that many of the same factors that enhance incentives to choose compliance also enhance incentives to revolt.

system parameters (i.e., M, V, D, and N) to gains from both compliance, Gc, and revolt, Gr. Thus, in each of four independent ways, efforts to induce compliance may potentially backfire by producing revolt instead.

Consider, by way of illustration, the delicacy of the agent's choice of a monitoring level (D). Figure 4 depicts the relationship between compliance and revolt gains, and the agent's detection capabilities for a representative CS system, corresponding to figure 2's CS system, where N = 10. As is apparent on inspection, the detection level that maximizes compliance gains is for the agent to sanction 35% of violations. If less

American Journal of Sociology

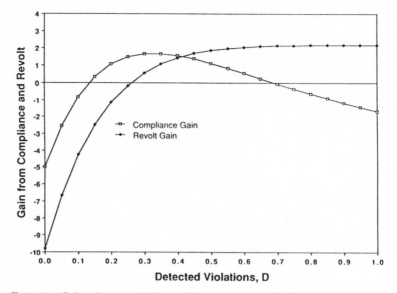

Fig. 4.—Gains from compliance (*Gc*) and revolt (*Gr*) as a function of the agent's detection of violations (*D*) for fig. 2's CS system, where group size *N* = 10, and *V* = .6. Gains from revolt are a monotonically increasing function of *D*. That is, better detection of violations enhances incentives to terminate sanctions by revolt. Gains from compliance are positive only if the agent detects between 15% and 65% of violations, and the optimal level of monitoring to maximize *Gc* is 35%.

than 15% are sanctioned, the group lapses into passivity, whereas if more than 40% of detected violations are punished, the group gives up on compliance and revolts.

An indirect but nonetheless significant conclusion results from the network of relations depicted in figures 3 and 4. Even within the admittedly simplifying confines of the proposed model, the informational demands on an agent that would construct a stable CS system are considerable. In the real world of imperfect information and bounded rationality, those demands can rarely be fulfilled except for those special circumstances where the conditions are especially favorable to CS-based control, for example, a small cohesive group faced with a nearly invulnerable agent with effective monitoring capabilities and strong sanctions, as in Gilham's example of a military boot camp. Hence, the finding reported by Slavin (1983) of inconsistency regarding the effectiveness of collective sanctions in schools is hardly surprising.

Collective Sanctions

CONCLUSION

By way of conclusion, let us consider the implications of the proposed model for understanding revolutionary tactics. The effect of CS may be to provoke revolt rather than submission. As a result, a potentially effective means of inducing revolt against an agent is to goad it into administering counterproductive collective punishments. In this vein, David Rapoport (1984) describes Nevhaev's *Revolutionary Catechism* as "suggesting devices for provoking governments to savage their peoples until the latter can bear it no longer," that is, devices for provoking governments into counterproductive repression.

One can understand in this light some of the factors contributing to the success of the Algerian revolution. According to Heggoy (1972, p. 235), the French army overreacted to terrorism in Algiers:

> The terrorist cells were dismantled and most of the members were arrested or killed. The strategic victory, however, belonged to the nationalists, who reaped immense political gains from the high-handed military tactics. [The French] created isolated Algerian ghettos whose occupants grew increasingly united in their hatred of France. . . . The difference between Algerians and Europeans living in Algeria became markedly clearer. . . . This development forced the two communities to drift further and further apart. The nationalists capitalized on the social fault thus created and undertook the leadership of the Algerian population as a whole.

In essence, the nationalists provoked the French colonial government to punish collectively and withhold collective rewards from the Algerian middle class and native Algerians in general. The result was to increase the incentives for previously procolonial Algerians to throw in their lot with the nationalists; so, too, did the Sicarri and Zealots who opposed the Roman Empire's rule of Judea employ, starting in the year A.D. 4, polarizing tactics based on terror with considerable effectiveness (see Rapoport 1984).

Collective punishment can be theoretically expected to fail when a vulnerable agent applies it to large or atomized groups. For example, the Nazi policy of taking reprisals against civilians had quite different effects, depending on their context. In some cases, it appeared to deter revolt such as in the Nazi occupation of Norway (see Wehr 1979). However, in France, it may have further motivated the underground resistance movement. When the already vulnerable Pakistani army used reprisals during the Bangladesh revolt, these appeared to fuel support for the rebellion. Here, the agent was conspicuously vulnerable, and the responsible groups were sizable. The question of the effectiveness of the Israeli policy of blowing up the family homes of accused terrorists has been much debated. Whereas it may deter some measure of terrorism, it may also

American Journal of Sociology

foster hostility toward the Israeli government and thus may increase rather than reduce resistance. According to the proposed model, the ultimate effectiveness of this policy would depend to an important extent on the cohesiveness of the Arab families involved.

In sum, CS systems may be highly effective at creating exogenous compliance norms. Alternatively, they may have the opposite effect and provoke passivity or even revolt. According to the proposed model, the effect of control depends quite sensitively upon both the attributes of the agent that controls collective incentives (i.e., the agent's monitoring capabilities, vulnerability to revolt, and the strength of the agent's sanctions) and the attributes of the group (i.e., the group's size, degree of intragroup control, proportion of potential violators, and the costliness of normative control and revolt).[8]

REFERENCES

Axelrod, Robert. 1984. *The Evolution of Cooperation.* New York: Basic.
————. 1986. "An Evolutionary Approach to Norms." *American Political Science Review* 80:1095–1111.
Barkun, Michael. 1968. *Law without Sanctions: Order in Primitive Societies and the World Community.* New Haven: Yale University Press.
Birenbaum, Arnold, and Edward Sagarin. 1976. *Norms and Human Behavior.* New York: Praeger.
Blau, Peter M. 1964. *Exchange and Power in Social Life.* New York: Wiley.
Brams, Steven J. 1983. *Superior Beings: If They Exist, How Would We Know?* New York: Springer-Verlag.
Bronfenbrenner, Urie. 1970. *Two Worlds of Childhood: U.S. and U.S.S.R.* New York: Sage.
Brubaker, E. R. 1975. "Free Ride, Free Revelation, or Golden Rule?" *Journal of Law and Economics* 18:147–61.
Buchanan, James M. 1975. *The Limits of Liberty.* Chicago: University of Chicago Press.
Chen, Phillip M. 1973. *Law and Justice: The Legal System in China 2400 B.C. to 1960 A.D.* New York: Dunellen.
Cherry, Richard R. 1890. *Lectures on the Growth of Criminal Law in Ancient Communities.* New York: Macmillan.
Chowdhury, Subrata Roy. 1972. *The Genesis of Bangladesh.* New York: Asia Publishing.
Coleman, James S. 1986. "The Emergence of Norms among Rational Actors in Groups with Varying Degrees of Closure." Sunbelt Social Network Conference, Santa Barbara, Calif.
Dallin, David, J., and Boris I. Nicolaevsky. 1947. *Forced Labor in Soviet Russia.* New Haven: Yale University Press.

[8] For a copy of a computer program that implements the mathematical model presented in this article and graphically represents the relationships among theoretic terms, send $3 to cover the cost of a floppy diskette and postage. This program will run on any IBM or compatible with at least 512K of RAM and either monochrome (Hercules) or color (CGA or EGA) graphics.

Collective Sanctions

Driberg, J. H. 1970. "The African Conception of Law." Pp. 162–73 in *Readings in African Law,* vol. 1. Edited by E. Cotran and N. N. Rubin. New York: Africana Publishing.

Emerson, Richard M. 1976. "Social Exchange Theory." *Annual Review of Sociology* 2:335–63.

Gilham, Steven A. 1982. "The Marines Build Men: Resocialization in Recruit Training." Pp. 231–41 in *The Sociological Outlook,* edited by Reid Luhman. Belmont, Calif.: Wadsworth.

Hardin, Russell. 1971. "Collective Action as an Agreeable *N*-Prisoners' Dilemma." *Behavioral Science* 16:472–81.

———. 1982. *Collective Action.* Baltimore: Johns Hopkins University Press.

Hasluck, Margaret. 1967. "The Albanian Blood Feud." Pp. 381–408 in *Law and Warfare: Studies in the Anthropology of Conflict,* edited by Paul Bohannan. Garden City, N.Y.: American Museum of Natural History Press.

Hechter, Michael. 1983. *The Microfoundations of Macrosociology.* Philadelphia: Temple University Press.

———. 1984. "When Actors Comply: Monitoring Costs and the Production of Social Order." *Acta Sociologica* 3:161–83.

Heckathorn, Douglas D. 1988. "Collective Sanctions and the Second Order Free Rider Problem." Paper presented at the annual meetings of the Public Choice Society and the Economic Sciences Association, San Francisco.

Heckathorn, Douglas D., and Steven M. Maser. 1987a. "Bargaining and Constitutional Contracts." *American Journal of Political Science* 31:142–68.

———. 1987b. "Bargaining and the Sources of Transaction Costs: The Case of Government Regulation." *Journal of Law, Economics, and Organization* 3:69–98.

Heggoy, Alf Andres. 1972. *Insurgency and Counterinsurgency in Algeria.* Bloomington: Indiana University Press.

Hirshi, Travis. 1969. *Causes of Delinquency.* Berkeley: University of California Press.

Hoebel, E. Adamson. 1968. *The Law of Primitive Man: A Study in Comparative Legal Dynamics.* New York: Atheneum.

Howell, Paul. 1954. *A Manual of Nuer Law.* London: Oxford University Press.

Irwin, John. 1980. *Prisons in Turmoil.* Boston: Little, Brown.

Johnson, Ana Guiterrez, and William Foote Whyte. 1977. "The Mondragon System of Worker Production Cooperatives." *Industrial and Labor Relations Review* 31: 18–30.

Kapferer, Bruce. 1973. "Social Network and Conjugal Role in Urban Zambia: Towards a Reformulation of the Bott Hypothesis." Pp. 83–110 in *Network Analysis Studies in Human Interaction,* edited by Jeremy Boissevain and J. Clyde Mitchell. The Hague: Mouton.

Karsden, Rafael. 1967. "Blood Revenge and War among the Jibaro Indians of Eastern Ecuador." Pp. 303–26 in *Law and Warfare: Studies in the Anthropology of Conflict,* edited by Paul Bohannan. Garden City, N.Y.: American Museum of Natural History Press.

Komorita, S. S. 1976. "A Model of the *N*-Person Dilemma-Type Game." *Journal of Experimental Social Psychology* 122:357–73.

Meijer, M. J. 1971. *Marriage Law and Policy in the Chinese People's Republic.* Hong Kong: Hong Kong University Press.

Michener, H. Andrew, and Edward J. Lawler. 1971. "Revolutionary Coalition Strength and Collective Failure as Determinants of Status Reallocation." *Journal of Experimental Social Psychology* 7:448–60.

Oliver, Pamela. 1980. "Rewards and Punishments as Selective Incentives for Collective Action: Theoretical Investigations." *American Journal of Sociology* 85:1356–75.

American Journal of Sociology

Oliver, Pamela, and Gerald Marwell. 1988. "The Paradox of Group Size in Collective Action: A Theory of the Critical Mass. II." *American Sociological Review* 53:1–8.

Olson, Mancur. 1965. *The Logic of Collective Action: Public Goods and the Theory of Groups*. Cambridge: Harvard University Press.

Opp, Karl-Deiter. 1982. "The Evolutionary Emergence of Norms." *British Journal of Social Psychology* 21:139–49.

Rapoport, A., and A. M. Chammah. 1965. *Prisoner's Dilemma*. Ann Arbor: University of Michigan Press.

Rapoport, Anatol. 1983. *Mathematical Models in the Social and Behavioral Sciences* New York: Wiley.

Rapoport, David C. 1984. "Fear and Trembling: Terrorism in Three Religious Traditions." *American Political Science Review* 78:658–77.

Rothschild-Whitt, Joyce. 1979. "The Collectivist Organization: An Alternative to Rational Bureaucratic Models." *American Sociological Review* 44:509–27.

Schellenberg, James A. 1982. *The Science of Conflict*. New York: Oxford University Press.

Schotter, Andrew. 1981. *The Economic Theory of Social Institutions*. New York: Cambridge University Press.

Scott, John Finley. 1971. *Internalization of Norms: A Sociological Theory of Moral Commitment*. Englewood Cliffs, N.J.: Prentice-Hall.

Scott, Robert A. 1976. "Deviance, Sanctions, and Social Integration in Small-Scale Societies." *Social Forces* 54:604–20.

Slavin, Robert E. 1983. "When Does Cooperative Learning Increase Student Achievement?" *Psychological Bulletin* 96:429–45.

Taylor, Michael. 1982. *Community, Anarchy, and Liberty*. Cambridge: Cambridge University Press.

Ullmann-Margalit, Edna. 1977. *The Emergence of Norms*. Oxford: Clarendon.

Wehr, Paul. 1979. *Conflict Regulation*. Boulder: Westview Press.

Yakir, Pyotr. 1972. *A Childhood in Prison*. New York: Macmillan.

Yamagishi, Toshio. 1986. "The Provision of a Sanctioning System as a Public Good." *Journal of Personality and Social Psychology* 51:110–16.

[24]

A Theory of Ethnic Collective Action[1]

Michael Hechter,

Debra Friedman and

Malka Appelbaum
University of Washington

This article presents a theory to explain the frequency of ethnic
collective action. Based on rational choice premises, it represents an alternative to currently popular structural theories.
We demonstrate why an individual will not necessarily join a
collective action even if its end is beneficial to him, and why
collective action does not always occur among the most seriously
disadvantaged ethnic groups. The strength of ethnically based
organizations is held to be an especially powerful determinant
of the likelihood of ethnic collective action.

We take collective action to be the concerted activity of a group of
individuals to pursue public goods.[2] As such it comes in many forms
(voting, lobbying, demonstrating or violent actions); occurs on
different social bases (classes, ethnic groups or sexes); and is
oriented toward achieving a variety of ends (material resources,
new laws or new positions). This article discusses the conditions
under which the members of ethnic groups will engage in collective
action. Little will be said about the specific ends that are pursued.
Rather, we are interested in posing two basic questions: under what
conditions is collective action likely to occur, and when it does take
place, why are some forms more common than others?

There has been considerable geographical and temporal variation
in the incidence of ethnic collective action, as well as in its forms.
Some ethnic groups rarely engage in it, whereas others regularly
seem to act in a corporate manner. Some groups vote in ethnic blocs;

[1] We are grateful for the comments of Charles Hirschman, Eric Leifer and an anonymous
reviewer.

[2] This definition excludes all instances of the concerted activity of a group to pursue purely
private goods (such as bank robberies), as well as spontaneous occurrences of social cooperation (such as those that follow natural disasters) or protest.

others support guerilla armies. We aim to set forth, in preliminary fashion, a theory capable of explaining variations in the incidence and form of ethnic collective action. Since there is nothing to distinguish the causes of ethnic collective action from the causes of any other kind, our analysis is anchored in a general theory of collective action.

We are hardly alone in seeking answers to questions of this sort. A vast literature on ethnic social movements and mobilization addresses similar concerns. While our approach is consistent with many of the findings in this literature, nonetheless it represents a departure from previous discussions. The most influential recent work is based on a structural theory of ethnic collective action. Though we sympathize with some of the premises of this structural theory, and though we prefer it to the normative theory that it has superseded, we have become increasingly aware of its inherent limitations.

THE STRUCTURAL THEORY OF ETHNIC COLLECTIVE ACTION

This theory assumes that when the members of ethnic groups occupy distinctive positions in the class or occupational structures, or in the labor market (especially disadvantaged positions), and when they become aware of their common plight, it will be only a matter of time before collective action ensues. True, there is debate about the precise kind of stratification necessary to promote collective action—whether this is best captured by the concepts of split (Bonacich, 1972, 1979) or segmented labor markets (Edwards, *et al.*, 1975), or by the cultural division of labor (Hechter, 1978). There is also debate about just how the individual members of ethnic groups become aware of their common plight—whether this is due to ecological variables (the classic formulation is Festinger, Schachter and Back, 1950) or to the catalytic role of competing groups who invade ethnically-protected spheres of economic activity (Blalock, 1967; Bonacich, 1972; and Hannan, 1979). Yet despite these quibbles, structural theorists presume that the more a group has to gain by collective action, the greater its incentive in embarking upon a collective strategy, and hence, the greater the probability that some collective action will follow.

Naturally, structuralists have devoted much effort to understanding the causes of ethnic stratification. Undoubtedly its primary cause emanates from the institutional arrangements that regulate and constrain economic, political and social activity in all societies, property rights and civil rights being the most significant examples. Thus, when ethnic groups are granted corporate rights over and above those granted to individuals, ethnic stratification is a necessary consequence (*See,* Van Dyke, 1977). But there are many other causes of ethnic stratification, some of which—like competitive labor markets—continue to be the focus of controversy. One the one hand, the competitive labor market was expected to diminish ethnic stratification by assuring that individuals would be allocated to occupations on universalistic rather than ascriptive grounds. This would increase the rate of interethnic contact, and, in the absence of corporate ethnic rights, would foster ethnic assimiliation and blur the boundaries between once-distinct groups (Parsons and Smelser, 1956; Smelser, 1969; Park, 1950). On the other hand, subsequent analyses revealed that the labor market often works to exacerbate ethnic stratification by fostering group, regional and international inequalities (Blumer, 1965; Bonacich, 1972, 1979; Castells, 1975; Hechter, 1975, 1976, 1978; Piore, 1975; Spence, 1973; Thurow, 1975).

Whereas this research on the origins of ethnic stratification systems is valuable in its own right, there is reason to doubt the nature of the link between stratification and collective action. If collective action merely resulted from differential stratification, there would be far more of it than the historical record reveals. The striking fact about any kind of collective action is its relative rarity (Olson, 1965; Hardin, 1982). To be sure, many distinctively stratified ethnic groups do vote in blocs and do have effective lobbying coalitions. Yet there is immense variation in the levels of mobilization of ethnic groups across time and place. In some societies where severe ethnic oppression should produce a strong collective interest in political change, according to the structural theory, there is a low incidence of ethnic collective action. The current situation in South Africa and in the southern United States during slavery are two well-known cases in point.[3]

[3] For the frequency of slave revolts in the antebellum South *See,* Aptheker, 1943. American blacks more frequently employed individual rather than collective tactics of opposition, such as working slowly or damaging tools or household articles. For the debate on slave opposition strategies, *See,* Elkins, 1959; Genovese, 1974; and Fogel and Engerman, 1974. In South

THEORY OF ETHNIC COLLECTIVE ACTION   415

How can this variation be explained? A theory that explains the occurrence of ethnic collective action solely by the existence of a common interest in change—and the collective benefits this would bring—cannot account for its nonoccurrence in the face of outright exploitation. Nor can it explain variation in the incidence and form of ethnic collective action among groups having the same interest in seeking political change. Such a theory can only explain the desirability of collective action rather than its actual occurrence. Clearly, this failure is due to the omission of other important factors that help account for these variations. Given this dilemma, one common solution is simply to add new variables to the theory in order to increase its explanatory power. But such *ad hoc* explanations have dubious value. In response to these serious shortcomings, we propose an alternative theory.

A RATIONAL CHOICE THEORY OF ETHNIC COLLECTIVE ACTION

The structural theory is inadequate because it ignores a central feature of all collective action: any acting that is done in the pursuit of collective goods is done by individuals. For this reason, any theory of collective action must consider individual level dynamics. Conditions affecting the average individual's decision about participation in a collective strategy will be decisive in determining the likelihood of ethnic collective action. Under certain conditions a rational individual will not participate in ethnic collective action even though he desires the collective benefits it is designed to obtain; however, under other conditions he will be likely to participate.[4]

This rational choice[5] theory of ethnic collective action is based on the assumption that individuals have given goals, wants, tastes or utilities. Since all goals cannot be equally realized because of scar-

---

Africa, blacks have usually relied on forms of passive resistance, Kuper, 1957—once again, an individual tactic.

[4] By convention, the pronoun "he" will be used to designate both male and female actors in this article. Although sex-specific pronouns can be avoided in the third-person plural, individual-level theories make heavy use of pronouns in the third-person singular. Unfortunately these are sex-specific (save for the inelegent "one").

[5] Recent surveys of the rational choice approach include Heath, 1976, March, 1978, and Elster, 1979. The latter two authors are particularly aware of the unresolved dilemmas facing current rational choice theory.

city, individuals will choose between alternative courses of action so as to maximize these wants and utilities. The resulting action may be seen as the end product of two successive filtering devices (*See*, Elster, 1979). The first is defined by structural constraints that limit the set of possible courses of action by reducing it to the vastly smaller subset of feasible actions. The second filtering device is the mechanism by which the actor chooses which course of action to take. Thus individuals choose the most efficient means of realizing desired goals. Ultimately individual action is seen to result from choices made in the face of changing structural constraints. If the individual's goals and the structural constraints he faces can both be specified in advance, testable hypotheses can be made about his likely course of action.

The major prediction of rational choice theory is that the individual will join in a collective action only when he expects the benefits of his participation to exceed the costs. While the previous discussion is cast wholly in individual terms, the theory aims to explain the choices made by large numbers of similarly situated actors to engage in ethnic collective action. It does so by specifying the structural conditions under which these actors come to define participation in some collective action as a net benefit. At first glance, this proposition appears little more than commonsensical and not that different from the structural theory we have rejected. Yet appearances can be deceiving. By formulating the problem of collective action in these terms, our theory must come to terms with a powerful obstacle to collective action, namely, the free-rider dilemma.

THE FREE-RIDER DILEMMA AND THE THEORY OF PUBLIC GOODS

The kind of collective action we seek to explain is concerted activity to obtain a public good, excluding, of course, all spontaneous and unplanned instances of collective action. Whereas the concept of a private good is self-evident, public goods differ from private ones in three respects.[6] First, they are indivisible: any given unit of the good can be made available to every member of the relevant public.

---

[6] On the characteristics of public goods, *See* especially, Samuelson, 1974, 1978; Olson, 1965; Riker and Ordeshook, 1973, Laver, 1980; Hardin, 1982; and Taylor, 1982.

Second, they are non-excludable: once provided, no member can be kept from consuming the public good. Third, they are non-rival: the consumption of a particular unit of the good does not affect the ability of other individuals to consume it. The basic point is that, once produced, such goods are available on a noncontingent basis to an entire public.

Common examples of public goods discussed by economists are clean air, lighthouses and public parks. While the theory of public goods has been extensively applied to questions of environmental quality, no one seems to have recognized its appropriateness for problems of ethnic mobilization. Mobilized ethnic groups nearly always seek public goods for their members: Affirmative Action legislation is only the latest of a long series of demands for public goods. (Full civil and political rights have been sought by disadvantaged ethnic groups for centuries.)

However, before a public good can be consumed, it must be produced. Collective action is first and foremost a problem of the production of public goods. Why individuals choose to consume public goods is no mystery: they generally contribute to the individual's welfare. But public goods are not automatically provided simply because people want them. The basic difficulty is that due to their very nature, it is unlikely that public goods will be produced in sufficient quantity, or even at all. Since no member of the public can be prevented from consuming them, in most cases a rational individual will not contribute to the production of public goods; instead he will act as a free-rider. Despite the fact that he has not helped provide the public good, the free-rider is in a position to consume it. Since the rationale for collective action is the production of some public good, it can be easily seen that the free-rider problem lies at the heart of any explanation of the phenomenon.

At first glance there seem to be easy solutions to the free-rider problem. Certain goods intrinsically require joint production—no individual can, by his own action, overthrow a political regime or form an ethnic lobby, and the production of others is clearly enhanced by cooperation. A person might be able to obtain a particular good solely through his own efforts, but the costs he would incur by doing do might outweigh the eventual benefits. Hence his costs would diminish significantly if the good were produced jointly. In such cases it would appear that cooperation is a rational strategy.

This solution seems attractive because it is obvious that individuals often have goals that cannot be satisfied through individual action alone. Nevertheless, it is insufficient to overcome the free-rider problem. Why should a revolutionary bear the costs of an action that is unlikely to succeed when many more people will benefit if he is successful, and none will bear the cost of failure? If he can induce other people to pursue this end, then what would prevent him from free-riding? In many cases the answer is nothing.[7] Goods that are jointly produced and jointly consumed will not be easily provided because each actor can usually convince himself that his individual utility is maximized not by participating but by shirking.

When formulated in this manner, the key problem for the theorist of collective action is to explain why some actors participate in concerted efforts to produce a public good when all members will benefit. Affirmative Action laws may represent a public good for all blacks, but any individual black's interest is served best by self-investment rather than investment in political activity. This is because his individual contribution to the passage of the law is negligible, and if Affirmative Action is enacted, he will benefit just as much as those who labored to get the legislation passed.

By now it should be clear that the first prediction of rational choice theory is that the incidence of any kind of collective action will be contingent. This helps explain the relative inactivity of some oppressed ethnic groups. On a statistical basis this prediction may be true, but how, then, can we explain those instances where ethnic collective action has, in fact, occurred? How did the Irish nationalists manage to create their own state? How can Zionism be accounted for? Why was there a civil rights movement in the American South?

While the free-rider problem only arises within the perspective of rational choice, the theory also tells us something about the conditions under which it can be overcome. Here its major prediction is that individuals will participate in collective action only when the private (rather than public) benefit of participating exceeds the private cost of doing so. This is why a theory of ethnic collective action must be concerned with the action of individuals on the behalf of public goods rather than with the situation of groups. While

---

[7] It is rational for actors not to free-ride if they are convinced that their comrades will simultaneously follow suit. But this is likely to occur only in highly interdependent groups which are small enough to enable members to monitor each others' behavior. This condition rarely holds in large ethnic groups, although it may exist in ethnically homogeneous neighborhoods.

groups (or publics) clearly benefit from the provision of public goods, they cannot be the focus of theoretical reasoning in any explanation of collective action itself.

When ethnic collective action does occur, we should be able to specify the conditions that make it probable.[8] The basic factors affecting the individual's benefit/cost calculation are expressed in the following equation:

$$Y = (X_1 \cdot Z + X_2)\, p + X_3 - (X_4)(1\text{-}p) - X_5 \cdot j + X_6$$

where Y is the individual's net benefit from participation in the collective action; X_1 is the amount of the public good he expects to obtain in the event that the collective action is successful; X_2 is the amount of private reward he expects to receive if collective action is successful; p is his estimate of the probability of successful collective action; X_3 is the amount of private reward expected for participation regardless of the probable outcome of the collective action; X_4 is the amount of private punishment he expects to bear if the collective action fails; X_5 is the cost of injury he expects to suffer through participation; j is the likelihood that injury will result from participation; and X_6 is the amount of private punishment the individual expects to receive if he fails to join the collective action.

The X_1 value, the individual's share of the public good, is multiplied by the dummy variable Z so that:

$$Z = 1 \text{ when } X_2 > X_1$$

$$Z = 0 \text{ when } X_2 \leq X_1$$

An individual can obtain the amount X_1 of the public good whether or not he contributes to its production. *Ceteris paribus,* if the amount of private reward the individual will receive should collective action be successful (X_2) is less than or equal to X_1, he will not participate in the production of the public good. Only when the private reward (X_2) is greater than his share of public good (X_1) does the latter influence his decision to participate in collective action.

In general, the approach specifies the conditions that affect and constrain the individual's calculations regarding participation in ethnic collective action. To the degree that group members face the same structural conditions or constraints, their individual cal-

[8] For an earlier attempt to specify the necessary conditions for collective action that is somewhat different from ours, *See,* Tullock, 1979.

culations will aggregate in such a way so as to predispose the group towards collective action. This is not to argue that most members actually engage in the kind of conscious calculation that the equation suggests. Rather, we claim merely that patterns of group action occur as if these kinds of calculations had been made.

The equation not only predicts when collective action is likely to happen; it also has implications for the forms it tends to assume. Forms of collective action that impose few personal costs on individual participants will take place more frequently than those that impose greater costs. This helps explain why ethnic voting and lobbying (which impose few costs) are so much more common occurrences than ethnically based guerilla wars.

Most of the terms in this equation seem immensely difficult to estimate—both for the individual who is presumably deciding whether or not to participate, and for the social scientist who is interested in knowing whether or not collective action will occur at all. Yet the situation is not as daunting as it first appears, for these costs and benefits are determined principally by various structural constraints. To the degree that we can adequately measure the structural constraints faced by different individuals, we are therefore in a position to estimate the Y values, their private interest in participating in collective action. Given the assumption that the structural constraints are properly identified and estimated, the procedure will yield testable hypotheses about the probability that individuals, will engage in collective action. Further, one of the terms in the equation (X_1) is nearly always a constant for each member of a given public. Thus X_1 can be estimated easily for groups that seek to obtain a public good.[9]

Essentially, the equation boils down to an enumeration of the individual's private benefits and costs. This has one implication that is worth repeating, for it is counterintuitive. According to this formulation the position of an ethnic group in the stratification system has no direct bearing either on any member's decision to participate or on the group's propensity to engage in collective action. Individuals in extremely exploited ethnic groups are neither more nor less likely to engage in collective action than those in privileged groups *(ceteris paribus)*. The claim is counterintuitive

---

[9] Thus, when a union promises to secure a $10 raise for each worker, if the collective action succeeds the value of X_1 will be $10 (Heath, 1976:31).

because it is evident that the members of exploited groups have a much greater interest in obtaining public goods (especially those that would preclude their future exploitation) than the members of non-exploited groups will ever have. The reason, of course, is that the rational actor, in a large group, has no incentive to participate in the production of public goods no matter how much he may desire them because of the free-rider dilemma. The central theoretical thrust of the preceding equation can now be restated: collective action will only occur to the degree that free-riding is prevented through the production of private rewards and punishments.

Does this imply that ethnic stratification is irrelevant in accounting for collective action? Not at all. The role of stratification in collective action is indirect; it operates principally through its effects on group solidarity (that is, the member's compliance with the group's normative obligations) and organization. To the degree the members of an ethnic group are dependent on one or a small number of affiliated organizations (such as ethnic associations of various kinds) for benefits that they cannot obtain elsewhere, they are likely to be highly solidary and have the potential to engage in collective action (Hechter, 1982). This situation occurs frequently among racial and ethnic groups that occupy distinctive positions in the stratification system.

Organizations are critical in promoting collective action for two basic reasons. First, they are the major source of the private rewards and punishments that prevent free-riding from taking place (in the equation, they have direct effects on the values of nearly all of the terms). Second, since we anticipate that the estimated probability of success for any collective action (p)—especially in its early stages— will tend to be low, organizations can play a key role in increasing the value of p by controlling the information available to their members. When members have few alternative sources of information, organizations can easily convince them that the success of a contemplated collective action is a real possibility, perhaps even a foregone conclusion. Linguistically distinct ethnic groups would appear to be especially liable to these influences.

THE EFFECTS OF ORGANIZATION ON COLLECTIVE ACTION

To this point we have argued that an individual is likely to participate in a collective action when the net value of doing so is positive, that is, when the benefits of such activity outweigh the costs. We have suggested further that ethnic stratification makes little or no difference for the likelihood of individual participation in collective action. What then changes the values of these terms so that an individual becomes predisposed to join in collective action? The single most powerful exogenous independent variable is the group's organization. By organization we mean, at the very least, an agency that can accommodate members and that can garner and distribute resources.

An organization can exert a systematic influence on the actor's decision concerning participation in collective action precisely because the individual's central consideration is the presumed private benefit he will gain minus the private costs he will be forced to bear. The organization supplies these private goods to the individual, over and above any collective benefit that he may share.

Excursus on the Genesis of Ethnic Organizations

Before discussing the role of organizations in facilitating ethnic collective action, one obvious question arises. If, as we claim, organizations are necessary for collective action to occur, how do public good seeking organizations (which themselves represent collective endeavors, and therefore are also prone to the free-rider dilemma) become established in the first place? Why is it in anyone's interest to build an ethnic organization if he can enjoy its fruits without having to contribute to its formation? To answer these questions we must distinguish between two different types of ethnic organizations: those whose *raison d'etre* is ethnic collective action and those which have been established for purposes other than ethnic collective action, but which nevertheless may serve as a basis for subsequent mobilization.

The formation of organizations that are in the business of seeking public goods (such as the I.R.A. or the P.L.O.) can be explained by the private interest of political entrepreneurs who supply the group with the desired public good at a profit (Frolich, Oppenheimer and Young, 1971). A group will often collectively value a good more than the cost of providing it. If the sum of the individual utilities attached to the good by each member exceeds the cost of providing it, then a potential surplus exists for political leaders who can arrange to provide the good to the group in exchange for contributions from them. Each member is prepared to pay a sum equal to or less than the utility he derives from the good in question. A political entrepreneur, then, can realize a surplus by setting up an organization at a cost which is less than the total value of contributions received. Once an organization is established the entrepreneur sets up a system of taxation and levies contributions from all members. He can punish recalcitrants by enforcing a penalty which exceeds the cost of the contribution required. This dramatically alters the cost-benefit calculation of a potential free-rider, since it becomes more costly to withhold a contribution than to make it. In other words, the leader offers members of the group a contract. He establishes an organization that will help in producing the public good in exchange for his private surplus. He collects revenues on the basis of a grant of coercive powers of taxation from the group which is conditional upon the satisfactory provision of public goods.

The formation of organizations whose main purpose is not the supply of public goods is much less problematic, however, and much more frequent. Ethnic organizations are often established voluntarily to supply valued private goods, like religious and economic services (such as credit and insurance). [10] Once such private good organizations are established in an ethnic community, they can play a crucial role in the mobilization of group members for collective ends. To the degree that members value the private benefits provided by ethnic organizations and to the degree that these benefits are not available to them elsewhere, they will be dependent on the organization. The greater their dependence the more willing they will be to engage in collective action. The existence of an ethnic organization that supplies private benefits enhances the likelihood of ethnic

---

[10]Thus, Thomas and Znaniecki (1920, 5:108) pointed to the importance of private benefits in establishing voluntary associations among immigrant Poles in the United States. "At first sight it is a rather baffling question how such a limited economic interest—limited both qualitatively and quantitatively—can serve as material foundation for such an important social structure as the super-territorial Polish American system, and even intelligent Poles, particularly the Socialists and the Sokols (who permit mutual insurance but do not consider it essential for their organizations), are inclined to regard with scorn the 'benefit' principle. However, it should be realized that the function of this business side of Polish American institutions is not to create a bond between the members—the real bond is the satisfaction of the 'social instinct'—but only to stabilize and extend a social cohesion which otherwise would manifest itself only irregularly and within narrower limits. In a word, mutual insurance is not a basis of association but of organization. It gives a minimum of rational order to those social relations which are the essential factor of the racial cohesion of American Poles."

mobilization for yet another reason. These organizations have an important effect on the stability and solidarity of ethnic communities since they become the focus around which extensive interaction on a regular basis takes place. When neighborhoods are institutionally complete (Breton, 1964)—with their own ethnic food stores, restaurants, taverns, schools, churches, mutual aid societies and newspapers—dense and cohesive interpersonal networks are likely to develop. These conditions enhance the prospects for ethnic collective action since the more extensive and regular the interaction is, the lower the costs of monitoring members' behavior to make sure they do not free-ride (Hechter, 1982).

To conclude, ethnic groups that successfully mobilize to pursue collective goods initially may have been organized to supply valued private goods. This is how they can reward rational actors for participating in collective action. As is the case in large interest groups with significant lobbying organizations, ethnic mobilization can be seen as a by-product of organizations that derive their strength from the provision of some benefits in addition to lobbying (Olson, 1965). A purely political ethnic organization that provides no benefits apart from the promise of a better future, and that has no taxation system set up by political leaders, also is not likely to have a supply of incentives with which to reward potential participants.[11]

On the Timing and Forms of Ethnic Collective Action

The first and probably the most critical calculation that the individual must make is the value of the private reward that he will gain if the collective action succeeds (X_2). This private reward may come in the form of a job, influence, power or money. Such rewards are drawn from the store of resources of existing organizations. This can be seen in the case of ethnic political parties that seek representation in a statewide legislative body. If their candidates are elected, they will immediately control additional resources—for example, jobs in the government—that can be used to reward loyal workers.[12] The individual who considers campaigning for this ethnic party candidate

---

[11] This helps explain why ethnicity serves as the basis for collective action far more frequently than does class. The relatively greater incidence of ethnic collective action is due to the fact that private good ethnic organizations are generally easier to establish and maintain than those based on the wider principle of class.

[12] The outstanding current example is provided by the success of the Parti Quebecois.

THEORY OF ETHNIC COLLECTIVE ACTION   425

will then compare the probability of receiving such a position as against his present situation; if the future promise is more attractive than the present reality, this may constitute a powerful inducement for his participation.

However, in order for this to be a realistic hope, three other conditions must be met. First, the individual needs evidence (or trust) that after successful collective action organizational resources will be sufficient to reward him adequately for his participation. Second, and even more important, the individual needs evidence (or belief) based on the prior actions of the organization (or its promise) that it possesses some reliable mechanism by which his contribution to the collective action can be recognized. He must have the sense that the monitoring mechanisms of the organization exist and are functioning fairly. In addition, it will be rewarded justly. Thus he requires some plausible expectations about the possible additional resources for private rewards and also confidence in the organization's distribution policies.

Therefore, we expect that an individual's estimate of the private rewards gained as a result of his participation in collective action (X_2) will increase when 1) the organization has a store of resources apart from those to be gained through action; 2) the organization's monitoring capacities are extensive; and 3) the organization has a proven record of justice in distribution. The last two expectations will be enhanced if the organization is long-established (and therefore predictable) and the individual has been a member for a considerable length of time. 4) Both the organization's ability to monitor and the individual's perception of the efficacy of the monitoring process will be increased when membership is small.

These assessments are significantly modified by a third factor, namely, the estimated probability of success (p). Although the individual may perceive that there are important private goods to be obtained through collective action, these are attractive only if there is a significant chance of obtaining them. The probability of success (that is, the probability that the public good will be obtained) is almost always low; this is why individuals rarely join collective action and why collective action in general is so rare.

However, the probability of success is always unknown and estimates of it may vary widely. Therefore, organizations have great opportunities for influencing the actor's estimate of this probability. An accurate assessment of this probabilty depends upon the adequacy of information about the relative strength of contenders for the public good and the strength of the opposition to any group seeking the public good. This information is hard to come by. To the extent that an organization can control the information available to its members and thereby present them with an optimistic reading of the evidence, the higher the value of this term.[13]

There is still another way that organizations can influence their members' perceptions of the likelihood of success. Every rational actor knows that the probability of success is dependent upon the organization's ability to prevent free-riding. In addition, each actor is personally interested in bearing as little of the cost of participation as possible. Therefore, the organization can increase the likelihood of individual participation if it has a high degree of solidarity. Consequently, we expect that the actor's perception of the estimated probability of success (p) will increase to the degree that: 5) the organization monopolizes information for its members; 6) and the organization is highly solidary.[14]

There are other types of rewards that the individual may also consider, particularly intra-organizational rewards such as honor, prestige, authority, power and position (X_3). Like the first type, these are rewards that come as compensation for individual conduct during collective action. They are easier to gauge and probably less enticing, but are nevertheless exceedingly powerful because they do not depend on the outcome of the collective action. A good soldier who has shown bravery and courage will be promoted whether the war is won or lost. Here again the individual must be able to count upon the organization's ability to recognize and reward a loyal performance. Obviously, the value of this heightened status varies with the individual's dependence on the organization.

---

[13] As noted above, this condition is easiest met in the case of linguistically distinctive ethnic groups. More precisely, to the degree that an ethnic group is monolingual and linguistically distinct, ethnic leaders have the best chance to control members' information. One suspects, therefore, that recent immigrants are most likely to fall into this category.

[14] By solidarity we refer to the degree of compliance that the group can expect to obtain from its members. An actor's compliance will increase to the degree that he values the resources of the group and they are not available to him elsewhere, and when he would suffer high costs in leaving the group. In a highly solidary group, by definition, each individual is more dependent on the group and therefore less likely to attempt to free-ride. However, given the chance, an actor will always try to free-ride so that a highly solidary group ensures the compliance of its members through monitoring mechanisms (*See*, Hechter, 1982).

THEORY OF ETHNIC COLLECTIVE ACTION   427

Given that the estimated probability of success for most collective actions is extremely low, the fact that the individual can count on some reward is very important. Regardless of the probable outcome of any collective action, the greater the intra-organizational rewards, the greater the organization's control over the behavior of its members. Therefore, we expect that the individual's perception of the private rewards to be gained within an organization by participating in collective action (X_3) will increase when: 7) the organization has resources to be distributed, aside from those gained as a byproduct of successful collective action, 8) the organization's monitoring capabilites are strong; 9) and the organization has a history of equitable distribution policies.

These are the benefits that the actor may be able to obtain as a result of participation. But there is also the important matter of costs. Two types of costs may be incurred by participation in collective action: personal injury during the fray and punishments that may be levied by outside agencies.

The likelihood of injury suffered in collective action (X_5) is primarily a function of two factors. First is the chosen strategy: injury is more likely in a terrorist attack than in a legal and peaceful demonstration. Second is the strength of the opponent and its repertoire of available countermeasures. There are several ways that an organization may influence the member's perception of these costs.

Obviously, an organization can choose a strategy that is designed to minimize the risk of personal injury. But sometimes organizations adopt tactics that increase the risk of injury, perhaps to demonstrate the seriousness of their demands. The rational actor is more likely to balk at participation under these conditions. The organization may try to reduce his perception of the significance of these costs by convincing the actor that its opponents are benign—for example, that the police will be restrained during a civil rights demonstration. Or it may cynically suggest that there is a very small probability of getting caught and therefore of getting punished.

An organization may try to convince members that risk-taking will be socially rewarded, but this is a dubious claim unless there is already high solidarity.[15] Thus, while the risk of personal injury may

---

[15] The greater the individual's dependence on the group, the more weight the group's social rewards will carry for him.

remain high, it need not be an absolute deterrent to participation in collective action.

Finally, an organization may try to reassure its members that if they do suffer personal harm, they will be cared for. They may offer to pay bail or hospital bills, have a fund for the survivors of those lost in battle or try to convince their members of their power to bargain with opponents for their members' safety.

Here as well, these appeals are convincing only if the organization is highly solidary. Individuals will be more willing to risk personal injury (X_5) when 10) the organization's strategy is nonviolent; and 11) the organization has resources and procedures to compensate members for injury resulting from their participation. From this point of view the reasons for the greater frequency of low-risk (*e.g.,* legal and nonviolent) collective action are obvious. Low-risk collective actions have fewer costs to dissuade the individual from participation and are less draining on organizational resources.

Opponents (especially the state and its various agencies) have several ways to make their influence known. They can advertise their strength: police patrols may be increased in a restless ethnic ghetto. Laws can be passed to prohibit all collective action, or only certain types.[16] Punishment can be threatened by the state or by opposing groups to participants: examples include jail sentences, the loss of a job or the loss of honor or social standing in the wider community. 12) If these are made clear and potential participants perceive that the opposition has sufficient authority to impose these punishments, they undoubtedly will constitute a powerful deterrent. Concomitantly, if participants in one locale are severely punished, this may dissuade individuals with similiar interests in other locales from participating.

Under certain conditions, however, these threats might actually induce people to participate. If someone believes that enough participants will engage in collective action so that each person's anonymity is preserved, this person may join if he can easily be identified as belonging to the same public whose interest the organization is pursuing. This is because he may expect to be punished even if he does not participate, because the opposition is either unable or unwilling to distinguish between participants and non-participants.[17] Thus, more southern blacks might have joined civil

---

[16] Curfews are an example of this type of law.

THEORY OF ETHNIC COLLECTIVE ACTION   429

rights marches in anticipation of blind reprisals by the white community against all blacks.

Therefore, we expect that 13) when the opposition promises to punish participants and the likelihood of failure of the collective action is high, individuals will be dissuaded from participating. Finally, 14) individuals may be indifferent to this cost if they believe that they will be punished even if they do not participate.

To reiterate, we have presented the following list of propositions:

A. The individual's estimate of the private rewards gained as a result of his participation in a successful collective action (X_2) will:

   1) increase when the organization has a store of resources aside from those to be gained through collective action;
   2) increase when the organization's monitoring capacities are extensive;
   3) increase when the organization has a proven record of justice in distribution; and
   4) increase when the organizational membership is small, thereby enhancing the efficacy of the monitoring process.

B. The individual's estimate of the probability of success (p) will:

   5) increase to the degree that the organization monopolizes information for its members; and
   6) increase to the degree that the organization is highly solidary.

C. The individual's estimate of the private rewards gained as a result of participation in collective action regardless of the outcome (X_3) will:

   7) increase when the organization has a store of resources aside from those gained through successful collective action;
   8) increase when the organization's monitoring capabilities are strong;
   9) increase when the organization has a history of equitable distribution policies.

D. The individual's willingness to risk personal injury (X_5) will be:

   10) greater when the organization's chosen strategy is legal

---

ᵛ This depends in good part on the phenotypical distinctiveness of the ethnic group.

and nonviolent; and

11) greater when the organization has resources and procedures to compensate members for injury resulting from participation.

E. The individual's estimate of the private punishment received as a result of not participating in collective action (X_6) will:

12) increase when the organization is highly solidary.

F. The individual's estimate of the private punishments received as a result of participating in a collective action that fails (X_4) will:

13) increase when the opposition promises publicly to punish participants; and

14) decrease if he believes that he will be punished even if he does not participate.

CONCLUSION

It is hardly news that ethnic collective action turns out to be a woefully complicated affair. None of the currently fashionable approaches in the sociological literature—including the so-called diffusion, reaction and competitive models of ethnic mobilization[18] are remotely up to the task. Further, the variables sketched above do not constitute anything like an exhaustive list of determinants. Using our approach it will never be possible to arrive at such a list. Perhaps the most we can claim is that any factor contributing to ethnic collective action will do so by altering the ethnic individual's perceived costs. While the theory seems to lack that wholesome sense of closure so dear to the hearts of many social scientists this is a necessary concession to the ambiguity and plasticity inherent in social life.

Yet, despite this openness, the theory does point away from certain types of factors discussed in the literature and directs attention towards others deemed more significant. It suggests that stratification has no direct effects on an ethnic group's propensity to engage in collective action, but that its influence is mediated by the establishment of ethnic organizations and quasi-groups. Whether these are formal structures or merely networks of social interaction

---

[18] *See,* Deutsch, 1965; Hechter, 1975; Hannan, 1979; Ragin, 1979; Nielson, 1980; Ritter, 1980; and Leifer, 1981.

THEORY OF ETHNIC COLLECTIVE ACTION   431

that persist over time, all such organizations have resources that may be employed to alter their members' private benefits. The amount of these resources is a critical determinant of subsequent collective action.

Resource-mobilization theorists of social movements (*cf.* Zald and McCarthy, 1979) have long insisted on the primacy of organizational variables for collective action; our approach concurs with their emphasis. Yet, while organizational resources are necessary preconditions of collective action, they are clearly insufficient ones. Here the theory directs special attention to the monitoring mechanisms of such organizations; these generally have not yet received their due. In the absence of effective monitoring mechanisms that control free-riders and reward loyal participants, no amount of organizational resources will be sufficient to create viable collective actions.

Finally, the individual's decision to participate will be constrained by threats of future punishment made by the group's opponents. To the degree that opponents can make such threats credible, the group's propensity for collective action will be diminished.

For the most part the determinants specified by the theory have a hallowed place in the sociological literature. What has been missing is a simple explanation of their efficacy. Too frequently analysis has halted with the demonstration of correlations between measured variables and the actual occurrence of events and types of collective action. By providing a theory that lays bare the elementary mechanisms of collective action we can begin to move beyond simple correlation towards the harder task of understanding. This article represents a first step toward that end.

REFERENCES

Aptheker, H.
1943 *American Negro Slave Revolts*. New York: Columbia University Press; London: P.S. Kings and Staples Ltd.

Blalock, H.M.
1967 *Toward a Theory of Minority-Group Relations*. New York: John Wiley and Sons, Inc.

Blumer, H.
1965 "Industrialization and Race Relations". In *Industrialization and Race Relations: A*

432   INTERNATIONAL MIGRATION REVIEW

Symposium. Edited by G. Hunter. London: Oxford University Press.

Bonacich, E.
1979 "The Past, Present, and Future of Split Labor Market Theory". In *Research in Race and Ethnic Relations*. Edited by C.B. Marett. Greenwich, CT: JAI Press.

――――
1972 "A Theory of Ethnic Antagonism: The Split-Labor Market", *American Sociological Review*, 37(5):533-47.

Breton, R.
1964 "Institutional Completeness of Ethnic Communities and the Personal Relations of Immigrants", *American Journal of Sociology*, 70(2):193-205.

Castells, M.
1975 "Immigrant Workers and Class Struggles in Advanced Capitalism: The Western European Experience", *Politics and Society*, 5(1):33-66.

Deutsch, K.W.
1966 *Nationalism and Social Communication*. Cambridge, MA: The MIT Press.

Edwards, R.C. and D.M. Gordon, eds.
1975 *Labor Market Segmentation*. Lexington, MA: Heath.

Elkins, S.M.
1959 *Slavery: A Problem in American Institutional and Intellectual Life*. Chicago: University of Chicago Press.

Elster, J.
1979 *Ulysses and the Sirens: Studies in Rationality and Irrationality*. New York: Cambridge University Press.

Fogel, R.W. and S.L. Engerman
1974 *Time on the Cross: The Economics of American Negro Slavery*. Boston: Little, Brown and Co.

Frolich, N., J. Oppenheimer and O. Young
1971 *Political Leadership and Collective Goods*. Princeton: Princeton University Press.

Genovese, E.G.
1974 *Roll, Jordon, Roll: The World the Slaves Made*. New York: Pantheon.

Hannan, M.T.
1979 "The Dynamics of Ethnic Boundaries in Modern States". In *National Development and the World System: Educational, Economic and Political Change, 1950-1970*. Edited by M.T. Hannan and J.W. Meyer. Chicago: University Press. Pp. 253-275.

Hardin, R.
1982 *Collective Action*. Baltimore: Johns Hopkins University Press.

Health, M.
1976 *Rational Choice and Social Exchange*. Cambridge: Cambridge University Press.

Hechter, M.
1982 "A Theory of Group Solidarity". In *Research in Supplement 1: Choice Models of Buyer*

Behavior: Research in Marketing. Edited by L. McAlister. Greenwich, CT: JAI Press.

———
1978 "Group Formation and the Cultural Division of Labor", *American Journal of Sociology,* 84(2):293-317.

———
1976 "Ethnicity and Industrialization: On the Proliferation of the Cultural Division of Labor", *Ethnicity,* 3(3):214-224.

———
1975 *Internal Colonialism: The Celtic Frings in British National Development, 1953-1966.* University of California Press.

———
1971 "Towards a Theory of Ethnic Change", *Politics and Society,* 2(1):29-45.

Kuper, L.
1957 *Passive Resistance in South Africa.* New Haven, CT: Yale University Press.

Laver, M.
1980 "Political Solutions to the Collective Action Problems", *Political Studies,* 28(2):195-209.

Leifer, E.
1981 "Competing Models of National Integration: The Role of Ethnic Ties", *American Journal of Sociology,* 87:(1):23-47.

March, J.G.
1978 "Bounded Rationality, Ambiguity, and the Engineering of Choice", *The Bell Journal of Economics,* 9(2):587-608.

Nielsen, F.
1980 "The Flemish Movement in Belgium After World War II: A Dynamic Analysis", *American Sociological Review,* 45:76-94. June.

Olson, M.
1968 *The Logic of Collective Action.* New York: Shocken.

Park, R.E.
1950 *Race and Culture.* Glencoe: Free Press.

Parsons, R. and N. Smelser
1956 *Economy and Society.* New York: Free Press.

Piore, M.
1975 "Notes for a Theory of Labor Market Stratification". In *Labor Market Segmentation.* Edited by R.C. Edwards *et al.* Lexington, MA: Health. Pp. 125-150.

Ragin, C.
1979 "Ethnic Political Mobilization: The Welsh Case", *American Sociological Review,* 44:619-635. Aug.

Riker, W. and P. Ordeshook
1973 *An Introduction to Positive Political Theory.* New York: Prentice-Hall.

434   INTERNATIONAL MIGRATION REVIEW

Ritter, K.
1980 *Natives and Settlers: The Cultural Division of Labor in Alaska, 1741-1970.* Ph.D. dissertation, Department of Sociology, University of Washington.

Samuelson, P.
1978 "Aspects of Public Expenditure Theories", *The Review of Economics and Statistics,* 40(3):332-6.

———
1974 "The Pure Theory of Public Expenditure", *The Review of Economics and Statistics,* 37(3):387-9.

Smelser, N.
1969 "Mechanism of Change and Adjustment to Change". In *Comparative Perspectives on Industrial Society.* Edited by W.A. Faunce and W.A. Form. Boston: Little, Brown and Co.

Spence, M.
1973 "Job Market Signaling", *The Quarterly Journal of Economics,* 87:355-375. Aug.

Taylor, M.
1982 *Community, Anarchy and Liberty.* Cambridge: Cambridge University Press.

Thomas, W.I. and F. Znaniecki
1920 *The Polish Peasant in Europe and America.* Boston: The Gorham Press.

Thurow, L.C.
1975 *Generating Inequality: Mechanisms of Distribution in the U.S. Economy.* New York: Basic Books.

Tullock, G.
1979 "The Economics of Revolution". In *Revolutions, Systems, and Theories.* Edited by H.J. Johnson, J.J. Leach and R.G. Muehlmann. Dordrecht, Holland: D. Reidel Publishing Company. Pp. 47-60.

Van Dyke, V.
1977 "The Individual, the State, and Ethnic Communities in Political Theory", *World Politics,* 29(3):342-369.

Zald, M.N. and J.D. McCarthy
1979 *The Dynamics of Social Movements: Resource Mobilization, Social Control and Tactics.* Cambridge, MA: Winthrop Publishers.

Name Index